EARLY MODERN THINGS

What can we learn about the past by studying things? How does the meaning of things, and our relationship to them, change over time? This fascinating collection taps a rich vein of recent scholarship to explore a variety of approaches to the material culture of the early modern world (c. 1500–1800).

Divided into six parts, the book explores: The Ambiguity of Things; Representing Things; Making Things; Empires of Things; Consuming Things; and, lastly, The Power of Things. Spanning across the early modern world, from Ming dynasty China to Georgian England, and from Ottoman Egypt to Spanish America, the authors provide a generous set of examples in how to study the circulation, use, consumption and, most fundamentally, the nature of things themselves.

Drawing on a broad range of disciplinary perspectives and lavishly illustrated, *Early Modern Things* supplies fresh and provocative insights into how objects – ordinary and extraordinary, secular and sacred, natural and man-made – came to define some of the key developments of the early modern world. This book will be essential reading for all those interested in the early modern world.

Paula Findlen is Ubaldo Pierotti Professor of Italian History and Co-Director of the Center for Medieval and Early Modern Studies at Stanford University, USA. Her previous works include *Possessing Nature: Museums, Collecting and Scientific Culture in Early Modern Italy* (1994), which was awarded the Marraro Prize in Italian History and the Pfizer Prize in the History of Science, and (co-edited with Pamela Smith) *Merchants and Marvels: Commerce, Science and Art in Early Modern Europe* (2001).

A cornucopia: a rich and valuable collection that ranges far and wide in its analysis of the dynamic and diverse powers – symbolic, material, economic, political and religious – of things in the early-modern world, and of the important questions that taking objects seriously raises for the historian of any era.

John Brewer, California Institute of Technology, USA

EARLY MODERN THINGS

Objects and their histories, 1500–1800

Edited by Paula Findlen

Routledge
Taylor & Francis Group

LONDON AND NEW YORK

First published 2013
by Routledge
2 Park Square, Milton Park, Abingdon, Oxon, OX14 4RN

Simultaneously published in the USA and Canada
by Routledge
711 Third Avenue, New York, NY 10017

Routledge is an imprint of the Taylor & Francis Group, an informa business

British Library Cataloguing in Publication Data
A catalogue record for this book is available from the British Library

Library of Congress Cataloging-in-Publication Data
Early modern things / edited by Paula Findlen.
        p. cm.
    Includes index.
    1. Material culture – History. 2. Ceremonial objects – History.
    3. Civilization, Modern. I. Findlen, Paula.
    GN406.E34 2012
    306.4–dc23   2012026865

ISBN: 978-0-415-52050-8 (hbk)
ISBN: 978-0-415-52051-5 (pbk)

Typeset in Bembo
by HWA Text and Data Management, London

To Jeff and Natalie,
who fill my life with love and laughter

CONTENTS

FIGURES

TABLES

CONTRIBUTORS

Renata Ago is Professor of Early Modern History at the University of Rome La Sapienza. She is the author of *Un feudo esemplare. Immobilismo padronale e astuzia contadina nel Lazio del '700* (Schena Editore, 1988), *Carriere e clientele nella Roma barocca* (Laterza, 1990), *La feudalità nell'età moderna* (Laterza, 1994 and 1998), *Economia barocca. Mercato e istituzioni nella Roma del Seicento* (Donzelli, 1998) and *Il gusto delle cose. Una storia degli oggetti nella Roma del Seicento* (Donzelli, 2006) (an English translation of this book is forthcoming from the University of Chicago Press, 2013). She is currently working on the quest for distinction in seventeenth century Rome.

Timothy Brook is a China historian at the University of British Columbia, where he holds the Republic of China Chair at the Institute of Asian Research. He has written eight books and edited nine, in addition to serving as editor-in-chief of the six-volume *History of Imperial China* published by Harvard University Press. *Vermeer's Hat: The Seventeenth Century and the Dawn of the Global Age* (Bloomsbury Press, 2008) was awarded the Mark Lynton Prize from the Columbia School of Journalism and the Nieman Foundation for Journalism at Harvard University. More recent are his co-authored *Death by a Thousand Cuts* (Harvard University Press, 2008), a study of Chinese historical executions, and *The Troubled Empire* (Belknap Press of the Harvard University Press), a survey of Chinese history from 1260 to 1644.

Paula Findlen is Ubaldo Pierotti Professor of Italian History at Stanford University where she has co-directed the Center for Medieval and Early Modern Studies, the Program in the History and Philosophy of Science, and the Science Technology and Society Program. Her publications include

Possessing Nature: Museums, Collecting and Scientific Culture in Early Modern Italy (University of California Press, 1994), *Merchants and Marvels: Commerce, Science, and Art in Early Modern Europe*, co-edited with Pamela Smith (Routledge, 2002), *Athanasius Kircher: The Last Man Who Knew Everything* (Routledge, 2004), and other books and essays on science, society, culture and collecting in early modern Italy. She has recently been writing about the history of the Uffizi.

Julie Hochstrasser is Associate Professor of Early Modern Northern European Art at the University of Iowa. She is the author of *Still Life and Trade in the Dutch Golden Age* (University of Chicago Press, 2007) and various essays on still life, landscape and the impact of Dutch visual culture throughout the world. For her research on 'the Dutch in the World,' she has circled the globe to investigate art and visual culture in key sites of early modern Dutch trade in Asia, Africa and the Americas. Another book on still life (at home in the Dutch Golden Age) is also currently in progress.

Erin K. Lichtenstein is a doctoral candidate in early modern European history at Stanford University. Her dissertation, tentatively titled '(Re)Forming Gender in the Textile Guilds of Genoa, Leiden, and Lyon, 1575–1650' explores how guilds forged a shared set of beliefs about social identities, especially gender, through an ongoing conversation among leaders, members and non-members.

Anne E. C. McCants is Professor of History and Director of the Concourse Program at MIT with research interests in the economic and social history of the Middle Ages and Early Modern Europe. She is the author of *Civic Charity in a Golden Age: Orphan Care in Early Modern Amsterdam* (University of Illinois Press, 1997), and numerous articles. She also serves as the Editor of *Social Science History*.

Alan Mikhail is Assistant Professor of History at Yale University. He is the author of *Nature and Empire in Ottoman Egypt: An Environmental History* (Cambridge University Press, 2011), which won the Roger Owen Book Award from the Middle East Studies Association and Yale University's Samuel and Ronnie Heyman Prize, and the editor of *Water on Sand: Environmental Histories of the Middle East and North Africa* (Oxford University Press, 2012). He is currently writing a book about the changing relationships between humans and animals in Ottoman Egypt.

Erika Monahan is Assistant Professor of Russian History at the University of New Mexico. She received her PhD from Stanford University in 2007. She is currently working on a book about commerce and empire in early modern Eurasia through the lens of merchant culture in Siberia.

Chandra Mukerji is Distinguished Professor of Communication and Science Studies at the University of California, San Diego, and has been both chair of the Communication Department and director of the Science Studies Program. In addition to many articles and book chapters, she is author of *From Graven Images: Patterns of Modern Materialism* (Columbia University Press, 1983), *A Fragile Power: Science and the State* (Princeton University Press, 1989), with Michael Schudson, *Rethinking Popular Culture* (University of California Press, 1991), *Territorial Ambitions and the Gardens of Versailles* (Cambridge University Press, 1997), and *Impossible Engineering: Technology and Territoriality on the Canal du Midi* (Princeton University Press, 2009), which won the 2011 Distinguished Book Award from the American Sociological Association. She is currently studying French Neoclassical architecture.

Carla Nappi is an Assistant Professor of History and Canada Research Chair in Early Modern Studies at the University of British Columbia. She is the author of *The Monkey and the Inkpot: Natural History and Its Transformations in Early Modern China* (Harvard University Press, 2009). Her current research explores the histories of translation across early modern Eurasia.

Marcy Norton is Associate Professor of History at George Washington University. She is the author of *Sacred Gifts, Profane Pleasures: A History of Tobacco and Chocolate in the Atlantic World* (Cornell University Press, 2008), winner of best book award from the Association for the Study of Food and Society, as well as *Chocolate and the European Internalization of Mesoamerican Aesthetics* (2006). She is currently writing a book about human–animal relationships in the Atlantic world.

Mark A. Peterson is Professor of History, University of California, Berkeley, is the author of *The Price of Redemption: The Spiritual Economy of Puritan New England* (Stanford University Press, 1997) and *The City-State of Boston, 1630–1865*, under contract with Yale University Press. His previous work in material culture includes 'Puritanism and Refinement in Early New England: Reflections on Communion Silver', *William and Mary Quarterly*, 3d ser., 58 (April, 2001): 307–346, and 'Theopolis Americana: The City-State of Boston, the Republic of Letters, and the Protestant International, 1689–1733', in *Soundings in Atlantic History*, ed. Bernard Bailyn (Harvard University Press, 2009).

Morgan Pitelka is Associate Professor of Asian Studies at the University of North Carolina at Chapel Hill, and Director of the Triangle Center for Japanese Studies. His publications include *Japanese Tea Culture: Art, History, and Practice* (RoutledgeCurzon, 2003), *Handmade Culture: Raku Potters, Patrons, and Tea Practitioners in Japan* (University of Hawaii Press, 2005), and *What's the Use of Art? Asian Visual and Material Culture in Context* (University of Hawaii Press, 2007), co-edited with Jan Mrázek. A new book on material culture and the politics of sociability in the career of Tokugawa Ieyasu (1543–1616) is forthcoming; his next project examines the history and archaeology of daily life and destruction in medieval Japanese castle towns.

Giorgio Riello is Professor of Global History at the University of Warwick and a member of Warwick's Global History and Culture Centre. He is the author of *A Foot in the Past* (Oxford University Press, 2006) and *Global Cotton: How an Asian Fiber Changed the European Economy* (Cambridge University Press, 2013). He has co-edited several books on the history of textiles, dress and fashion including *The Spinning World* (Oxford University Press, 2009), *How India Clothed the World* (Brill, 2009) and *Global Design History* (Routledge, 2011). In 2009 he received the Newcomen Prize in Business History, and in 2010 he was awarded the Philip Leverhulme Prize.

Jessica Riskin teaches in the History Department at Stanford University. She is the author of *Science in the Age of Sensibility: The Sentimental Empiricists of the French Enlightenment* (University of Chicago Press, 2002) and the editor of *Genesis Redux: Essays in the History and Philosophy of Artificial Life* (University of Chicago Press, 2007). She is currently finishing a book about the history of scientific accounts of life and mind entitled *The Restless Clock*, under contract with Basic Books.

Pamela H. Smith is Professor of History at Columbia University, and the author of books on alchemy, artisans and the making of knowledge; most recently, *The Body of the Artisan: Art and Experience in the Scientific Revolution* (University of Chicago Press, 2004) and *Making Knowledge in Early Modern Europe: Practices, Objects, and Texts, 1400–1800* (with Benjamin Schmidt, University of Chicago Press, 2008). Her present research reconstructs the vernacular knowledge of the early modern European metalworkers.

Corey Tazzara is currently a postdoctoral Harper Fellow at the University of Chicago. He received his PhD from Stanford University in 2011 and will begin as Assistant Professor of History at Scripps College in Fall 2013. His book project is entitled *The Masterpiece of the Medici: Commerce, Politics, and the Making of the Free Port of Livorno*.

Amanda Vickery is Professor of Early Modern History at Queen Mary, University of London. She is the author of *Behind Closed Doors: At Home in Georgian England* (Yale University Press, 2009) and *The Gentleman's Daughter: Women's Lives in Georgian England* (Yale University Press, 1998) which won the Wolfson, the Whitfield and the Longman/History Today prizes. She is the editor of *Women, Privilege and Power: British Politics 1750 to the Present* (Stanford University Press, 2001) and *Gender, Taste and Material Culture in Britain and North America* (Yale University Press, 2006). She writes and presents documentaries for BBC2 and BBC Radio 4. In 2011, she judged the Samuel Johnson prize.

ACKNOWLEDGMENTS

The idea for this project emerged in the early stages of working with Renata Ago on the English translation of her *Gusto for Things: A History of Objects in Seventeenth-Century Rome*. It also has grown from my own desire to return to issues that first interested me in the history of collecting and subsequently in the relations between commerce, science, and art, following the project I developed with Pamela Smith that became *Merchants and Marvels*. More broadly, I saw this project as an opportunity to bring together a group of colleagues who represent some of the exciting new directions in the history of objects, material culture, and – that elephant in the room – things.

My first thanks go to the many entities that made a large international workshop and the ensuing publication possible: Stephen Hinton, then Senior Associate Dean of Humanities at Stanford University, the Department of Art and Art History, the Center for East Asian Studies, the Center for Russian, Eastern European, and Eurasian Studies, the Clayman Institute for Gender Research, and my two home bases at Stanford: the Department of History (where colleagues humored my good intentions to attempt to do the job of department chair during the period when this project was underway) and the Program in the History and Philosophy of Science and Technology. Both have been marvelous environments in which to think and learn for over fifteen years, and for this I am most grateful. The History Department materially supported this project by bringing both Renata Ago and Amanda Vickery for an extended stay on campus as Kratter Visiting Professors in 2009–10. The Stanford Humanities Center not only provided funding but also opened its doors to host several days of boisterous conversation about nothing but early modern things and subsequently provided me with a supportive and enjoyable environment in which to complete this book as the Ellen Andrews Wright Fellow at the Stanford Humanities Center in 2011–12.

No collaborative project ever happens without the goodwill of many people. Shari Haun from History and Rosemary Rogers from History and Philosophy of Science ensured that all travel and conference arrangements went without a hitch. I also wish to thank many of the participants in the workshop who might otherwise be an invisible presence in the conversation: Jan de Vries, Morten Steen Hansen, Bissera Pentcheva, Londa Schiebinger, Randolph Starn, Daniel Stolzenberg, Kären Wigen, Caroline Winterer, and especially Luca Molà and Evelyn Welch who presented at the conference but were unable to contribute to the volume. Their comments and suggestions during the workshop considerably improved the final product. All the participants in my 'Early Modern Things' seminar that took place in winter 2010 attended the workshop, read the work of many participants, and engaged in our debates about the meaning of things in a different world. I thank this talented group of students, undergraduate and graduate, for sharpening my own sense of how historians write about objects. A warm note of appreciation goes to Kyle Lee-Crossett who, as a Stanford Humanities Center Undergraduate Research Assistant, took out an ungodly number of books about early modern material culture on my behalf to assist in my completion of this book.

At Routledge all of the editors involved with this project – Vicky Peters, Michael Strang and Laura Mothersole – have been most supportive, firm about deadlines, and just plain helpful in wrapping up the final details and thinking about how best to present the project. Three anonymous readers were kind enough to look at an early proposal for this project and all of them offered excellent suggestions to improve the final version. I thank John Hodgson and Sarah Mabley for their role in overseeing the production of this volume as it went to press, and Barbara Eastman for her copyediting.

My final and most heartfelt thank you goes to Erin Lichtenstein. She has been an inspired collaborator not only for the workshop but also during the final editing of this volume. Every paper in this volume has benefited from her careful, critical reading and the overall project could not have been completed in such a timely fashion without her incredible organizational skills. She has the last word on this volume not only to contribute an important perspective from her own research on early modern women artisans but because no one else has thought as much about the whole with me.

In the early stages of this project I had the bittersweet experience of watching my daughter Natalie take the first steps towards a new phase of life, starting kindergarten, as my mother became ill and passed away. I will always think of them both in relation to the period in which I lived and breathed *Early Modern Things*, each cycling through a different moment in life's journey. As I complete this acknowledgment, Natalie is graduating second grade, and Jeff and I marvel at the girl she has become. Life is full of many things but the best ones are usually immaterial.

Stanford, June 2012

ILLUSTRATION SOURCES AND PERMISSIONS

Figure 0.1 *Source*: The Oba with Europeans, Benin Plaques, brass, lost wax cast, made in Benin City, 16th–17th centuries, 43.5 × 41 × 10.7 cm. AN249473001. © Trustees of the British Museum.

Figure 0.2 *Source*: Hans Burgmair the Elder, standing black youth dressed in a feather skirt, cape, and head-dress and holding a club and shield, 1520–30, pen and black ink, with brown, black and grey wash, the verso in pen and brown ink, 235 × 160 mm. AN211381001. © Trustees of the British Museum.

Figure 0.3 *Source*: *Buckles and buttons. I am the thing dem-me* (London, 1777), hand-colored engraving, 349 × 246 mm. AN112679001. © Trustees of the British Museum.

Figure 0.4 *Source*: Porcelain bottle with underglaze blue, overglaze yellow enamel and silver mounts, made in Jingdezhen, *c*.1628–60, 29.7 cm. AN141459001. © Trustees of the British Museum.

Figure 0.5 *Source*: Anon., Florentine costume book owned by the Doni family, 17th century, pen and brown ink drawing, with watercolor, heightened with gold, 294 × 211 mm. AN683879001. © Trustees of the British Museum.

Figure 1.1 *Source*: Li Zhongli 李中立, *Bencao yuanshi* 本草原始 (Shanghai: Shanghai guji chubanshe, 2002), 992:602.

Figure 2.1 *Source*: Fra Angelico School, *Pope Clement V on horseback with a hawk on his fist, riding away from a female saint (the Holy Church)*, 1402–1455, British Museum, pen and ink, 16 × 15.5 cm. © Trustees of the British Museum.

Figure 2.2 *Source*: 'Indian of Trinidad,' f. 83r in *Histoire Naturelle des Indes* (Drake Manuscript), c. 1586, The Pierpont Morgan Library, New York, MA 3900. Courtesy of the The Pierpont Morgan Library, New York; Bequest of Clara S. Peck, 1983. Photo by David A. Loggie.

Figure 2.3 *Source*: Detail from 'Southeastern South America, Straits of Magellan,' f. 12 in 'Vallard Atlas,' 1547, Huntington Library, HM 29. Reproduced by permission of The Huntington Library, San Marino, California.

Figure 2.4 *Source*: Barthel Beham, *Bildnis einer Frau mit Papagei* (*Woman with a Parrot*), 1529, Kunsthistorisches Museum, Vienna, GG 3483. Courtesy of the Kunsthistorisches Museum, Vienna.

Figure 3.1 *Source*: Leeuwenhoek's drawing of a dog's uterus, in a letter to the Royal Society of London, 30 March 1685, published in *Philosophical Transactions of the Royal Society of London* 15 (1685), Fig. 1, after 1134. Courtesy of Stanford University Libraries.

Figure 3.2. *Source*: Christopher Wren's drawing of a brain, in Thomas Willis, *Cerebri anatome, cui accessit nervorum descriptio et usus* (London: J. Martyn & J. Allestry, 1664), Fig. Ia, between 24 and 25. Courtesy of Stanford University Libraries.

Figure 3.3 *Source*: Thomas Dallam's organ, King's College Chapel, Cambridge University. Photo: David Vernon.

Figure 3.4 *Source*: Thomas Willis, drawing of nerves, in Thomas Willis, *Cerebri anatome, cui accessit nervorum descriptio et usus* (London: J. Martyn & J. Allestry, 1664), Tab. IXa, between 424 and 425. Courtesy of Stanford University Libraries.

Figure 4.1 *Source*: Clara Peeters (1594–c.1657), *Still Life with Goblets and Flowers*, 1612, Staatliche Kunsthalle, Karlsruhe, oil on panel, 59.5 × 49 cm, inv. 2222. Printed by permission of the Staatliche Kunsthalle, Karlsruhe.

Figure 4.2 *Source*: Pieter Claesz (c.1597–1660), *Still Life with Roemer, Oysters, Saltvat, and Roll*, 1633, Staatliche Kunstsammlungen, Kassel, oil on panel, 37.8 × 53.2 cm, inv. GK 437. Photo Credit: bpk, Berlin/Staatliche Kunstsammlungen, Kassel/Art Resource, NY.

Figure 4.3 *Source*: Willem Kalf (1619–1693), *Still Life with a Chinese Porcelain Bowl, Glasses, and Fruits*, 1662, Staatliche Museen zu Berlin, Gemäldegalerie, oil on canvas, 64 × 53 cm., inv. 948 F. Photo Credit: bpk, Berlin/Staatliche Museen zu Berlin/Jörg P. Anders/Art Resource, NY.

Figure 4.4 *Source*: Pieter Claesz, *Still Life with Violin and Glass Ball*, c.1628, Germanisches Nationalmuseum, Nuremberg, oil on panel, 59 × 36 cm, inv. GM 1409. Printed by permission of the Germanisches Nationalmuseum, Nuremberg.

Figure 4.5 *Source*: Clara Peeters (1594–c. 1657), *Still Life with Goblets and Flowers* (detail), 1612, Staatliche Kunsthalle, Karlsruhe, oil on panel, 59.5 × 49 cm, inv. 2222. Printed by permission of the Staatliche Kunsthalle, Karlsruhe.

Figure 4.6 *Source*: Samuel van Hoogstraten (1627–1678), *Augenbetrüger*, c.1666–1678, Staatliche Kunsthalle Karlsruhe, oil on canvas, 63 × 79 cm, inv. 2620. Printed by permission of the Staatliche Kunsthalle, Karlsruhe.

Figure 5.1 *Source*: Private collection.

Figure 5.2 *Source*: London Metropolitan Archives, WJ/SP/D/078. Courtesy of the Corporation of London.

Figure 5.3 *Source*: London Metropolitan Archives, DL/AM/PI/1/1675/3. Courtesy of the Corporation of London.

Figure 5.4 *Source*: Lichfield Record Office P/C/11 (Ellesmere, 1734). Courtesy of the Staffordshire Record Office.

Figure 5.5 *Source*: Domenico Ghirlandaio (1449–1494), *Inventory of a Legacy of the Magistrates*, second half of the fifteenth century, fresco at San Martino dei Buonomini, Florence, Italy. © Photo SCALA, Florence.

Figure 5.6 *Source*: London Metropolitan Archives, ACC/0446/H001. Courtesy of the Corporation of London.

Figure 5.7 *Source*: Private Collection.

Figure 5.8 *Source*: Private Collection.

Figure 6.1 *Source*: Nicolay, *Le navigationi et viaggi nella Turchia, di Nicolo de Nicolai del Delfinato, Signor d'Arfevilla… : con diuerse singolarità in quelle parti dall'autore viste & osseruate* (Anversa [i.e. Antwerp]: Guiglielmo Siluio, 1576), f. 166. Courtesy of Mandeville Special Collections Library, University of California, San Diego.

Figure 6.2 *Source*: Nicolay, *Le navigationi et viaggi nella Turchia, di Nicolo de Nicolai del Delfinato, Signor d'Arfevilla… : con diuerse singolarità in quelle parti dall'autore viste & osseruate* (Anversa [i.e. Antwerp]: Guiglielmo Siluio, 1576), f. 160. Courtesy of Mandeville Special Collections Library, University of California, San Diego.

Figure 6.3 *Source*: Nicolay, *Le navigationi et viaggi nella Turchia, di Nicolo de Nicolai del Delfinato, Signor d'Arfevilla… : con diuerse singolarità in quelle parti dall'autore viste & osseruate* (Anversa [i.e. Antwerp]: Guiglielmo Siluio, 1576), f. 254. Courtesy of Mandeville Special Collections Library, University of California, San Diego.

Figure 7.1 *Source*: Leipzig University Library, Ms. 1479, fol. 3r. Courtesy of Leipzig University Library.

Figure 7.2 *Source*: Wenzel Jamnitzer, writing box, 1560–1570, Kunsthistorisches Museum, Vienna, cast silver, 6.0 × 22.7 × 10.2 cm, inv. no. 1155/64. Courtesy of the Kunsthistorisches Museum, Vienna. Photo: Tonny Beentjes and Pamela H. Smith.

Figure 7.3 *Source*: Wenzel Jamnitzer, writing box (detail), 1560–1570, Kunsthistorisches Museum, Vienna, cast silver, 6.0 × 22.7 × 10.2 cm, inv. no. 1155/64. Courtesy of the Kunsthistorisches Museum, Vienna. Photo: Tonny Beentjes and Pamela H. Smith.

Figure 7.4 *Source*: Reproduction and photo: Tonny Beentjes and Pamela H. Smith

Figure 7.5 *Source*: BnF Ms. Fr. 640, fol. 122v. Reproduction from Bibliothèque nationale de France.

Figure 7.6 *Source*: Reproduction and photo: Tonny Beentjes and Pamela H. Smith.

Figure 7.7 *Source*: Reproduction and photo: Tonny Beentjes and Pamela H. Smith.

Figure 7.8 *Source*: Wenzel Jamnitzer (attributed), life-cast lizard (detail of hind foot), *c*.1540–1550, Germanisches Nationalmuseum, Nuremberg, silver, 7.0 × 4.1 cm., inv. HG 11135. Courtesy of Germanisches Nationalmuseum, Nuremberg. Photo: Tonny Beentjes and Pamela H. Smith.

Figure 7.9 *Source*: Wenzel Jamnitzer (attributed), life-cast lizard (detail of tail), *c*.1540–1550, Germanisches Nationalmuseum, Nuremberg, silver, 7.0 × 4.1 cm., inv. HG 11135. Courtesy of Germanisches Nationalmuseum, Nuremberg. Photo: Tonny Beentjes and Pamela H. Smith.

Figure 7.10 *Source*: Reproduction and photo: Tonny Beentjes and Pamela H. Smith.

Figure 7.11 *Source*: Wenzel Jamnitzer, writing box, 1560–1570, Kunsthistorisches Museum, Vienna, cast silver, 6.0 × 22.7 × 10.2 cm, inv. no. 1155/64. Courtesy of the Kunsthistorisches Museum, Vienna. Photo: Tonny Beentjes and Pamela H. Smith.

Figure 7.12 *Source*: Bibliothèque nationale de France, Ms. Fr. 640, fol. 138v. Reproduction from Bibliothèque nationale de France.

Figure 8.1 *Source*: Archivio di Stato di Firenze, LCF 3937, f. 12v. Courtesy of the Ministero per i Beni e le Attività Culturali. Further reproduction or duplication by any means is prohibited.

Figure 8.2 *Source*: Archivio di Stato di Firenze, LCF 3937, f. 14r. Courtesy of the Ministero per i Beni e le Attività Culturali. Further reproduction or duplication by any means is prohibited.

Figure 9.1 *Source*: Pill-pot of tin-glazed earthenware, oviform body with out-turned rim and flared foot, pinkish-white glaze painted in blue. *Pitulae imperialis* were pills containing syrup of violets, aloes, rhubarb, agaric, senna, cinnamon, ginger, nutmeg, clove, spikenard and mastic all rolled together, cut and rounded to form pills, made in London for an apothecary with the initials E. P., 1675, 9.2 cm h, 5.5 diam. AN226801001. © Trustees of the British Museum.

Figure 9.2 *Source*: Anon., *Von der tugent und krafft der edlen wurtzel Rebarba*, *c*.1520–1600, German letterpress woodcut, 298 × 205 mm. AN76716001. © Trustees of the British Museum.

Figure 10.1 *Source*: Spanish 8 Real Cob Coin, Obverse and Reverse, Philip IV (1625–1665), Potosi, weight 27.09 grams, diameter 44 millimeters. Courtesy of the Robert H. Gore, Jr., Numismatic Collection, Department of Special Collections, University of Notre Dame Libraries.

Figure 10.2 *Source*: Massachusetts 'Pine Tree' Shilling, large planchet, Noe 1, 1652, Obverse and Reverse, weight 4.33 grams, diameter 29.5 millimeters. Courtesy of the Robert H. Gore, Jr., Numismatic Collection, Department of Special Collections, University of Notre Dame Libraries.

Figure 10.3 *Source*: Spanish ½ Real Cob Coin, clipped, Obverse and Reverse, West Indies, weight, 1.80 grams, diameter 17.5 × 13.8 millimeters. Courtesy of the Robert H. Gore, Jr., Numismatic Collection, Department of Special Collections, University of Notre Dame Libraries.

Figure 10.4 *Source*: Peace medal or gorget, Boston, 1676, Brass, 13.3 × 8.9 centimeters. Courtesy of the Museum of the American Indian/Heye Foundation, New York

Figure 11.1 *Source*: Made by Stacey D. Maples, 2012.

Figure 11.2 *Source*: 'Ottoman Rhodes,' Pirî Reis, *Kitabi Bahriye* (Istanbul: Devlet Basimevi, 1935).

Figure 12.1 *Source*: Tea bowl named 'Araki,' Chinese, Ming Dynasty, 16th century, Tokugawa Art Museum, flower scroll design, blue and white porcelain. Courtesy of the Tokugawa Art Museum, Nagoya, Japan. Photo © Tokugawa Art Museum Image Archives/DNPartcom.

Figure 13.1 *Source*: Japanese bottle, blue glazed ceramic porcelain, made in Hizen Province, Japan, 1651–1700, 19 × 10 × 10 cm. AN40073001. © Trustees of the British Museum.

Figure 14.1 *Source*: Thomas Chippendale, *The Gentleman and Cabinet Maker's Director*, 3rd ed (London: T. Chippendale, 1762), plate 116. Courtesy of the British Library Board.

Figure 14.2 *Source*: William Ince and John Mayhew, *The Universal System of Household Furniture* (London: n.p., 1762), plate 37. Courtesy of the British Library Board.

Figure 14.3 *Source*: William Ince and John Mayhew, *The Universal System of Household Furniture* (London: n.p., 1762), plate 40. Courtesy of the British Library Board.

Figure 14.4 *Source*: Thomas Sheraton, *The Cabinet Dictionary* (London: W. Smith, 1803), plate 71. Courtesy of the British Library Board.

Figure 14.5 *Source*: Thomas Sheraton, *The Cabinet Dictionary* (London: W. Smith, 1803), plate 69. Courtesy of the British Library Board.

Figure 14.6 *Source*: Advertisement for 'The Queen's Royal Furniture Gloss,' *c*.1798, British Museum, London, D2–1281, printed engraving. © Trustees of the British Museum.

Introduction

EARLY MODERN THINGS

Objects in motion, 1500–1800

Paula Findlen

> Material life is made up of people and things.
>
> (Fernand Braudel)

In 2010 the British Museum embarked upon an experiment with the BBC and Radio 4 to narrate a history of the world with one hundred objects selected from their collection. The result is a fascinating account of humanity from the Egyptian mummy and the Tanzanian hand axe to the American (but now global) credit card and Chinese solar lamp.[1] Imbedded in this history are eighteen artifacts belonging to the early modern era, *c*.1500–1800. Each object has its own biography but, taken together, they offer a version of global early modernity.[2] What do these things tell us about this fundamental moment when all the different parts of the world found themselves, to differing degrees and with dramatically different consequences, knit together more tightly than ever before?

Opening Neil MacGregor's *A History of the World in 100 Objects* is not unlike the experience of finding oneself inside an early modern cabinet of curiosities, or better yet perusing the pages of a catalogue with its idiosyncratic vision of how to collect across cultures.[3] A sultan's signature dances across the page with calligraphic flourish, a talisman of Ottoman bureaucracy. A golden Inca llama figurine and an Aztec double-headed serpent, beautifully rendered from thousands of tiny pieces of turquoise and shell, provide tangible reminders of bygone American empires just as a Hawaiian chieftain's brilliantly feathered helmet recalls the era before Captain Cook's voyage when Pacific island kings confidently invoked their gods. In the Kingdom of Benin (today Nigeria) the Portuguese traders who exchanged brass bracelets for pepper, palm oil, ivory, and gold found themselves immortalized in plaques depicting the stately

FIGURE 0.1 Portuguese merchants trading brass bracelets (*manilas*) with the Oba in the Kingdom of Benin

majesty and power of the Oba rulers at the moment of encounter, transforming a European commodity into African art (Figure 0.1).[4] An Indian rhinoceros that arrived in Lisbon in 1515, only to drown en route to Rome, is forever eternalized in Albrecht Dürer's famous engraving of an animal he never saw. In the British Museum he is in good company – a European cousin of porcelain elephants exquisitely crafted by late seventeenth-century Japanese artisans who learned the secrets of Chinese pottery from Koreans but not the anatomy of a pachyderm.

The durability of seemingly fragile objects, with many afterlives that have taken them halfway round the world, never ceases to amaze. A miniature galleon crafted by late sixteenth-century Augsburg artisans sends the Holy Roman Emperor Rudolf II and the seven German electors on a perpetual voyage of state to the sounds of blaring trumpets, exploding cannons, and a clock's rhythmic chiming. This imaginary journey across a European banquet table finds its counterpart in Spanish pieces of eight that rapidly circumnavigated the globe in the same era, depositing silver coins wherever ships landed. Their purchasing power – far more than Chinese bronze coins and paper currency, the Florentine florin, the Venetian ducat, or the Ottoman *akçe* – sent porcelain, lacquer ware, silks, and other Asian commodities on equally long voyages to fulfill the demand for novel and exotic luxuries. Long after the mines had reached peak production and the Spanish empire was under strain, Potosí's wealth continued to serve as a seemingly perpetual medium of exchange.[5] Numerous examples of coins re-stamped in China, Indonesia, Europe, Great Britain, and eventually Australia transformed this token of the silver century into local currencies, a credit card for an earlier age.

The early modern era was a transformative moment, a world set in motion on a new and larger scale. To paraphrase Timothy Brook, it was 'an age of second contacts,' as a world defined by medieval trade routes and tentative encounters in the era of Columbus gave way to new connections with far more transformative consequences.[6] The early modern world was an expansive landscape of interconnected people and things whose relations were increasingly defined by long-distance trading ventures, overseas colonies, and dreams of empire. Envisioning this period through objects, we see the cultural hybridity of many things engendered at this particular moment. A sixteenth-century Mexican map of Tlaxcala painted on bark, records in Spanish and Nahuatl an intertwined world of peoples, places, and faiths. A Javanese shadow puppet depicts Bima, one of the great heroes of Hindu epic, for an Indonesian audience converted to Islam. Both artifacts testify to the new geography of religion in an age of commerce. An eighteenth-century map sketched on North American buckskin captures negotiations between Piankashaw Indians and British settlers regarding the disposition of territory between the Great Lakes and the Mississippi after the defeat of the French during the Seven Years' War. It is an artifact of the middle ground.[7] Each of these objects is a product of new relations among peoples expressed in their material culture.

Other early modern objects do not explicitly connect cultures but reinforce the particularities of local power, knowledge, and faith. The painted miniature of a Mughal prince in conversation with a Muslim holy man around 1610 elegantly portrays the virtues of a ruler guided by the wisdom of Allah in a predominantly Hindu world. A Leipzig broadsheet commemorates Luther's famous critique of the sale of papal indulgences that sparked the Protestant Reformation exactly one hundred years earlier, recreating a signal episode that has become part of the landscape of historical memory. The Iranian Shi'a brass standard (*'alam*) from around 1700, inscribed with the names of martyred imams, testifies to the power and purity of belief. It is an early modern artifact with a medieval genealogy that publicly proclaims the religion of an early modern state. Each of these things helps us to understand the divisions of this world as well as its points of contact.

Repeatedly we see how the same object can have dramatically different uses at each moment of its existence. The West African drum covered in North American deerskin, found in Virginia and acquired by the British Museum's founder Hans Sloane around 1730, has had multiple lives. This simple wood instrument evokes the ghostly specter of slaves forced to dance on the ships that carried them across the Atlantic and, later, slave music suppressed in the British colonies to prevent its subversion of a society whose prosperity depended on the subordination and objectification of other humans. This singular artifact bears witness to a wide range of human experience – capture and coercion, resistance and memory, curiosity and collection – and makes the history of this moment tangible and concrete. Like the bark shield left behind by fleeing aborigines in Botany Bay in 1770 and brought to London by Cook, it is an object virtually without words that nonetheless speaks volumes by inviting us to find its history.[8]

By contrast, the final artifact in the British Museum's history of the early modern world is literally covered with writing. It is an ancient jade ring dating to *c.*1200 BCE inscribed by the Qianlong emperor in 1790 when he declared it to be a stand for an ancient Ding bowl that he also inscribed to make the complementary and commemorative function of these two objects transparent. The words of a Manchurian emperor about his vision of Chinese antiquity *are* the early modern object.[9] As antiquarians have long known, remaking the past does indeed produce new things or, put a different way, a new use for an old artifact. Like Heidegger's proverbial earthenware jug, it turns out to be meaningless if we cannot grasp the void inside the vessel, the empty, protean space that may be the thing itself.[10] We can never see this Chinese artifact simply as an ancient *Bi*.

Theorizing early modern things

How do objects reveal their histories? What can we learn about the past by studying things? This volume explores the material culture of the early modern world with these questions in mind. It offers a rich and culturally diffuse set of examples for how to study the making, circulation, and consumption of things. The dynamic and mutable nature of things as well as their representations and meaning are also a central feature of this project. While primarily emphasizing historical approaches to material culture, *Early Modern Things* does not privilege any single perspective. It is not a methodological manifesto for how to study things in any specific sense but a historical sampler of what we can learn by writing the history *of* objects as well as histories *from* objects.[11]

The contributors to *Early Modern Things* invite readers to consider the benefits of social, economic, and cultural perspectives as well as insights from the history of science, technology, and medicine in understanding material culture. At the same time, they have participated in an experiment to be more explicit about the benefits of continuing to expand the range of the conversation by contributing to a volume that, with no claim to thematic, temporal, or geographic comprehensiveness, nonetheless brings together a series of chapters that reach from Tokugawa Japan, Ming China, Renaissance Italy, and Spanish Americas to the Ottoman empire, early modern Siberia, colonial North America, and Georgian England. We have engaged in this conversation in the belief that the history of material culture is one of the most productive areas in which to develop intersecting narratives of the past, some of them local and comparative, others cross-cultural, transnational, and global. This volume reflects the growing awareness of the importance of writing about early modern material culture in light of developments in different parts of the world. Without insisting that all histories must be global or cross-cultural, it takes up Peter Burke's call for productive comparisons by juxtaposing interesting case studies.[12]

Things multiply across time and space. Certain objects become visible because they are essential, necessary ingredients of daily life but hardly unique. Others emerge into view when they become objects of desire, only to recede to the point of invisibility as they become ordinary, unfashionable, even obsolete. Virtually every society vacillates between the euphoria of its materialism and episodes of introspective anxiety about the passion for stuff. Even materially impoverished societies nonetheless have complex relationships to things. Yet things need not be entirely concrete or material; even objects cannot be solely defined by their materiality. 'Isn't man the thing of a billion things?'[13] With this simple question, the eleventh-century philosopher Shao Yong invited his readers to calculate humanity as the sum of all other entities, the final thing at the end of a very long list.

This metaphysical definition of thing stands in marked contrast to Diderot's insistence in his *Encyclopédie* article on 'thing' (*chose*) that neither God nor man can be a thing. He opposed words to things, *res* and *verba*, declaring that a simulacra or apparition could not be a thing (neither his Chinese nor Japanese contemporaries would have agreed with him about the necessity of this division).[14] In developing his understanding of the meaning of things, Diderot expressed the eighteenth-century western idea of things as a series of binary opposites. Having grappled with the concept of thingness, Diderot subsequently considered the legal, economic, and religious criteria for classifying things. 'Things are corporeal or incorporeal, mobile or immobile; they belong to our patrimony or they are common and public; they are sacred or profane, fungible or irreplaceable, possible or impossible.' At the heart of Diderot's crisply articulated definition lay the tension between those things that were unique, immutable possessions and the realm of objects that were constantly used as a medium of exchange. 'Fungible things, *res fungibiles*,' he observed, 'are those that one can replace with others of the same species, like silver coin, grain, liquors, etc. They are opposed to those that one calls in law *non fungibiles* that one cannot replace with other similar things…like a house, a horse, etc.'[15] As historians and anthropologists have long observed, the vast majority of things are fungible. Nothing can be permanently removed from this category nor can anything be absolutely inalienable. Every object takes its place in a system of use and meaning in which value is constantly being renegotiated.

A great deal of what we know about early modern things is not found inside dictionaries and encyclopedias, however. These 'lavish lists,' to invoke Beth Berry's description of the early modern Japanese propensity for enumerating things, are an essential resource for understanding writing about things but they need to be measured against our knowledge of objects in practice as well as theory.[16] A wide range of documentation – surviving artifacts, representations of things that are themselves objects (paintings, drawings, engravings, inventories, wills, catalogues, advertisements), and inquiries into things (mercantile assessments of production, use, and value, artisanal how-to books, and learned books about objects) – allows us to reconstruct past material worlds, or what Chandra Mukerji has called 'patterns of materialism.'[17] Diaries, account books, travel and trade journals, guild and shop records provide us with other crucial ingredients to create a more dynamic account of the role of objects in lived experience: what people acquired, inherited, rented, sold, and exchanged; whether they cherished old things or craved new ones; and their first encounters with unfamiliar objects such as the 'things transformed in fire in a barbarian company' that the painter Li Rihua described in the early seventeenth century, observing the different properties of European-made glass.[18]

The early modern period was repeatedly defined and redefined by episodes in which different societies became familiar with each other's things. When Columbus and ninety sailors landed on Hispaniola on October 11, 1492 they carried barter goods that he described as 'things of small value,' hoping to lubricate the flow of the 'things of the Indies' into the Spanish treasury. Imagine their disappointment when all they received in return were 'other little things that it would be tiresome to write down' and not the fabled treasures of Cathay.[19] The quest for Asian commodities would continue to fuel overseas voyages for the next few centuries and ultimately stimulate the creation of an entirely new world of goods.

The Spaniards who unearthed the wealth of the Indies observed crucial differences between European and American attitudes towards possessions. They took note of Inca 'storage systems,' described by anthropologists and archeologists as essential to the pre-conquest American economy.[20] They recorded the Aztec New Fire Ceremony, an elaborate ritual of cosmic renewal that occurred every fifty-two years. In his *General History of the Things of New Spain* the sixteenth-century Franciscan ethnographer Bernardino de Sahagún captured the European response to the Aztec disposal of all their things by depicting this ceremony not as a moment of ritual cleansing but as an act of demonic possession. Who but the devil could compel someone to break and burn all the household goods, and even throw oneself at the fire? While certain strands of European Christianity, especially the teachings of the Franciscans, encouraged a simple life relatively devoid of material possessions, they nonetheless considered the collective annihilation of material existence to be a disturbingly pagan ritual. The New World gifts that Hernan Cortés presented to Charles V became a cornucopia of glittering objects to amaze Dürer when he saw them in Brussels in August 1520 (Figure 0.2). Although the Habsburgs eventually melted most of them down, this was not about the negation of things but an acknowledgment of their pecuniary value.[21] They were indeed fungible.

Two centuries later, Robinson Crusoe's realization that money is really pretty 'stupid stuff' on a Caribbean island – more useless than the tobacco pipe in his pocket, or a pair of mismatched shoes that floated ashore without their

FIGURE 0.2 African slave wearing a Brazilian feathered skirt and holding an Aztec mosaic shield, possibly the one Cortès gave to Charles V in 1519

owners – became the canonical European example of the mutability of things. Once marooned, he discovers the value of artisanal tools, raw materials, and a copy of the Bible, and learns to make clay pots. In the company of a parrot, Defoe's adventurer realizes that a life profiting from slaves, sugar, and tobacco is actually worth very little in comparison to the world he has made from a ship's salvage and his native ingenuity. Robinson Crusoe's 'many things' of 1719 were removed from normal cycles of production, trade, profit, and consumption.[22] His mental inventory of a ship's cargo not only reflects his reassessment of the value of things but offers a pungent critique of the meaning they used to have. Had the mercer Defoe, whose business life revolved around the sale of early modern merchandise, actually taken a trans-Atlantic voyage, he might have been surprised to discover how valuable some of the seemingly less useful things in the ship's cargo could turn out to be in another world. British and Europeans in North America observed that Native Americans clamored for 'many Things that they wanted not before.'[23] The currency Robinson Crusoe found so useless was fast becoming a global medium of exchange. If Defoe's hero had been on an island in the China seas, he would have surely grasped the value of silver coins in seemingly remote locations.[24]

In 1719 Defoe invited his readers to gain critical perspective on the expanding world of early modern goods by displacing them. Yet, as Giovanni

BUCKLES and BUTTONS
I AM THE THING. DEM-ME.

FIGURE 0.3   An English macaroni who has become what he wears, 1777

Botero remarked after observing the acquisitive habits of late sixteenth-century Italians, the vast majority of his contemporaries remained 'admirers of our own things.'[25] This habit of taking pleasure and pride in material culture was not an exclusive trait of late Renaissance society, but found its expression in different genres of writing in praise of things throughout the early modern world. In late Ming China the learned Wen Zhenheng assembled a portrait of his society's material culture to ensure that its 'superfluous things' might not be forgotten. In eighteenth-century Japan encyclopedias of the *Dappled Fabric of Our Famous Things* educated schoolchildren in the virtues of domestic production and consumption.[26] At this same moment, cosmopolitan inhabitants of the Ottoman Empire struggled with the meaning of an age embodied by the tulip and the coffeehouse while insisting that neither of them truly defined who they were or what they valued.[27]

'Buckles and Buttons. I am the Thing,' declared an English macaroni caricatured in a 1777 engraving (Figure 0.3). The imaginary fop's taste for the latest luxuries so defines him that he has become the objects of his desire.[28] In retrospect, Diderot was wrong to proclaim that people were not things. The objectification of humanity occurred not only when people became commodities, as the trans-Atlantic slave trade infamously reveals, but also in the process by which people constructed identities through things.[29] Like animals, humans are both subjects and objects. So what in the end is a thing? We can only sympathize with the editor of the *Oxford English Dictionary* who, after offering myriad useful statements about this slippery word, finally threw up his hands and declared that *thing* was, more often than not, 'a vague definition for an object which it is difficult to denominate more exactly.'[30]

Finding history in objects

Things may be hard to define in any language, but they contain multiple histories. For the past few decades historians, anthropologists, and literary critics have joined forces with art historians, museum curators, and archeologists to make objects the subject of study. In the late 1970s cultural anthropologists began to rethink the status of goods and commodities as bearers of meaning and artifacts of exchange.[31] In this same era the material culture of everyday life also emerged as a centerpiece of a new kind of social history pioneered by leading members of the French Annales school, most notably Fernand Braudel who reconsidered earlier accounts of the origins of capitalism and the rise of conspicuous consumption offered by influential early twentieth-century economists and sociologists such as Thorsten Veblen, Max Weber, and Werner Sombart.[32]

Braudel's magisterial study of civilization and capitalism was the historian's response. His three volumes demonstrated the importance of capturing the ordinary fabric of daily experience – what the Tang dynasty poet Wu Tzu-mu, describing the seven necessities of life, called 'the things that people cannot do without every day' – through patient empirical research that allowed him to trace the history of the chair, the chest, the table, the knife, the fork, and many other essential artifacts and foodstuffs.[33] Braudel's research project assembled a vast quantity of information about the material culture of early modern Europeans that we are still sifting through. While no one today would subscribe to Braudel's overly teleological and simplistic understanding of the differences between the West and the Rest, as expressed through food, clothing, and furniture, his innovative work spawned a number of subsequent projects, including the sophisticated cultural history of material life practiced by more recent Annalistes such as Daniel Roche who combined a multiplicity of sources to map important changes in the possessions, habits, and desires of early modern Parisians.[34]

Braudel's research emphasized the importance of a full-scale material reconstruction of daily life; subsequent work focused more explicitly on questions of demand, taste, and the market. By the late 1980s consumption had become a key word in the early modern cultural historian's vocabulary. John Brewer's influential volumes outlined a history of consumption that, while situating developments in eighteenth-century England in a broader European context, largely reinforced the understanding that England had a special role in giving birth to a modern consumer society on the eve of the Industrial

Revolution.[35] His projects generated a cornucopia of information about the expanding world of commercial goods, luxuries, and collectibles in the capital cities and prosperous towns of England and Europe, while also making visible new methodologies such as the use of probate inventories to explore the material culture of the middling classes, the new social history of art, literary materialism, and the courtly fascination with rare and exotic things. Historians and art historians working on the eighteenth century have also played a central role in defining the 'sex of things' – gendered objects, either in the making, marketing, or use; gendered patterns of consumption and inheritance; and of course questions of fashion and taste.[36]

The visibility of Brewer's history of consumption made it the focal point of a lively debate about the birth of modern consumer society. Italian Renaissance historians and art historians and scholars of the Dutch Golden Age challenged French and British narratives of eighteenth-century commercial modernity, moving the origins of consumer culture backwards in time. In this same period Simon Schama's ingenious use of images with texts created an enduring portrait of the 'embarrassment of riches' of the Dutch Golden Age. Subsequent work offered a more nuanced reading of Dutch still lifes and prints and the moralizing themes of Dutch society, but the virtuous prosperity of the seventeenth-century Netherlands continues to embody what Jan de Vries aptly calls the age of 'new luxury' – a moment when purchasing power created a demand for new household goods that commerce and long-distance trade fulfilled by filling the warehouses of the Dutch East India Company with the world's commodities.[37] A considerable body of research has confirmed that the early modern Dutch burghers were a new and different kind of consumer.

If Amsterdam embodied the Dutch cornucopia of global things – in 1631 Descartes described the city as 'an inventory of the possible' where the world's curiosities and commodities converged[38] – late medieval and Renaissance cities such as Genoa, Florence, and Venice defined the apogee of 'old luxury' for the preceding age in western Europe. In the same period in which Brewer and Schama debated the relative modernity of the English and the Dutch, Richard Goldthwaite artfully deployed the methodologies of social, economic, and cultural history to create a new image of the Italian Renaissance as an 'empire of things.'[39] He rightfully insisted on the role of cities in creating a dynamic world of artisans, patrons, consumers, markets, and commodities that gave the Italian peninsula its distinctive and precocious material culture. It was only a matter of time before Renaissance Studies produced a worthy counterpart to Schama's project. In the mid-1990s Lisa Jardine's interpretation of the Renaissance as an age of 'worldly goods' combined the insights of social and cultural history with the approach of new historicism, portraying the age of the Renaissance as a pan-European orgy of wealth, power, and conspicuous consumption.[40] Jardine's Renaissance not only led Dürer to draw the Indian elephant and gawk at Aztec treasure, but also travel to Venice to see how well regarded the things he made were in a society that celebrated its most successful artists, artisans, and patrons. It was a world of fabulous artifacts made for powerful and wealthy patrons.

As Samuel Cohn recently observed, the emphasis on exceptional things runs the risk of creating a static and relatively undifferentiated portrait that reflects only a small segment of Renaissance society.[41] What can we know about the totality of a society from a singularly expensive and unique artifact in comparison with the information we glean sifting through hundreds, even thousands of documents recording the entrance and exit of myriad things in households? What does the bejeweled clock tell us that the broken chair does not reveal? Recent work on the 'material Renaissance' by Evelyn Welch, Marta Ajmar, Flora Dennis, and others has expanded the range of sources from which to reconstruct the history of consumption and the material life of the household.[42] It also has helped to erode barriers between curators who study history to understand objects in the museum, and historians who study objects to write about the past from things.[43] Cohn encourages art historians and cultural historians to pay greater attention to the work of economic historians on production, living standards, and most importantly patterns of consumption. His comments reflect new efforts to create a dialogue between several distinct and well-developed perspectives on material culture that can indeed be fruitfully combined to address a broader range of questions. Renata Ago's recent study of the meaning of objects in seventeenth-century Rome is an excellent demonstration of how to use wills, inventories, account books, and correspondence in relation to paintings and proscriptive literature to understand the system of things and the role of objects as a dynamic form of capital as well as tokens of identity in an early modern capital city.[44]

One of the primary goals of this volume is to invite readers to think about the insights gleaned from different methodologies and kinds of sources. In recent years historians have become far more conversant with the methodologies of art history in order to understand how to use objects as historical evidence with greater sophistication.[45] At the same time, art historians have expanded their understanding of the material culture of art to include a wider repertoire of objects. This development has not been without its methodological anxieties. Joseph Koerner once divided his fellow art historians into two categories: 'those who study what objects mean and those who study how objects are made.'[46] Over a decade later, the art historical literature on making things has grown considerably. There is an active dialogue underway between historians and art historians about the role of artistic representation in creating a vocabulary of things, not only in great works of painting and sculpture but also in more humble artifacts whose material production and decorative elements enrich our understanding of the meaning of things. As Mary Sheriff recently observed, 'the realms of commerce and art have never been distinct.'[47]

Historians are not regularly in conversation with literary scholars about how we approach the past, but we should pay closer attention to developments in literary materialism, especially as it pertains to the Renaissance and Early

Modern, because this has also become a rich and vibrant field of inquiry.[48] The 'new new historicism,' practiced most notably by scholars such as Margreta de Grazia, Peter Stallybrass, Ann Rosalind Jones, and Patricia Fumerton, has taken the object as a focal point for research since the mid-1990s. No longer content to forage in the Renaissance *Wunderkammer*, they have reclaimed the 'everyday' as an important subject. Clothing, food, pots, pans, pins, feathers, and other quotidian artifacts have now emerged from the archive of English Renaissance literature and theater.[49] This literary engagement with social history has begun to create common ground with the material history of Italian Renaissance art and the cultural history of artifacts.[50] As a result, the contours of Shakespeare's 'material London' have been made visible through a literary archeology of writing and performance to rival art historians' use of images and social historians' use of archives.[51] We need to understand better how to consider literary sources as a record of material culture that goes beyond the history of the book, or the occasional quotation deployed to illustrate how materialism became a literary preoccupation that might rehearse on stage the anxieties and passions invoked by a world of things.

The study of early modern material culture also needs to integrate the findings of historians of science, medicine, and technology about the role of objects in making knowledge. For over a decade, there has been growing interest in the material culture of knowledge and invention. Early work focused on questions of collecting and consumption, exploring subjects such as the collecting and display of natural objects, the role of artisanal virtuosity in the *Wunderkammer*, and the development of a commercial marketplace for nature, instruments, experiments, and medicines.[52] This approach has created fruitful intersections with both the history of art and economic history by exploring how nature and knowledge became important commodities in the era of the Scientific Revolution.

More recently, historians of science have become interested in the materiality of knowledge. How does the very nature of things shape scientific inquiry? How is it reflected in efforts to observe, describe, and represent? Lorraine Daston's fascinating interdisciplinary conversation between historians of science and art historians about 'things that talk' represents an important step in developing longstanding interest in the relations between science and art into a new approach to think more specifically about questions of embodiment.[53] An important strand of the history of science has taken up the history of objects as a dimension of the history of ideas. Interpreting nature is fundamentally a project about looking at things and deriving knowledge from them, or what the Chinese called *gewu* (the investigation of things), creating a venerable literature devoted to this subject that would eventually accommodate a new fascination with 'concrete things' by the end of the Ming era.[54] Neither nature nor the instruments with which we interpret it are universals. Mastering nature's infinite variations and calibrating instruments requires careful attention to the particularities of things. Trying to make the least visible parts of nature materialize before our eyes and seeing nature not only with an instrument but *like* an instrument were fundamental preoccupations of early modern science.

One of the most exciting new approaches to understanding early modern things has emerged from efforts to understand artisanal mentalities and practices. A series of projects by scholars such as Chandra Mukerji, Domenico Bertoloni Meli, Pamela Long, Lissa Roberts, Simon Schaffer, Dagmar Schäfer, and Pamela Smith have explored what it means to embed knowledge in artifacts.[55] How are things made? How is knowledge of their making conveyed to others? Such work has stimulated new research in what might be described as early modern 'materials science.' It not only emphasizes the importance of understanding the stuff from which things are made but also encourages a more hands-on investigation of things themselves, including the replication of recipes, techniques, and experiments from written guidelines for the making of things as well as more careful and sustained inspection of surviving artifacts. In many respects, historians now have a greater appreciation for the kind of object-based knowledge museum curators, restorers, and craftsmen possess as an essential component of understanding things. Writing history without artifacts misses this level of understanding of the thing itself. We are indeed fortunate whenever we can include an object in our analysis; in the vast majority of instances, words are all that remain of long-vanished artifacts. How then do we conjure up the thing itself?

The world in small things

The single most important new development in the history of early modern things concerns the geography of objects and its implications for seeing the history of material culture as an essential component of global history. Over a decade ago, the distinguished art historian Craig Clunas, whose work on the material culture of late Ming China has been so important to understanding Asian art, commodities, and culture, lamented the inability of most historians of Great Britain and western Europe to see beyond the confines of their subject. He rightfully observed that while research on early modern European consumption was highly sophisticated, its findings explained but a tiny corner of the world, venturing outwards only to the extent to which Europeans themselves traveled, conquered, and colonized.[56] Clunas' research on the Chinese appreciation for 'superfluous things' in the late Ming has offered an important and illuminating counter-narrative to efforts to locate the birth of modern consumer society in some western moment between the Renaissance and the Industrial Revolution.[57]

The 'material Renaissance,' the Dutch 'embarrassment of riches,' the French 'history of everyday things,' and the Anglo-American 'birth of a consumer society' continue to evolve in light of new research and methodologies but they do so in a much broader context in which materials from other societies – for instance, Ihara Saikaku's detailed literary account of *The Japanese Family Storehouse* (1688), a witty satire of the world of wealthy arrivistes, spending their fortune and filling the family storehouse to the brim with desirable goods[58] – play an important role in understanding patterns of early modern acquisition, display, and consumption. There is by now a considerable body of literature on the history of objects, their uses and their meaning in East Asia, and a growing interest in this subject for South Asia, making Chinese 'superfluous things' and the 'Japanese storehouse' essential categories for understanding the full range of early modern commerce, consumption, and collecting.[59] Equally important work has been done on colonial and revolutionary North America and colonial Latin America.[60] Contours of this history also have begun to emerge for the 'tulip age' of the Ottoman Empire and the age of ivory, pepper, gold, slaves, 'guinea cloth,' and a growing list of exchangeable commodities that reshaped material life in coastal African societies starting in the mid-fifteenth century.[61] In short, we are at a propitious moment in which to begin to take stock of the histories we are writing of and from early modern things.

Material culture is now a central preoccupation of scholars interested in global patterns of production, consumption, and commodification. Observing how things travel has spawned a considerable amount of research that combines the economic historians' attention to trade, investment, and profit with a curatorial attention to objects. There has been much greater attention to the degree to which different societies participated in the globalization of the early modern economy, with the case of Japan's trade restrictions in the 1630s being a well-cited instance of a policy that limited but by no means halted the influx of foreign goods, since the lists of things people could buy and sell in coastal cities continued to grow, creating the image of the storehouse as a tangible sign of a new sort of prosperity.[62] Economic history has often struggled with how to measure desire, but the new histories of consumption in recent years have developed a productive approach to integrating cultural history into traditional economic analysis while insisting on the need to understand the constraints of trade – Jan de Vries famously summarized the cost of one pound of Asian commodities for every early modern European as an annual tribute of approximately 6000–7000 lives and circa 150 tons of silver – since desire and necessity, curiosity and commerce together created a converging world.[63] From such insights, it is now possible to write what Francesca Trivellato has called 'global history on a small scale,' a history that follows the movement of people and things through illuminating case studies of how economic practices, mentalities, and trading communities emerge.[64]

How should we write the history of the world in small things? In an important essay Robert Finlay reconstructs the decline of the late medieval 'ceramic route,' the exportation of approximately 73 million pieces of Chinese porcelain to Great Britain and western Europe between 1600 and 1800 along new trade routes, and the creation of the Royal Saxon Porcelain Manufactory in Meissen in 1709. In his analysis, porcelain is the harbinger of early modern globalization; it was an everyday item in late Ming China that subsequently became a hybrid global artifact. Produced and used in many different parts of

FIGURE 0.4 Seventeenth-century Chinese porcelain made for Mughal India decorated in imitation of Indian cotton patterns

the world, porcelain became the container of choice for coffee, tea, chocolate, and sugar (see Figure 0.4).[65] Seventeenth-century merchants transported so many Chinese ceramics and silks between Acapulco and Mexico City that this route became known as the 'China Road.' Thanks to the annual voyage of the Manila Galleon after 1571, there was more porcelain in New Spain than Spain. Even before Spanish ships made the first voyage from the Philippines to Mexico, there were more than 22,000 porcelain wares stockpiled in Manila.[66] They had been looking for new markets.

Porcelain became part of life's daily refinement in capital cities such as Istanbul, Paris, and London; it could be found even in seemingly remote locations far removed from the major porcelain trade routes. Wan Li porcelain cups have been unearthed near the Jamestown settlement in Virginia, leaving no doubt that the English settlers who crossed the Atlantic did so with a few Asian commodities packed in their chests. Thousands and thousands of pristine pieces have resurfaced in recent decades thanks to salvage operations of ships that sank on various routes between Europe and Asia.[67] In 1710 Defoe marveled at the 'china warehouses' setting up shop in London and subsequently fantasized about a house entirely made of porcelain when he sent Robinson Crusoe to China in his *Further Adventures*. Later in the eighteenth century, Benjamin

Franklin recalled the moment when porcelain first made its appearance in his home in the 1730s: 'being call'd one morning to breakfast, I found it in a China bowl, with a spoon of silver.'[68] His growing prosperity permitted the purchase of additional pieces, allowing his family to develop a taste for such things, as the Dutch had done a century before. Franklin embodied the process eloquently described by Maxine Berg that would lead Britain to create the new luxury goods of the late eighteenth century, capturing a market previously dominated by Eastern commodities and further entangling different parts of the world in a new system of commerce and consumption.[69]

The westward path of porcelain also marked the eastward flow of silver, one of the other truly significant commodities of the early modern period. As Kenneth Pomeranz reminds us, silver was not simply money but a western manufactured good that became the object of China's desire as Spain surpassed Japan as the source of its silver.[70] The Chinese preferred it in bars though they also traded goods for currency. It was the primary European export to China before the late eighteenth century, a commodity made primarily from Potosí's wealth, moved throughout the world along trading routes, deposited in different locations where Europeans used it to acquire other things, and then recycled within various local markets. When Spanish reals were in short supply, the Dutch began minting their own silver coins, starting in 1659. The Latin motto of the Dutch Republic, frequently embossed on their currency, seemed especially fitting for their new role connecting the world through trade: *concordia res parvae crescunt* (In harmony small things grow).[71] This phrase defined the peaceful confederation of Dutch provinces but, when stamped on a coin bound for the Dutch West Indies, it became a token of how small things generated large profits. If China was the graveyard of the world's silver, it is little wonder that inhabitants of Boston considered silver to be a rare and precious thing since so little of it migrated from Potosí to New England, unlike the flow of porcelain. The Caribbean became their Philippines, a mercenary trading zone where people and things converged.

While porcelain and silver have long enjoyed pride of place as especially hybrid objects, greater attention to the history of fabrics and fashions such as silks, brocades, furs, and especially cotton has expanded our understanding of how and why things traveled and what they became in the process. Calling cotton 'the first global commodity,' Giorgio Riello and Prasannan Parthasarathi put together a team of scholars to trace how an Indian fabric became a material staple in China, the Middle East, and Africa before making inroads into European, Japanese, and American markets in the eighteenth century.[72] In his work with Beverly Lemire, Riello has insisted on the importance of fashion as a window into global history that requires both economic and cultural analysis.[73] Their research does not attribute innovation solely to the European sector but instead describes how the desire for Indian cotton and growing appreciation of its methods of production stimulated a new industry and created new products. A mid-seventeenth century porcelain vase made for the Mughal

FIGURE 0.5 A seventeenth-century Florentine woman in a brocaded dress dyed red and blue

market effectively captures the importance of cotton in an age of porcelain by working patterns that imitate Indian printed cotton into its design (Figure 0.4). It is a talisman of the exchange of commodities between two different parts of the world.

Identifying the artifacts that circulated most widely through overlapping networks of global exchange has produced a significant body of research on commodities such as sugar, tobacco, cacao, tea, coffee, black pepper, cochineal, and fur.[74] Following the history of individual commodities is essential to understanding material culture, not only because their singularity lends itself to writing biographies of objects but also because through objects we can connect histories. Marta Ajmar-Wollheim and Luca Molà's analysis of Italian Renaissance brocaded fabric made of Asian silk and Syrian thread, colored with Asian or South American dye, fixed with Turkish or Italian alum, and finished with African gold thread beautifully illustrates the way in which early modern objects became global (Figure 0.5).[75] It needs to be juxtaposed to the kind of experiments in writing global economic history practiced by Timothy Brook for the seventeenth century and Maxine Berg and Giorgio Riello for the eighteenth century as well as recent work in the history of collecting that helps us to understand what Benjamin Schmidt calls 'the mobility of global icons.'[76] Representations of things also migrate. Retracing their itinerary helps us to understand the production of meaning that frequently has a separate life from the object in question. Describing an Aztec codex in a mid-seventeenth century cabinet of curiosities in Bologna that was repeatedly called a 'Book on China,' Daniela Bleichmar concludes that the first way to understand this curious artifact was to categorize it as a product of Oriental wisdom, eventually relabeled a 'Book on Mexico.'[77] The passage from Asia to America marked a shift in consciousness that was still unfolding, two centuries after Columbus' quest for the East. In this respect, connections are not only tangible reminders of human contact but also intellectual presuppositions about objects as a reflection of how the world ought to be rather than what it is.

In this volume some of the canonically exotic objects of early modern commerce – chocolate, tea, porcelain, and their representations in Dutch still lifes – find their place next to objects that have not enjoyed the same level of attention. New World birds, Japanese weapons and tea bowls, Chinese ginseng, a French recipe book, Ottoman clothing, Tuscan shoes and glassware, Russian rhubarb, Boston shillings, Anatolian timber, Egyptian grain, and Georgian furniture for men and women complete the panoply of things we have assembled in our own version of the British Museum's virtual cabinet of the early modern. This work emerges from several generations of interdisciplinary scholarship on early modern things and is highly indebted to the literature discussed in this introduction as well as in individual essays. While exploring the state of the conversation in general, including the diversity of methodologies now deployed to study material culture, it also brings together recent work that has largely been the product of parallel conversations. In all instances, the goal is to make the history of early modern things more explicitly the protagonist of the story and to observe the early modern world from this perspective.

Giorgio Riello recently has argued that by 'connecting objects and narratives' it is possible to write a new history of the early modern.[78] This volume is one step towards a more deliberate conversation about what that history might reveal and how it might lead us to redefine certain aspects of the early modern world where Africans dressed in Chinese silk and adorned themselves with Venetian glass beads, where Japanese drank from Chinese porcelain and reinvented European firearms, and where Chinese first encountered the American turkey and planted New World sunflowers, maize, sweet potatoes, and tomatoes while successfully monopolizing the Indonesian tortoiseshell trade to the consternation of the Dutch.[79] The early modern era was also a world in which the Ottomans wore Indian cotton and English broadcloth and sipped coffee from Chinese porcelain, while Creole Spaniards filled their homes with Genoese pottery and seasoned their chocolate with Sri Lankan cinnamon, and the 'Baubles of Britain' that filled the corner cupboards of North American colonists became objects of loathing on the eve of revolution, producing a ritual sacrifice of goods worthy of the Aztec New Fire Ceremony that would indeed create a world born anew in this one corner of the globe.[80]

Notes

1 Neil MacGregor, *A History of the World in 100 Objects: From the Handaxe to the Credit Card* (New York: Viking Penguin, 2010).
2 Igor Kopytoff, 'The Cultural Biography of Things: Commoditization as Process,' in *The Social Life of Things: Commodities in Cultural Perspective*, ed. Arjun Appadurai (Cambridge: Cambridge University Press, 1986), 64–91.
3 Daniela Bleichmar and Peter C. Mancall, eds., *Collecting Across Cultures: Material Exchanges in the Early Modern Atlantic World* (Philadelphia, PA: University of Pennsylvania Press, 2011).
4 Claire Farago, 'On the Peripatetic Life of Objects in the Era of Globalization,' in *Cultural Contact and the Making of European Art since the Age of Exploration*, ed. Mary D. Sheriff (Chapel Hill, NC: University of North Carolina Press, 2010), 17–41.
5 Dennis O. Flynn, Arturo Giráldez, and Richard von Glahn, eds., *Global Connections and Monetary History, 1470–1800* (Aldershot: Ashgate, 2003).
6 Timothy Brook, *Vermeer's Hat: The Seventeenth Century and the Dawn of the Global World* (New York: Bloomsbury Press, 2008), 8.
7 Richard White, *The Middle Ground: Indians, Empires, and Republics in the Great Lakes Region, 1650–1815*, 2nd ed. (Cambridge: Cambridge University Press, 2011; 1991).
8 Lorraine Daston, ed., *Things That Talk: Object Lessons from Art and Science* (New York: Zone Books, 2004).
9 Craig Clunas, *Empire of Great Brightness: Visual and Material Culture of Ming China, 1368–1644* (Honolulu, HI: University of Hawai'i Press, 2007), 91.
10 Martin Heidegger, 'The Thing,' in idem, *Poetry, Language, Thought*, trans. Albert Hofstadter (New York: Harper Collins, 1971), 174–182; Bill Brown, 'Thing Theory,' *Critical Inquiry* 28 (2001): 1–16.
11 Giorgio Riello, 'Things That Shape History: Material Culture and Historical Narratives,' in *History and Material Culture*, ed. Karen Harvey (London: Routledge, 2009), 24–46, esp. 25–26; Steven D. Lubar and W. David Kingery, eds., *History from Things: Essays on Material Culture* (Washington DC: Smithsonian Institute Publications, 1993).
12 Peter Burke, '*Res et verba*: Conspicuous Consumption in the Early Modern World,' in *Consumption and the World of Goods*, ed. John Brewer and Roy Porter (London: Routledge, 1993), 148–161.
13 In Clunas, *Empire of Great Brightness*, 115; Daniel Roche, *A History of Everyday Things: The Birth of Consumption in France, 1600–1800*, trans. Brian Pearce (Cambridge: Cambridge University Press, 2000), 2.
14 See the discussion of *wu* (things or matter) in Clunas, *Superfluous Things: Material Culture and Social Status in Early Modern China* (Cambridge, MA: Polity Press, 1991); and the discussion of *koto* in Michael F. Marra, 'On Japanese Things and Words: An Answer to Heidegger's Question,' *Philosophy East and West* 54 (2004): 555–568.
15 Denis Diderot, 'Chose,' *Encyclopédie, ou dictionnaire raisonné des sciences, des arts et des métiers* (Paris, 1751–1772), 3:374–375.
16 Mary Elizabeth Berry, *Japan in Print: Information and Nation in the Early Modern Period* (Berkeley, CA: University of California Press, 2006), 163.
17 Chandra Mukerji, *From Graven Images: Patterns of Modern Materialism* (New York: Columbia University Press, 1983).
18 Clunas, *Empire of Great Brightness*, 80. See also Alan Macfarlane and Gerry Martin, *Glass: A World History* (Chicago, IL: University of Chicago Press, 2002).
19 In Marcy Norton, *Sacred Gifts, Profane Pleasures: A History of Tobacco and Chocolate in the Atlantic World* (Ithaca, NY: Cornell University Press, 2008), 95, 142. See also Paul Freedman, *Out of the East: Spices and the Medieval Imagination* (New Haven, CT: Yale University Press, 2008).
20 Terry Y. LeVine, ed., *Inka Storage Systems* (Norman, OK: University of Oklahoma Press, 1992).

21 Arnold J. Bauer, *Goods, Power, History: Latin America's Material Culture* (Cambridge: Cambridge University Press, 2001), 38; Carinna Johnson, 'Aztec Regalia and the Reformation of Display,' in *Collecting Across Cultures*, ed. Bleichmar and Mancall, 83.

22 Daniel Defoe, *Robinson Crusoe* (London: W. Taylor, 1719); Kenneth Pomeranz and Steven Topik, *The World that Trade Created: Society, Culture, and the World Economy, 1400 to the Present*, 2nd ed. (Armonk, NY: M. E. Sharpe, 2006), 158–160.

23 In Peter N. Stearns, *Consumerism in World History: The Global Transformation of Desire*, 2nd ed. (New York: Routledge, 2006; 2001), 41.

24 Richard von Glahn, *Fountain of Fortune: Money and Monetary Policy in China, 1000–1700* (Berkeley, CA: University of California Press, 1996).

25 Giovanni Botero, *Della ragion di stato* (1589), II.12, in Richard A. Goldthwaite, 'The Empire of Things: Consumer Demand in Renaissance Italy,' in *Patronage, Art, and Society in the Renaissance*, ed. F. W. Kent and Patricia Simon (Oxford: Clarendon Press, 1987), 173.

26 Clunas, *Superfluous Things*, 164; Berry, *Japan in Print*, 159.

27 Ariel Salzmann, 'The Age of Tulips: Confluence and Conflict in Early Modern Consumer Culture (1550–1730),' in *Consumption Studies and the History of the Ottoman Empire, 1550–1922*, ed. Donald Quataert (Albany, NY: State University of New York Press, 2000), 83–106; Dana Sadji, ed., *Ottoman Tulips, Ottoman Coffee: Leisure and Lifestyle in the Eighteenth Century* (London: Tauris Academic Studies, 2007); and Leslie Pierce, 'The Material World: Ideologies and Ordinary Things,' in *The Early Modern Ottomans*, ed. Virginia H. Aksan and Daniel Goffman (Cambridge: Cambridge University Press, 2007), 213–232.

28 Giorgio Riello discusses this image in *A Foot in the Past: Consumers, Producers and Footwear in the Long Eighteenth Century* (Oxford: Oxford University Press and the Pasold Research Foundation, 2006), 77.

29 Trevor Burnard, 'Collecting and Accounting: Representing Slaves as Commodities in Jamaica, 1674–1784,' in Bleichmar and Mancall, eds., *Collecting Across Cultures*, 177–191.

30 'Thing,' *Oxford English Dictionary*, 3291.

31 Mary Douglas and Barry Isherwood, *The World of Goods: Towards an Anthropology of Consumption* (Harmondsworth, UK: Penguin, 1978); Appadurai, ed., *The Social Life of Things*; Nicholas Thomas, *Entangled Objects: Exchange, Material Culture, and Colonialism in the Pacific* (Cambridge, MA: Harvard University Press, 1991); Daniel Miller, ed., *Material Culture: Why Some Things Matter* (Chicago, IL: University of Chicago Press, 1998); idem, ed., *Materiality* (Durham, NC: Duke University Press, 2005); and idem, *Stuff* (Cambridge: Polity, 2010).

32 Thorsten Veblen, *Theory of the Leisure Class: An Economic Study of Institutions*, ed. Martha Banta (Oxford: Oxford University Press, 2007; 1899); Max Weber, *The Protestant Ethic and the 'Spirit' of Capitalism and Other Writings*, trans. Peter Baehr and Gordon C. Wells (London: Penguin, 2002; German original, 1905); and Werner Sombart, *Luxury and Capitalism*, trans. W. R. Dittmar (Ann Arbor, MI: University of Michigan Press, 1967; German original, 1913). For an interesting critique of this early literature, see Mukerji's *From Graven Images*; Jan de Vries, 'Luxury and Calvinism/Luxury and Capitalism: Supply and Demand for Luxury Goods in the Seventeenth-Century Dutch Republic,' *Journal of the Walters Art Gallery* 57 (1999): 73–85; and Maxine Berg and Elizabeth Eger, eds., *Luxury in the Eighteenth Century: Debates, Desires, and Delectable Goods* (Basingstoke: Palgrave, 2002).

33 Fernand Braudel, *Civilization and Capitalism, 15th–18th Centuries*, trans. Siân Reynolds (New York: Harper & Row, 1979), 3 vols. Wu Tzu-mu is quoted in Stearns, *Consumerism in World History*, 8.

34 Daniel Roche, *The People of Paris: An Essay on Popular Culture in the 18th Century*, trans. Marie Evans with Gwynne Lewis (Leamington Spa: Berg, 1987); idem, *The Culture of Clothing: Dress and Fashion in the Ancien Régime*, trans. Jean Birrell (Cambridge: Cambridge University Press, 1994); and idem, *A History of Everyday Things*.

35 Brewer and Porter, eds., *Consumption*; John Brewer and Susan Staves, eds., *Early Modern Conceptions of Property* (London: Routledge, 1994); and Ann Bermingham and John Brewer, eds., *The Consumption of Culture, 1600–1800: Image, Object, Text* (London: Routledge, 1995). On England's consumer revolution, see Neil McKendrick, John Brewer, and J. H. Plumb, *The Birth of a Consumer Society: The Commercialization of Eighteenth-Century England* (Bloomington, IN: Indiana University Press, 1982); Lorna Weatherhill, *Consumer Behavior and Material Culture in Britain, 1660–1760* (London: Routledge, 1987); Maxine Berg, *Luxury and Pleasure in Eighteenth-Century Britain* (Oxford: Oxford University Press, 2005); and Amanda Vickery, *Behind Closed Doors: At Home in Georgian England* (New Haven, CT: Yale University Press, 2010). For a synthetic account of the European history of consumption, placed in a global context, see Stearns, *Consumerism in World History*.

36 Victoria de Grazia with Ellen Furlough, eds., *The Sex of Things: Gender and Consumption in Historical Perspective* (Berkeley, CA: University of California Press, 1996); David Kuchta, *The Three-Piece Suit and Modern Masculinity: England, 1550–1850* (Berkeley, CA: University of California Press, 2002); Renata Ago, *Gusto for Things: A History of Objects in Seventeenth-Century Rome*, trans. Bradford Bouley and Corey Tazzara with Paula Findlen (Chicago, IL: University of Chicago Press, 2013); Dena Goodman and Kathryn Norberg, eds., *Furnishing the Eighteenth Century: What Furniture Can Tell Us about the European and American Past* (London: Routledge, 2006); Vickery, *Behind Closed Doors*; and Maureen Daly Goggon and Beth Fowkes Tobin, eds., *Women and Things, 1750–1950: Gendered Material Strategies* (Farnham, Surrey: Ashgate, 2009).

37 Simon Schama, *The Embarrassment of Riches: An Interpretation of Dutch Culture in the Golden Age* (New York: Knopf, 1987). See also Anne Goldgar, *Tulipmania: Money, Honor, and Knowledge in the Dutch Golden Age* (Chicago, IL: University of Chicago Press, 2007); Julie Hochstrasser, *Still Life and Trade in the Dutch Golden Age* (London: Yale University Press, 2007); de Vries, 'Luxury and Calvinism,' and idem, *The Industrious Revolution: Consumer Behavior and the Household Economy, 1650 to the Present* (Cambridge: Cambridge University Press, 2008), esp. 1–184.

38 In Brook, *Vermeer's Hat*, 8.

39 Richard A. Goldthwaite, *The Building of Renaissance Florence: An Economic and Social History* (Baltimore, MD: Johns Hopkins University Press, 1981); idem, 'The Empire of Things'; and idem, *Wealth and the Demand for Art in Italy 1300–1600* (Baltimore, MD: Johns Hopkins University Press, 1993).

40 Lisa Jardine, *Worldly Goods: A New History of the Renaissance* (London: Macmillan, 1996).

41 Samuel Cohn, Jr., 'Renaissance Attachment to Things: Material Culture in Last Wills and Testaments,' *Economic History Review* (2011): 1–22. For an early example of the kind of project he suggests, see Duccio Balestracci, *The Renaissance in the Fields: Family Memoirs of a Fifteenth-Century Tuscan Peasant*, trans. Paolo Squatriti and Betsy Merideth (University Park, PA: The Pennsylvania State University Press, 1999).

42 Evelyn Welch, *Shopping in the Renaissance: Consumer Cultures in Italy 1400–1600* (Oxford: Oxford University Press, 2005); Marta Ajmar-Wollheim and Flora Dennis, eds., *At Home in Renaissance Italy* (London: Victoria & Albert Museum, 2006); and Michelle O'Malley and Welch, eds., *The Material Renaissance* (Manchester: Manchester University Press, 2007).

43 Laurel Thatcher Ulrich's *The Age of the Homespun: Objects and Stories in the Creation of American Myth* (New York: Knopf, 2001) is a fascinating experiment in what a historian can do with museum artifacts.

44 Ago, *Gusto for Things*.

45 For example, David Freedberg and Jan de Vries, eds., *Art in History, History in Art: Studies in Seventeenth-Century Dutch Culture* (Los Angeles, CA: The Getty Center, 1991); Pamela H. Smith and Paula Findlen, eds., *Merchants and Marvels: Commerce, Science, and Art in Early Modern Europe* (New York: Routledge, 2002); and Brook, *Vermeer's Hat*.

46 Joseph Leo Koerner, 'Factura,' 36 *Res* (1999): 5; James Elkins, *What Painting Is* (London: Routledge, 1999).

47 Mary D. Sheriff, 'Introduction: Cultural Contact and the Making of European Art, 1492–1930,' in *Cultural Contact*, ed. idem, 6.

48 While beyond the scope of this volume, Bill Brown's pioneering work on modern materialism has been central to understanding literary materialism; for example, *A Sense of Things: The Object Matter of American Literature* (Chicago, IL: University of Chicago Press, 2003).

49 Margreta de Grazia, Maureen Quilligan, and Peter Stallybrass, eds., *Subject and Object in Renaissance Culture* (Cambridge: Cambridge University Press, 1996); Ann Rosalind Jones and Stallybrass, *Renaissance Clothing and the Materials of Memory* (Cambridge: Cambridge University Press, 2000); and Patricia Fumerton and Simon Hunt, eds., *Renaissance Culture and the Everyday* (Philadelphia, PA: University of Pennsylvania Press, 1999). For an interesting reflection on this work, see Jonathan Gil Harris, 'The New New Historicism's *Wunderkammer* of Objects,' *European Journal of English Studies* 4 (2000): 111–123.

50 Tara Hamling and Catherine Richardson, eds., *Everyday Objects: Medieval and Early Modern Material Culture and Its Meanings* (Farnham, Surrey: Ashgate, 2010) combines elements of these different projects. See also Roberta J. M. Olson, Patricia L. Reilly, and Rupert Shepherd, eds., *The Biography of the Object in Late Medieval and Renaissance Italy* (Oxford: Blackwell, 2006).

51 Lena Orlin Cowen, ed., *Material London ca. 1600* (Philadelphia, PA: University of Pennsylvania Press, 2000). See also Linda Levy Peck, *Consuming Splendor: Society and Culture in Seventeenth-Century England* (Cambridge: Cambridge University Press, 2005).

52 See the articles by Roy Porter and Simon Schaffer in *Consumption and the World of Goods*, ed. Brewer and Porter, 58–81 and 489–526; Colin Jones, 'The Great Chain of Buying: Medical Advertisement, the Bourgeois Public, and the Origins of the French Revolution,' *American Historical Review* 101 (1996): 13–40; Smith and Findlen, eds., *Merchants and Marvels*; David Gentilcore, *Medical Charlatanism in Early Modern Italy* (Oxford: Oxford University Press, 2006); Mario Biagioli, *Galileo's Instruments of Credit* (Chicago, IL: University of Chicago Press, 2006); and Harold Cook, *Matters of Exchange: Commerce, Medicine, and Science in the Dutch Golden Age* (New Haven, CT: Yale University Press, 2007).

53 Daston, ed., *Things that Talk*. See also Matthew Jones, 'Descartes' Geometry as Spiritual Exercise,' *Critical Inquiry* 28(2001): 40–71; reprinted in Bill Brown, ed., *Things* (Chicago, IL: University of Chicago Press, 2004), 40–71.

54 See especially Carla Nappi, *The Monkey and the Inkpot: Natural History and Its Transformations in Early Modern China* (Cambridge, MA: Harvard University Press, 2009); and Dagmar Schäfer, *The Crafting of the 10,000 Things: Knowledge and Technology in Seventeenth-Century China* (Chicago, IL: University of Chicago Press, 2011). The phrase 'concrete things' is from Fang Yizhi's *Wuli xiao zhi* (Notes on the Principles of Things, 1631–1634) discussed by Schäfer.

55 Pamela H. Smith, *The Body of the Artisan: Art and Experience in the Scientific Revolution* (Chicago, IL: University of Chicago Press, 2004); Domenico Bertoloni Meli, *Thinking with Objects: The Transformation of Mechanics in the Seventeenth Century* (Baltimore, MD: Johns Hopkins University Press. 2006); Lissa L. Roberts, Simon Schaffer, and Peter Dear, eds., *The Mindful Hand: Inquiry and Invention from the Late Renaissance to Early Industrialisation* (Amsterdam: Edita, 2007); Smith and Benjamin Schmidt, eds., *Making Knowledge in Early Modern Europe: Practices, Objects, Texts, 1400–1800* (Chicago, IL: University of Chicago Press, 2008); Chandra Mukerji, *Impossible Engineering: Technology and Territoriality in the Canal du Midi* (Princeton, NJ: Princeton University Press, 2009); Pamela O. Long, *Artisan/Practitioners and the Rise of the New Sciences 1400–1600* (Corvallis, OR: Oregon State University Press, 2011); Schäfer,

The Crafting of the 10,000 Things; and Smith, Amy Meyers, and Harold Cook, eds., *Ways of Knowing: The Material Culture of Empirical Knowledge* (forthcoming).

56 Clunas, 'Modernity Global and Local: Consumption and the Rise of the West,' *American Historical Review* 104 (1999): 1497–1511.

57 Clunas, *Superfluous Things*. For a comparative approach, see S. A. M. Adshead, *Material Culture in Europe and China, 1400–1800: The Rise of Consumerism* (London: MacMillan, 1997); and Kenneth Pomeranz, *The Great Divergence: Europe, China, and the Making of the Modern World Economy* (Princeton, NJ: Princeton University Press, 2000).

58 Ihara Saikaku, *The Japanese Family Storehouse*, trans. G. W. Sargent (Cambridge: Cambridge University Press, 1959); Burke, '*Res et verba*,' 154; and Susan B. Hanley, *Everyday Things in Premodern Japan: The Hidden Legacy of Material Culture* (Berkeley, MD: University of California Press, 1997), esp. 45.

59 In addition to the work of Clunas, see Timothy Brook, *The Confusions of Pleasure: Commerce and Culture in Ming China* (Berkeley, MD: University of California Press, 1998); Lothar Ledderose, *Ten Thousand Things: Module and Mass Production in Chinese Art* (Princeton, NJ: Princeton University Press, 2000); Michael Marmé, *Suzkou: Where the Goods of All the Provinces Converge* (Stanford, CA: Stanford University Press, 2005); and Schäfer, *The Crafting of the 10,000 Things*. On Japan, see Hanley, *Everyday Things*; Morgan Pitelka, *Handmade Culture: Raku Potters, Patrons, and Tea Practitioners in Japan* (Honolulu, HI: University of Hawai'i Press, 2005); Berry, *Japan in Print*; and Fujita Kayoko, 'Japan Indianized: The Material Culture of Imported Textiles in Japan, 1550–1850,' in *The Spinning World: A Global History of Cotton Textiles, 1200–1850*, ed. Giorgio Riello and Prasannan Parthasarathi (Oxford: Oxford University Press and the Pasold Research Fund, 2009), 181–203. On South Asia, see Anthony Reid, *Southeast Asia in the Age of Commerce 1450–1680*, vol. 1: *The Lands Below the Winds* (New Haven, CT: Yale University Press, 1988); Eric Tagliacozzo and Wen-Chin Chang, eds., *Chinese Circulations: Capital, Commodities, and Networks in South Asia* (Durham, NC: Duke University Press, 2011); and more tangentially, Sanjay Subrahmaynam, *The Political Economy of Commerce: Southern India, 1500–1650* (Cambridge: Cambridge University Press, 1990).

60 On colonial and revolutionary British North America, see James Deetz, *In Small Things Forgotten: An Archeology of Early America*, rev. ed. (New York: Anchor Books, 1996; 1977); Bernard Bailyn, *The New England Merchants in the Seventeenth-Century* (Cambridge, MA: Harvard University Press, 1979); Thatcher Ulrich, *The Age of the Homespun*; and T. H. Breen, *The Marketplace of Revolution: How Consumer Politics Shaped American Independence* (Oxford: Oxford University Press, 2004). On colonial Latin America, see Alfred W. Crosby, *The Columbian Exchange: Biological and Cultural Consequences of 1492* (Westport, CT: Greenwood Press, 1972); Bauer, *Goods, Power, History*; Norton, *Sacred Gifts, Profane Pleasures*; Marta V. Vicente, *Clothing the Spanish Empire: Families and the Calico Trade in the Early Modern Atlantic* (New York: Palgrave Macmillan, 2007); and Elvira Vilches, *New World Gold: Cultural Anxiety and Monetary Disorder in Early Modern Spain* (Chicago, IL: University of Chicago Press, 2010).

61 On Africa, see James F. Searing, *West African Slavery and Atlantic Commerce: The Senegal River Valley, 1700–1860* (Cambridge: Cambridge University Press, 1993); Stanley B. Alpern, 'What Africans Got for Their Slaves: A Master List of European Trade Goods,' *History in Africa* 22 (1995): 5–43; John K. Thornton, *Africa and Africans in the Making of the Atlantic World, 1400–1800*, 2nd ed. (Cambridge: Cambridge University Press, 1998; 1992); Judith A. Carney, *Black Rice: The African Origins of Rice Cultivation in the Americas* (Cambridge, MA: Harvard University Press, 2001); Carney and Richard Nicholas Rosomoff, *In the Shadow of Slavery: Africa's Botanical Legacy in the Atlantic World* (Berkeley, CA: University of California Press, 2009); Collen E. Kriger, '"Guinea Cloth": Production and Consumption of Cotton Textiles in West Africa before and during the Atlantic Slave Trade,' in *The Spinning*

World, ed. Riello and Parthasarathi, 105–126. Recent work on Ottoman material culture is discussed in note 27.

62 Hanley, *Everyday Things*, 17.

63 Jan de Vries, 'Connecting Europe and Asia: A Quantitative Analysis of the Cape-route Trade, 1497–1795,' in *Global Connections*, ed. Flynn et al., 82.

64 Francesca Trivellato, *The Familiarity of Strangers: The Sephardi Diaspora, Livorno, and Cross-Cultural Trade in the Early Modern Period* (New Haven, CT: Yale University Press, 2009), 7–10. For an earlier literature, see Philip D. Curtin, *Cross-Cultural Trade in World History* (Cambridge: Cambridge University Press, 1984); and Pomeranz and Topik, *The World that Trade Created*.

65 Robert Finlay, 'The Pilgrim Art: The Culture of Porcelain in World History,' *Journal of World History* 9 (1998): 141–187.

66 Luke Clossey, 'Merchants, Migrants, Missionaries, and Globalisation in the Early-Modern Pacific,' *Journal of Global History* 1 (2006): 44; Robert Batchelor, 'On the Movement of Porcelains: Rethinking the Birth of Consumer Society as Interactions of Exchange Networks, 1600–1750,' in *Consuming Cultures, Global Perspectives: Historical Trajectories, Transnational Exchanges*, ed. John Brewer and Frank Trentmann (Oxford: Berg, 2006), 106.

67 Riello, 'Things That Shape History,' 34–35; Maxine Berg, 'In Pursuit of Luxury: Global History and British Consumer Goods in the Eighteenth Century,' *Past and Present* 182 (2004): 85; Brook, *Vermeer's Hat*, 59–77.

68 Batchelor, 'On the Movement of Porcelains,' 110; Daniel Defoe, *Further Adventures of Robinson Crusoe* (London: W. Taylor, 1719), ch. 14; Benjamin Franklin, *Autobiography*, in Breen, *Marketplace of Revolution*, 154.

69 Berg, 'In Pursuit of Luxury.'

70 Pomeranz, *The Great Divergence*, 160. See also Dennis O. Flynn and Arturo Giráldez, 'Born with a "Silver Spoon": The Origins of World Trade in 1571,' *Journal of World History* 6 (1995): 201–221; and Flynn and Giráldez, 'Cycles of Silver: Global Economic Unity through the Mid-Eighteenth Century,' *Journal of World History* 13 (2002): 391–427.

71 Brook, *Vermeer's Hat*, 160; Batchelor, 'On the Movement of Porcelains,' 108.

72 Riello and Parthasarathi, eds., *The Spinning World*, 2; Giorgio Riello and Tirthanker Roy, eds., *How India Clothed the World: The World of South Asian Textiles, 1500–1850* (Leiden: Brill, 2009).

73 Beverly Lemire and Giorgio Riello, 'East & West: Textiles and Fashion in Early Modern Europe,' *Journal of Social History* 41 (2008): 887–916. See also Berg, 'Asian Luxuries and the Making of the European Consumer Revolution,' in idem, *Luxury in the Eighteenth Century*, 228–244, among her many articles on this subject.

74 For example, see Sidney Mintz, *Sweetness and Power: The Place of Sugar in Modern History* (New York: Viking, 1985); Ralph S. Hattox, *Coffee and Coffeehouses: The Emergence of a Social Beverage in the Medieval Near East* (Seattle, WA: University of Washington Press, 1985); Wolfgang Schivelbusch, *Tastes of Paradise: A Social History of Spices, Stimulants, and Intoxicants*, trans. David Jacobson (New York: Pantheon, 1992); Piero Camporesi, *Exotic Brew: The Art of Living in the Enlightenment*, trans. Christopher Woodhall (Oxford: Polity Press, 1994); Amy Butler Greenfield, *A Perfect Red: Empire, Espionage, and the Quest for the Color of Desire* (New York: HarperCollins, 2005); Brian Cowan, *The Social Life of Coffee: The Emergence of the British Coffeehouse* (New Haven, CT: Yale University Press, 2005); Freedman, *Out of the East*; Norton, *Sacred Gifts, Profane Pleasures*.

75 Marta Ajmar-Wollheim and Luca Molà, 'The Global Renaissance: Cross-Cultural Objects in the Early Modern Period,' and Dana Liebsohn, 'Response,' in *Global Design History*, ed. Glenn Adamson, Giorgio Riello, and Sarah Teasley (London: Routledge, 2011), 11–20, 21–24. See also Lisa Jardine and Jerry Brotton, *Global Interests: Renaissance Art between East & West* (Ithaca, NY: Cornell University Press, 2000).

76 Brook, *Vermeer's Hat*; Berg, *Luxury and Pleasure*; Riello, 'Things That Shape History'; and Benjamin Schmidt, 'Collecting Global Icons: The Case of the Exotic Parasol,' in *Collecting Across Cultures*, ed. Bleichmar and Mancall, 53.
77 Bleichmar, 'Seeing the World in a Room: Looking at Exotica in Early Modern Collections,' in *Collecting Across Cultures*, ed. Bleichmar and Mancall, 15–30.
78 Riello, 'Things That Shape History,' 36.
79 On this last subject, see Heather Sutherland, 'A Sino-Indian Commodity Chain: The Trade in Tortoiseshell in the Late Seventeenth and Eighteenth Centuries,' in *Chinese Circulations*, ed. Tagliacozzo and Chang, 172–199.
80 In Breen, *The Marketplace of Revolution*, 28.

PART I

The ambiguity of things

1

SURFACE TENSION

Objectifying ginseng in Chinese early modernity

Carla Nappi

Object lessons: failing to do the history of a global commodity

One night during the reign of Emperor Wen of the Sui Dynasty (r. 581–604), a man walked out of his home to look for the baby he heard crying his backyard.[1] The man was soon joined by his family and neighbors as they all searched, in vain, for the wailing child that screamed through their Shangdang hometown.[2] Eventually they located the source of the crying: it was not an infant, but instead a small herb growing within a mile of the man's house. They dug a deep pit around the herb and pulled out a root shaped like a man, complete with arms and legs. The crying stopped, though the story continues to ring through the literature of Chinese *materia medica*.

The root dug up by the Shangdang man, known as *tujing* 土精 or 'essence of the earth,' has come to be identified with the more common name *renshen* 人參, popularly translated as 'ginseng.' Present in Chinese texts on *materia medica* (known collectively as *bencao* literature) from the earliest instantiations of the genre, ginseng became one of the most tightly regulated commodities in early modern China, Korea, and Japan, and an extraordinarily important commodity in the contemporary global drug market. Prized globally as a pharmaceutical, ginseng has inspired many attempts to understand the history of this 'traditional' medical drug.

The rise of commercialism, commodification, and connoisseurship in the late Ming (1368–1644) and early–mid Qing (1644–1911) has been widely treated in recent years, and the story of ginseng could be written as one of many object histories in this expanding literature of the material and visual culture of early modern China.[3] Early modern ginseng would consequently be a character in a kind of vegetable *bildungsroman*: the story would trace its development from a very local item of *materia medica* in northeast China, through its star turn as a North American supply of the drug was discovered after Jesuits and other European interlocutors wrote from China and the Royal Society published accounts of its seemingly magical qualities.[4] Finally, ginseng's story would close with its triumphant coming of age as it matured into a global commodity with a continuing history into today's pharmaceutical and consumable market.

Though I had begun this work thinking that I was going to tell such a story about ginseng as a commodity, about networks of exchange and the circulation of objects in global history, there was a problem: all of these ideas presuppose the existence of a stable entity, a coherent object that does the circulating. The main character may transform and morph over the course of its lifetime, but it remains recognizable on some level as the same individual we knew at the start of the story. However, when we attempt to trace ginseng through early modern history and its sources, it starts slipping through our grasp. Indeed, if we consider an object to be a recognizable entity that exists and persists across time and space, there was no trans-historical ginseng. What was there, then, if not a stable object that can be read back into early modernity and beyond?[5]

Early modernity in China was characterized by new modes of thinking about locality, new ways of observing, and new forms of translation. Taken together, these combined to form new ways of identifying objects, and thus new kinds of objects. Ginseng as we know it (an object with many varieties and names, a type of thing that can be sought and found in different localities) emerged in this period as a new kind of object.

This chapter is a history of the practices of identification (via location, observation, and translation) that created a new form of early modern objecthood from which ginseng emerged. It explores how what had previously been a collection of stories, images, names, and resemblances coalesced during early modernity into a coherent, individual whole. Whereas before the late sixteenth century there was an assemblage of names, images, and descriptions linked through statements of resemblance and comparison, by the eighteenth century we see an 'it' with varieties differentiated by locality and by comparison and observation of new, named parts of the object. This change was made possible through new modes of identification and a new system of standards and criteria, along with a shift from identification-through-resemblance to identification through new modes of observation geared toward judgments of quality.

The two main goals of this chapter are first, to introduce a case study that raises important issues surrounding the history and circulation of objects in early modern China; and second, to explore those broader issues as they speak to the larger field of object histories or studies of material culture. The turn to thinking about materiality in object histories, while productive and important, has obscured the need to understand and question the epistemic nature of the 'object' itself, considered not only as a physical thing but as an instantiation of a concept or a class of things. In telling a history of an object, we are always simultaneously creating and re-creating both that history and the object itself.

The problem, then, is one of the form of historical practice as well as the context of the historical narrative that such a practice seems to create. This story of the early modern objectification of ginseng is an invitation to think about the *instability* of objects, the lack of coherence of things, and what this might mean for the study of material culture in early modernity.

The modern 'ginseng' category subsumes and erases a vast set of names and objects and ideas and knowledge systems. In contemporary terms the descriptor is used to name any number of plant species, and in early modernity terms in Chinese, Jurchen, Mongolian, and Manchu texts were also used to describe several different kinds of plants. I've decided to use 'ginseng' here (when I don't use *renshen* or *shen* to indicate the specific language of some Chinese texts) *not* to imply that the entities described in this chapter can be unproblematically equated with modern objects and categories, but to give a name to the contemporary analytic object that emerges from the set of practices and enunciations outlined below. To put it another way, this paper is a kind of archaeology or genealogy of 'ginseng.'[6]

The early modern object

Scholarship on material culture reminds us that objects are physical things that exist in space. Less obvious is the fact that objects also exist in time: things are always in flux, and not just on the scale of centuries, but also in a moment. In his work on Shakespearean things, Jonathan Gil Harris emphasizes the 'diachronic dimensions of materiality,' describing materiality as a process, and things both *in* and *as* motion.[7] Harris and others have insisted that things always exist – to the extent that we may say they exist at all – in flux. Conceiving of things in this way, they might be described as parasites or quasi-objects,[8] as palimpsests,[9] as multiplicities or machines,[10] as turbulent fluids or unstable networks.[11] Arjun Appadurai has conceived of objects as 'things-in-motion,' possessed of lives and biographies that trace the transformations in their meaning and value.[12] Despite their flux, there are still ways to study the histories of such objects. Historians have attempted to do so under the rubrics of historical ontology[13] or 'applied metaphysics,'[14] focusing historico-philosophical attention not on some presumed solidity of an object, but rather on the coming into being and receding of the thing in historical time.

The trans-historical object does not exist. Even if there is a stable material entity that persists over time, its meaning, identity, and thing-ness change, sometimes dramatically, in different (historical, geographic, epistemic) contexts.[15] One way to understand this is to understand that the particular ways of being in motion, the particular types of practice that constitute objects, are specific to particular times and place. Each of the authors discussed above acknowledges, on some level, the importance of historically situating their particular studies. However, in thinking about objects, that historical specificity ends to take a back seat to the idea of flux and motion as constituting objects.

A history of objects is a history of practices: in writing the history of a thing, we essentially write a history of resemblances, of practices of identification and similitude, of objectification, of translation, of the forming and re-forming of objects in the context of different rationalities.[16] But these practices emerge in particular historical contexts. This chapter will show that there was a particular way of being in motion, and a new way that the particular forms of motion constituted new modes of objecthood, in China's early modernity. The early modern object was constituted, I will argue, by practices of identification characterized by new modes of location, observation, and translation.

Identification as location: locating early modernity

An abundant secondary literature treats the role of localities and local histories in early modern China.[17] Among the several types of 'place' that acted as coherent entities or identifying categories for the purposes of scientific and medical trade were linguistic communities; named states identified in Chinese texts; and named locations or location-terms that recurred as important textual categories of analysis, including several ways of describing 'foreign,' 'overseas,' or barbarian goods and peoples. Many of these latter location-terms operated as identifiers of places, peoples, and objects in texts about natural knowledge in the Ming and Qing.[18] Local identity was a crucial aspect of any description of *materia medica*, for example: place of origin was used to distinguish among varieties of a drug, to interpret its medicinal efficacy, and to determine its market value.

The nature of locality changed over the course of early modernity in China, and the practice of identification of natural objects through location transformed along with it. First, the surfaces of more types of bodies were mapped and used to identify entities – not just geographic bodies, but human and drug bodies as well. In addition, location was used to identify more places upon those bodies. The number of named localities in early modern texts about natural objects increased, both on the map of the empire and on the bodies of natural objects themselves, and as a result objects could exist in new and multiple localities. They also contained new spaces within themselves, and their boundaries and surfaces were defined more clearly, more firmly, and in more detail. As more drugs were cultivated, 'wildness' became a defining characteristic of natural objects (especially those regulated as commodities). Finally, more locations of all types were brought into relation with each other, and came to mutually define one another. Ginseng emerged as an early modern object in this context.

Surface

The surface of the earth became knowable in a new way through the early modern period. This has been documented in studies of the importance of mapping geographic and political space to Qing imperial expansion.[19] This conceptual move to a privileging of knowing, seeing, and identifying surface over depth extends to the literature of *renshen* (later translated as 'ginseng') in Chinese texts. As the spatial reach of *renshen* moved from a primarily vertically defined set of localities (defined in terms of depth) in the Ming to a more wide-ranging horizontal reach (defined in terms of extension across space) in Qing texts, the spatiality of *renshen* lore changed as well. Stories of deep-rooted crying *renshen* at the tops of mountains gave way to tales of wandering tigers protecting *renshen* supplies from the gatherers who roamed the Northeast and tried to spot the plant emerging from the ground's surface.[20] Folklore moved from a vertical dimensionality to a more horizontal one as the Qing expanded in the same direction and characterizations of botanical rootedness were replaced by concerns with herbal spread over surface terrain. A similar move out of the earth and across its surface can be noted in the change from pre-Qing textual characterizations of *renshen* that emphasized the anthropomorphism of its roots (the best kind resembled a man when it was in the earth) to a mid–late Qing focus on surface qualities of the plant and its root in evaluating its quality.

The surface of *renshen* itself also was mapped and identified in a new way, increasingly prioritizing surface-level characteristics in diagrams and verbal descriptions that characterized the object.[21] *Bencao* and other medical texts from the Ming and earlier typically described *renshen* in terms of extension in vertical space: its habitat in shady or shadowy areas, its presence being marked by clouds, the particular configuration of stalks and leaves and limbs popping out from its body. The highest grades of the drug were described as looking like a human body, and that was particularly manifest by the protrusion of limbs and a head from its central core. Emphasis was placed on the importance of digging to extract the buried drug from within the earth. In contrast, texts from the eighteenth century and later tend to (though this is not universal) start emphasizing more surface-level qualities: the wrinkle of the skin of the root, the number of rings or indentations on the surface, the shade of the markings on the body of the plant. In addition, diagrams of ginseng in late Ming and Qing *bencao* tend to emphasize surface detail more so than earlier representations of the drug, generally incorporating more hairs, markings, and protrusions evident on the outside of the object than earlier images had done (Figure 1.1).[22]

Multiplying localities

During the early modern period more named localities were identified upon drug bodies, paralleling a similar process upon geographic bodies on maps of the empire and beyond. This transformation was reflected in texts about natural objects and *materia medica*, and extended across the early modern period and well into the nineteenth century.

Ginseng (usually as *renshen*) had been an important item of trade and tribute throughout the Ming, and featured prominently in texts on *materia medica* and medical prescriptions.[23] It was also frequently commented upon in *bencao* texts. Through the Song, *bencao* texts and the medical records cited within them tended

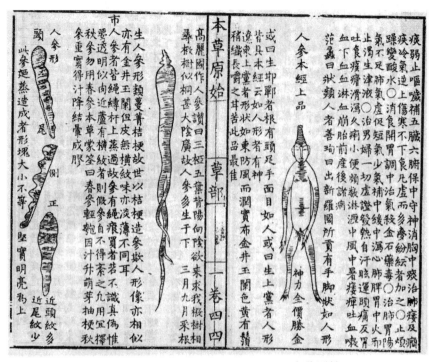

FIGURE 1.1   Image of ginseng from the Bencao yuanshi 本草原始

to locate the center of ginseng production (and the origin of the top quality of the drug) in the mountainous areas of Shangdang. The second most often-discussed area of production was Liaodong, in the area of the Northeast now known as Manchuria. Other localities associated with ginseng production included Handan (in what is known today as Hebei), Hedong, and mountainous regions including Mt. Taishan. A very famous variety of the plant praised by several Song *bencao* authors was *zituanshen* found on Mount Zituan (located in today's Luzhou, Sichuan), close *relatives* of which were found in other mountainous regions associated with the Taihang range. Several authors mentioned ginseng from areas now translated as 'Korea,' but they did not emphasize its importance or quality with respect to the material from the areas listed above.

A distinct change in the localities associated with top-quality and plentiful ginseng appears to have taken place by the late Ming, away from Shangdang and toward the Northeast. Justifications for the change vary: according to Li Shizhen, for example, local production in Shangdang stopped when area people began blaming ginseng harvesting for recent disasters in the area.[24] Another explanation for the shift has also been proposed. From the twelfth century on, Jurchen and Mongol medical practices had stimulated demand for ginseng by prolific prescription of the drug as an item of *materia medica*. This apparently led to the depletion of ginseng supply in Shangdang (the famous area of *renshen* production mentioned in the crying-baby anecdote that opened this paper) and other parts of China, precipitating an increase in demand for Jurchen ginseng and ultimately its establishment as one of three treasures of Manchuria, along with sable skins, and wu-la grasses used to make footwear.[25] Shifting geopolitical relationships from the Song to the Ming also undoubtedly played a role in the move to the Northeast as the reputed seat of optimal ginseng production: the region had been enemy territory outside Song control. With the Northeast under control of a Ming rulership with a capital in Beijing, locations therein (and thus potential localities of ginseng production) came under the ambit of Chinese textual practices. Whatever the explanation, the center of production and harvesting as reflected in late Ming *bencao* was focused in three localities on the Liaodong peninsula: Gaoli 高麗, Baiji 百濟, and Xinluo 新羅. These three terms were sometimes invoked independently in late Ming and early-mid Qing *bencao* texts to identify contemporary locations in Korea; were sometimes explicitly equated with Korea 朝鮮 or with the products sold in Ming and Qing markets after being brought by Korean traders; and were sometimes treated as a unit.[26]

The history of the plant changed dramatically with the rise of Manchu rule in China. The Ming court had stipulated ginseng as a tribute good from Choson Korea, and it was used as currency by Korean travelers to the Ming court.[27] In 1636 (after the second Manchu invasion of Korea), however, Taizong removed it from the list of tribute goods expected from Korea. The Qing didn't consider the root a local Korean product (*fangwu*); since the Ming couldn't access ginseng in the Northeast frontier region they considered it a Korean product, but the Manchus were used to the stuff growing in their homeland and it had contributed immensely to their rise in power.[28] Two recent scholars have argued that this drug was largely responsible for shifting the territorial boundaries of the Qing Empire in the Northeast: borders that were relatively porous in the Ming became marked and reinforced in the Qing, both shaping and in turn influenced by the ginseng trade.[29] Changbaishan, the sacred mountain on the border between China and Korea and the legendary birthplace of the Aisin Gioro family, was a particularly contested border area and space for ginseng gathering.[30] Ethnic identities were reinforced in Qing policy, as ginseng collection permits were selectively given out based on Manchu or Mongol identity, and Han collectors were barred from gathering and selling the valued trade item.[31]

Differentiation and identification of ginseng by the place in which it was collected was a central feature of Ming and Qing descriptions of the plant. Qing ginseng was graded, in part, on location of origin: Manchurian ginseng, especially from the Changbaishan area, was top quality; Korean material was next; Japanese material was considered less desirable (and fetched lower prices on the Qing market); and finally (as of the mid-eighteenth century), North American ginseng rounded out the list.[32] This represented a marked shift in identification of the location in which top-quality ginseng could be found.

Eighteenth-century discussions of ginseng characteristically included extended discussions of the geographical history and provenance of the drug(s). Texts devoted to *renshen*, including Huang Shucan's 黃叔燦 (1722–1806) *Shen pu* 參譜,[33] Lu Xuan's 陸烜 (fl. 1769) *Renshen pu* 人參譜, and Tang Bingjun's 唐秉均 (eighteenth century) *Renshen kao* 人參考 each provide focused attention to spaces famed for producing the drug. Together with Qing *bencao* accounts from the same period, they illustrate a very different spatial profile for ginseng. Zhao Xuemin's (1719–1805) *Bencao gangmu shiyi* (composed *c.*1800, published in 1871), for example, significantly extends earlier discussions of the plant. Zhao identifies (as separate, individual drugs) not only more parts of the plant than were typically prescribed in earlier *bencao* (including leaves, stalks, seeds, and small 'hairs'), but also includes separate entries for many locally defined *shen* varieties.[34] In an important move, Zhao typically refers to *renshen* from the Northeast as *Liaoshen* (Liaodong *renshen*), and differentiates it from the shen produced in Gaoli and Xinluo, which he describes alongside other 'foreign' (*yang* 洋) shen from Japan and France. Here, we have a reflection in Qing *bencao* of the kind of change described above: by the late eighteenth century, material from the contested Northeast territory was no longer considered by one of the terms we might today translate as 'Korean.' Once the Qing solidified its boundaries in the Northeast, place terms that were commonly used in Ming *bencao* alongside other locations within the empire (Gaoli, Baiji, Xinluo, Chaoyang) were now used to describe varieties of ginseng that were considered foreign (and of relatively lower quality), while *Liaoshen* (Liaodong *renshen*) was coined to identify local, top-quality Qing ginseng from the Northeast.[35]

The core of localities associated with ginseng in Ming and earlier texts was transformed and expanded, now including markers of place like Ningguta and Fenghuang (in today's Hunan), *min* 閩, Ao 奧, Yunnan, Dongchuan (a province in today's Yunnan), Luofu 羅浮 (a mountain in today's Guangdong), France, and Japan (including a discussion of Suzhou stores specializing in Japanese *renshen*), in addition to many others.[36] Local 'ginsengs' were increasingly being produced in the late seventeenth and early eighteenth centuries, as scholars attempted to identify local variants of the drug. Attempts to cultivate local ginseng varieties in Japan resulted in the creation and regulation (by pharmaceutical authorities) of a local Japanese product.[37] Jesuit missionaries stationed in Qing China were also interested in discovering new varieties of the drug. After Pierre Jartoux (1669–1720) found 'Tartars' gathering ginseng in the early eighteenth century while surveying Manchuria for the Kangxi court, he wrote a letter to the Procurator General of the Missions of India and China, touting the benefits of the drug (after having tried it himself), and speculating that a type of ginseng could probably be identified in Canada as well. It was.[38]

From Ming to Qing, locality entered drug descriptions in a new way. Many Ming *bencao* authors had used local provenance to identify, characterize, understand, and grade medical drugs and their varieties. Texts such as the *Bencao gangmu*, *Bencao mengquan*, and *Bencao yuanshi* often distinguished herbal drugs by place of origin. The *Bencao gangmu* by Li Shizhen (1518–1593) reflects a strong concern with mapping locality in time as well as space.[39] The ways in which locality was manifest in Qing *bencao*, in contrast, tended to differ from discussions in Ming texts. New genres focused on locality gained textual authority in the natural history canon, as Qing *bencao* relied much more heavily on gazetteers and travel accounts as credible sources of medical knowledge than was previously the case, including works on local *materia medica* in Tibetan, Manchu, Mongolian, and Uyghur scripts. In medical texts, identification and characterization became linked with locality in a new way in the late seventeenth and early eighteenth centuries. Texts included more types of locations associated with the drug, and these new spaces of ginseng – the plant, the human body, the garden, the empire, the borderlands – became crucial to its identification. Increasing number of local 'ginsengs' were sought, cultivated, and named.

Wildness

In mid-Qing texts, 'wildness' became a defining characteristic of natural objects. Eighteenth- and nineteenth-century texts began to distinguish wild ginseng from cultivated varieties, and to describe practices instituted to regulate ginseng production as a commodity. In general, wild ginseng was treated as vastly superior in quality to (and commanded a much higher price in the marketplace than) the cultivated drug. Still, enough enterprising farmers kept hidden ginseng gardens that the Qing law code outlawed ginseng gardening until the end of the nineteenth century.[40] This was apparently a particular problem in the area of Jilin, on the northeastern borderlands of the empire. Supplies of wild ginseng gathered in Jilin and sent to the Qing court were largely deemed unacceptable, and from the early nineteenth century local farmers attempted to recover their losses by hiding ginseng plants deep inside garden plots devoted to other crops and selling the resulting cultivated drug as a wild variety. In roughly 1879, supplies of wild Manchurian ginseng were so low, and the returns on wild ginseng from other areas were so inconsequential, that the Qing reversed their earlier policy and started encouraging cultivation of the plant in order to have enough supplies available from which to collect decent tax revenue.[41]

In sum, by the eighteenth century, a single object with varieties emerged from a collection of resemblances. Ginseng became 'Chinese' in European writings,[42] it became effectively 'foreign' or 'local' in Chinese texts, and other local varieties were named and regulated both within and outside of China. It could also be 'wild' or 'cultivated' (and was regulated as such). With an explosion of new varieties and features identified on the plant, more locations of all types were brought into relation with each other, and used to mutually define one another. Texts began arguing anew whether different names, images, and descriptions did indeed refer to a single object, and people who worked with and wrote about ginseng began to observe the object in new ways.

Identification as observation: observing early modernity

Observation practices changed in early modern China, and the practice of identifying objects through observation transformed along with it. This became manifest in the case of natural objects in at least two ways. First, the observation of an object increasingly entailed observing it within and in relation to a network of other objects. In addition, the trained observation of objects, especially of commodities, became a way to authenticate and characterize them, while (where possible) still keeping them intact.[43]

The earliest accounts of the names and images that early modern authors later identified as 'renshen' (and that later were subsumed under 'ginseng') defined types of the drug, and discussed its observable qualities, using levels of resemblance – to a human being, to other plants, to other drugs. The various materials described under the *renshen* rubric were fundamentally understood in relation to bodies and to other local varieties, and its medicinal effects described in terms of the effects of other simple drugs or forms of treatment. This way of conceptualizing *renshen* extended to the ways that it was observed, and the ways those observations were recorded.

In the late seventeenth and early eighteenth centuries, modes of observing ginseng shifted from merely observing likeness and resemblance to observing via a set of criteria used to characterize both the drug and the new network of objects associated with it. Ginseng consequently emerged as a new kind of object defined by a network of other various objects (paper certificates and inscriptions, texts, roots, skin, leaves, cauldrons, trees, maps, images, animals, people, recipes, names, boxes and packaging, gifts, grain) that were each meant to be observed (when gathering, preparing, buying, and selling) in a specific way. The collection of ginseng, for example, was to be undertaken in a prescribed way: when found, if a ginseng plant was too young for harvesting it was surrounded by a fence and watered. If it was deemed to be mature enough (discerned from visual evidence by the trained eye of collectors), bone or wood implements were used to carefully extract the root, and measurements of the plant's location were taken with respect to the ground and nearest tree.[44] In order to prepare the ginseng specimen for the next phase of its life as a gift, form of tax payment, or commodity, it went through a rigorous process of treatment that involved using specific implements to clean and process the root, watching carefully for evidence of changes in qualities like color, moisture, and surface imperfections caused by insects. Each step of this process involved special kettles, specific grains the root was to be steamed with, and a carefully dictated set of other objects that were to be used to make raw ginseng into a specimen suitable for use. It was then dried and packaged with similar care. Every step in the unearthing and production of this object was regulated and made possible by informed and trained observation.

The second change was in the types of observations made. Observers of ginseng were instructed to examine the size and form of the roots (slender and firm roots with rings, knobs, and a close-fine grain were most highly prized); whether the material was wild or cultivated (as discussed above, wild was considered vastly superior); the age of the root (it was not considered fully developed before six or seven years of growth); the season of gathering (late fall was best); and whether the material was worm-eaten or improperly dried or stored. As emphasis shifted to the new localities on the surface of the object, eighteenth-century texts tended to identify and describe more parts of the drug as well: leaves, skin, nodules, etc. There is no doubt that some of this training was a kind of folk knowledge, and that folk knowledge of some sort was involved in finding and preparing the root prior to early modernity in China. However, the observable criteria for deeming a specimen of ginseng suitable for use as a commodity within the empire and beyond, along with textual codification of this knowledge in written inscriptions, largely emerged in the Qing period. Identification became a form of trained observation practices that were regulated and textualized.

As of the eighteenth century, observation of ginseng was more dependent on visually discerning complex surface images, and less so on perceiving characteristics of the object through smell, taste, and sound. Whereas in Ming texts, you altered the material body of a drug and used your sensory apparatus to observe changes in its color, smell, sound, or texture in order to authenticate it, in Qing texts, authentication of drugs maintained the integrity of the object to a greater degree.[45] Highly valuable objects such as ginseng were treated as commodities that needed to remain intact.

As the processing and market for ginseng became much more tightly regulated, new standards and criteria for assessing the quality of ginseng emerged. Government assessors were trained to observe the object for evidence of quality based on processing, color, moisture, timing of collection, storage, and other markers of authentication. Thus, producers and sellers of the drug needed to train themselves to look at the root in this way as well if they wanted to make money from their wares. These criteria were codified through inscriptions that circulated through a tightly controlled market and administrative system. As ginseng moved more, it accreted inscriptions and other objects that moved with it.

In sum, there was a shift from identifying an object through narration-based resemblances to identifying it through notions of quality emphasized and created by new forms of inscription (maps, rules, permits, quotas). Through these new practices of observation, ginseng became an object, the integrity of which needed to be maintained (especially in the case of the higher-grade specimens used as commodities in gift and market networks). Trained observation allowed people to differentiate samples based on surface characteristics. The possibility of varieties of ginseng (discerned visually, even distinguishing between specimens from a single locality) in turn helped create the idea that these varieties were different instantiations of a single object.

Identification as translation: translating in early modernity

We have seen that two modes of identification, new attributions of locality and new kinds of observation, developed in the late seventeenth and early eighteenth centuries, and both helped to concretize ginseng as a new kind of object. In an increasingly multilingual empire with a ramifying bureaucracy devoted to translation, along with an increasing number of natural history texts translated from non-Chinese sources, translation was also an increasingly important mode of identifying and characterizing objects. As more objects entered Chinese texts from foreign languages, seventeenth- and eighteenth-century authors celebrated the coexistence of multiple names for an object. In this context, ginseng became a translated object.

Under the reigns of the Kangxi, Yongzheng, and Qianlong emperors, Qing landholdings doubled in size between 1660 and 1760. At its height, the Qing ultimately controlled an empire larger than the modern People's Republic of China and brought new peoples with new languages and ways of understanding the natural world into its borders.[46] As its imperial boundaries shifted, relationships of exchange shifted along with them, and translation became exceptionally important both as a strategic and administrative tool of the court, and to scholars who rendered texts (including natural history texts) into Chinese and Manchu. In these contexts, at least three important types of text were concerned with and reflective of the naming, identification, and equation of natural objects across spatial, temporal, and linguistic divides: dictionaries or glossaries, *bencao* texts, and monographic treatises (or *pulu*). All of these texts were not only concerned with 'translation' in a broad sense, but specifically with identifying and characterizing plant, animal, stone, and other material entities. The practices they used to identify and translate these entities took a number of forms, all of which were on some level concerned with practices of etymology or synonymy. In addition to reconciling Chinese lexicographical history with the terminology in official documents in many languages, translators compared stories, observations, and literary accounts in Chinese, Manchu, Mongolian, Tibetan, and Uyghur.

The Qing Empire was ruled by a Manchu-speaking, non-Chinese people, and many of its rulers both insisted on the use of the Manchu language in official court communications and celebrated multilingual rule. The phenomenon of Qing multilingualism has been addressed by historians of China in recent years, but its ramifications for the history of medicine are just beginning to be explored, and its significance for understanding transformations in natural history is largely unwritten.[47] As landholdings expanded through the seventeenth and eighteenth centuries, texts on the natural and medical resources of the Qing translated the names and knowledge of plants, animals, and stones from the borderlands into Chinese, Manchu, and other Qing languages.[48] Local gazetteers listed and described the products and customs of the areas coming under Qing rule. On the heels of a commercial publishing boom in the mid-sixteenth century, many printed editions of medical books and encyclopedias were available, and they often included lists of recipes and medical drugs available in the pharmacological marketplace.[49]

Many of the institutions that mediated and facilitated multilingual activities in the early Qing were modified forms of institutions that had predated Qing rule. A number of official organizations were set up in the Ming in an attempt to manage and control the translation and interpretation of official documents and foreign texts. At least one Interpreters' Station (*Huitong guan* 會同館) in the capital was charged with accommodating, entertaining, and keeping tabs on the movements of foreign envoys. A Translators' College (*Siyi guan* 四夷館), established in 1407 under the aegis of the Hanlin Academy, was responsible for translating foreign (*fan* 番) scripts and languages.[50] With the onset of Qing rule in 1644, the name of the Bureau of Translators was changed from *Siyi guan* 四夷館 to Siyi guan 四譯館 (with the *yi* changed to reflect a shift from 'Barbarian' to 'Translation'). The Qing moved the *Siyi guan* to a new building in 1653, and finally absorbed it into the *Huitong guan* to create a single *Huitong siyi guan* in 1748.

Dictionaries and glossaries

The *Siyi guan* and *Huitong guan* left a number of memorials, glossaries, and manuals that were concerned with identifying and naming early modern objects. The *Siyi guan* texts included accounts of raw materials and aromatics, plant and animal trade, culinary habits, and the general organization of people responsible for translating between *fan* states and China. These manuals were generally of two or three types: *zazi* 雜字 and *yiyu* 譯語 manuals were glossaries of important terms arranged by categories, while *laiwen* 來文 manuals were meant as guides for translating official memorials from foreign to Chinese script and vice versa.[51] The *laiwen* manuals include paired memorials in Chinese and other scripts recording the tribute of goods like jade, coral, metals, horses, daggers, and camels by envoys from these countries, in exchange for Chinese tea leaves, ceramic vessels, cloth, gold-flecked paper, and medicines.[52] The *zazi* and *yiyu* glossaries include lists of plant, animal, mineral, astronomical, and other terms of interest to Chinese translators, categorized according to major topics based on traditional Chinese lexicographical categories. The *Huitong guan* also left a series of glossaries, largely without foreign scripts and consisting solely of Chinese terms and transliterations of their foreign equivalents. These latter manuals, often named *yiyu*, covered different languages than those treated at the *Siyi guan* and were probably intended for oral communication.[53] They are similarly divided into topical categories.[54]

In addition to the manuals produced by official bureaus, the Qing also commissioned dictionaries from a wide range of other sources.[55] One of these, the [*Yuzhi*] *Wuti Qingwenjian* (often translated as the 'Qing Pentaglot'), appearing in 1708 and revised through the eighteenth century, included 18,671 entries rendered in Manchu, Mongolian, Tibetan, Uyghur, and Chinese script.[56] This dictionary included several extensive topical sections devoted to terminology for plants, animals, and other natural objects used as drugs and foodstuffs.

Interestingly, few accounts of *renshen* or other *shen* varieties are recorded in late Ming and early Qing polyglot dictionaries in any languages other than Jurchen, Manchu, and Mongolian. The only *Siyi guan* or *Huitong guan* manuals to record ginseng synonyms were the Mongolian-Chinese *Huayi yiyu*, a Mongolian manual of the *Siyi guan*, and a Jurchen glossary from the *Huitong guan*.[57] This relative lack actually tells us something interesting. Since the manuals were compiled from official court documents, including records of the items traded and offered in tribute, it seems clear that ginseng was not an item of trade or tribute by the peoples administered by the other states controlled by the bureaus. The relative silence on ginseng in glossaries thus speaks to another way of construing the importance of locality to ginseng textual history, confirming that early modern ginseng was identified with a very specific set of regional localities.[58]

By the Qing, in contrast, countless names were devised for ginseng varieties and instantiations, in Chinese as well as many of the other languages that were used in the period. The *Wuti Qingwenjian* was created for a different purpose than the manuals and records a very different range of ginseng names, including separate names for ginseng in addition to at least two additional surface features of the plant. In eighteenth-century texts, individual parts of the plant were increasingly differentiated by separate-but-related terms.[59]

In part thanks to lexicography and the efforts of translators, ginseng was translated into an early modern object. Dictionaries, however, were not the only early modern texts in which ginseng and other natural objects were reconstituted through identification as translation.

Materia medica *and monographic natural history texts*

Proper naming was a central goal of any naturalist. Confucius had urged students to study the *Shijing* to learn the names of plants and animals, and was famous for urging scholars to pay heed to the 'rectification of names' (*zhengming*).[60] Medical authors in the Ming and early Qing regularly used their prefaces to accuse earlier scholars of misnaming drugs, often using this accusation to justify the need for a new text. *Bencao* texts typically included discussions of alternate names for each of the drugs described in the text, often explaining their derivation or source. Scholars collected these names wherever they could find them: local dialects, oral vernacular and slang, and (increasingly as of the late Ming) a wide range of medical and non-medical texts, including foreign-language texts.[61] Qing pharmaceutical works increasingly incorporated materials from the borderlands of the empire, making greater use of gazetteers than earlier collections of *materia medica* had done and often emphasizing the importance of local variation in drug types, names, and usage.[62] Medical recipes worked as empires in microcosm, blending individual ingredients into compound wholes and reflecting a new medical cosmopolitanism.

The late Ming and early Qing also saw the flourishing of a genre of monographic texts devoted to individual natural and artificial objects. These *pulu*, often translated as 'treatises' or handbooks, covered a great deal of information on the history and use of whatever object they treated.[63] Several *pulu* were devoted to ginseng, and all of them contain some discussion of naming or treatment of alternate names. In both *bencao* and *pulu*, early modern treatments of *materia medica* tended to identify objects with an assemblage of synonyms.

While identification and synonymy were key concerns throughout the Ming and Qing, a significant shift in the way synonymy was constituted, and in the characteristics that were used to identify and name objects, emerged in late Ming and early Qing literature and lexicography. There was a shift in this period from a primarily historical and narrative-based etymology to a locality-based synonymy, or to naming and identification practices based largely on locality and local identities.

The treatment of names and multilingual descriptions of ginseng paralleled the development of observable characteristics of its body: similar to the way a plurality of visually distinguishable varieties created an epistemic whole (or type) of which they were parts, an individual 'ginseng' emerged from a plurality of synonyms. Ginseng became a composite object in early modernity: a collection of synonyms textually equated to each other.

Conclusion: disassembling the early modern object

This chapter has begun to trace the emergence of an early modern object (ginseng) from a network of practices and texts that were in some way concerned with identification. From its early turn as a subterranean being that mimicked a crying baby to its later existence as a tightly regulated global commodity, ginseng was at the same time ordinary and extraordinary, natural and supernatural, local and global. It epitomized the new ways of moving across time and space characterized by early modern objects in China. Natural objects were constituted through practices of identification, and ginseng was simultaneously created through new modes of location and observation and through translation out of a collection of synonyms. Changing notions of locality and local identity helped bring about new synonyms and identities for ginseng in the context of the Qing Empire. Ultimately, there was no single ginseng.

How early modern is this phenomenon, and how specific is it to ginseng? This is a preliminary investigation into one of potentially many similar early modern objects. Similar practices may have operated in forming other early modern objects, especially ones that functioned as highly regulated commodities, like tea.[64] Many of the practices described here were no doubt present before the Ming and Qing periods. It is their combination and degree that was particular to early modernity, and that led to the formation of new objects. The example of ginseng encourages us to supplement existing object histories with a history of practices and processes of identification and characterization, reconceptualizing what an object is, how it emerges, and what kind of access we have to it.

If we think of objects in general, and early modern objects in particular, as constantly in the process of coming into and out of being through epistemic, perceptual, and discursive practices, this replaces the notion of an object as singular with that of an object as always multiple. This construction raises several questions for the early modern historian. Whence the materiality of objects in this history of objectification? If there is no singular object, what does this do, if anything, to discourses about 'circulation' of objects in early modernity? (What is doing the circulating?)

In the end, this is not a history of ginseng as a stable object, but as a thing constantly in flux, in fact *produced by* that flux and meaningless outside of it. It is a history of the practices that bring into being, albeit momentarily, something that allows people to speak to and interact with each other, but it is also the beginning of a history of what it has meant in one early modern context to identify and characterize things.

Notes

1 A brief account of this story can be found in Li Shizhen, *Bencao gangmu, juan* 12 (*renshen.shiming*). There are a great many editions of the *Bencao gangmu* available, and citation to the text is most useful for readers when presented in terms of sections of the text rather than page numbers in any single edition. For this chapter I have consulted (and I recommend to interested readers) Li Shizhen, *Bencao gangmu*, ed. Liu Hengru and Liu Shanyong (Beijing: Huaxia chubanshe, 2002), 2 vols. For a detailed study of Li's text, see Carla Nappi, *The Monkey and the Inkpot: Natural History and its Transformations in Early Modern China* (Cambridge, MA: Harvard University Press, 2009). Similarities between *renshen* and mandrake lore in global history have been noted by previous authors. See, for example, Berthold Laufer, 'La Mandragore,' *T'oung Pao* 18.1/2 (March–May 1917): 1–30; and John T. Appleby, 'Ginseng and the Royal Society,' *Notes and Records of the Royal Society of London* 37.2 (1983): 121–145 (esp. 124).
2 Shangdang is a town in southeastern Shanxi, a province bordering Inner Mongolia in northeastern China.
3 For examples of this flourishing field, see Craig Clunas, *Superfluous Things: Material Culture and Social Status in Early Modern China* (Honolulu, HI: University of Hawai'i Press, 2004); Timothy Brook, *The Confusions of Pleasure: Commerce and Culture in Ming China* (Berkeley, CA: University of California Press, 1998); and Jonathan Hay, *Sensuous Surfaces: The Decorative Object in Early Modern China* (Honolulu, HI: University of Hawai'i Press, 2010). On the rise of trade networks in the context of Ming maritime relations, see for example Angela Schottenhammer, ed., *The East Asian Mediterranean: Maritime Crossroads of Culture, Commerce and Human Migration* (Wiesbaden: Harrassowitz, 2008).
4 On the Royal Society's interest in ginseng, see Appleby, 'Ginseng and the Royal Society.'
5 The 'early modern' in China is itself a relatively new object. It has been located anywhere from the tenth through the nineteenth centuries: some locate Ming trade networks or Qing imperial expansion within a globalizing early modern world, while others cite Song commercialization as evidence of a dynastic early modern identity.

For the purpose of this chapter, 'early modernity' in Chinese history roughly covers the sixteenth through eighteenth centuries, or the late Ming through high Qing periods. For an excellent introduction to the debates on early modernity in China, see Lynn A. Struve, ed., *The Qing Formation in World-Historical Time* (Cambridge, MA: Harvard University Asia, 2004).

6 In thinking of this phenomenon as a history of practices, I've been inspired by Paul Veyne, 'Foucault Revolutionizes History,' in *Foucault and his Interlocutors*, ed. Arnold Davidson (Chicago, IL: University of Chicago Press, 1997), 146–182.

7 Jonathan Gil Harris, 'Shakespeare's Hair: Staging the Object of Material Culture,' *Shakespeare Quarterly* 52.4 (Winter 2001): 479–491, especially 483.

8 Michel Serres, *The Parasite* (Minneapolis, MN: University of Minnesota Press, 2007).

9 Jonathan Gil Harris, *Untimely Matter in the Time of Shakespeare* (Philadelphia, PA: University of Pennsylvania Press, 2009).

10 Gilles Deleuze and Félix Guattari, *A Thousand Plateaus: Capitalism and Schizophrenia*, trans. Brian Massumi (Minneapolis, MN: University of Minnesota Press, 1987).

11 Serres, *The Parasite*.

12 Arjun Appadurai, 'Introduction: Commodities and the Politics of Value,' in *The Social Life of Things: Commodities in Cultural Perspective*, ed. idem (Cambridge: Cambridge University Press, 1986), 3–63.

13 See especially Ian Hacking, *Historical Ontology* (Cambridge, MA: Harvard University Press, 2002); and Ursula Klein and Wolfgang Lefèvre, *Materials in Eighteenth-Century Science: A Historical Ontology* (Cambridge, MA: MIT Press, 2007).

14 Lorraine Daston, 'The Coming into Being of Scientific Objects,' in *Biographies of Scientific Objects*, ed. idem (Chicago, IL: University of Chicago Press, 2000), 1–14.

15 In his treatment of commodification as part of the life cycle of objects, Appadurai makes this point nicely.

16 Paul Rabinow, *Essays on the Anthropology of Reason* (Princeton, NJ: Princeton University Press, 1996), x.

17 Examples of this abundant and growing literature include Peter Bol, 'The Rise of Local History: History, Geography, and Culture in Southern Song and Yuan Wuzhou,' *Harvard Journal of Asiatic Studies* 61.1 (2001): 37–76; and idem, 'The "Localist Turn" and "Local Identity" in Later Imperial China,' *Late Imperial China* 24.2 (2003): 1–51. The importance of medical regionalism in particular has been recently treated in Marta Hanson, *Speaking of Epidemics in Chinese Medicine: Disease and the Geographic Imagination in Late Imperial China* (New York: Routledge, 2011). Ethnological studies of regional medical knowledge (or myths thereof) on the southwestern Chinese frontier include Norma Diamond, 'The Miao and Poison: Interactions on China's Southwest Frontier,' *Ethnology* 27.1 (1988): 1–25 (a spirited historical context for which can be found in H. Y. Feng and J. K. Shryock, 'The Black Magic in China Known as Ku,' *Journal of the American Oriental Society* 55.1 [1935]: 1–30). On local identities in Ming China, see also Leo Shin, *The Making of the Chinese State: Ethnicity and Expansion on the Ming Borderlands* (Cambridge: Cambridge University Press, 2006).

18 For a list of some general works of this type see Wolfgang Franke, *An Introduction to the Sources of Ming History* (London: Oxford University Press, 1968), 201–207.

19 For examples of this literature see Peter Perdue, *China Marches West: The Qing Conquest of Central Eurasia* (Cambridge, MA: Belknap Press of Harvard University Press, 2005); Laura Hostetler, *Qing Colonial Enterprise: Ethnography and Cartography in Early Modern China* (Chicago, IL: University of Chicago Press, 2001); and James Millward, '"Coming onto the Map": "Western Regions" Geography and Cartographic Nomenclature in the Making of Chinese Empire in Xinjiang,' *Late Imperial China* 20.2 (1999): 61–98.

20 For an account of these sorts of more horizontally defined stories, see V. K. Arseniev, *Dersu the Trapper* (Kingston, NY: McPherson, 1996). Van J. Symons draws heavily

from this text in his assessment of late-nineteenth and early-twentieth century ginseng gathering culture in Manchuria in Van J. Symons, 'The Ch'ing Ginseng Monopoly' (PhD diss., Brown University, 1974).

21 In relating built (or in this case, grown) structures to the architecture of the human body, I am building on the work of Gaston Bachelard, *Poetics of Space* (Boston, MA: Beacon Press, 1994), especially his treatment of nests and shells; and Juhani Pallasmaa, *The Eyes of the Skin* (Hoboken, NJ: John Wiley & Sons, 2005).

22 Of course exceptions can be found, but a survey of visual and textual images of *renshen* seems to indicate this general trend. One example of an attention to surface detail is found in the *Bencao yuanshi* 本草原始 (1612) by Li Zhongli 李中立 (*jinshi* 1595) (Figure 1.1). This text often mentions place of origin as one of the defining characteristics of *materia medica* and the images included are striking. Often bearing little resemblance to the depictions included in previous *bencao*, the images in the *Bencao yuanshi* frequently depict cross sections of plants and animal parts, and feature a high degree of interplay between text and image on its pages. For a brief description of the *Bencao yuanshi*, see Paul Unschuld, *Medicine in China: A History of Pharmaceutics* (Berkeley, CA: University of California Press, 1986): 248–249. After its initial publication it was later reprinted in a small, pocketbook edition (1754) and then with significant revisions in 1844. The copy that I've used is a reprint of a Wanli era edition, included in *Xuxiu Siku quanshu* (Shanghai: Shanghai guji chubanshe, 2002), vol. 992–993.

23 For a brief account of Ming *renshen* policy and trade, see Seonmin Kim, 'Borders and Crossings: Trade, Diplomacy and Ginseng between Qing China and Choson Korea' (PhD diss., Duke University, 2006), 41–47.

24 See Li, *Bencao gangmu, juan* 12 (*renshen.jijie*).

25 On the 'three treasures' of Manchuria, see Cong Peiyuan 丛佩远, *Dongbei sanbao jingji jianshi* 东北三宝经济简史 (Beijing: Nongye chubanshe, 1989). *Renshen* is treated on pp 1–174. See also Symons, 'The Ch'ing Ginseng Monopoly,' 14–21. Prior to the rise of the Qing, revenue from the Jurchen ginseng trade was a key factor in the rise of Jurchen power that ultimately made the establishment of Qing rule possible.

26 *Xinluo* is often translated as 'Silla' today, though care should be taken to understand the terms *Xinluo*, *Gaoli*, and *Baiji* in a late Ming and early-mid Qing *bencao* context as place markers and not as dynastic names. On 'Silla' ginseng in Chinese texts, including its presentation to Tang court as tribute, see Soyoung Suh, 'Korean Medicine between the Local and the Universal: 1600–1945' (PhD diss., UCLA, 2006), 39–42.

27 On Ming–Korean tributary relations, see Donald N. Clark, 'Sino-Korean Tributary Relations under the Ming,' in *The Cambridge History of China, Volume 8: The Ming Dynasty, 1368–1644, Part 2*, ed. Denis Twitchett and Frederick W. Mote (New York: Cambridge University Press, 1998), 272–300.

28 Kim, 'Borders and Crossings,' 73–74.

29 Kim, 'Borders and Crossings,' 93. This argument was also featured in Symons, 'The Ch'ing Ginseng Monopoly.'

30 Seonmin Kim, 'Ginseng and Border Trespassing Between Qing China and Choson Korea,' *Late Imperial China* 28.1 (2007): 37–38. On Jurchen and Qing *renshen* gathering in the Changbai area, see *Qing dai Dongbei shen wu* (Jilin wen shi chubanshe, 1991).

31 Prior to 1730, ginseng collection was largely managed by Manchu bannermen. After 1730, regulation of ginseng trade was primarily conducted by the Ministry of Finance. This particular attention to the ethnicity of ginseng gatherers is discussed in several works, including Kim, 'Ginseng and Border Trespassing,' 37–38.

32 On the emergence of a Canadian ginseng trade as a result of Jesuit investigations in northeast China, see Appleby, 'Ginseng and the Royal Society,' 136–140.

33 The edition I have dates from Renzong 13 (1808).

34 These include *nansha shen*, *fangfeng dang shen*, *shangdang shen*, *turen shen*, *jian shen*, *xiyang shen*, and *dongyang shen*, among others. The descriptions run for several pages. On the change of emphasis in Qing texts from Shangdang *renshen* from the Shanxi area to *renshen* from the Northeast, see Jiang Zhushan 蒋竹山, 'Qingdai de renshen shuxie yu fenlei fangshi de zhuanxiang 清代的人參書寫与分类方式的转向,' *Journal of Huazhong Normal University (Humanities and Social Sciences)* 47.2 (March 2008): 69–75. Jiang characterizes a shift from pre-Qing discussions of *renshen* as a curiosity of natural history to Qing emphasis on the drug as a commodity. That perceived shift might, however, be an artifact of the very different type of sources of evidence invoked in many Qing *bencao* when compared with Ming and earlier *bencao*.

35 In its extended discussion of local *renshen* production, Tang Bingjun's *Renshen kao* (see esp. 1–3) also invokes *Liaoshen* as a particularly good variety of the drug.

36 'France' in these texts may well have referred instead to North America, indicating ginseng variants from Quebec.

37 By the late eighteenth century, ginseng was an expensive and highly sought-after drug in Japan, and doctors worried about counterfeiting. On the regulation and effort to control the quality of ginseng, and on the relationship between Korean imports and locally produced ginseng in early modern Japan, see Guillaume Carré and Christian Lamouroux, 'Faux produits et marchandises contrefaites dans la Chine et le Japon prémodernes: réglementations, corps de métiers et contraintes éthiques,' *Extrême-Orient, Extrême-Occident* 32 (2010): 115–161.

38 An English translation of Jartoux's French letter (dated 12 April 1711) can be found in *The Travels of Several Learned Missioners of the Society of Jesus, into Divers Parts of the Archipelago, India, China, and America* (London: R. Gosling, 1714), 215–225. Symons, 'The Ch'ing Ginseng Monopoly,' 1 provides an account of early eighteenth-century writings by Jesuits Pierre Jartoux and Jean Baptiste Regis, whose account of their survey of Manchuria for Kangxi included descriptions of meeting 'Tartars' gathering ginseng for 'mandarins.' The first western-language account of ginseng was reportedly published in French in 1643, but perhaps the most famous such account was recorded in Jean-Baptiste Du Halde, *Description de la Chine* (1736). See also Appleby, 'Ginseng and the Royal Society.'

39 In this massive late Ming encyclopedia of the practice and natural history of *materia medica*, Li frequently invoked chronological lists of precursors, arranging accounts of medical drug history by publication date and (where previous *bencao* had not included accounts of materials, such as when discussing clothing and tools) explicitly historicizing local lore in some of the chapters of his work.

40 See Symons, 'The Ch'ing Ginseng Monopoly,' 110–118, including a brief account of Jilin *renshen* guilds.

41 By 1750, returns on *renshen* and animal trapping in Mongolia were so inconsequential that Mongol gatherers were instructed to focus on collecting bee honey instead. Symons discusses this ('The Ch'ing Ginseng Monopoly,' 28), but an extended treatment of these rules is also available in (and Symons largely bases his analysis on) the *Da Qing Huidian*.

42 See Appleby, 'Ginseng and the Royal Society.'

43 On connoisseurship in early modern China, see Clunas, *Superfluous Things*. On the language of observation as applied to visual artifacts, see Craig Clunas, *Pictures and Visuality in Early Modern China* (Princeton, NJ: Princeton University Press, 1997), 111–133. On the language of observation as applied to pharmaceuticals, see Nappi, *The Monkey and the Inkpot*, 34–44.

44 Symons, 'The Ch'ing Ginseng Monopoly,' 53–58 provides a detailed treatment of this process and of the qualities used in grading Qing ginseng.

45 On changing objects to authenticate them in Ming drug literature, see Nappi, *The Monkey and the Inkpot*, 41–44.

46 See Hostetler, *Qing Colonial Enterprise*.

47   On Qing multilingualism see Pamela Kyle Crossely, 'Manchu Education,' in
     Education and Society in Late Imperial China, 1600–1900, ed. Benjamin A. Elman
     and Alexander Woodside (Berkeley, CA: University of California Press, 1994),
     340–378; and Evelyn S. Rawski, 'Qing Publishing in Non-Han Languages,' in
     Printing and Book Culture in Late Imperial China, ed. Cynthia Brokaw and Kai-
     wing Chow (Berkeley, CA: University of California Press, 2005), 304–331,
     and citations therein. On Manchu medical sources see Marta Hanson, 'On
     Manchu Medical Manuscripts and Blockprints: An Essay and Bibliographic
     Survey,' *Saksaha* 8 (2003): 1–32; and idem, 'The Significance of Manchu Medical
     Sources in the Qing,' in *Proceedings of the First North American Conference on Manchu
     Studies* (Portland, OR, May 9–10, 2003), ed. Stephen Wadley et.al. (Wiesbaden:
     Harrassowitz, 2006), 131–176.
48   A number of these texts in Tibetan and Manchu, with occasional texts in Uyghur
     and other scripts, have been reprinted in *Zhongguo bencao quanshu* (Beijing: Huaxia
     chubanshe, 1999), esp. vol. 395–398.
49   On publishing in the late Ming, see Lucille Chia, 'Of Three Mountains Street:
     The Commercial Publishers of Ming Nanjing,' in *Printing and Book Culture*, 107–
     151, esp. 135–136 on medical works; and Joseph McDermott, *A Social History
     of the Chinese Book: Books and Literati Culture in Late Imperial China* (Hong Kong:
     Hong Kong University Press, 2006), which treats the late Ming in each of its
     thematically organized chapters. On the wide distribution and circulation of daily-
     use encyclopedias in the late Ming, see Wei Shang, 'The Making of the Everyday
     World: Jin Ping Mei Cihua and Encyclopedias for Daily Use,' in *Dynastic Crisis and
     Cultural Innovation: From the Late Ming to the Late Qing and Beyond*, ed. Der-wei Wang
     and Wei Shang (Cambridge, MA: Harvard East Asian Monographs, 2005), 67–74.
50   1407 was also the year that Zheng He returned from his first voyage. There were
     initially eight bureaus of the Siyi guan: Mongol (*Dada* 韃靼), Jurchen (*Ruzhen* 女
     真), Muslim (*Huihui* 回回), Tibet (*Xifan* 西番), Uyghur (*Gaochang* 高昌), *Baiyi*
     百夷, Burma (*Miandian* 緬甸), and India (*Xitian* 西天). A *Babai* 八百 bureau was
     added in 1511, and a Siam (*Xianluo* 暹羅) bureau was added in 1578. The most
     complete treatment of these organizations in western languages can be found in F.
     Hirth, 'The Chinese Oriental College,' *Journal of the China Branch of the Royal Asiatic
     Society* New Series, 27 (1887): 203–219; Paul Pelliot, 'Le Hoja et le Sayyid Husain
     de l'histoire des Ming,' *T'oung Pao* Second Series 38.2/5 (1948): 81–292 (esp. 207–
     292); and Norman Wild, 'Materials for the Study of the Ssu I Kuan (Bureau of
     Translators),' *BSOAS* 11.3 (1945): 617–640.
51   The *yiyu* translation manual also includes a *Huihui* section, though it provides only
     Chinese transliterations for *Huihui* words, rather than Arabic or Persian script. For
     the *Huihui* material in Chinese transcription, see *Yiyu* 譯語, in *Beijing tushuguan guji
     zhenben congkan* 北京圖書館古籍珍本叢刊 (Beijing: Shumu wenxian chubanshe,
     1987), *Jing bu* 經部, vol. 6, 607–612. For a brief introduction to the *Yiyu*, see Hu
     Zhenhua 胡振华, 'Zhengui de huizu wenxian Huhuiguan yiyu 珍贵的回族文献
     《回回馆译语,' *Zhongyang minzu daxue xuebao* 中央民族大学学报 2 (1995): 87–
     90.
52   Several paired memorials (Chinese/Persian) are collected in *Huihui guan laiwen*.
     Among briefer accounts are more extensive memorials recording, for example,
     envoys asking for imperial blessing on a recently built mosque, and an envoy who
     had not eaten cooked food in several years, subsisting only on fruit and seeds,
     paying tribute.
53   The surviving *yiyu* glossaries include Japanese, Ryukyu, Tibetan, Korean,
     Vietnamese, Persian, Uyghur, Jurchen, and several southeast Asian languages.
     Some of these have been studied by scholars interested in linguistic reconstruction
     of past spoken dialects. See, for example, Daniel Kane, *The Sino-Jurchen Vocabulary
     of the Bureau of Interpreters* (Bloomington, IN: Indiana University Research Institute
     for Inner Asian Studies, 1989), esp. 90–98.

54 These dictionaries were often produced in stages over time, and by many hands. Each language in the manuals was written by a different individual, and the responsible scribes may never have known or come into physical contact with each other. Some were clearly copying from other texts, and seem not to have mastered the script they were writing.

55 On court patronage of translation and dictionary projects under the Kangxi, Yongzheng, and Qianlong emperors, see Rawski, 'Qing Publishing,' 305–306. For an excellent introduction to polylinguistic dictionaries in the Qing, see ibid., 314–317.

56 A three-volume, 1957 Beijing reproduction of a late eighteenth century manuscript edition is widely available in North American libraries. On this text and the other dictionaries to which it was related, see Pamela Kyle Crossley and Evelyn S. Rawski, 'A Profile of the Manchu Language in Ch'ing History,' *Harvard Journal of Asiatic Studies* 53.1 (1993): 83–87.

57 Specifically, these were the late Ming *Zengdang Hua Yi yiyu: Dada guan* (ostensibly from the *Siyi guan*), the late Ming *Hua Yi yiyu*, and the (likely early Qing) *Ruzhen guan yiyu* (a Jurchen-language transliteration manual ostensibly from the *Huitong guan*). The dating and provenance of these manuals is debated.

58 All three texts simply record equivalents for the term *renshen*, without specifying any further types of *shen* or parts of the plant. The Mongol manuals both include the Chinese term, a rendering in Mongol script, and a transliteration of the Mongol term into Chinese: *gu-wen-hu-er-ban-ha-er-a-li* 古溫忽兒班哈兒阿力. The Jurchen glossary includes simply the Chinese term and a Chinese transliteration of the Jurchen term: *O-r-ho-da* 斡兒火苔, or Orhoda, being orho (grass, or *cao* 草) + da (root, or *gen* 根). For the translation of this term see Kane, *Sino-Jurchen Vocabulary* (a study and translation of the same Jurchen manual that I discuss here), 210.

59 Further specification or identification of parts of other plants, especially grains and aromatics, was relatively common in these texts.

60 On naming in early Chinese thought, see John Makeham, *Name and Actuality in Early Chinese Thought* (Albany, NY: SUNY Press, 1994). On naming in Chinese thought and history see the articles in *Extrême-Orient, Extrême-Occident* 15: *Le Just Nom* (1993), and Christoph Harbsmeier, *Science and Civilisation in China, Volume 7.1: Language and Logic* (Cambridge: Cambridge University Press, 1998), esp. 52–60 and 311–326.

61 The *Bencao gangmu*, for example, included discussions of names from Sanskrit, as well as local oral dialects.

62 For one example of this trend, see Zhao Xuemin (1719–1805), *Bencao gangmu shiyi* (Shanghai: Shanghai guji chubanshe, 1995).

63 For an extensive treatment of *pulu* literature, see Martina Siebert, *Pulu: 'Abhandlungen und Auflistungen' zu Materieller Kultur und Naturkunde im Traditionellen China* (Wiesbaden: Harrassowitz, 2006). *Pulu* topics included plants (the *Luoyang mudan ji* [Treatise on Luoyang tree peonies] by Ouyang Xiu, the *Zhupu* [Treatise on bamboo] by Dai Kaizhi); animals (The *Xiepu* [Crab treatise] by Fu Hong, the *Qin jing* [Bird classic] by Shi Kuang); implements (the *Mojing* [Ink classic] by Zhao Guanzhi, the *Xiangpu* [Treatise on incense] by Hong Chu); and foodstuffs (the *Chajing* [Tea classic] by Lu Yu), to name but a few examples. Many of these have been collected and published in modern collectanea.

64 The literature on early modern objects as commodities in Chinese history is young, vibrant, and growing. Recent studies on commodities such as gingko, rhubarb, tea, opium, and other materials include Kuang-chi Hung, 'Within the Lungs, the Stomach, and the Mind: Convergences and Divergences in Medical and Natural Histories of *Ginkgo biloba*' (unpublished talk presented at the Princeton Workshop on Medical Commodities in Early Modern East Asia, Princeton, New Jersey, February 11–12, 2012); Chang Che-Chia, 'Origins of a Misunderstanding: The Qianlong Emperor's Embargo on Rhubarb Exports to Russia, the Scenario and

its Consequences,' *Asian Medicine* 1.2 (2005): 335–354; Yangwen Zheng, *The Social Life of Opium in China* (Cambridge: Cambridge University Press, 2005); and Frank Dikötter et. al., *Narcotic Culture: A History of Drugs in China* (Chicago, IL: University of Chicago Press, 2004). My work tends to differ from these (excellent) studies by taking an approach that problematizes the methodology enabling a historian to identify a commodity in texts across time and space.

2

GOING TO THE BIRDS

Animals as things and beings in early modernity

Marcy Norton

Introduction

Let us compare a hawk trained for falconry and a chicken raised as poultry.[1] In early modern Europe people believed, approached, and celebrated the beingness of the hawk, its identity as a noble, collaborative predator. On the other hand, avian husbandry was organized around chickens as things (edible flesh, useful feathers) and as producers of things (eggs). Hunting and husbandry can be thought of as meta-structures, or what I term 'modes of interaction,' that emphasize respectively the beingness and thingness of animals. We find rather different circumstances in pre-Hispanic America, where there were practices and beliefs around animals in which thingness and beingness constituted one another. In Caribbean, Amazonian, and Mesoamerican societies, predation and adoption operated as modes of interaction that existed on a continuum of incorporation: one took on the attributes of a consumed animal, or one made it into a family and community member. The eagle's awesome ferocity and predatorial acumen manifested in its feathers; accordingly a human ritually outfitted in eagle feathers embodied these qualities. Baby parrots were taken from their nests and became adopted kin.

This is a micro-global history of avian–human relationships with two nested objectives. The first is to demonstrate how modes of interaction produce particular subjectivities; in other words, to identify and investigate the contexts in which humans relate to birds as vassals, foodstuff, marvels, sacred beings, kin, and, finally, pets. The second is to explore how the entanglement of the cultures of Native America and Europe, inaugurated by Columbus' arrival in the Americas, mutually affected European and Amerindian modes of interaction. In particular, this chapter will focus on the transmission of Amerindian featherworks and parrots into Europe.[2]

This chapter develops and builds as a key concept 'modes of interaction,' meta-structures that organize how people relate to and think about animals. These modes are comprised of entrenched customs, patterns of behavior, and institutions. These modes do a lot of work: among other things, they create categories of participants, produce knowledge, and structure relationships between and among different species of animals. In particular, they condition the kind of subjectivity ascribed to the different animal participants; as we will see, the subjectivity of the nameless chicken is very different from that of the cherished hawk. Ontologically, modes of interaction possess the determining power of other structures such as gender, so that they organize production and ideology but are also circumvented, defied, and transgressed.[3]

Birds in Europe

As modes of interaction, hunting and husbandry were the meta-structures that organized human–animal relationships in Europe over millennia. Elite hunting, defined as the chase and slaughter of prey, consisted of two main types: venery and falconry, the former with the assistance of horses and dogs, and the latter with the assistance of raptors (as well as dogs and horses in many cases). In husbandry, animals provided labor (for plowing fields, providing security, transporting goods and people, etc.), became materials (meat, hides, feathers, tallow), and interfered with production (the wolf who dined on a sheep, the cat who snared a chicken). Hunting was defined as a noble activity, serving as preparation and proxy for war, where husbandry was plebian, the direct involvement with laboring and livestock animals being only fit for the third estate. Despite varied political formations and ecological and social changes, these structures manifested fundamental continuity across time (the medieval and early modern periods) and commonalities across space (Western Europe).

Hunting

Falconry was a subset of elite hunting practices that spanned Eurasia for centuries.[4] Falconry likely originated in Mesopotamia several centuries BCE, arrived in Western Europe with the Celts or Goths via the Balkans, and began to flourish with the elite Muslim influence in the wake of the Crusades and the Christian *reconquista* of Muslim Iberia. Falconry, then and now, involves three stages. First, raptors were captured in the wild, either as 'nestlings' or young adults, often lured with prey such as a pigeon and then seized in nets. The captured birds belonged to an array of different species of falcons and hawks, and it was prestigious to have diverse kinds and numerous birds in one's mews. Particularly fashionable in the medieval and early modern period were birds procured from northernmost regions of Europe such as Norway and Ireland; the birds could be bought by agents or arrive as gifts.[5] Hawks were among the prized gifts that traveled among diplomatic channels throughout Eurasia. Second, after being caught, the birds had to become 'manned' (also called 'reclaimed' or *amansado*) or made comfortable and familiar with human company. To accomplish this, birds were deprived of sight by having their eyes temporarily sewn shut or covered by a hood, and over a period of time (often as long as a year), the birds were hand-fed, usually by one handler alone, so that what we now call 'pair-bonding' could take place between bird and human. Third, after being tamed, the raptors were trained to kill and retrieve live prey (many kinds of birds – among them partridges, pheasants, herons, storks, swans, cranes, and geese – but also small mammals[6]) and return to their handlers with their quarry. The professional falconers who tended to raptors were key staff in royal and noble households.[7]

The ideology of elite hunting in Europe insisted on two things: that it offered training for war, and that it was a noble leisure pursuit. It was distinguished from the hunting of commoners, pursued for ignoble purposes such as obtaining food (noble hunters would eat their prey, but that was not the *reason* that they hunted). In the words of the noble author of a Spanish hawking treatise, 'the exercise of war is nothing to the knight who is a practitioner of this hunt.'[8] Hunting in general and falconry in particular reflected and promoted the neo-feudal legitimacy of the aristocracy by naturalizing might as a legitimate source of power; the strong overpowering the weak is naturalized in hunting and so legitimated in war.

Hunting produced categories of participants: namely the lords (the chief hunters), the vassals, and the enemies. Vassals included humans (professional huntsmen, kennel keepers, hired falconers) and non-humans: the horses, dogs, and birds who collaborated in the pursuit, capture, and slaying of the prey. I term these animals 'vassals' because the language of the hunt figured them as faithful dependents, hierarchically below the human hunters (though not necessarily below the boys who cleaned the kennels and mews, etc.), and owing them obedience, but bound to them through mutual bonds of service. It is hard to overemphasize the prestige and value of animals who assisted in the hunt (Figure 2.1). Birds employed in falconry, and dogs and horses bred for hunting, enjoyed a status in many ways superior to humans of lower classes.[9] Like the other vassal animals, raptors were recipients of expensive diets, fine living quarters, and intensive training. It was advised that if one purchased one's raptor from a 'rustic,' one should be sure it was not being fed from the customary, inferior meat of peasants, which would hazard the hawk's health. This suggests that hawks in captivity consumed a more expensive diet than did human 'rustics.'[10]

Hunting ascribed a subjectivity of vassalage that encompassed the birds of prey employed in falconry. This subjectivity was produced by the emphasis on individuality, collaboration, and the merger between self and other that falconry produced. Falconers such as the seventeenth-century Simon Latham insisted on their birds' individuality:

FIGURE 2.1   Fra Angelico School, *Pope Clement V on horseback with a hawk on his fist, riding away from a female saint (the Holy Church)*, 1402–1455. This drawing illustrates how a hawk, as well as a horse, contributes to the dignity of the papal potentate and how the man and his animals blend their bodily space

> all Hawkes be not alike in their disposition, but are of contrary natures, and therefore will require great and diligent attendance, and skill to finde out their properties: and the same being perfectly knowne, you may order your Hawke accordingly.[11]

Latham not only took for granted that each hawk had her or his own character, but that it was the responsibility of the falconer to study his raptor, as the individual personality emerged only over time, not instantly on first sight.[12] In contemporary terms we might call this 'anthropomorphism,' but another way of understanding this is to see it (rightly or wrongly) as the attribution of fellow subject status to another being. The individuality of hawks was also recognized through naming practices; for instance the Castilian grandee Pedro López de Ayala, author of a fifteenth-century falconry treatise, mentioned a barbary falcon named Botafuego (Fireboot), who despite his diminutive size, was renowned for his ability to kill a crane without any assistance.[13]

Vassalage depended on and organized the mutual engagement of humans and animals, and hunting depended on the cooperation of non-human animals for success. Hunters fully recognized the agency of both their vassals and prey, underscored by the insistence that mutual affection was the foundation for animal–human collaboration. In English falconry manuals the language of love is most pronounced. According to Latham, the only way for

> those kind of wilde Creatures to be at his command and familiar with him, that by nature and kinde are altogether shye and fearfull of him, [is that] he must... draw and win them by his continuall loving and courteous behavior towards them, in his art and outwardly manner of dealing with them.[14]

Gervase Markham advised the falconer to approach taming his hawk in terms suggestive of lovers' attentions, describing the process as

> a continual carrying of them upon your fist, and by a most familiar stroaking and playing with them, with the Wing of a dead Foule or such like, and by gazing often and looking of them in the face, with a loving and gentle Countenance, and so making him acquainted with the man.[15]

To effect collaboration, communication between people and their vassal animals was critical. Latham explained that a successfully trained hawk will 'always and inwardly in her mind [be] attending and listening for your voice, and some other pleasing reward from you.'[16] He described the process of training a hawk to stay close when outside:

> walke with her to the young woods or groves... walking along from her into the winde, using your voice unto her softly... let it be especially with your tongue in whistling and chirping unto her; by which meanes to cause her to draw and follow after you with little noise.[17]

Finally, avian vassalage produced a very particular kind of merger between human and bird, the blending of bodily space (Figure 2.1). The process of taming a wild raptor depended on constant physical contact and touch, as well as food rewards and soothing vocals. Falconer Edmund Bert strongly believed that in the first day of reclaiming, as taming was known, a hawk should always be on the fist of a trainer – 'she should sit and walke all that day... either upon my fist or upon some man's else,' warning that even momentarily setting her 'downe upon a pearch but whilest I should change my Glove, she would be more impaired thereby then she would profit in tenne days travaile.'[18] During the entirety of taming period, he wrote, 'for the most part my fist is her perch,' even when eating, and he took care not 'to hasten to bed for love of my Hawke.' The end result was to 'make her love me as her perch.'[19] The purpose of having the hawk become a virtual appendage of the falconer during the 'reclaiming' process was to utterly habituate the bird to its human handler.

Yet, it seems likely that these practices had profound consequences for the human's psychological experience of the bird. Neuroscientists have proposed that the brain experiences 'peripersonal space' – the immediate space around the body – as part of the body; that 'through a special mapping procedure, your brain annexes this space to your limbs and body,' so that 'your self does not end where your flesh ends, but suffuses and blends with the world, including other beings,' such as one's lover, one's horse, or, the hawk perched on one's arm for hours on end.[20]

Husbandry

The birds and people brought into husbandry were assigned markedly different relationships than those produced by hunting. Where hunting was coded as elite, direct involvement in husbandry was fundamentally plebian – though with the important caveat that though nobility disdained and eschewed hands-on involvement in husbandry, they depended on its products for food, clothing, lighting, etc., and received income from it through tithes, taxes, and estates. The aristocrat performed his nobility by practicing falconry and the professional falconer raised his social standing through his service; conversely, raising chickens, or even killing avian 'pests,' was work for commoners.

Husbandry manuals – in particular the Spanish *Libro de agricultura* and the French *L'agriculture et maison rustique*, both of which appeared in multiple editions in the sixteenth and seventeenth centuries – provide a gateway into the underlying logic of this mode of interaction.[21] Husbandry produced four categories of participants. First, there were the human masters responsible for producing goods and services. While much of husbandry was gendered male, raising poultry was considered women's work across Western Europe. Gabriel Alonso de Herrera, in his *Libro de agricultura*, stated that 'for the most part there is hardly a woman who does not know how to raise chickens (as Palladius says),' invoking the fourth-century Roman author. He did qualify this statement with the observation that 'in some parts not women, but men, raise them,' such as in monasteries.[22] Jean Liebault, too, in *L'agriculture et la maison rustique*, asserted that the 'government of chickens…is the principal employment of the farm woman.'[23] Second was the category of servants, which included the human laborers (shepherds, farm hands), horses, mules, oxen, and dogs – and as will be seen, roosters and mothering hens – who provided labor for transportation, plowing, shepherding, protection, and reproduction, among other services. Third, livestock were those animals bred, raised, managed and killed for their products when dead and alive: namely, cows, sheep, pigs, and goats. In the avian domain, livestock were poultry: chickens, but also ducks, doves, and geese. Husbandry, as it pertained to birds, did not involve only domesticated fowl but also the capture and keeping of wild ducks and geese.[24] Fourth, vermin were the wolves who preyed on sheep and calves;

the foxes and snakes who consumed chicks; even the geese who grazed on the seed sown by farmers.[25] Birds thus appear not only as domesticated and tamed fowl in husbandry, but also as 'vermin' that pillaged fields.[26]

The different categories of animals produced by husbandry led to different kinds of subjectivities. Servants – human and animal – figured as subordinate subjects, while livestock and vermin were constituted more as objects. Where vassal animals were subjectified in hunting, poultry were 'objectified' in husbandry, viewed as collectives rather than individuals, as objects to be managed rather than subjects with whom to collaborate. Their beingness was neglected in favor of their thingness.

Poultry, the quintessential avian livestock, were constituted as objects through the processes of collectivization, management, and alienation.[27] The individuality of singular animals was effaced in husbandry through their organization into herds and flocks. Unlike the hawk deployed in falconry, chickens, geese, ducks, and other tamed and domesticated fowl were almost always viewed in the plurality. For livestock, the terminology suggests generic categories and interchangeability, not only of individuals of a species, but among species: for instance Alonso de Herrera treated ducks and geese together in one chapter and used 'gallina' generically to refer to a female of either of these species, as well as a chicken.[28] While falconry treatises referred to particular avian individuals and insisted on their unique personalities, no hen emerged as an individual in the pages of the husbandry manuals.[29] Hens were distinguished into subsets by color (Alonso de Herrera suggested that black and blonde ones were favored as egg-layers, and white ones were to be avoided for not 'fattening as much nor are they as flavorful' as well as for too easily attracting the unwanted attention of hawks; Liebault asserted that red ones were best).[30] In contrast to the way in which vassal animals were *engaged*, livestock were *managed*. Whether hens produced enough or the right size of eggs, whether they thrived and fattened well, how to choose breeders, when to breed them, and how to get them to lay eggs[31] – all this depended not on an active relationship between woman and bird but almost solely on the actions of the person (with a few exceptions discussed below). There is no sense of the chickens being 'loved' or 'taught' in the way that the hawks brought into falconry were.

If identification underpinned the ways that hunters related to vassal animals, alienation was a common principle in the way humans related to livestock in Western Europe. In alienation, the emphasis is on animals as products or producers of products. The logic of alienation construed creatures as vessels of disenchanted *things*. Cow bodies contained beef, candles, and leather; sheep bodies, mutton, milk, and yarn. In this way, the living animal – cow, sheep, pig, goat, chicken – was (is?) a living carcass (it is interesting to note that there are today computerized tomography scanners that 'analyze the "carcass quality" of live animals, so the best can be selected for breeding'[32]). Nowhere is this seen more clearly than in the preface of Edward Topsell's *The Fowles of Heauen;*

or History of Birdes (a partial translation of Ulisse Aldrovandi's *Ornithology* that remained unpublished until last century). Topsell wrote,

> without fowles we should lodge hard not having feathers in our beds, fare hard without many rare delicates, live sick without many singular remedies and parts of physicik, and many places would be eaten up or so annoyed with flies (especially our fens) that it were impossible for men to dwell in them.[33]

In his chapters concerning chickens and capons, Aldrovandi devoted ample space to how the birds were to be fed depending on the desired use of their carcasses. The principle of alienation underlay the recommended management of poultry in *Libro de agricultura* and *L'agriculture et la maison rustique* in order to ensure the best meat and eggs. The live chicken was regarded as a byway to producing 'flesh' of 'a particular taste.'[34] Feeding and fattening instructions pertained to how to deliver the best-producing flesh or the best egg-layers, as suggested by the chapter title of 'The sustenance that hens need to have in order to lay many eggs.'[35]

The skeptical reader might object that the view of poultry so far described emerges from elite records; might not the farm woman have seen her avian charges as individuals and feel affection for them? The answer is clearly 'yes,' and though so far I have not been able to find a farm woman's view of her poultry, Aldrovandi did reveal a special, mutual affinity between himself and a particular hen when discussing 'tame chickens so gentle and mild in nature that they cannot live without human companionship.' He recalled that

> A few years ago in my country home I raised a hen who, in addition to the fact that she wandered the whole day alone through the house without the company of other hens, would not go to sleep at night anywhere except near me among my books, and those the larger ones, although sometimes when she was driven away she wished to lie upon her back.[36]

In this reminiscence, we see that Aldrovandi developed a relationship with a chicken based on her individuality and mutual affection that belies the lack of subjectivity I've proposed for livestock. Yet this instance of a special man–chicken bond does not undermine the argument about livestock subjectivity. Rather, it reveals its limits. A prescribed subjectivity does not preclude relationships that thwart its contours, but these become exceptions rather than normative. Through this small window, we see the agency of both man and chicken thwarting the normative subjectivity for poultry. But the passage makes clear that the norm was for a hen to be part of a flock, in 'the company of other hens,' and not to be spending the night with a nobleman and his books (he made clear that 'she was driven away,' after all).

Servant animals

Not all of the animals brought into husbandry were livestock. A significant minority were servant animals. The servant class of animals in husbandry shared with the vassal class in hunting a subjectivity organized around their individuality, capacity for collaboration, and commonalities with people. Roosters, along with oxen and working dogs, exemplified the servant class of animal. In the many pages Alonso de Herrera devoted to poultry, birds appear as undifferentiated livestock – except when he touched on the subject of roosters. He explained the 'principal signs that make a rooster very good,' identifying

> much courtliness and generosity and for this reason there is the old adage, 'courtly like the rooster,' and for this it seems to me noteworthy that God put [him] in our homes before our eyes so that we can learn the way the rooster with one mouth calls in a loud voice and entertains such a multitude of chickens.[37]

In their roles as reproductive agents, the common subjectivity roosters shared with people was recognized. Similarly, a servant subjectivity organized around identification and collaboration emerged in the work of Liebault when he described the process by which a capon (a castrated rooster) could substitute for the biological mother after she hatched her chicks. According to him, this substitution not only would make the hen 'ready to hatch eggs' sooner, but would also ensure, due to the superior caretaking skills of the capon, that the chicks were 'best nourished and defended from hawks and other birds of prey.' He instructed his readers to choose a capon 'with the strongest and sharpest nettles.' The capon was then to be enclosed

> in the basket with the little ones, along with bread doused in wine, leaving them there sometime, until at last he *feels love for them such that even in liberty he will raise them, watch them, lead them and become more crazily in love with them than their own mother*.[38]

As with the reproductive role of the rooster, the maternal role of the capon highlights the shared investment in caretaking and affection for young shared by humans and birds alike.

Finally, it needs to be said that while distinct, the structures of hunting and husbandry were by no means wholly separate. The practices of hunting influenced the conduct of husbandry, and, in turn, the practices of husbandry shaped the development of hunting over generations. For instance, the process of training hawks in medieval and early modern Europe depended on an accessible and abundant supply of domesticated chickens and doves which were fed as food and rewards.[39] And cock-fighting was organized around domesticated roosters but imported many of the values of hunting (simulated war, contest, naming practices).[40]

Menageries

Hunting and husbandry were not the only modes that organized European people's interactions with birds, to be sure. But they predominated, and so influenced and conditioned other contexts. One such context was the menagerie. By definition menageries were rare; only those with great wealth and extraordinary diplomatic connections – popes, princes, Medici – were able to develop them, as they possessed the wherewithal to obtain and sustain cheetahs, leopards, and rhinos from overseas.[41] Following classical antecedents, princes and nobles displayed their power by flaunting goods and animals that had been procured from far-flung places. The menagerie was a subset of a potentate's other collections of natural and artificial wonders[42] and so in some ways quite different than animals bred, captured, and procured in hunting and husbandry operations.

The exemplary bird of the menagerie was the parrot. Though parrots were quite prevalent in the Roman Empire due to extensive networks that allowed access to those of the Far East, with the collapse of Rome they largely disappeared, at least in the flesh. In the words of Bruce Boehrer,

> living parrots seldom appear in the historical records of medieval Europe. … The story of parrots in medieval Europe is in large part the story of their absence. Yet, paradoxically, as they grow less visible in the feather, they loom larger in the cultural imagination, often in ways that bear no discernible relation to biological reality.[43]

In the visual and textual iconography of the Middle Ages, parrots were sacred emblems, portrayed as symbols of Christ, companions of the Virgin Mary and residents of the Holy Land.[44] In the thirteenth century Frederick II acquired an umbrella cockatoo from the Sultan of Babylon, and in the fourteenth century Charles IV of France had an Alexandrine parakeet in his aviary.[45] Parrots arrived into Europe in increasing numbers with fifteenth-century Portuguese expansion into West Africa,[46] and became increasingly commonplace in menageries; Pope Pius II taught his parrot to orate Latin verses and Martin V maintained in his retinue two men who attended 'the parrot of His Holiness with its cage.'[47] They were flaunted during processions, along with elephants and leopards and other exotic animals, and occupied honored places in royal aviaries.[48] The subjectivity of parrots of medieval and Renaissance royal and aristocratic menageries was that of an objectified wonder. The animal in the menagerie was valued primarily as a symbol, and not for its individual personality and affinity for others – which is not to deny that individual humans and parrots formed strong attachments to one another.

Birds in the Americas

In exploring and colonizing parts of native America, Europeans encountered societies even more bird-obsessed than their own. Among the ways Amerindians related to birds were hunting, taming, eating, and/or enjoying the songs of wild birds; raising and eating domestic birds; harvesting and trading feathers from which to create art and adornment; mimicking them in ritual performances; and auguring and deifying birds.

Just as European hunting and husbandry were linked in practice and ideology to aristocratic rule and to dynastic and colonial warfare, so Amerindian modes of interaction were cognate to forms of social life and inter-group conflict. In both Mesoamerican and Caribbean and Amazonian societies (the latter two possessing strong cultural affiliations),[49] a major objective of warfare was to obtain captives.[50] Such captives were assimilated into the host communities in two ways that, to European eyes, appeared dramatically opposed, but actually seem to have operated on a similar logic. Some individuals (primarily though not exclusively children and women) were incorporated as adoptive kin or slaves, depending on contingencies and the community; other individuals (primarily men) were killed, and in many places ritually cannibalized, and so also incorporated in another fashion. Charles de Rochefort, a French missionary who lived among the Caribs of the Lesser Antilles in the early seventeenth century, described this phenomenon:

> [T]hey bring home [a] Prisoner of War from among the *Arouagues* [Arawaks], he belongs of right to him who either seized on him in the Fight, or took him running away; so that being come into his Island, he keeps him in his house; and that he may not get away in the night, he ties him in an *Amae*, which he hangs up almost at the roof of his dwelling; and after he has kept him fasting four or five days, he produces him upon some day of solemn debauch, to serve for a publick Victim to the immortal hatred of his Country-men towards that Nation. ... They design for slavery only the young Maids and Women taken in the War: They do not eat the Children of their She-prisoners, much less the Children they have by them themselves.[51]

Though Mesoamerican communities differed in many important aspects from Amazonian and Caribbean groups, captive-oriented warfare was a central and shared element. Among the Aztecs and others in Central Mexico, warrior captives were fed to the solar deity; others were chosen to incarnate deities, and so treated as gods until their sacrifice. Later on the family of the warrior who took the captive in battle – the captor – ritually consumed the flesh of the captive.[52] Some women and children taken captive in war were also sacrificed, but others were spared; the great ethnographic compendium known as the *Florentine Codex* states that

If a woman [slave] could embroider, or if she prepared food well, or made cacao—from her hand good food, good drink came—[of if she were] a clear speaker she was also set aside. The nobles took [women like her] as wives.[53]

Predation

The two sides of captive warfare, predation and adoption, also mediated Caribbean, Amazonian, and Mesoamerican relationships with non-humans. In predation, whether in war or hunting, a central element was the transformation of the warrior – or shaman or priest acting in the warrior role – into an apex predator. *Naguallism* refers to those practices related to the assumption of animal properties in which aspects of deity, animal, and human were interchangeable. In Nahuatl a *nagualli* (or *nahaulli*) referred to a shamanic type who could shape-shift into an animal.[54] Studies of South American shamanism (including Amazonian and Caribbean) likewise focus on the importance of shape-shifting.[55] Naguallism encompassed a constellation of beliefs and practices around animal metamorphosis; the inextricability of 'matter' (pelts, skins, feathers) and 'spirit' (essences of preciousness, beauty, power, courage, etc.); and the instantiation of the divine through animal accoutrements. Nagual subjectivity presupposed absolute identification between subject and object and an understanding of subjectivity based not on the bounded, essential subject but rather entities comprised of the sum of their appurtenances.

The relationship between transitive animal properties and an amorphous and contingent subjectivity dependent on an identity between matter and essence can be seen through Mesoamericans' conceptualizations of their deities. The 'costume' or 'adornment' was essential to the god's very being; outer display was identical to essence itself: 'for the Mexica—as for Amerindian more generally— it was the skin, that most external and enveloping "appearance," which constituted a creature's essence, and so stored the most formidable symbolic power.'[56] Eagle feathers' special power was exemplified in the patron deity of the Mexica, Huitzilopochtli (or Uitzilopochtli), that manifestation of the divine associated with creative and destructive powers of the sun, and so war, death, and creation.[57] Huitzilopochtli as the sun incarnate gave life, yet to do so required a steady diet of hearts and blood. The property of life-giving sacrificial killing could be found in the falcon (or eagle) who 'gives life to Uitzilopochtli because, they said, these falcons, when they eat three times day, as it were give drink to the sun; because when they drink blood they consume it all,' explained a native informant to who contributed to the *Florentine Codex*.[58] The raptor as much begot the divinity as it was begot from it. These correspondences were enacted in ritual. In a festival typical of the Mexica, the hearts of sacrificed prisoners were named 'precious eagle-cactus fruit'; 'they lifted [the hearts] up to the sun, the turquoise prince, the soaring eagle. They offered it to him; they nourished him with it. And when they had been offered, they placed it in the eagle-vessel.

And the captives who had died they called "eagle men."' The warrior who took the prisoner in battle was celebrated and reified as the eagle: 'And [as for] the captor, they there applied the down of birds to his head and gave him gifts. They named [the captor] the sun, white earth, the feather, because [he was] as one whitened with chalk and decked with feathers.'[59] The characteristic of sacrificial killing migrated transitively between god, sun, bird, and man, and in fact made each entity itself an embodiment of that quality.

The fungibility of feathers and pelts and the conviction that substance and essence were identical also underlay the many sets of practices in which humans took on or displayed animal attributes. An example of this 'transforming capacity of the donned skin' can be seen in the elite coteries of distinguished warriors known as 'Eagle Warriors' and 'Jaguar Warriors.'[60] The warriors were empowered by wearing the eagle pelt through which they channeled the animal's distinct prowess, as articulated by those interviewed for the *Florentine Codex*: 'The eagle is fearless, a brave one; it can gaze into, it can face the sun.'[61] Stone sculptures survive of the eagle helmets – fashioned out of wood and covered in the raptor's feathers – young warriors would wear. The raptors' importance in Mexica rituals is also suggested by the live eagles levied from tributaries.[62]

The Caribbean and Amazonian rituals in which warrior-hunters and shamans transformed into jaguars and fierce birds of prey bear striking resemblances to those described for Mesoamerica. Raymond Breton, a Dominican missionary who participated in the French settlement of Guadeloupe and lived among the Dominica Island Caribs for extended periods between 1652 and 1654 – oftentimes the only European in their midst – included invaluable ethnographic information in his *Dictionaire caraibe-françois* (1665).[63] In several places in the *Dictionaire*, he described a feast, 'one of their most solemn,' in which boys and men took on the qualities of a certain raptor.[64] Preparations began several months before the event, when men sought out the birds in their nests ('little ones for the little ones, and for the married men, big and heavy ones') to raise for this *mystère* (rite). On the feast day, the chief warrior killed the bird he had raised by crushing it against his head, letting the blood trickle down and leaving it there for the duration of the ceremony. The boys were prepared for their participation by having their flesh incised; then the men who 'have had a child or killed an Arawak' crushed the other birds with red chili who had been captured and kept for that purpose. The bloodied, chili-covered raptor carcasses were smeared over the cuts of the boys and men. The ritual culminated when each boy and man consumed the heart of 'his bird,' followed by a vomit-inducing tobacco infusion.[65] By letting the raptor's blood seep under his skin, and eating its heart, each boy and man was imbued with the raptor's essence, giving him the virile vigor necessary for fatherhood and predation in war and hunt.

The importance of identification with the raptor for the Dominica Island Caribs reverberates throughout Breton's dictionary, and in several places he refers to this rite as well as a gourd filled with the flesh of the *mansfenix* 'that they wear around their neck like a relic in order to become strong and valiant.' Elsewhere, he elaborated that

> our savages/natives sometimes have on their necks collars of little gourds… full of the flesh of *mansfoenix*, and other times, the fur of jaguars, claws of raptors and other similar things, that they wear like relics, especially at feasts and outside their feasts they always have them attached to their neck.[66]

Colonial ethno-historical sources, as well as nineteenth- and twentieth-century ethnographies, document similar rituals among Amazonian and mainland Caribbean groups.[67]

Adoption

One kind of incorporation was that which happened when one assumed the attributes of another by wearing its skin, enshrouding oneself in its feathers or ingesting its flesh and organs. Another kind of incorporation took place when an outsider animal or human became adopted into a kin network or other grouping. 'Adoption' as a mode was organized around the capture and adoption of birds and other animals (including humans in war). These adopted animals would be assimilated in host societies as 'fictive kin.'

Throughout South America, the Caribbean, and Mesoamerica, individual parrots were captured, tamed, and brought into households. Colonial texts, archaeological evidence, and modern-day ethnographies all point to widespread and ancient practices of capturing wild parrots and related birds throughout Amazonia, the Andes, the circum-Caribbean, Mesoamerica, and even as far as New Mexico in earlier periods.[68] Writing in the early sixteenth century, Peter Martyr d'Anghiera wrote of the Indians on the coast of Venezuela that 'these natives also keep numbers of birds which they rear either for food or for their pleasure.'[69] The anonymous author and artist of the sixteenth-century manuscript *Histoire Naturelle des Indes* devoted ample space to describing the ingenious methods of parrot capture among Native Americans in Trinidad and Nicaragua[70] (Figure 2.2). French missionary Charles de Rochefort characterized the Caribs of the Lesser Antilles as 'great Lovers of divertissements and recreation. … [T]o that purpose they take a pleasure in keeping and teaching a great number of Parrots and Paraquitos.'[71] Breton included at least seven varieties of parrots, noting which ones were particularly adept at speaking.[72]

The *Florentine Codex* attests to adoption practices in Mesoamerica: the 'young yellow-headed parrot… is captured [to be] tamed,' and the 'white-fronted parrot… is a singer, a constant singer, a talker, a speaker, a mimic, an answerer, an imitator, a word-repeater. It repeats one's words, imitates one, sings, constantly sings, chatters, talks.'[73] The importance of adoption is reflected in its incorporation into practices at the highest level. Among tributes levied by Aztec

FIGURE 2.2 An 'Indian of Trinidad' captures live parrots in *Histoire Naturelle des Indes*, c.1586

rulers were live birds, some intended for sacrifice, and others to be maintained in royal aviaries.[74] 'Live birds,' according to the missionary Diego Durán, were 'sent by these different nations, the most highly esteemed and those of the finest plumage. Some were green, some red, others blue; parrots, large and small.'[75]

The Frenchmen who spent time among the Amazonian Tupinamba in the mid-sixteenth century offer the earliest 'thick descriptions' of Amerindian bird adoption practices. André Thevet, who served as a Franciscan missionary in the failed French colony in Brazil, wrote:

> The savages of this land hold [these parrots] very dear, because three or four times a year they pluck their feathers to make hats [and] decorate shields, wooden swords, tapestries, and other exquisite things that they make customarily. They keep these birds in their lodgings, without having to enclose them, as we do here. … The women in particular nourish them…they hold them very dear, to the point of calling them in their language 'their friends.' Moreover our Americans teach these birds to speak in their language how to ask for the flour that they make or roots, or they very often teach them to say and exhort that they must wage war against their enemies, capture them so as to eat them.[76]

Jean de Léry, his Protestant rival, made similar observations about a parrot 'trained by a savage woman,' who called her bird 'thing that I love.'[77]

Colonial ethno-historical sources and more recent anthropological ethnographies of Amazonian groups alike confirm the value placed on such adopted birds, that it was women's work to tame and raise them, and that the birds belonged in the domestic space.[78] When Henry Bates, a nineteenth-century English naturalist who journeyed in the Amazon, could not get an intractable green parrot who fell out of a tree to cooperate in becoming a pet, he was referred to 'an old Indian woman…who was said to be a skilful bird-tamer.' In two days time his parrot was returned to him 'as tame as the familiar love-birds of our aviaries.' Bates speculated on 'what arts the old woman used,' having been told that 'she fed it with her saliva,' and he concluded that 'the chief reason why almost all animals become so wonderfully tame in the houses of the natives is…their being treated with uniform gentleness, and allowed to run at large about the rooms.'[79] Catherine Howard, an anthropologist who lived among the Amazonian Waiwai in the 1980s, described how parrots

> were treated like children in numerous ways. Both were ornamented, painted, befeathered, or otherwise "dressed" by those responsible for their care and 'socialization.' … A naked parrot seen in public—like a naked child—reflected badly on its caretakers, as if they nurtured neither its physical nor social growth.[80]

Christopher Crocker, an anthropologist who did fieldwork among the Brazilian Bororo, also attested that 'ownership of macaws is almost entirely limited to women,' and the birds are often seen as replacements for lost children.[81] Adoption ascribed a particular subjectivity to parrots and macaws assimilated into Amerindian communities. The adopted parrots' status as kin is suggested by their place 'in the lodgings,' by being the beneficiaries of women's 'nourishment,' and by being trained in common enmities (such as calling to 'eat' their foes).

A final, vital aspect of Amerindian practices that demands attention was adopted parrots' role as suppliers of feathers for ritual objects, those 'hats,' 'tapestries,' weapons and shields referred to by Thevet.[82] Ritual feather objects were comprised of feathers from both beloved pet birds and those hunted for that purpose; in both cases the connection between the living bird and the power that it transmitted to its human wearers in rituals were of vital importance. Howard explains how feathers were necessary for Waiwai men to 'construct a "beautiful" persona, while it was women who convert[ed] the birds into either "food or humanized pets."'[83] And Crocker writes that 'all domesticated macaws are living banks of rare and critical ritual material,' and that 'it is almost axiomatic that every man of status has either a full box of macaw feathers, or is related by consanguinity or alliance to a woman with a tame macaw, or both.[84]

The featherworks worn and deployed by Caribbean, Amazonian, and Mesoamerican peoples most often featured feathers from multiple bird species and displayed layered and multivalent meaning. John Ogilvie, a European adventurer who lived among Waiwai in British Guiana in the early twentieth century, complained that in order to purchase a feather headdress he was 'subjected [to] the history of the hat itself. I was taken on a verbal hunt after each bird, just who was at the hunt, how and where it was shot, and countless long-winded details.'[85] Later in the century, an anthropologist described how the feathered costume worn by a Waiwai displayed 'a microcosm of the cosmology charted out on the body.'[86] For the Bororo, the red macaw feathers of adopted birds resonated with fertility.[87] It has already been seen that humans wearing raptors' skin or ingesting their hearts was a means to manifest predatorial prowess. The feathers from the non-raptorial birds, including adopted parrots, seemed to connect to a different set of avian qualities, such as those of beauty, preciousness, fertility, and transcendence.

The lengthy and highly specific descriptions of feathered regalia in the *Florentine Codex* offer some clue to the way that particular birds were associated with essential properties: the ear pendants of coatinga feathers of Huitzilopochtli, the 'heron-feather spray with a single quetzal feather' of Opochtli, and the 'white heron feather headdress' and 'fan-shaped ornament of red arara feathers' that belonged to Tezcatzoncatl;[88] they also speak to how much meaning has been lost, as most European chroniclers spoke indiscriminately of 'feathers.' Yet, the descriptions of gods and religious festivals in the *Florentine Codex* leave no doubt that the gleaming green feathers of the quetzal, above all, were indispensible in these instantiations of divinity.[89] The feathers – 'green, herb-green, very green, fresh green, turquoise-colored…the ones which glisten, which bend'[90] – of the quetzal summoned, evoked, or created the life-giving rain, the transforming wind, and the transcendent beauty of the divine. The property of precious beauty, shimmeringness, belonged to the quetzal in its feathers, and that property inhered in the feathers themselves. Art historian Alessandra Russo writes that birds in general and the quetzal in particular were the way through which sacred 'essence…can manifest itself in the body of ordinary men.'[91] Quetzal feathers were also necessary for the costumes worn by Mayan and Aztec rulers. Like the parrots in the Amazon and Caribbean valued for their feathers, quetzal birds were not killed (though they were also not kept in captivity; they were caught and released).[92]

Cultural encounter and exchange

An inflow of both parrots and featherworks into Europe was an almost immediate consequence of Columbus' arrival in the Americas and the voyages of exploration and campaigns of conquest that followed in his wake. Explorers and soldiers readily accepted gifts of parrots and then sought them as trade goods throughout the Americas. In accepting or trading for such goods and animals,

Europeans entered into Amerindian trade and gift networks that involved exchanges of live birds, feathers, and featherworks.[93] The cross-cultural and trans-Atlantic migration of birds and featherworks begs the question: what exactly was moving when these birds and featherworks moved? Raw materials? Technologies? Ideas? Active agents?

In thinking about the transfer of objects – sentient and inanimate, conscious and unconscious, silent and talking – there is a range of potential processes. First, there may be universal elements, such as an intrinsic potential in both parrots and humans to form strong attachments, or for humans to find colorful, glimmering things, such as feathers, alluring. Second, there may be cultural convergence: shared elements in European and Amerindian societies may allow the same object to be valued and attributed meaning similarly. Third, there may be what Marshall Sahlins termed 'commodity indigenization,' or the way that a receiving culture will assimilate a foreign object on its own terms. Fourth, there may be transmission with the object, when due to qualities within an object and/ or contexts in which an object is transmitted, elements of the 'giving' culture's use and practices migrate with the object. Of course, in actuality, some or all of these processes can and do coexist, and often the result is local interpretations of a syncretic, hybrid, or mestizo phenomenon.[94]

In the case of the featherworks, along with other precious objects that Cortes received from Moctezuma and then presented to Charles V, who, in turn, 're-gifted' them to other sovereigns,[95] there seems to have been mostly cultural convergence and commodity indigenization at play. In considering the Aztec objects that became part of Habsburg collections, Carina Johnson writes that 'the feather helmets, weapons, and shields could be easily read as military and sumptuary. ... [T]he feather helmets approximated European feather plumes decorating the hats and helmet of lords, soldiers, and elite commoners.' Yet there were also major shifts in use and meaning as 'sacral and inalienable objects were transformed into desacralized and alienable items. ... Preconquest nonmetal objects, particularly feather and stonework, could gain new desacralized roles as *Kunstkammern* exemplars of Mexican craftsmanship.'[96] Amy Buono, in her study of the movement of Tupinamba featherworks in the early modern world, argues that as these sacred objects moved through 'Kunst- und Wunderkammern, and early natural history collections... they were transformed into commodities to be bought and sold, gifted and bartered.'[97]

Another kind of cultural transfer occurred with the creation of featherworks as Christian ritual objects, or when traditional featherworks were deployed in Christian rites. The *Salvator Mundi* was such a Christian featherwork, commissioned by missionaries in post-conquest Mexico and created by *amanteca* (the skilled Mexica featherworkers) using traditional Mesoamerican skills, technologies, and materials. Russo finds the persistence of pre-Hispanic aesthetic, spiritual, and iconographic elements: the feathered mosaic 'evokes not only the metonymic liturgical base of Christianity, the Eucharist (the host-victim as part of the Son and the Father) but also the pre-Hispanic concept of the *ixiptatl* understood as part and emanation of the thing represented.'[98] Buono likewise reveals feathered *mestizaje* in her discovery that in the mid-sixteenth century Tupi men and women in a Bahia mission were 'baptized in the feathered adornments of their own cultural practices,' finding feathers accommodated 'in the new Jesuit Christian complex of colonial Brazil.'[99] But overall far more was lost than maintained in the transmission from native America to Europe. There is no indication that any aspect of nagual subjectivity traveled with the feathers; the Amerindian conviction that featherworks transmitted a living avian essence to humans or gods who were bedecked with them did not translate. Instead we see the logic of alienation that undergirded husbandry: feathers were raw materials, alienated from their connection to the living bird. This cultural disconnect is on display when the adventurer John Ogilvie was interminably bored by having to hear the 'history' of featherworks he wanted to buy, this very 'history' being what made it so valuable to the Waiwai on the other end of the transaction.

What about the parrots who migrated across the Atlantic on ships? This migration was one of the earliest among the Columbian Exchanges. According to Bartolomé de las Casas, on December 13, 1492, during Columbus' first voyage and the exploration of the island that would become Hispaniola, 'the Indians that [Columbus] had brought to the ship had understood that the Admiral wanted to have some parrots, it seems that the Indians who went with the Christians told the natives something about this, and so they brought parrots to them and gave as many as they were asked for,' reportedly amassing at least forty.[100] On his subsequent voyages he procured more parrots on Guadalupe, the Venezuelan littoral, and probably elsewhere.[101] Conquistador-turned-chronicler Gonzalo Fernández de Oviedo wrote in his 1526 *Sumario* that he had 'presented to his Majesty thirty or more parrots representing ten or twelve different species,' most of whom 'could speak very well.' By that date it had become so common to bring parrots across the Atlantic that Oviedo could write, 'since so many species have been carried to Spain, it is hardly worthwhile to take time to describe them here.'[102] Portuguese and French traders were systematically importing macaws and other parrots procured from Tupi in Brazil by the early sixteenth century.[103] It is notable that the depiction of an exchange of Amazonian parrots and monkeys for European goods served to characterize the essence of European–Brazilian relations in the 1547 *Vallard Atlas* (Figure 2.3).[104]

Over the course of the following centuries, the influx of parrots accompanied and/or generated two interrelated transformations in European parrot culture, one 'quantitative,' and the other 'qualitative.' First, there was an expansion of parrot ownership. Parrots were no longer reserved for princes' menageries; parrot keeping extended to mariners, wealthy merchants, and nobles, and encompassed artisan classes by the eighteenth century[105] (Figure 2.4). Second, the parrot metamorphosed from mystical marvel to family pet. If, in the Middle Ages, parrots featured mainly as decorations on illuminated manuscripts and, rarely, as living entities in royal aviaries, in the early modern period they became

FIGURE 2.3 Tupi men and women exchange tamed parrots and monkeys with Europeans for metal tools in the *Vallard Atlas,* 1547

increasingly common in urban households.[106] The defining relationship of the modern 'pet' to its human keepers is that of kin; it is a family member.[107] Georges Buffon, in the *Histoire naturelle des oiseaux* (1778), eloquently articulated this notion when he described the special attractiveness of parrots:

> It entertains, it distracts, it amuses; in solitude it is company; in conversation it is an interlocutor, it responds, it calls, it welcomes, it emits peals of laughter, it expresses a tone of affection... [it] seems to be moved and touched by caresses; it gives affectionate kisses; in a house of mourning it learns to moan, and accustomed to repeating the dear name of a deceased person, it reminds sensitive hearts of their pleasure and sorrows.[108]

Buffon rendered the parrot as the ideal family member, offering and receiving affection, amusement, and solace, sensitive to the energies and vicissitudes of the household as a whole. This role helps explain why parrots were so commonly linked in text and image with female domesticity. Taken too far, female parrot keepers might elevate their parrots over human objects of affection, such as the lady of the satirical verse who claimed that she loved her parrot 'more than her life, and for which she would have given all of her loves.'[109]

What accounts for the metamorphosis of parrots from rare, sacred wonder to family pet? Was it an inevitable consequence of a 'universal' impulse among humans to have pets, and among parrots to bond with their captors?[110] Was it a consequence of the fact that a ready supply of American and African parrots initially fulfilled the fantasy of the magical Orient, but the subsequent fact of their abundance led to their devaluation into quotidian companion species? Or did the parrot's metamorphosis – and even the emergence of the modern category of the pet – owe something to the Amerindian mode of interaction of

FIGURE 2.4 Barthel Beham, *Woman with a Parrot*, 1529

adoption? The answer likely lies in a combination of all three of these, and so we have yet another example of modern *mestizaje*.

There is doubtless a component which could be characterized as a universal impulse. Or, as a skeptic of cultural explanations could put it: parrots' enmeshment in the European home had less to do with culturally constructed subjectivities and more to do with a 'universal' attraction among humans to intelligent, speech-capable, attachment-forming birds. Yet a universal impulse cannot fully account for the intensification and extensification of parrot bonding in Europe, for Europeans did have access to home-grown intelligent avian candidates who could be tamed and taught to speak: crows and magpies. The seventeenth-century English ornithologist Francis Willughby, following Aldrovandi, acknowledged that crows are 'capable of humane speech, and hath been taught to pronounce several words, both we our selves do certainly know,' and he wrote of the magpie that 'the Bird is easily taught to speak, and that very plainly. We ourselves have known many, which had learned to imitate man's voice, and speak articulate with that exactness.'[111] However, there is no evidence that crows and magpies were brought into the realm of pethood in the systematic and celebrated way that parrots were.

What about the second explanation, one that would consider the metamorphosis of parrots in Europe from marvel to pet as a mostly internal story – that Europeans had a pre-existing classical and medieval interest in parrots, and overseas regions only supplied birds but not cultural or social contexts? There is some truth to this as well. Clearly, parrots' lofty presence in the medieval imagination and princes' menageries predisposed Mediterranean explorers and soldiers to accept gifts of parrots, and, before long, demand them.

While the universal and Eurocentric explanations of the parrot sea change should not be dismissed, it does seem that European entanglement with Native American parrot-heavy culture catalyzed a juncture in the history of human–parrot relationships. Parrots crossed the Atlantic with elements of the Amerindian mode of incorporation in tow. First, Europeans did not, for the most part, pluck parrots out of trees; rather they bought or received them as gifts from Amerindians who had captured and tamed them, as depicted in contemporary sources (Figures 2.2 and 2.3). Anghiera wrote tellingly that 'the Spaniards are indifferent bird-hunters, and are neglectful in catching them.'[112] Europeans were brought into ritual gift and trade exchanges that long pre-dated their arrival. Europeans acquired their parrots – and many of them – from Amerindians who had century-old skills and traditions honed for the capture of live birds. So, at the very least, we should see that there was no such thing as raw supply of parrots; these birds were captured and tamed by technologies and practices developed over millennia.

Furthermore, tantalizing traces suggest that Amerindian adoption contributed to the emergence of modern pethood. The existing scholarship emphasizes the eighteenth and nineteenth centuries as the period in which the modern 'pet' originated. For Marc Shell this development links to the rise of secular cosmology in the late seventeenth and eighteenth centuries; for Kathleen Kete it evolved with the rise of romanticism and bourgeois domesticity.[113] There is no reason to doubt these factors were seminal in the emergence of the modern pet. But alongside these developments, Amerindian practices around adoption should be considered as well. The arrival of the kin subjectivity that characterized Amerindian parrot adoptions contributed to the genesis of the subjectivity of the modern pet. Parrots arrived not just as *tabula rasa* animals, ready to be made over into European pets, but rather already tamed and trained, already made into kin.

The processes by which European ideas and practices surrounding parrots changed as a result of sustained contact with Amerindian cultures are largely out of view. However, the French Dominican Jean-Baptiste Labat, who lived in the Caribbean (mostly in Martinique) between 1694 and 1706, offered a glimpse of this process in his *Nouveau voyage aux isles de l'Amerique*. In a chapter on parrots, he wrote first of a fellow cleric whose pet parrot was so loyal, affectionate, and protective that he threatened to bite anyone who came near him, including Labat's own friendly dog. 'I don't think one could see in the world an animal more affectionate to his master,' Labat wrote. He also praised the parrot's speaking ability, 'when we heard its voice without seeing it, it was difficult to distinguish if it was one of a bird or of a man.'[114] Perhaps inspired by this bird,

Labat himself purchased three parrots during his stay in the Caribbean, one from Guadeloupe and two from Dominica.[115] The one from Guadeloupe came as a big disappointment; because of his size Labat thought he was 'old and so he would never learn to talk. He would only screech and because he had an extremely loud voice, it broke my ears, and this obligated me to have him killed.' Labat soon 'repented' this act. Just as his slave was plucking feathers from the parrot's carcass, a few of his parishioners paid him a visit. They informed him that the deceased parrot had been

> still young and that his cries are what we call *cancaner* in the language of the islands, that he would have learned to speak in short time, and would have surpassed the others. As the bad deed was without remedy, I put it in a stew; his flesh was very good, delicate and succulent.[116]

(This recollection led to a lengthy digression on different preparations for parrot – young ones on the grill, older ones in soup – and their similarity and superiority to the flavor of European partridges). Labat learned from his mistake, so he decided to 'pension' the other two parrots, a male and a female, with a woman in his parish so they would learn to talk, offering the aside that 'we know that women have the gift of speech, and they like to use it.' Despite their advanced age, the Dominica parrots returned able to speak 'to perfection,' having 'attended such a good school.' They became so tame that they would fly at liberty in the woods but return at the sound of a whistle. The parrots lived four years in Labat's care until 'the husband' was crushed by a window shutter; his death 'having left him with a little bit of sadness (*un peu de chagrin*), I got rid of the female so as not to have it for a second time.'[117]

Labat's text offers a view of a distinctly Creole and mestizo space in which Amerindian parrot adoption was becoming European parrot pethood. The presence – political, social, and cultural – of Amerindians was still actively shaping parrot practices in seventeenth-century Lesser Antilles; the first parrots owned by European settlers were captured and tamed by Indians. Then, it seems, capturing and taming technologies were transferred to Creoles and settlers themselves, such as the woman to whom he sent his parrots to be educated, and his fellow cleric. As with all translations, in the process of transmission there were changes, including new dangers, like window shutters. For Labat the boundary between food and pet was porous, and quite unlike that of Amerindians in that and other areas. Labat's willingness to eat his own parrot – and perhaps also the decision to rid himself of a parrot to avoid grieving twice – would have been shocking to Amazonian and Caribbean Indians,[118] as it might have also been to his visiting parishioners and his colleague. Similarly, Jean de Léry described a range of practices and attitudes toward eating shipboard parrots when confronted with famine conditions; there were those who had 'eaten theirs' at the beginning of the food scarcity, others 'who still had monkeys and parrots…which they had kept so as to teach them to speak a language that they did not yet know,' but as starvation increased 'now put them into the cabinet of their memory, and made them serve as food,' and finally himself, who 'in spite of this inexpressible suffering and famine...nevertheless up to that time kept one, as big as a goose, that uttered words freely like a man, and was of excellent plumage.' Then he too finally succumbed to eating his bird, 'discard[ing] nothing but the feathers, so that not only the body but also the tripes, feet, claws, and hooked beak served me and some of my friends to keep ourselves alive for three or four days.' But then he 'regretted it' when they soon after 'saw land,' and felt 'distress.'[119]

The notion that there was a connection between European and Amerindian parrot keeping was not foreign to early modern observers. In the *Ornithology of Francis Willughby* (1678), the naturalist described a parrot,

> one of those great ones in the house of the illustrious Lady Mary of Bremen, Dutchess of Croy and Areschot. ... [T]his Bird was so in love with Anna the Dutchesses Neece, now Countess of Meghen and Barronness of Grosbeke, that where ever she walked about the Room it would follow her, and if it saw any one touch her cloaths, would drinke at him with its Bill; so that it seemed to be possessed with a spirit of jealousie.[120]

After discussing the 'love' a pet parrot felt for Duchess Anna he mused about 'a certain Brasilian woman,' and quoted the passage in Jean de Léry about this woman and the bird 'which she made much of, which seemed to be endowed with that understanding and reason,' and who did her bidding.[121] Though separated by distance and time, Willughby saw in both relationships a parrot devoted to a woman, familial closeness characterized by jealousy and loyalty.

Conclusion

In the burgeoning interdisciplinary field of human–animal studies, 'anthropocentrism' tends to be the gauge by which humans' practices and attitudes toward other animals are evaluated.[122] But this heuristic is not a fine enough tool to do justice to the multiplicity and diversity of the ways people have related to non-human beings over time. And those approaches that focus on universal features in human–animal relationships are also wanting; while acknowledging a shared universal nugget in human–avian attachments, it should also be recognized that these attachments take very specific cultural forms: both the European falconer and the Tupinamba woman formed intense bonds with his hawk and her parrot, respectively, but these attachments had strong cultural inflections. At first glance, the kinship subjectivity of Amerindian adoption may look quite similar to the vassalage of European hunting, but there was an important difference: while hawks might be tamed in the household, they were not represented as part of the domestic space, any more than a human vassal would be. The ideal of vassalage and pethood also differed. In vassalage, affection and communication were byproducts of a common pursuit of conquest. In pethood, affection and communication were/are the objective itself, the connection between bird and human the very point.

The subjectivity produced by naguallism shares many qualities with that of vassalage produced by the European mode of hunting. In both cultures, the warrior's prowess was manifested and articulated through identification with fearsome predators. Yet, there was an important difference, namely that of the absolute identification that took place in naguallism. Because of the understanding that material and essence were inextricable, the subject and object could become one in native America in ways inconceivable in European cultures. The difference is not – as some have argued – that Europeans were more anthropocentric and Native Americans less so, but rather that Amerindians had a more porous sense of self and, correlated, a greater confidence in the interpenetration of thingness and beingness.

Exploring the transmission of featherworks and parrots across the Atlantic adds further complexity to our understanding of the Columbian Exchange. Once again we see that such exchanges were much more than cross-transfers of 'biota' across hemispheres. Cultural structures were essential in mediating the reception on both sides. Before the integration of the Atlantic world, Europeans had home-grown traditions that produced enduring human–avian relationships. Yet, in coming in contact with Amerindians and parrots, Europeans experienced directly a human–bird relationship organized around notions of kinship not previously experienced in their society. The role of Amerindian practices as a significant factor in European parrot adoption and consequently in the broader realm of human–animal relationships has not been adequately recognized. Europeans, conditioned through their direct and indirect relationships with persons in the New World, learned not only how to train and teach parrots, but perhaps also to follow Amerindians in seeing birds as kin.

Notes

1 I am grateful to Lauren (Robin) Derby, Paula Findlen, Margaret Garber, Erin Lichtenstein, Susanah Shaw Romney, and Zeb Tortorici for reading versions of this chapter and offering useful comments and encouragement.

2 The flourishing of European chickens and African guinea hens in the Americas, and American turkeys in Europe were, of course, no less interesting and consequential aspects of the Columbian Exchange.

3 For more on this concept, Marcy Norton, 'Animals in Spain,' in *Lexikon of the Hispanic Baroque: Technologies of a Transatlantic Culture*, ed. Evonne Levy and Ken Mills (Austin, TX: University of Texas Press, forthcoming).

4 This paragraph follows Thomas T. Allsen, *The Royal Hunt in Eurasian History* (Philadelphia, PA: University of Pennsylvania Press, 2006), 58–67, as well as the sources cited below. Under falconry, I am including 'hawking,' but contemporaries distinguished between these activities. Richard Grassby, 'The Decline of Falconry in Early Modern England,' *Past & Present* 157 (November 1997): 37.

5 Fadrique de Zúñiga y Sotomayor, *Libro de cetreria de caça de açor* (Salamanca: Juan de Canoua, 1565), f. 4v; Pedro López de Ayala, *Libro de la caça de las aves (British Library, Londres)*, ed. John G. Cummins (London: Tamesis, 1986), 71 (14r), 63 (10r), 82 (20r); Allsen, *Royal Hunt*, 243; Grassby, 'Decline,' 43.

6 For training a gyrfalcon to pursue hares, López de Ayala, *Libro*, 72 (14v), 80 (18v).

7 Grassby, 'Decline,' 56.

8 Zúñiga y Sotomayor, *Libro*, f. 1r; on hunting generally, Pedro Núñez de Avendaño, *Auiso de caçadores y de caça* (Alcala: Joan de Brocar, 1543), f. 28v.

9 Michel de Montaigne, 'Apology for Raymond Sebond,' in *The Complete Essays of Montaigne*, trans. Donald Murdoch Frame (Stanford, CA: Stanford University Press, 1976), 338.

10 Zúñiga y Sotomayor, *Libro*, f. 21v; on expensive medicines, López de Ayala, *Libro*, 150–152 (56v–57v); Allsen, *Royal Hunt*, 61.

11 Simon Latham, *Lathams New and Second Booke of Falconrie* (London: Roger Jackson, 1618), 74–75.

12 Simon Latham, *Lathams Falconry or The Faulcons Lure* (London: R. Jackson, 1615), 27.

13 López de Ayala, *Libro*, 69 (13r), 80 (18v); Grassby, 'Decline,' 47.

14 Latham, *Second Booke*, 3.

15 Gervase Markham, *Country Contentments: Or, The Husbandmans Recreations*, 5th ed. (London: John Harison, 1633), 37; López de Ayala, *Libro*, 118–119 (32v–33r).

16 Latham, *Second Booke*, 27.

17 Ibid., 41, 42.

18 Edmund Bert, *An Approued Treatise of Hawkes and Hawking* (London: Richard Moore, 1619), 13.

19 Ibid., 21, 22; see also Latham, *Second Booke*, 27, López de Ayala, *Libro*, 85–88 (43v–44r), 99–100 (22r–v); Zúñiga y Sotomayor, *Libro*, 32r.

20 Sandra Blakeslee and Matthew Blakeslee, *The Body Has a Mind of Its Own: How Body Maps in Your Brain Help You Do (Almost) Everything Better* (New York: Random House, 2007), 4, 133–137.

21 Gabriel Alonso de Herrera, *Libro de agricultura de Alonso de Herrera* (Pamplona: Mathias Mares, 1605) (this edition is nearly identical to the 1563 edition as concerns poultry); Charles Estienne and Jean Liebault, *L'agriculture et maison rustique* (Lyon: Jaques du Puys, 1583). Alonso de Herrera's work appeared in thirteen editions in Spanish during the sixteenth and seventeenth centuries, Antonio Palau y Dulcet, *Manual del Librero Hispano-Americano* (Barcelona: Libreria anticuaria, 1923), 6: 574–575.

22 Alonso de Herrera, *Libro de agricultura*, 149r.

23 Liebault, *Maison rustique*, 39v.

24 Alonso de Herrera, *Libro de agricultura*, 133v; Liebault, *Maison rustique*, 46v.

25 Alonso de Herrera, *Libro de agricultura* 149v, 150v; Liebault, *Maison rustique*, 40v, 46v.

26 Grassby, 'Decline,' 47.

27 For a general history of the chicken, Page Smith and Charles Daniel, *The Chicken Book* (Athens, GA: University of Georgia Press, 2000).

28 Alonso de Herrera, *Libro de agricultura*, 142r–143v.

29 Ibid., 142r–143v, 150r–155v; Liebault, *Maison rustique*, 39v–51r.

30 Alonso de Herrera, *Libro de agricultura*, 150v; Liebault, *Maison rustique*, 40v.

31 Alonso de Herrera, *Libro de agricultura*, 150v–151v; Liebault, *Maison rustique*, 39v–51r.

32 Evan Ratliff, 'Taming the Wild,' *National Geographic*, March 2011, 54–55.

33 Edward Topsell, *The Fowles of Heauen; or History of Birdes*, ed. Thomas Perrin Harrison and F. David Hoeniger (Austin, TX: University of Texas, 1972), 19.

34 Liebault, *Maison rustique*, 41r.

35 Alonso de Herrera, *Libro de agricultura*, 151r, also 143r; Liebault, *Maison rustique*, 43v–44r, 46r.

36 Ulisse Aldrovandi, *Aldrovandi on Chickens: The Ornithology of Ulisse Aldrovandi*, ed. and trans. L. R. Lind (Norman, OK: University of Oklahoma Press, 1963), 36.

37 Alonso de Herrera, *Libro de agricultura*, 150r.

38 Liebault, *Maison rustique*, 43r. My emphasis.

39 For example, López de Ayala, *Libro*, 87 (44v).

40 Smith and Daniel, *Chicken Book*, 71–75, 77–82; George Wilson, *The Commendation of Cockes, and Cock-Fighting* (London: Henrie Tomes, 1607).

41 Classic and unsurpassed is Gustave Loisel, *Histoire des ménageries de l'antiquité à nos jours* 3 vols. (Paris: O. Doin et fils, 1912), vol. 1; for menageries of Renaissance popes and other powerful Italians, Silvio A. Bedini, *The Pope's Elephant* (Manchester: Carcanet Press, 1997); for those of the Portuguese court, Annemarie Jordan-Gschwend, *The Story of Süleyman: Celebrity Elephants and Other Exotica in Renaissance Portugal* (Zurich: A. J. Gschwend, 2010).

42 Lorraine Daston and Katharine Park, *Wonders and the Order of Nature, 1150–1750* (New York: Zone Books, 2001), 34, 67, 88; Jordan-Gschwend, *Story of Süleyman*, vi.

43 Bruce Thomas Boehrer, *Parrot Culture: Our 2,500-year-long Fascination with the World's Most Talkative Bird* (Philadelphia, PA: University of Pennsylvania Press, 2004), 3–15, 24–29, especially 23.

44 Ibid., 32, 35–39; Bruce Boehrer, 'The Cardinal's Parrot: A Natural History of Reformation Polemic,' *Genre* 41.1/2 (2008): 3–4; Donald F. Lach, *Asia in the Making of Europe* (Chicago, IL: University of Chicago Press, 1970), 179–180.

45 Boehrer, *Parrot Culture*, 23, 28; see also idem, 'Cardinal's Parrot,' 5; Loisel, *Histoire*, 1: 232.

46 Boehrer, 'Cardinal's Parrot,' 4; Jordan-Gschwend, *Story of Süleyman*, 7; Lach, *Asia*, 178–179.

47 Boehrer, 'Cardinal's Parrot,' 5; Loisel, *Histoire*, 1: 202.

48 Bedini, *The Pope's Elephant*, 19, 28; Jordan-Gschwend, *Story of Süleyman*, 7.

49 Neil L. Whitehead, 'Ethnic Plurality and Cultural Continuity in the Native Caribbean,' in *Wolves from the Sea: Readings in the Anthropology of the Native Caribbean*, ed. idem (Leiden: KITLV Press, 1995), 91, 96–97. For a recent overview of the ethno-histories of these groups, see relevant essays in *The Cambridge History of the Native Peoples of the Americas*, Vol. III: *South America*, ed. Frank Salomon and Stuart B. Schwartz, 2 parts (Cambridge: Cambridge University Press, 1999), 2: 864–903.

50 For Caribbean and South America, Neil L. Whitehead, 'The Crises and Transformations of Invaded Societies,' in *Cambridge History of the Native Peoples*, 882–888; idem, *Lords of the Tiger Spirit: A History of the Caribs in Colonial Venezuela and Guyana 1498–1820* (Dordrecht: Foris Publications, 1988), 182 and ch. 8 generally; Juan Villamarin and Judith Villamarin, 'Chiefdoms,' in *Cambridge History of the Native Peoples*, 2: 600. For northeastern North America, see Daniel K. Richter, 'War and Culture: The Iroquois Experience,' *The William and Mary Quarterly* Third Series, 40.4 (October 1983): 528–559; for southeastern North America, Christina Snyder, *Slavery in Indian Country: The Changing Face of Captivity in Early America* (Cambridge, MA: Harvard University Press, 2010), 36–44.

51 Charles de Rochefort, *The History of the Caribby-Islands*, trans. John Davies (London: T. Dring and J. Starkey, 1666), bk. 2, ch. 21, 326 (emphasis in the original), also 266, 271, 323, 325, 327–331. See also Pietro Martire d'Anghiera, *De Orbe Novo, the Eight Decades of Peter Martyr d'Anghera*, trans. Francis Augustus MacNutt, 2 vols. (New York: G. P. Putnam's Sons, 1912), 1: 63, 71.

52 Frances Berdan and Patricia Rieff Anawalt, eds., *The Codex Mendoza*, 4 vols. (Berkeley, CA: University of California Press, 1992), 3: 64r, 4: 188–189; Inga Clendinnen, *The Cost of Courage in Aztec Society: Essays on Mesoamerican Society and Culture* (New York: Cambridge University Press, 2010), especially chs. 1 and 3.

53 Bernardino de Sahagún, *The Florentine Codex: General History of the Things of New Spain* (hereafter FC) 12 books in 13 volumes, trans. Arthur J. O. Anderson and Charles Dibble (Santa Fe, NM: School of American Research and the University of Utah Press, 1950), 1: 44; Marcy Norton, *Sacred Gifts, Profane Pleasures: A History*

of Tobacco and Chocolate in the Atlantic World (Ithaca, NY: Cornell University Press, 2008), 16.

54 Marie L. Musgrave-Portilla, 'The Nahualli or Transforming Wizard in Pre- and Postconquest Mesoamerica,' *Journal of Latin American Lore* 8.1 (1982): 3–62; Martha Few, *Women Who Live Evil Lives: Gender, Religion, and the Politics of Power in Colonial Guatemala* (Austin, TX: University of Texas Press, 2002), 58–61; Daniel G. Brinton, 'Nagualism,' *Proceedings of the American Philosophical Society* 33.144 (1894): 11–73.

55 Gerardo Reichel-Dolmatoff, *The Shaman and the Jaguar: A Study of Narcotic Drugs among the Indians of Colombia* (Philadelphia, PA: Temple University Press, 1975); Nicholas J. Saunders, ed., *Icons of Power: Feline Symbolism in the Americas* (London: Routledge, 1998), 16–21; Carlos Fausto and David Rodgers, 'Of Enemies and Pets: Warfare and Shamanism in Amazonia,' *American Ethnologist* 26.4 (1999): 933–956. On Tupi bird transformation, Amy Buono, 'Crafts of Color: Tupi Tapirage in Early Colonial Brazil,' in *The Materiality of Color: The Production, Circulation, and Application of Dyes and Pigments 1400–1800*, eds. Andrea Feeser, Maureen Daly Goggin and Beth Fowkes (Aldershot: Ashgate Press, 2012), 28, 31.

56 Inga Clendinnen, *Aztecs: An Interpretation* (Cambridge: Cambridge University Press, 1991), 228, 346, n. 51. See also Elizabeth H. Boone, 'Incarnations of the Aztec Supernatural: The Image of Huitzilopochtli in Mexico and Europe,' *Transactions of the American Philosophical Society* 79.2 (1988), 4; Arild Hvidtfeldt, *Teotl and *Ixiptlatli: Some Central Conceptions in Ancient Mexican Religion* (Copenhagen: Munksgaard, 1958), 98–99; Alessandra Russo, 'Plumes of Sacrifice: Transformations in Sixteenth-Century Mexican Feather Art,' *RES: Anthropology and Aesthetics* 42 (2002): 234–235.

57 FC, 1: 1, Clendinnen, *Aztecs*, 22.

58 FC, 11: 43–44.

59 Ibid., 2: 47–48.

60 Ibid., 2: 49; Clendinnen, *Aztecs*, 228–229.

61 FC, 1:41.

62 Manual Aguilar-Moreno, *Aztec Art* (Crystal River, FL: Foundation for the Advancement of Mesoamerican Studies, 2007), http://www.famsi.org/research/aguilar/Aztec_Art.pdf, 32, fig. 43; *Codex Mendoza*, 3: 31r, 55r.

63 Sybille de Pury, 'Le Pere Breton par lui-meme,' in Dictionnaire caraïbe-français (Paris: KARTHALA Editions, 1999), xvi–xvii; Raymond Breton, Dictionaire Caraibe-François: Meslé de quantité de remarques historiques pour l'esclaircissement de la langue (Auxerre: Gilles Bouquet, 1665).

64 Breton identified the 'mansfenix,' as a *milan*, or a kite. Breton, *Dictionaire*, 1: 202, 132.

65 Ibid., 1: 202.

66 Ibid., 1: 21, 192. See also 31, 255, 290. For the identification of the bird as a kite, see 1: 37.

67 Lawrence Waldron, 'Like Turtles, Islands Float Away: Emergent Distinctions in the Zoomorphic Iconography of Saladoid Ceramics of the Lesser Antilles, 250 BCE to 650 CE,' (PhD diss., City University of New York, 2010), 183; Arie Boomert, 'Raptorial Birds as Icons of Shamanism in the Pre-Historic Caribbean and Amazonia,' in *Proceedings of the XIX International Congress for Caribbean Archaeology*, ed. Luc Alofs and Raymundo Dijkhoff (Aruba: Archaeological Museum, 2001), 123; Catherine V. Howard, 'Feathers as Ornaments Among the WaiWai,' in *The Gift of Birds: Featherwork of Native South American Peoples*, ed. Ruben E. Reina and Kenneth M. Kensinger (Philadelphia, PA: University of Pennsylvania Museum of Archaeology, 1991), 66–67; Peter T. Furst, 'Crowns of Paper: Bird and Feather Symbolism in Amazonian Shamanism,' in *Gift of Birds*, 106–107.

68 Reina and Kensinger, eds., *Gift of Birds*; John O'Neill, 'Featherwork,' in *Costumes & Featherwork of the Lords of Chimor: Textiles from Peru's North Coast*, ed. Ann P. Roe (Washington, DC: Textile Museum, 1984), 146; Elizabeth P. Benson, *Birds and Beasts of Ancient Latin America* (Gainesville, FL: University Press of Florida, 1997),

69, 74–75; Boehrer, *Parrot Culture*, 50–55; FC, bks. 11, 12: 22–23; Darrell Creel and Charmion McKusick, 'Prehistoric Macaws and Parrots in the Mimbres Area, New Mexico,' *American Antiquity* 59.3 (July 1994): 510–524.

69 Anghiera, *De Orbe Novo*, 1: 344; he also mentioned that the inhabitants of Paria had 'talking parrots,' which they readily offered as gifts, 1: 254.

70 Anonymous, *Histoire naturelle des Indes: the Drake manuscript in the Pierpont Morgan Library*, intro. Verlyn Klinkenborg and trans. Ruth S. Kraemer (New York: Norton, 1996), f. 83, 88.

71 Rochefort, *The History of the Caribby-Islands*, bk. 2, ch. 17, 307.

72 Breton, *Dictionaire*, 1: 25, 218–219; 2: 286–287. See also Anghiera, *De Orbe Novo*, 1: 72; Jean Baptiste du Tertre, *Histoire generale des Antilles habitées par les François* (Paris: Thomas, 1667), 2: 248. For Panamian Cuna, Lionel Wafer, *A New Voyage and Description of the Isthmus of America* (Cleveland, OH: Burrows, 1903), 120.

73 FC, 11: 22, 23.

74 H. B. Nicholson, 'Montezuma's Zoo,' *Pacific Discovery* 8 (1955): 3–17.

75 Diego Durán, *The History of the Indies of New Spain*, trans. Doris Heyden (Norman, OK: University of Oklahoma Press, 1994), 203.

76 André Thevet, *Les singvlaritez de la France antarctiqve* (Paris: Heritiers de Maurice de la Porte, 1558), 92v–93v. My translation in consultation with sixteenth-century English translation quoted in Boehrer, *Parrot Culture*, 54, 52. Thevet and Léry (see below) are often problematic as sources for Tupinamba culture, but these particular descriptions are corroborated by other kinds of ethno-historical sources. On their status as sources, Neil L. Whitehead and Michael Harbsmeier, Introduction to *Hans Staden's True History: An Account of Cannibal Captivity in Brazil*, ed. and trans. Whitehead and Harbsmeier (Durham, NC: Duke University Press, 2008), xxxi–xxxiii.

77 Jean de Léry, *History of a Voyage to the Land of Brazil, Otherwise Called America*, trans. Janet Whatley (Berkeley, CA: University of California Press, 1990), 88.

78 In addition to sources below, see Amy J. Buono, 'Feathered Identities and Plumed Performances: Tupinambá Interculture in Early Modern Brazil and Europe' (PhD diss., University of California, Santa Barbara, 2008), 109–113.

79 Henry Walter Bates, *The Naturalist on the River Amazons*, 2nd ed. (London: J. Murray, 1864), 256–257.

80 Howard, 'Feathers as Ornaments,' 50.

81 J. Christopher Crocker, 'My Brother the Parrot,' in *The Social Use of Metaphor*, ed. J. David Sapir and J. Christopher Crocker (Philadelphia, PA: University of Pennsylvania Press, 1977), 33.

82 Reina and Kensinger, eds., *Gift of Birds*; the articles in 'Feather Creations: Materials, Production and Circulation,' *Nuevo Mundo Mundos Nuevos*, Coloquios (2006), http://nuevomundo.revues.org/1234#newyork; Buono, 'Feathered Identities'; Russo, 'Plumes of Sacrifice'; Breton, *Dictionaire Caraibe-François*, 1: 80, 88, 180, 203, 2: 299; Roe, ed., *Costumes & Featherwork*.

83 Howard, 'Feathers as Ornaments,' 56, 60–61.

84 Crocker, 'My Brother the Parrot,' 34.

85 John Ogilvie quoted in Howard, 'Feathers as Ornaments,' 54

86 Citing Peter Roe, Howard, 'Feathers as Ornaments,' 58. For Tupinamba, Buono, 'Feathered Identities,' 90; for South American feather symbolism generally, see also Benson, *Birds and Beasts*, 73–74.

87 Elizabeth Netto Calil Zurur, 'Social and Spiritual Languages of Feather Art: The Bororo of Central Brazil,' in *Gift of Birds*, 31.

88 FC, 1: 1, 2, 3, 14–15, 17, 24.

89 Ibid., bk. 1, passim, and 2: 82, 86, 113, 149, 196. See also Francisco Hernández, *Historia natural de Nueva España*, ed. Germán Somolinos d'Ardois, 2 vols. (Mexico: Universidad Nacional de Mexico, 1959), 2: 319; Russo, 'Plumes of Sacrifice,' 230–236.

90 FC, 11: 19; Clendinnen, Aztecs, 218. For quetzal feathers in deities' regalia, FC, 1: 2, 3, 5, 12, 13, 14, 16, 20. Quetzal and parrot feathers were among tribute levied by Aztecs (*The Codex Mendoza*, 3: 28r, 43r, 47r, 49r).

91 Russo, 'Plumes of Sacrifice,' 236.

92 Benson, *Birds and Beasts*, 75–76; Hernández, *Historia natural*, 2: 319.

93 Reina and Kensinger, eds., *Gift of Birds*; Roe, ed., *Costumes & Featherwork*; Villamarin and Villamarin, 'Chiefdoms,' 2: 619, 621, 649; Frances Berdan, 'Circulation of Feathers in Mesoamerica,' in 'Feather Creations,' http://nuevomundo.revues.org/1387.

94 I offer an in-depth analysis of different models for the transmission of goods between cultures in Marcy Norton, 'Tasting Empire: Chocolate and the European Internalization of Mesoamerican Aesthetics,' *The American Historical Review* 111 (2006): 661–670, and *Sacred Gifts*.

95 Carina L. Johnson, 'Aztec Regalia and the Reformation of Display,' in *Collecting Across Cultures: Material Exchanges in the Early Atlantic World*, ed. Daniela Bleichmar and Peter C. Mancall (Philadelphia, PA: University of Pennsylvania Press, 2011), 88–92, 97–98. For European reception of Mesoamerican ideas about hummingbirds, see Iris Montero Sobrevilla, 'Transatlantic Hum: Natural History and the Torpid Humminbird, *c.*1500–1800' (DPhil thesis, University of Cambridge, 2012).

96 Johnson, 'Aztec Regalia,' 90–91, 97.

97 Buono, 'Feathered Identities,' 302. See also Buono, 'Crafts of Color.'

98 Russo, 'Plumes of Sacrifice,' 245.

99 Buono, 'Feathered Identities,' 195.

100 Christopher Columbus, *The Diario of Christopher Columbus's First Voyage to America, 1492–1493*, transcribed and trans. Oliver Dunn and James E. Kelly, Jr. (Norman, OK: University of Oklahoma Press, 1989), 223.

101 Anghiera, *De Orbe Novo*, 1: 64, 72, 154, 254.

102 Gonzalo Fernández de Oviedo y Valdés, *Natural History of the West Indies*, trans. Sterling A. Stoudemire (Chapel Hill, NC: University of North Carolina Press, 1959), 60.

103 Léry, 72, 88, 197, 201, 208; *Hans Staden's True History*, 82, 96; Buono, 'Feathered Identities,' 106, 153, n. 287.

104 Surekha Davies, 'Depictions of Brazilians on French Maps, 1542–1555,' *The Historical Journal* 55:2 (2012), 1–32. I thank Peter Mancall for telling me about this image.

105 Louise E. Robbins, *Elephant Slaves and Pampered Parrots: Exotic Animals in Eighteenth-Century Paris* (Baltimore, MD: Johns Hopkins University Press, 2002), 10, 122, 136, 150; Boehrer, *Parrot Culture*, 56.

106 Boehrer, *Parrot Culture*, 50, 55–73; Erwin Stresemann, *Ornithology from Aristotle to the Present* (Cambridge, MA: Harvard University Press, 1975), 24–26.

107 Marc Shell 'Family Pet,' *Representations* 15 (1986): 121–153, esp. 123, 126, 129.

108 Quoted in Robbins, *Elephant Slaves*, 129.

109 Ibid., 142, 143; Boehrer, *Parrot Culture*.

110 James Serpell, *In the Company of Animals: A Study of Human–Animal Relationships* (Cambridge: Cambridge University Press (Canto), rev. ed. 1996), 72.

111 Francis Willughby and John Ray, *The Ornithology of Francis Willughby* (London: John Martyn, 1678), 123 and 128; Wafer, *A New Voyage*, 120.

112 Anghiera, *De Orbe Novo*, 265.

113 Shell, 'Family Pet,' 134–135; Kathleen Kete, *The Beast in the Boudoir: Petkeeping in Nineteenth-Century Paris* (Berkeley, CA: University of California Press, 1994), chs. 2 and 3, esp. 40. Keith Thomas writes that 'by 1700 all the symptoms of obsessive pet-keeping were in evidence,' (117) but I think he was including those animals that I consider 'vassals' in this category (*Man and the Natural World: Changing Attitudes in England, 1500–1800* [London: Allen Lane, 1983]).

114 Jean-Baptiste Labat, *Nouveau voyage aux isles de l'Amerique* (The Hague: P. Husson, 1724), 2: 155–156.
115 Ibid., 2: 157.
116 Ibid., 2: 157–158.
117 Ibid., 2: 158–159.
118 Breton, *Dictionaire*, 2: 290; Jorge Juan and Antonio de Ulloa, *A Voyage to South America*, trans. John Adams, 5th ed. (London: J. Brettell, 1807), 1: 409.
119 Léry, *Voyage*, 208, 213, also 210.
120 Willughby and Ray, *Ornithology*, 117.
121 Ibid., 118.
122 The classic is Thomas, *Man and the Natural World*; see, for instance, the recent Nathaniel Wolloch, *Subjugated Animals: Animals and Anthropocentrism in Early Modern European Culture* (Amherst: Humanity Books, 2006).

3

THE RESTLESS CLOCK

Jessica Riskin

The clock was an early modern thing of particular salience. During the sixteenth and seventeenth centuries, clocks constituted a socially, economically and culturally crucial technology, a philosophical and cultural point of reference, and a very visible object in the landscape, adorning churches, clock towers in town squares, houses and, in ever more miniature forms, people. As a philosophical and cultural point of reference, the clock provided a ubiquitous metaphor for natural systems of all kinds, from the clockwork cosmos of the heavens down to the clockwork microcosm of the smallest living creatures.

However, clocks in these usages did not always mean 'clockwork' in the senses of the term that later became dominant: rigid, passive, rote, constrained. On the contrary, particularly as models of living beings, clocks and other machines often signified very different and sometimes opposite things from these later meanings: responsive, interactive, surprising, funny.[1] A twenty-first-century reader of clockwork and other machine metaphors in early modern natural science must therefore read most alertly and suspend any preconceptions regarding the figurative meaning of 'clockwork' and 'machinery,' especially in relation to comparisons of clockwork machines to living bodies.

This chapter examines how actual machines (especially clocks, but also automata, organs, gears, pipes, hydraulic pumps...) informed philosophical conversations about the workings of living beings in unexpected ways. It focuses more attention upon philosophical developments than do the other contributions to this volume, but this does not make it an intellectual history rather than a history of things. Instead it is a history of things in their engagement with ideas and vice versa, a material history of ideas and an intellectual history of objects, on the principle that things and ideas must be no more separate in historical understanding than they are separable in lived experience.[2]

William Harvey, author of the hydraulic pump model of the heart, invoked automata – moving mechanical figures of people and animals – to describe the process of animal generation. Poring over the development of a chick embryo, Harvey observed that a great many things happened in a certain order 'in the same way as we see one wheel moving another in automata, and other pieces of mechanism.' But, Harvey said, the parts of the mechanism were not moving, as some natural philosophers claimed, in the sense of changing their places. Rather, the parts were remaining in place, but transforming 'in hardness, softness, colour, &ce.'[3] It was a mechanism made of *changing* parts.

Here was an idea to which Harvey regularly returned. Animals, he surmised, were like automata whose parts were perpetually transforming: expanding and contracting in response to heat and cold, imagination and sensation and ideas.[4] The image of a mechanism of changing parts echoes one in Harvey's earlier treatise on the motion of the heart. 'Mechanical contrivance' in the earlier passage, as in the later one, signified a succession of connected developments that were also all occurring at once. In the earlier passage, Harvey had famously likened the heart to a 'piece of machinery in which one wheel gives motion to another, yet all the wheels seem to move simultaneously.'[5] Geared mechanisms represented constellations of motions that seemed at once sequential and simultaneous, a congress of mutual causes and effects.[6] The first appearance of life itself, as Harvey described it, seemed to happen both all at once and as a sequence of events. With casual poetry, Harvey wrote of seeing the chick first as a 'little cloud,' and then,

> in the midst of the cloudlet in question there was a bloody point so small it disappeared during the contraction and escaped the sight, but in relaxation it reappeared again, red and like the point of a pin; so that betwixt the visible and the invisible, betwixt being and not being, as it were, it gave by its pulses a kind of representation of the commencement of life.[7]

A gathering cloud and, in its midst, a barely perceptible movement between being and not being: the origin of life. Clockwork and firearms offered models to depict a defining feature of this cloudy pulse that was life: the fusion of causation and simultaneity.

Chick embryos inspired another close observer, a couple of generations younger than Harvey, to think in terms of interacting machines. The Italian doctor and physiologist Marcello Malpighi differed from Harvey in that he viewed the embryo as 'preformed' within the egg, so that its growth took the form of a development rather than an accretion of parts.[8] But like Harvey, Malpighi saw tiny, organic machinery at work in the process. He described the development of the embryo as a sequence of 'machinelets' (*machinulæ*) giving rise to one another.[9] When he called the structures 'machinelets' and the process mechanical, he meant that it was rule-governed and preordained, an unfolding of material forms. Malpighi also recommended that anatomists reason by analogy from the larger and simpler natural machines, which they were able to see, to understand the invisibly tiniest and most complex machinery.[10]

Elsewhere, Harvey invoked an analogy that would become commonplace by the end of the century, the analogy between an animal body and a church organ. Muscles, he suggested, worked like 'play on the organ, virginals.' Under James I, English churches had resumed the use of organs in services, so they were once again a feature of the landscape and available as a source of models for living systems.[11] But the organ did not signify for Harvey what it later came to signify in such analogies: a complex sequence of mechanically enacted movements. Rather, Harvey meant that the muscles performed their actions by 'harmony and rhythm,' a kind of 'silent music.' Mind, he said, was the 'master of the choir': 'mind sets the mass in motion.'[12]

The particular ways in which Harvey invoked artificial mechanisms indicate a critical problem with classifying him, as historians have been inclined to do, either as a 'mechanist' or otherwise,[13] namely that the meaning of 'mechanism' and related terms was very much in flux. Lecturing at the College of Physicians in London in April of 1616, Harvey told his anatomy and surgery students that anatomy was 'philosophical, medical and mechanical.'[14] But what did he mean, and what did his students understand, by 'mechanical'? In part, he likely meant that there was no need to invoke ethereal or celestial substances in explaining physiological phenomena, because the mundane elements patently transcended their own limits when they acted. The 'air and water, the winds and the ocean' could 'waft navies to either India and round this globe.' The terrestrial elements could also 'grind, bake, dig, pump, saw timber, sustain fire, support some things, overwhelm others.' Fire could cook, heat, soften, harden, melt, sublime, transform, set in motion and produce iron itself. The compass pointing north, the clock indicating the hours, all were accomplished simply by means of the ordinary elements, each of which 'exceeded its own proper powers in action.'[15] Here was a form of mechanism that was not reductive, but really the reverse: a rising of mechanical parts to new powers.

Similarly, Harvey elsewhere defined 'mechanics' as 'that which overcomes things by which Nature is overcome.' His examples were things having 'little power of movement' in themselves that were nonetheless able to move great weights, such as a pulley. Mechanics, understood in this way, included natural phenomena that overcame the usual course of nature: Harvey again mentioned the muscles. Therefore to say, as Harvey did, that the muscles worked *mechanically* in this instance meant that the muscles, like artificial devices such as a pulley, overcame the usual course of nature and moved great weights without themselves being weighty.[16]

Motion, relatedly, was a term with various meanings, as Harvey himself emphasized. He noted many different kinds of local movement: the movement of a night-blooming tree and that of a heliotrope; the movements caused by a magnet and those caused by a rubbed piece of jet.[17] In what were likely notes for a treatise on the physiology of movement, Harvey jotted down any form of local movement that came to mind, such as the presumably peristaltic and undeniably graphic '[s]hit by degrees not by squirts.' He identified too, as a distinct form of movement, a kind of controlled escalation, as '[i]n going forward, mounting up, with the consent of the intellect in a state of emotion.'[18]

Harvey drew upon another form of causal motion to resolve another critical mystery in the generation of life. This was action at a distance, which, like the apparently simultaneous occurrence of causally connected events, seemed to pose a problem for a properly 'mechanical' anatomy. Invoking Aristotle, Harvey proposed that embryos arose from a kind of contagion, 'a vital virus' with which the sperm infected the egg.[19] But after the initial moment of contact, once the contaminating element had disappeared and become 'a nonentity,' Harvey wondered, how did the process continue. '[H]ow, I ask, does a nonentity act? How does a thing which is not in contact fashion another thing like itself?'[20] Aristotle invoked 'automatic puppets' to explain precisely this seeming mystery of action at a distance. He had surmised that the initial contact at conception set off a succession of linked motions that constituted the development of the embryo.[21] According to Aristotle's model, Harvey explained, the seed formed the fetus 'by motion' transmitted through a kind of automatic mechanism. Harvey rejected this explanation along with the whole host of other traditional explanations by analogy: to clocks, to kingdoms governed by the mandates of their sovereigns, and to instruments used to produce works of art. All, he thought, were insufficient.[22]

In their place, Harvey proposed a different analogy: one between the uterus and the brain (Figures 3.1 and 3.2). The two, he observed, were strikingly similar in structure, and a mechanical anatomy should correlate structures with physiological functions: 'where the same structure exists,' Harvey reasoned, there must be 'the same function implanted.' The uterus, when ready to conceive, strongly resembled the 'ventricles' of the brain and the functions of each were called 'conceptions.' Perhaps, then, these were essentially the same sort of process.[23] The brain, Harvey taught his anatomy and surgery students, was a kind of workshop, the 'manufactory of animal spirits.'[24] Brains produced works of art by bringing an immaterial idea or form to matter. Perhaps a uterus produced an embryo in the same way, by means of a 'plastic art' capable of bringing an idea or form to flesh. The form of an embryo existed in the uterus of the mother just as the form of a house existed in the brain of the builder. This would solve the problem of action at a distance. The moment of insemination endowed the uterus with an ability to conceive embryos in the same way that education endowed the brain with the ability to conceive ideas. Once the seed disappeared, it no longer needed to act: it was the uterus itself that took over the task of fashioning the embryo.[25] The idea that the uterus functioned like a brain, actively fashioning an embryo the way a brain fleshes out an idea, was for Harvey not only within the bounds of the 'mechanical,' but a model that could actually rescue mechanism by eliminating the need for action at a distance.

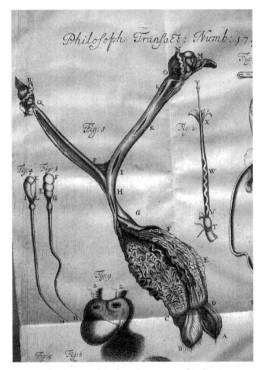

FIGURE 3.1 Antonie van Leeuwenhoek's drawing of a dog's uterus

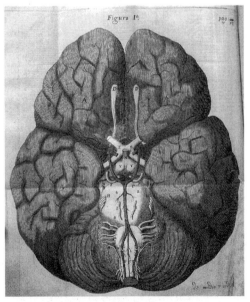

FIGURE 3.2 Christopher Wren's drawing of a brain

In keeping with his inclusion of purposeful action – the womb's fashioning of an embryo – within the mechanisms of life, Harvey disliked arguments from design, which instead referred all order to the rational foresight of an external engineer. This did not discourage Harvey's admirer Robert Boyle from later trying, nevertheless, to represent Harvey as a natural theologian. 'I remember that when I asked our famous Harvey,' Boyle reminisced, what had ever induced him to think of a circulation of the blood,

> He answer'd me, that when he took notice that the Valves in the Veins of so many several Parts of the Body, were so Plac'd that they gave free passage to the Blood Towards the Heart, but oppos'd the passage of the Venal Blood the Contrary way: He was invited to imagine, that so Provident a Cause as Nature had not so Plac'd so many Valves without Design.[26]

Yet Harvey himself maintained that Nature did not work by design, skill, foresight or reason but rather by 'a connate genius or disposition.' The existence of a higher agency was generally apparent in the excellence of natural phenomena, according to Harvey, but these did not operate *by means of* that higher agency. Natural phenomena operated by an inherent agency. Therefore, those who would 'refer all to art or artifice are to be held indifferent judges of nature or natural things.'[27]

During the Civil War, taking refuge in Oxford, Harvey lived briefly in Merton Street, where he became a neighbor of a younger doctor and anatomist, Thomas Willis, an early cartographer of the brain and nervous system. Like Harvey, Willis resisted the central tenets of brute mechanism. He understood Descartes, with his account of animals as automata, to have meant that animals were 'meerly passive': they moved only when set in motion by 'other Bodies, striking some part of the Soul' so that their actions were nothing but the 'artificial Motion of a Mechanical Engine.'[28] This was the standard construal of Descartes' theory by the 1650s and the one toward which Descartes himself (ambivalently) tended. Willis disliked the passivity of this view of the animal machine. Why, after all, must matter be incapable of agency and perception? God could surely have endowed matter with these capacities. Willis therefore described a 'self-moving' animal-machine possessed of a fully material soul common to both beasts and humans. This material soul was responsible, he reckoned, for life, sensation and motion.[29]

Willis's account of animals was thus as rigorously materialist as Descartes', but in Willis's view, the material soul of animals was also 'Knowing and Active.' It was even capable of learning by means of the 'Accidents' it encountered as it stumbled through the world in the course of its day. By means of these contingencies, the soul acquired new knowledge and skills. Its capabilities accordingly increased in complexity. To his knowing, active, educable, yet fully material soul, Willis ascribed physical 'Members' and 'Organical Parts.' He singled out two parts in particular, a vital component in the blood and a sensitive component in the animal spirits, which traveled throughout the 'Pipes and other Machines' of the brain and nerves.[30] The animal soul as Willis described it was coextensive with the body and made of particles of the same matter, but the choicest among these: the most 'subtle and highly active.' These most 'nimble and Spirituous Particles' played a principal role in the formation of the animal body. Gathering together in dynamic, 'Turgid' heaps, they jostled, stirred and steered the other, grosser particles into their proper places.[31]

Artificial machinery offered Willis plenty of models on which to base his idea of a vital, perceptive, active animal-machine. He went beyond the clockmaker's assemblage of wheels and gears, which was, after all, but a narrow domain in the growing expanse of human-made devices. 'Mechanical things,' Willis pointed out, required 'Energetical' components: 'Fire, Air, and Light.' Any smith, chemist, glassmaker, lens-grinder, or instrument maker could easily testify to the truth of this. Likewise the 'Great Workman,' in creating the animal-machine, 'did make the greatly active, and also most subtil Souls of Living Creatures' out of the most active and energetic particles of matter. The movements of these particles through the body were like 'a blast of Wind in a Machine': when struck, they ran 'hither and thither, and so produce[d] the Exercises of Sense and Motion in the whole Body.'[32] Willis too had organs in mind: his drawing of the nerves of the trunk, indeed, strikingly resembled the symmetrical geometry of an organ (Figures 3.3 and 3.4).

However, when Willis looked at automatic organs, he saw constraint, to be sure, but not passivity. If the soul of a man was like a musician playing any tune he liked on his instrument, the 'Soul of the Brute' was rather like a 'water

FIGURE 3.3   Thomas Dallam's organ, King's College Chapel, Cambridge University

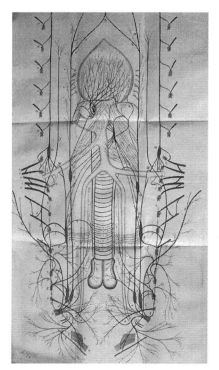

FIGURE 3.4 Thomas Willis, drawing of nerves

Organ': it could play only a limited repertoire of tunes 'regularly prescribed by a certain Rule or Law,' and yet it nevertheless 'Institute[d], for Ends necessary for it self, many series of Actions.'[33] Artificial mechanisms provided models not only for agency, but also for indeterminate, variable and responsive activity. Guillaume Lamy, a member of the Paris Medical Faculty,[34] invoked a weathervane, for example, in his rigorously mechanist account of the sensitive soul, to show how a mechanism could behave as unpredictably as a young man's passions. These would turn and shift according to the prevailing winds like a cock on a church tower.[35]

The person who probably went the farthest toward establishing the mechanism of the new philosophy along a different trajectory was the committed optimist, G. W. Leibniz. In his view, neither animals nor, indeed, machines were brutes. Leibniz figured prominently among the many who rejected Descartes' claim that animals lacked souls. But in his case, it was part of a more general refutation of Cartesian physics: to Leibniz, nothing really lacked a soul. To be sure, no sort of brute machinery, no matter how subtle, could by itself account for perception. But neither could it account for 'the principle of action and motion' under any circumstances.[36] Descartes' clockwork, to Leibniz, was implausible even as an account of a clock, let alone of a dog. Mere '*extended mass*' could never suffice. Mechanics required something more: 'the notion of *force*, which is very intelligible, even though it springs from Metaphysics.' Matter drained of spirit could explain nothing, not even inanimate machinery.[37]

Leibniz elaborated his idea of a *vis viva* or 'living force' in all mechanical phenomena during the so-called *vis viva* controversy of the 1680s and 90s. Here he defended a view of conservation of *vis viva*, mathematically equivalent to the later notion of kinetic energy, against Cartesians who argued for Descartes' principle of conservation of motion, equivalent to the later notion of momentum.[38] Motion, Leibniz argued, was 'not something entirely real' because it consisted merely of relations among objects, whereas force, a 'force of acting,' was 'something real,' belonging to a given body in itself.[39] Moreover, he said, no one had ever explained force,[40] and he rejected what he saw as the current tendency to instead 'summon God *ex machina*, and withdraw all force for acting from things.' This was a marionette-mechanism with God as the puppeteer, such that 'when a person thinks and tries to move his arm, God moves the arm for him,' an idea so absurd it 'ought to have warned these writers they were depending on a false principle.'[41]

On the other hand, Leibniz also disliked Henry More's and others' appeal to 'an Archaeus,' or Paracelsian vital spirit, which he found 'unintelligible': 'as if not everything in nature can be explained mechanically, and as if those who try to explain everything mechanically are thought to eliminate incorporeal things.'[42] Rather, Leibniz was after a third way: neither marionette-mechanism nor alchemical abandonments of mechanism, but a fully mechanist account of nature that incorporated immaterial 'active force.'[43]

These principles were not purely abstract, but constituted a fully alternative approach to physics and engineering. Leibniz's notion of *vis viva* informed a tradition of physics and engineering growing through the eighteenth century and into the nineteenth. In 1740, the French marquise, mathematician, philosopher, and lover of Voltaire, Emilie du Châtelet, used Leibniz's notion of living force to present a revised version of Newtonian physics. As the translator of Newton's *Principia* into French, and one of a select few able to read and understand that text, du Châtelet was influential in shaping the promulgation and development of physics in the eighteenth century, and she saw Leibnitz's living force as its salvation.

Both Descartes and Newton, she wrote, had tried and failed to describe a force in the universe that would remain constant and undying. If one equated force with the motion of a moving body, one could not avoid the terrible conclusion that the universe was winding down, losing force, and would one day need to be set in motion again. But if one took the living force in a moving body to be proportional to the square of its velocity, the problem was solved. In that case one would immediately see that this force, 'which is something real, and which endures like matter' would 'remain steadfast' and never perish.[44] Leibniz's active mechanism, with the understanding of force and motion that du Châtelet promoted, was no idle speculation, but had momentous scientific and practical consequences. The Leibnitzian tradition in physics and engineering also included such people as Lazare and Sadi Carnot, Gaspard Monge, Jean-Victor Poncelet and John Smeaton, whose work culminated in the development of an energistic physics and the concepts of energy and work around the middle of the nineteenth century.[45]

To Leibniz and his followers in this tradition, the limits of brute mechanism seemed glaringly obvious. Boyle, Leibnitz judged, had failed to distinguish ultimate from proximate causes when he presented his vision of nature as machinery. When Boyle and the other argument-from-design natural theologians exiled perception and agency to a position fully outside their world-machine, it appeared to Leibniz to be a kind of blinkering, a refusal to see the obvious: the machinery could never work without metaphysical forces driving it.[46] Everywhere in material events one found an active agency working from within: 'a flare that runs the length of a cord or a fluid that runs in a channel.' In the 'last analysis of the laws of mechanics, and the nature of substances,' Leibniz argued repeatedly, one had ultimately to appeal 'to active indivisible principles.'[47] In his world-machine, perception and agency were not banished but active within the very works.

Metaphysical principles played at the crux of Leibniz's mechanical systems. His guiding axiom, for example, that 'there is nothing without a reason' was a mechanical as well as a metaphysical principle. This principle of sufficient reason, Leibniz reckoned, constituted the very connection between mechanical causes and their mechanical effects. The Archimedean principle of equilibrium, in which two equal weights sat in a balance in the same relation to its axis, provided Leibniz with an example: since the situation was perfectly symmetrical, the balance had no reason to tip to one side rather than the other, and therefore it remained in equilibrium.[48] Not only physiology but physics itself required perceptive agency. Moreover, since the 'entrails' of nature, the movements of her internal parts, were all hidden from view, understanding could come more easily through a study of her 'designs' than of her structural 'movements.'[49]

Perhaps Leibniz's search for alternative models for a mechanist natural science helped to motivate the great interest he took in Chinese philosophy.[50] In pursuit of this interest, he studied written Chinese and acquired a limited knowledge of its structure. He also read the history of China and translations of Chinese classical texts that Jesuit missionaries had produced during the 1670s and 80s, published as *Confucius Sinarum philosophus sive scientia Sinensis latine exposita* (1687). Shortly afterward, during a trip to Rome, Leibniz met Claudio Grimaldi, a Jesuit who had served as a diplomatic aide at the imperial court in Beijing and been involved in various mathematical and astronomical pursuits there. After their meeting, Leibniz sent Grimaldi a list of thirty questions, largely about Chinese natural sciences, resources and practical arts.[51] And he did in fact find, in Chinese approaches to nature, concepts that he thought traversed the traditional philosophical categories in Europe.

When Leibniz wrote the 'Discourse on the natural theology of the Chinese' (1716) during his last year of life, his project was accommodationist in the tradition of the sixteenth-century Italian Jesuit Matteo Ricci, a founder of the Jesuit China Mission. Like Ricci, rather than urging that the Chinese must renounce their ancient beliefs in favor of doctrinal Christian ones, Leibniz meant to demonstrate the reconcilability, indeed the essential sameness, of Christianity and Confucianism.[52] To that end, he argued against the allegations leveled by some Europeans of Chinese materialism, focusing particular attention on the Confucian notion of *Li*, which Jesuit interpreters had rendered as equivalent to the Scholastics' prime matter.[53]

One must not interpret *Li* that way, Leibniz cautioned, since the Scholastics' prime matter was 'purely passive, without order or form.' *Li* in that case could not possibly be 'the origin of activity,' as Confucianism taught. 'I do not believe [the Chinese] to be so stupid or absurd,' Leibniz wrote, as to attribute 'the active power, and the perception that regulates this active power' to so passive and inert a thing as the Scholastics' prime matter.[54] *Li*, he emphasized, in Chinese usage denoted not only 'the material basis of Heaven and Earth and other material things,' but also 'the moral basis of virtues, customs, and other spiritual things.'[55] In Confucianism (as rendered by European commentators), Leibniz identified a principle that was at once active and mechanical, material and moral: one which violated, in other words, the increasingly entrenched injunction of philosophical mechanism that segregated the moral from the mechanical.

In reacting against the brute mechanism of his contemporaries, Leibniz began with its insufficiency to account for life and mind. He appealed to internal experience, the inner consciousness of 'this *me*' not explicable by 'figures or movements.'[56] A sentient, thinking being, he argued in this instance, was 'not a mechanical thing like a watch or a mill': 'one cannot conceive of sizes and shapes and motions combining mechanically to produce something which thinks, and senses too.'[57] In a thought experiment designed to show the non-mechanical nature of thought, he instructed his reader to imagine a big machine, the size of a mill, that could think, feel and perceive. Imagine, he wrote, walking into this great factory of thought and looking around. You would find only 'pieces that push each other and never anything to explain a perception.' You would understand consciousness no better than before entering the mill of mind. Looking at the machinery, the pushing and pulling, the moving parts, the thing you would be led to understand was that perception and consciousness were not that. Perception, Leibniz wrote, resided not in the operation of the mechanism but in its very substance. Indeed, perception *was* the primary substance: mind was the stuff of the machine.[58]

But Leibniz ultimately decided that if sentient beings could not be made of pure clockwork, neither could clocks. Living creatures and human selves were inexplicable by means of brute mechanics, but that was only the tip of the iceberg. Matter itself, Leibniz decided, could not be made of inert chunks: '*atoms of matter* are contrary to reason.' Any corporeal entity, no matter how 'invincibly attached,' must still be composed of parts: one could imagine dividing it further.

The indivisible atoms that made up the world, therefore, must be something else: '[w]e could call them *metaphysical points*: they have something *vital* and a kind of *perception*.'[59] Over the course of his career, Leibniz thus developed an increasingly distinct understanding of mechanism.[60] Since extended chunks of matter on their own, in his view, explained nothing, he replaced extension with perception and offered an equal and opposite philosophy to Hobbesian materialism: a reduction of matter to spirit. In place of chunks of matter, he put perceiving subjects. The building blocks of his cosmos were not blocks but little souls. Any material thing could be divided, whereas to be simple meant to be indivisible. Therefore the simplest substances, Leibniz reasoned, must by definition be spirits.

No difference in substance, therefore, divided material from spiritual things. By the time he wrote the *Monadology* (1714), Leibniz had decided that both were made of 'Monads,' elementary spiritual substances whose defining attribute was perception. The difference between material and spiritual things resided only in the laws governing them: laws of force and transfer of motion for material things, laws of justice for spirits. Animals were material in the sense that God governed them as a 'machinist.' Rational souls, able to think, to recognize God and eternal and necessary truths, were spiritual in the sense that God governed these as a 'Prince' or 'Legislator.'[61]

Leibniz described the cosmos and everything within it, including living animals and humans, as a great nesting of machines within machines within machines, all built out of little perceiving spirits. What Leibniz now meant by 'machinery' was therefore, in a key sense, not just different from, but in fact opposite to what Hobbes and the Cartesians meant. There was no actual pushing and pulling, no action by impact, but only the appearance of these mechanical causes. Indeed, matter itself was an appearance, a secondary effect of the perceptual substance out of which the world was composed. Monads could not change one another, having no extension, no parts: as Leibniz famously described it, no 'windows' through which anything could come in or go out. Rather, each little soul followed its own internally directed sequence of changes that had been set in motion at the beginning of time, and a pre-established harmony coordinated all these sequences so as to follow the laws of mechanics.[62]

The same eternal, harmonious order also correlated the laws of matter and spirit such that 'the internal springs of bodies are ready to act of themselves, as they should, at the very moment when the soul has a conforming desire or thought,' and the mechanical laws of nature would always bear out the moral order of justice.[63] Thus, when Leibniz compared God to a watchmaker and his creations to automata, when he wrote that the bodies of men and animals were 'no less mechanical' than watches,[64] he meant something profoundly different from the very same statement by a Cartesian or a Hobbesian.

To see how very different his meaning was, consider the image from which this chapter takes its title, Leibniz's image of the 'restless clock':

> In German, the word for the balance of a clock is *Unruhe*—which also means disquiet; and one can take that for a model of how it is in our bodies, which can never be perfectly at their ease. For if one's body were at ease, some new effect of objects—some small change in the sense-organs, and in the viscera and bodily cavities—would at once alter the balance and compel those parts of the body to exert some tiny effort to get back into the best state possible; with the result that there is a perpetual conflict which makes up, so to speak, the disquiet of our clock; so that this [German] appellation is rather to my liking.[65]

Nowhere in this passage, among the metaphorical significations of 'clock,' do we find what had by then become, and still remain, the expected connotations: regularity, imperturbability, precision. Instead we have something like their opposites: disquiet, unease, exertion, conflict. Wherever Leibniz returned to the notion of an animal as a machine his meaning was similarly exotic. He described natural machinery as 'entangled,' waxing and waning, enfolding and unfolding, 'frail' and yet capable of self-maintenance.[66]

In the conversation surrounding Leibniz's writing, too, machinery held implications strikingly different from those, such as absolute uniformity, that were even then becoming ever more firmly associated with clockwork. The French Calvinist Pierre Bayle, for example, who engaged Leibniz on the subject of human machinery during the late 1690s, argued that a machine was distinctive in its capacity to act variously, and that it differed in this regard from a simple entity, which was constrained always 'to act uniformly if no foreign cause divert[ed] it.' Being composed of several pieces, a machine 'would act diversely, because the particular activity of each piece could at any moment change the course of the others.'[67] To Bayle, a machine was something made of active parts whose actions generated possibilities.

Likewise, when Leibniz called a process 'mechanical,' he did not mean that it was drained of spirit, agency and perception. Rather, such a process followed entirely from its own internal principles, with no appeal to a *Deus ex machina*.[68] The motions of the celestial bodies, the formation of plants and animals, the organism of a living being, all of these were divinely formed mechanisms, their only miracle being at their origin, and '[w]hat follows upon it purely natural and entirely mechanical.'[69] Leibniz's great objection to the Newtonian system, which he voiced concertedly during the last couple years of his life in an intense epistolary debate with Newton's friend and translator, Samuel Clarke, was that Newton described the cosmos as an artifact, a device, of brute mechanism. Like any such device, it required its Maker to step in and adjust it, to rewind it and keep it running. The very running of Newton's cosmic Clock, therefore, rested upon an extra-natural cause, an actor intervening from outside the system.

In Leibniz's view, this was not only to denigrate God's handiwork but also to violate the principles of naturalism and mechanism. A thoroughly naturalist, mechanical theory of nature, he argued, could accommodate no such interventions from outside. Rather, such a theory would need to include the ultimate causes as well as the proximate ones; it must encompass the metaphysical principles governing force and the laws of motion. According to Leibniz's ideal of science, there should be one single system encompassing all of nature, with nothing outsourced, nothing rendered exceptional or external. The authors of the mechanical philosophy – Galileo, Descartes, Hobbes, Gassendi – had 'purged inexplicable chimera from philosophy' but they had left a metaphysical gap and filled it with a meddlesome God who acted supernaturally. 'I,' wrote Leibniz, 'tried to fill this gap, and have at last shown that *everything happens mechanically in nature, but that the principles of mechanism are metaphysical*.'[70]

We return, at last, to the clock, that early modern thing of momentous, but ambiguous, connotation. When considering its significance as a universal metaphor for natural systems of every kind, from cosmos to creature, only keep in mind that a clock could mean nature's mystery naturalized, a demonstration that mechanism is metaphysics and vice versa. It could mean an unquiet and restless thing, in the same state of perpetual flux and conflict that is life.

Notes

1   The first mechanical clocks appeared on European abbeys and churches in the late twelfth and early thirteenth centuries, but clock-making developed rapidly in the fifteenth and sixteenth centuries, generating not only smaller and more accurate clocks, but elaborate clockwork displays of moving mechanical figures: angels, devils, saints, animals, and religious and earthly scenes of every kind. Key sources in the history of clocks and clockwork automata include Carlo Cipolla, *Clocks and Culture, 1300–1700* (New York: Norton, 2003 [1st edition 1967]); David S. Landes, *Revolution in Time: Clocks and the Making of the Modern World* (Cambridge, MA: Harvard University Press, 1983); and Klaus Maurice and Otto Mayr, *The Clockwork Universe: German Clocks and Automata, 1550–1650* (Washington, DC: The Smithsonian Institution, 1980). See also Jessica Riskin, 'Machines in the Garden,' *Republics of Letters: A Journal for the Study of Knowledge, Politics, and the Arts* 1.2 (2010): http://rofl.stanford.edu/node/59.

2   A thriving recent and current literature has been exploring the history of the material culture of science in relation to scientific ideas and theories, including especially the work included in two volumes edited by Lorraine Daston: *Biographies of Scientific Objects* (Chicago, IL: The University of Chicago Press, 2000) and *Things That Talk: Object Lessons From Art and Science* (Cambridge, MA: MIT Press, 2004). These volumes take up the problem of combining material culture and intellectual history in various ways. The things under consideration in the first volume, *Biographies*, are all objects in the sense of being objects of scientific study, but they include as many intellectual things as physical ones (and, indeed, quite a few whose status, intellectual or physical, would be hard to decide): mathematical entities, dreams, the self, economic theories of value, society, culture, the ether. The *Things that Talk* of the second volume are more straightforwardly physical—architectural columns, soap bubbles, photographs, glass flowers—and here the project is to show how such things 'talk' in the sense that they contain messages that they press upon their human interlocutors and thereby shape the conversation around them. This essay represents a further instance of the current interest in the history of material culture in relation to intellectual history and vice versa. In this case, both the things in question and the nature of their relations to ideas are straightforward. The things

are physical things – mechanical contraptions – and they are inseparable from ideas because people incessantly used them as models and examples to think with and, reciprocally, designed and built the machines on the basis of (implicit and explicit) philosophical principles. The historiographical novelty here, if any, lies not in any general claim about how things and ideas are related, then, but rather in seeing how one's understanding of each transforms when one regards their history as conjoined rather than separate.

3 William Harvey, 'Anatomical Exercises on the Generation of Animals, to which are added essays on Parturition; on the Membranes, and Fluids of the Uterus; and on Conception' (1651), in *The Works of William Harvey, M.D.*, trans. Robert Willis (London: Syndenham Society, 1847), 417.

4 Harvey, *De motu locali animalium* (*c.*1627), ed. and trans. Gweneth Whitteridge (Cambridge: Cambridge University Press, 1959), 99, 153: 'Or as muscles in automata: in action movement is effected while the parts become greater and less by turns...'

5 Harvey, 'An Anatomical Disquisition on the Motion of the Heart' (1628) in *Works*, trans. Willis, 31. In the original Latin: *una rota aliam movente, omnes simul movere videantur.*

6 In the same way, Harvey also found the heart to be like the mechanism in firearms, in which the sequence of trigger, flint, steel, spark, powder, flame, explosion, and shot all seemed to take place 'in the twinkling of an eye,' Harvey, 'The Motion of the Heart,' 31–32.

7 Ibid., 30–31.

8 The debate between 'preformationists' and 'epigenicists' has been much studied. For some landmark and some recent treatments, see Peter Bowler, 'Preformation and Pre-existence in the Seventeenth Century: A Brief Analysis,' *Journal of the History of Biology* 43 (1971): 221–244; idem, 'The Changing Meaning of 'Evolution,' *Journal of the History of Ideas* 36 (1975): 95–114; Stephen Jay Gould, 'On Heroes and Fools in Science,' *Natural History* 83.7 (1974): 30–32; Shirley Roe, *Matter, Life, and Generation* (Cambridge: Cambridge University Press, 1981); Jane Maienschein, 'Competing Epistemologies and Developmental Biology,' in *Biology and Epistemology*, ed. Richard Creath and Jane Maienschein (Cambridge: Cambridge University Press, 2000).

9 Marcello Malpighi, 'Dissertatio epistolica de formatione pulli in ovo' (1673), in *Opera omnia* (London: Robert Scot, 1686). See François Duchesneau, 'Leibniz's Model for Analyzing Organic Phenomena,' *Perspectives on Science* 11.4 (2003): 399. On Malpighi, see also Howard B. Adelmann, *Marcello Malpighi and the Evolution of Embryology*, 5 vols. (Ithaca, NY: Cornell University Press, 1966); and Walter Bernardi, *Le metafisiche dell'embrione: Scienze della vita e filosofia da Malpighi a Spallanzani* (Florence: L. S. Olschki, 1986).

10 Malpighi, 'Anatome plantarum' (1675–1676), in *Opera omnia*, 1: 1.

11 On organs and their role in early modern philosophical discussion, see Penelope Gouk, *Music, Science and Natural Magic in Seventeenth-Century England* (New Haven, CT: Yale University Press, 1999), esp. chs. 3 and 4; and Michael John Gorman, 'Between the Demonic and the Miraculous: Athanasius Kircher and the Baroque Culture of Machines,' in *The Great Art of Knowing: The Baroque Encyclopedia of Athanasius Kircher*, ed. Daniel Stolzenberg (Stanford, CA: Stanford University Libraries, 2001), 59–70.

12 Harvey, *De motu locali animalium*, 145, 147.

13 For some recent treatments of this question, see Roger French, *William Harvey's Natural Philosophy* (Cambridge: Cambridge University Press, 1994), esp. ch. 8; and Jole Shackelford, *William Harvey and the Mechanics of the Heart* (New York: Oxford University Press, 2003), esp. pp. 109–110.

14 Harvey, *Lectures on the Whole of Anatomy* [*Prelectiones Anatomiae Universalis*] (1616), ed. and trans. C. D. O'Malley, F. N. L. Poynter and K. F. Russell (Berkeley, CA: University of California Press, 1961), 22.

15 Harvey, 'The Generation of Animals,' 508–509.

16 Harvey, *De motu locali animalium*, 127.

17 Ibid., 43.

18 Ibid., 143.

19 The passage in Aristotle to which Harvey referred was *History of Animals*, bk. 6, part 13; Harvey, 'The Generation of Animals,' 359.

20 Ibid., 359–360.

21 Aristotle, *Generation of Animals*, bk. 2: 734b3–734b18; 741a32–741b24.

22 Harvey, 'The Generation of Animals,' 345–346, 350, 359–360. See also *De motu locali animalium*, 147 and 151, where Harvey canvasses the various models of order: a well-governed state; the work of masons, bricklayers and carpenters; the working of a ship, an army and a choir.

23 Harvey, 'The Generation of Animals,' 372, 577–579, 585.

24 Harvey, *The Whole of Anatomy*, 219.

25 Harvey, 'The Generation of Animals,' 577–579, 585.

26 Robert Boyle, *A Disquisition about the Final Causes of Natural Things* (London: John Taylor, 1688), 157–158. See also Richard A. Hunter and Ida Macalpine, 'William Harvey and Robert Boyle,' *Notes and Records of the Royal Society of London* 13.2 (1958): 115–127.

27 Harvey, 'The Generation of Animals,' 367–369.

28 Thomas Willis, *Two Discourses Concerning the Souls of Brutes* (London: T. Dring, C. Harper, and J. Leigh, 1683), 3. Willis attributed the same view to the Spanish doctor and philosopher Gomez Pereira before Descartes and to Kenelm Digby afterward.

29 Ibid., preface, 56.

30 Ibid., 34, 24.

31 Ibid., 6.

32 Ibid., 24, 56.

33 Ibid., 34.

34 On Lamy and his relations to Willis, see Ann Thomson, *Bodies of Thought: Science, Religion, and the Soul in the Early Enlightenment* (Oxford: Oxford University Press, 2008), 86–88.

35 Guillaume Lamy, 'Explication méchanique et physique des fonctions de l'âme sensitive' (1677), in *Discours anatomiques: Explication méchanique et physique des fonctions de l'âme sensitive*, ed. Anna Minerbi Belgrado (Paris: Voltaire Foundation, 1996), 167.

36 G. W. Leibniz, 'Reflections on the Souls of Beasts' (1710?) in *G.W. Leibniz: Texts and Translations* ed. and trans. Donald Rutherford (San Diego, CA: University of California, San Diego, 2001).

37 Leibniz, 'Système nouveau de la nature et de la communication des substances' (1695), in *Système nouveau de la nature et de la communication des substances et autres textes*, ed. Christiane Frémont (Paris: Flammarion, 1994), 66.

38 On the *vis viva* controversy, see Carolyn Iltis, 'Leibniz and the Vis Viva Controversy,' *Isis* 62.1 (1971): 21–35; and Daniel Garber, 'Leibniz: Physics and Philosophy,' in *The Cambridge Companion to Leibniz*, ed. Nicholas Jolley (Cambridge: Cambridge University Press, 1995), 309–314.

39 Leibniz, 'A Discourse on Metaphysics' (1686), in *Philosophical Essays* (hereafter PE), ed. and trans. Roger Ariew and Daniel Garber (Indianapolis, IN: Hackett, 1989), 51. Leibniz first presented his refutation of Descartes' principle of conservation of motion in 'Brevis demonstratio erroris memorabilis Cartesii …,' in *Acta Eruditorum* (March 1686): 161–163; see also Leibniz, 'Specimen Dynamicum' (1695), in PE, 130.

40 Leibniz, 'Specimen Dynamicum,' 119, 123.

41 Ibid., 125, 130.

42 Ibid., 126.

43 Leibniz, 'Essay de dynamique sur les loix du mouvement, où il est monstré, qu'il ne se conserve pas la même quantité de mouvement, mais la même force absolue,

ou bien la même quantité de l'action motrice,' *Mathematische Schriften*, ed. C. I. Gerhardt, 9 vols (Halle: H. W. Schmidt, 1860), 6: 215–231.

44 Gabrielle-Émilie le Tonnier de Breteuil, marquise du Châtelet, *Institutions de physique* (Paris: Prault fils, 1740), ch. 21, cited passages on 446 and 449–450.

45 On the role of *vis viva* in eighteenth- and nineteenth-century physics and engineering, see Erwin Hiebert, *Historical Roots of the Energy Principle* (Madison, WI: University of Wisconsin Press, 1962); D. S. L. Cardwell, 'Some Factors in the Early Development of the Concepts of Power, Work and Energy,' *The British Journal for the History of Science* 3 (1967): 209–224; Pierre Costabel, *La signification d'un débat sur trente ans (1728–1758): La question des forces vives* (Paris: Societé Francaise d'Histoire des Sciences et des Techniques, 1983); Ivor Grattan-Guinness, 'Work of the Workers: Advances in Engineering Mechanics and Instruction in France, 1800–1830,' *Annals of Science* 41 (1984): 1–33; Jean-Pierre Séris, *Machine et communication: Du théâtre des machines à la mécanique industrielle* (Paris: J. Vrin, 1987); Olivier Darrigol, 'God, Waterwheels, and Molecules: Saint-Venant's Anticipation of Energy Conservation,' *Historical Studies in the Physical and Biological Sciences* 31.2 (2001): 285–353. I am grateful to Robert Brain for urging me to consider the physical and practical importance of *vis viva* and the Leibnizian tradition that formed around it.

46 Leibniz, 'On Nature Itself, Or, on the Inherent Force and Actions of Created Things, Toward Confirming and Illustrating Their Dynamics' (1698), in PE, 156.

47 Leibniz, 'Réponse aux réflexions continues dans la seconde edition du Dicionnaire critique de M. Bayle, article Rorarius, sur le système de l'harmonie préétablie' (1702), in *Système nouveau*, ed. Frémont, 194, 197–198.

48 Leibniz, 'Plus ultra' (1679), *Leibniz: Philosophical Papers and Letters*, ed. and trans. Leroy E. Loemker (Dordrecht: Reidel, 1969), 227.

49 Leibniz, 'Doutes concernant la Vraie Théorie Médicale de Stahl' (1709), in *La controverse entre Stahl et Leibniz sur la vie, l'organisme et le mixte*, ed. Sarah Carvallo (Paris: J. Vrin, 2004), préambule, 81.

50 I thank Tim Brook for drawing my attention to Leibniz's interest in Chinese natural philosophy in relation to his search for an alternative, active form of mechanism.

51 See Daniel J. Cook and Henry Rosemont, Jr., 'The Sources of Leibniz's Knowledge of China,' in Leibniz, *Writings on China*, ed. Cook and Rosemont (Chicago, IL: Open Court, 1994), 10–18; Franklin Perkins, *Leibniz and China: A Commerce of Light* (Cambridge: Cambridge University Press, 2004), ch. 3.

52 On Matteo Ricci, accommodationism and Leibniz, see Cook and Rosemont, 'Sources,' 13–14.

53 See Leibniz, 'Remarks on Chinese Rites and Religion' (1708), in *Writings on China*, ed. Cook and Rosemont, 68; Leibniz, 'Discourse on the Natural Theology of the Chinese' (1716), in *Writings on China*, ed. Cook and Rosemont, 77–80.

54 Leibniz, 'The Natural Theology of the Chinese,' 85.

55 Ibid., 80.

56 Leibniz, 'Réponse aux réflexions,' 197.

57 Leibniz, *New Essays on Human Understanding*, ed. and trans. Peter Remnant and Jonathan Bennett (Cambridge: Cambridge University Press, 1996 [c 1690–1705]), bk. 2, ch. 20: 66–67. See also Leibniz, 'Letter to Queen Sophie Charlotte of Prussia, On What is Independent of Sense and Matter' (1702), in PE, 192: 'Perception cannot be explained by a mechanism.' For secondary treatments of Leibniz's view of selfhood in relation to bodily mechanism, see Benson Mates, *The Philosophy of Leibniz: Metaphysics and Language* (Oxford: Oxford University Press, 1986), 206–208; Christia Mercer, *Leibniz's Metaphysics: Its Origins and Development* (Cambridge: Cambridge University Press, 2001), especially chs. 2 and 4; and Catherine Wilson, *Leibniz's Metaphysics: A Historical and Comparative Study* (Princeton, NJ: Princeton University Press, 1990), esp. 238–243. For a comparison of Leibniz's to Descartes' views in this matter, see François Duchesneau, *Les modèles du vivant de Descartes à Leibniz* (Paris: J. Vrin, 1998).

58 Leibniz, 'Principes de la philosophie (Monadologie)' (1714), in *Principes de la nature et de la grâce, Monadologie et autres textes*, ed. Christiane Frémont (Paris: GF Flammarion, 1996), para 17.
59 Leibniz, 'Système nouveau,' 71.
60 On this trajectory in Leibniz's thinking, see especially Duchesneau, *Les modèles du vivant*, 315–372.
61 Leibniz, 'Monadologie,' paras 19, 89; Leibniz – Arnauld, 6 October 1687, in *Discourse on Metaphysics, Correspondence with Arnauld, Monadology* (hereafter DCM), trans. George Montgomery (LaSalle: Open Court, 1902), 230–231.
62 Leibniz, 'Monadologie,' paras 1–15.
63 Leibniz – Arnauld, Göttingen, 30 April 1687, in DCM, 187; Leibniz, 'Monadologie,' paras 78, 81, 85–89.
64 Leibniz, *Essais de théodicée* (Amsterdam: I. Troyel, 1710), para 188; Leibniz, 'From the Letters to Clarke' (1715–1716), in PE, 344. See also Leibniz, *New Essays*, bk. 3, ch. 6, 328: 'organic bodies are really machines'; and Leibniz, 'Monadologie,' para 64: 'Thus each organic body of a living being is a sort of divine machine, or a natural Automaton, that infinitely surpasses all artificial automata.'
65 Leibniz, *New Essays*, bk. 2, ch. 20, 166. Leibniz was responding in these passages to John Locke's discussion of pleasure and pain in the *Essay Concerning Human Understanding* (London: S. Manship, 1690), bk. II, chs. 20–21. Leibniz was departing from Locke's notion of 'uneasiness,' which Leibniz translated as 'inquietude' or 'unruhe,' and building it into a physical yet non-reductive theory of the basis of human behavior. The key element in this transformation was Leibniz's idea of unconscious perceptions, which made a continuity between bodily and conscious responses.
66 Leibniz, *On Body and Force, Against the Cartesians* (May 1702), in PE, 253; 'Système nouveau,' 72; *Essais de théodicée*, para 14.
67 Pierre Bayle, 'Rorarius (Jerôme),' in *Dictionnaire historique et critique* (1st ed. 1695–1697), 5th edition (Amsterdam: Brunel, 1740), 4: 82, note H.
68 See, for example, Leibniz, 'Système nouveau,' 72; and 'Postscript of a Letter to Basnage de Beauval' (1696), in PE, 147.
69 Leibniz, 'Letters to Clarke' (1715–1716), in PE, 344.
70 Leibniz, 'Toward a Philosophy of What There Actually is and Against the Revival of the Qualities of the Scholastics and Chimerical Intelligences' (1710–1716?), in PE, 318–319.

PART II
Representing things

4

STIL-STAENDE DINGEN

Picturing objects in the Dutch Golden Age

Julie Hochstrasser

Still-life painting brings the world of things to center stage. What anthropologist Bronislaw Malinowski called the 'imponderabilia of everyday life' can suddenly reveal great depths of meaning under the clear light of careful composition and virtuoso rendering. Natural objects hold within them the mystic creative forces of the universe: the shell bespeaks its ocean; the flower contains the energy of soil and sun that brought it into being, and will as quickly reclaim it (Figure 4.1). The contemplation of these objects, prompted by the painter's labor, introduces cosmic life cycles into the diurnal rhythms of human understanding. Man-made objects may be defined by their functionality, but this infuses them also with the micro-narratives of their daily use. The knife bears within it the lifting and cutting of a thousand repasts, the glass its sipping of the wine, day after day, week after week, month after month, year after year – and so is built a history of residual memories that may rest unnoticed until the artist's brush directs insistent focus, to rouse reflective contemplation in the viewer, awaken and inspire recollection or imagination (Figure 4.2). Such prompting to contemplation, such intense concentration of visual attention through the work of art, was always true of artistic rendition, of course – but the invention of the genre of still life turned this spotlight yet more intensely upon the material world of *things*.

This picturing of objects as subjects in their own right emerged as an independent genre during the first decades of the seventeenth century in Europe, and nowhere more prolifically than in The Netherlands.[1] From the fifteenth century, and particularly with the mastery of the medium of oil painting by the brothers Van Eyck, Netherlandish painters had been perfecting the art of depicting the material world with riveting illusionism. Objects of all sorts had played a role within the larger context of figural paintings, but artistic production was predominantly devoted to religious subjects and portraiture. At the turn of

FIGURE 4.1   Clara Peeters, *Still Life with Goblets and Flowers*, 1612

FIGURE 4.2   Pieter Claesz, *Still Life with Roemer, Oysters, Saltvat, and Roll*, 1633

the seventeenth century, however, Netherlandish painters began to focus upon tabletop arrangements of objects – flowers, fruits, banquets, even just assemblages of precious objects that would later be referred to as *pronken* (Dutch: to show off) – without any further pretense for their presence in the spotlight of artistic attention. In fact, these paintings – as objects which simultaneously also represent other objects – inveigle us doubly within the universe of early modern things. What can it tell us, this conspicuously material evolution, at this particular time and place? Art historians have long debated how precisely to understand it. In what follows, we will review this development, and what contending scholarship has made of it, to probe ultimately more deeply into the fascination of not only what these pictures signify, but perhaps more intriguingly, *how* they do, for they have much to tell us about the world of early modern things.

Material objects played only supporting roles within the sacred and mythical narratives of Medieval and Renaissance painting, but in turn these contexts imbued objects with rich symbolic allusions. In Hugo van der Goes' *Portinari Altarpiece* of 1476, for example, the center panel presents, beneath the nativity, a lovely little still life in which symbolism was explicit for viewers of the time: the wheat stands for the bread of the Eucharist that was the flesh of Christ; seven blue columbines presage the sorrows of the Virgin; the red lily represents the blood of Christ; the violets strewn on the ground connote humility; and so on.[2] But at the turn of the seventeenth century those kinds of narrative excuses fell away, leaving early modern things to stand independent before the viewer's eye. So the pertinent interpretive question becomes: how much of this sort of symbolic reference lingered on in the emerging genre of still life? Without a doubt, certain objects continued to convey symbolic content: bread and wine still constituted the Eucharist, but when bread and wine appeared within the context of a banquet scene, how much of that meaning continued to inhere?[3]

The conventional interpretation of seventeenth-century Dutch painting long held that this religious and other symbolism dictated the interpretation of still-life painting as a genre, giving a moralizing or *vanitas* cast to all Dutch still life.[4] Such an approach taken to extremes sometimes so clearly exceeded the bounds of common sense that it prompted protest even from the very scholar who had himself initiated the emblematic interpretation of seventeenth-century Dutch painting.[5] Other commentators countered that the most cogent import for these pictures was instead the extraordinary attention to descriptive rendering that came still more preeminently to the fore in the absence of narrative contexts for their depiction.[6] Debate between these two interpretive poles preoccupied the scholarship for some time, but eventually other aspects of Dutch daily life that had remained unexamined inspired yet further discoveries in the many allusions of things depicted.[7]

Although the Dutch term *stilleven* did not appear in an inventory until 1650, more specific topical descriptions marked the development of the genre, as inventories registered not only *vanitas* but also *bloemetjes* (flower pieces), *fruitages* (fruit pieces), *banketjes* (banquets), *ontbijtjes* (breakfasts), *toebackjes* (a still life

FIGURE 4.3 Willem Kalf, *Still Life with a Chinese Porcelain Bowl, Glasses, and Fruits,* 1662

with smoking implements), and many more particular designations such as *hammetje* (a ham banquet) or *oestertje* (an oyster meal).[8] In the first decades of the century, Clara Peeters in Antwerp contributed significantly to many of its formative types, in additive arrangements that articulated each object distinctly (Figure 4.1).[9] In the 1630s, Haarlem painters Pieter Claesz and Willem Claesz Heda developed a more compact compositional style in the monochrome palette that prevailed in that town throughout the mid-century (Figure 4.2).[10] By the 1660s, arrangements of more splendid objects figured forth the height of the century's prosperity, as epitomized in Willem Kalf's dramatic chiaroscuro renditions in Amsterdam (Figure 4.3).[11]

Stilstaende dingen (still-standing things) had become a secure subject in their own right; the phrase was employed by Joost van den Vondel in a witty poem celebrating the painter and his wife Cornelia Pluvier (penned within their lifetime), in which he wrote that Kalf…

> *…heeft stilstaende dingen lief:*
> *Banketten, dischgerecht, en brief,*
> *Limoen, citroen en glas en schael,*
> *Cieraet, en overdaet en prael…*

[...likes still-standing things:
Banquets, tableware, a letter,
Lemon, citron and glass and bowl,
Finery, and excess and splendor...][12]

Another sort of still life was designated in period inventories as *vanitas* – the only moniker to associate a particular meaning to the pictures it labeled, in reference to Ecclesiastes 1:2, *Vanitas vanitatum, et omnia vanitas* (vanity of vanities; all is vanity). In that context particularly, some objects still invoked familiar symbolic associations with insistent clarity: one still life by Jan de Heem contains a crucifix, which renders the written words on the page beneath it superfluous, so clear is its message to Christian eyes.[13] Skulls likewise retained their inevitable semantic charge of memento mori (remember your death) even without an accompanying inscription.[14] But for most objects, meaning remained more ambiguous with their transposition into still life. So in recent years, a whole generation of scholars could tussle over the presence or absence of symbolic content in the genre: did the *vanitas* message inhere even in pictures that were not so identified? Were depictions of richly laid tables moralizing admonitions against the medieval sin of *luxuria*, as the conventional interpretation would have it, or proud celebrations of the trading prowess and economic success of a newly minted republic?[15]

It is indeed 'the magic of things' (*die Magie der Dingen*, as a recent German still-life exhibition dubbed it), that both these poles can be held in simultaneous suspension within the pictorial realm of still life. But what is undeniably striking is the coincidence of the emergence of this new genre with a key moment in the birth of consumer society.[16] Surely it is no coincidence at all. In The Netherlands, early modern things came to this unprecedented focus of painterly attention just at a moment when material culture was burgeoning within the life of an increasingly affluent society, registering once again (as art is wont to do) the themes and issues at the forefront of broader societal concern.

This becomes still clearer when one tallies the appearance of these new still-life subjects in *boedelinventarissen* (Dutch: household inventories) of the period. Data from the Dutch town of Leiden, when arranged decade by decade, show that in sheer numbers of pictures as compared with other genres, the popularity of still life peaked in the decade of the 1660s, which also happened to be the height of the country's prosperity (Figure 4.4).[17] This rise, peak, and decline is equally obvious when viewed in percentage terms (Figure 4.5). Amsterdam data specific to still life likewise clearly indicate a steady increase to the 1660s (Figure 4.6).[18] Elsewhere throughout the country, this finding remains consistent: a compilation of attributed paintings in inventories from various Dutch cities once again indicates that the percentage of still-life paintings relative to other genres reaches its height in that prosperous decade of the 1660s (Figure 4.7) – right when Kalf was producing those tour de force renderings of luxury objects.[19]

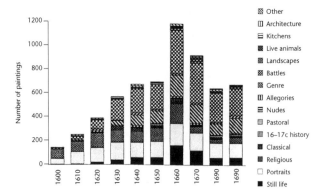

FIGURE 4.4   Numerical breakdown of genres of paintings in Willemijn Fock's selected sample of Leiden inventories

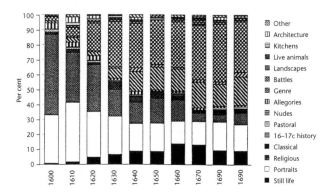

FIGURE 4.5   Percentage breakdown of genres of paintings in Willemijn Fock's selected sample of Leiden inventories

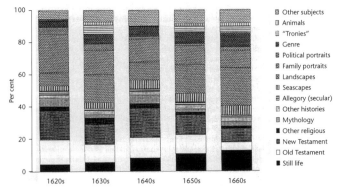

FIGURE 4.6   Percentage breakdown of genres of paintings in Montias's random sample of Amsterdam inventories

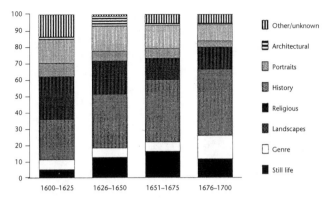

FIGURE 4.7 Percentage breakdown of genres of attributed paintings in Chong's collected sample of Dutch inventories

So this rising popularity of the picturing of things is amply clear; still, it cannot be understood sheerly as a celebration of the new Republic's financial successes. The sudden rise and rapid proliferation of the genre of still life at this historical moment relates as well to the emergence of the public art market in The Netherlands in the wake of iconoclasm and Protestant attitudes toward religious idolatry.[20] As burgeoning prosperity fueled the general flowering of artistic activity, the loss of the church as major patron for artistic commissions meanwhile prompted painters to develop other subjects – landscape, genre, still life – that appealed to the *breede middenstand*, this broad middle class newly and increasingly empowered to consume art for their own pleasure.

Yet this still returns us to the question: why objects? What was it that prompted painters to turn their focus to the material world in and of itself, seemingly devoid of narrative content? The socio-economic circumstances of the time do further illuminate the intense popular interest in material culture in such a milieu: a high degree of social mobility made burghers keenly aware of the levels of affluence registered by material culture, which played throughout the compositions of still-life objects; the pride of the nascent Dutch Republic would surely have reinforced such interests as well.[21] Nonetheless, precisely what these pictures tell us, either about societal attitudes toward material surfeit in general, or about the more particular and personal experiences of individuals within the world of goods, remains within the domain of interpretation – hence its susceptibility to endless debate.

What exactly, then, *can* we learn from these particular selections of things as they are pictured? Answers vary widely according to the questions one poses. From banquet pieces we might hope to learn something of what people ate; indeed, comparison with the dietary advice in period physicians' treatises does reveal some surprising discoveries. This dietary lore was still governed by the medieval theory of the four humors, so that for example if one wished to eat oysters, which are cold and slimy, then one was to balance them with something

FIGURE 4.8 *Pieter Claesz, Still Life with Violin and Glass Ball,* c. 1628

hot and dry, like pepper; sure enough, nearly every one of these painted oyster banquets is accompanied by pepper – often presented spilling out of a little paper cone (Figure 4.2).[22] If we are in search of real indices of Dutch diet, we are well advised to take these artful compositions with the proverbial grain of salt – as, at best, representations of what *certain* people *might* have eaten at *particular* times. Yet the correlations are striking enough to call into question the conventional interpretation of these still lifes as negative examples of the luxury one should avoid: instead, they are consistent with accepted and even *recommended* dietary practice in a great many details.[23]

We learn what people valued – though within this context we don't necessarily learn why: for their beauty, or their sheer visual fascination, or their intrinsic monetary worth itself? The arrival of exotic objects within the intimate space of Dutch still life bears witness to the global trade network the Dutch commanded during their Golden Age: the pepper on Claesz's table was prized cargo of the spice trade from the Indies that made the fortunes of the Dutch East India Company (the Vereenigde Oostindische Compagnie or VOC), while Kalf's covered porcelain bowl came all the way from China, and the sugar probably served therein was imported by the West India Company, early on from the Dutch colony in Brazil, and after its loss, from Suriname.[24] Yet the elegant presentation of these commodities (often on silver platters – at least metaphorically, and often quite literally) also conceals the darker shades of violence and exploitation that were the true social cost of many of these luxuries. The overseas trade took a severe toll on the Europeans who manned the ships, the spice trade devastated the social fabric of the East Indies, and sugar was cultivated by slaves brought from Africa by the West India Company to 'the hell of the sugar mills.' All the

FIGURE 4.9   Clara Peeters, *Still Life with Goblets and Flowers*, detail of Figure 4.1, 1612

while, still life served up these sumptuous goods in a world utterly apart from such grave externalities.[25] Every commodity pictured in still life holds a complex story of its own; unpacking those takes one vast distances outside the borders of The Netherlands, and far beyond the reach of this chapter.[26]

Another conspicuous theme elicited by the objects chosen runs throughout these pictures: a preoccupation – even an obsession – with the passage of time. Stated forthrightly in so many still-life compositions by the inclusion of a pocket-watch, not only in overtly *vanitas* pictures, but also beside a vase of flowers, or right in the midst of a banquet table (Figure 4.3), and hinted at more subtly by the fading flowers themselves, or the fleeting pleasures of the perishables on offer at table, this theme had, of course, a grounding in that biblical notion of *vanitas*, and medieval roots in memento mori. But even there, a distinctly early modern development of the notion of 'time as money' casts this preoccupation in another light: the concern with the painter's *own* time, spent crafting the valuable object that is this painting (Figure 4.8).[27] Pieter Claesz underscores just such a self-reflexive allusion by juxtaposing the pocket-watch and other typical components of *vanitas* with a self-portrait, perfectly mirrored in the reflective sphere on the left. This same conceit was displayed by other painters as well: close examination of Peeters' 1612 still life reveals no fewer than nine self-reflections, painstakingly registered in the various nodes of the gilt goblet (Figure 4.9), while in the latter half of the century Abraham van Beyeren would repeatedly capture his likeness on the side of a silver pitcher in his lavish banquets, each artist thus insistently reminding the viewer that art outlasts even death.

So with regard to individual objects, the things depicted in still life have much to show us about early modernity: maybe about daily eating habits, or fashions surrounding them; surely about trade and its countless commodities; about surfeit and lack and the subtly differentiated aesthetic continuum that spans them; about time and morality and art and death. Those are all lines of inquiry that I have explored elsewhere, and they do address the many questions posed for this collective inquiry in diverse and fascinating ways, but we haven't the space to pursue them further here; suffice it to say they are each rewarding windows onto early modernity by means of various facets of its material culture.[28]

But leaving aside those myriad things taken separately, *collectively*, too, the picturing of things in and of itself has something very important to tell us. The *phenomenon* of still life, arising as it does at this particular historical moment: what does it tell us that artists decided (rather suddenly in fact, in art historical terms) to paint things as subjects in their own right? – not in the context of an overt narrative, religious or otherwise, but there in the light of day, depicted in minute detail, exclusively, it would seem, for the inspection and admiration of the attentive viewer?

What happens when we look at a still life? The self-reflexive cues from Dutch painters are suggestive. For oddly enough, just as their own mirror imaging subtly proposes, the elimination of human agents from within the pictorial space of still life has a curiously inverse effect: it is precisely this absence that turns attention back upon the viewer, transforming a conglomeration of inert objects into this singularly self-reflexive exercise in introspection. Instead of dictating an exterior narrative, still life prompts the viewer to engender interior narratives of one's own.

In a somewhat uncanny echo of the Dutch painters' idiosyncratically self-reflexive motif, recent theory surrounding vision and 'the gaze' has also reanimated the world of objects, in ways strict science cannot account, and these thought experiments have had an impact on our ways of conceiving picture theory as well. Lacan's formulation of the gaze as *objet petit a*, as reflection and projection of the self, infused the material world with his own psychoanalytical concerns with primal separation and lack – he does not share the fisherman Petit Jean's self-delighted certainty that the sardine can bobbing and glinting out in the water 'doesn't see you!'[29] The surrealists with whom Lacan associated heavily in 1930s Paris expressed this theoretical construct in their visual imagery as well: Man Ray's 1923 *Indestructible Object; or Object to be Destroyed*, is a metronome endowed with a human eye that does quite literally stare back at the viewer.[30] That disconcerting notion that 'the object stares back' has reverberated throughout the theoretical fields of material culture and art history alike, reinvesting the material world with something of the very power and animation it once commanded in earlier belief systems infused with magic or other supernatural associations.[31]

Without attributing to Dutch still life any such anachronistically surrealist or postmodern posturing, in their presence, one cannot help but concede that Lacan's eccentric formulation takes on its eerie force: the objects assembled do indeed take on a life of their own, and in turn, as he contended, the awareness of an object prompts one's own self-awareness in relation to it. In fact, Lacan himself thinks of Dutch painters just a bit further on in his own discussion, albeit adducing landscape rather than still life: in these pictures that do not contain any human figures he finds precisely that presence of the gaze that he identifies as this powerful projection of self.

> Looking at pictures, even those most lacking in what is usually called the gaze, and which is constituted by a pair of eyes, pictures in which any representation of the human figure is absent, like a landscape by a Dutch or Flemish painter, you will see in the end, as in filigree, something so specific to each of the painters that you will feel the presence of the gaze.[32]

Lacan continues, 'But this is merely an object of research, and perhaps merely illusion.' Merely, perhaps, for Lacan's critical purposes – but for ours, this convergence of 'mere illusion' with powerful presence is precisely the point. One delights of course in the particularities of masterful technical handling – the painter's 'lead-tin-yellow trick' that builds the nubbly texture of lemon peels with a binder of whipped egg whites, the umber glaze that renders the translucency of oysters – so that the agency of the human hand might vanish like magic in the stunning presence of these objects – but in the end we recall that it is indeed that human hand that has assembled them, that chose them and composed them and then mixed and applied just these colors in just this way to conjure the vision before us.[33]

Yes, there is routine in the production behind it. The ceaseless permutations of the same objects arranged and restlessly rearranged throughout the oeuvre of any given painter were rigorously structured by an overwhelming consistency of format for still-life compositions overall. Even technical reproductive formulae were replicated to an extraordinary degree, as one detects for example in the remarkable consistency of the patterns of reflection on the many *roemers* Pieter Claesz depicts in his various assemblages; countless other examples he produced over the years nevertheless match up to an extraordinary degree with the pattern visible in Figure 4.2.[34]

But the novelty of this *phenomenon* of the independent still-life painting obliges us to step back, to consider the larger historical developments that could have allowed this individual's perception, this one man sitting before a glass of wine, to find such a privileged place within the artistic landscape. It is a particularly striking development given that in the Italian hierarchy of the genres, still life had been relegated to the bottom rung of the ladder. Even as late as 1678, Rembrandt's pupil Samuel van Hoogstraten, recording theory for his *Inleyding tot de Hooge Schoole der Schilderkonst* (Introduction to the Academy of Painting), still echoes that Renaissance judgment, denigrating still-life painters as the 'common foot-soldiers in the army of art.'[35] *Historia* was supposed to be the most noble subject for a painter to address.

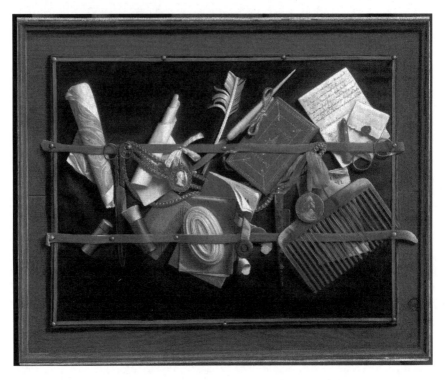

FIGURE 4.10 Samuel van Hoogstraten, *Augenbetrüger*, c. 1666–1678

Yet we have already witnessed the proof that still lifes enjoyed great popularity among the Dutch public, painted and purchased in growing numbers, to peak in Dutch household inventories in the very decade of the 1660s that also saw the greatest prosperity in the Dutch Republic overall. Evidently, the Dutch populace cared not a whit for the hierarchy of the genres or art theory per se – instead, the very intimate personal vision put forward in still life apparently spoke to them in a way that struck a chord. Indeed, rather ironically, Hoogstraten himself painted still lifes, including a number of cleverly *trompe-l'oeil* 'letter-rack' compositions (Figure 4.10). As assemblages of objects, these are among the most personal one could imagine: a comb, a shaving-brush, eyeglasses, a personal note, a medal he was awarded for his proficiency in his art – all sorts of playful self-references that assert the painter's most direct involvement, in a sort of self-portrait represented now through the very objects of his daily life.[36] Gone are the last vestiges of religious and other traditional symbolism, but at the heart of the genre, the painter remains: here is an iconography of the self, pure and simple. Witty and sometimes quizzical, to be sure, here the fascination with objects has transcended the iconographical imperatives of the past to compose its own, intimately personal narrative.

So at this level of analysis too, then, just what does it tell us, this early modern discovery of, and fascination with, the picturing of things? Although this was hardly the intentional focus of Foucault's 'archaeology of the human sciences,' his famous study of *The Order of Things* provides one way to apprehend the question.[37] Foucault contends that the tectonic shift from the late sixteenth century into the seventeenth granted a new legitimacy to the role of the individual perceiver. His extended exegesis of Vélazquez's *Las Meninas* illustrates this through the painter's provocative problematization of point of view in this royal portrait: is that the king and queen we see reflected in a mirror on the back wall? But if so, they must be standing where *we* are! And what is on the massive canvas that we see only from behind? Velazquez only ever painted one canvas that we know of on such a grand scale, and it was the very picture we are looking at – yet given the painter's orientation, it ought to be a portrait of the king and queen, who *seem* to be the target of the painter's gaze – except that he is actually looking out at *us*! And the picture we are viewing depicts instead the Infanta Margarita and her coterie, so the conundrums multiply. In the end, the painter's view is privileged above all: he commands the center, and he alone views the massive canvas that turns its back to us.

The phenomenon of still life asserts this same control: whether the things depicted be humble or precious, breakfast or banquet, fish or fowl or shell or flower, it is the painter's point of view that has set the stage, that forms the very *raison d'être* of this art – even if no further meaning were to be invested in the objects assembled for our attentive contemplation. If there is any doubt about this, the painters themselves assert it visually. In the first decades of the seventeenth century, Clara Peeters played this game quite assertively; the multiple self-reflections in her Karlsruhe still life capture her image again and again as it is reflected, each time altered ever so slightly, in each of the nodes of the gilt goblet: here am I, this is *my* view (Figure 4.9). And they were not unique – she records her reflection on an object in the composition in other pictures too. This young woman from Antwerp boldly inscribes her place within the long tradition of precise Netherlandish illusionism with this highly personal form of signature.[38]

Likewise, the silver ball in Pieter Claesz's Nuremberg still life captures his image with extraordinary clarity – at his easel, insisting upon his presence, his agency, right there on the surface of this very self-reflexive work (Figure 4.7). At first glance, this appears to be a conventional *vanitas* painting, complete with many familiar ingredients: the skull that irrevocably intones memento mori, echoed by the up-ended *roemer* that also connoted death through a popular adage, and the pocket-watch that alludes inescapably to the passage of time. But by juxtaposing his own image so decisively in this assemblage of objects, Claesz redefines their context in a very insistent way. The quill pen of practice, the oil lamp of assiduity, the violin that was thought of as a popular cure against the melancholy to which artists were said to be notoriously prone – all now respond to the traditional message of the transience of earthly life with a robust reply: the painter's art has the power to outlast death. And like Peeters, Claesz too claims his place by imbedding this self-portrait within the very fabric of the work of art itself, though once again it is subverted in this curious way to the material object on which it is reflected.

Other painters did the same: Pieter van Roestraten even focused one entire painting on such a reflective sphere with an even more elaborately detailed reflection of himself at work in his studio.[39] Abraham van Beyeren includes his image again and again, in one after another of his banquet pieces, with his self-portrait reflected this time on the surface of a costly silver pitcher.[40] Even Jan de Heem, considered the preeminent practitioner of still life in his time, plays at this game – in an unusually grand still life that traces its provenance to King Charles I of England, he sneaks in his reflection not only on the node of a goblet just as Peeters had done before him, but also again, ever so tiny, on a brass nail head on a chair back.[41]

But even when painters did not explicitly insist that we acknowledge their presence through overt self-reflection, their individual points of view remain present through the consistency of their personal vision – as Lacan's remark asserted as well. Vondel singles out Kalf's *stil-staende dingen* in part because of the tour de force of sheer painterly skill displayed in their rendering, but also, it seems, for the quirkiness of the painter's idiosyncratic choices of subject. As an early modern thing, a still-life painting – this object that in turn invokes so powerfully a whole array of *other* early modern objects – bespeaks that shifting of the episteme that Foucault proposes. It establishes incontrovertibly that the perception of this individual is not only legitimate, but even valuable – maybe even beyond price. Goethe's oft-quoted remark before another Kalf painting states this in another way:

> One must see this picture in order to comprehend the sense in which art dominates nature, and what the spirit of man lends to the objects, when he beholds them with creative eyes. For me at least there is no question, if I had to choose between the golden vessels and the picture, that I would choose the picture.[42]

Ironically, the particular work Goethe was referring to has since been disattributed, as perhaps a copy of another work by Kalf – several versions exist of the painting he was apparently praising in these remarks. It is currently believed to be a copy after a Kalf in a private collection, which might be autograph, or one in Rouen, which has been judged to be – but so much the more impressive, then, that Goethe was so deeply moved even by what proved to be only a copy.[43] In any case, it is Goethe's *point* that is of the essence here: that paintings like these, which take objects as their subjects, compound the fascination of the objects they depict with their *own* materiality and, more particularly, with the crafting that produced them. But also, a second point remains (however ironically, given the case of the copy): that Goethe holds Kalf's own individual point of view as valuable in the extreme, and at the very least, most worthy of our sustained attention.

Foucault's thesis is of interest for our consideration of still life in a second very important way as well: in the fundamental nature and status of the 'things' we find 'ordered' in still life. At its most essential, his central argument in *The Order of Things* is that the sixteenth-century episteme conceived of the relationships between things of the world in terms of profound resemblance: the great chain of being linked the entire universe into this continuum of similitudes. In the world of art, this was clearly true of the complex symbolism of Renaissance visual language; like Hugo van der Goes' bouquet in the *Portinari Altarpiece*, many of the 'things' that would subsequently find their way into still life were infused with these sorts of associations – the kinds of fruit and flower symbolism that Sam Segal has recorded so exhaustively in his exhibition catalogues for Netherlandish still life of various types: a fruitful past, a flowery past, a prosperous past.[44]

But then comes a seismic shift: Foucault contends that a great rift occurred in the seventeenth century (what he calls the 'classical' period – most applicable, of course, to the French case), in which this sense of universal resemblance fell (or was traded) away, in favor of what was hailed as a more lucid principle of structure for the world: classification, cleansed of such complex connections of association. In Foucault's formulation there would also come a third tectonic shift, with the eighteenth century, into the organic structure of analogy that he assigns to the episteme he labels as modernity – a separate discussion that might pertain for some of the other cases in this volume. However, since, *pace* Foucault, scholars today do see even the seventeenth century within the scope of early modernity, it is that first shift, from the late sixteenth century into the seventeenth, from 'resemblance' to 'classification,' that concerns us here.

As we have seen, it is precisely during these years, at that juncture, that the rise of the independent genre of still life occurs; and interestingly enough, the open debate among art historians as to the interpretation of these pictures hinges upon the very dichotomy that Foucault outlines for the two sides of the divide. It is the question put forward by Bergström in his seminal book on Dutch still life: how much symbolism still inheres, survives, lingers, in these objects? This very same debate long fueled Dutch art historiography more broadly as well: do these paintings narrate or describe?[45] Or for still life, do the things in these pictures still contain within them the kind of associative symbolism that Foucault tracks through the sixteenth century's great chain of being? The same kind of associative symbolism that, within the more pertinent context of Dutch art, was codified in moralizing emblem books? Or are they now drained of that associative aura, classified like Linnaeus's taxonomies: breakfasts, banquets, flowers; types or species, methodically described? Are Rachel Ruysch's blossoms still invested with symbolism, or are they instead strictly scientific description of an exceptionally high degree of quality, worthy of this daughter of an eminent professor of anatomy and botany?

Perhaps one could argue that with such images, the trajectory away from symbolic objects is complete; but in the end, the answer, of course, is that they teeter on that divide: yes and no – or as Norman Bryson put it, both, or neither.[46] That is their complexity, their richness – these objects hold within them *both* resemblance (in Foucault's deep Renaissance sense) *and* classification. Even the verbal distinctions (and that means also the philosophical discriminations they articulate) confine far too strictly the profusion of associations that objects can contain and convey – most certainly in the medium of the visual realm. Foucault might have protested, but it remains as vital a point today as ever: Bruno Latour argues in his own animistic analysis that 'we have *never* been modern.'[47] *Pace* Foucault once more, by contemporary scholars' lights, the significatory brink on which early modernity teetered will always be with us. It returns through the exposure to other cultures, through the revisitation of one's own past, probably most of all through the irrepressible human urge to find meaning – for then of course, even the impulse to classify is invested with meaning of its own. With Hoogstraten's letter-racks, it seems the objects he depicts have been thoroughly purged from that older universe of symbolic associations, and yet – by virtue of their obvious personal significance for the artist himself, through this more private iconography, they are as pregnant with meaning as ever.

In the end, what still life tells *us* is inevitably a product of our times, inasmuch as we ourselves are rooted in an episteme, however uncertain its boundaries or its very nature as viewed from within its midst. Without a doubt, the rise of this genre within European painting attests to a new self-consciousness about the materiality of the early modern world. But these pictures also embody the complexity of associations these material objects inspire when we are prompted, so eloquently by these extraordinary representations, to ponder them awhile.

Notes

1 Ingvar Bergström's seminal study *Dutch Still-Life Painting in the Seventeenth Century* put forward the first ideas about the origins of Dutch still life: originally *Studier i holländskt stillebenmåleri under 1600-talet* (Götheborg: Rundqvist, 1947); revised English edition trans. Christina Hedström and Gerald Taylor (London and New York: Faber and Faber, 1956). But the general bibliography on still life has been growing as well; for very broad overviews see Sybille Ebert-Schifferer, *Still Life: A History* (New York: Abrams, 1999) and Norbert Schneider, *Still Life: Still Life Painting in the Early Modern Period* (Köln: Taschen, 1999). For a more intensely theoretical meditation on Dutch still life in particular, see Hanneke Grootenboer, *The Rhetoric of Perspective: Realism and Illusionism in Seventeenth-Century Dutch Still-Life Painting* (Chicago, IL: University of Chicago Press, 2005).

2 Religious flower symbolism, like all religious symbolism during this period, could get extremely elaborate: while the three irises in Van der Goes' foreground still life (white for purity and purple for the royal ancestry of Christ) could refer here to the trinity of the Father, Son, and Holy Ghost, the iris, as 'little sword,' also invokes Simeon's address to Mary at the Presentation in the Temple: 'And you yourself a sword will pierce so that the thoughts of many hearts may be revealed' (Luke 2:35).

3 Quint Gregory explored the proposition that representations of bread and wine in banquet pieces by Catholic painters such as Pieter Claesz and Willem Claesz Heda make deliberate allusions to the Eucharist, strategically veiled precisely by the

absence of explicit doctrinal context that still life provides. Henry Duval Gregory V, 'Tabletop Still Lifes in Haarlem, *c.*1610–1700: A Study of the Relationships between Form and Meaning' (PhD diss., University of Maryland, College Park, 2003).

4   Bergström opined that still life's development out of the religious contexts of Medieval and Renaissance imagery of earlier centuries continued to hold the key to its interpretation in the seventeenth. Bergström, *Dutch Still-Life Painting*, passim.

5   The emblematic interpretation of Dutch art first pioneered by Edy de Jongh continued the earlier trend toward finding moralizing symbolism in still life as elsewhere in Dutch painting – until de Jongh himself called for common sense to constrain over-interpretation in this mode. Edy de Jongh, 'The Interpretation of Still-Life Paintings: Possibilities and Limits,' in *Still-Lifes in the Age of Rembrandt*, exh. cat. (Auckland: Auckland City Art Gallery, 1982), 27–36; also reprinted in De Jongh, *Questions of Meaning: Theme and Motif in Dutch Seventeenth-Century Painting* (Leiden: Primavera Pers, 2000), 129–148. To Josua Bruyn's interpretation of the cheese in a Haarlem picture invoking Tertullian calling cheese 'heavenly milk,' De Jongh protested that 'cheese…was rarely consumed on an allegorical level in the seventeenth century,' ibid., 67.

6   Svetlana Alpers advanced this argument for Dutch painting in general; see Svetlana Alpers, *The Art of Describing: Dutch Painting in the Seventeenth Century* (Chicago, IL: University of Chicago Press, 1983). Specifically for still life, N. R. A. Vroom made the case for a more 'modest message' to the monochrome banquet pieces of Claesz, Heda, and their circle – that they were painted for humble human interest and nothing more; see N. R. A. Vroom, *A Modest Message as Intimated by the Painters of the Monochrome Banketje*, trans. Peter Gidman (Schiedam, The Netherlands: Interbook International, 1980). Originally published as *De schilders van het monochrome banketje,* (Amsterdam: Kosmos, 1945).

7   This was the central thrust of my research for 'Life and Still Life: A Cultural Inquiry into Seventeenth-Century Dutch Still-Life Painting' (PhD diss., University of California, Berkeley, 1995): to vault the horns of that old stalemated dilemma and, acknowledging the centrality of description to the endeavor of still life, to explore other meanings derived from Dutch daily life, aside from religious and literary symbolism.

8   The term *stilleven* is found in the inventory of Judith Willemsdr. van Vliet in Delft: 'Een stilleven van Evert van Aelst'. Abraham Bredius, *Künstler-Inventare: Urkunden zur Geschichte der holländischen Kunst des XVIten, XVIIten und XVIIIten Jahrhunderts*, 8 vols. (The Hague: Nijhoff, 1915), 1439; A. P. A. Vorenkamp, 'Bijdrage tot de geschiedenis van het Hollandsch stilleven in de zeventiende eeuw' (PhD diss., University of Leiden, 1933), 7; Lydia de Pauw-de Veen, *De begrippen 'schilder', 'schilderij' en schilderen' in de seventiende eeuw* (Brussels: Paleis der Academiën, 1969), 141; and Alan Chong, 'Contained Under the Name of Still Life: The Associations of Still-Life Painting,' in Alan Chong and Wouter Kloek, *Still Life Paintings from The Netherlands, 1550–1720* (Zwolle: Waanders Publishers, 1999), 10–37, n. 8, 32.

9   Peeters made seminal contributions in nearly all the major categories of still life: scenes of flowers, fruit, banquets, game, and fish. See Pamela Hibbs Decouteau, *Clara Peeters 1594–ca. 1640 and the Development of Still-Life Painting in Northern Europe* (Lingen: Luca Verlag, 1992).

10   See Martina Brunner-Bulst, *Pieter Claesz: der Hauptmeister des Haarlemer Stillebens im 17. Jahrhundert* (Lingen: Lucca, 2004), and *Pieter Claesz: Master of Haarlem Still Life* (Zwolle: Waanders, 2004).

11   See Peter van den Brink et al., *Gemaltes Licht: die Stilleben vom Willem Kalf 1619–1693* (Munich, Berlin, et al.: Deutscher Kunstverlag, 2007).

12   Joost van den Vondel, *Raetsel*; while undated, the poem appears in: *J. v. Vondels Poëzy; of, Verscheide gedichten, De complete werken van Joost van Vondel*, vol. 2 (Leonard Strik, 1682), 397–398 (though *not* in the 1650 edition of his *Poëzy*). In *De Complete werken van Joost van den Vondel*, vol. 2 (s-Hertogenbosch and Amsterdam: Henri Bogaerts,

1870), it appears between two other works both dated 1663. Vondel calls the poem a 'puzzle' because he plays on the names of Kalf and Pluvier by writing about them as an actual calf and plover.

13   The text on the paper reads: *Maer naer d'Alders[c]oonste Blom\ Daer en siet' men niet naer' om* [But no one looks upon the fairest bloom of them all]. Sam Segal, *Jan Davidsz de Heem und sein Kreis* (Braunschweig: Herzog Anton Ulrich Museum, 1991), 188.

14   See Alain Tapié et al., *Les Vanités dans la peinture au XVIIe siècle: méditations sur la richesse, le dénouement et la redemption* (Cannes: Le Musée des Beaux-arts, 1990).

15   Norman Bryson calls them the 'Pan-Allegorists' and the 'Anti-Allegorists' of Dutch art; see *Looking at the Overlooked: Four Essays on Still Life Painting* (Cambridge, MA: Harvard University Press, 1990).

16   Jochen Sander, *Die Magie der Dingen / The Magic of Things: Stillebenmalerei 1500–1800* (Ostfildern: Hatje Cantz Verlag, 2008).

17   This data is drawn from transcriptions by Willemijn Fock in an exhaustive analysis of the contents of houses along Leiden's elegant canal Het Rapenburg. I thank her for generously sharing data on still life with me independently of the published volumes, but see also Theodoor Herman Lunsingh Scheurleer et al., *Het Rapenburg: geschiedenis van een Leidse gracht* (Leiden: Afdeling Geschiedenis van de Kunstnijverheid, Rijksuniversiteit Leiden, 1986–1992).

18   The still life particulars have been extracted for this table from John Michael Montias' database generated from his extensive archival work in Amsterdam. This study goes only up to the decade of the 1660s and not further. For more of his inventory findings, see Montias and John Loughman, *Public and Private Spaces: Works of Art in Seventeenth-Century Dutch Houses* (Zwolle: Waanders, 2000).

19   This analysis formed part of a study of period ownership of various genres in Alan Chong, 'The Market for Landscape Painting in Seventeenth-Century Holland,' in Peter Sutton, ed., *Masters of 17th-Century Dutch Landscape Painting* (Boston, MA: Museum of Fine Arts, 1987), 104–120. See also Chong, 'Contained Under the Name of Still Life,' Appendix, 37.

20   Compare Åke Bengtsson, *Studies on the Rise of Realistic Landscape Painting in Holland, 1610–1625* (Stockholm: Almqvist and Wiksell, 1952), passim.

21   See Bryson, 'Abundance,' ch. 3 in *Looking at the Overlooked*, 96–135.

22   See Johan van Beverwyck, *Schat der Gesontheyt* (first published Dordrecht: for Mathias Havius, by Hendrick van Esch, 1636); these citations from a later edition (Amsterdam: widow of J. J. Schipper, 1672), 135–136, and 172.

23   See Julie Berger Hochstrasser, 'Food Lore: The Dictates of Use,' in idem., 'Life and Still Life,' 29–154.

24   The bowl in Kalf's painting dates from the Tianzi period (1621–1627) of the Ming Dynasty. Van den Brink et al. aver that it cannot be stated with certainty that the bowl contains sugar, but the presence of a spoon in the similar bowl in Kalf's Thyssen Bornemisza painting lends further credence to that possibility. Van den Brink et al., *Gemaltes Licht*, cat. 30, 127–128. For a still-life painting depicting rock-crystal sugar served in a similarly shaped porcelain bowl, see Pieter van Roestraeten, *Still Life with Tea Things*, private collection, The Netherlands, reproduced in Julie Berger Hochstrasser, *Still Life and Trade in the Dutch Golden Age* (New Haven, CT and London: Yale University Press, 2007), 191, fig. 104. Kalf's own connections with these overseas trades are intriguing: his younger brother Govert died in 1640 on a trip to India, and in July 1653 Kalf was living in the home of his wife's aunt, who was married to Johan le Thor, one of the Directors of the West India Company (van den Brink et al., *Gemaltes Licht*, 11, 15).

25   Ad van der Woude calculated that of all the men who set sail with the VOC over its long lifetime, over half never returned; see Jan de Vries and Ad van der Woude, *The First Modern Economy: Success, Failure, and Perseverance of the Dutch Economy, 1500–1815* (New York: Cambridge University Press, 1997), 642. On the damage wrought by the spice trade, see Charles R. Boxer, *The Dutch Seaborne Empire 1600–1800* (London:

Hutchinson & Co. Ltd., 1965). On the 'hell of the sugar mills,' see Ruud Spruit, *Zout en slaven: de geschiedenis van de Westindische Compagnie* (Houten: De Haan, 1988), 46.

26 For in-depth studies on a selection of commodities frequently depicted in seventeenth-century Dutch still life, including further history on their social costs, see Hochstrasser, *Still Life and Trade.*

27 See Julie Berger Hochstrasser, '*Goede Dingen Willen Tijd Hebben* (Good Things Take Time): Time as a Meditation on Painting in Dutch Still Life of the Seventeenth Century,' in *Symbols of Time in the History of Art (Papers presented at the Thirtieth International Congress of the History of Art (CIHA), London 2000)*, ed. Christian Heck and Kristin Lippincott (Turnhout, Belgium: Brepols, 2002), 117–135.

28 For a brief sampling of this research, see Julie Berger Hochstrasser, 'Feasting the Eye: Painting and Reality in the Seventeenth-century "*Bancketje*,"' in Chong and Kloek, eds., *Still-Life Paintings*, 72–85. For more comprehensive explorations see Hochstrasser, 'Life and Still Life.'

29 See Jacques Lacan on the *objet petit a* in *The Four Fundamental Concepts of Psychoanalysis* (New York; London: W. W. Norton, 1998, *c.*1973), 67–122; for the anecdote about Petit Jean and the sardine can, see 95.

30 See Man Ray, *Indestructible Object, or Object to be Destroyed*, 1964 (replica of 1923 original), 22.5 x 11 x 11.6 cm. Museum of Modern Art, New York.

31 For studies in material culture, Arjun Appadurai's contribution has proven seminal: *The Social Life of Things: Commodities in Cultural Perspective* (Cambridge: Cambridge University Press, 1986). The convergence between material and visual culture has generated crossovers between anthropology and art history; see for example Christopher Pinney, *Camera Indica: The Social Life of Indian Photographs* (Chicago, IL: University of Chicago Press, 1997). Within the field of art history strictly speaking, see James Elkins, *The Object Stares Back: On the Nature of Seeing* (New York: Harcourt Brace, 1997).

32 '...The function of the picture—in relation to the person to whom the painter, literally, offers his picture to be seen—has a relation with the gaze.' Lacan, *Four Fundamental Concepts*, 101.

33 For familiarity with these techniques I am deeply grateful to Renate Woudhuysen-Keller of the Hamilton-Kerr Institute at the University of Cambridge, England, and René Hoppenbrouwers and Hélène Dubois (then) of the Stichting Restauratie Atelier Limburg, for the course on 'Sixteenth- and Seventeenth-century Dutch and Flemish Painting Techniques' presented by the Amsterdam Maastricht Summer University in 2001.

34 For multiple examples, see Hochstrasser, 'Life and Still Life.'

35 Samuel van Hoogstraten, *Inleyding tot de Hooge Schoole der Schilderkonst* (Rotterdam: Francois van Hoogstraten, 1678; reprint [Doornspijk]: Davaco, 1969).

36 On Hoogstraten's art and art theory, see Celeste Brusati, *Artifice and Illusion: the Art and Writing of Samuel van Hoogstraten* (Chicago, IL: University of Chicago Press, 1995).

37 Michel Foucault, *The Order of Things: An Archaeology of the Human Sciences* (New York: Pantheon Books, 1971, *c.*1970); originally *Les Mots et les choses* (Paris: Gillimard, 1966).

38 Peeters captured her reflection in other works as well; see Decoteau, *Clara Peeters*, for the catalogue raisonné. Brusati points out moreover that with this she may be claiming her heritage within the Netherlandish tradition of Jan van Eyck, who depicted his own reflection in the armor of St. George in the Madonna with the Canon van der Paele; see Celeste Brusati, 'Stilled Lives: self-portraiture and self-reflection in seventeenth-century Netherlandish still-life painting,' *Simiolus* 20.2/3 (1990/1991): 168–182, for a fuller exploration of the implications of this work and others that display these self-reflections.

39 See Lindsay Bridget Shaw, 'Pieter van Roestraeten and the English "vanitas,"' *Burlington Magazine* 132, (1990): 402–406.

40 Compare still lifes with self-reflections by Abraham van Beyeren in collections of the Cleveland Museum of Art, Toledo Museum of Art, Indianapolis Museum of Art, and the Ashmolean Museum at Cambridge University, among others; several reproduced in Segal, *A Prosperous Past: The Sumptuous Still Life in The Netherlands, 1600–1700* (The Hague: SDU Publishers, 1989). For further discussion of self-reflection and other forms of self-reference incorporated into seventeenth-century Dutch still-life paintings, see Hochstrasser, 'The Self-Conscious Painter: Time and the Still Life,' in idem., 'Life and Still Life,' 456–540.

41 See Segal, *Jan Davidsz de Heem*, 72, fig. 7, and catalogue entry, 132–134.

42 *Man muss dieses Bild sehen um zu begreifen, in welchem Sinne die Kunst über die Natur sei und was der Geist des Menschen den Gegenstanden leiht, wenn er sie mit schöpferischem Auge betrachtet. Bei mir wenigstens ist's keine Frage, wenn ich die goldnen Gefässe oder das Bild zu wählen hätte, dass Ich das Bild wählen würde.* Johann Wolfgang Goethe, *Schriften zur Kunst*, Erster Teil, *dtv Gesamtausgabe*, 33 (1962): 63–64.

43 See van den Brink et al., *Gemaltes Licht*, 82–87.

44 See Sam Segal, *A Flowery Past: A Survey of Dutch and Flemish Flower Painting from 1600 Until the Present* (Amsterdam: De Boer; 's-Hertogenbosch, Noordbrabants Museum, 1982); *A Fruitful Past: A Survey of the Fruit Still Lifes of the Northern and Southern Netherlands from Brueghel till Van Gogh* (Mijdrecht, The Netherlands: Drukkerij Verweij, 1983); and Segal, *A Prosperous Past*.

45 The two poles of the debate were defined respectively by Eddy de Jongh's essay *Zinne- en minnebeelden in de schilderkunst van de zeventiende eeuw* ([n.p.] 1967), now also available in De Jongh, *Questions of Meaning*; and Alpers, *The Art of Describing*.

46 Bryson, *Looking at the Overlooked*.

47 Bruno Latour, *We Have Never Been Modern*, trans. Catherine Porter (Cambridge, MA: Harvard University Press, 1993).

5

'THINGS SEEN AND UNSEEN'

The material culture of early modern inventories and their representation of domestic interiors

Giorgio Riello

Inventories have long been considered the panacea of historians. They are not only available in large quantities but belong to that category of sources from which, as Peter Burke puts it, historians are 'filling their buckets from the stream of Truth.'[1] Inventories have been used to learn about crops and agrarian practices, the evolution of buildings and architectural structures, the appearance of shops, the possession of goods and their associated social practices, and the history of everyday life, but also about language, calligraphy, colonialism, money demand, book collecting and the spreading of Arab numerals.[2] Put in a very simplistic way, the drawback of inventories has never been deemed to be their particular nature, but their complex and demanding processing (Figure 5.1). The archival work of transcription, compilation, standardization, and – with the beginning of the information age – database design has been central to the use of inventories.[3]

It would be unfair to say that there have not been dissenting voices. Margaret Spufford and Jeff and Nancy Cox, among others, have gathered not only a wider range of information about inventories, their creation, their nature, and their purpose, but have also warned against their straightforward use.[4] More recently, Mark Overton has admitted that, although 'inventories overcome many of the limitations of individual documents, we need to be aware of how inventories may give a distorted picture of household production and consumption.'[5] These caveats in the use of inventories as sources are now accepted by most historians who consider these documents as useful but at times opaque tools for historical research. This chapter examines the relationship between inventories and the material reality that they captured, and in doing so argues that inventories should not be solely seen as sources. Today, few would agree with Fernand Braudel's definition of inventories as *documents de vérité*.[6] They are neither uncontaminated

FIGURE 5.1 Inventory of Philipp Watkins of Dorstone in the English county of Hertfordshire, taken on October 30, 1695

records of an objective reality, nor simple literary manifestations divorced from materiality. They are instead forms of representation that are influenced by social and legal conventions and by the specific economic and financial values attributed to artifacts and commodities in the early modern period.[7]

This chapter starts by charting the ways in which inventories have been used in historical research. In the past fifty years, inventories have been of particular use in the writing of early modern economic and social histories. Yet, their use as sources has conditioned our understanding of their nature and value. As part of their re-evaluation, this paper addresses three main issues: their creation; their power of representation; and their declining importance over time. The act of 'inventorying' allows us to glimpse the material world that an inventory represents: the estate, the household, the actions of the appraisers, and lastly the intentions of the owners of the goods described. The aim is to show that inventories are not 'snapshots of reality,' but the result of strategies, biases and representational intentions. By the very action of *representing* (rather than *presenting*) a domestic space and its contents, inventories are complex and difficult texts to decipher. They are also forms of representation that are time-specific. Omnipresent in the Renaissance and the early modern period, their number and usefulness diminished from the eighteenth century: a conundrum that can only be addressed by considering their nature and reason of production.

The use of inventories as historical sources

The word 'inventory' comes from the Latin *inventarium* that approximately means 'what is found in.' Inventories are lists of household or stock goods that were drawn up for a variety of legal and administrative procedures in early modern Europe. In Finland after 1734 and in the Austrian city of Salzburg until 1803, inventories were taken for all people who died over the age of eighteen. In Central European cities like Württemberg there was a legal obligation to produce an inventory before marriage.[8] In Burgundy, Brie, Westphalia, Austria, Holland, and Crete, inventories were compulsory when minors were among the inheritors.[9] Inventories were at times taken in cases of bankruptcy; the sale of an estate; loss from fire (Figure 5.2); admittance to mental hospitals, old people's homes, or orphanages; wardship; or when a poor house or hospital claimed a resident's properties.[10] The most common event in which an inventory was produced was the death of a property owner. In this case, what is called a 'probate inventory' could be created to protect the patrimony, eventually tax it, and – as in the case of England between the early sixteenth and the end of the eighteenth century – start the process by which a will was probated.[11]

An inventory can be anywhere from a few lines (Figure 5.3) to several hundred pages long. While most sixteenth- and seventeenth-century Florentine inventories are one or two pages long, the 1531 inventory of Alessandro de Medici's palace in via Larga in Florence lists over eighty pages of goods.[12] Inventories provide a wide range of information about the goods' owner; his/

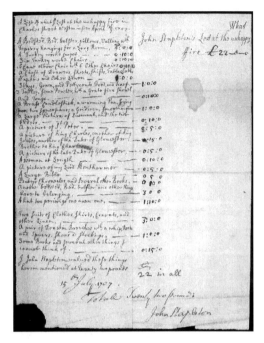

FIGURE 5.2 'A List of what I lost at the unhappy fire in Charles Street Westminster,' April 9th 1707

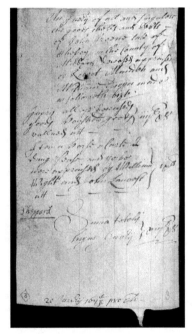

FIGURE 5.3 'An Inventory of all and singular the goods, chatles and debts of John Greene,' 1675

her furniture, taste, and religious values; where he/she lived; the cause of death; the family, business, credit, and debit relationships; and sometimes his/her wardrobe, social standing, and occupation. Even the most synthetic inventory often provides additional information about the color, material and the state of objects listed.[13]

Inventories are not only qualitatively rich but they are also numerically abundant in European and, to a certain degree, North American archives.[14] Estimates put the number of surviving inventories at two to three million in England and a staggering seven million for sixteenth-century France.[15] The usefulness of inventories is aided by the fact that they cover a wide range of social groups, although they only rarely include the lower orders.[16] In Britain – and in some cases on the continent – their analysis is facilitated by the fact that they are organized as separate bodies of sources in central and local archives. The inventories of the Prerogative Court of Canterbury, now deposited at the National Archives in Kew; the Court of Orphans of the City of London, now at the Corporation of London Archives; the Prerogative Court of York, now at the Borthwick Institute in York; the Minutier Central of the Archives Nationales in Paris; the Giudici di Petizion and del Proprio in Venice; or the Magistrato dei Pupilli in Florence are some of the major repositories of inventories in Europe.[17]

Late nineteenth-century antiquarians and local historians across Europe praised the qualities of inventories and provided the first transcriptions of 'selected' and 'curious' ones. Since the 1950s the field of economic history took inventories to be good historical sources to be used in large samples. The field of agrarian history made particular use of the information that inventories provided on livestock and crop prices.[18] Two areas of research, however, turned out to be extremely influential in the use of inventories as sources to investigate what today we call material culture: the history of architecture and building, and the history of consumption.

Inventories helped the history of architecture and building in addressing important issues concerning the relationship between the physical structure of buildings and the social and economic functions that they performed. The focus was not on the meaning of things, but on their capacity (as well as the capacity of their setting) to respond to new patterns of family life and to shape new types of social relations.[19] One example is the parlor changing from a public to a private space in early modern England, which can be analyzed according to a functional agenda (number of objects and their function); access and the permeability of rooms (distance from the non-domestic environment); and social requirements (what happened in the room and how this connected to changing social practices).[20] In turn, the history of the built environment has provided an enormous contribution to the understanding of inventories because it has connected the classic information provided by these documents (what is there and what is not) with new information gleaned from the study of family patterns, social behavior, history of leisure, and the emerging theme of the birth of comfort.[21] Studies on Italian and French inventories, in particular, have emphasized the material richness – and at the same time the uniformity – of early modern urban living. These studies have focused on the description of the household interiors of specific social classes, their transformations over time, and the interrelationship of towns, provinces, and states in shaping notions of taste, style and desirability.[22]

It was the renewed interest in consumption in the 1980s that instigated new approaches to the use of inventories. Studies by Carole Shammas, Lorna Weatherill and Annik Pardailhé-Galabrun, among others, provided a wide range of data on the variety and quantity of goods in pre-modern households; the relationship between wealth and consumption; the role of new goods; the differences between rural and urban consumption patterns; and the link between the acquisition and the production of goods.[23] Inventories were powerful methodological tools when used to criticize a wide range of consumption theories, including the very concept of a 'consumer revolution' for the early modern period.[24] While previous studies had confined themselves to studying the economic and social values of demand and consumption, the use of a large sample of inventories allowed us to investigate issues of emulation, fashion, respectability, separate spheres, public versus private, and innovation or conservatism in taste.[25]

The process of inventorying

The ways in which an inventory took shape informs its representational value. I call the act of drawing up an inventory the process of 'inventorying.' Inventorying was a common occurrence in early modern Europe and some people were involved in their compilation and transcription several times in their lives, either as inheritors, offspring, or appointed executors or administrators. A series of legal acts regulated all instances in which inventories were required and, as in the case of England, they established that the executors or administrators were responsible for producing two copies of each inventory, one of which had to be deposited with the local authority (Figure 5.4).[26] The law, however, did not provide any significant guidance for the persons who had to 'materially' produce an inventory. It clearly stated that an inventory was needed to assess the movable goods of a person, but did not specify the particular aim, skills, or knowledge of appraisers – all factors influencing the structure, level of detail, thoroughness and usefulness of an inventory.[27] Legal standards for the production of inventories must have been very flexible, as can be inferred by the fact that only a small number of inventories were questioned in court.[28]

Stephen Porter suggests that the structure and layout of inventories were the results of conventions adopted by the appraisers more than any established rule.[29] But who did create an inventory? In Continental Europe, notaries were in charge of drawing up inventories because these were public acts governing private legal matters (Figure 5.5). In this case established legal practices might have been important, as indicated by their relative stability over time and by the

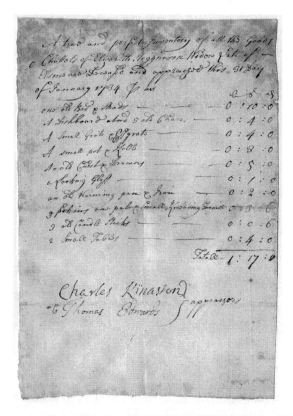

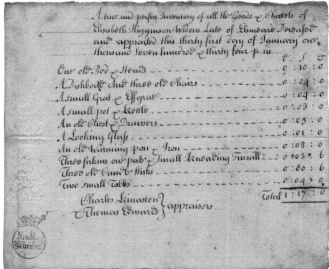

FIGURE 5.4   'A true and perfect Inventory of all the Goods & Chattles of Elizabeth Higginson Widow Late of Elsmeare Deceased and appraised this 31 Day of January 1734'

FIGURE 5.5   Domenico Ghirlandaio, *Inventory of a Legacy of the Magistrates*, second half of the fifteenth century

presence of regional difference. Notaries were absent, however, in common law countries such as England. Here, an act of 1529 established that the appraisers had to be chosen from among the creditors or persons to whom a legacy was due. A second choice could be one of the next of kin of the deceased or 'two other honest persons,' normally chosen from among the neighbors.

Appraisers therefore typically belonged to the community in which the deceased was living, although occasionally they might have been appointed for the task in a professional capacity.[30] This was probably the case in the Parish of Chelsea and Kensington in London. Here a sample of sixty inventories for the period 1672–1734 presents 120 appraisers, most of whom were men. Twelve of them appear to have appraised more than one household.[31] Thomas Harding was the appraiser of five inventories between 1672 and 1682, and William Freeman appraised four inventories between 1672 and 1691. They appraised together the inventory of Edward Smith in 1672 and that of William Smith in 1676. It is important to observe how these two inventories, although describing rather different households, present similar features such as identical sequences of rooms (the kitchen, followed by the chamber, followed by the yard) and a similar use of adjectives such as 'old' or 'small.'[32] John Hartshorne of Broseley of Shropshire during the 1740s and 1750s acted as an appraiser on eighteen different occasions, suggesting again that this task might have been carried out in at least a semi-professional manner.[33] The Lewes shopkeeper and diarist Thomas Turner appraised five estates between 1759 and 1764. These tasks could have been the result of his social standing within the local Sussex community, where he served as churchwarden, overseer of the poor, surveyor of the highway and, for a short period, keeper of the school. In May 1759 he appraised his mother's estate, a task that he carried out meticulously over three days as befitted a man with his business acumen and knowledge of the values of stocks and household goods. By contrast, a couple of years later he appraised 'the stock on the ground, household furniture and husbandry' of a late Mr. Piper and took 'a rough kind of inventory' of the little possessions of the deceased valued at a modest £7 2s.[34]

References to the taking of an inventory such as those of Thomas Turner are rare. Inventories themselves are usually the only surviving testimony of their own making, and must thus serve as a guide to how they were created. Their most common layout presents a room-by-room division, which suggests that the process of appraising was based on a perambulation of the house (Figures 5.6 and 5.7). The inventory presents each room's contents, from one to half a dozen items, normally through 'classic' groups of goods such as 'fire hearths, fire shovells & tongues' or 'one feather bed two bolsters & three feather pillowes.'[35]

FIGURE 5.6   'An inventorie of all maner & stuff remayning in Paget Place at London the xxth of february 1552, Anno E VI VIII'

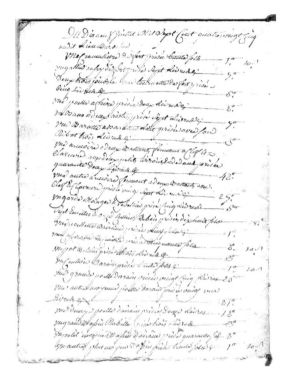

FIGURE 5.7 'Inventory of the goods of Gilles Neveu of Roches in the Parish of Plouasne'

In cases in which the body still lay in the house, appraisers probably started by paying their respects to the deceased and evaluating his/her most personal items such as money and apparel.[36] The task that appraisers had to accomplish was therefore influenced by the physical layout of a building. The place where the deceased's body was positioned and the interconnections between this space and the rest of the building structured the inventory. Lena Orlin argues that the deceased's family could cluster most goods into one room for the convenience of the appraisers, thus eliminating any conception of the physical space where these items were originally located.[37] This was common practice in pauper inventories or in the drawing up of inventories of large estates where objects were 'de-contextualized.' In these cases objects were often distinguished by types.[38]

The final result of the process of appraisal was the construction of a document that followed different conventions:

- A 'logical' or 'German' model, used also in Finland and Westphalia, that was based on different typologies of objects according to their use and/or the material they were made of: wood, metals, textiles, etc., or groups of objects destined for cooking, sleeping, entertaining, etc.[39]

- A 'piece-by-piece' or 'English' model that is also common in French and Dutch inventories and is based on the listing of individual items room by room or randomly.
- A 'mixed model' in which all pieces are listed one after the other, but within each piece there is a logical order. This is particularly used in sub-spaces such as chests and wardrobes.
- Finally there is a 'poor model' that has no logical order. This is present in sale inventories or inventories of people living as lodgers.[40]

Each of these models was regional or national, an indication that the drawing up of an inventory followed widely accepted rules. Yet, these models are ideal types based on the assumption that the main aim of an inventory was to represent the material culture of a household. This might in fact have been far from the appraisers' intentions. When drawing up an inventory, the appraisers had limited concern about the house, the household, or the family. Their task was to assess 'goods and chattels' and value them. In doing so, the inventory did not always take the bounded domestic space as its natural limit. Inventories often extend into the sheds and fields to count cattle and value crops. While they hardly convey the more 'human' side of domestic life, they often provide precious insights on the early modern notion of life, which was much less linked to the space that we would today define as domestic.

A subjective representation

Moving from the action of inventorying to the document called an inventory, Lena Orlin warns us that 'probate inventories are less innocent than they appear' as they are seldom uncontaminated by narrative. She argues that inventories should be seen as works of 'fiction' (or better said, they contain fictional elements) and presents a long list of cases in which specific goods were not included in inventories and many others in which entire rooms disappear from the record.[41] This useful perspective might be integrated here by adding three simple points. First is the fact that if inventories are considered 'fiction,' they surely belong to a *genre* which follows established rules. Among the various ways to represent physical space, inventories were constructed with specific aims. Second, inventories cannot be taken as simple works of fiction as they are not entirely detached from what they describe.[42] Appraisers connected inventories to social and cultural attitudes and values. Third, and perhaps most importantly, if we consider the uses of inventories in historical research, most 'distortions' should disappear when large samples of inventories are considered together. If inventories are particular representations of 'the real,' each of them is a unique document. Historians, however, have been more interested in making sense of inventories as groups or samples, rather than as individual documents. In large samples, distortions only rarely become systematic.[43]

Because of these points, instead of 'fiction' I prefer to argue that inventories are 'subjective representations.' Like a painting or a picture, inventories are 'framed.' They have clear limits in the type of information that they convey and the ways in which such information is presented. In short, my argument is that the subjective quality of inventories is not necessarily about *what* they include or exclude (and therefore how much they differ from a model inventory) but *who* and *how* they include/exclude. There is no model inventory, but each of these documents is per se 'subjective' because it is conditioned by specific sets of social and cultural values, assumptions, conventions and beliefs.[44]

Inventories are – in the first instance – subjective representations because they favor a notion of a stable society. The world of vagrants, migrants, or the large strata of early modern society that is defined in French as *sans feu, sans lieu, sans aveu* (without hearth, without place, without morals) is neglected by inventories.[45] Only about 20–40 percent of the eighteenth-century Swedish population left an inventory; in Colonial America from one fourth to two thirds of all households; and with sensible regional and local variations, from 10 to 40 percent of the population in England.[46] A partial correction of this bias comes from recent work on so-called paupers' inventories. They were created via the obligation of local parishes in connection with the poor law legislation.[47] As for the lower strata of society, women too are normally under-represented in inventories. Husbands and wives could hold property individually or jointly, but the right of husbands was deemed to be the most important.[48] Women appear as widows or as spinsters, but their share of all surviving inventories does not exceed 20 percent of the total.[49]

Inventories are also static documents that were drawn up at specific times, whereas – as Nancy Cox puts it – 'the home was a living entity constantly being reshaped to make closer the correspondence between image and reality and in response to events of fortune and misfortune.'[50] While account books, diaries or probate accounts are able to capture change – the flux of objects, events, and people that shape the physical structure of a house and create the social meaning of a household – inventories are fixed in time.[51] Probate inventories, for instance, are not only the result of a specific situation/event, but are also placed in time according to very specific demographic trends (i.e. life expectancy). The static picture of the household they provide is connected to personal and familial life cycles. This is not always true for individual inventories, but it does hold for aggregates or, in other words, for the 'big picture' that inventories provide to historians. Typically, before marriage a couple saved to purchase clothes, textiles and furnishings; after marriage they bought kitchen utensils and a piece of land that was sold when their children had left home.[52] Furnishings and jewelry served as a pension, and by the time a couple died and inventories were drawn up, the house contained only the articles needed by a two-person family.[53] It is very difficult to identify the age of the deceased in most European inventories and therefore it is an impossible task to analyze if there is a connection between the way inventories were constructed and the circumstances of death.[54]

Inventories are also subjective because they are not exhaustive records of the contents of a domestic space. Objects like the deceased's apparel are normally included in sixteenth and early seventeenth-century English inventories, but become less frequent in the later seventeenth and eighteenth centuries, often summarized under the label 'his/her own apparrell.'[55] The definition of a probate inventory itself, a list 'of goods belonging to people valued on oath by their neighbors or executors after their death as part of the process of obtaining probate of their "moveable" estate, i.e. all their possessions other than freehold or copyhold land,'[56] implies a wide range of omissions, as underlined by contemporary legal texts.[57] The appraisers included all personal holdings (personal goods, credits, livestock and equipment), but excluded real estate (land and buildings) – although the produce of the real estate (leases or crops in the fields) and the remaining part of the so-called realty holdings (improvements) were included in inventories.[58]

There is a second category of objects that, although with differences across Europe, are more or less systematically excluded from inventories: objects of low value.[59] This was not necessarily the result of appraisers' negligence.[60] The law only required accuracy in valuation, not in listing the complete contents of a household. While a cow or an ox (animals that can be sold) in the stable are listed in the inventory, the cat or dog (without financial value) are not; clothing that can be resold is included, but old shoes or French sabots of little monetary value are not.[61] As Jan de Vries notices, historians interested in analyzing the role of newspapers or children's toys in family life would find little help from inventories.[62] Similarly, inventories exclude non-durable goods. A chunk of cheese would be considered valuable enough to be included in the inventory, but the other food in the kitchen is normally not. Inventories also sometimes exclude valuable objects such as jewelry, silver or glass. It could be claimed that these were 'personal' objects that could not only be excluded from an inventory, but also disposed of before the inventory was taken.[63] Wills are rich in legacies and gifts that were only rarely included in inventories.

A special category of goods whose inclusion in inventories is a subject of debate is widows' property.[64] Margaret Spufford underlines the difficulty of knowing whether the wife's belongings were excluded or not in the husband's inventory. Only in rare cases was the wife's original dowry separately listed at the end of an English inventory.[65] Italian archives, by converse, contain large numbers of dowry inventories taken either at the husband's death or, more frequently, at the moment of the restitution of the dowry to the bride's family. One such case is the inventory of Beatrice Sottomanzo's dowry. The inventory was requested by Margherita Barletta:

> Margherita Barletta of Monopoli, wife of Angelo Intino, her second husband, says that in the years past she married her daughter Beatrice Sottomanzo, child of her first husband, Donato Sottomanzo, with Angelo di Nicola Brescia. It was established that if Beatrice were to die before

Margherita, her dowry would have gone back to the mother. Beatrice died and left a three-year old son. Beatrice's husband married again and Margherita has obtained the custody of the child. She produces the inventory of Beatrice's possessions.

In this case the inventory becomes a document surveying the domestic life of a household whose existence already ceased. It thus distinguishes between *beni mobili che esistono* (goods still present) and *beni mobili venduti* (goods that have been sold).[66]

Inventories also vary in space and time, making the notion of a model inventory even more problematic. In places like England or Scotland they list only movable property. In other places, such as Quebec, inventories provide more information on the real estate of the deceased and include debts, deeds and business properties.[67] Even more challenging for historians is the fact that inventories vary over time. Legal and cultural practices underwent profound modifications during the early modern period, so the process of inventorying did not remain stable. Changes in the structure of inventories and in their contents are of fundamental importance in explaining changes in the way the domestic interior and its belongings were viewed and represented. The changing structure, degree of detail, and language of inventories are the outcomes of a changing material reality that they tried to capture, an increase in literacy, and the transformation of the early modern economy.

Perhaps the most challenging aspect of understanding inventories is the fact that the very spaces and objects that they represented changed over time. This was not just a physical change, but also a change of their meaning. An example might be the changing priorities of English inventories. Early inventories expressed a clear concern with the body – the physicality of the deceased. This is why many sixteenth-century inventories start with the deceased's clothing (normally a high percentage of his/her estate) and the 'money in purse,' something that becomes less common over time.[68] Rural inventories, by converse, retain their concern with the non-domestic and place cattle and husbandry implements at the very beginning of the inventory. The relationship between natural and social environments is thus best captured in sixteenth-century inventories rather than the inventories of an urbanizing country such as England in the late seventeenth century.

Entering inside the space of a house, a cottage, or a palace, inventories are subjective records because they embrace specific ways of categorizing the domestic. Inventories produced in the southwestern English region of Cornwall in the seventeenth and early eighteenth centuries, for instance, rarely distinguish different rooms. Is this a result of specific architectural or material conditions, or of specific space-embedded ways of representing the household? When we compare those that do list rooms with the inventories of another English county like Kent, where most inventories distinguish rooms, we find that the mean number of rooms is similar in the two counties. This means that there is not a relationship between the number of rooms and their listing in inventories.[69]

The problem of representation offered by inventories is not only related to *how*, but also *how well* they represent the domestic. Inventories, for instance, are not good at representing 'what is in between' spaces. The connectivity of the domestic spaces is often lost in inventories since doors, corridors and stairs are only rarely mentioned. The room disposition and the interior arrangement, although not recorded in inventories, are suggested in other ways. When the listing is room by room, inventories show the movement of the appraiser, the path followed through the building, and the way in which the built environment was seen and experienced by appraisers.

At a more microscopic level, inventories are often considered to be simple lists of objects. But are inventories simply 'descriptive?' As Antonia Malan observes,

> the categorization of artifacts also reflected the organizing principles used in daily life. Organizing principles included named room-by-room lists, categorization by composition (different metals or ceramic bodies), the condition of the object (broken, new, old) and the function and capacity of vessels.[70]

Do groupings of objects have meanings per se or are the objects simply put together because of their proximity in space? Are these associations based on functional complements or according to personal choices? And is this a process of association that changed over time as a result of shifting social practices? Inventories, for instance, show that in the early modern period the hearth lost its role as the center of the house and that a decreasing number of objects revolved around the fireplace. Objects started to be stored in cupboards and drawers, to be associated in new ways, and to be positioned according to new functional principles. Individual inventories can only partially illuminate the ways in which these new practices were understood and expressed.[71] This is why single inventories have to be accompanied by the analysis of extensive samples. The repetition of similar nomenclatures or locations of objects suggest the existence of a shared way of thinking about the domestic space that is conveyed in inventories.

This leads me to a final point about the medium used by inventories: language. Even if I do not go as far as to say that inventories are fictional, their written nature makes it necessary to assess them as texts. Historians who use inventories are aware of the difficulty of interpreting specific words, not just in transcribing but also in attributing a meaning to them.[72] Semantic variations over space and time and the different national languages in which inventories are written has so far made a comparative analysis of inventories from different areas of Europe impractical. The problem of inventories, however, is not confined to specific words: 'inventories are texts, and like other texts, they

[are] require[d] to be understood in their entirety.'[73] The grammar, syntax, and literary style of inventories are all elements that need to be taken into consideration. Inventories, for instance, are often redundant: the repetition of the Latin word *item* to denote a new topic, line, or category, commonly used in English and other languages and only rarely transcribed by historians, is one example. They are also often redundant in the use of adjectives. The longer the inventory, the more common is the use of adjectives attempting to distinguish similar items and at the same time justifying different values.[74] The fact that most analyses of inventories have produced databases that do not consider the inventories' layout, structure, and spelling, and rarely reflect on the qualitative information that they provide, means that it is still difficult for historians to appreciate them as texts.

The disappearance of inventories

Why did inventories disappear at the end of the *ancien régime*? This is a problem that has no unilateral answer since, to a limited extent, inventories are still taken today. This is true not only for countries such as Sweden where inventories started to be taken relatively late, in the 1730s, and continue to the present, but also in other European countries in which they are still commonly taken for rented accommodations, repossessions, and legal causes. It is, however, correct that by the mid-nineteenth century the practice of taking inventories came more or less to an end. For countries like Italy, the demographic and economic stagnation of the seventeenth and eighteenth centuries coincided with a slow but steady decline in the number of inventories taken. Inventories also faded out in countries such as France, although over a longer period and at an even slower pace than in Italy. In Britain, however, their disappearance is much more of an enigma for historians. Instead of lessening in number over a long period of time, English inventories died out over the course of just a few decades during the second quarter of the eighteenth century. This phenomenon has been explained in different and contradictory ways.[75]

A 'legal explanation' has emphasized the specific nature of British common law. Praxis rather than legislative initiative guaranteed that inventories were taken. Since inventories were present before the 1529 Act that regulated them, their existence was only partially due to legal reasons.[76] Historians, unable to identify a specific act establishing the end of inventories as a legal requirement, have emphasized instead how the 1529 Act became obsolete and how by the early eighteenth century new legal practices promoted novel ways of protecting the estate of a deceased.[77] This explanation sees inventories as documents aimed at protecting the totality of the estate. But judging by the formula 'All and Singular Goods and Chattels,' the inventory was also supposed to be an insurance that 'singular' goods would not be removed. This function seems to be particularly important for all those inventories that had no valuations associated with specific items. Moreover, this legal explanation is at odds with what can be defined as the emergence of the 'bureaucratic state' during the early modern period. If the state, rather than private interests, is seen as the reason for the drawing up of inventories, it is particularly difficult to explain why a document with such an important regulative function in the translation of wealth stopped being produced in the precise historic moment in which the state started to have an active interest in controlling and measuring the production and distribution of wealth.

A second set of explanations has addressed these critiques by emphasizing the importance of changing practices. According to these theories, inventories disappeared not because of a centralized legislative initiative, but because of changes in the practices shared by local communities. This explanation underlines the importance of understanding who made the inventories, who paid for them, and what role they played within society. It does not try to specify the reason why inventories disappeared, but simply suggests that long-established practices could become obsolete not only in the wider world of legal fiction, but also in everyday life. This model, however, would predict a smooth process in which inventories faded out with the same degree of slowness as in other European countries, not the rapid decline that actually occurred.

Even more puzzling is the fact that inventories not only disappeared fairly quickly (probably in less than one generation), but that they also disappeared from most archives.[78] In fact, some historians have argued that inventories continued to be taken well into the nineteenth century, and that they do not survive because of the result of an archival policy that privileged the keeping of other documents instead of inventories. While for the late eighteenth century large numbers of wills survive, the same cannot be said about inventories, which were no longer kept with their respective wills. The pressure applied by the bureaucratic state to create a new system of recording society and the economy was not matched by the physical space of archives. If a choice had to be made, the documents related to the wealth and wishes of the deceased had to be kept, rather than those related to his or her personal belongings.[79]

This 'archival' explanation cannot simply be dismissed as a plot of archivists against historians. One of the elements that it implicitly underlines is the changing nature of wealth and possessions in the early modern world. The early modern period, and especially the seventeenth and eighteenth centuries, was characterized by an increasing level of material welfare. What has been defined as a 'revolution of objects' made it difficult to record belongings as analytically as had been traditionally done.[80] Early eighteenth-century inventories are more synthetic than sixteenth or seventeenth-centuries ones, normally only listing rooms and associating values to their contents. If objects are listed, they are usually subsumed under generic categories, such as 'furniture,' 'pewter,' or 'linen,' or with residual expressions such as 'other lumber' or 'other things.' It might be counterintuitive that higher levels of material culture of the eighteenth century produced shorter rather than longer inventories. This conundrum can be easily explained if we consider that the value of individual objects declined steadily both in absolute and relative terms. Real prices show that most goods became cheaper in the course of the seventeenth century. Similarly, the increase in the average number of belongings made each of them a smaller proportion of the total wealth of an individual.

The valuation of goods proposed in inventories and their relationship with market prices has been the subject of detailed research, especially in Britain where inventories normally include a monetary evaluation of the goods.[81] Inventories systematically undervalued goods as a form of precaution against price fluctuations. This was also a way to protect the executor as well as the parties inheriting the estate.[82] A balance between a possible value of the estate and the interests of the creditors, whose credits were guaranteed by the estate itself, was carefully negotiated through a thorough evaluation of the market possibilities, the conditions of the goods, and the level of the debts to be repaid.[83] This is why special knowledge was required in the valuation of particular goods, especially business stocks. Yet, their financial function might provide a good explanation as to why inventories became redundant in the course of the late seventeenth and eighteenth centuries. As the economy became increasingly market-based, information about real, nominal, and monetary values were no longer part of specialized knowledge, but could be inferred by a larger and less educated crowd of people. If prices are signs and inventories were constructed to convey meanings of value, their function in a highly dynamic market economy might have been of little importance. One could force this explanation and say that inventories became obsolete because they conveyed a meaning that was transparent to everyone.

The simpler the credit–debit relationships or the legacies created by the will, the simpler would have been the inventory required. This is a rational approach that underlines how inventories maintained their ability to provide basic financial data that was useful in assessing legal fees and in ensuring the solvency of the estate. Eighteenth-century Italian inventories, for instance, provide several examples of this transformation in the nature and purpose of inventories. The inventory of Vincenzo Chiarugi of Florence, who died in 1786, presents more similarities with an account book than with an inventory. The *Attivo* includes a description of the *Beni stabili* (buildings and fixtures) with their associated values. This is followed by the *Mobili delle case del patrimonio in Empoli* and *Mobili in Firenze* (classic inventories of two households in Empoli and Florence with their movable goods) very briefly listed and valued. The *Passivo* is composed of gifts and debts, while the final part of the inventory includes the *Ipoteche* (mortgages).[84] It is not uncommon to find inventories listing the contents of a series of buildings. The *beni e registro* of the Contess Giulia Margherita Mora of Barge provides in four pages a detailed overview of all her belongings including a house, an orchard, woodland, etc. (Figure 5.8).

An explanation for the disappearance (or mutation) of inventories based on the relationship between values, prices, and market information is, however, weak at addressing changing social attitudes to materiality and material culture.

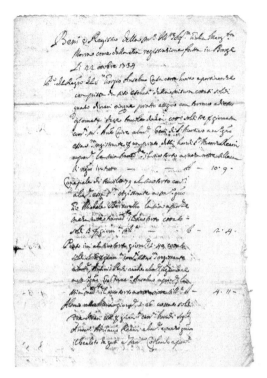

FIGURE 5.8 Goods and List of Goods belonging to Countess Giulia Margherita Morra as from the registrino taken place in Barge on the 22 October 1734

The 'rise of material culture' did not merely imply an increase in the number of objects possessed by an individual. Research has underlined how social and cultural attitudes towards material culture also changed profoundly. Material goods have value beyond the market. Lorna Weatherill in her study of consumer behavior in Britain has particularly emphasized the non-monetary value of possessions.[85] The affective and personal value of goods is only rarely conveyed in inventories; wills are much more suitable documents to make material culture tangible and meaningful. They are personal documents that explain and contextualize the actions of the deceased and often refer to his or her belongings in the forms of presents and bequests to friends and family. Values in this case become unnecessary because objects are invested with emotional and personal meanings.

The material culture and market approaches to the understanding of inventories' disappearance clearly set the problem within the much broader context of what is traditionally called the 'rise of capitalism.' Markets became more integrated and exchange acquired momentum, providing cheaper and more abundant quantities of goods. However, one can hardly take these processes as the reason for the disappearance of inventories. In many parts of Europe, where the level of material welfare was high, inventories remained very detailed throughout the seventeenth and eighteenth centuries. In general, the increasing level of material goods could have two opposing effects on inventories. On the one hand, a wider spectrum of goods made it difficult to record each item with the same degree of precision. On the other hand, however, there was more ground to be covered by an inventory. As Van der Woude and Schuurman point out, identical material cultures in two geographic areas of The Netherlands had completely different effects on inventories. While in Frisia inventories were common in the sixteenth and seventeenth centuries, but declined in the eighteenth century, in Groningen inventories became widespread only in the eighteenth century.[86]

Conclusion

Inventories were documents designed to prevent goods from being spirited away from the deceased's residence by relatives or creditors.[87] They have been used by historians to reconstruct the lives, and in particular the patterns of consumption and material wealth, of early modern people, rich and poor alike. This paper provides a critical view of what an inventory is and what it might do for historians. By arguing that inventories are representations of the domestic (and in many cases also of what is beyond the domestic), I have underlined their importance in relation to the materiality that they wished to capture but also the intentions and circumstances in which they took shape. Critical awareness of the structure, language, form, and content of an inventory should not be seen in opposition to their use in large samples or large data sets. In many ways historians using this methodology respond to issues stemming from the idiosyncratic nature of each individual inventory. Yet, inventories can be a lens through which to see more than mere lists of goods. They provide unique insights on how contemporaries thought about material things, addressed and assessed their value, and dealt with an increasingly complex material world.

Acknowledgments

I would like to thank Richard Butler, Donal Cooper, Nancy Cox, Karin Dannehl, Mark Overton, Sarah Pennell, Liliane Pérez, John Styles, Alessandra Tessari, and Amanda Vickery for their help and comments. This paper was part of the research carried out by the Arts and Humanities Research Council (AHRC) Centre for the Study of the Domestic Interior, active at the Royal College of Fashion between 2002 and 2006. Previous versions of this paper were presented at the conference 'Inventories in Renaissance and Early Modern Europe,' held at the Victoria and Albert Museum in May 2004; at the AHRC International Network on 'Global Commodities' workshop held at Istanbul Bilgi University in September 2011; and at the European University Institute in Fiesole, Italy in March 2012.

Notes

1 Peter Burke, *Eyewitnessing: The Uses of Images as Historical Evidence* (Ithaca, NY: Cornell University Press, 2001), 13.

2 Edmund Weiner, 'Local History and Lexicography,' *Local Historian* 24.3 (1994): 164–173; Swati Chattopadhyay, 'Goods, Chattels and Sundry Items: Constructing 19th-Century Anglo-Indian Domestic Life,' *Journal of Material Culture* 7.3 (2002): 243–271; Alison Bell, 'Emulation and Empowerment: Material, Social, and Economic Dynamics in Eighteenth and Nineteenth-Century Virginia,' *International Journal of Historical Archaeology* 6.4 (2002): 253–298; Renata Ago, 'Collezioni di quadri e collezioni di libri a Roma tra XVI e XVIII secolo,' *Quaderni Storici* 37.2 (2002): 379–403; Esteban A. Nicolini and Fernando Ramos, 'A New Method for Estimating the Money Demand in Pre-Industrial Economies: Probate Inventories and Spain in the Eighteenth Century,' *European Review of Economic History* 14 (2009): 145–177; Peter Wardley and Pauline White, 'The Arithmeticke Project: A Collaborative Research Study of the Diffusion of Hindu-Arabic Numerals,' *Journal of the Family and Community Research Society* 6.1 (2003): 5–17.

3 Anton Schuurman, 'Probate Inventories: Research Issues, Problems and Results,' in *Probate Inventories: A New Source for the Historical Study of Wealth, Material Culture, and Agricultural Development*, ed. Ad van der Woude and Anton Schuurman (Wageningen: Wageningen Landbouwhogeschool, 1980), 21; R. J. Morris and Ann McCrum, 'Introduction: Wills, Inventories and the Computer,' *History and Computing* 7.3 (1995): iv–xi; Mark Overton, 'A Computer Management System for Probate Inventories,' *History and Computing*, 7.3 (1995): 135–142.

4 See Jeff Cox and Nancy Cox, 'Probate 1500–1800: A System in Transition,' in *When Death do Us Part: Understanding and Interpreting the Probate Records of Early Modern England*, ed. Tom Arkell, Nesta Evans, and Nigel Goose (Oxford: Leopard's Head Press, 2000), 13–37; Margaret Spufford, 'The Limitations of the Probate Inventory,' in *English Rural Society, 1500–1800: Essays in Honour of Joan Thirsk*, ed. John Chartres and David Hey (Cambridge: Cambridge University Press, 1990), 139–174; idem, 'The Cost of Apparel in Seventeenth-Century England, and the Accuracy of Gregory King,' *Economic History Review* 53.4 (2000): 677–705.

5 Mark Overton et al., *Production and Consumption in English Households, 1600–1750* (London: Routledge, 2004), 13.

6 Fernand Braudel, *Civilisation matérielle et capitalisme, XVe–XVIIIe siècle* (Paris: Colin, 1967) 1: 212.

7 This perspective is shared by Adrian Evans, 'Enlivening the Archive: Glimpsing Embodied Consumption Practices in Probate Inventories of Household Possessions,' *Historical Geography* 36 (2008): 40–72.

8 Peter Borscheid, 'Les inventaires wurtembergeois: une chance pour l'histoire sociale: programme et premiers résultats,' in *Les actes notariés: sources de l'histoire sociale XVIe–XIXe siècles*, ed. Bernard Vogler (Strasbourg: Istra, 1979), 208; Dominik Gross, 'Marriage Strategies and Social Prestige of Barber-Surgeons in 19th-Century Württemberg: A Quantitative Evaluation of Marriage and Probate Inventories,' *Historical Social Research* 23.4 (1988): 94–108.

9 Micheline Baulant, 'Typologie des inventaires après décès,' in *Probate inventories*, ed. van der Woude and Schuurman, 33–34; Jan Kuuse, 'The Probate Inventory as a Source for Economic and Social History,' *Scandinavian Economic History Review* 22.1 (1974): 23.

10 Thera Wijsenbeek, 'Delft in the Eighteenth Century,' in *Probate inventories*, ed. van der Woude and Schuurman, 162; Catherine Gaeng, 'Noblesse et bourgeoisie au Luxembourg au XVIIIe siècle: ce que nous apprennent les inventaires et ventes de mobilier,' *Hémecht* 47.3 (1995): 339–370.

11 Overton et al., *Production and Consumption*, 15.

12 See Giovanni Lazzi, 'Giovanna Bigalli Lulla, Alessandro de' Medici e il palazzo di via Larga: l'inventario del 1531,' *Archivio Storico Italiano* 150.2 (1992): 1201–1233.

13 Occasionally inventories mention age, date of marriage, or place of origin. See Baulant, 'Typologie des inventaires,' 38–39.

14 This analysis limits itself to early modern Western Europe with some occasional references to North America. Inventories were also common in the Ottoman Empire and Eastern Europe and could be found also in Asia, as in the case of requisition inventories in eighteenth-century China. See Gilles Veinstein, 'Note sur les inventaires après décès ottomans,' in *Quand le crible était dans la paille: hommage à Pertev Naili Boratav*, ed. Rémy Dor and Michèle Nicolas (Paris: Maisonneuve et Larose, 1978), 383–395; Colette Establet and Jean-Paul Pascual, 'Damascene Probate Inventories of the 17th and 18th Centuries: Some Preliminary Approaches and Results,' *International Journal of Middle East Studies* 24.3 (1992): 373–393; Yan Yun, 'The Daily Life of Official-Elite Families in Eighteenth-Century China: A Case Study of Property-Confiscation' and Elif Akçetin, 'Objects on the Move: Gifts, Commodities and Corrupt Objects in the Qianlong Reign (1736–1795)' (papers presented at the AHRC International Network on Global Commodities conference, 'The Material Culture of Everyday Living: Ottoman Consumption in a Comparative Perspective,' Bilgi University, Istanbul, Turkey, September 15–16, 2011).

15 Madeleine Jurgens and Jean Favier, *Documents du Minutier central des notaires de Paris: inventaires après décès, tome premier (1483–1547)* (Paris: Archives Nationales, 1982), 9.

16 James A. Johnston, 'The Probate Inventories and Wills of a Worcestershire Parish, 1676–1775,' *Midland History* 1.1 (1971–1972): 21.

17 On the Prerogative Courts of Canterbury and York inventories see J. S. W. Gibson, 'Probate Inventories in the Records of the Prerogative Court of Canterbury,' *Local Historian* 14.4 (1981): 222–225. On the Minutier central see Jurgens and Favier, *Documents du Minutier central*.

18 Mark Overton, 'English Probate Inventories and the Measurement of Agricultural Change,' in *Probate Inventories*, ed. van der Woude and Schuurman, 205–216; Nancy Cox and Jeff Cox, 'Valuations in Probate Inventories: Part I,' *Local Historian* 16.8 (1985): 467–478; Nancy Cox and Jeff Cox, 'Valuations in Probate Inventories: Part II,' *Local Historian* 17.2 (1986): 85–100; Mark Overton, 'Prices from Probate Inventories,' in *When Death do Us Part*, ed. Arkell, Evans and Goose, 120–141. For Italy, see Maria Serena Mazzi and Sergio Raveggi, *Gli uomini e le cose nelle campagne fiorentine del Quattrocento* (Florence: L. S. Olschki, 1983). For Spain, José M. Perez Garcia, 'Los inventarios post-mortem como indicadores de la riqueza Ganadera, Galicia occidental (1600–1669),' in *La documentación notarial y la historia. Actas del Coloquio de Metodologia Histórica Aplicada* (Madrid: Junta de Decanos de los Colegios Notariales de Espana, 1984), 1:297–315.

19 Frank E. Brown, 'Continuity and Change in the Urban House: Developments in Domestic Space Organisation in Seventeenth-Century London,' *Comparative Studies in Society and History* 28.3 (1986): 559–561; John Bedell, 'Archaeology and Probate Inventories in the Study of Eighteenth-Century Life,' *Journal of Interdisciplinary History* 31.2 (2000): 223–245. See also Nicholas Cooper, 'Rank, Manners and Display: The Gentlemanly House, 1500–1750,' *Transactions of the Royal Historical Society* 12 (2002): 291–310.

20 Ursula Priestley and P. J. Corfield, 'Rooms and Room Use in Norwich Housing, 1580–1730,' *Post-Medieval Archaeology* 16 (1982): 93–123.

21 See in particular John E. Crowley, *The Invention of Comfort: Sensibilities and Design in Early Modern Britain and Early America* (Baltimore, MD: Johns Hopkins University Press, 2000). See also Matthew Johnson, *An Archaeology of Capitalism* (Oxford: Blackwell, 1996), 170–174; Sara Pennell, '"Pots and Pans History": The Material Culture of the Kitchen in Early Modern England,' *Journal of Design History* 11.3 (1998): 201–216.

22 For France see for instance Bertrand Gautier, 'L'habitat des marchands bordelais au XVIIe siècle d'après les inventaires après décès,' *Annales du Midi* 216 (1996): 505–520. For Italy: Paola Pavanini, 'Abitazioni popolari e borghesi nella Venezia Cinquecentesca,' *Studi Veneziani* 5 (1981): 63–126; Laura Megna, 'Comportamenti abitativi del patriziato veneziano (1582–1740),' *Studi Veneziani* 22 (1991): 253–324.

23 Carole Shammas, 'The Domestic Environment in Early Modern England and America,' *Journal of Social History* 14.1 (1980): 3–24; idem, *The Pre-Industrial Consumer in England and America* (Oxford: Clarendon Press, 1990); Annik Pardailhé-Galabrun, *The Birth of Intimacy: Privacy and Domestic Life in Early Modern Paris* (Philadelphia, PA: University of Pennsylvania Press, 1991); Lorna Weatherill, 'Consumer Behaviour and Social Status in England, 1660–1750,' *Continuity and Change* 1.2 (1986): 191–216; idem, *Consumer Behaviour and Material Culture in Britain, 1660–1760* (London: Routledge, 1988).

24 Neil McKendrick, John Brewer and John H. Plumb, *The Birth of a Consumer Society: The Commercialization of Eighteenth-Century England* (London: Europa, 1982).

25 See for instance Overton et al., *Production and Consumption* and the recent analysis of the reception of global commodities by Anne McCants, 'Poor Consumers as Global Consumers: The Diffusion of Tea and Coffee Drinking in the Eighteenth Century,' *Economic History Review* 61.S1 (2008): 172–200.

26 This is the specific case of Britain, though regulations varied widely across Europe. Tom Arkell, 'The Probate Process,' in *When Death do Us Part*, ed. Arkell, Evans and Goose, 11.

27 Bedell, 'Archaeology and Probate Inventories,' 228–229.

28 John S. Moore, 'Probate Inventories: Problems and Prospects,' in *Probate Records and the Local Community*, ed. Philip Riden (Gloucester: A. Sutton, 1985), 16. The few legal causes related to inventories complained about the intentions of appraisers, rather than low standards of appraisal.

29 Stephen Porter, 'The Making of Probate Inventories,' *Local Historian* 12.1 (1976): 36.

30 Cox and Cox, 'Probate inventories: Part I': 134–135. The study by Jeff and Nancy Cox of the Severn Gorge's inventories shows that 145 inventories were appraised by at least one person with the same surname of the deceased. See Barrie Trinder and Nancy Cox, eds., *Miners and Mariners of the Severn Gorge: Probate Inventories for Benthall, Broseley, Little Wenlock and Madeley, 1660–1764* (Chichester: Phillimore, 2000).

31 B. R. Curle, ed., 'Kensington and Chelsea Probate Inventories, 1672–1734,' unpublished transcript held at the London Metropolitan Archives (1970).

32 Corporation of London, London Metropolitan Archives (hereafter LMA), AM/PI/1/1672/73b; AM/PI/1/1676/30.

33 Nancy Cox, 'Retailing and Consumption 1550–1820: An Analytical and Methodological Approach' (PhD diss., University of Wolverhampton, 2001). I thank Nancy Cox for providing me with an extract of her thesis. See also the original inventories in Trinder and Cox, eds., *Miners and Mariners*.

34 David Vaisey, ed., *The Diary of Thomas Turner, 1754–1765* (Oxford: Oxford University Press, 1984), xxii, 182, 224.

35 LMA, AM/PI/1/1686/78: 'A True & perfect Inventory of All & Singular Goods & Chattles of John Wyseman…,' 25 October 1686.

36 Most inventories were made within a few days from the death, but there are cases of inventories produced ten or even twenty years after the death. Trinder and Cox, eds., *Miners and Mariners*, 8.

37 Lena Cowen Orlin, 'Fictions of the Early Modern English Probate Inventory,' in *The Culture of Capital: Property, Cities, and Knowledge in Early Modern England*, ed. Henry S. Turner (New York: Routledge, 2002), 60.

38 Pewter, for instance, is normally listed at the end of an inventory as it had to be removed from its original setting to be weighted.

39 English inventories also follow this model when they divide household and stock goods, when they group together objects with similar functions present in a single room, or when they list specific categories such as 'pewter,' 'linen,' 'silver,' or 'books.'

40 This classification is proposed in Baulant, 'Typologie des inventaires,' 38–40.

41 Cowen Orlin, 'Fictions,' esp. 53.

42 Micheline Baulant, 'Necessité de vivre et besoin de paraitre: les inventaires et la vie quotidienne,' in *Inventaires après-décès et ventes de meubles: apports à une histoire de la vie économique et quotidienne, XIVe–XIXe siècle*, ed. Micheline Baulant, Anton J. Schuurman, and Paul Servais (Louvain-la-Neuve: Academia, 1988), 9.

43 Daniel Roche is conscious of this and reminds us that it is not the content of the inventory to be 'distorted,' but the act of creation of inventories. He distinguishes four types of *lacunes*: economic, legal, fraud, and under-evaluation of goods. Daniel Roche, Rémy Arnette, and François Ardellier, 'Inventaires après décès parisiens et culture matérielle au XVIIIe siècle,' in *Les actes notariés*, ed. Vogler, 233.

44 Kevin M. Sweeney, 'Furniture and the Domestic Environment in Wethersfield Connecticut, 1639–1800,' in *Material Life in America, 1600–1860*, ed. Robert Blair St. George (Boston, MA: Northeastern University Press, 1988), 232–233.

45 Joël Cornette, 'La revolution des objets: le Paris des inventaires après décès (XVIIe–XVIIIe siècles),' *Revue d'Histoire Moderne et Contemporaine* 36 (1989): 480.

46 For Sweden see Carl-Johan Gadd, 'Swedish Probate Inventories, 1750–1860,' in *Probate Inventories*, ed. van der Woude and Schuurman, 229–231. For Colonial America: Daniel S. Smith, 'Underregistration and Bias in Probate Records: An Analysis of Data from Eighteenth-Century Hingham, Massachusetts,' *William and Mary Quarterly* 32.1 (1975): 101; Bruce C. Daniels, 'Probate Court Inventories and Colonial American History: Historiography, Problems, and Results,' *Histoire Sociale/Social History* 9 (1976): 394. For Britain: Johnston, 'Probate Inventories,' 21.

47 Peter King, 'Pauper Inventories and the Material Lives of the Poor in the Eighteenth and Early Nineteenth Centuries,' in *Chronicling Poverty: The Voices and Strategies of the English Poor, 1640–1840*, ed. Tim Hitchcock, Peter King, and Pamela Sharpe (London: Macmillan, 1997), 155–191.

48 Cox and Cox, 'Probate 1500–1800,' 22.

49 Inventories have been used to study specifically gendered possession and work. See Lorna Weatherill, 'A Possession of One's Own: Women and Consumer Behaviour in England, 1660–1740,' *Journal of British Studies* 25.2 (1986): 131–156; Maxine Berg, 'Women's Consumption and the Industrial Classes of Eighteenth-Century England,' *Journal of Social History* 30.2 (1996): 415–434; Alison A. Smith, 'Gender, Ownership and Domestic Space: Inventories and Family Archives in Renaissance Verona,' *Renaissance Studies* 12.3 (1998): 375–391; Jane Whittle, 'Housewives and Servants in Rural England, 1440–1650: Evidence of Women's Work from Probate Documents,' *Transactions of the Royal Historical Society* 15 (2005): 51–74.

50 Cox, 'Retailing and Consumption.'

51 Jan de Vries, 'Purchasing Power and the World of Goods,' in *Consumption and the World of Goods*, ed. John Brewer and Roy Porter (London: Routledge, 1993), 102.

52 See John Styles, 'Custom or Consumption? Plebeian Fashion in Eighteenth-Century England,' in *Luxury in the Eighteenth Century: Debates, Desires and Delectable Goods*, ed. Maxine Berg and Elizabeth Eger (London: Palgrave, 2003), 103–115.

53 Schuurman, 'Probate Inventories,' 22–23.

54 The shortness of the inventories taken during catastrophic occurrences – such as the plague in London of 1665 – clearly expresses the difficult task of appraisers called into infected households whose life would have probably been touched again by death. I thank Sara Pennell for such information.

55 This contrasts with the practices in other European countries where inventories continued to itemise clothing until the end of the *ancien régime*. See for instance, Fernando Ramos, 'Patterns of Textile Consumption in Pre-Industrial Spain:

Castille, 1750–1850. Consumption Revolution Without Industrial Revolution?' (paper presented at the Economic History Society Conference, University of London, April 2–4, 2004). I thank Fernando Ramos for providing me with a copy of his paper.

56 John S. Moore, ed., *The Goods and Chattels of our Forefathers: Frampton Cotterell and District Probate Inventories, 1539–1804* (London: Phillimore, 1976), 1. This definition applies to English inventories. Eighteenth-century New England inventories, for instance, included land as well as all other possessions. Daniels, 'Probate Court Inventories,' 393.

57 Richard Burn, *Ecclesiastical Law*, 2nd ed. (London: H. Woodfall and W. Strahan, 1767), 4: 204–221.

58 Shammas, *Pre-Industrial Consumer*, 19; Overton et al., *Production and Consumption*, 14–18.

59 Bedell, 'Archaeology and Probate Inventories,' 224.

60 I thank Nancy Cox for clarifying this point for me. Things of low value could be lumped under a final heading of 'things forgotten and unseen' or 'all the lumber.'

61 Wijsenbeek, 'Delft in the Eighteenth Century,' 164.

62 de Vries, 'Purchasing power,' 99–102.

63 Baulant, 'Necessité de vivre,' 14.

64 For a more exhaustive analysis of the widow's property see Cowen Orlin, 'Fictions,' 67.

65 Spufford, 'Limitations,' 145. See also idem, *The Great Reclothing of Rural England: Petty Chapmen and Their Wares in the Seventeenth Century* (London: Hambledon, 1984), 40–41.

66 Archivio di Stato di Bari, 'Atto 4111: Inventarium, 28 settembre 1727.' I thank Alessandra Tessari for providing me with the text of this inventory.

67 Morris and McCrum, 'Wills, Inventories and the Computer,' iv; Jean-Pierre Wallot, 'Les inventaires après décès à Montreal au tournant du XIXe siècle: preliminaires à une analyse,' *Revue d'Histoire d'Amerique Français* 30.3 (1976): 163–221.

68 By converse, Schuurman notices how nineteenth-century Dutch inventories become increasingly vague when approaching the person. Anton Schuurman, 'Some Reflections on the Use of Probate Inventories as a Source for the Study of Material Culture of the Zaanstreek in the Nineteenth Century,' in *Probate Inventories*, ed. van der Woude and Schuurman, 177.

69 Overton et al., *Production and Consumption*, 121–136.

70 Antonia Malan, 'The Archaeology of Probate Inventories,' *Social Dynamics* 16.1 (1990): 2.

71 Pennell, 'Pots and Pans History,' 209.

72 Baulant, 'Necessité de vivre,' 16.

73 Weiner, 'Local History,' 164.

74 Overton et al., *Production and Consumption*, 114–116.

75 Moore, 'Probate Inventories,' 19.

76 Act of Parliament (England), Public Act, 21 Henry VIII, c. 5: 'What Fees ought to be taken for Probate of Testaments' http://familyrecords.dur.ac.uk/nei/NEI_21Henry8c5.htm (accessed August 2012).

77 The common way of protecting the estate and interests of the various parts was to bind the executor to a maximum level of liability that was commonly established as twice the total value of the estate. This means that the only necessary element was the total evaluation of the estate that could be stated in the probate accounts.

78 There are sporadic exceptions for dioceses and archdeaconries such as Bangor in Gwynd and Ratby in Leicestershire where inventories continued to be taken and preserved until the 1850s.

79 Moore, 'Probate Inventories,' 19–20.

80 van der Woude and Schuurman, eds., *Probate Inventories*, 'Editors' Introduction,' 4.

81 Cox and Cox, 'Valuations in Probate Inventories.'

82 This was not the case when the executor had to take care of the estate for a long period, as in the case of the presence of minors. In this specific case the under-evaluation of goods would have allowed the executor to gain benefits from the management of the estate.

83 We could perhaps imply that in very simple cases of credit–debt relationships, inventories, and in particular their evaluations, were of no use in protecting the estate and were therefore not necessary.

84 Archivio di Stato di Firenze, Magistrato dei Pupilli del Principato, 2706, f. 607–613.

85 Weatherill, *Consumer Behaviour*, ch. 8.

86 van der Woude and Schuurman, 'Editors' Introduction,' 4.

87 Ross W. Jamieson, 'Bolts of Cloth and Sherds of Pottery: Impressions of Caste in the Material Culture of the Seventeenth Century Audiencia of Quito,' *The Americas* 60.3 (2004): 433.

6

COSTUME AND CHARACTER IN THE OTTOMAN EMPIRE

Dress as social agent in Nicolay's *Navigations*

Chandra Mukerji

Nicolas de Nicolay, one of France's leading cartographers during the Renaissance, published a book in 1567 describing his travels with the French Ambassador to the court of Suleiman the Magnificent, the center of the Ottoman Empire.[1] Many thinkers of the time wrote about the Ottomans,[2] but Nicolay's *Navigations et pérégrinations en la Turquie* was distinctive because it contained extensive illustrations: portraits of Ottoman peoples dressed in local costume.

The *Navigations* was enormously popular: translated and reprinted in many editions in England, Germany, The Netherlands and Italy as well as France.[3] It was a beautiful book, lavish with pictures, and described an empire that was rapidly expanding into Europe. The popularity of the *Navigations* helped to stimulate a proliferation of costume books over the next few decades, including Vecellio's famous work (which even reproduced one of Nicolay's illustrations).[4] But the value of Nicolay's work lay not in its success as an exotic costume book, but as work of social and moral analysis of the Ottoman world based on patterns of clothing.

Nicolay's attention to dress was not – as might be supposed – a product of an Orientalist curiosity about Ottoman 'others.'[5] Costume was deemed an important social and moral force in Europe, and Nicolay wanted to understand how it worked among the Ottomans. He had learned early that Europeans like himself could find appearances in the empire deceptive. Janissaries who looked like Europeans were in fact mostly hostile and dangerous to Western visitors, and warriors like Delli horsemen who dressed in animal skins could act like gentlemen in social encounters. His book was a tutorial in Ottoman appearances and material practices, providing pictures and text for identifying social differences within the empire, and characterizing the groups that lived there. Nicolay studied dress as an object with moral agency in Ottoman social life, part of a material order designed to enhance moral bonds.[6]

Nicolay was concerned with the question of how character was shaped by the environment, and looked to the social environment as a determinant of group qualities. Clothes not only provided vivid evidence of cultural diversity, but also were understood in the Renaissance as tools of moral and social entanglement.[7] Certainly, some of the geographer's pictures in the *Navigations* depicted people in exotic costumes, and Nicolay often praised Christianity while derogating Islam. He also spoke of open sexuality among women as a moral flaw in Ottoman culture. But while Nicolay was clearly chauvinistic about Western culture and ethnocentric in his moral judgments, he nonetheless focused in the text of the *Navigations* on material exchanges and formations that carried moral obligations *within* Ottoman society.[8]

There was a good sociological reason why Nicolay thought he could recognize moral significance in patterns of dress in the Ottoman Empire. He and the Ottomans both lived in patrimonial societies in which favors and material exchanges were central to the political and moral order. Ottoman clothing may have looked different than European dress and carried distinct social symbolism, but it had similar moral import. So while Nicolay may have started simply projecting European ideas about clothing onto Ottoman people, he ended with a useful technique for taking the moral and political measure of Ottoman culture, precisely because dress *did* imply moral commitments in Ottoman life. The geographer could judge people in the empire not on their appearance, per se, but on their willingness to 'fit' their clothes – whatever those clothes might be.

Social geography and the question of dress

That Nicolay would draw images of Ottoman people in local costume was not in itself surprising, given that he was one of France's leading chorographers,[9] and European chorographers in the sixteenth century were beginning to depict costumes on their maps. Regional maps and city plans by convention recorded social activity, displaying political or tax boundaries, roads, walls, gardens, landmark buildings, religious sites and habitations. Social types represented on their borders simply added another layer of information, associating social types with geographical homelands.[10]

Nicolay had served as a military cartographer, too, and translated Pedro de Medina's *Arte de navegar* (1545) into French (1569)[11] before he went to the Ottoman Empire, demonstrating his learned and deep interest in geographical discoveries. When he left on his voyage to the eastern Mediterranean, Nicolay probably assumed he would draw social portraits to illustrate a book of voyages filled with the maps and elevations of ports, towns and citadels – although this turned out not to be the case. Political events intervened, and made his voyage into the Ottoman world too problematic to dwell on using the conventions of a travel book.

The politics of Empire

Nicolay did not go to the Ottoman Empire out of a desire to understand Ottoman culture, power and clothing. He was sent as navigator for the French ambassador, Gabriel de Luels sieur d'Aramont or d'Aramon, who had convinced the king to join the Turks in attacking Hapsburg strongholds around the Mediterranean. The French were politically weak and geographically surrounded by the Hapsburg Empire; there was Spain to the south, The Netherlands to the north, and southern Italy and North Africa to the southeast. France needed the Turks as allies, d'Aramont suggested, to counter Hapsburg power.

Nicolay was sent with the ambassador because of his navigational abilities, and also probably because he had been a soldier/spy. He engaged in intelligence-gathering while accompanying d'Aramont, making hundreds of drawings of ports, coasts, and fortresses that had strategic value as well as geographical import. He did not publish his maps and drawings in the end – maybe because of their strategic sensitivity, but most likely because the alliance with the Ottomans turned into a diplomatic disaster the French wanted to forget.[12] The Ottomans not only attacked Hapsburg strongholds in North Africa with French help, but also coastal towns in Italy where they took large numbers of Christian slaves. The attacks were condemned by the Pope, and the French king had to apologize for them. Nicolay had no reason to want to chronicle these events with maps and drawings that would detail his complicity, so his maps and drawings became more an embarrassment than an asset. This left the geographer with only portraits of Ottoman social types, and these provided material for the *Navigations*.[13]

A work of geography

The first book of the *Navigations* was written like a conventional travel account, and reiterated ideas from classical geography about the connection between different creatures and their geographical location – commonplaces that would establish his standing as a credible observer.

> All [animals] according to their types are confined and limited to particular elements… like fish in water, birds in the air, and beasts on the earth. I also argue that they are located not only in their proper elements, but in certain parts or regions of them. As Pliny says, it is admirable that nature distributes diverse animals not only on the earth and sea, but also in certain places.[14]

But influenced by Christian principles, Nicolay did not believe as Pliny the Elder did that geographical determinism extended to human groups.[15] He believed in free will, or at least human superiority to other creatures. He made the case that human groups were clearly distinctive because they were mobile, and could flourish in geographical regions where they migrated. As descendents of Adam, people were meant to exercise sovereignty over nature, and not be determined by it:

> The archetype of human being [was] Adam, name signifying land or earth, not only because his body was formed from earth, but more because the earth was given to him for his possession and habitation as monarch of the animals. ... [For] man as seigneur and prince of the whole sphere, both earth and sea, all lands and seas are open to discovery. And by all climates, all airs and under whatever part of the heavens, man by prerogative from God, his Creator, can live. ... Such that on all *terra firma*, there is no place without human habitation.[16]

The geographer suggested that while the character of people was not determined by geographical environment, it could be shaped by *social* environment. Social life placed moral demands on human beings – opportunities for loyalty, sacrifice, and service – to which they had to respond. Although he did not argue the case, Nicolay treated clothing as a material infrastructure for bringing people into moral relation with one another. He *assumed* that groups were supposed to submit to the moral imperatives of their clothing, and he believed people of virtue and modesty did. Clothing mediated between the moral obligations of people and their free will as descendents of Adam.

In reasoning this way, Nicolay brought traditions of Christian humanist geography to the problem of social analysis, considering the moral power of material environments and gift-giving as a means of cultural formation. Costume for him was continuous with the environment, part of social worlds where human beings lived and pursued moral lives. Looking at clothes and material life in terms of moral exchanges, the geographer could study Ottoman people and their social differences, using the moral obligations of their costumes as a measure of their actions.

Clothes as moral agents in Renaissance Europe

Nicolay's views of clothes were very similar to those described by Jones and Stallybrass as typical in literature from this period. They argue that costume was not a superficial covering or 'expression' of the self in the Renaissance, but quite the opposite, a tool for deep personal transformation. Clothes (defined broadly as all things that were worn) were meant to shape people. They were not simply meant to mark rank, gender, and occupation, but to serve as moral demands on persons to acquire the virtues that their stations in life demanded.[17]

A uniform or livery was used to define social roles and responsibilities to others, but dress generally meant more than that. The costume was something for a body and soul to adjust to (in the same sense that gender is understood today by Judith Butler as a means of disciplining not only the contemporary female body but also the inner life of women[18]). According to Jones and

Stallybrass, material constraint produced not only the Renaissance body, but also its moral essence.[19] And it was this essence that Nicolay hoped to understand in the Ottoman Empire by studying costume and character among its different social types.

This view of clothing supported the patrimonial order in Europe in the Renaissance. Patrimonial authority depended on the exchange of favors and gifts to cement social ties up and down the hierarchy. By regulating patterns of mutual obligation, they fashioned emotional as well as functional ties. Obedience to superiors alone was not enough of a commitment in this system. Loyalty was required – a bond that was personal and emotional. Elites could not simply supervise their subordinates, either. They were responsible for them and their families, and were supposed to give them the basic resources they needed for life as well as rewards for higher degrees of service. These social obligations were also emotionally grounded. And although some people evaded their responsibilities and were in fact uncaring, this cultural constellation of patrimonialism remained authoritative. So the use of clothes in the system of patrimonial exchange to mark rank and responsibilities to others served as infrastructure of social order and personal discipline.

Jones and Stallybrass describe well the constellation of value(s) that surrounded clothing in the patrimonial order, and appropriately disparage the view of costume only as fashion in the Renaissance, but they also illustrate ways that stable understandings of costume came under duress where political pressures were disturbing the patrimonial system.[20] Political conflicts that threatened clienteles began also to undermine the moral imperatives of clothes. Struggles among vying groups with different sartorial markers started to dissociate dress from the moral obligations of rank, and to associate styles of clothing with other constellations of power.[21]

Modesty as a taken-for-granted value was imperiled, and as a result, started to matter more to defenders of the patrimony. Nicolay appeared to be one of them. Since he lived near Lyon, one of the most active trading cities in Europe, Nicolay certainly would have been aware of some of the sartorial politics of the mid-sixteenth century. And he was deeply troubled by those who refused to see their clothing as entailing personal obligations. This anxiety, while palpably ethnocentric, may well have spurred him to pay closer attention to dress and patterns of moral discipline in the Ottoman Empire.

In Nicolay's estimation, virtuous people with true modesty exhibited self-containment, fitting their clothes with appropriate patterns of virtue.[22] In contrast, frauds put on clothing that they did not have the inner qualities to 'deserve.' Clothes made moral demands and required appropriate responses, and where these responsibilities were systematically evaded, Nicolay attributed this to a moral weakness of group character. This became his method for assessing the strengths and failings of the Ottoman Empire.

Because he worked from the assumption that clothes should and could serve as moral agents, Nicolay wrote about dress in a way his European readers could understand. He gave them pictures with characterizing details of costume, and commentaries on the people in the pictures that clarified the cultural significance of their material attributes.

The result was certainly not an undistorted picture of Ottoman life, but neither was it a simple psychological projection of Nicolay's fears and desires. Nicolay recognized a moral order of clothing in Ottoman culture, and its importance to Suleiman and his court. He explained uniforms as items of extra-monetary exchange, marks of merit that stood for virtues and carried obligations. He also pointed to the tradition of charity in Islam that endowed material exchanges with deep spiritual as well as social import, and helped sustain the culture of fellow-feeling so important to Islamic cultures.[23] His deeply European view of the social agency of clothes nonetheless tapped something important in Ottoman life and revealed qualities of the Ottoman Empire to European readers that began to make sense of its overwhelming power by exploring its social diversity.[24]

Peichs or lackeys

The Peichs of the Great Turk (also known as his lackeys) exemplified for Nicolay the highest level of personal grace, gentility, and modesty. They wore costumes appropriate not only to their high service to 'the Great Turk,' but also to their moral discipline (Figure 6.1). As members of this royal guard, they were meant to run ahead of Suleiman the Magnificent to announce his arrival, and to protect him during his travels.[25] Nicolay described them this way:

> There are eighty to one hundred 'Peichz or Laquais Persiens.' The best of these are as able and courtly as one could imagine. They wear multi-color damask robes. They wear a shirt of fine cotton under this. They have a high hat made of pounded silver and with fine or false stones, according to their means. These are decorated with ostrich or other fancy feathers, according to their fantasy. They march with the grand Seigneur into the countryside, crying for God to keep his powers great.[26]

While Peichs dressed in costumes that marked their high service to their master, they also honed their moral character with the physical difficulty of their service and the spiritual intonations of their voices. They had to run as long as necessary – sometimes for days on end without sleep – verbally calling on God to protect the Great Turk. Their service was part of a long, difficult tradition of sacrifice.

> In times past… [they] traveiled and ranne barefooted without any shoes, or any other thing on their feet having that the soles of their feete were shod like unto horses, the skin under the plant of their feet being so hard that easily they could forbeare the nailes and irons… and being thus shod

So Peich ò Peicler di natione Perfica, Lachai del gran Signore.

FIGURE 6.1   Peich or Lackey from a 1576 Italian edition of Nicolas de Nicolay's *Navigations*, 1567

the better to counterfait the horses, did wear in their mouths a bal of silver, perced and made with holes in divers places, like unto the bit of a bridle, & is for to keep their mouth fresh & the longer to sustain their breath. Round about their girdle, which was very large and very wel wrought of leather, they hung divers cymbals or belles, which by moving and shaking in their running made a very plesant and delectable noyce.[27]

The Peichs had symbolized the animal power of men, but also had risen above their animal being through moral service, embracing their spiritual duty with moral dignity. They were proud of their Persian past, but accepted Ottoman rules and habits, submitting themselves to Byzantium's conquerors. They became Ottomans by sporting facial hair like Turks – adopting what the geographer described as a fearsome mask of mustache and beard. This mode of grooming covered and controlled their expressions, but was not just a matter of masking. Beards and mustaches gave Ottomans what Nicolay described as a gruesome, inhuman appearance designed to terrorize enemies. Thus this mode of grooming more vividly made manifest the Peichs' deep moral commitment to the rule of Suleiman the Magnificent and the power of the empire.

Water carriers

The moral power invested in objects and moral obligations entailed through their exchange in Ottoman culture were illustrated most vividly by Nicolay in his description of water carriers. These men provided water in Ottoman cities, and most notably along the routes pilgrims used going to Mecca. They gave water away as a spiritual practice, a form of gift-giving that served Islam and demonstrated their devotion to the faith.[28] Water carriers had become common in many cities of the empire, according to Nicolay, in large part because drinking alcohol was forbidden by Islam, and in dry parts of the empire, water was crucial to life and difficult to find. They were engaged in helping others to observe religious rules either through pilgrimage or by keeping away from alcohol. They went to wells and fountains in the morning to fill their leather pouches, and carried them to parts of the city where water was scarce. These water carriers did not work for money, but lived only from the gifts they received in exchange from those they served. They added to their services by carrying perfumed water to splash on the faces of those who asked for it. Cynically, Nicolay suggested some distributed small gifts of fruit or the like to stimulate reciprocal gift-giving. But they were never assured of an income in providing this service, and most, Nicolay suggested, dedicated themselves to their moral discipline of service.[29]

Although poor, they signified the value of their work with the care they gave to their clothing and the implements of their service. Those who could afford it carried the pouches of water on straps made with embroidery or covered with other decorations. They would carry a beautiful cup, too, leafed with gold and etched with decorations, with which they would offer water to those passing by. To make the water taste better, some carried semi-precious stones that they would place in the cup. And to add to the spiritual content of the exchanges, some carried a decorated mirror that they would hold up to those who approached them, reminding them of the imminence of death and the depth of their moral weaknesses. In spite of the service to Muslims they provided, water carriers would provide water to anyone who wanted it, no matter their religion. They were driven by norms of service and the pursuit of fellow-feeling that were parts of the culture of Islam. In this way, they underscored with their actions the importance of material exchange to the moral economy of the Ottoman Empire, and the power of service in the moral order of Muslim life.[30]

Janissaries

The Ottoman social type that most concerned and fascinated Nicolay was the Janissary. Janissaries began their lives, according to the geographer, as four-year old sons of Christian slaves, taken away from their families and trained in Islam. Their parents gave up their boys in the hope they would enjoy a better life as officials in the army. The geographer explained that Europeans might infer from the stature and dress of Janissaries that they were potential allies or friends, but the opposite was true. They were dangerous and powerful. When they fit their clothes and fulfilled their duties, they were awe-inspiring models of discipline, trained to attack European enemies. If Janissaries started drinking, as they sometimes did in secret, they could become more dangerous and unpredictable, and so they were important for Europeans to avoid.[31]

There were four types of Janissary depicted and described by Nicolay. The first was an ordinary soldier, shown as tall and stately with a sword, musket, and great uniform. The second was a policeman or keeper of the peace for Constantinople. The third was a cavalry officer. And the fourth was an Aga or captain general of the Janissaries, who was the head of the Janissary army. The military tradition of the Janissaries, according to Nicolay, was the Macedonian phalanx that the Turks learned about by occupying their land. While the Janissaries did not imitate the uniform or the selection of arms used by the Macedonians, they did arm themselves amply and used facial hair to control their countenance while shaving the rest of their bodies (like wrestlers).[32]

Nicolay described how Janissaries were shaped for military service not only through physical training, but also through wearing uniforms that carried the moral obligation to serve the ruler in return.

> They are dressed two times a year with a great blue cloth, like all the azamoglans, or Christian converts. And on their head, by special prerogative, they wear a felt hat with a piece of pelt or thin material in front with a gold disk in the middle adorned with a (false?) ruby, turquoises or other precious stones of small price, on the top of which are placed plumes. These are not chosen by each but given to those who have proven themselves most worthy in war.[33]

The Janissaries also received pensions according to their rank and service, gaining higher pensions for valor in battle. Janissary soldiers of lower ranks lived and worked together collectively without rancor, having no other family with which to live and respecting the use of valor as the basis of hierarchy.[34]

The Janissary Aga or simply Aga was the highest ranking officer in the Janissary army (Figure 6.2). He was a man of great dignity and political importance to the empire who was showered with gifts and material assets from clothing to slaves, homes, servants, followers, and pensions. The extent of these material assets not only marked the scope of his social and political importance, but also pointed to the range of his obligations, the history of his prowess, and the moral imperative of his service.[35]

Nicolay described such exchanges of things in detail. The Aga received a thousand *aspres* per day for his expenses, and would receive a guaranteed pension of six thousand ducats. Five times a year, he was outfitted with new clothes made of gold cloth – perhaps crimped or velour or fine satin. He was supplied with a fine Barbary or Turkish horse, decorated with precious stones, and dressed in gold. He had a Janissary in his personal service and another as his secretary, and

FIGURE 6.2 Janissary Aga from a 1576 Italian edition of Nicolas de Nicolay's *Navigations*, 1567

in addition he was supplied with two to three hundred slaves. Other Janissaries would come to his house every day to ask what he needed from them.[36]

As much as he received gifts, the Aga was required to give not only service to Suleiman, but also gifts to those below him, binding them to him with obligations created through material exchange. He was expected, for example, to open his house twice a week to feed any Janissaries who would come. The Aga carried huge responsibilities, and the scale of his service was indicated by the assets given his household, and the frequent gifts he took and gave that reiterated on a regular basis the patrimonial obligations and responsibilities that formed the social order of Janissaries.[37]

To Nicolay, most Janissaries fit their uniform well, and developed the valor that matched their material gifts. They could be brutal in war, but it was their obligation as warriors, and in this way, too, most fit their clothes.

Delli horsemen

The Delli seemed at first glance to Nicolay the opposite of the disciplined Peichs and Janissaries. He wore an animalistic costume and had an appearance that made him look in his portrait like a European fantasy of barbaric exoticism

FIGURE 6.3 Delli horseman from a 1576 Italian edition of Nicolas de Nicolay's *Navigations*, 1567

(Figure 6.3). But the geographer explained the Delli's appearance approvingly in his text.

Nicolay first met the man he drew while traveling with the ambassador, d'Aramont. The ambassador and his entourage needed a place to stay for the night, and asked a local Bascha for help. The man invited them into his house, preparing a feast for his guests, and a Delli who was in his service appeared at the dinner, startling Nicolay with his appearance.[38]

> [His] jacket, long-sleeved shirt and leggings…were from the pelt of a young bear with the hair on the outside and ankle-length boots of yellow leather, pointed in front and high in the back, steel-tipped and with long and large spurs. On the head, [Dellis] wear a long, Polish or Georgian-style headpiece, dangling toward the shoulders made from the skin of a spotted leopard; and on top of this, in front of the forehead, to make himself appear more terrible, was attached a large tail of an eagle and the two wings attached with gold studs to his shield that he tied to his side with a sash.[39]

Nicolay not only drew the Delli as he appeared at dinner, but also took the opportunity to interview the horseman with the help of a translator. Nicolay questioned the man about his cultural and religious background as well as his clothing, summarizing what he learned this way:

> Delli horsemen are adventurers, like light horsemen, who make a profession of searching adventures in the most hazardous places, where, made bellicose with their weapons, they prove their virtue and prowess. And, in this way, they voluntarily follow the armies of the grand Turk without any pay, much like Anchises [in Greek mythology],[40] except that most of them are fed and maintained at the expense of the Baschas [and other notables] who keep the most brave and valiant of them among their followers. ... [They are] of great stature, well-shapen, and with big feet, their color being yellowish, but they are naturally malicious, and easy to deceive. Notwithstanding this, they were greatly esteemed by Alexander the great.[41]

Nicolay learned, too, that the Turks called Dellis madmen ('delli' meaning both 'bold' and 'crazy,' according to Nicolay). But the geographer found the Delli not mad at all, but very courteous. Nicolay reported that horsemen of his type called themselves by a different name, Zataznicis, meaning 'challengers of men.'[42] To become warriors, they had to beat ten other men in hand-to-hand combat, and did it using ruses and tactics of fighting passed down for generations. They could only dress as warriors after they completed this challenge, so the clothes were a badge of honor and evidence that their animal tendencies had been disciplined, not a mark of madness.

> I asked him why he dressed so strangely, and with such large feathers. The response was that it was to make him look more ferocious and unbeatable to his enemies. ... And as to the feathers, this costume was theirs and no others were permitted to wear it to make themselves memorable, because between them the headdress was esteemed as the true mark of a valiant man of war. Which was all that I could learn from this nice Delli.[43]

The Delli also said that he had been raised as a Christian, although he followed the laws of the Turks because he lived under them. Perhaps it was his Christian background that encouraged Nicolay to accept the Delli's animal appearance. In any case, the geographer argued the costume was not a sign of moral degradation, but indicated instead his willingness to serve without recompense, not for personal advantage.

Religious Turks

Nicolay found many social types in the Ottoman Empire that he considered modest and disciplined, but he also encountered groups – mainly in Constantinople and other centers of luxury – that he found immoral. Although many of these types appeared virtuous to European eyes because of their fine clothing and careful habits, he considered them decadent deceivers. Nicolay often found these urban denizens lazy and manipulative (echoing ideas common in the Arab world and derived from Ibn Khaldun).[44] Whatever the source of his ideas, Nicolay inventoried the chicanery of the streets and markets of Constantinople and the decadence of elites in urban centers throughout the empire.

Nicolay's prime example of urban mendacity was a man the geographer labeled a 'religious Turk.' This self-proclaimed hermit was depicted in his portrait as a beautiful, serene, and elegant man, walking peacefully with a deer, but Nicolay described him as a fraud. While acting as a spiritual seeker, he was really just part of a community of con men and beggars:

> There are moreover throughout the whole of Turkey another sect of religious [men] dwelling within the towns and villages in certain shops, the walls of which they cover with skins of diverse wild beasts. … To show themselves more strange and marvelous, they bring up and feed certain wild beasts, such as wolves, deer, eagles and ravens to declare that they have abandoned the world, to live a solitary life amongst the beasts. But in this, their hypocrisy is openly shown, for…they do not dwell in hermitages, but in towns full of people, and likewise they do not live among wild beasts, …rather their animal companions are tame.[45]

Members of this sect maintained shrines filled with animals and animal skins that they sold, but they worshipped Mohamed. They based their spiritual authority on a religious relic they maintained: the sword of a successor to Mohamed named Haly, which they claimed he had used to cut mountains and rocks asunder.[46] But while pretending to be moral guardians of the faith, Nicolay said, they were in fact greedy self-promoters that preyed on the innocence of others.

> These good religious people thus live on the profit of their shops…and leave their shops as a wolf leaves the woods for hunger, and [they] go to town to ask for alms, taking with them a bear or a deer with a bell hung from its neck. … And there under the mask of religion they disguise their damnable and too evident hypocrisy.[47]

The geographer helped readers of the *Navigations* to 'see' this deceit with the details of his illustration. The man in the portrait had the appropriate demeanor and accessory (the deer companion) that denoted his sect, but he was wearing clothes more like that of an urban merchant than a self-effacing hermit. Neither poor nor disheveled, he hid behind his mustache.[48] The religious Turk was deceptive and abusive because he did not live up to the obligations of his office. His appearance did not serve his inner discipline and service, but was used for the manipulation of others for personal gain.

Turkish women of Constantinople

Turkish women in Constantinople were to Nicolay deceivers of another and more interesting sort. They did not so much dissemble in their dress as evade the agential power of costume altogether in their patterns of dressing and undressing. They made no *public* moral commitments with their clothes and actions because they had to veil themselves and live behind closed doors. This shielding of the body from the public suggested a certain modesty, but Nicolay argued that Turkish women in Constantinople, on the contrary, simply learned to live outside the moral constraints of public life.[49]

This was illustrated most clearly, according to the geographer, when Turkish women went to public baths. They spent many days every week in the baths naked, attending to their pleasures – unconstrained by clothes or public decorum. Women who were lesbians openly expressed their sexual feelings for one another in this hidden world. And even women of high standing would bring their servants to clean them, and apply potions to their skin, pursuing pleasure rather than modesty.[50]

Nicolay was clearly not allowed in women's baths, and may well have been projecting his own fantasies and desires on the women.[51] He had repeated other false reports in the book, so this could easily have been another. Still, Nicolay had an informant who had explained to him the lives of women – a man he called a friend who had been raised in the Serail. Given this testimony, it is hard to assess whether the basis of his writings about the baths was shaped more by information or desire.

In the end, the description of the baths in the *Navigations* was concerned less about gender and sexuality than the role of clothing and nakedness in social and moral order. The freedom of the baths reflected what happened without the moral constraint of clothing. If forms of dress were public commitments that people made about their moral intent, those who were hidden behind veils and walls never made such commitments, and could more readily discard the moral demands of clothing – corrupted by their public obscurity. This made them symbols of erotic alterity.

Calenders

The Calenders were another group in the Ottoman Empire whose explicit attention to sexuality – even in the pursuit of celibacy – provided Europeans with material for imagining an erotic alterity. The Calenders were a religious sect of men who pierced their penises with large iron or silver rings to denote and enforce virginity. Nicolay drew a graphic image of the practice in his portrait of the Calender that emphasized the public (although discreet) display of the rings. Still, the geographer respected the spiritual commitment of the Calenders, and treated the large penis ring as a part of their public costume, denoting celibacy.[52]

> The Calenders dress in a short, sleeveless robe, a sort of hair shirt made of wool and horsehair. They do not let their hair grow [like other sects] but shave their heads, covering them with a kind of felt hat like that of Greek priests with stiff fringe the length of an apple around the brim. They adorn their ears with heavy iron earrings and place similar iron pieces around their neck and arms, and through the skin of their virile member, they pierce a large and heavy ring of iron or silver, looped in such a way to make them unable to exercise any lust if they still had the desire or ability.[53]

The Calenders did not evade the power of costume, but quite the contrary, used iron or silver rings as agents to enforce chastity. They dressed the part of religious seekers, enforcing their spiritual obligations with their mode of dress and piercing. What disquieted Nicolay was the contrast between their sartorial denial of sexuality and their practices of singing. By religious tradition, Calenders sang bawdy songs, perhaps as a test of their rejection of lust. The songs were sacred in the sense that they were written by the man the geographer described as the first martyr of their faith. This leader of the Calenders had been expelled from the empire because his religious beliefs contradicted Islam.[54]

Nicolay treated Calenders as bewildering, but serious moral actors. They seemed bizarre in their choice of costume, but also models of sexual restraint. Their conduct also illustrated the moral authority given to objects in the Ottoman Empire – a practice that made sense to Nicolay no matter how odd he may have found its manifestation.

Conclusions

The beauty of Nicolay's lavish illustrations and the attention to dress in his commentaries on Ottoman life has helped obscure the social analysis in the *Navigations*, leaving this work to languish misunderstood as an entertaining picture book and site of European fantasy about exotic 'others.' Perhaps as Renaissance understandings of the moral agency of costume were replaced by the logic of the fashion system, his method of studying Ottoman life was rendered invisible. Still, Nicolay's attention to dress made sense in his own time, when the moral force of costume was accepted as crucial to forging social bonds and creating solidarity. Studying patterns of dress could reveal flows of power, too, since costume could serve as a measure of cultural integration and trace lines of authority and obedience. Renaissance Europeans who believed in the moral agency of dress could readily accept the sociopolitical use of costume in the Ottoman Empire, and recognize it as a point of convergence between the patrimonial cultures of Europe and the eastern Mediterranean. The differences in costumes between France and Constantinople might have been profound, but their uses implied a similar moral logic.

Attention to costume was a good way to enter the culture of the Muslim world, where fellow-feeling was highly valued, and gift exchange was widely practiced to produce a sense of solidarity.[55] The Ottoman government relied particularly heavily on material exchanges, too, since officials like the Janissaries were given power precisely because they were slaves who had no independent source of living apart from the benefits of their offices. This made them not only socially dependent on patrimonial networks, but also beneficiaries of gifts that made them emotionally dependant on Suleiman and the other members of the Janissary army who protected and fed them. The court and army became their family, as Iban Khaldun noted, supplying them with their emotional and material needs, and giving them rewards for their loyalty and moral courage.

If their success as Janissaries resulted from prowess in battle, their military bravery was nonetheless more than a test of their courage. It was an expression of their moral allegiance to the Sultan, and their willingness to die for their 'family.' Their uniforms were not just outer signs of rank, then, but also personal reminders of their social obligations to the community of Janissaries and to their patron and ruler.

Personal commitment, beyond simply behavioral norms, was meant to propel Janissaries to ask the Aga how they could serve him. And in principle, it was a reflection of his fellow-feeling for those in his service that the Aga provided meals in his own home. These personal exchanges conveyed the depth of the obligations and personal feelings in patrimonial relations.[56] Like the gifts described by Mauss, such exchanges brought the whole being of the giver to the recipient, making debts a matter of personal responsibility and social obligations a matter of honor.[57]

The patrimonial materialism of Ottoman society was comprehensible in Europe, where patrimonial relations had similar forms and effects. European offices were also supposed to entail personal commitments between members linked by patrimonial networks. Offices were meant to carry the moral weight of a gift, in principle binding the official not only to a job, but to the well-being of the prince who allocated the office. Thus the moral order of the Ottoman world translated into the moral order of Europe despite differences of religion.

The *Navigation* gained popularity in this period, I would argue, not by titillating readers with lavish and exotic pictures, but rather by making Ottoman social types seem comprehensible. Fear of the Ottomans not only drove Europeans like Nicolay to be concerned about the empire's power, but also spurred them to try to assess its strengths and weakness. Because the book was translated into many vernaculars, printers clearly assumed people wanted to read it as well as look at the pictures. So the text as well as the illustrations mattered.

The text and pictures together allowed Renaissance readers to 'see' Ottoman types as carriers of cultural logics that had political implications. Even though some portraits looked exotic, Nicolay's textual descriptions of Ottoman types portrayed them as more than just the alien barbarians of the Crusader tradition. Of course, the *Navigations* also conveyed many prejudiced and irrational views derived precisely from this narrative heritage. Still, by studying clothes,

Nicolay also disrupted the simple repetition of some of its language. He drew attention to the moral reasoning of Ottoman people around material gifts and social obligations, making it harder to typify them as immoral barbarians. He showed that costume was as socially weighty in the Ottoman world as it was in Renaissance Europe, and by conveying this, Nicolay brought Ottoman culture closer to European readers. The result was a surprisingly compelling window for Europeans onto the Ottoman Empire, using period understandings of the agency of clothing as a tool for the analysis of a culture's vulnerabilities and threat.

Notes

1 Nicolas de Nicolay, *Les quatre premiers livres des navigations et pérégrinations orientales* (Lyon: G. Rouille, 1567).
2 See, for example, Andrea Cambini, *Two Commentaries the One of the Originall of the Turcks the Other of the Warre of the Turcke against George Scanderbeg. London 1562* (Amsterdam: Da Capo, [1562] 1970).
3 For example: Nicolay, *Navigations*, op. cit.; idem., *Les quatre premiers livres des navigations et pérégrinations orientales, de N. de Nicolay, … avec les figures au naturel tant d'hommes que de femmes selon la diversité des nations, & de leur port, maintien & habitz [avec une élégie de P. de Ronsard à N. de Nicolay]* (Lyon: G. Roville, 1568); idem., *Vier Bucher von de Raisz und Schiffart in die Turckey* (Antorff [Antwerp]: Wilhelm Silvium, 1576); idem., *Le navigationi et viaggi nella Turchia, di Nicolo de Nicolai del Delfinato, Signor d'Arfevilla…: con diuerse singolarità in quelle parti dall'autore viste & osseruate* (Anversa [Antwerp]: Guiglielmo Siluio, 1576); idem., *De schipvaert ende reysen gedaen int landt van Turckyen* (Antwerp: Willem Silvius, 1577).
4 Cesare Vecellio, *Vecellio's Renaissance Costume Book: All 500 Woodcut Illustrations from the Famous Sixteenth-Century Compendium of World Costume* (New York: Dover, 1977), particularly 459; Donald F. Lach, *Asia in the Making of Europe* (Chicago, IL: University of Chicago Press, 1965). There was a revival of costume books in the nineteenth century that has perhaps led to an elision of Orientalist literature from that period, and the early costume books. See for example M. Breton, *China: Its Costume, Arts, Manufactures, &C*, 4th ed. (London: Howlett and Brimmer, 1824).
5 Orientalism is premised on power relations that did not exist in sixteenth-century France. See Edward W. Said, *Orientalism* (New York: Pantheon Books, 1978), 31–110. The Ottoman Empire was strong and France was weak, so the sense of natural superiority of Europe that developed in the nineteenth century and was the foundation of Orientalism was not part of Renaissance thinking. The frame used by humanists to explain the alterity of the Ottomans, their brutal ferocity and military efficacy, came from the Crusades rather than an emergent Orientalism. Margaret Meserve, *Empires of Islam in Renaissance Historical Thought* (Cambridge, MA: Harvard University Press, 2008), 65–116.
6 Compare to Marcel Mauss, *The Gift: Forms and Functions of Exchange in Archaic Societies* (Glencoe, IL: Free Press, 1954).
7 Compare to Ann Rosalind Jones and Peter Stallybrass, *Renaissance Clothing and the Materials of Memory* (Cambridge: Cambridge University Press, 2000). For an explanation of patrimonial societies and patterns of moral obligation based on exchanges of favors, see Sharon Kettering, *Patrons, Brokers, and Clients in Seventeenth-Century France* (Oxford: Oxford University Press, 1986). The period Kettering studies is later, but the patrimonialism she describes was widespread in the sixteenth century.
8 Mauss, *The Gift*.

9 He had drawn a famous set of maps of Scotland, and also was working on detailed regional surveys of the region around Lyon that were later printed in Ortelius' atlas. Robert W. Karrow, Museum Plantin-Moretus, and Bibliothèque royale de Belgique, *Abraham Ortelius (1527–1598): cartographe et humaniste* (Turnhout: Brepols, 1998).

10 Trevor Morgan Murphy, *Pliny the Elder's Natural History: The Empire in the Encyclopedia* (Oxford: Oxford University Press, 2004), particularly 43, 80–88.

11 Pedro de Medina and Nicolas de Nicolay, *L'art de naviguer de M. Pierre de Medine, Espagnol: contenant toutes les reigles, secrets, et enseignemens necessaires à la bonne nauigation* (Lyon: Gvillavme Roville, 1569).

12 Nicolas de Nicolay, Marie-Christine Gomez-Géraud, and Stéphane Yérasimos, *Dans l'empire de Soliman le Magnifique* (Paris: CNRS, 1989), introduction.

13 Ibid.

14 Ibid., 44.

15 Murphy, *Pliny the Elder's Natural History*, 80–88. It is interesting that Ibn Khaldun shared this idea, associating climate with differences among groups and defining a hierarchy of human types. See Ibn Khaldun, *The Muqaddimah: An Introduction to History* (Princeton, NJ: Princeton University Press, 2005), 49–64.

16 Nicolay, *Navigations*, 43.

17 Jones and Stallybrass, *Renaissance Clothing and the Materials of Memory*, particularly 15–58.

18 Judith P. Butler, *Bodies That Matter: On the Discursive Limits Of 'Sex'* (New York: Routledge, 1993).

19 Jones and Stallybrass, *Renaissance Clothing and the Materials of Memory*, particularly 15–33.

20 Ibid., 15, 71–77.

21 Compare to Chandra Mukerji, *From Graven Images: Patterns of Modern Materialism* (New York: Columbia University Press, 1983), particularly ch. 5. This chapter describes some interconnections between fashion and politics in this period both in the competition among elites and the movement of fashion centers.

22 Nicolay, *Navigations*. Compare to Khaldun, *Muqaddimah*, 214–216.

23 Khaldun, *Muqaddimah*, 123–128, 145–148.

24 Ibn Khaldun associated luxurious dress with the decline of empires precisely because it accompanied a loss of group feeling. What Nicolay saw in Ottoman society was that group feeling could be supported by these exchanges when they produced deep personal feelings of moral obligation. It is hard to know if he misread Ottoman society because of his own ethnocentrism, or that his understanding of patrimonialism allowed him to recognize when moral authority could be sustained through things, and particularly forms of gift-giving. Ibid., 123–128, 145–148. Compare to Kettering, *Patrons, Brokers, and Clients*.

25 Albert Lybyer, *The Government of the Ottoman Empire in the Time of Suleiman the Magnificent* (New York: Russell and Russell, 1966), 129–130.

26 Nicolas Nicolay, 'Les annales des sultans ou grand seigneurs des Turcs, traduites de la version latine de Jean Leonclavius,' in *Annales des Turcs qui va jusques à l'an de Mahomet DCCCXVI...*, ed. Jean Leonclavius (Paris: 1568), 13–14.

27 Nicolas de Nicolay, Thomas Washington, and John Stell, *The Nauigations, Peregrinations and Voyages, Made into Turkie by Nicolas Nicholay Daulphinois, Lord of Arfeuile, Chamberlaine and Geographer Ordinarie to the King of Fraunce, Conteining Sundry Singularities Which the Author Hath There Seene and Obserued: Deuided into Foure Bookes, with Threescore Figures, Naturally Set Forth as Well of Men as Women, According to the Diuersitie of Nations, Their Port, Intreatie, Apparrell, Lawes, Religion and Manner of Liuing, Aswel in Time of Warre as Peace* (London: Thomas Dawson, 1585), 84.

28 Compare to the values of shared moral culture in Islam as described in Ross E. Dunn, *The Adventures of Ibn Battuta: A Muslim Traveler of the 14th Century* (Berkeley, CA: University of California Press, 1989), 7–12.

29 Nicolay et al., *Dans l'empire de Soliman le Magnifique*, 204–206.

30 Ibid.
31 Lybyer, *The Government of the Ottoman Empire*, 79–82, 91–97; Nicolay et al., *Dans l'empire de Soliman le Magnifique*, 153–165.
32 Nicolay et al., *Dans l'empire de Soliman le Magnifique*, 153–165.
33 Ibid., 156–157.
34 Ibid., 157.
35 Ibid., 165.
36 Ibid.
37 Ibid.
38 Ibid., 227.
39 Ibid.
40 Anchises was the father of Aeneas. What Nicolay means with this metaphor is not entirely clear, but perhaps Anchises' devotion that led him to Troy with his son. See Virgil, *The Aeneid, an Epic Poem of Rome*, trans. Levi Robert Lind (Bloomington, IN: Indiana University Greek and Latin classics, 1963), 41.
41 Nicolay et al., *Dans l'empire de Soliman le Magnifique*, 226.
42 Ibid.
43 Ibid., 227, 229.
44 Khaldun, *Muqaddimah*, 109–122.
45 Nicolay et al., *Dans l'empire de Soliman le Magnifique*, 197–199.
46 Ibid., 197.
47 Ibid., 199.
48 Ibid., 198.
49 Ibid., 137–143. Compare to the Persian women who do not have to hide themselves completely, but still are beautiful and modest in covering their heads, 217.
50 Ibid., 135–140.
51 Ruth Yeazell, *Harems of the Mind: Passages of Western Art and Literature* (New Haven, CT: Yale University Press, 2000). Compare to Mary Montagu Wortley's description of going to the baths more than a century later. She spoke mainly of the beauty and gentility of the women. See Shirley Foster and Sara Mill, eds., *An Anthology of Women's Travel Writings* (Manchester: Manchester University Press, 2002), 28–29.
52 Nicolay et al., *Dans l'empire de Soliman le Magnifique*, 190–192.
53 Ibid.
54 Ibid., 192.
55 Khaldun, *Muqaddimah*, 123–154.
56 Kettering, *Patrons, Brokers, and Clients*; Mauss, *The Gift*; Khaldun, *Muqaddimah*.
57 Mauss, *The Gift*.

PART III

Making things

7

MAKING THINGS

Techniques and books in early modern Europe

Pamela H. Smith

Words and things

Since at least the seventeenth century, when Descartes proclaimed that being able to make a machine was tantamount to true knowledge of the machine, understanding the process by which objects are made has come to be another approach both to things and to knowledge. Indeed, historians and museum curators are often confronted with objects, and they are increasingly of the opinion that no longer is it enough to understand how an object participated in commercial networks or the role it played in patronage relationships; an appreciation of the meaning, function, and operation of a historical object can also be gained by a knowledge of how it is made. As many cases of early modern industrial espionage have demonstrated, however, knowledge of making processes can often be difficult to obtain because it often cannot be conveyed effectively in written description, but rather must be learned on site by careful and conscious observation. Even then the observer cannot necessarily replicate the knowledge gained, with the result that the history of industrial espionage is more a history of trying to steal away experienced craftspeople and their embodied knowledge than of written accounts detailing pilfered techniques. All these problems are felt with particular intensity by the historian when dealing with objects made in the past. Sometimes the maker's knowledge is written down, but technical writings seldom convey sufficient information to actually engage in making an object. How, then, might the historian come to gain knowledge of making processes?[1]

Early modern views of words and things

The contrast between words and things and writing and doing seemed particularly acute to some early modern thinkers. As Theophrastus von Hohenheim, called Paracelsus (1493–1541), put it with characteristic vehemence:

> For who could be taught the knowledge of experience from paper?, since paper has the property to produce lazy and sleepy people, who are haughty and learn to persuade themselves and to fly without wings. ... Therefore the most fundamental thing is to hasten to experience.[2]

Paracelsus made 'experience' central to his reform of medicine and learning in the early sixteenth century. As this passage illustrates, he viewed paper, writing, and texts as standing in opposition to hands-on experience. By experience, Paracelsus meant the bodily labor of the craftsperson in engaging with the materials of nature and in drawing out of them their 'active ingredients,' which give pharmaceutical preparations their potency and efficacy, for example, or which cause ores to yield up their metals. Paracelsus viewed experience as essentially of the body:

> The art of medicine cannot be inherited, nor can it be copied from books; it must be digested many times and many times spat out; one must always rechew it and knead it thoroughly, and one must be wide awake while learning it.[3]

Paracelsus believed that true knowledge could be apprehended only with the whole body: the mode of those who worked with their bodies to redeem and refine matter, namely artisans and handworkers. By imitating the processes of nature, they brought forth tangible works that proved the certainty of their knowledge.

In Paracelsus's view, potters, weavers, carpenters, miners, and masons all created from matter products that made visible the revelation to human beings of God's mercy: 'In the sweat of thy face shalt thou eat bread, till thou return unto the ground' (Genesis 3:19). When Adam and Eve ate from the tree of knowledge, thereby launching the great trajectory of human history, their progeny had to labor through handwork to gain the means of living that they would have had in Paradise without toil and sickness. It was the labor of agriculture and the crafts and, above all, the work of the healer that Paracelsus believed made possible the escape from physical debility and untimely death that began the great saga of redemption for human beings. Paracelsus believed that the Creation was God's first Revelation, even before the Word, and that God continued to reveal himself through the generative, creative, and healing powers of nature. Following the light of Nature (analogous to Luther's light of Grace) rather than the written and textually codified logic of the pagan Aristotle, craftspeople could harness these powers, thereby revealing God in the world – 'making visible,' as Paracelsus phrased it, 'the invisible.'[4]

Paracelsus repeated many times that the means to true healing and knowledge, and to reform of human life on earth lay through the work of the hands and the crafts. This meant learning with all the senses, by means of conversing with, listening to, and gaining knowledge orally from others, through travel and wandering, but, above all, through 'experience' in the great Book of Nature:

> I think it praiseworthy and no shame to have thus far journeyed cheaply. For this I would prove through nature: He who would explore her, must tread her books with his feet. Scripture is explored through its letters; but nature from land to land. One land, one page. Such is the Codex Naturae; thus must her leaves be turned.[5]

Paracelsus himself worked among craftspeople, particularly among miners, learning their lore and collecting their proverbs and their medicinal recipes, as well as writing, lecturing, and preaching in the vernacular. 'Künden [Können],' he maintained, 'ist mer dan wissen' ('Doing is more than knowing'), by which he meant that the how-to knowledge (*Können,* or *Kundschaft*) of the craftsperson, gained through constant practice, observation, and experience, amounted to a higher order of philosophical knowledge. The craftsperson, he claimed, would know when he has attained Können because he will be able to produce well-formed and useful things over and over again.[6]

In his philosophy of laborers, Paracelsus was trying to capture on paper the essence of handwork and skill. His endeavor was not easy – we still do not entirely know what to make of handwork, for much of it involves tacit knowledge, which is hard to codify in writing because it requires acute observation and attention to the circumstances of the ephemeral moment. As Paracelsus wrote, the craftsperson must be wide awake, must learn to pay attention with all the senses, to 'overhear' matter, just as the metal caster seizes the moment at which bronze is ready to pour, and the mason reads the signs of the vein at which the slab in the quarry can be broken away. Such is the hard-earned bodily knowledge of all artists and artisans.

More recently, anthropologists, historians and sociologists of science, and others have scrutinized bodily knowledge. Echoing phenomenology and pragmatism, anthropologist Tim Ingold writes that skill is a constant and active perceptual engagement with the world, and that learning to attend is the essence of skill. Indeed, as he claims, skill grows out of human interaction with the natural environment, and out of this attentive and collective experience comes all the remarkable products of human culture – stone tools, cuneiform record-keeping, iron smelting, glass-working, indigenous and commercial medicines, and nuclear weapons.[7] Recently, educational psychologists have wondered how we might teach skill, how we can transmit the practice of 'attending,' this mode of active, perceptual engagement with the world. In *The Craftsman*, sociologist

Richard Sennett has written a sensitive plea for valuing craft, seeing in it a model for shaping our dealings with others in a democratic society. He argues that the skills of the craftsperson – the focus, the intuitive leaps, and the improvisation – in a word, *experience* – can be taught through encouraging the innately human capabilities of concentrating on and working through situations of resistance and ambiguity, just as craftspeople do in manipulating physical materials.[8]

Recipes and how-to books

Given the antithesis posed by Paracelsus between experience and books, and the paradox that Paracelsus incarnated when he composed his polemic about experience *in writing*, what are we to make of the boom in the writing down of techniques, indeed, the writing of whole books, by European craft practitioners beginning around 1400? What were these writings meant to convey about embodied experience? Technical writings are seldom able to provide sufficient information to actually engage in making an object. Why, then, were such techniques written down? What indeed, is the relationship between making and writing?

The first problem is what to call these books about lived experience. They have much in common with collections of recipes gathered together in a book – lists of ingredients and a narrative of techniques for handling those ingredients in order to produce something tangible. The term 'recipe' indicates the action-oriented nature of these books, for it simply transposes onto the whole process the first word of the instructions: 'Take… (these ingredients).' Historians have called them how-to manuals, didactic texts, books of secrets, and technical writing. But books themselves can also function as tools, such as the *Theorice novella* from the 1400s, used to calculate planetary position, which was really a computing device in book form (Figure 7.1). Such a 'book' makes clear that we should not hold fast to a binary dichotomy between books and things. Indeed, in the past generation, book historians have rediscovered the book as material thing.[9]

But the question still remains: why around 1400 did artisans take up pen and paper with such gusto? Well-known names spring to mind – Lorenzo Ghiberti (1378–1455), Leonardo da Vinci (1452–1519), and Albrecht Dürer (1471–1528) – but many more less-prominent craftspeople also began to write accounts of their trades: gunpowder makers, gunners, fortification experts, navigators, and, even more surprising, a galley oarsman in the service of the Venetian navy. Why did these individuals, who previously had been happy to live out their lives without recording their experiences and knowledge, simply creating and producing in relative obscurity, suddenly begin to write? This sudden increase in the writing down of experience took place in the context of increasingly powerful territorial rulers and their need of artisans for war technologies and the theater of state; it also took place in an increasingly urbanized culture, with concentrations of artisans who experimented with different media and engaged

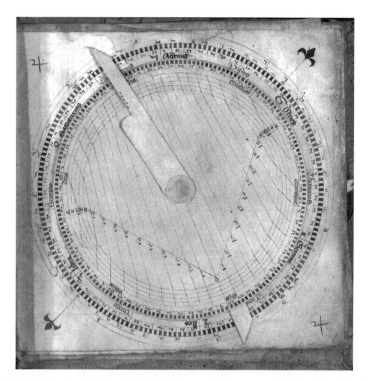

FIGURE 7.1 *Theorice novella, c.*1400. This paper instrument, contained in a book, was used to calculate planetary position. Leipzig University Library, Ms. 1479, fol. 3r

in an intense exchange of skills and ideas with their fellow craftspeople and other social groups.

The wave of technical writing that followed on this beginning rippled out still further with the invention of printing in the 1460s, as recipe collections and technical treatises were some of the earliest works off the presses and among the best sellers, growing larger and larger with each reprinting as material was added and the pseudonymous names of the authors were changed. Early works in the vernacular appear in astounding numbers: *Distillir-Bücher* in the 1490s, the *Kunstbüchlein* in the 1500s, assaying and metalworking treatises (known as *Probir-Büchlein*) in the 1530s, and the pseudonymous Alessio Piemontese's *Book of Secrets*, which burst onto the scene in 1555, first in Italian, then quickly in many other European languages, going through ninety editions by the seventeenth century.[10] This boom in technical writing continued through the seventeenth and eighteenth centuries, which saw the publication of many more books on the making of all kinds of things, from beehive construction to saltpeter making, and from embroidery to cannon casting.[11]

Why did practitioners move so suddenly from lived experience to the written word, from the orality and tacit knowledge of artisans to the written word of books? Not surprisingly, there is no single reason for writing a how-to book.

Collections of recipes and techniques are quite varied: they run the gamut from straightforward instructions to advertisements for a practitioner's abilities, to wonder-working promises, among many other forms. The appearance of these technical guides has been associated with the growth of urban culture and the cities' increased population of a 'middling sort,' who in their social mobility were more isolated from familial sources of technical knowledge and more desirous of new information that might be useful in their emulation of their social betters.[12] If we examine these books, however, we find a variety of reasons why they appear to have been written, and they have many different – often singular – origins: for example, the preparation of copy for printing, the keeping of workshop texts and working notes, artisans' exchanges (sometimes simply aspirational) with patrons, a desire to inform and attract investors (especially in mining), and the attempt of administrators to wrest control of production processes.[13] One vernacular writer, the Venetian galley oarsman Michael of Rhodes (the subject of a recent three-volume study),[14] seems to have been responding to a particularly intense competition for positions of command in the Venetian fleet, believing that a book gave him the edge in this competition.[15] Still other technical writers were trying to establish an identity – for example as architects – or ally their trade with the liberal, rather than mechanical, arts. Simon Werrett has recently shown how gunners sought to raise their status by writing how-to books about fireworks, not for their fellow gunners but for a noble audience.[16] Engineers sought both to create an identity for themselves as practitioners of a liberal art who possessed a type of knowledge that could be the basis of decision making and, more generally, to reform pedagogy.[17] The writings of some practitioners are particularly visible to us because they are more numerous, such as those of metalworkers, or because they are more ambitiously self-conscious, such as goldsmiths like Benvenuto Cellini (1500–1571) or painters such as Giorgio Vasari (1511–1574). Technical writings sometimes sought to teach how to do something, but often they just proclaimed that 'doing' is a legitimate activity, of high status, which can be expressed in written form. Some functioned simultaneously as 'how-to-do' and 'how-to-be' books,[18] and many of them seem to be compilations put together by entrepreneurial printers. Many European how-to books of the late seventeenth and the eighteenth centuries seem designed to be employed mostly by connoisseurs taking the measure of the burgeoning world of material goods.[19] In other words, one must examine such technical writings on a case-by-case basis to understand their genesis.

These varied origins and functions help to explain why the information in them often does not seem very useful as a 'how-to guide,' compiled as it often is from other texts and arrayed with little conceivable order, sometimes including bare-bones recipes, magic tricks, and undigested, out-of-date, and inaccurate information that could not possibly be useful to actual production. So many of the ways in which we think of knowledge as powerful – innovative, oriented to formulating general rules, precise, accurate, and useful – seem frequently to be absent from technical writing. But even those technical writings which seem to be more akin to instruction books suffer from the problem of conveying information in writing: although a few of these books deliberately conceal processes, they more often simply suffer from the fact that technical writing can be descriptive only; it points to bodily activity, but cannot accomplish that activity, teach it completely, or often even describe it fully. Embodied 'gestural,' 'artisanal,' or 'craft' knowledge, as it has been termed, is often unwritten and tacit. In the early modern period, artisans learned their craft not by following written instructions or even sometimes by language at all, but rather by working alongside experienced practitioners and observing and imitating. Their experiential knowledge was acquired through observation and imitation rather than through texts; written descriptions could never sufficiently take into account the always-changing conditions of the workshop, or the sometimes-unpredictable qualities of the materials. A book is not an optimal means for conveying technique.

Making objects and writing books

What, then, is the relationship between making objects and writing books, between craft production, experience, and writing? In order to explore this subject in more detail, I shall focus on one such book, an anonymous manuscript from the late sixteenth century that includes all kinds of making processes. It can help us to begin to answer this question, but it also points to some of the challenges of using such texts as historical sources. The text, Ms. Fr. 640, is held by the Bibliothèque nationale de France (BnF) and was written in French at the very end of the sixteenth century.[20] It contains recipes for pigments, varnishes, magic tricks, the grafting and growing of plants, and medicines, and many other subjects; in some respects it resembles the *Secrets* of Alessio Piemontese. Much of the manuscript is devoted to metalworking and, especially, to sand-casting medals and plaster casting from life. Ms. Fr. 640 diverges from this and other collections of recipes and books of secrets, however, in its detailed descriptions, its constant reference to the writer's own experiences, its seeming lack of formulaic recipes (although much research remains to be done on the possible sources for the manuscript's recipes), its extensive observations of animal behavior, its illustrations, and its apparent function as a set of working notes. In the molding and casting sections, the author records his experiments and even reminds himself to 'try this!' A sense of the scale of experimentation of this manuscript can be grasped by a comparison to Piemontese's *Secrets*: where Piemontese contains seven recipes for sand casting, Ms. Fr. 640 has about forty recipes. It seems likely that Ms. Fr. 640 is the first or second draft of a collection of recipes and techniques the writer-compiler-practitioner planned to publish.

What problems do we encounter in this odd combination, namely, a *book* on *techniques*? The first thing that stands out is that it cannot be read in a linear way because the writer loops around and around various techniques and includes recipes for similar processes widely spaced throughout the text; thus it is not organized to be used as a work of reference – it is in fact wholly impractical for such a purpose. Second, of great importance for the historian, it is difficult to assess whether the manuscript deals with authentic practices because the materials used and the techniques contained in it are no longer entirely comprehensible to either a modern reader or a modern maker. This raises an important point: in thinking about things made in the past or in dealing with texts that tell us how to make things, we have to find a way to assess whether they are in any way related to practice, let alone whether they are actually the results or records of practice.

The most obvious means of assessment is to compare such accounts to other records of practice. Cennino Cennini, in his book of painting practices, briefly mentions casting from life, but it is only more than a century later that Hugh Platt (1552–1608), a brewer's son and irrepressible collector of recipes, records in somewhat more detail processes for casting plants and animals in *The Jewell-House of Art and Nature Conteining Divers Rare and Profitable Inventions, Together With Sundry New Experimentes in the Art of Husbandry, Distillation, and Molding* (1594), roughly contemporaneous with the manuscript writer. Book IV of *The Jewell-House*, 'The Art of molding, or casting of any live bird, or little beast, hearbe, or flower, or of any patterne of mettall, wax, &c. into gold, silver, plaister, &c,' contains detailed instructions for casting a branch of rosemary as a lost-pattern cast and two-piece molds 'if you woulde save your patternes' that are very similar to, but generally not as detailed as, those of Ms. Fr. 640.[21] Johann Kunckel (1630–1703) and an anonymous author (possibly Kunckel himself) who reprinted Kunckel's recipes also incorporate instructions for casting from life.[22] Kunckel's recipes continued to be printed into the eighteenth century in increasingly attenuated forms. Both these authors provide similar instructions for life casting, if with nowhere near the same detail as Ms. Fr. 640.

Another means by which we might assess the practical authenticity of a text about making things is to engage in 'remaking,' that is, to reconstruct or replicate the procedures described in the text. I contend that such reconstruction can be used as a source by historians to gain insight not only into the material world of techniques and materials, but even into the way in which an artisan explained to him- or herself the behavior of natural materials – the maker's 'philosophy' or 'vernacular science' (Paracelsus's 'philosophy of laborers'). As we shall see, it can also help us to reconstruct some unsuspected aims of technical writing.

Reconstruction

In proposing remaking or reconstruction as a technique, I am not breaking new ground: object-based inquiry and the techniques of reconstruction are familiar to museum scholars, curators, conservators, and archaeologists, especially those dealing with prehistoric artifacts, but historians are still unfamiliar with the idea of reconstruction of technique, reenactment, and bodily knowledge.[23]

Some have ridiculed reconstruction as 'subjective' and inauthentic, and there is no doubt that we can never have true empathy with figures in the past – we cannot feel what they felt, nor can we ever get inside someone else's mind. But there is a difference about handwork that I think justifies reconstruction, and that is the production of the material object – we might say the intervening and representing – which gives us a firmer handhold on the past than would be the case for non-externalized mental processes. But, more fundamentally, I think we have to accept that experience is a different form of knowledge from discursive or propositional knowledge that can be written down and codified, thus it demands different methods of investigation and analysis. Indeed, anthropologist Timothy Ingold has questioned the subject–object divide posited in the difference between maker and made thing, and has suggested that objects can be viewed more as interventions in the flows of the cosmos. Seen in this light, reconstruction allows us to act as both participant in and observer of that flow, resulting in a type of knowledge that simply cannot be obtained in other ways.[24]

The focus on 'things' has also opened up new modes of inquiry in history. For example, historian Leora Auslander has eloquently made the point that

> people do different things with words and with things and that... difference has to do with embodiment and its corollaries of complex sensory perception and mortality. ... A narrative of origins can be sewn into a quilt or woven into a basket. Joys and sorrows can be expressed in how clothing is made, worn, preserved, or destroyed. Sometimes words and things come together; things are written about in diaries, inventories, letters, or songs, but the 'truth' of the object is not more to be found in the words than in the thing itself...[25]

Perhaps at the simplest level, historians have praised reenactment for its pedagogical efficacy: it is an extremely efficient way to gain knowledge about techniques; reading an account of a technique is quite inefficient in comparison. From my own experience, for example, when taking a course on historical techniques of oil and tempera painting, and following the practice by early modern artists of tracing over the lines of an experienced artist, I suddenly realized how powerful such imitation could be: what we would call 'rote' copying actually turned out to be a shortcut to seeing the function, and being able to replicate the swelling and diminishing of lines, as well as to coming to understand the most effective techniques of shading and perspective. This kind of tracing and copying is anathema today in art instruction, bound up as current instruction generally is with the idea of individual creativity.

Reconstruction also has another benefit for historians of the early modern period (and perhaps of all periods), for we scholars, steeped in text-based sources and trained from an early age in reading, writing, and propositional knowledge, actually may fail to understand the greater part of human experience in the preindustrial world, when most learning and knowledge was experiential and acquired by observation.

A few examples of what historians have learned by means of the reconstruction of experiential knowledge will demonstrate its potential. Historians of science have a long tradition of reconstructing crucial scientific experiments. One recent example is Otto Sibum's reconstruction of James Joule's 1840s experiments to determine the mechanical equivalent of heat, which were crucial to the development of thermodynamics. By recreating Joule's machines and processes, Sibum came to understand the high level of skill and expertise Joule had learned as the son of a Manchester brewer, and why other scientists were still having trouble replicating Joule's experiments as late as 1875. Sibum concludes that Joule left out the bodily work and the workers in his account of these experiments partly in order to represent himself as a disembodied observer of nature, reading off precision measurements from an instrument, thus acting in accord with the emerging standards of 'science' and 'scientific' practice, as opposed to the bodily, sensory, and site-specific knowledge of the brewery.[26]

Historian of science Peter Heering recently reconstructed an eighteenth-century solar microscope and found that historians could understand the significance of solar microscopes in the Enlightenment only by seeing them in action. Such instruments fell out of favor in the nineteenth century when they were reported as producing fuzzy images unfit for scientific activity. Heering's reconstructions show that these instruments actually produced strikingly clear magnifications. He concludes that solar microscopes were thus excluded from scientific research because they were associated with nonprofessional social gatherings of amateurs, which did not mesh with new ideas about the professionalized and exclusivist nature of science.[27]

In the Newton Project, historians of chemistry William Newman and Lawrence Principe have reconstructed alchemical practices such as the 'the tree of Diana,' a treelike silver structure described as being grown in a laboratory vessel. Similarly, they have produced a 'silica garden' and a 'star regulus,' both phrases in alchemical texts that historians have previously taken to be allegorical or metaphorical, but which these historians have proven to have actual material correlates that can be reproduced in the laboratory.[28]

From a different discipline, literary scholar Peter Stallybrass and book historian Roger Chartier worked with book curators and conservators to puzzle out what Shakespeare meant when he referred to 'erasable tables' in Hamlet and in various sonnets. Most scholars have understood Shakespeare's use of this phrase to refer to printed books or metaphorically to ideas written in the mind, but, through reconstructing inks and gessoes, the group found that Shakespeare meant actual erasable tablets – paper painted with a gesso ground and bound into very small codices or notebooks. This very material referent adds another layer of complexity to Hamlet's utterances about memory and forgetting, and completely transforms Shakespeare's meanings in some of his sonnets.[29]

One of the most important results of reconstruction has been the insight into the original appearance of works of art. In many works, colors have faded or otherwise degraded so much that we no longer know how an artwork originally appeared. This is especially true for sculpture, which has also been the victim of modernist aesthetics that have taken the essence of sculpture to be form, rather than color. Roberta Panzanelli notes that the 'history of art has tended to dismiss polychrome sculpture as quirky and not quite true to the essence of sculpture.'[30] But color, which has been used on statuary since the most ancient times, always formed an essential part of the sensory and affective experience of the work of art. Without having a realistic idea of the appearance of an object, we cannot hope to understand the artistic aim of the maker or the sensory and affective experience of a work of art in the past. Indeed, reconstructions of polychrome wood statuary and oil paintings have revealed that one important component of the artistic aim in the Middle Ages was to achieve a variety of surface textures that reflected light in different ways – for example, the sparkling glazes playing off each other and contrasting with the areas of burnished and matte leaf gilding.[31] None of this can be fully appreciated solely from texts or, due to their various states of disrepair or nineteenth-century cleaning campaigns, from the surviving objects.[32] In addition, reconstructions of polychromy on statuary, as was undertaken in a recent exhibition at the Getty Museum, can tell historians much about period conceptions of the body and of gender, and about notions of vitality and life.[33] Without a realistic idea of the appearance of an object, we can understand neither the intentions of the maker nor the viewer's experience.

Finally, reconstruction can show us how collaborative practice operated. The garden historian Mark Laird has been instrumental in the reconstruction of Painshill Park, an eighteenth-century garden southwest of London in Surrey, which included some of the first plantings of North American species. His experience has brought into focus two important points: first, the aesthetic aims of the garden to which we have no access now (without verbal or visual descriptions of these early gardens); and second, the recognition that the gardens were really a result of a collaborative process among designer, gardeners, plants, *and* the environment. If one worked only from written plans and designs for the garden, this fact would never emerge.[34] This insight is more significant than it sounds because, like other sources from the crafts, it gives evidence that distributed cognition and collaborative working methods are the norm, in contrast to conventional models of cultural production. As historians, we are used to thinking in terms of sources authored by mostly identifiable individuals, thus it is more difficult for us to 'think outside the author' and to understand an alternative model for the creation of cultural products.

Casting from life

There are many further examples of reconstruction that might be offered, but I will conclude with my own attempt at reconstructing experiential knowledge,

FIGURE 7.2 Wenzel Jamnitzer, writing box, 1560–1570. Cast silver, 2.36 × 8.93 × 4.02 in. (6.0 × 22.7 × 10.2 cm)

or, as Paracelsus admonished, I shall 'hasten to experience.' Over the past five years, I have been working with Tonny Beentjes, a practicing silversmith and conservator based in Amsterdam, to reconstruct the techniques of casting from life by trying the recipes and instructions in Ms. Fr. 640, the extraordinarily detailed sixteenth-century manuscript written by a French practitioner of metalworking. We began this project with the aim of understanding the life-casting techniques of the contemporaneous master goldsmith of Nuremberg, Wenzel Jamnitzer (1510–1585), famed for his remarkable life casting (Figure 7.2), as well as for his instrument making and his 1567 model book and philosophical presentation of rendering solid forms, *Perspectiva Corporum Regularium, das ist ein fleyssige Fuerweysung/wie die Fünff-Regulirten Cörper....*

Casting from life seems to have been a widespread and fairly well-known artisanal technique from 1400. The earliest reference to life casting in the Renaissance appears in the fourteenth-century painter Cennino Cennini's *Libro dell'Arte*, which includes entries on casting faces, whole bodies, 'a bird, a beast, and any sort of animal, fish, and other such things.'[35] Lorenzo Ghiberti cast plants from life on the doors of the Florence Baptistery, and Donatello (1386/87–1466) used wax-impregnated fabrics to model the draperies on some of his sculpture.[36] Life casts were produced in great numbers in northern Italy in the sixteenth century; many are believed to have been produced in sixteenth-century Padua, previously attributed to Andrea Briosco, called Riccio (1470–1532), or to Severo da Ravenna (*fl. c.*1496–1543).[37] Life casting was carried out on a perhaps even grander scale in northern Europe, particularly in Nuremberg. Nature casts of textiles were made in the Vischer workshop in Nuremberg, where life casting was a well-known technique by the first half of the sixteenth century, reaching a high point in the work of Wenzel Jamnitzer.[38]

Casting from life is accomplished by pouring a plaster mold around fresh plants or recently killed animals, then burning out or removing the plant or animal (the pattern) by heating in a kiln, and, finally, casting hot liquid metal into the void left by the animal or plant. The French manuscript contains instructions for making nature casts of flowers, plants, lizards, snakes, crabs and crayfish, shells, turtles, frogs and toads, bats, several species of birds, eagle talons, rats, moths and butterflies, beetles, flies, spiders, and even spider webs.[39] While instructions for casting from life were collected, printed, and reprinted into the eighteenth century, Ms. Fr. 640 contains the most detailed description yet known.

From the number of printed sources and life-cast objects in sixteenth-century collections, it is clear that this was a widely known and much-desired technique for at least three centuries. Life casts filled the collections of the sixteenth and early seventeenth centuries. The inventories of the Habsburg and Bavarian Wittelsbach *Kunstkammern* were full of hundreds of life casts in silver, tin, lead, plaster, and other media, and the eagerness with which they were sought can be detected in the anxious letters between Wenzel Jamnitzer and Archduke Ferdinand of Austria (1529–1595) between 1556 and 1562 about a commission to build a fountain with life-cast animals around the base.[40] Another example of this interest can be found in a letter from an official of the court of Grand Duke Francesco I de' Medici (1541–1587) to Duke Wilhelm V of Bavaria (1548–1626) that details a 'Pergkhwerckhstuckh,' or *Handstein*, that the grand duke was sending to Wilhelm. It included life-cast lead patterns for plants that were to be attached to the work, and a postscript to the letter states that the live frogs, snakes, plants, and other animals that the duke desired could not be obtained due to the cold weather.[41] According to this evidence, life casts were sometimes regarded as more valuable than objects modeled by the hand.

Life casts in these collections possessed multiple levels of meaning: they could prove rare and odd natural phenomena, such as the crippled and seven-fingered hands of peasants and the misshapen lemons cast in plaster in the Bavarian Wittelsbach *Kunstkammer*.[42] They could stand in for the real objects that soon withered and died, and they could display the talent of the artist in producing fine molds and in understanding the casting properties of metals. Metalworkers demonstrated their ability to imitate nature – and thereby lay claim to an unmediated knowledge of nature and an ability to harness the processes of nature.[43] More important, life casting connected nature and art, demonstrating the human ability to imitate the transformative powers of nature. In the seventeenth century Gottfried Wilhelm Leibniz came to view life casting as demonstrating the formation of fossils in the earth,[44] just one example of the manner in which making objects eventually came to be descriptive of natural processes and synonymous with knowing in a scientific sense.

There is much in Ms. Fr. 640 of great interest and much yet to be discovered, including the possible identity of its author and the location of its composition, but for the purposes of this article I will focus only on what we have learned in attempting to replicate life-casting recipes contained in the manuscript.

Try this!

Since sixteenth-century castings of most of the flora and fauna used in the manuscript are still extant in European and American museums, the first stage of our investigation involved examining life-cast objects in those institutions. This examination showed that the techniques described in the manuscript matched precisely with the traces of making on the objects. These techniques included the use of two-piece molds. Until the recent work of Edgar Lein and confirmation in this manuscript, it was not clear to scholars that casting from life was done in two-piece molds. Life casts were believed to have been accomplished by encasing the animal or plant entirely in plaster, which was then heated in a furnace to burn out the animal, with metal then being poured into this one-piece mold. Our reconstructions showed that two-piece casting allowed the opening of the molds before casting the metal in order to take out the animal's or plant's ashes. Even some insects, such as stag and rhinoceros beetles, which no one would have suspected of being molded in a two-piece mold, show molding lines and are formed very well in two-piece molds (Figures 7.3 and 7.4).

The similarly obscure technique of positioning the animal or plant to be cast – which is described in the manuscript and confirmed by traces on museum objects – has been clarified by our reconstruction. The technique of casting the metal into the thinnest portion of the animal (the tail of the lizard, for example,

FIGURE 7.3 Rhinoceros beetle (detail of Figure 7.2).

FIGURE 7.4 Reconstruction of Rhinoceros beetle, cast in silver by Tonny Beentjes and Pamela H. Smith

or the stem of a buttercup) is counterintuitive to the modern metal caster, who holds that a massy weight of metal must charge the channels of the mold all at once in order to fill all the narrowest parts of the mold. The manuscript instead instructs the metalworker to position the gate for the metal in the most delicate area of the plant or animal, and then heat the metal and the mold much hotter than a modern metalworker would normally do. Our reconstruction of this procedure, in which we tested the casting of silver into insect molds, demonstrated the efficacy of this combination of techniques in reproducing the most delicate features of an animal or plant (Figures 7.5–7.7).[45]

These examples show that our reconstruction has revealed important components of the techniques employed in early modern European life casting. But the reconstruction has also allowed a greater understanding of the function and significance of the objects. For example, the technique of casting the metal from the smallest part of the mold afforded extremely fine detail and the almost complete lack of an obvious point of entry for the metal (Figures 7.8 and 7.9). This was, of course, essential for *Kunstkammer* objects, prized in early modern Europe for their liveliness in imitating nature. A wide gate for the metal constructed into the underside of the animal, as a modern metalsmith would do, would leave an unsightly area of afterwork where the sprue had been clipped, filed, and polished. Such obvious traces of facture would have been jarring to the collector and his guests who handled these objects, turning them over and around in their hands to admire them. This underscores just how much the

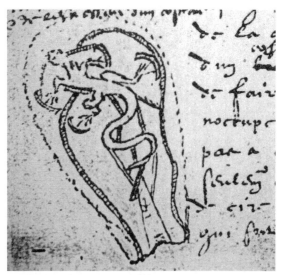

FIGURE 7.5   Sketch illustrating the posing and casting infrastructure for a lizard in BnF Ms. Fr. 640, fol. 122v. Note the arrangement of gate, sprues, and vents

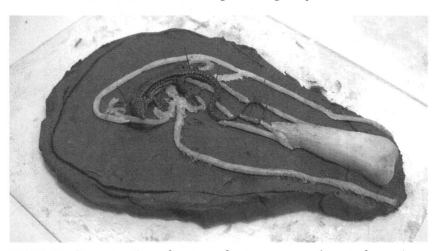

FIGURE 7.6   Reconstruction of system of gate, sprues, and vents for casting a lizard from life, using arrangement sketched in BnF Ms. Fr. 640 (see Figure 7.5). Reconstruction by Tonny Beentjes and Pamela H. Smith

relationship of the early modern person with the things of a collection differed from that of the modern viewer, who would never notice afterwork on the underside of a life cast because the object would be displayed sitting statically on a shelf behind glass. Reconstruction of technique thus afforded us insight into the interaction and experience with objects in early modern Europe.

Reconstruction also gave us a new kind of attention to objects and a new way to see things we would not otherwise have noticed on an object. This is the

FIGURE 7.7 Detail on underside of neck of cast silver lizard, using the mold reconstructed from the system illustrated in Figure 7.6. Casting by Tonny Beentjes and Pamela H. Smith

FIGURE 7.8 Wenzel Jamnitzer (attributed), life-cast lizard (detail of hind foot), *c*.1540–1550. Silver, 2.76 × 1.61 in. (7.0 × 4.1 cm)

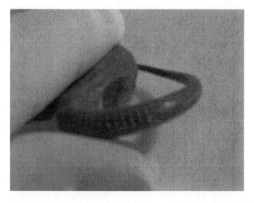

FIGURE 7.9 Wenzel Jamnitzer (attributed), life-cast lizard (detail of tail), *c*.1540–50. Silver, 2.76 × 1.61 in. (7.0 × 4.1 cm). Oval area on tail shows location of the main sprue (clipped off and filed), through which the metal was poured into the mold

result of the different kinds of reading in which one must engage depending on whether one is simply reading for information or reading for the purpose of carrying out a technique. This became especially clear to us in trying to follow the description for posing an animal on a clay base. The animal must be held in position as the plaster is poured into the mold, otherwise it will float up as the liquid plaster fills the mold. The author of Ms. Fr. 640 describes the process of passing pins through the animal's feet to the clay beneath and either threading wire through these holes or leaving the pins in place (Figure 7.10). The pins are then removed when the plaster for the second half of the two-piece mold is poured. These pins leave a very small void in the plaster, which then fills with metal and which must be clipped off after casting. During our reconstruction in January 2008, we had just finished this delicate procedure on the basis of the manuscript descriptions when we were scheduled to fly to Vienna to examine one of the most impressive sixteenth-century examples of life casting as it came out of one exhibition and was going the next day into another: a writing box attributed to Wenzel Jamnitzer (Figure 7.2). As we looked attentively at the box, we realized with mounting excitement that we could see the traces of this procedure on the frogs and lizards on the box (Figure 7.11). They revealed tiny protrusions of metal on their feet – the traces of pins that had once held the animal to the clay base. We would never have noticed or recognized these small protrusions for what they were unless we had been laboring over this very technique the day before.

Working with the manuscript also made clear the polyvalent quality of materials. For example, many early modern recipes, including those in Ms. Fr. 640, specify iron oxide as an ingredient in mold material in order to 'make it strong.'[46] By this, our metalworker might have meant giving the mold 'strength' by its blood-red color, a 'belief' that modern editors of some recipe books have ridiculed, thereby dismissing the technique as well. But when we tested the addition of iron oxide in January 2011, we found that using it not only gave the mold a rich blood-red color, but also did indeed make it tremendously hard.[47] We thus cannot dismiss the technique, but we should not ridicule the belief either, for as I have argued in other work, red was one of the nodes of a relational web of interlinked homologies among red, blood, gold, and lizards that underlay metalworking practices and techniques, a kind of 'vernacular science' of matter and transformation.[48] This web was not a theory that could be formulated as a set of propositions, but rather it was a lived and practiced theory. The writer of Ms. Fr. 640 seems to have been working within this framework, viewing red and iron oxide as 'strong as blood,' because elsewhere he specifies adding a lizard to molten metal in order to color it gold. In a similar way, he used the *pater noster* prayer as a time-measuring tool – a perfectly normal practice in his day – and at the same time as a prophylactic when mixing ingredients for a burn salve.[49] It should not surprise us that such practices could be simultaneously efficacious and part of a more systematic understanding of nature. Artisanal practices could be mundane and oriented to the production of goods, and at the same time give

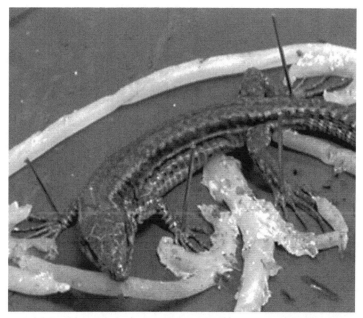

FIGURE 7.10 Reconstruction of process by which pins were employed to hold dead lizard to clay base, using arrangement described in BnF Ms. Fr. 640. Reconstruction by Tonny Beentjes and Pamela H. Smith

FIGURE 7.11 Detail of Figure 7.2, showing lizard with traces of pins in its feet.

access to the greater powers of nature and the cosmos. Again and again in this manuscript, we see just what embodied knowledge meant in the metalsmith's workshop: using urine and excrement, warning that the practitioner's bad breath could prevent the adhesion of metal gilding, using the humidity of damp cellars as a tool in many processes, employing the constant slow heat produced by thermophilic bacteria in rotting horse manure for metalworking procedures (and incubating silkworms), and admonishing readers to undertake certain kinds of work only when the weather was still and dry. All these examples point to the bodily entanglement of the practitioner with his lifeworld, but this entanglement with matter and environment obviously did not prevent him from either working with great efficacy or at the same time understanding his materials as what we might call epistemic things – things that embodied concepts and knowledge systems.[50]

Working through resistances

Reconstruction also taught us about the nature of acquiring experiential knowledge – that it is a process of working through resistances of matter. Disasters such as our mold walls collapsing, which caused liquid plaster to spill in all directions, taught us to make the walls thicker next time. Our molds failed during burnout of the organic material within them, and we poured lead and tin too hot and silver too cold – among myriad other learning opportunities. We came to appreciate the process of experimentation, doing things over and over using different materials, that is vividly evinced by the author's unceasing trials in the manuscript. Indeed, the author apparently could not stop experimenting and recording, as the entire margins of many pages are taken up with notes on the techniques, including more trials of different materials with accounts of successes and failures. Eventually we learned that working through resistances was part of the process of knowledge getting. We marveled at the length of time it took to acquire experiential knowledge. Any experimentation with molds that must dry for days or weeks is necessarily the work of months and years. We came to truly understand Bernard Palissy's descriptions in his 1580 *Admirable Discourses on the nature of waters and fountains, …on metals, salts and salines, on rocks, earths, fire and enamels* of his almost unceasing bodily tribulations in experimenting with ceramics. We especially appreciated his dialogue in which Theory attempts to pry out of Practice the secret of his glaze making. Practice tells Theory that he (Theory) is not 'wide awake, quick, sympathetic and hard working' enough to understand his secrets. Theory retorts that if Practice teaches him *in writing* the fruit of his experience, he will not need these prerequisites. To this Practice replies: 'Even if I used a thousand reams of paper to write down all the accidents that have happened to me in learning this art, you must be assured that, however good a brain you may have, you will still make a thousand mistakes, which cannot be learned from writings, and even if you had them in writing, you would not believe them until practice has given you a thousand afflictions.'[51]

In our impatience to let the metal cool so we could open the mold and see the fate of our casts, we understood the metalworker Vannoccio Biringuccio's comments in Book 6 of his 1540 *Pirotechnia* on the art of casting:

> I say that the greatest labors of both mind and body are required for its operations in the beginning, middle, and end. It is indeed true that these labors are endured with pleasure because they are associated with a certain expectation of novelty, produced by the greatness of art and awaited with desire. ... As a result, as if ensnared, he [the metal caster] is often unable to leave the place of work.[52]

He goes on that the mind is held in suspense and fear regarding the outcome; the spirit is disturbed and continually anxious. 'For this reason they are called fanatics and are despised as fools. But, with all this, it is a profitable and skillful art and in large part delightful.' To avoid becoming frustrated and left 'discouraged, worn out, and often ruined,' the caster must do 'everything with exactness.'[53] Without our own experience of these contradictory emotions in casting, we might have read Biringuccio as writing rhetorically, when he actually sought to convey the bodily and mental absorption of the caster.

In these vicissitudes of experimentation, we came to realize that metal casting is not primarily about the *metal*, but about experimentation on *mold* materials. The composition of the 'sand' (as the author of Ms. Fr. 640 calls the mold mixture), both for sand casting and for plaster, is key to the entire process of producing a life cast, for the mold material must be fine enough to take the imprint of the animal's delicate surface texture; light enough not to flatten the animal; durable enough to withstand the burnout, the heating of the mold before casting, and the pouring of the red-hot metal; and friable enough to crumble easily when breaking the mold to reveal the finished cast object. It goes without saying that the investment materials for sculpture of any sort are of supreme importance in creating the work. The essential qualities of the investment medium are easy removal of the mold from the metal-cast object, a sharp impression, and an absence of flaws that would necessitate afterwork. Such qualities could be discovered only by repeated experiment with natural materials, and the literature of the sixteenth century, including Ms. Fr. 640, testifies to this constant experimentation by metalworkers with clays, sands, and other materials.[54] Nevertheless, only our own trials and tribulations made us able to understand what these metalworkers meant by their repeated claim that nature and art, and labor and ingenuity, came together in the knowledge of mold materials, for these could either be sought from nature or made by art, and thus constant observation, experiment, and experience were crucial.[55]

We were helped in our struggles by the fact that, unusually, Ms. Fr. 640 contains sketches to describe the design of gates, channels, and vents for the molds. It would have been nearly impossible to follow a written description of such a design, for it would have necessitated long-winded accounts of many small details. The principle that a picture is worth a thousand words is of course a commonplace, but this was brought home to us with great immediacy as we compared our experience of struggling to follow the text and the sketches. Indeed, our experience of the sketches may also provide a clue to the purpose of Ms. Fr. 640. We can compare it to the pictures of the fitting out and construction of ships included by the Venetian Michael of Rhodes in his 1430s book, for which the audience was likely patrician youths whose merchant families sent them to sea at their own expense to learn about commerce. Michael taught them to recognize different ships and the loads they carried by means of his colorful drawings and his oral instruction.[56] It appears, indeed, that almost all how-to manuscripts on shipbuilding written at this time by practitioners were not intended to furnish instructions for other craftsmen, but instead were employed by practical men explaining the tools and expertise of their trade to the social group above them, administrators or patrons, who needed both the illustrations and the book to understand the spoken presentation and to take it seriously as 'knowledge.'[57] Pictures are especially effective in organizing technical knowledge into an abbreviated form because the processes described are extremely tedious and confusing to follow in writing, especially for the uninitiated. Images supplemented with verbal elaboration are undoubtedly even better than pictures alone at transmitting complicated procedures. Michael's pictures thus tell us about one of the aims of a how-to book – for use with patrons and officials as a basis for oral presentation to non-experts. It may be that Ms. Fr. 640 involved such a relationship – perhaps instruction of a high-status student or dialogue with a humanist collector of sculptures and techniques.

Our reconstruction also gave me insight into my tacit expectations of what a text should be and what it should do, and just how widely my expectations diverged from those of the author of Ms. Fr. 640. One cannot read the manuscript in a linear manner. The 'reading' of Ms. Fr. 640 necessitates doing and reenacting in order to understand it as a record of practice and to follow it. We came to see how 'reading' the manuscript was not a simple matter of drawing out passages that dealt with mold materials or metal alloys. Rather, every recipe for molding plaster was embedded in instructions for all kinds of other techniques, sometimes specific to the animal or object being molded, and one had to return again and again to pore over whole sections of the manuscript. Reading and using the manuscript came to seem not a familiar linear textual experience so much as a kind of holistic experimentation in casting materials, even a meditation on trial and error itself. Indeed, reading the manuscript could not be separated from trying the methods recorded in it. From the evidence of the manuscript – in which a fair copy has been set down, but then more trials have been made and the maker has filled the margins with additions, further observations, and notes to himself to 'try this' – it would appear that the composition of the manuscript itself could not be divorced from the lived experience of actually performing the actions (Figure 7.12). This is, I believe, an

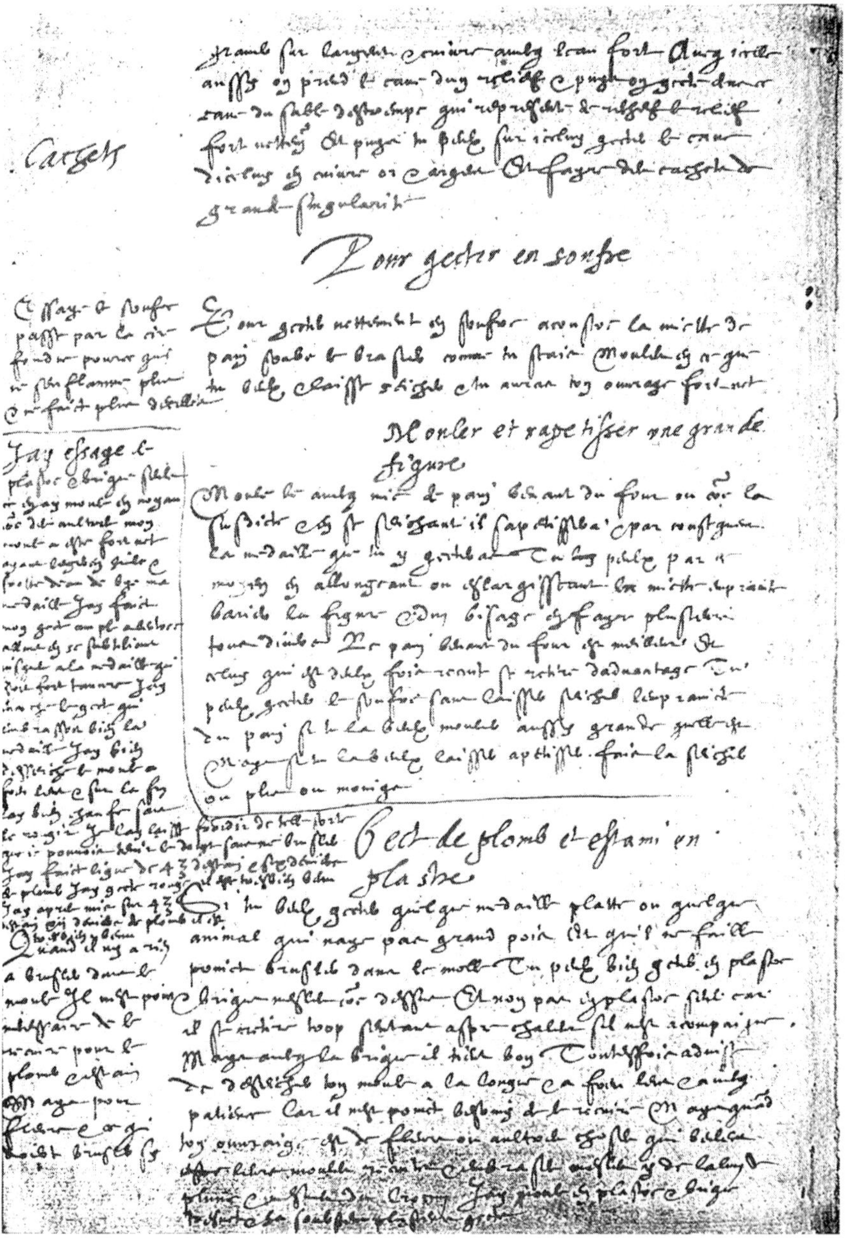

Cargets

Pour gecter en soufre

Mouler et rapetisser une grande figure

Cest de plomb et estaim en plastre

FIGURE 7.12 Text page from BnF Ms. Fr. 640, fol. 138v, showing marginal additions and rethinkings

important piece of information for understanding the compilation character and nonlinearity of much technical writing of the early modern era.

Skill

In *The Craftsman*, Richard Sennett has suggested that recipes are not about producing something or teaching a sequence of actions, but rather they are an altogether different sort of education: they are about educating the attention, transmitting attitudes to work and to matter, conveying the lessons of experience – thus the 'try this' or 'tried' in recipes – and fostering improvisation and intuitive action. Recipe collections, then, can form a meditation on the material; they develop a habit of regarding matter and its manipulation. By their very repetition, often listing different variations of ingredients or different methods of doing something, they can encourage and model the processes of trial-and-error testing. Such trial-and-error procedures teach that matter is something to work through, something in which to explore resistances, in which to seek out the characteristics of a material in different situations. The metalworking sections of Ms. Fr. 640 are overwhelmingly about exploring resistances of different materials, and the looping back again and again over similar procedures reproduces the process of repeated trials.

Repeated experimentation with materials results in a knowledge of the behavior of matter that allows for an ability to intuit, improvise, and innovate in materials (for example, in searching out suitable sands and clays for mold material) and techniques. Indeed, improvisation based on long experiment is the stock-in-trade of the artisan/maker: in the smoke and heat of the workshop, with dangerous and molten materials all around him, the metal caster must make the split-second determination at which exact moment the metal is ready to pour. As a modern Japanese silversmith trained in traditional methods put it:

> Remember, our work is not done by measuring and talking. The hammering, the forging, all the processes are performed by intuition. It's the split-second intuitive decision to remove the iron from the fire, when and how to bring up the flame, to immerse the blade in the water now – it is these acts of intuition that produce.[58]

As Biringuccio put it in his 1540 book on metalworking: the practitioner must

> understand well what you wish to do in this operation, and…adapt the force to overcome the resistance that is offered according to the qualities of the materials. … But…the light of judgment cannot come without practice, which is the preceptress of the arts.[59]

And, as the assay master of a 1604 manuscript, the 'Goldsmith's Storehouse,' phrased it:

a p[erfec]t Assay Master, [is one] whose perfection [is] grounded upon Artificiall Exercise, for these thinges doe rather consiste in doing them in referringe, for they are not easelye reduced to matter of Argument...the trade asketh a good Judgment, gotten rather by years & experience, then by speculation & dispute.[60]

The goal of a practitioner's repeated trial and error was 'skill,' that is, a capacity of 'judgment' that made him able to improvise in response to the contingencies of the workshop and the materials. Biringuccio noted that a caster must use the judgment born of experience in designing vents and gates. He provided his reader with as much as he could, ending with 'I neither know nor am able to say any more about this.'[61] To learn more, the reader would have to 'flee to experience.' In *Personal Knowledge*, Michael Polanyi draws a distinction between subsidiary awareness and focal awareness, giving the example of the pianist who shifts her attention from a subsidiary awareness of the movement of her hands in relation to the notes and music to a focus on the individual movements of her fingers. Such a shift in attention often leads to a disastrous performance and stage fright. This kind of focal awareness on the particulars of a skill, whether the hammering of a carpenter, the skilled handling of a tennis racket, or the abilities of the average car driver, moves in the course of repeated practice from a focus on particular components of the skill to an increasing unconscious of the particular actions, and finally results in attainment of the ability to hold in subsidiary awareness the particulars while performing a series of integrated movements and procedures to bring about a whole skilled performance or result. Polanyi says,

> [i]n the exercise of skill and the practice of connoisseurship, the art of knowing is seen to involve an intentional change of being: the pouring of ourselves into the subsidiary awareness of particulars, which in the performance of skills are instrumental to a skilful achievement, and which in the exercise of connoisseurship function as the elements of the observed comprehensive whole.[62]

How can writing convey this embodied amalgam of action, sensory apperception, and cognition? I would argue that some technical writings, including Ms. Fr. 640, and many recipe collections, attempt just that: that is, to convey essential components of skill and its acquisition. First and foremost is the constant trial and error, the trying again and again, the necessity to practice, practice, practice – the essential need to proceed by experimentation. Second, these texts necessitated imitation and reenactment of the techniques in order to be comprehensible, thus pointing to the indispensability of learning a skill by 'doing' and imitation. Third, they sought to make clear the necessity of educating the attention: the need to be alert to the signs of matter and for close observation, and the state of being attuned with body and senses to the material, while simultaneously transcending these particulars to attain the higher-order awareness that allows the skilled practitioner to respond to the contingencies of the workshop.

Ms. Fr. 640 seems to be an attempt to capture in writing – perhaps to teach by modeling – the tacit, bodily knowledge of the manipulation of matter by the human hand – in other words, to capture that elusive human ability, skill. Skill is the essence of craft knowledge, and I would argue that it represents a higher-order form of knowledge, perhaps analogous to generalization in propositional knowledge. In addition to everything else they are, then, 'how-to' texts can also form an attempt to 'think about thinking,' to think about embodied cognition and how it is to be acquired, as well as about the foundations of knowledge.

A craftsperson like Lorenzo Ghiberti, at the beginning of the great boom in artisanal writing, experimented in a great diversity of media, including writing. For Ghiberti, paper and writing upon it could be just another medium, one that required a different kind of attention and discipline, but simply one more arena of experimentation. For Leonardo and some other fifteenth- and sixteenth-century artisans, writing became another site of experimentation and a tool of craft. In the final analysis, Ms. Fr. 640 forms such a site of experimentation in a double sense: as a compilation of 'technical writing,' Ms. Fr. 640 is an account of the practice of a workshop, where materials were tested, experiments undertaken, skills learned, and things made. But as that oxymoronic kind of thing, a *book* of *practice*, it forms an experiment in rendering a written account of handwork and skill, which at the same time makes real the impossibility of using words alone to do the job.

Notes

1   I have published a slightly different version of this chapter as 'In the Workshop of History: Making, Writing, and Meaning,' *West 86th: A Journal of Decorative Arts, Design History, and Material Culture* 19 (2012): 4–31.
2   Theophrastus von Hohenheim (called Paracelsus), *On the Miners' Sickness and Other Miners' Diseases*, in *Four Treatises of Theophrastus von Hohenheim called Paracelsus*, ed. Henry E. Sigerist, trans. George Rosen (Baltimore, MD: Johns Hopkins University Press, 1941), 91.
3   Paracelsus, *Die große Wundarznei* (1536), in *Sämtliche Werke: Medizinische, naturwissenschaftliche und philosophische Schriften*, ed. Karl Sudhoff, vol. 10 (Munich: Oldenbourg, 1928), 225.
4   Paracelsus, *Astronomia Magna: oder die gantze Philosophia sagax der großen und kleinen Welt/des von Gott hocherleuchten/ erfahrnen/und bewerten teutschen Philosophi und Medici* (finished 1537–1538; first published 1571), in *Sämtliche Werke*, ed. Sudhoff, vol. 12 (1929), 59.
5   Paracelsus, 'Fourth Defense,' (1538), part of *The Seven Defensiones*, in *Four Treatises*, ed. Sigerist, trans. C. Lilian Temkin, 29.
6   Paracelsus, *Die große Wundarznei*, 210.
7   Tim Ingold, *The Perception of the Environment: Essays in Livelihood, Dwelling and Skill* (London: Routledge, 2000).
8   Richard Sennett, *The Craftsman* (New Haven, CT: Yale University Press, 2008).

9 For an introduction to recent book history, see David Finkelstein and Alistair McCleery, *The Book History Reader*, 2nd ed. (London: Routledge, 2006).

10 William Eamon, *Science and the Secrets of Nature: Books of Secrets in Medieval and Early Modern Culture* (Princeton, NJ: Princeton University Press, 1994), 130. Alessio Piemontese may have been Girolamo Ruscelli (1500–1566), whose 'secrets' came out of what seems to have been an attempt at the reform of knowledge in Naples. According to Girolamo Ruscelli, *Secreti nuovi di maravigliosa virtù* (Venice: Gli heredi Marchiò Sessa, 1567), a group of Neapolitan gentlemen founded an 'Accademia Segreta,' which aimed 'to make the most diligent inquiries and, as it were, a true anatomy of the things and operations of nature itself.' The center of this academy was the Filosofia, or laboratory. The group of scholars and gentlemen of Naples employed eleven specialized artisans to set up and carry out the experiments that produced medicines, dyes, metals, and other useful products. See William Eamon and Françoise Paheau, 'The Accademia Segreta of Girolamo Ruscelli,' *Isis* 75 (1984): 327–342, quotation 339.

11 The literature on these books includes: John K. Ferguson, *Bibliographical Notes on Histories of Inventions and Books of Secrets*, 2 vols. (London: Holland Press, 1959 [originally 1898]); Eamon, *Science and the Secrets of Nature*; Pamela O. Long, *Openness, Secrecy, Authorship: Technical Arts and the Culture of Knowledge from Antiquity to the Renaissance* (Baltimore, MD: Johns Hopkins University Press, 2001); Natasha Glaisyer and Sara Pennell, eds., *Didactic Literature in England 1500–1800: Expertise Constructed* (Aldershot: Ashgate, 2003); Alison Kavey, *Books of Secrets: Natural Philosophy in England, 1550–1600* (Urbana, IL: University of Illinois Press, 2007); Elizabeth Spiller, *Seventeenth-Century English Recipe Books: Cooking, Physic, and Chirurgery in the Worlds of Elizabeth Talbot Grey and Aletheia Talbot Howard* (Aldershot: Ashgate, 2008); Pascal Dubourg Glatigny and Hélène Vérin, *Réduire en art: la technologie de la Renaissance aux Lumières* (Paris: Éditions de la Maison des sciences de l'homme, 2008); and Elaine Leong and Alisha Rankin, eds., *Secrets and Knowledge in Medicine and Science, 1500–1800* (Aldershot: Ashgate, 2011). For an excellent introduction, see Jo Wheeler (with the assistance of Katy Temple), *Renaissance Secrets, Recipes and Formulas* (London: V&A, 2009). On women's technical writing, see Elizabeth Tebaux, 'Women and Technical Writing, 1475–1700: Technology, Literacy and Development of a Genre,' in *Women, Science and Medicine, 1500–1700: Mothers and Sisters of the Royal Society*, ed. Lynette Hunter and Sarah Hutton (Thrupp: Sutton, 1997), 29–62.

12 A thorough study of these practical guides would have to include conduct manuals, exemplified by Baldassare Castiglione's *The Courtier* (Venice: Aldus Manutius, 1528) and imitated in numerous vernacular texts, as well as the *Hausväterliteratur*, which seems to have been partly aimed at managers of estates. Rudolf Bell, *How to Do It: Guides to Good Living for Renaissance Italians* (Chicago: Chicago University Press, 1999), examines guides for married couples published in the sixteenth century. A complete study of this genre would need to be quite expansive.

13 Jacob Eyferth, 'Craft Knowledge at the Interface of Written and Oral Cultures,' *East Asian Science, Technology and Society* 4 (2010): 185–205, deals with craft knowledge in China, but his inventory of written forms of craft knowledge is extremely useful.

14 Michael of Rhodes, *The Book of Michael of Rhodes: A Fifteenth-Century Maritime Manuscript*, ed. Pamela O. Long, David McGee, and Alan M. Stahl, transcription by Franco Rossi, trans. Alan M. Stahl, 3 vols. (Cambridge, MA: MIT Press, 2009).

15 Alan M. Stahl, 'Michael of Rhodes: Mariner in Service to Venice,' in ibid., 3: 87–91.

16 Simon Werrett, *Fireworks: Pyrotechnic Arts and Science in European History* (Chicago, IL: University of Chicago Press, 2009).

17 Hélène Vérin, *La gloire des ingénieurs: l'intelligence technique du XVIe au XVIIIe siècle* (Paris: Albin Michel, 1993).

18 Bradin Cormack and Carla Mazzio, *Book Use, Book Theory, 1500–1700* (Chicago, IL: University of Chicago Library, 2005), 84.

19 I gained this insight from Craig Clunas' discussion of Chinese how-to books: 'Luxury Knowledge: The *Xiushilu* ('Records of Lacquering') of 1625,' *Techniques and Culture* 29 (1997): 27–40.

20 For more information on this manuscript, see Pamela H. Smith and Tonny Beentjes, 'Nature and Art, Making and Knowing: Reconstructing Sixteenth-Century Life Casting Techniques,' *Renaissance Quarterly* 63 (2010): 128–179.

21 These instructions can be found, respectively, in Hugh Platt, *The Jewell-House of Art and Nature* (London: P. Short, 1594), 49–53, 53–54, 56–57, 58, 59, 64–65, 66, 67. In addition, Gualtherus H. Rivius (Walther Ryff), *Der furnembsten notwendigsten der gantzen Architectur angehörigen Mathematischen und Mechanischen künst eygentlicher bericht und vast klare verstendliche unterrichtung zu rechtem verstandt der lehr Vitruvij* (Nuremberg: Petreius, 1547), fol. 41r (pt. 1), claims to have treated casting from life in another treatise, which, if ever published, is no longer extant.

22 See Edgar Lein, *Ars Aeraria: Die Kunst des Bronzegießens und die Bedeutung von Bronze in der florentinischen Renaissance* (Mainz: P. von Zabern, 2004), 42–45; idem, '"Wie man allerhand Insecta, als Spinnen, Fliegen, Käfer, Eydexen, Frösche und auch ander zart Laubwerck scharff abgiessen solle, als wann sie natürlich also gewachsen wären": Die Natur als Modell in Johann Kunckels Beschreibungen des Naturabgusses von Tieren und Pflanzen,' in *Das Modell in der bildenden Kunst des Mittelalters und der Neuzeit: Festschrift für Herbert Beck*, ed. Peter Bol and Heike Richter (Petersberg: M. Imhof, 2006), 103–119; and idem, 'Über den Naturabguss von Pflanzen und Tieren,' in *Goldglanz und Silberstrahl*, ed. Karin Tebbe, vol. 2 (Nuremberg: Germanisches Nationalmuseum, 2007).

23 For a very illuminating exchange among historians about this topic, see Leora Auslander, Amy Bentley, Leor Halevi, H. Otto Sibum, and Christopher Witmore, 'AHR Conversation: Historians and the Study of Material Culture,' *American Historical Review* 114 (2009): 1355–1404. See also the special issue of *Rethinking History* 11.3 (2007), especially Vanessa Agnew, 'History's Affective Turn: Historical Reenactment and Its Work in the Present,' 299–312. For a robust defense of reconstruction as necessary to writing the history of cooking, taste, and food, see Ken Albala, 'Cooking as Research Methodology: Experiments in Renaissance Cuisine,' in *Renaissance Food from Rabelais to Shakespeare: Culinary Readings and Culinary Histories*, ed. Joan Fitzpatrick (Aldershot: Ashgate, 2010), 73–88. See also the recently published Peter Heering and Roland Wittje, eds., *Learning by Doing: Experiments and Instruments in History of Science Teaching* (Stuttgart: Franz Steiner Verlag, 2011); and Klaus Staubermann, ed., *Reconstructions: Recreating Science and Technology of the Past* (Edinburgh: National Museums Scotland, 2011). See also the remarkable account of colonial woodworking in North America by Robert Tarule, *The Artisan of Ipswich: Craftsmanship and Community in Colonial New England* (Baltimore, MD: Johns Hopkins University Press, 2004).

24 Tim Ingold, 'Showing Making: Materials, Movements, Lines' (paper presented at 'Showing Making,' Amsterdam, June 18, 2009). See also his 'Materials Against Materiality,' *Archaeological Dialogues* 14.1 (2007): 1–16. For accounts by anthropologists who acted as participant observers in various crafts, see Michael W. Coy, ed., *Apprenticeship: From Theory to Method and Back Again* (Albany, NY: State University of New York Press, 1989), and Trevor H. J. Marchand, ed., *Making Knowledge: Explorations of the Indissoluble Relation Between Mind, Body and Environment* (Chichester: Wiley-Blackwell, 2010).

25 Auslander et al., 'AHR Conversation': 1356–1357.

26 Heinz Otto Sibum, 'Reworking the Mechanical Value of Heat: Instruments of Precision and Gestures of Accuracy in Early Victorian England,' *Studies in History and Philosophy of Science* 26 (1995): 101–103.

27 Peter Heering, 'The Enlightened Microscope: Re-Enactment and Analysis of Projections with Eighteenth-Century Solar Microscopes,' *British Journal for the History of Science* 41 (2008): 345–367.

28 See the work of William Newman, 'Multimedia Lab: Newton's "Chymistry" of Metal Solubilities,' accessed June 2, 2011, http://webapp1.dlib.indiana.edu/newton/reference /chemLab.do.

29 Peter Stallybrass, Roger Chartier, J. Franklin Mowery, and Heather Wolfe, 'Hamlet's Tables and the Technologies of Writing in Renaissance England,' *Shakespeare Quarterly* 55.4 (2004): 379–419.

30 Roberta Panzanelli, ed., with Eike D. Schmidt and Kenneth Lapatin, *The Color of Life: Polychromy in Sculpture from Antiquity to the Present* (Los Angeles, CA: Getty, 2008), 2.

31 Jill Dunkerton, *Giotto to Dürer: Early Renaissance Painting in the National Gallery* (New Haven, CT: Yale University Press, 1991), 174–175.

32 Arie Wallert, 'Makers, Materials and Manufacture,' in *Netherlandish Art in the Rijksmuseum 1400–1600*, ed. Henk van Os, Jan Piet Filedt Kok, Ger Luijten, and Frits Scholten (Amsterdam: Waanders, 2000), 268, points to the widespread nineteenth-century practice of stripping off paint from polychromed statuary.

33 Panzanelli et al., *Color of Life*.

34 Mark Laird, *The Flowering of the Landscape Garden: English Pleasure Grounds, 1720–1800* (Philadelphia, PA: University of Pennsylvania Press, 1999).

35 Cennino D'Andrea Cennini, *Il libro dell'Arte (The Craftsman's Handbook)*, trans. Daniel V. Thompson, Jr. (New York: Dover, 1960), 129 (ch. 167). On casting from life, see Ernst Kris, 'Der Stil "Rustique": Die Verwendung des Naturabgusses bei Wenzel Jamnitzer und Bernard Palissy,' *Jahrbuch der Kunsthistorischen Sammlungen in Wien*, n.s., 1 (1928): 137–208; idem, *Le style rustique* (Paris: Macula, 2005); Norberto Gramaccini, 'Das genaue Abbild der Natur—Riccios Tiere und die Theorie des Naturabgusses seit Cennini,' in *Natur und Antike in der Renaissance* (Frankfurt: Liebieghaus Museum Alter Plastik, 1985), 198–225; and, more recently, idem, 'Ideeler Besitz: Paduaner Gipsabgüsse des Quattrocento,' in *Reproduktion: Techniken und Ideen von der Antike bis Heute, Eine Einführung*, ed. Jörg Probst (Berlin: Dietrich Reimer Verlag, 2011): 58–83; Andrea Klier, *Fixierte Natur: Naturabguss und Effigies im 16. Jahrhundert* (Berlin: Reimer, 2004); Georges Didi-Huberman, *L'Empreinte* (Paris: Centre Georges Pompidou, 1997); Ingrid Stöckler, 'Die Entwicklung des Naturabgusses von Padua bis Nürnberg: Eine nähere Betrachtung des silbernen Schreibzeugkästchens des Wenzel Jamnitzer' (Lic. phil. diss., University of Zurich, 1990); and Edgar Lein's works cited above.

36 On Ghiberti, see Gramaccini, 'Das genaue Abbild,' 207–210; on Donatello, see Richard Stone, 'A New Interpretation of the Casting of Donatello's *Judith and Holofernes*,' in *Small Bronzes in the Renaissance*, ed. Debra Pincus, Studies in the History of Art Series 62 (New Haven, CT: Yale University Press, 2001), 55–67.

37 Richard Stone, 'Antico and the Development of Bronze Casting in Italy at the End of the Quattrocento,' *Metropolitan Museum Journal* 16 (1982): 111, notes 'that stylistic wastebasket called the School of Padua.'

38 Dorothea Diemer, 'Handwerksgeheimnisse der Vischer-Werkstatt: Eine neue Quelle zur Entstehuung des Sebaldusgrabes in Nürnberg,' *Münchner Jahrbuch der bildenden Kunst*, third series, 47 (1996): 24–54.

39 BnF Ms. Fr. 640, fol. 169r, includes casting fish from life in a list of topics at the end of the manuscript, but there are no instructions for it. There are apparently no extant examples of bats or rats cast from life.

40 See David von Schönherr, 'Wenzel Jamnitzers Arbeiten für Erzherzog Ferdinand,' in *Mitteilungen des Instituts für Oesterreichische Geschichtsforschung*, ed. Ritter von Sickel, H. Ritter von Zeissberg, and E. Mühlbacher ([1888]; facs. repr., Amsterdam: Swets & Zeitlinger, 1971), 289–305. Lein, 'Johann Kunckels Beschreibungen,' 112–114, enumerates the objects recorded in the Bavarian Wittelsbach and Habsburg collections. See also Katrin Achilles-Syndram, ed., *Die Kunstsammlung des Paulus Praun: die Inventare von 1616 und 1719* (Nuremberg, Germany: Stadtrat, 1994), for the inventory of the Nuremberg Praun collection. A letter from the Bishop of Arras

to Leone Leoni written between 1550 and 1556 mentions a Roman goldsmith who produced a fine medal and taught his men to cast plants: Eugene Plon, *Leone Leoni sculpteur de Charles-quint et Pompeo Leoni sculpteur de Philippe II* (Paris: Plon, Nourrit, 1887), 86. My thanks to Regina Seelig-Teuwen for this reference.

41 Dorothea Diemer, 'Bronzeplastik um 1600 in München: Neue Quellen und Forschungen,' *Jahrbuch des Zentralinstituts für Kunstgeschichte* 2 (1986): 159–160 (document 8). See also Lein, 'Johann Kunckels Beschreibungen,' 112.

42 Johann Baptist Fickler, *Das Inventar der Münchner herzoglichen Kunstkammer von 1598*, part of *Bayerische Akademie der Wissenschaften, Philosophisch-Historische Klasse Abhandlungen,* ed. Peter Diemer, new series, 125 (Munich: Verlag der Bayerische Akademie der Wissenschaften, 2004), 130, contains inventory entries cataloguing these rarities.

43 Smith, *The Body of the Artisan* (Chicago: University of Chicago Press, 2004).

44 Gottfried Wilhelm Leibniz, *Protogaea*, ed. and trans. Claudine Cohen and Andre Wakefield (Chicago, IL: University of Chicago Press, 2008), 49 (entry 18).

45 We poured with the molds at temperatures of 500 °C and the silver higher than 1150°C, near 1200°C.

46 Ms. Fr. 640, fols. 107v, 150r, 161v.

47 Similarly, modern metalworkers told us that instead of the pulverized roof tiles called for in the manuscript, we could use any kind of 'chamotte' or 'grog' used by modern mold makers to produce molds that stand up to the heat (refractory qualities), but in our July 2009 and January 2011 experiments, we found that pulverized tiles (the making of which is an extremely time-consuming activity) produced far stronger molds than the use of generic grog. This is in line with Ken Albala's claim that you will not be able to predict an outcome according to modern methods or ideas, but rather you just have to try the recipe and see what happens; in Albala, 'Cooking as Research Methodology.' Conservators have also found this to be the case. See for example, Fachhochschule (Köln), Fachbereich Restaurierung und Konservierung von Kunst- und Kulturgut, 'Die Farben des Mittelalters,' *Restaurieren heißt verstehen: Zerstörungsfreie Untersuchung und Restaurierung in der Studienrichtung Restaurierung und Konservierung von Schriftgut, Graphik und Buchmalerei* (Cologne: Fachhochschule Köln, 2001).

48 See Pamela H. Smith, 'Vermilion, Mercury, Blood, and Lizards: Matter and Meaning in Metalworking,' in *Materials and Expertise in Early Modern Europe: Between Market and Laboratory*, ed. Ursula Klein and Emma Spary (Chicago, IL: University of Chicago Press, 2010): 29–49; idem, 'What is a Secret? Secrets and Craft Knowledge,' in *Secrets and Knowledge in Medicine and Science, 1500–1800*, ed. Elaine Leong and Alisha Rankin (Surrey: Ashgate, 2011): 47–66; and idem, 'The Movement of Knowledge: Following Itineraries of Matter in the Early Modern World,' in *Cultures in Motion*, ed. Daniel Rogers, Bhavani Raman, and Helmut Reimitz (Princeton, NJ: Princeton University Press, forthcoming).

49 Ms. Fr. 640, fol. 103r.

50 On epistemic things, see, for example, Hans-Jörg Rheinberger, *Toward a History of Epistemic Things: Synthesizing Proteins in the Test Tube* (Stanford, CA: Stanford University Press, 1997).

51 Bernard Palissy, *The Admirable Discourses* (1580), trans. Aurele la Rocque (Urbana, IL: University of Illinois Press, 1957), 188–203.

52 Vannoccio Biringuccio, *The Pirotechnia* (1540), trans. Cyril Stanley Smith and Martha Teach Gnudi (New York: Basic, 1943), 213.

53 Ibid., 214–215.

54 The following writers discuss, in greater or lesser detail, recipes for heat-resistant molding sands and plaster: Pomponius Gauricus, *De sculptura* (1504), ed. André Chastel and Robert Klein (Geneva: Droz, 1969), 224–230 (in the book titled *Chēmikē*); Biringuccio, *Pirotechnia*, 324–328 (bk. 8, 'The small art of casting'); Rivius, *Architectur*, fols. 40v–42v, drawing heavily from Gauricus; Giorgio Vasari, *Le Vite de*

più eccellenti architetti, pittori e scultori (Florence: L. Torrentino, 1550), esp. 148–167, and Benvenuto Cellini, *I Trattati dell' Oreficeria e della scultura* (1568) – see Benvenuto Cellini, *Traktate über die Goldschmiedekunst und die Bildhauerei (I Trattati dell' Oreficeria e della scultura di Benvenuto Cellini)*, ed. Erhard Brepohl, trans. Ruth Fröhlich and Max Fröhlich (Cologne: Böhlau, 2005), 103–105 (bk. 1, ch. 13), 167 (bk. 2, ch. 1).

55 As Gauricus, *De sculptura*, 227, notes, 'which powder is the best has already been incessantly investigated by many.' Biringuccio says about clays, 'aside from actual trial, I believe that there is little that can help you, since the clay in itself has no color or visible sign that I know of to show how satisfactory it is. … But all I can say about it is to show you by their effects how the good ones should be in their nature; and so by trial you will choose among those that come into your hands' (Biringuccio, *Pirotechnia*, 218 [bk. 6, ch. 1]).

56 David McGee, 'The Shipbuilding Text of Michael of Rhodes,' in *The Book of Michael of Rhodes*, 3: 238–241. Many sixteenth-century mining texts could well possess the same function.

57 I develop this point in Pamela H. Smith, 'Why Write a Book? From Lived Experience to the Written Word in Early Modern Europe,' *Bulletin of the German Historical Institute* 47 (2010): 25–50, http://www.ghi-dc.org/files/publications/bulletin/bu047/bu47_025.pdf.

58 Suzanne B. Butters, *The Triumph of Vulcan: Sculptor's Tools, Porphyry, and the Prince in Ducal Florence*, 2 vols. (Florence: Olschki, 1996), 1: 286–287, quoting from Edward Lucie-Smith, *The Story of Craft: The Craftsman's Role in Society* (Oxford: Phaidon, 1981), 85.

59 Biringuccio, *Pirotechnia*, 280. This point is emphasized by Peta Motture, *Bells & Mortars and Related Utensils, Catalogue of Italian Bronzes in the Victoria & Albert Museum* (London: V&A, 2001), 23: 'It is clear from the variations in the recipes…that they merely provided a guideline, and that the knowledge and experience of the founder formed a key part of the process. This can also be deduced from different descriptions of how to prepare the metal for pouring and how to tell when it is ready. Gauricus, for instance, who did not have first-hand knowledge of the processes, recounts how the foundrymen themselves stressed the need to understand the nature of the metals, how they flow in the mould and when they become liquid or boil.'

60 H. G., 'Goldsmith's Storehouse,' *c.*1604, Folger Shakespeare Library, Washington, DC, ms. V.a. 179, fols. 5v–6v.

61 Biringuccio, *Pirotechnia*, 249. Many early modern attempts to teach skills in writing end abruptly in such a statement.

62 Michael Polanyi, *Personal Knowledge: Towards a Post-Critical Philosophy* (1962; repr. London: Routledge, 1998), 64.

8

CAPRICIOUS DEMANDS

Artisanal goods, business strategies, and consumer behavior in seventeenth-century Florence

Corey Tazzara

Historians of material culture are fascinated with the particularities of early modern economic life. They have argued that reducing prices to a single abstract figure or a purchase to a single transaction in time are dangerous simplifications because prices for apparently identical goods varied according to the buyer's social status or relationship with the seller, and because many transactions were spread out over weeks or even months.[1] This chapter joins the chorus by arguing that the aggregate numbers often used to portray production and sales figures over the long run mask stunning variation in the short run. Artisans in Florence faced a volatile demand environment in which sales varied widely from month to month. Recognizing this fact helps account for the inventory stockpiling habitual among many artisans in seventeenth-century Italy.

Scholars have argued that the seventeenth and eighteenth centuries witnessed a consumer revolution that involved a steady diversification of demand throughout Europe.[2] New manufactures and colonial products multiplied to meet the desires of consumers. But despite their love of material things, the middling classes of Baroque Italy as elsewhere in Europe were unable to accumulate many of the objects they desired, at least until households began allocating more of their time and labor to purchasing new goods in what Jan de Vries has termed the Industrious Revolution.[3] Local artisans, unlike their high-flying colleagues who produced for international markets, have largely been assigned a passive role in this narrative. They are portrayed first as victims of weak demand, vainly producing new objects until the mid-seventeenth century, and thereafter as beneficiaries of an increasingly strong demand.[4] However, though an examination of the retail journals of Florentine artisans reveals that consumer demand in the short term was highly variable and hence unpredictable, artisans were hardly docile worker bees producing goods that nobody could afford. The strategies they employed to overcome this capricious demand included stockpiling of inventories and the diversification of goods and services. Ultimately, their efforts to create a more regular market were not merely a consequence of growing demand, but may help explain the development of demand itself.

Although the Florentine economy was stagnant during the long seventeenth century, Florentine patricians continued to purchase consumer goods and were eager participants in the proliferation of material objects observed elsewhere in Europe. The wealth of Florence ultimately rested on the city's famous, if troubled, wool and silk industries, and on banking. Profits from these industries constituted the basic source of spending for consumer goods in Florence. Wealthy families invested in consumer articles partly because they lacked attractive alternatives for more productive investments. They were the main consumers of objects produced by the burgeoning ranks of artisans in Florence, many of whom were making the new consumer goods for which the seventeenth century is celebrated: fancy glassware, coaches, cutlery, ceramics, elaborate furnishings, and the like. Florence produced almost all of the luxury items consumed in the city and, indeed, in Tuscany as a whole.[5] The case of Florence shows that the spread of consumer culture and the diversification of the artisanate need not be accompanied by an expanding local economy. But it does raise the question of how readily the business practices studied in the markets of the major European cities, London and Paris first among them, can be mapped onto Florence.

Early modern artisans did not often write about their approach to business in this growing world of goods. When artisans did discuss their work, their goal was often to celebrate their self-worth and professional identity rather than to enter into the minutiae of their businesses.[6] If anything, craftsmen prized secrecy and feared to commit their practices to print. As the French potter Bernard Palissy put it in his *Admirable Discourses* (1580), when Theory asked Practice for information about ceramics:

> The secrets of agriculture must not be kept secret. The hazards and dangers of navigation must not be kept secret. The word of God must not be kept secret. The sciences that serve the whole state must not be kept secret.

Artisanal knowledge was another matter altogether, however, and Practice was reluctant to disclose the arcana of the ceramics industry: 'Many charming inventions are contaminated and despised because they are too common.'[7] Palissy feared that unveiling his technical secrets would result in the overproduction of goods and the immiseration of craftsmen. Although many artisans have left us their diaries and account books, we have few explicit discussions of business practices until the mid-eighteenth century. We must thus infer their strategies from their practices and by examining the statements of other, more loquacious observers.

Florentine merchants produced a vibrant body of literature that promoted a common vocabulary and set of operating procedures among agents in far-flung commercial ventures.[8] The dangers of business life particularly troubled them. Leon Battista Alberti was not merely recasting a literary trope when he noted that the mercantile life is

> fraught with a thousand risks, carries with it a mass of suspicions and trouble, and brings numerous losses and regrets. There is trouble in purchasing, fear in transporting, anxiety in selling, apprehension in giving credit, weariness in collecting what is due you, deceit in exchange.[9]

The city's diarists offered a wealth of advice to their readers about how to cope with pervasive risk. Remedies included hard work, always keeping one's money active and invested in a variety of ventures, and, above all, good planning. Paolo da Certaldo remarked that 'foresight is a beautiful thing.'[10] Even so, merchants knew that it was impossible to secure themselves completely from the vicissitudes of *fortuna*.

It is unclear whether artisans faced as tumultuous a business environment as merchants. Benedetto Cortugli (*c.*1416–1469) thought that 'it was almost impossible for [artisans] who worked hard and diligently to be poor.'[11] According to Cotrugli, they had an easier time because they worked within a guild framework that regulated production processes and access to the profession. Scholars have speculated, moreover, that the frequent holidays of the pre-Tridentine calendar prevented overproduction and regularized the relationship between supply and demand.[12] In any case, the political and economic changes of the sixteenth century wrought key transformations on the Florentine artisanate. The Medici grand dukes relied on guilds for social and political control, but circumscribed their capacity to regulate economic activity. Local artisans produced a greater variety of goods than their ancestors, in other words, and they did so with fewer of the labor restrictions of the old Catholic calendar and guild-dominated political sphere. If artisans had been shielded from the whims of *fortuna* during the heyday of Florentine merchant capitalism, as Cortugli believed, their situation was different by the close of the Renaissance.[13]

The glass industry was one of the expanding industries of early modern Florence. Although glassmakers primarily served the local market, post-mortem inventories of three artisans reveal that they kept substantial stocks of wares that would appear to be far in excess of their immediate business needs. For instance, the shop of the glassmaker Giuseppe Coscietti (d. 1602) contained about 46,000 pieces of glasswork and was valued at about 5,600 lire – an impressive sum, although it excludes debits and credits and therefore does not reflect all of Coscietti's assets. Of that, only 7 percent represented fixed capital such as benches and tools. The other 93 percent comprised raw materials, semi-finished products, and finished goods (Table 8.1). Coscietti was not alone in possessing a large stock of unsold products and only modest capital goods. Fellow Florentine

TABLE 8.1   Giuseppe Coscietti (d. 1602), value of shop inventory by category. From Gabriella Cantini Guidotti, *Tre inventari di bicchierai toscani fra cinque e seicento* (Firenze: L'Accademia della Crusca, 1983). My calculations.

	Lire	Percent
Finished goods	2,846	51
Semi-finished	77	1
Raw materials	2,270	40
Fixed capital	413	7
Total	5,605	100

glassmakers Lorenzo d'Orlando and Baccio Rustichelli had similarly large stockpiles, 53,000 and 32,000 items respectively.[14] Lorenzo even had a storage magazine in his house for what could not be kept in his workshop.[15]

Perhaps these large inventories explain why the contemporary observer Tomaso Garzoni accused the more unscrupulous glassmakers of foisting friable glass on their customers.[16] Garzoni's monumental *Universal Marketplace* (1585) surveys some 150 professions, ranging from poets to prostitutes and from merchants to chimney sweeps. It provides the best guide to the artisanal world of late-Renaissance Italy. The need to move merchandise off the shelves was one that Garzoni frequently mentioned as a source of the dishonesty of artisans in business matters. Cobblers, for instance, often lied about the kind of material their shoes contained (sheepskin instead of calfskin), fobbed off an old shoe as a new one, or performed shoddy repair jobs so that customers had to return more often. 'Dithering and lying are common among them, as they are among all people who serve others,' he remarked. 'Work today is so fraudulent that we scarcely meet anybody who tells the truth.'[17] Craftsmen burdened with large stocks might well be tempted to indulge in dishonest practices to move merchandise.

Historians have cautioned against inferring the business practices of any single artisan from inventories, however. While a large number of inventories may reveal something of the structure of the industry, they do not shed light on crucial dimensions of stock flow.[18] One may wonder how long the wares of Coscietti, d'Orlando, and Rustichelli sat on their shelves. How much business did artisans do? How rapidly did they turn over inventory? Probate inventories, whatever they tell us about consumer demand from the point of view of the consumer, are bad at revealing what demand looked like to the producers.

I have examined the journals of five craftsmen who worked between 1570 and 1680: a glassmaker, two shoemakers, a glover, and a leather gilder. These individuals were chosen because they produced for the domestic Tuscan market and worked on their own account rather than on behalf of merchants, unlike the well-studied wool and silk artisans; because they sold primarily at the local retail level; and because their journals survive.[19] The journals record transactions in chronological order and so are unusually useful for the study of businesses over the short run. Typically, transactions were recorded first in a journal and ordered chronologically to provide a continuous record of the shop's business activities. Entries would also be listed in the ledger, the *libro di creditori e debitori*, organized by individual customer. Ledgers exist in great abundance and are good for studying business relationships between an artisan and specific individuals. The journals are more useful, however, for building a chronologically nuanced picture of an artisan's activities.

The journals enabled me to compile various measures for gauging the variability of demand such as the number and value of transactions in a given period. My figures do not necessarily express all the income a tradesman received, since only transactions that involved credit appear to have been recorded with consistency. This caveat should not distort my results, however. Scholars have shown that recourse to credit was the norm in most transactions, even if an article was ultimately purchased with cash. More importantly, there is no reason to imagine a systematic bias in favor of cash at certain times of the year.[20] Finally, it is worth reiterating that this paper is less concerned with total values than with measuring variability. At stake is not how a business fared over the long haul, but reconstructing what an artisan could expect as he developed his plans in the short and medium terms. It is about imagining how artisans made predictions and judged variability.

Before examining my artisans in detail, it is useful to compare their businesses with the silk and wool manufacturers who have received more scholarly attention. The textile sector in Florence was directed toward export and organized by a handful of rich families. Unlike retail artisans, textile manufacturers did not engage in stockpiling. Capitalist entrepreneurs (*lanaioli* for wool and *setaioli* for silk) operated on a brief time horizon guided by the dictates of cash flow, seeking to maintain liquidity above all. They created a fluid, decentralized labor market wherein artisans contracted in the short or medium terms to produce a fixed quantity of goods. These workers specialized in one of many manufacturing stages: woolens, for instance, had a discrete labor force for processing, spinning, weaving, finishing, and dyeing. Such methods enabled the *lanaioli* and *setaioli* to stay responsive to demand in the international markets where they did business.[21] Subcontracting was common in export-oriented industries throughout Western Europe, even in heavily guilded industries, in order to cope with volatility in distant markets.[22] By contrast, retail artisans in local sectors produced and sold on their own account directly to consumers. Guilds had little authority to regulate production and trade within the city, and artisans were free to respond to business conditions as they deemed best.

Giovanni Fidani was a glassmaker active in Florence between 1640 and 1671. During the first decade of his career, he specialized in the production of wine flasks and sold to a restricted but lofty clientele. In the 1640s his biggest and most regular customer was the Marquis Lorenzo de' Medici. Fidani effected several sales without immediate payment, merely trusting in the promises of one of

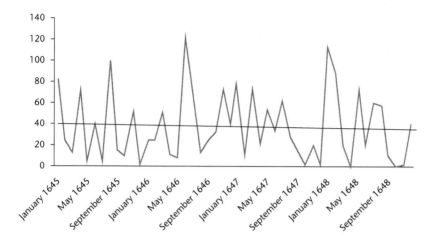

FIGURE 8.1   Giovanni Fidani, glassmaker, monthly sales in lire, 1645–1648. From ASF, LCF, 2223. Mean = 37; median = 25; standard deviation = 32; average coefficient of variation = 0.86

Medici's agents. Most of his other patrons were members of the aristocratic Capponi, Magalotti, and Strozzi families.[23] As substantial landowners, these families needed flasks for the wine produced on their estates. Perhaps owing to this limited base of patrons, his sales show a high degree of variability over time (Figure 8.1). For example, the only transaction recorded for August 1643 was the purchase by Battista Mancini of ninety lire worth of flasks and 'other stuff from my shop' – but though Mancini's was the only transaction that August, it was the single largest purchase in the entire four-year period I studied.[24] The high variability of the demand faced by Fidani helps explain why post-mortem inventories of glassworkers often abounded in unsold merchandise: such accumulation was necessary for meeting occasions of unusual demand.

To produce Fidani's graph, I compiled a table of sales in lire by totaling the amount of money paid or debited for handiwork per month. From this table I also calculated the mean, median, and standard deviation. To gauge variability, I used a simple measure called the coefficient of variation (CV). This is the ratio of the standard deviation to the mean, thus relating the data set's overall dispersion to the average monthly sales. A CV approaching zero indicates low variation, while a figure approaching one signifies high variation. Since the coefficient of variation is a ratio, it also allows me to compare the variation in sales between my artisans. I have omitted the graphs for the other artisans to conserve space, but I list the descriptive statistics in the endnotes, and further data are available online.[25]

The variable demand structure was not unique to glassmakers like Fidani, but was shared by two cobblers from vastly different socio-economic worlds. Ridolfi Montini was a Florentine cobbler who specialized in quality footwear such as silver slippers and shoes in the Roman or French style.[26] Almost all the shoes he sold were described with precise adjectives: purled, made of hay, made of chammy, made of cork, etc.[27] As Garzoni said,

> [i]t is important for everybody to appear nimble and elegant with a beautiful pair of shoes, be they in the Spanish or Neapolitan or Savoyard style, or with a lovely pair of slippers or high-heels as are worn in our age.[28]

Important clients included Count Lione Nerli and his wife, the Countess Caterina, but most of his other customers were artisans or their wives. Perhaps Montini was one of those uppity shoemakers who liked to debate about the Scriptures, 'which is about as decorous in his mouth as a beret is on the head of an ass.'[29]

Shoes were not all vanity, of course. Even poor people needed shoes. They were necessary bulwarks against 'the excessive cold of winter, the burning heat of summer, the wetness of water, the thorns of the earth, the bites of snakes, the hardness of rocks,' and anything else that could harm one's foot.[30] Antonio Achiani, who lived in the impoverished hamlet of Chianni near Pisa, sold primarily to 'laborers,' as they were described in his journal. His wares were characterized simply as 'shoes' or 'slippers,' without any fancy adjectives.[31] At times he accepted payment in kind, as when one laborer bought shoes in exchange for their equivalent in rice.[32] Like Montini, Achiani sold ready-made shoes, described as 'di bottega' or 'of the shop' in the journals, and also made money on repairs and second-hand sales. And though Achiani's shoes were less refined than those of Montini and much cheaper, they both faced a highly mercurial demand environment. It seems that seventeenth-century Italians were not as shoe-crazy as their twenty-first century descendants – or at least cobblers were not selling them shoes as often as they might have wished.[33]

Perhaps not surprisingly given the limited number of people capable of affording their goods, luxury artisans also contended with variable demand. I examined the account books of Alessandro Pesi, a leather gilder of the early seventeenth-century.[34] Pesi sold to the cream of Florentine society, including the high Medici functionary Curzio Picchena, and had a few connections to markets outside Tuscany. As a gilder, his primary ware consisted of extremely expensive *corami* or leather wall hangings, often patterned and dyed as well as gilded. Pesi probably subcontracted key components of his business. Garzoni praised one Neapolitan master for 'possessing the entire art,' but his achievement was rare in such a complicated industry: it required perfectly tanned leather, silver or gold leaf, and engraved wooden stamps, and sometimes the pieces were painted as well. The final product was nonetheless 'incredibly lucrative' for master artisans and merchants. The average wall hanging that Pesi sold cost about two hundred lire but could cost upwards of nine hundred if he provided all the materials. Even his labor fees were steep.[35] His profession was very different from the common run of leather workers described as 'base plebs' by Garzoni a few decades earlier:

Leather masters have an incredibly dirty, reeking, and fetid trade. For this reason they are the first to be expelled during times of plague. ... But those practitioners who discovered the art of gilded wall hangings, so noble and prized in our times, certainly merit the highest praise and honor for having shown themselves to be wise and singular men by perfecting an art which had otherwise been of little value in itself.[36]

Perfecting such a noble art did not result in more regular sales, however, at least not for Pesi. Despite a general rise in sales over the two years I studied, he faced the usual highly unpredictable demand described above.

Domenico Signorini was a glover and perfumer of the late seventeenth century. 'The principal labor of glovers consists of tanning gloves,' Garzoni notes, 'so that whoever knows best how to tan and perfume them earns even more money.'[37] Perfume concealed the reek of tanned leather, and some of the delicate scents Garzoni recorded were jasmine, amber, musk, and bezoar oil. For all that they 'earn even more money,' however, these craftsmen were not blessed with more regular business: Signori's journal shows somewhat less though still substantial variation in sales.[38] Like Pesi, Signorini sold to some of the city's richest families, such as Tornaquinci, Salviati, and Ricasoli, and he enjoyed a few ties to markets beyond the grand duchy. Signorini's products cost less but were equally refined: calfskin gloves, fans with ivory handles, and vases of rose-scented perfume. He employed an innovative practice to woo customers by offering samples to both individual buyers as well as distributors in Rome and Lucca. Sometimes his samples were returned, but often customers agreed to buy them outright. He also sold a greater variety of goods than my other artisans. Perhaps these two techniques – offering samples and a greater variety of wares – helped regularize his monthly sales somewhat. It would be rash to reach this conclusion on an analysis of only twenty-four months of business of a single artisan, but if true would provide evidence of a gradual transition to more regular sales among late-seventeenth century tradesmen even in as restricted a market as Tuscany.[39]

Recall that a coefficient of variation approaching one indicates high variability in a data set. By this measure, all five of the artisans I studied contended with substantial variation in month-to-month demand (Table 8.2). It did not matter whether their sales were in general growth or decline, or whether they were producing luxury or ordinary goods. Indeed, even the durability of goods did not matter. The artisans I studied produced items ranging from the relatively durable (glassware and leather hangings) to the relatively impermanent (shoes), with Signorini's gallantries falling somewhere in the middle. One might have

TABLE 8.2 Coefficients of variation. From Figure 8.1; footnotes 26, 31, 34, and 38.

Fidani	Achiani	Montini	Pesi	Signorini
0.86	0.81	0.86	0.81	0.69

expected that producers of durable goods would have faced a more variable demand than producers of ephemeral goods, since their products lasted longer and were presumably replaced less frequently. I did not find this. Perhaps this distinction is not valid since seventeenth-century artisans did not produce objects for 'consumption' in the literal sense of the word. Impermanent goods such as shoes were repaired or recycled. The rag-dealers that scoured people's closets for old clothing were the most eloquent testimony of a society that recycled everything it could.[40] A craft economy made reuse and repair much more viable than the modern factory system.

Historians who have examined the short-term ups and downs of business life in the seventeenth century have pointed to the seasonal nature of production or its connection to the calendar of civic and religious holidays.[41] But while my data do show some tendency toward seasonal consumption, variation within months – by comparing, for instance, May of one year to May of the following year – was almost as pronounced as variation between months. For example, the glassmaker Giovanni Fidani sold merely five lire worth of flasks in May 1645 and only eight in May 1646, but then he made an impressive fifty-four lire in May 1647 and seventy-two in May 1648. The vast difference between the first two years and the latter two years is accounted for by the decisions of a few wealthy patrons like Lorenzo de' Medici and Filippo Magalotti to buy their flasks from Fidani in May 1647 and again the following year. Another example: in May 1616 the gilder Alessandro Pesi made a (for him) meager fifty-nine lire. The following May, however, was his second-biggest grossing in the entire two-year period. He sold goods worth 2,700 lire thanks to three large and expensive wall hangings bought by Niccolò Asigetti, as well as significant purchases by members of the Bracci and Rinuccini families. The other artisans faced similar variation within rather than between seasons.[42] These considerations indicate that erratic variation, not variation according to the seasons or holidays, was the lot of the artisans I have studied.

Why was demand so unpredictable from their point of view? An under-monetized economy should probably not bear the brunt of the blame, since historians have argued that networks of credit and pawning mitigated the problems of a limited diffusion of currency.[43] Instead, these data point to the real limits not of money, but of credit and consumption – in other words, they reveal the general weakness of consumer demand in Florence during the long seventeenth century. This explanation seems particularly persuasive in light of the relatively few big patrons that my artisans enjoyed. Almost 40 percent of all the glassmaker Fidani's revenues owed to the purchases of just one customer, Lorenzo de' Medici, and most of his other sales were shared by a handful of customers. With the exception of the provincial cobbler Achiani, who sold to laborers, the other artisans I studied depended for most of their sales on a restricted set of aristocratic patrons. This made them susceptible to the consumption patterns of a few members of the Florentine elite and probably accounts for much of the capricious demand they faced. Perhaps their remaining, if less frequent, customers hailed from the upper rungs of the middling sort, who increasingly had wealth to put into the credit markets or to deposit with the Monte di Pietà.[44]

Other sources confirm that aristocratic expenditure remained erratic even as occasions for making purchases multiplied alongside the objects of the new material world. At the beginning of the fifteenth century, Leon Battista Alberti identified only four things worth hoarding: silver, tapestries, clothing, and gems. Otherwise all value resided in a family's lands, shops, and palazzo. By the end of the sixteenth century, however, a writer such as Sabba da Castiglione celebrated more luxury goods than he could conveniently list.[45] New sumptuary legislation in Tuscany in 1562, 1568, and 1637 permitted Tuscans to lead a nobler lifestyle in accordance with the 'de-republicanization' of society, while also regulating specific markers of identity, particularly clothing and jewelry.[46] Nevertheless, even the rich did not buy objects as often as one might expect for a society that had developed a new appreciation of material goods. Account books show that many consumption expenditures remained linked to special occasions for aristocrats deep into the seventeenth century: weddings of course, but also baptisms, funerals, travel, accession to office, and a host of public ceremonies. Gifts and tips occupied an especially important place in the account books of wealthy families, while the purchase of luxury objects for decoration or consumption remained infrequent.[47] If the local Florentine market was as dependent on elite consumption as historians like Richard Goldthwaite and Paolo Malanima have argued, then it makes sense that the artisans who supplied their wants were beholden to the special occasions that characterized the consumption patterns of the nobility.[48]

Now, to return to the problem of artisan inventories with which this paper began. The gilder Alessandro Pesi's records provide an unusual window into his business thanks to an inventory that was taken of his shop when he formed a partnership in June 1617, which can be read in conjunction with his journal (Figures 8.2 and 8.3). As expected, the inventory reveals that the most valuable items consisted of raw materials and semi-finished goods: these two categories comprised about four fifths of the value of the shop or nearly two thousand lire (Table 8.3). That figure appears low in light of the business Pesi did: in the previous three months, he had sold goods valued at twice that figure, and in June itself he grossed another 3,300 lire – his largest-netting month in my data set and substantially more than the appraisal of the entire shop done the same month. These facts appear especially strange in light of the glassmaker Giuseppe Coscietti's inventory (Table 8.1): although a glassmaker who had to maintain a furnace and its associated expenses, shop capital constituted only 7 percent of the value of his workshop. By contrast, Pesi's amounted to more than three times that figure, 22 percent. I would interpret these figures by suggesting that in the month of June, when Alessandro Pesi formed his partnership, his stocks were depleted due to several months of high demand. This inventory depletion is the corollary of unpredictable demand: overstocked inventories served precisely to

TABLE 8.3   Alessandro Pesi's inventory from June 1617

	Lire	Percent
Semi-finished goods	828	33
Raw materials	1,118	45
Fixed capital	553	22
Total	2,499	100

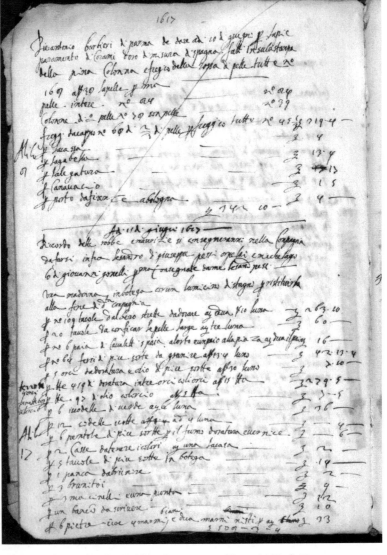

FIGURE 8.2   Alessandro Pesi's Shop Inventory of June 1617, f. 12v

meet demand in those fortunate though fickle moments when customers placed a lot of orders with a shop.

Over-stocking was a sensible response for an artisan facing frequent slow spells punctuated by periods of intense sales. Their large inventories were not merely a sad consequence of an inadequate market, in other words, but part of a strategy that ensured they would capture as much business as possible during sudden deluges of demand. No artisan wanted to turn away a customer who could not wait for a commission and instead sought a ready-made object.

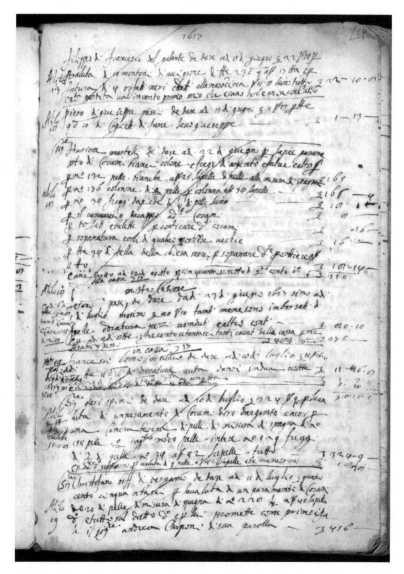

FIGURE 8.3   Alessandro Pesi, Shop Inventory, f. 14r

Stockpiling does not mean that artisans worked continuously, of course, or would amass as much inventory as possible. Contemporaries saw laziness as a characteristic vice of artisans. Perhaps this 'laziness' was actually a function of the significant periods of slowdown that afflicted most artisans no matter what the size of their inventories. Artisans themselves certainly valued hard work and did not see themselves as sloth-ridden. A learned Florentine shoemaker wrote a playful dialog between a shopkeeper and his soul. The soul, complaining loudly of neglect, said that the shopkeeper was too busy with business to tend to his spiritual needs: 'Always afraid that you'll lose what you have, like other greedy old men, you never give me a moment's rest. As soon as you are done eating or sleeping, you run off to work.'[49]

Stockpiling served artisans in other ways, too. The goods stored in their workshops were as money- or credit-convertible as the goods accumulated in the dowries and family patrimonies that historians have studied in recent decades. Giuseppe da Modena's account of his travails as a second-hand dealer in Siena suggests that neither shopkeepers nor the larger community distinguished between shop goods and credit on the one hand, and personal wealth and credit on the other.[50] A large stock served as a kind of treasury, as part of the family patrimony itself.[51] As such, artisans or their heirs could use their stock of wares to pay for debts or purchase goods. At the broadest level, then, a large stock enabled a tradesman to participate more fully in the credit networks that greased the wheels of seventeenth-century commerce. But whereas families accumulated wealth for hard times, artisans stored up treasure for good as well as bad times.[52]

There are key limitations to this study. First, with the exception of one moment in Alessandro Pesi's career, we do not have inventories for the five artisans studied. While my interpretation is based on the general phenomenon of stockpiling noted among artisanal inventories in early modern Italy, it is possible that these artisans did *not* stockpile but rather confronted their capricious demand in other ways. Second, my argument makes broader assumptions about the economic lives of these artisans drawn from the secondary literature: their embeddedness in networks of credit, the relative infrequency of (unrecorded) cash transactions, the role of shop inventories as treasury, and the relationship of their shops to family strategy. If they had survived, the diaries, wills, and ledgers of my artisans might have provided information about these topics. Above all, my interpretation offers an inductive view of craft strategy based not on the words of artisans, for they have not left us many, but on the structural conditions of their business life.

Whatever the larger contours of their economic lives, however, these artisans certainly had to confront a predictably unpredictable demand for their goods. Artisans could pursue two avenues for making revenue more regular: either they could increase the frequency with which they sold to their patrons, or they could increase the number of their patrons. Probably they sought to do both. Variable demand spurred artisans to increase the range of products they sold and to multiply their connections with other artisans in their quest to build a more regular and predictable market.[53] That was as true in smaller local scenes such as Florence as in the large international markets that historians have examined. Variability also encouraged artisans to extend credit to buyers of limited means, to run informal pawnshops out of their shops, and to deal in second-hand goods as well as their own products.

Scholars have contrasted the supposedly pre-modern amassing of inventory with the more modern spread of specialization and subcontracting (in which an artisan farmed out an order to another craftsman). They have suggested that these practices were responses to a long-term, steady rise in aggregate demand. Instead, these strategies are best viewed alongside stock accumulation within the context of the short-term unpredictability that was the real time horizon of the artisan or shopkeeper. Why did some artisans prefer inventory stockpiling rather than subcontracting for coping with uncertain demand? Subcontracting networks made sense when distant markets, though uncertain, were large enough to enable some masters to focus on marketing. Secondly, industries that involved a complex of disparate skills were ripe for specialization, such as coach- and watch-making.[54] Florence's textile exports fit both those bills. Although inventory stockpiling has received less attention, it seems that many Florentine artisans were not busy enough to sustain subcontracting arrangements. They could meet demand by producing on their own account.

Although export industries have attracted the lion's share of research, scholars should pay more attention to artisans who produced for a local market. These masters participated in the same burgeoning world of goods as the celebrated artisan–entrepreneurs who manufactured for the international scene. If their business strategies differed according to the volatility and small size of local markets, local artisans nonetheless contributed to deep changes in European production and consumption. My approach helps resolve the paradox of why even Florence, one of Western Europe's most stagnant economies in the seventeenth century, witnessed an increasingly diverse artisanate and a host of new goods appearing on the local market. By pushing new wares onto customers and increasing the range of goods they sold, these retail artisans sought to create a more regular market for themselves. And in doing so, they played an active role in cultivating the transformation in demand that helped drive Europe toward the Industrious Revolution.

Notes

1 Evelyn Welch, *Shopping in the Renaissance* (New Haven, CT: Yale University Press, 2005); Michelle O'Malley and Evelyn Welch, eds., *The Material Renaissance* (Manchester: Manchester University Press, 2007). Economic historians in recent decades have also sought to move beyond what Michael Sonenscher called 'the uniformities generated by calculations of averages' in his book on the French craft economy in the eighteenth century (*Work and Wages. Natural Law, Politics, and the Eighteenth-Century French Trades* [Cambridge: Cambridge University Press, 1989], 145). The rediscovery of the short term has also affected historical economists

interested in game theory, as with Avner Greif, *Institutions and the Path to the Modern Economy: Lessons from Medieval Trade* (Cambridge: Cambridge University Press, 2006); and sociologists or anthropologists influenced by Pierre Bourdieu's ideas about practice. Short-term strategy is having its own Renaissance.

2 Neil McKendrick et al., *The Birth of a Consumer Society: The Commercialization of Eighteenth-Century England* (Bloomington, IN: Indiana University Press, 1982); John Brewer and Roy Porter, eds., *Consumption and the World of Goods* (New York: Routledge, 1993); Domenico Sella, 'Peasants as Consumers of Manufactured Goods in Italy around 1600,' in *The European Peasant Family and Society: Historical Studies*, ed. Richard L. Rudolph (Liverpool: Liverpool University Press, 1995); James R. Farr, *Artisans in Europe, 1300–1914* (Cambridge: Cambridge University Press, 2000), 62–66; Joel Mokyr, 'Demand as a Factor in the Industrial Revolution: A Historical Note,' in *Escaping Satiation: The Demand Side of Economic Growth,* ed. Ulrich Witt (Heidelberg: Springer, 2001); Pamela H. Smith and Paula Findlen, eds., *Merchants & Marvels: Commerce, Science and Art in Early Modern Europe* (New York: Routledge, 2002); Jan De Vries, *The Industrious Revolution: Consumer Behavior and the Household Economy, 1650 to the Present* (Cambridge: Cambridge University Press, 2008).

3 Renata Ago, *Il gusto delle cose: una storia degli oggetti nella Roma del Seicento* (Roma: Donzelli, 2006) (English translation as *Gusto for Things: A History of Objects in Seventeenth-Century Rome*, trans. Bradford Bouley and Corey Tazzara with Paula Findlen [Chicago. IL: University of Chicago Press, forthcoming]); idem, *Economia barocca: mercato e istituzioni nella Roma del Seicento* (Roma: Donzelli, 1998). In Tuscany, the lower classes could purchase very few luxury goods until the late eighteenth century. Paolo Malanima, *Il lusso dei contadini: consumi e industrie nelle campagne toscane del Sei e Settecento* (Bologna: Il Mulino, 1990), esp. 36–49.

4 Scholars who have considered the role of the producer in the spread of consumer culture have focused on artisan–entrepreneurs who manufactured on a large scale or for international markets. In Neil McKendrick's original formulation of the theory of consumer revolution, eighteenth-century entrepreneurs such as Josiah Wedgwood played a critical role in manipulating consumer demand. Cissie Fairchilds argues that the system of production and marketing that 'populuxe' goods entailed – eluding guild regulations in production, illicit subcontracting, and black-market sales – conditioned the direction of growth in France. Neil McKendrick et al., *The Birth of a Consumer Society*; Cissie Fairchilds, 'The Production and Marketing of Populuxe Goods in Eighteenth-Century Paris,' in *Consumption and the World of Goods,* ed. Brewer and Porter, 228–248. Artisan–entrepreneurs have come into their own as innovators in the export-oriented guilds surveyed in Stephan R. Epstein and Maarten Prak, eds., *Guilds, Innovation, and the European Economy, 1400–1800* (Cambridge: Cambridge University Press, 2008). Not by chance, a recent volume on the Italian guilds focuses almost entirely on the fate of such export-oriented guilds: Alberto Guenzi, Paola Massa, and Fausto Piola Caselli, *Guilds, Markets, and Work Regulations in Italy, 16th–19th Centuries* (Brookfield, VT: Ashgate, 1998). Carlo Poni's work has focused on the minor guilds, but deals with norms for resolving disputes rather than with business strategies or innovation. See Carlo Poni, 'Norms and Disputes: The Shoemakers' Guild in Eighteenth-Century Bologna,' *Past and Present* 123 (1989): 80–108; idem, 'Local Market Rules and Practices: Three Guilds in the Same Line of Production in Early Modern Bologna,' in *Domestic Strategies: Work and Family in France and Italy 1600–1800,* ed. Stuart Woolf (Cambridge: Cambridge University Press, 1991), 69–101.

5 Malanima, *Il lusso dei contadini*; idem, *La decadenza di un'economia cittadina: l'industria di Firenze nei secoli XVI–XVIII* (Bologna: Il Mulino, 1982); idem, *I Riccardi di Firenze: una famiglia e un patrimonio nella Toscana dei Medici* (Firenze: L. S. Olschki, 1977). For the earlier period see Richard A. Goldthwaite, *The Economy of Renaissance Florence* (Baltimore, MD: Johns Hopkins University Press, 2009), esp. 322–340; idem, *Wealth and the Demand for Art in Italy, 1300–1600* (Baltimore, MD: Johns Hopkins

University Press, 1993); idem, *The Building of Renaissance Florence: An Economic and Social History* (Baltimore, MD: Johns Hopkins University Press, 1980); and recently, Samuel Cohn, 'Renaissance Attachment to Things: Material Culture in Last Wills and Testaments,' forthcoming in *The Economic History Review*. On the craft economy, see Alfred Doren, *Le Arti Fiorentini*, trans. G. B. Klein, 2 vols. (Firenze: Le Monnier, 1940); Goldthwaite, *The Economy of Renaissance Florence*, ch. 5. Brown and Goodman draw on censuses from 1631 and 1642 to demonstrate that the Florentine artisanate continued to diversify deep into the seventeenth century. They argue that women moved into the stagnating textile fields as men shifted toward more highly paid luxury fields. Judith C. Brown and Jordan Goodman, 'Women and Industry in Florence,' *Journal of Economic History* 40.1 (1980): 73–80. See also R. Burr Litchfield, *Florence Ducal Capital, 1530–1630* (New York: ACLS Humanities E-Book, 2008).

6 James S. Amelang, *The Flight of Icarus: Artisan Autobiography in Early Modern Europe* (Stanford, CA: Stanford University Press, 1998), 119–126, 214.

7 Bernard Palissy, *Discours admirable de l'art de terre* (Geneva: Jules-Guillaume Fick, 1863), 2–3; this translation is from *The Admirable Discourses of Bernard Palissy*, trans. Aurèle La Rocque (Urbana, IL: University of Illinois, 1957), 188–189. Secrecy functioned to prevent the spread of techniques beyond the local community; individual artisans in the same town or guild did share their practices. See Pamela O. Long, *Openness, Secrecy, Authorship: Technical Arts and the Culture of Knowledge from Antiquity to the Renaissance* (Baltimore, MD: Johns Hopkins University Press, 2001); Stephan R. Epstein, 'Property Rights to Technical Knowledge in Premodern Europe, 1300–1800,' *American Economic Review* 94.2 (2004): 382–387; and Francesca Trivellato, 'Guilds, Technology, and Economic Change in Early Modern Venice,' in *Guilds, Innovation, and the European Economy*, ed. Epstein and Prak, 221–227.

8 For instance, the *Pratica della mercatura* of Francesco Balducci Pegolotti (*c.* 1340) originated as an in-house manual for merchants of the Bardi banking company; see the edition edited by Allen Evans (Cambridge: The Mediaeval Academy of America, 1936). Gunnar Dahl, *Trade, Trust, and Networks* (Lund, Sweden: Nordic Academic Press, 1998) provides an analysis of this literature during the Renaissance. The seventeenth century saw the culmination of this tradition throughout Europe with the publication of works such as Gerard Malynes, *Consuetudo, vel, Lex Mercatoria* (London: Adam Islip, 1622), Giovanni Domenico Peri, *Il negotiante* (Genova: P. G. Calenzano, 1638), and Jacques Savary, *Le parfait négociant* (Paris: Jean Guignard fils, 1675). On the importance of common business practices and a shared discursive language, see Francesca Trivellato, *The Familiarity of Strangers: The Sephardic Diaspora, Livorno, and Cross-Cultural Trade in the Early Modern Period* (New Haven, CT: Yale, 2009), ch. 6–7.

9 Leon Battista Alberti, *I libri della famiglia*, ed. Girolamo Mancini (Firenze: Carnesecchi e Figli, 1908), 185; the translation is from *The Family in Renaissance Florence*, trans. by R. N. Watkins (Long Grove, IL: Waveland Press, 1994), bk. 3, 61.

10 Paolo da Certaldo, 'Libro di buoni costumi,' in *Mercanti scrittori: ricordi nella Firenze tra Medioevo e Rinascimento*, ed. Vittore Branca (Milano: Rusconi, 1986), 30 n. 139.

11 Benedetto Cotrugli, *Il libro dell'arte di mercatura*, ed. Ugo Tucci (Venezia: Arsenale, 1990), 178.

12 Armando Sapori, *Il mercante italiano nel medio evo* (Firenze: Univcrsitaria editrice, 1945), 31–32. We may wonder how effective such work prohibitions were. On January 1, 1403, the merchant Gregorio Dati confessed that for forty years he had failed to abide by the commandments of the Lord and resolved to be more pious in the future: 'I resolve from this day forward to refrain from going to the shop or conducting business on solemn Church holidays, or from permitting others to work for me or seek temporal gain on such days.' If urgent business required him to work even on holidays, Dati promised to give a florin to the poor the following day. *Il libro segreto di Gregorio Dati*, ed. Carlo Gargiolli (Bologna: Gaetano Romagnoli, 1869), 69; the translation is from Gene Brucker, ed., *Two Memoirs of Renaissance*

Florence, trans. Julia Martines (Long Grove, IL: Waveland Press, 1991), 124. In any case, after the Council of Trent the Church began to curtail the number of holidays from about ninety to sixty (in 1568–1570) and finally to thirty-five in 1642, although communities long maintained feast days for their local saints. Overall, while the number of feast days may have declined during the long seventeenth century, artisans' compliance with work prohibitions probably increased. See Arnaldo D'Addario, *Aspetti della Controriforma a Firenze* (Roma: Pubblicazioni degli Archivi di Stato, 1972); and Robert Bireley, *The Refashioning of Catholicism, 1450–1700* (Washington, DC: The Catholic University of America Press, 1999). I am grateful to Brad Bouley for his expertise on the Catholic Reformation.

13 Apart from the textile industries, the relationship between guilds and the artisanate in early modern Florence remains to be studied. But there is good reason to doubt the older historiography that stressed the *vincolismo* or corporate constraints of Medici political economy. For the traditional view, see Furio Diaz, *Il Granducato di Toscana: i Medici* (Torino: UTET, 1976), 127–148. For work that has redefined our sense of the flexibility of Medici industrial policy, see Malanima, *La decadenza di un'economia cittadina*; idem, 'L'economia toscana nell'età di Cosimo III,' in *La Toscana nell'età di Cosimo III*, ed. F. Angiolini, V. Becagli and M. Verga (Florence: Edifir, 1993), 3–38; idem., 'La Firenze degli artigiani nell'economia Toscana,' in *La grande storia dell' artigianato*, ed. Franco and Gloria Fossi Franceschi (Florence: Giunti, 1998–2002), 5: 25–35; and Luca Molà, 'Artigiani e brevetti nella Firenze del Cinquecento,' in *La grande storia dell' artigianato*, ed. Franceschi, 3: 57–79. See also n. 4 above.

14 Antonio Neri, *Arte vetraria*, ed. Rosa Barovier Mentasti (Milan: Il Polifilo, 1980 [1612]); Guido Taddei, *L'arte del vetro in Firenze e nel suo dominio* (Firenze: Le Monnier, 1954); Francesca Trivellato, *Fondamenta dei vetrai: lavoro, tecnologia e mercato a Venezia tra Sei e Settecento* (Roma: Donzelli, 2000). On the growth in the local glass industry between 1561 and 1642, see Litchfield, *Florence Ducal Capital*, para. 267. On the diversification of glass products and the creation of 'mass consumption' in the seventeenth century, see Trivellato, *Fondamenta dei vetrai*, 138–142. Economic historians have explained the 'inventory gap' in several ways. They have noted that pre-modern manufacturing was labor rather than capital intensive. As a result, fixed capital played a small role in their inventories because shops' assets consisted mostly of stock-in-trade rather than capital goods. Scholars have also argued that big stocks were symptomatic of a weak demand environment: goods accumulated in shops because nobody was buying them. Accordingly, Trivellato found that annual expenditures on shop capital by Murano glassmakers accounted for about 6 or 7 percent of ongoing expenses (ibid., 210–224); cf. Jan De Vries, *Economy of Europe in an Age of Crisis, 1600–1750* (Cambridge: Cambridge University Press, 1976), 86–90.

15 Storing wares in the home was a common practice among early modern shopkeepers. Rosa Tamborrino and Evelyn S. Welch, *Shopping and Housing: Shops, Merchants' Houses and the Market Place in Europe in the Early Modern Age* (Roma: Università Roma Tre, 2008).

16 Tomaso Garzoni, *La piazza universale*, ed. Paolo Cherchi and Beatrice Collina, vol. 2 (Torino: Einaudi, 1996), Discorso LXIV, 869–873. See George W. McClure, *The Culture of Profession in Late Renaissance Italy* (Toronto: University of Toronto Press, 2004).

17 Garzoni, *La piazza universale*, Discorso CXXXI, 1348.

18 On the Italian inventories, see Maria Serena Mazzi, 'Gli inventari dei beni: storia di oggetti e storia di uomini,' *Società e storia* 3 (1980): 203–214; on the stock-flow problem, see in particular Jan De Vries, 'Between Purchasing Power and the World of Goods: Understanding the Household Economy in Early Modern Europe,' in *Consumption and the World of Goods*, ed. Brewer and Porter, 104–106.

19 This paper exploited the records found among the Libri di Commercio e di Famiglia (LCF) in the Archivio di Stato di Firenze (ASF). This large collection comprises letters, journals, and ledgers as well as *ricordanze*.

20 This would not have been true for cities like Livorno, Genoa, and Venice, where the rhythms of the sailing season might have created a bias in favor of cash at certain times of year.

21 Goldthwaite, *The Economy of Renaissance Florence*, ch. 4.

22 See Catharina Lis and Hugo Soly, 'Subcontracting in Guild-Based Export Trades, Thirteenth–Eighteenth Centuries,' in *Guilds, Innovation, and the European Economy*, ed. Epstein and Prak, 81–113.

23 ASF, LCF, 2223.

24 Ibid., 3v.

25 Currently http://chicago.academia.edu/CoreyTazzara.

26 ASF, LCF, 3531. Sales in lire from June 1616 through December 1617: mean = 61; median = 39; standard deviation = 53; coefficient of variation = 0.86.

27 The terms are *rovesciato, pagliato, di comosco,* and *sugerato.*

28 Garzoni, *La piazza universale*, Discorso CXXXI, 1346.

29 Ibid., 1348.

30 Ibid.

31 ASF, LCF, 9. Sales in lire from January 1572 through December 1573: mean = 25; median = 22; standard deviation = 21; coefficient of variation = 0.81. The economies of Chianni and nearby Rivalto for a somewhat later period (beginning in 1629) are discussed in Malanima, *I Riccardi di Firenze*, 144–153.

32 ASF, LCF, 9, 93r.

33 Most people among the middling classes did not own more than one or two pairs of shoes. Ago, *Il gusto delle cose*, 101; Daniel Roche, *The People of Paris: An Essay in Popular Culture in the Eighteenth century* (Berkeley, CA: University of California Press, 1987), 166; Giorgio Riello, *A Foot in the Past. Consumers, Producers and Footwear in the Long Eighteenth Century* (Oxford: Oxford University Press, 2006), 18–29. Riello also argues that some shoemakers amassed substantial inventories of shoes (165). On the diffusion and appearance of shoes, see also Carlo Poni, 'Norms and Disputes'; and Andrea Vianello, 'Maglie e calze,' in *Storia d'Italia, Annali,* ed. Carlo Marco Belfanti and Fabio Giusberti (Torino: Einaudi, 2003).

34 ASF, LCF, 3937. Sales in lire from January 1616 through December 1617: mean = 1126, median = 774, standard deviation = 914; coefficient of variation = 0.81.

35 On the decorative role of leather hangings in wealthy seventeenth-century households, see Ago, *Il gusto delle cose*, ch. 3.

36 Garzoni, *La piazza universale*, Discorso LXXXV, 1038–1040. The brief quotations earlier in the paragraph are from the same source.

37 Ibid., Discorso LXXXVI, 1041.

38 ASF, LCF, 4765. Sales in lire from January 1677 through December 1678: mean = 442, median = 446, standard deviation = 305, coefficient of variation = 0.69. I counted only *deve dare* entries, that is, ordinary payments or extensions of credit. This misses some of the samples he sent out and later marked as 'paid' (*pagato*), but such transactions were both less frequent and of smaller value than other transactions. Interestingly, Signorini seems not to have given a price to the samples ahead of time.

39 Signorini's business strategies resemble those found among luxury artisans in Paris and London during the well-studied eighteenth century, despite a fluctuating demand that belies the seasonal regularities observed in those contexts. Sonenscher suggests that artisanal enterprises grew as much by diversifying products and markets, like Signorini, as by sheer market expansion (*Work and Wages*, 146).

40 Patricia Allerston, 'Clothing and Early Modern Venetian Society,' *Continuity and Change* 15.3 (2000): 367–439; and Laurence Fontaine, ed., *Alternative Exchanges: Second-Hand Circulations from the Sixteenth Century to the Present* (New York: Berghahn Books, 2008).

41 Karl Gunnar Persson, *Grain Markets in Europe, 1500–1600* (Cambridge: Cambridge University Press), 65–72; L. D. Schwarz, *London in the Age of Industrialisation: Entrepreneurs, Labour Force and Living Conditions, 1700–1850* (Cambridge: Cambridge

University Press, 1992), ch. 4. In *Work and Wages*, Michael Sonenscher speaks in ch. 5 of the 'generally erratic rhythms of employment' in the Rouen tailoring trade, typical for other crafts as well (163), and his account of wage variations in ch. 6 tells a similar story. Riello likewise discusses the seasonality of shoe production (*A Foot in the Past*, 188), although his monthly averages for the number of shoes produced by John Edwards between 1751 and 1757 provides evidence for more erratic than seasonal variation (180). I am indebted to Cameron Hawkins for some of these references. His forthcoming book *Work in the City: Roman Artisans and the Urban Economy* models the ancient Roman craft economy through a sensitive reading of industry and craft in eighteenth-century Europe.

42 See my webpage, currently http://chicago.academia.edu/CoreyTazzara, for the evidence.

43 In Florence credit was provided by pawnbrokers such as the Monte di Pietà and by the ubiquitous practice of 'offsetting' in which tradesmen extended small loans to their customers and thereby served as sources of microcredit on the market. Goldthwaite, *The Economy of Renaissance Florence*, 462–463. For Rome, Ago, *Economia barocca*, 57–60, 108–109; for England, Craig Muldrew, *The Economy of Obligation, The Culture of Credit and Social Relations in Early Modern England* (New York: St. Martin's Press, 1998). The articles in *Quaderni storici* 136.2 (2011) are also devoted to credit.

44 On the increase of wealth among the middling sort in the sixteenth century, see Goldthwaite, *The Economy of Renaissance Florence*, 574–582. The seventeenth century is less certain. The development of the silk industry and new luxury production on the one hand, and the decline of the wool industry on the other, probably led to further stratification within the middling class, with some artisans becoming wealthier and most becoming poorer.

45 Ago, *Il gusto delle cose*, 53–54.

46 Diane Owen Hughes, 'Sumptuary Law and Social Relations in Renaissance Italy,' in *Disputes and Settlements*, ed. John Bossy (Cambridge: Cambridge University Press, 1983), 69–99; Giulia Calvi, 'Abito, genere, cittadinanza nella Toscana moderna (secc. XVI–XVII),' *Quaderni storici* 110 (2002): 477–503; Franco Franceschi, 'La normativa suntuaria nella storia economica,' in *Disciplinare il lusso: la legislazione suntuaria in Italia e in Europa tra Medioevo ed Età moderna*, ed. Maria Giuseppina Muzzarelli and Antonella Campanini (Roma: Carocci, 2003). Franceschi makes the point that our understanding of the economic effects of sumptuary legislation, particularly on artisans and shopkeepers, remains in its infancy (171–174). Perhaps the laws that regulated public display served to promote investment in interior spaces?

47 Ago, *Il gusto delle cose*, 37–44. The festivities of the Medici court probably stimulated demand once the court's schedule became known. Not all dealers benefited, however. For example, when the grand duke visited Siena in 1625, his officials 'requested' a donation of goods from the community's Jewish shopkeepers. Giuseppe da Modena had to fork over a pair of sheets, a bed-canopy, a blanket, and a pillow. He claimed that these articles amounted to more than ten *scudi* – 'twice as much as they imposed upon any one else' – for which he was not compensated. Cecil Roth, 'The Memoirs of a Siennese Jew,' *Hebrew Union College Annual* 5 (1928): 361, 379.

48 Sales were highly variable, but does that mean they were unpredictable? It is unlikely that the spending sprees of aristocrats or the movements of the Medici court were known far enough in advance to have enabled Florentine artisans to plan their production schedules ahead of a purchase. Those scholars who have acknowledged the fluctuations of short-term demand have rightly insisted on the importance of information for artisans. Collegial relations, whether through guilds or less formal institutions, helped craftsmen stay abreast of 'fleeting opportunities,' to use Sonenscher's phrase, and possibilities for subcontracting. Nevertheless, although Italian artisans were notorious gabbers, it is doubtful that they could transform rumors of aristocratic spending into definite business plans. Information

swapping was more useful in fulfilling recent orders than in anticipating new ones. Sonenscher, *Work and Wages*, 138. Epstein and Prak emphasize the role that corporate bodies played in providing information about business opportunities and in spreading innovative practices in their introduction to *Craft Guilds*.

49 Giambattista Gelli, *La Circe e i Capricci del bottaio*, ed. Severino Ferrari (Firenze: Sansoni, 1957), 157. The Piedmontese blacksmith Giovan Battista Fongio (1631–1694) did not let severe gout get in the way of his trade but worked without letup during an illness that beset his last twelve years of life. Bice Mortara Garavelli, 'Scrittura popolare: un quaderno di memorie del XVII secolo,' *Rivista Italiana di Dialettologia: scuola società territorio* 3–4.1 (1979–1980): 172.

50 For instance, when Giuseppe purchased a piece of muslin for twenty-three lire from a Donna Fiore Galletti, his lodger Raffaele Nepi stood surety for him. Later, when Raphael went on a trip to Grosetto, Giuseppe gave him some goods from his shop to sell 'at fixed prices.' Raphael sold the goods while he was away, but when he returned to Siena, he refused to turn over the money until Giuseppe had paid back Donna Fiore (thus releasing Raphael from the surety). The lodger's move appeared idiotic to Giuseppe: 'I replied that it was not right for him to do such an affront to me and to avenge himself on me, seeing that he had not yet received either harm or insult from me and that, even though he were to have to pay, he was lodging in my house and could anyhow have deducted what he paid from the rent.' Whatever Raphael's motivations in this episode, it is clear that neither Giuseppe nor Raphael clearly distinguished between shop accounts and personal accounts. Cecil Roth, 'The Memoirs of a Siennese Jew': 367, 385.

51 Welch, *Shopping in the Renaissance*, 147; Paula Hohti, "Conspicuous' Consumption and Popular Consumers: Material Culture and Social Status in Sixteenth-Century Siena,' *Renaissance Studies* 24.5 (2010): 654–670. For England, see Peter Earle, *The Making of the English Middle Class: Business, Society and Family Life in London, 1660–1730* (Berkeley, CA: University of California Press, 1989), 112–114, 120–122. Earle calculates that about 20 percent of the assets of English manufacturers, wholesalers, textile retailers, and artisans came from stock-in-trade in the period 1665–1720. He suggests that the convertibility of their inventory may have been a problem in periods of slack demand, although it seems that it could still have served as collateral for loans, albeit at reduced prices.

52 It is worth contrasting the inventory strategies of these Florentine artisans with modern firms. 'Inventory theory' enables companies to optimize the size of their stocks by minimizing the costs of keeping more goods on hand than necessary (storage costs, lost investment opportunities), on the one hand, and not having enough on the other (lost sales). A key dimension of inventory control is forecasting future demand, however. Although there are methods for predicting demand under uncertain conditions, the certainty of the erratic demand faced by my Florentines is not common enough in the modern world to have merited extensive research; on the contrary, the refrain among inventory scholars is that it is often possible for companies to make educated guesses about future demand. In addition, a critical assumption in most inventory theory is the separation of the finances of the firm from that of the executives. This assumption helps guard against excessively risk-averse decisions by firms, but it does not describe the situation faced by pre-modern artisans. For inventory theory, see the influential textbook by Martin K. Starr and David W. Miller, *Inventory Control: Theory and Practice* (Englewood Cliffs, NJ: Prentice-Hall, 1962).

53 On the active role played by clothiers in developing demand, see Elizabeth Currie, 'Diversity and Design in the Florentine Tailoring Trade, 1550–1620,' in *The Material Renaissance*, ed. O'Malley and Welch, 154–173; idem, 'Fashion Networks: Consumer Demand and the Clothing Trade in Florence from the Mid-Sixteenth to Early Seventeenth Centuries,' *Journal of Medieval and Early Modern Studies* 39.3 (2009): 483–509. This was a problem that even the export-oriented textile industry

had to cope with. Goldthwaite notes that the chief advantage of large size for the silk weaver Jacopo di Tedesco was in being able to offer his clients (*setaioli*) a greater range of products. Goldthwaite, *The Economy of Renaissance Florence*, 333.

54 See Lis and Soly, 'Subcontracting in Guild-Based Export Trades;' Giorgio Riello, 'Strategies and Boundaries: Subcontracting and the London Trades in the Long Eighteenth Century,' *Enterprise and Society* 9.2 (2008): 243–280. Riello argues that subcontracting developed not so much with a rise and diversification of demand in general, but with an increase in the frequency of transactions. One may wonder whether some subcontractors also stockpiled. Subcontracting networks developed to cope with volatility in international markets by allowing a master–entrepreneur to subcontract with other masters during times of great demand. Perhaps he sloughed the problem of volatility onto the shoulders of the lesser artisans who produced for him, some of whom may have faced an environment similar to that of my Florentine artisans: a small number of buyers, an unpredictable demand structure, and a limited range of wares. What did the subcontractor do when business was slow?

PART IV
Empires of things

9

LOCATING RHUBARB

Early modernity's relevant obscurity

Erika Monahan

In the spring of 1653 Fedor Ivanov syn Krisovo, a Russian peasant from the Urals town of Verkhotur'e, petitioned Tsar Aleksei Mikhailovich to reduce his tax burden. He explained that in the past year he had spent so much time assisting state convoys in the search for and extraction of rhubarb that he could not farm his own land enough to meet his tax burdens.[1] That same summer in distant Deptford, England, a gardener named John Evelyn was growing rhubarb in his own one-hundred-acre garden. Evelyn had also spotted it growing in the Oxford Botanic Garden.[2] At first glance these two events do not appear to be remotely connected. John Evelyn and Fedor Krisovo, men of completely different backgrounds with wildly different world views half a world apart, knew nothing of each other. They worked their respective patches of soil with different means and different ends, but their actions share a common denominator: they reflect the growing popularity of rhubarb in early modern Europe.

Locating rhubarb

Today we mostly think of rhubarb as the pleasing filling in pies and jams. However, making those sour stalks taste pleasant requires a heavy dose of sugar, a commodity that was neither widely available nor inexpensive for most of human history, so stalks were not the focus of early modern enthusiasm. Nor were the leaves, which contain oxalic acid, poisonous to humans. This fact was discovered through trial and error, such as in Elizabethan England when rhubarb leaves were tried as table greens. A cook at Versailles, ignorant of their toxicity, allegedly experimented with a soup using rhubarb leaves.[3] We can only wonder what befell that gastronomically bold but probably not regicidal cook. No, it was neither the leaf nor the stalk that early moderns coveted, but the root of the rhubarb plant.

Rhubarb's medicinal history dates to ancient times. Although the oldest Egyptian medicinal text does not mention rhubarb, it does appear in the Greek Dioscorides' seminal *De Materia Medica*, which was written in the first century CE and circulated throughout the Christian and what became Muslim worlds in Ancient and medieval times. At the other end of Eurasia, knowledge of rhubarb's medicinal value may have dated back farther; rhubarb is listed in the earliest Chinese herbal, *The Divine Farmer's Materia Medica* (*Shen Nong Ben Cao Jing*), which was probably compiled between 300 BCE and 200 CE.[4] Both texts prescribe rhubarb to treat a wide range of maladies, from hypochondria to sciatica, malaria to nosebleeds.[5] The thirteenth-century polymath from Andalusia, Ibn al-Baitar (d. 1248), included among rhubarb's medicinal benefits 'strengthening the stomach, improving its smell, softening the faeces, cessation of thirst and vomiting,[6] relieving jaundice, regulating the heart beat and improving the appetite.'[7] In Christian Europe it was used to treat all manner of illness, including jaundice, various skin complaints, fevers, even syphilis. It was also used as a diuretic and accompanied most bloodletting treatments in seventeenth-century France.[8]

But where rhubarb really earned its mass appeal was in the gastrointestinal business, as a gentle purgative. Dioscorides had credited rhubarb with acting 'against laxity' and al-Baitur acknowledged that rhubarb could 'strengthen the stomach' and 'softened the faeces' but neither considered it foremost as a laxative or purgative. The Greeks understood rhubarb's binding abilities, but not its purgative properties. The evacuative attribute became most strongly associated with rhubarb imported from the Far East. Gradually – over the course of the twelfth to the fourteenth centuries – it became recognized that the rhubarb that came from the east was far more potent than the rhubarb of Dioscorides.[9] For example, by the early sixteenth century when the Portuguese doctor Garcia d'Orta visited Samarkand, a flourishing market in Central Asia to which Chinese merchants had brought rhubarb since at least the fourteenth century, he reported that 'lesser' sorts of rhubarb grew in the region of Samarkand, indicating his awareness of varying potencies among different rhubarb species.[10]

This Chinese rhubarb was not just any purgative. What made this rhubarb so special was its combined aperient *and* astringent qualities: it catalyzed a catharsis that was followed by constipation – a little binding action on the end (astringent). Paradoxically, rhubarb could effect essentially opposite actions – relieving diarrhea (small dose) and cleansing the system (larger dose). These qualities made it nothing short of a wonder drug. In early modern medicine generally the power of the cleansing principle reigned supreme. Laxatives, purging, and bloodletting were prescribed for most maladies: rhubarb was used in all three. Relative to other purgatives, it was popular for being effective yet mild enough that small children and pregnant women could take it.[11] Thus, rhubarb's particular characteristics in the midst of widespread market demand set the stage for a highly coveted, albeit extremely distant, commodity.

Obstacles other than distance complicated definitively 'locating' rhubarb. Rhubarb was accompanied by uncertainties that challenged entrepreneurs and horticulturalists alike. To begin with, making sense of the various names applied to rhubarb requires some untangling.[12] Geography informed the naming of rhubarb in ways that could confuse as much as clarify. The rhubarb known to ancient Greeks was named based on presumed origin, but by the sixteenth and seventeenth centuries appellations generally reflected the trade route it traveled to European markets: Turkish, Indian, Chinese, and Russian rhubarb sold at European markets was probably often the same species and had come from China.[13] Although the name only reflected the route traveled, that route could impart meaningful qualitative differences, even for rhubarb of the same sort. For example, the Russian state established a rhubarb monopoly and instituted a quality control system (called the *brak*) that resulted in 'Russian' rhubarb garnering the highest prices and best reputation in eighteenth-century Europe.[14] Astute buyers knew that Russian rhubarb came from China (*Rhubarbus palmatum*) but having traversed Russia added real value.

Confusions about rhubarb were hardly limited to transit route. Botanical unknowns stumped enthusiastic naturalists and mercantilists for centuries. Ambassadors to China, medics in Central Asia, missionaries traversing Eurasia, and trade agents in India brought back conflicting or ambiguous reports on the question of whether medicinal rhubarb grew only in the wild or was cultivated.[15] Part of the problem was that different species of rhubarb existed. Determining what was *Rha rhabarbarum*, *Rheum officinale*, 'true rhubarb,' *R. rhaponticum*, *R. palmatum*, *R. undulatum*, etc. made for a complicated story. From the seventeenth to nineteenth centuries naturalists and druggists struggled to determine which variety or varieties was/were 'true rhubarb,' identifying over fifty different species that spanned much of the globe in the process. Pharmacological challenges were no less acute than botanical ones. Chinese rhubarb had long been brought to the markets of the Near East and Mediterranean in miniscule quantities.[16] Demand for it accelerated when it became clear that Chinese rhubarb held the desired potency. What remained unclear, however, was just what made Chinese rhubarb so effective – a question that would remain unanswered well into the nineteenth century.[17]

Indeed, the state of early modern technology made species identification, to say nothing of manipulation or application, a substantive challenge. Before the first documented chemical analyses of rhubarb were done in 1803, appearance, color, smell, and taste were the merchant's and the druggist's best tools of recognition.[18] Lacking modern tools of preservation, representation, reproduction, and communication, even the matter of physical description was not trivial. Early modern botanists–horticulturalists sometimes had samples, but often relied only on descriptions and drawings by others in order to make their classifications. The vagaries of transport and dehydration easily rendered samples unrecognizable. Indeed, rhubarb was typically sold in dehydrated form after being dried by various processes: Mongols reportedly hung it on their sheep's

FIGURE 9.1   English apothecary jar for Imperial Pills, laxative containing rhubarb, 1675

horns and let it dry in the wind and sun of steppe pasture.[19] Obviously, the problem of recognition made merchants vulnerable and they armed themselves at market with descriptions of how to identify good rhubarb.[20] Ultimately, dried rhubarb root would make its way to some European apothecary's shop where the druggist would pulverize it and mix rhubarb root powder with other substances to prepare a tincture or pill that patients would then purchase and take in the apothecary shop (Figure 9.1). Given rhubarb's great expense – the most expensive purges in Italian apothecaries were made with rhubarb – clients with ties to long-distance commerce who were trying to economize might obtain the rhubarb for their prescribed tincture or pill directly and bring it to the apothecary themselves.[21]

As if visual recognition, species variation, preservation and transport were not challenging enough, variations in potency among individual plants and during phases of growth, medical practices, and patient particulars left much wiggle room in determining definitively rhubarb's efficacy. The apothecary's expertise and/or integrity was another variable at which the following seventeenth-century verse took aim:

His Skill in *Physick* did his Fame advance,
Tho some accuse him of dull Ignorance:
Powder of Post may sometimes do the Trick,
As well as *Rhubarb, Senna, Agarick*;
For let the sad Disease be what it will,
The Patients Faith helps more than Doctors Skill;[22]

Such difficulties were as daunting as they were typical in the development of botanical taxonomy and knowledge of medicinal plants in the early modern period. Early modern medicine was always a fuzzy business, and such challenges did not keep demand for rhubarb from rising.

Growing demand

Though knowledge about rhubarb's properties only crept along, consumption exploded in the early modern period. Like most commodities of long-distance medieval trade, rhubarb consumption was initially concentrated in elite niches. Rhubarb appears routinely in lists of court expenses for the Kingdom of Aragon in the fourteenth century.[23] An elixir containing rhubarb powder was administered to England's failing Henry VIII in the sixteenth century.[24] The Scottish doctor to the royal court in Moscow prescribed rhubarb for Prince Mikhail Dolgorukov in December 1665.[25] But in the early modern period, exclusive consumption patterns began to broaden as more Europeans became global consumers. Imports and consumption rose significantly throughout the sixteenth and seventeenth centuries. In seventeenth-century England, rhubarb consumption increased as the use of imported curatives became more common. In the late sixteenth century a small fraction (estimated 14 percent) of drugs were imported to England from outside Europe. By 1669, despite nativization efforts, 70 percent of pharmaceutical drugs in Britain were imported, mostly from India and the East Indies.[26] In the early eighteenth century the British East India Company imported over 10,000 lbs. of rhubarb annually. In the next decades London imports averaged more than 18,000 lbs. per annum, peaking in 1768 at about 67,764 lbs.[27] If a typical rhubarb dose was 1 dram, or about 4 grams, such a volume of import could have supplied approximately 30.7 million grams or nearly eight million doses.[28]

Growing popular demand was not confined to England.[29] Rhubarb appears as one of the top fifteen commodities in an inventory from an apothecary in early sixteenth-century Italy.[30] Venetian merchants continued to seek rhubarb in the markets of Aleppo, while in Russia commercial agents from England, Sweden, The Netherlands, Italy, and the Ottoman Empire kept their nose to the ground for inside information on the rhubarb trade.[31] Rhubarb sailed from St. Petersburg to northern European ports while Greek merchants bought rhubarb in Moscow to resell in Constantinople.[32] Meanwhile, the Dutch East India Company (Vereenigde Oost-Indische Compagnie, or VOC) and British East India Company (EIC) competed with the Russian state's overland trade for rhubarb market share. In recent years, scholarship eschewing Eurocentrism has challenged the traditional interpretation that the emergence of global maritime trade effected the decline of Eurasian caravan trade.[33] The case of rhubarb may offer an instructive example for the debates in the 'decline' thesis, for this commodity may have traveled better by land than sea. Historian Wilhelm Heyd reported that merchants preferred to transport rhubarb over land despite available maritime options.[34] At the end of the sixteenth century Dutchman Jan van Linschoten directly averred that rhubarb that traveled over land 'is most esteemed & best sold.'[35] Nonetheless, many company men filled their return ship-carriage allotments from India with rhubarb: private decisions that reflect the profitability of the rhubarb trade.[36]

Profitable it was. Rhubarb was among the most expensive drugs and it grew more expensive as it moved westward. In Siberia, rhubarb could cost 10 or 18 rubles per pud (1 pud weighs 36.1 lbs., slightly more than four gallons of water), which was about three times what a home, a camel, a fine horse, or a slave could cost. The precious root cost easily five times that in Moscow and many times more than that in Western Europe.[37] An Italian Jesuit Matteo Ricci, who lived in Macao from 1582 to 1601, reported that in Peking one could 'buy a pound of rhubarb for ten cents, which in Europe would cost six or seven times as many gold pieces.'[38] Another Italian, P. A. Mattioli, asserted that rhubarb was worth its weight in gold. In Renaissance Florence a pound of rhubarb could retail at almost 6,000 soldi per pound, which was almost seven times as expensive as manna and eighty times as expensive as pudding pipe, other popular purgatives.[39]

The increased demand for rhubarb was a European-wide phenomenon. Typical of many introduced and exotic commodities (e.g. tea, coffee, pineapple) that often retain the same word across multiple languages, the word for rhubarb in most European languages was quite similar. Although it bears no resemblance to the Chinese term *da huang*, it was usually translated as some variation derived from the Ancient Greek appellation, *Rha barbarer*, meaning 'from the barbarian lands beyond the Volga': *rabarber* in Dutch, Danish, Estonian, and Polish; *rhubarbe* in French; *rabarbaro* in Italian; *ruibarbo* in Spanish and Portuguese.[40] Reminding us that language is historically contingent is the Greek example. The contemporary Greek word for rhubarb is *raventi*, which bears little resemblance to the cognates it helped birth. Rather, *raventi* is similar to the Turkish form, *ravent*. *Raventi*, understandably, seems to have found its way into the Greek language during the period of Ottoman control post-1453.[41] However, since the Greek language persisted, it was not a foregone conclusion that the word for rhubarb would become Turkish; the geography of commerce helps explain these cognate appellations. *Raventi* resembles the terms of its neighbors to the north and east: in Persian, rhubarb is *rewas* and in Russian, *reven'*.[42] Much Persian trade moved westward through the Ottoman Empire in times of war and peace. In the sixteenth century Russia had more extensive commercial relations with the Muslim world than Christendom.[43] Indeed, English merchant Arthur Edwards, scoping out the commercial scene in Persia in 1566, advised the directors of the Muscovy Company in London that they should have someone 'on the ground' in Persia who knew Russian.[44] This example invites consideration of ways in which the shifting orientation of economic and political hegemony away from the Mediterranean and Near Eastern worlds mapped itself onto linguistic idiosyncrasies.

Rhubarb's efficacy alone did not assure its market success. Rather, its ascendance reflected the convergence of numerous monumental developments that define early modern dynamism and helped catapult this exotic medicinal to the forefront of apothecary inventories. European markets were increasingly stimulated by increased supply of Eastern products and increased consumer spending. Overland trade caravans and newly established maritime trading companies delivered increasing supplies of rhubarb. Global commercial expansion fed and was fed by developments in Europe that further stimulated demand for rhubarb. Importantly, new discretionary spending facilitated emergent patterns of consumption, of which more apothecaries were one manifestation.[45]

A host of interrelated developments helped channel consumer choices to the apothecary's shop. Emergent imperialism along with the development of scientific thinking and the popularization of natural sciences like botany transformed the intellectual landscape. Entrepreneurial investors, collection-obsessed elites, and naturalists alike attended keenly to new developments at the farthest reaches of global discovery. For its part, scientific discovery often occurred outside the laboratory, as taxonomy was young and the whole world presented itself to be catalogued. Thus began a botanical revolution as naturalists and botanists endeavored to name, catalogue, reproduce, and understand all manner of flora and fauna. The increase in scientific study of the natural world stimulated the growth of medicinal knowledge, which in turn galvanized the discovery of new treatments, and commercial opportunities were not far behind. The popularization of the printing press also played a role, enabling broader dissemination of medical knowledge (Figure 9.2). More herbal and pharmaceutical guides were produced – the Smithsonian Institute libraries' digital collection has compiled a list of 149 herbals published between 1470 and 1745, and this list is incomplete – fixing declarations of rhubarb's efficacy in print and helping to channel consumer choices.[46] '[F]or purging this rhubarb is the best herb of all other purgatives,' read one fifteenth-century Florentine herbal.[47] Although more famous for describing the novel coffee plant, the Italian physician–botanist Prospero Alpini also composed *De rhapontico*, a treatise devoted to rhubarb, in the early seventeenth century.[48] In this way, pharmacological knowledge disseminated via print technology and urban apothecaries helped drive demand for the distant root.

Managing rhubarb

It was in this context that this sour-stalked tuber became the object of an English gardener's and Siberian peasant's digging in the dirt. John Evelyn, along with other seventeenth-century gardners, had a hard time producing medicinally potent rhubarb. In such failures to reproduce 'true rhubarb,' the Russian state found opportunity. If Europe could not properly grow potent medicinal rhubarb, it would have to import it from the east. Russia, so famously poised

FIGURE 9.2 Sixteenth-century German imperial broadsheet advertising the wonders of rhubarb

between Europe and Asia, endeavored to profit considerably by facilitating East–West transit trade. By the middle of the seventeenth century the Russian leadership had noted that the price of rhubarb increased fivefold from Siberia to Moscow and even more abroad. Considering it a good investment, the state regulated the rhubarb trade by instituting policies that fluctuated between a monopsony and a monopoly on rhubarb for over two centuries. The state was so serious about garnering the rhubarb trade that it decreed the death penalty for anyone caught smuggling the precious root. Practice, predictably for an over-extended empire, was less draconian; for example, when merchants caught with illicit rhubarb in Siberia in 1656 explained that they had not heard about the law, customs officials merely confiscated the rhubarb and allowed the 'smugglers' to proceed freely.[49]

The Russian state did not limit its enterprising efforts to the regulation of trade. It also sought to procure rhubarb domestically, which is how our Siberian peasant Fedor ended up on rhubarb detail. He was commandeered to help in the state's attempt to source rhubarb within the empire's borders. The domestic procurement program was ultimately unsuccessful because the rhubarb growing wild in Siberia didn't have the right medicinal punch.[50] Ironically, the rhubarb that did grow so well and wild in Siberia – which Russian soldier–Cossack bands, with the help of peasants like Fedor, actually harvested but ultimately rejected – was a predecessor to or variant of *Rhaponticum*, the rhubarb sort that has become the popular pie plant. In fact, an early recipe for rhubarb tart, mailed from England to America in 1739, called specifically for 'Siberian stalks.'[51] Although prevalent, *Rhaponticum* was not what early modern consumers wanted. *Rhaponticum* would have its day in the sun (even as it grows best with healthy doses of shade) but that was still far off in the future while Fedor was digging up Siberian plants.

Following rhubarb in and across the Russian empire sheds light on the vast geographic extent of the rhubarb trade and on the nature of Muscovy's integration into European culture and economy. Rhubarb entered on the Eurasian steppes of the southern Siberian border towns or Astrakhan. That which was not used domestically, which was probably most of it, was re-exported through Astrakhan, routes to Poland, or Arkhangel'sk and later, St. Petersburg. History books long presented Russia as isolated from Europe and the rest of the world until that innovating tempest, Peter the Great, opened a 'window on the West.' In fact, many channels connected Russia to its neighbors prior to the Great Westernizer Peter I. Novgorod and the Bulgar kingdom on the Volga River were part of trade networks that supplied 'to all ends of the earth' in the medieval period.[52] Fine sables from (what became) Russian lands graced the elite courts of Christendom and Dar es Salaam, and lower classes donned squirrel pelts well before the discovery of the New World.[53] In the sixteenth century, Russian forest products essential to the bourgeoning maritime industry – hemp, tar, potash – supplied the tacking for the British navy and East India companies, which meant that Muscovy was already fairly integrated into the European economy in the seventeenth century.[54] While forest products dominated Muscovy's export profile, rhubarb was also part of the mix. In 1568 an English ship sailed from Arkhangel'sk with 20 pounds of rhubarb in its hold.[55] Finally, Russia played a role in decisive developments in the early modern commercial scene. Even though it would be overshadowed by the East India Company, the Muscovy Company, founded in 1555 by Englishmen looking to pass through Muscovy en route to the riches of the Orient, was the first joint-stock trading company Europeans formed.[56]

The Russian state's policies towards rhubarb – establishment of a monopoly, domestic procurement program, quality control system – demonstrate the Russian state operating according to mercantilist principles that animated western European empires. It took the interventionist step of establishing a state monopoly in an effort to channel revenue to state coffers. It instituted a program to source rhubarb domestically in order to minimize specie export. While domestic procurement proved unsuccessful, the Russian state had more success increasing rhubarb profits through its inspection system, known as the *brak*. Beginning in the early eighteenth century, rhubarb was inspected upon import and again when leaving Russia for Europe; unfit specimens were destroyed. Consequently, as noted above, 'Russian rhubarb' garnered the highest prices in European markets.[57] Most basically, the lexical existence of coveted 'Russian rhubarb' throughout Europe illustrates contact between Europe and Muscovy.

Relative to rhubarb's transit through the Russian empire, much less is known about rhubarb's use in Russia. If the popularity rhubarb enjoyed in early modern Europe was not *as* widespread in Russia – a hypothesis based on absences which may be due more to sources than practice[58] – the picture of domestic use of rhubarb in Russia may present an example of the limits of integration. We know that expatriate European doctors at the Russian court prescribed rhubarb in the seventeenth century. Samuel Collins, personal physician to Tsar Aleksei Mikhailovich from 1659–1666, wrote a prescription for Prince Mikhail Dolgorukov in December 1665.[59] A prescription for rhubarb by a different European doctor written for the Princess Maria Alekseevna in January 1674 also survives in the Apothecary archive in Moscow.[60] That prescriptions for rhubarb were written by expatriate court physicians demonstrates that Muscovites appreciated certain Western ways even as the doctors' expatriate status and the lack of additional evidence of rhubarb's medicinal use in Russia suggests a lack of cultural integration. By a similar token, efforts to find and cultivate rhubarb place Russia on the map of the 'republic of letters' of botanists and naturalists sharing seeds and information about valuable and newly discovered flora.[61] However, it was expatriate Europeans in Russia that dominated those early modern correspondences.

Some clues suggest a variety of domestic uses for rhubarb in Russia. Archdeacon Paul of Aleppo visited Moscow in the 1650s and reported that Russians drank glasses of vodka with small chunks of rhubarb root in it for their good health (demonstrating the food–medicine hybridity discussed below).[62] Croatian exile Yuri Krizhanich, however, also writing during Tsar Aleksei Mikhailovich's reign, listed rhubarb as a dye, not a medicine.[63] Russians reportedly used rhubarb to dye wool. Although the practice does not seem to have been widespread, rhubarb was also used as a dye in German lands. Rhubarb was used as a red, and possibly yellow, colorant to illuminate the fifteenth-century German manuscript *Barlaam and Josephat*.[64]

While rhubarb's profitability to the state lay in its role as a transit medicinal commodity, it is unlikely that rhubarb was only ferried across the Russian empire. Interestingly, two types of rhubarb (*kopytchatyi* and *cherenkovyi*) were trafficked through Russia, according to Russian customs records. Even after it became clear which sort (*kopytchatyi*) was the highly valued medicinal rhubarb, the lesser sort (*cherenkovyi* = *Rhapontic*) continued to appear in customs records, together with and independent of the more valuable sort. There is the possibility that merchants tried to disguise the *cherenkovyi* as the official Chinese rhubarb. Adulteration and smuggling seem to be cost-cutting measures as old as commerce itself. However, the idea that all the *cherenkovyi* recorded at customs posts was passed off as *kopytchatyi and* that Russian rhubarb maintained its premiere reputation in such competitive markets seems to attribute far too much savvy to the smugglers and too little to the consumers. Perhaps merchants continued to ship the *cherenkovyi* rhubarb repeatedly found in customs post declarations because it enjoyed a certain demand, perhaps as the rhubarb Russians used as dye, tanning agent, or veterinary medicine.[65] Perhaps these uses did not require the particular potency of Chinese rhubarb and were satisfied by the lesser sort. While the matter of domestic consumption requires further research I suspect that the 222 lbs. (6 puds and 5 pounds) of Crown rhubarb sold in state-owned apothecaries in 1777 does not account for all domestic consumption.[66]

As noted above, Russia was not the only nation to pursue nativization in the seventeenth century.[67] Indeed, both John Evelyn and the Russian state, in their efforts to domesticate a profitable commodity, were typical of their mercantilist age. And they had much company in their failure to successfully domesticate rhubarb. In the eighteenth century the Swedish botanist Carolus Linnaeus called for European countries to domesticate rhubarb, and the British Society of Arts patronized that objective by distributing seeds and offering prizes (money and gold medals) for the best rhubarb grown in order to 'benefit the nation and all mankind by stimulating inventiveness, industry, and commerce.'[68] Despite such incentives the effort to nativize 'Chinese' rhubarb remained unrealized. The journal of *Economic Botany* in 1947 reported that, 'For rhubarb root we still look to China.'[69]

The reason that rhubarb nativization efforts failed has much to do with the nature of the plant itself. For much of the eighteenth century botanists puzzled over what – soil, climate, age of individual plants, or genetic/ontological variation – accounted for a failure to cultivate on European soil a rhubarb with the same look and potency of Chinese rhubarb.[70] They gradually came to understand that rhubarb tends not to breed 'true.' This proclivity towards bastardization not only made the establishment of an accurate botanical genealogy more challenging, but could also complicate each of the problems enumerated above.[71]

From medicine to food

Alongside the story of the rise and ultimate decline of rhubarb roots, rhubarb underwent an identity shift – from medicinal root to sour-stalked food ingredient, with a protracted period in which it was recognized as both.[72] In broad strokes, in Ancient and medieval times rhubarb root was medicine and from around the eighteenth century rhubarb stalks have been a food. For the most part these are separate stories, for the potent root that was used for medicine did not come from the same variety of plant whose sour stalks were stewed for pies and tarts. Where these separate stories do intersect is in Siberia: the rhubarb that has become popular as a pie plant was a version of the rhubarb cultivated and rejected by the Russian state as the true medicinal rhubarb. Recall that the earliest known rhubarb tart recipe called for 'Siberian rhubarb.'

Although this chapter is most concerned with the intense interest of early moderns in medicinal rhubarb and the vast lengths they went to in order to obtain it, it is worth considering briefly how rhubarb transitioned to a food item.

In a word, sugar largely accounts for rhubarb's reinvention as a dessert food. In the fifteenth century Europeans may have consumed on average one teaspoon of sugar each year.[73] That changed dramatically over the next two centuries, as sugar went from exotic to quotidian on the commodity continuum. Between the 1660s and 1750s total sugar exports to Europe grew by 2.2 percent per annum, more than doubling the per capita sugar consumption in France and Britain. By the 1770s the volume of New World sugar shipments to Europe alone measured over four times the volume of all Asian goods shipped to Europe.[74] Indeed, by the eighteenth century New World plantations had begun to feed (and simultaneously rot) the 'sweet tooth' of the European commoner. It is no coincidence that it is in this same century that the first sweet rhubarb recipes appear, such as the above-mentioned tart recipe calling for the stalks of 'Siberian rhubarb,' which was mailed across the Atlantic Ocean in 1739.[75] Thus, from the eighteenth century onward, recipes for tarts, pies, compotes, and other sweet concoctions gradually began to supplant the common notion of rhubarb's purpose. Sugar's diffusion from the exotic to quotidian ferried rhubarb's transformation from medicine to food.

But it was not quite that cut and dry. One does find rhubarb described concurrently as food and medicine in Mediterranean medieval Europe. It seems to have made its way into European kitchens first via Muslim Spain. A thirteenth-century cookbook from Andalusia contains two recipes for beverages calling for Chinese rhubarb; they are descriptively titled 'The Great Drink of Roots' and 'The Great Cheering Syrup.'[76] This Andalusian cookbook likely drew on well-established food ways from the Arabic world. Centuries earlier and far to the east a tenth-century 'cookbook' from the Abbasid empire, the *Kitab al-Tabikh*, contains several recipes that call for rhubarb.[77] Tellingly, much of the cookbook is organized not according to types of foods or meal genres, as modern customs prescribe, but according to recipes appropriate to treating various health ailments. Rhubarb is typically mentioned in chapters dealing with humoral health. 'Juice of rhubarb (*ribas*) is astringent and good for yellow bile,' it instructs,[78] and adds that 'rhubarb is cold and dry. It controls bowel movements and quenches yellow bile and blood.'[79] Chapter six, on 'Foods recommended for the Young and the Elderly,' suggests that 'a person whose dominant humor is yellow bile may eat...ribasiyya (stew soured with rhubarb)'[80] (while some recipes are not at all sweet, ribasiyya did call for some sugar, though the dish was sour overall[81]). Thus the question is not whether rhubarb was either food or medicine: it was both.

Italy, stereotypically cutting-edge in fine cuisine, appreciated rhubarb as food earlier than most of Europe. The chef Bartolomeo Scappi served rhubarb root to the clerical elite both as a vegetable and in a thick soup.[82] Meanwhile, the Badia of Florence purchased purgative pills of rhubarb from a nearby apothecary several times in the 1490s.[83] Consumption was not confined to elite clerics and monks. When a sixteenth-century Italian woman wrote to a friend recommending Indian rhubarb to treat a fever, she differentiated it from the rhubarb used for cooking, demonstrating that both conceptions were possibilities in Renaissance Italy.[84] Only gradually did recipes containing rhubarb make their way north. The earliest northern European recipe calling for rhubarb I have encountered is a seventeenth-century recipe for the beverage meade.[85] In the late eighteenth century, a time when rhubarb sold speedily at local markets to Londoners who made sweet tarts from it, a book on Ancient cookery was published in England; it contains a recipe for 'An excellent approved medicine both for the stomach and head of an elderly person' that contains rhubarb.[86]

What all these examples so clearly demonstrate is that food and medicine were not neatly distinct categories in the pre-modern world. Just as *Merchants and Marvels* demonstrated that we do better to abandon stark dichotomies between science and art in the early modern world, this examination into cookery has the same message for the categories of cuisine and medicine.[87] We moderns recognize that eating well is important for good health, but beyond what would be deemed alternative niches, food is not medicine. In the pre-modern period it very much was. Not all medicine was food (think witches' brews of special stones and lark eyelashes, etc.). Food, on the other hand, was quite typically medicine, considered not with respect to calories or nutrients (a twentieth-century neologism) but in terms of its effects on physical health, typically according to Gallenic theories of humoral health.

Sugar accounts for why rhubarb stalks became a food, but it does not account for why rhubarb stopped being a medicine. Despite all of its desirable and arguably survivalist qualities – a highly adaptable morphology should bode well for species survival and reproduction, should it not? – rhubarb did not retain its place as an internationally traded commodity of major importance. Why not? In answering this question the matter of rhubarb's history may help illuminate an underappreciated aspect of the rise of capitalism.

In part, the explanation lies in rhubarb's biology. Though one author affectionately describes rhubarb as a plant that resisted being known or tamed – a 'wondrous drug' that refused to offer up its essence[88] – such characteristics only frustrated early modern botanists. For starters, rhubarb bastardized easily. It manifested differently at different altitudes, in different soils and climates. As a result, attempts to determine species type and efficacy were repeatedly confounded because the same plant transplanted and subjected to different conditions could change substantially. Seeds were particularly susceptible to bastardization. It took early botanists quite some time to understand that the plant reproduced 'more true,' that is, more like its parent, by planting sprigs instead of seeds. In modern times, most people who have planted rhubarb have probably done so by digging up the plant from a friend's garden to replant in a new place. Yet, what is common wisdom for us was hard won in ages without photographic reproduction or rapid transportation. When written descriptions, drawings, or long dead specimens that shrank and deteriorated during transcontinental transport were the best resources that botanists, gardeners, and doctors had as reference, determining generational metamorphosis was no trivial task. The pace of growth further put rhubarb at odds with modernity's checklist of horticultural desirability. One plant would take four to nine years to mature to a point where its roots contained a desirable medicinal potency. In other words, it was the plant's fault.

But the nature of the plant accounts for only part of the explanation. These qualities became insurmountable disadvantages in the context of an emerging capitalist system. Rhubarb's particularities meant that rhubarb did not lend itself to large-scale, systematic, controllable, predictable reproduction. The long turnaround time for a rhubarb plant to reach a profitable efficacy made it a harder choice in which to invest capital. Even incentives to investment offered by some botanical societies, whose mission statements would hardly have stood up to venture capitalist scrutiny, were insufficient to ensure sustained entrepreneurial efforts at mass production. As processes of production became systematized, regularity and predictability became increasingly important. It was far more efficient to transport and plant seeds than sprigs. Recall that it was not the product but the *process* that made Henry Ford's Model T so successful, and garnered that thoroughly modern capitalist his fortune. Plants conducive to systematic, large-scale production, such as corn, were the agricultural equivalent of Ford's Model T.[89] To make a closer comparison, in the seventeenth century, rhubarb and tobacco were commodities of comparable market importance. Centuries later, the notion that the two plants might hold comparable market significance sounds absurd.[90] Tobacco, like corn, with its regularity and reproductive predictability, is highly conducive to large-scale plantation production. Rhubarb is not.

Of course, another possible explanation for rhubarb's obsolescence is that a better or equivalent substitute emerged. Indeed, it is impressive that the root's medicinal popularity spanned so many centuries, even into modern times. Still consonant with Ancient and medieval understandings, the late eighteenth-century *Universal Dictionary on Trade and Commerce* lauded rhubarb root for its:

> double virtue of a cathartic and astringent; it readily evacuates particularly the bilious humors, and afterwards gently astringes and strengthens the stomach and intestines. It is given with great success in all obstructions of the liver, in the jaundice, in diarrhoeas, and in the fluor albus and gonorrhoeas; it is also an excellent remedy against worms. It is sometimes given as a purgative, sometimes as only an alterant; and which way ever it is taken it is an excellent medicine, agreeing with almost all ages and constitutions.[91]

More than a century later, in the age of modern chemical laboratories and drug development, and despite attempts at synthetic production, no obvious alternative had yet emerged. Numerous pharmaceutical guides of the late nineteenth and early twentieth centuries continued to regard rhubarb as an important medicine, 'used in large amounts, having been long accepted as a household remedy in syrup and tincture form the world throughout.' With an endorsement that echoes Guido Panciroli's enthusiasm (see below), one 1921 guide reads, 'Rhubarb is one of the great gifts of empiricism to the medical profession.'[92] Even after World War II (WWII), chemists still wrote that, '[f]or rhubarb root, we still look to China.'[93] It was only later in the twentieth century that scientists developed reliable purgative alternatives.

Concurrently, modern chemists looked for alternative product ends for rhubarb. One such opportunity arose from the fact that lemon juice cleaned teeth wonderfully but unfortunately its ascorbic acid (like Coca Cola) also dissolved teeth. In post-WWII America some saw in the lemon's fatal flaw an opportunity for rhubarb when it was discovered that the oxalate in rhubarb counteracted the corrosive properties of lemon juice. In 1947, the *Science News Letter* optimistically speculated, '[a]t present no one can anticipate how much these discoveries will expand the market for rhubarb and its juice, but a new industry may arise...'[94] Alas, in the modern West, rhubarb has yet to be decoupled from sugar, so it maintains its new identity as a food, in a niche at odds with excellent dental hygiene.

The importance of rhubarb

Commodities' histories are not new, but they have enjoyed something of a renaissance in recent years, focusing on culture surrounding a particular commodity rather than on traditional economic indicators like price and volume. In this sense 'commodity' refers not to the bulk goods of commodities markets but to particular objects whose pathways and life ways authors intricately explicate. Recent commodity studies generally follow one of two different narratives. First, there is the story of a commodity that moves from exotic to quotidian. These histories explain how an object that holds a basic and ubiquitous place in our quotidian affairs was once upon a time a rare and exotic product. Academic and popular presses have produced studies on commodities such as sugar, coffee, chocolate, tobacco, and the potato following this narrative line.[95] The second main narrative charts the move from precious to obsolete. Authors identify a product that once was quite important to many people, an object of competition and desire, but is now essentially unknown. Examples of these studies include cochineal, musk, and ostrich feathers.[96] Historians value these histories of obsolescence – the history of ignorance and absence, explanations of what got left behind and why. They remind us of lost possibilities, projects unpursued, of trajectories not taken. And historians – through training or inclination – intrinsically recognize a value in that.

The story traced in this chapter fits neither of these typical narratives, but nevertheless this root's history illuminates fundamental early modern economic and cultural changes.[97] Rhubarb was accompanied by a certain obscurity in early modern times, not because it was unimportant, but because it was perplexing, as shown above. In early modern texts, however, rhubarb is anything but obscure. It was a valuable medicine embedded in time and tension, place and process, indifferent to the historian's scrutiny and understanding, just like other historical people, places, and things. One need not dig deep in the early modern Eastern travel literature to find rhubarb. In 1403 the Castillian King Henry III sent his ambassador Ruy Gonzales de Clavijo to Samarkand, who reported back that he encountered there, 'silks, which are the best in the world, (more especially the satins), and musk, which is found in no other part of the world, rubies and diamonds, pearls and rhubarb, and many other things.'[98] From their first forays into Russian lands in the mid-sixteenth century, the English Muscovy Company wanted to gain access to the East. In 1620 when the Russian boyars asked English Muscovy Company representative John Merrick why the English desired transit access to Persia, he answered that, among other things, they wanted to buy 'silk, dyes, rhubarb' and other products, in that order.[99] As a rule, early modern travelers to the Far East – Jesuits no less than ambassadors – did not fail to include rhubarb in their observations.[100] They recorded where they found it, where they purchased it, what they learned of its trafficking and processing. The Jesuit Matteo Ricci, mentioned above, reported on the price of rhubarb in Peking.'[101] Another Jesuit, Diego de Pantoia, in 1601 wrote a letter to Spain reporting that 'Turkes and Moores' brought rhubarb to Peking to sell and exchange. Michel Boym, a Polish Jesuit who lived in China from 1643–1659, left a detailed description of rhubarb's appearance and methods of processing along with a detailed picture of rhubarb growing *in situ*. The Jesuit Ferdinand Verbiest traveled in Tartary in 1683 and noted that Uzbeks and Mongols had rhubarb.[102] In the 1710s the Scottish doctor John Bell reported his rhubarb sightings in Eurasia.[103] Russian ambassadors en route to China consistently kept their eyes out for rhubarb.[104] In fact, rhubarb literally defined the bounds of China for one Russian ambassador who traveled to China 1654–1658. The report submitted to the tsar said of the Great Wall: 'And that wall goes from rhubarb China, where the root of *"kopytchatoi"* rhubarb grows...across the Chinese kingdom to the sea.'[105] Travelers to the New World were similarly on the lookout for rhubarb. In 1541 the Genovese Pascual Cataño brought the Iberian merchant-scholar Nicolás Monardes a new rhubarb that he had found in New Spain, an 'excellent medicine' called 'rhubarb of Mechoacan.'[106] A law professor from Padua, Guido Panciroli (1523–1599), at the end of the sixteenth century, took inventory of what the world had gained and lost in his *The History of Many Memorable Things Lost...and An Account of many Excellent Things Found*. Of his twenty-two chapters on the wonders of modernity, he listed rhubarb fourth![107]

That seventeenth-century Jesuits trekking across Eurasia mentioned rhubarb in their journals hardly persuades that rhubarb belongs in the 'not obscure' category. And the suggestion that it was one of the most valuable things of the modern world sounds downright absurd. Yet, if the steppe-traversing missionaries and a relatively unknown academic do not qualify rhubarb as 'not obscure,' it turns out that rhubarb was quite relevant to several well-known historical figures. Rhubarb enhusiasm was on the tongue and in the texts of personages throughout the centuries who are historical household names far beyond specialized historian circles. Aristotle recommended to his pupil, Alexander the Great, to take rhubarb.[108] Marco Polo noted that rhubarb grew in 'great abundance' in the province of Sukchur and that 'thither merchants come to buy it, and carry it thence all over the world.'[109] It is well known that Christopher Columbus's New World adventures brought pineapple, tomatoes, and tobacco to the Old World, but the journal entry and letters exclaiming his discovery of rhubarb have gotten far less attention.[110] Rhubarb's charms and popularity did not escape the attention of that ever-observant Old World playwright, William Shakespeare.[111] The famous Swedish botanist Carolus Linnaeus chose rhubarb as the subject of his dissertation.[112] We know well about storied founding father Benjamin Franklin's experiments with lightning and electricity; yet that he facilitated the first attempt to grow Chinese rhubarb on what would become American soil remains unpublicized. In 1770, he mailed from London 'some of the true rhubarb seeds' to his horticulturalist friend John Bartram in Philadelphia.[113]

Nor does rhubarb as a mainstream concern remain confined to the pre-modern period. In the lead-up to the Opium Wars (1839–1842), the Chinese state threatened to cut off the westbound rhubarb trade, warning that the constipated of Europe would suffer without relief.[114] Perhaps the ironic icon of imperialism, Rudyard Kipling, intimated the political implications that accompanied rhubarb's medicinal use when he wrapped a tiger cub in rhubarb leaves to symbolize India under medical treatment in his 'Masque of Plenty.'[115] Dr. Livingstone, the famous nineteenth-century explorer of the African continent, was no stranger to malaria in his travels. His favorite remedy for the malady was a concoction of quinine, calomel, rhubarb, and resin of julep, which he called 'Livingstone pills.'[116] These examples demonstrate that rhubarb figured in the margins of mainstream historical events, operative in bits of 'History' that few would call obscure. Rhubarb was not merely a simple pie plant, but a matter of tremendous profit and risk, an object of grand imperial policies and mass appeal. In the early modern world rhubarb mattered to everyone from Columbus to Linnaeus to an obscure peasant or diarrheal miller.

Rhubarb, then, seems to straddle the categories of commodity narrative described above. Rhubarb stalk, the food, has become widespread and common, while rhubarb root, the medicine, has gone from precious to obsolete. The reinvention of this tart stalk as a complement to pies and jams means that 'everyone' knows what rhubarb is, but very few people think of it as medicine. Hence, there is a double disconnect. First, it is not a highly coveted medicine in our world. A search for rhubarb on the Internet (a resource tailor-made for unearthing obscurity) locates references to *da huang* and other products marketing themselves as Ancient Chinese medicine, but rhubarb does not loom large in the healing consciousness of MDs, pharmacists, or even of acupuncturists, homeopathophiles, or hippies. It is found in the medicine cabinets of neither mainstream nor alternative healers in twenty-first century America. Second, rhubarb's diachronic transmutation – that its contemporary function is entirely different from its historical one – makes the historical study of rhubarb strike some as actually funny because in today's world, rhubarb is something else, something of decidedly less importance – an unexpected incongruity, which is, after all, the very essence of humor.

Conclusion

A history of rhubarb root invites us, in every sense, to unearth it, and not just for the pleasure of enjoying a good pun. Delving into its strangeness forces us to recognize – to put it most basically – that the early modern economy differed profoundly from the modern. As we proceed towards a better understanding of the origins of capitalism – a historical problem that despite centuries of inquiry retains its vitality – the strange history of rhubarb highlights the criteria and consequences of an efficiency-driven economic system.[117] Jan de Vries' proposal of an 'industrious revolution' preceding the Industrial Revolution has importantly complicated the periodization of this momentous phenomenon. His work, along with that of others in the past decades, has profoundly changed the way we understand the early modern world. When we look at the early modern economy now we see consumer demand instead of inert masses; marketing strategies of some sophistication; and an insurance industry. We are now aware of complicated finance as part and parcel of 'exchanges' in centuries past. Historians have shown us that such contemporary phenomena as investor mania, ruinous speculation, and economic crashes also shook the worlds of early modern subjects; the South Sea Bubble fiasco in the 1720s is one prominent example.[118] Much of this historical scholarship cultivates an appreciation for the complexity and sophistication of early modern economies. We see a world that increasingly is filled with motivations, institutions, tools, and practices that we know to be part of our own contemporary economic landscape. Thus, the early modern period appears increasingly modern. But rhubarb's heyday, of root drying on sheep's horns in the steppe sun, traversing Eurasia in leather bundles on camels' backs or in the holds of Dutch or English caravels, pounded in the mortar of an apothecary's shop, and administered during leeching, does not seem modern at all.

This chapter has glimpsed ways in which rhubarb was relevant to a Russian in China, a Scotsman in Siberia, a Portuguese in Samarkand, a Dutchman in India, an Italian in the New World, an Iberian at home, and many others spanning a vast geography during the early modern period. The point here is not to suggest that we have missed rhubarb as a motor of history. While there can be a tendency towards big claims in recent cultural histories of commodities, this chapter makes no such claims.[119] Magellan would have sailed east and Columbus west even if there had been no such thing as rhubarb. Nor is the intention to stake a revisionist claim against seeing sophistication and complexity in the early modern economy. On the contrary, I think the point to be made is that the early modern economy *was* complex and sophisticated *and* that the rhubarb trade flourished. As Martha C. Howell has written,

> By paying close attention to these practices, we stand not only to grasp the distinctive character of this period in European history but also to appreciate the ways that this age did—and did not—lay groundwork for the modern western market society.[120]

This contribution, which has followed rhubarb from the highlands of China and trading posts of Siberia to the kitchen gardens of England and apothecaries of Amsterdam and Andalusia, serves to check notions of linear economic development and fortify a concrete sense of difference. Rhubarb did not change the world; the world changed around rhubarb, making the once coveted medicinal root obsolete.

Acknowledgments

I am grateful to Paula Findlen, Sebastian Barreveld, Vera Keller, Marcy Norton, Clare Griffin, Nikolaos Crissidis, Evgenii Rychalovskii, and Delia Gavrus for their invaluable encouragement and suggestions.

Notes

1 Sankt-Peterburgskii Institut istorii RAN (formerly LOII), f. 28, op. 1, d. 562, l. 1.
2 Clifford M. Foust, *Rhubarb: The Wondrous Drug* (Princeton, NJ: Princeton University Press, 1992), 21.
3 Foust, *Rhubarb*, 214.
4 *The Divine Farmer's Materia Medica: A Translation of the Shen Nong Ben Cao Jing*, trans. Yang Shou-zhong (Boulder, CO: Blue Poppy Press, 1998), 47, 69, 97, 117, 145.
5 Dioscorides, *De material medica*, trans. T.A. Osbaldeston (Johannesburg: IBIDIS Press, 2000), 3: 364, http://www.cancerlynx.com/BOOKTHREEROOTS.PDF.
6 In China in the first century BC it was prescribed to induce vomiting in order to combat poisoning.
7 Efraim Lev and Zohar Amar, *Practical Materia Medica of the Medieval Eastern Mediterranean According to the Cairo Genizah*, Sir Henry Wellcome Asian Series, vol. 7 (n.p.: Brill, 2008), 259–261.
8 Laurence Brockliss and Colin Jones, *The Medical World of Early Modern France* (Oxford: Clarendon Press, 1997), 307.
9 See Guido Panciroli (1523–1599), from Henrico Salmuth, *The History of Many Memorable Things Lost, Which Were in Use Among the Ancients: And An Account of Many Excellent Things Found, Now in Use Among the Moderns, Both Natural and Artificial* (London: J. Nicholson, 1715), 292–294.
10 Ibid., 10. For rhubarb in fourteenth-century Samarkand see B. G. Kurts, *Russko-kitaiskie snosheniia v XVI, XVII, i XVIII stoletiiakh* (Dnepropetrovsk: Gosudarstevnnoe izdatel'stvo Ukrainy, 1929), 5.
11 Researchers have recently concluded that *R. rhapontic* is effective and acceptable for use in menopausal women. See M. Kaszkin-Bettag, et al., 'Efficacy of the Special

Extract ERr 731 from Rhapontic Rhubarb for Menopausal Complaints: A 6-Month Open Observational Study,' *Alternative Therapies in Health and Medicine* 14.6 (2008): 32–38.

12 For example: *Rha ponticum, Rha barbarum, Rhapontic verum* ('true rhubarb'), *R. palmatum, Ravend cind, kopytchatyi, cherenkogo* are some names used. See Erika Monahan, 'Trade and Empire: Merchant Networks, Frontier Commerce and the State in Western Siberia, 1644–1728' (PhD diss., Stanford University, 2007), 356.

13 Foust, *Rhubarb*, 123.

14 Ibid., 59–61.

15 On ambassadors Fedor Baikov and Izbrandt Ides, see Natalja F. Demidova and Vladimir S. Mjasnikov, *Pervye russkie diplomaty v Kitae (Rospis' I. Petlina i stateinyi spisok F.I. Baikova)* (Moscow: Glavnaia redaktsiia vostochnoi literatury, 1966), 125, 154; Mark I. Kazanin, 'Introduction,' in *Izbrant Ides i Adam Brand, Zapiski o russkom posol'stve v Kitai (1692–1695)* (Moscow: Glav. red. vostochnoĭ lit-ry, 1967), 150; on seventeenth-century Jesuits Michael Boym and Ferdinand Verbiest and Simon Pallas' observations, see Foust, *Rhubarb*, 23–24, 160. Scottish doctor John Bell reported that rhubarb grew wild without cultivation. See John Bell, 'A Journey from St. Petersburg to Peking,' in *Travels from St. Petersburg in Russia to Diverse Parts of Asia in Two Volumes* (Glasgow: R. & A. Foulis, 1763), 1: 281.

16 Wilhelm Heyd, *Histoire du commerce du Levant au moyen-âge*, vol. 2 (Leipzig: Otto Harrassowitz, 1886), 2: 665–667, http://www.archive.org/details/histoireducomme 00heydgoog.

17 Margery Rowell, 'Medicinal Plants in Tsarist Russia,' *Janus* 63.1–3 (1976): 85–93; Foust, *Rhubarb*, 181.

18 Foust, *Rhubarb*, 180–182.

19 Audrey Burton, *The Bukharans: A Dynastic, Diplomatic, and Commercial History, 1550–1702* (New York: St. Martin's Press, 1997), 384, 428, 442.

20 John E. Dotson, *Merchant Culture in Fourteenth-Century Venice: The Zibaldone da Canal* (Binghamton: Medieval and Renaissance Texts & Studies, 1994), 130; G. F. Miller, *Conquest of Siberia and the History of the Transactions, Wars, Commerce, &c. &c. Carried on Between Russia and China*, trans. Peter Simon Pallas (London: Smith, Elder, and Co. Cornhill, 1842), 90–93.

21 James Shaw and Evelyn Welch, *Making and Marketing and Medicine in Renaissance Florence* (New York: Rodolfi, 2010), 240, 242, 255.

22 Richard Ames, *An Elegy on the Death of Dr. Thomas Safford Who Departed this Life May the 12th 1691* (London: A. Turner, 1691), http://xtf.lib.virginia.edu/xtf/view?docId=chadwyck_ep/ uvaGenText/tei/chep_2.0009.xml;query=rhubarb.

23 Michael R. McVaugh, *Medicine before the Plague: Practitioners and their Patients in the Crown of Aragon, 1285–1345* (Cambridge: Cambridge University Press, 2002), 151.

24 Foust, *Rhubarb*, 16, 19.

25 Russian State Archive of Ancient Acts (hereafter referred to as RGADA), f. 143, op. 2, ed. khr. 748. I thank Clare Griffin, email correspondence November 24, 2010, December 2, 2010.

26 Denis Leigh, 'Medicine, the City and China,' *Medical History* 18 (1974): 54.

27 Foust, *Rhubarb*, 90–91; idem, 'Customs 3 and Russian Rhubarb: A Note on Reliability,' *Journal of European Economic History* 15 (1986): 555.

28 67,764 lbs × 453.6 grams/lb = 30,737,750 grams/4 grams per dose = 7,684,437.6 doses. This figure is very approximate. Rhubarb doses were often 2 grams, too. Shaw and Welch, *Making and Marketing Medicine*, 242–244, 250. The population of Europe in 1750 is estimated to have been about 163 million.

29 Foust, *Rhubarb*, 57.

30 Shaw and Welch, *Making and Marketing Medicine*, 66, Fig. 3.1.

31 Suraiya Faroqhi, 'The Venetian Presence in the Ottoman Empire (1600–1630),' *Journal of European Economic History* 15 (1986): 379; Foust, *Rhubarb*, 9–10; Iu.N. Il'ina, 'Novye perevody. Iz knigi *Puteshchestvie v Rossiiu*,' *Zviezda* 5 (2003): 84, 86.

32 B. G. Kurts, *Sochinenie Kil'burgera o russkoi torgovle v tsarstvovanie Alekseia Mikhailovicha* (Kiev: Tip. I.I. Chokolova, 1915), 288.

33 See Morris Rossabi, 'The "Decline" of the Central Asian Caravan Trade,' in *The Rise of Merchant Empires: Long Distance Trade in the Early Modern World, 1350–1750*, ed. James D. Tracy (Cambridge: Cambridge University Press, 1990), 351–370; Scott Levi, 'India, Russia, and the Transformation of the Central Asian Caravan Trade,' in *India and Central Asia: Commerce and Culture, 1500–1800*, ed. Scott C. Levi (New York: Oxford University Press, 2007): 93–122.

34 Heyd, *Histoire du commerce du Levant au moyen-âge*, 2: 667.

35 Foust, *Rhubarb*, 11.

36 Leigh, 'Medicine, the City and China,' 54–55.

37 Monahan, 'Trade and Empire,' 359; Foust, *Rhubarb*, 50.

38 Quoted in Foust, *Rhubarb*, 23.

39 Shaw and Welch, *Making and Marketing Medicine*, 242–243.

40 Dioscorides called the plant *Rha*, footnoting a longer appellation of *Rha barbarum*, which referred to its origins in the land of barbarians beyond the Volga. He gave *Rheon* as an alternative name and noted that the Romans called it *Rhapontic* (meaning literally, 'beyond the Volga' and Pontic steppe stretching from western Ukraine to Kazakstan). Foust, *Rhubarb*, 3–4. Surprisingly, in the typically isolated Basque and Georgian languages: rhubarb = *rhubarb*; in Macedonian, it is *karanitsa*.

41 I thank Nikolaos Chrissidis for his generous Greek language help.

42 M. V. Fekhner, *Torgovlia russkogo gosudarstva so stranami vostoka v XVII veke* (Moscow: Izdatel'stvo gos. Istoricheskogo muzei, 1952).

43 Janet Martin, 'Muscovite Travelling Merchants: The Trade with the Muslim East,' *Central Asian Survey* 4.3 (1985): 31; Rudi Matthee, 'Anti-Ottoman Politics and Transit Rights: The Seventeenth-century Trade in Silk between Safavid Iran and Muscovy,' *Cahiers du monde russe* 35.4 (1994): 739–761.

44 M. Arthur Edwards, Letter of April 26, 1566 in *Principal Navigations, Voyages, Traffiques and Discoveries of the English Nation Collected by Richard Hakluyt*, ed. Edmund Goldsmid, vol. 3, part 2, *The Muscovy Company and the North-eastern Passage* (Adelaide: Adelaide ebooks, 2006).

45 Foust, *Rhubarb*, 21, 34. The importation of exotic drugs gave the apothecary industry a major boost. See E. F. Woodward, 'Botanical drugs: A Brief Review of the Industry with Comments on Recent Developments,' *Economic Botany* 1.4 (1947): 402–414.

46 See http://www.sil.si.edu/digitalcollections/herbals/Titles_chron.cfm., accessed May 2, 2012. See also Edward Kremers and Glenn Sonnedecker, *Kremers and Urdang's History of Pharmacy* (Philadelphia, PA: Lippincott, 1976 [1st ed. 1940]), 32–33, 96; Leigh, 'Medicine, the City and China,' 54; Foust, *Rhubarb*, 21, 35, 253, 255; Shaw and Welch, *Making and Marketing Medicine*, 313–316.

47 Shaw and Welch, *Making and Marketing Medicine*, 242.

48 http://www.summagallicana.it/lessico/a/Alpino%20o%20Alpini%20Prospero.htm, accessed May 3, 2012.

49 Monahan, 'Trade and Empire,' 358–365.

50 See Erika Monahan, 'V poiske revenia: Ob odnom zabytom episode torgovok politiki Rossii serediny XVII v.,' in *Sosloviya, instituty i gosudarstvennaya vlast' v Rossii. Srednie veka i rannee Novoe vremya. Sb. statei pamyati akad. L.V. Cherepnina* (Moscow: Yazyki slavyanskih kul'tur, 2010): 765–771; idem, 'Trade and Empire,' ch. 9.

51 Foust, *Rhubarb*, 214. For a study on the globalization of the sugar trade see Sidney W. Mintz, *Sweetness and Power: The Place of Sugar in Modern History* (New York: Viking, 1985).

52 Janet Martin, *Treasure in the Land of Darkness: The Fur Trade and Its Significance for Medieval Russia* (New York: Cambridge University Press, 1986), chs. 1–2.

53 Marie Schiller, 'The Fur Trade in Fourteenth Century Novgorod,' John Bell Library, University of Minnesota, http://www.lib.umn.edu/bell/tradeproducts/squirrel, accessed April 28, 2012.

54 Artur Attman, *The Russian and Polish Markets in International Trade 1500–1650* (Göteborg: Institute of Economic History, 1973), 6. See also Inna Liubimenko, *Istoriia torgovykh otnoshenii Rossii s Anglieiu*, vol. 1, *XVI vek* (Iur'ev: Tip. K. Mattisena, 1912); Jarmo T. Kotilaine, *Russia's Foreign Trade and Economic Expansion in the Seventeenth Century: Windows on the World* (Boston, MA: Brill, 2005), ch. 3.

55 T. S. Willan, *The Early History of the Russia Company, 1553–1603* (New York: Augustus M. Kelley Publishers, 1968), 82.

56 Kotilaine, *Russia's Foreign Trade*, 94. I thank Paul Bushkovitch for pointing out to me that many of the founding shareholders of the Muscovy Company went on to be involved in the East India Co. In fact, in the 1610s an unsuccessful merger of the Muscovy and East India Companies was proposed.

57 Ultimately, Crown rhubarb did not outcompete East Indian rhubarb as chronic oversupply and maneuverability problems undercut profits. Foust, *Rhubarb*, ch. 3.

58 For an introduction to the debate about Russia's sources see the debate on the 'Intellectual Silence of Russia' in *Slavic Review* 21.1 (1962); Simon Franklin, 'Literacy and Documentation in Early Medieval Rus,' *Speculum* 60.1 (1985): 1–38; William R. Veder, 'Old Russia's "Intellectual Silence" Reconsidered,' *California Slavic Studies* 19 (1994): 18–28; Simon Franklin, 'On the "Intellectual Silence" of Early Rus,' *Russia Mediaevalis* 10 (2001): 262–270; idem, *Writing, Society and Culture in Early Rus, c.950–1300* (New York: Cambridge University Press, 2002).

59 RGADA, f.143, op. 2, ed. khr. 748. I thank Clare Griffin.

60 RGADA, f. 143, op. 2, ed. khr. 1093 retsepty dlia tsarskikh osob 13th Jan 1674. I thank Clare Griffin, email correspondence November 24, 2010, December 2, 2010.

61 John Appleby attributes the first successful cultivation of *R. palmatum* on European soil to the Scottish physician John Bell who grew it in his garden in St. Petersburg, Russia, even though the British Society of Arts credited James Mounsey (1710–1773) with this achievement. John H. Appleby, '"Rhubarb" Mounsey and the Surinam Toad: A Scottish [sic] Physician-Naturalist in Russia,' *Archives of Natural History* 11.1 (1982): 141–145.

62 Kurts, *Sochinenie Kil'burgera*, 288.

63 Kh. Trusevich, *Posol'skiia i torgovyia snosheniia Rossii s Kitaem* (Moscow: Tip. T. Malinskago Moroseika, 1882), 109. W. F. Ryan's encyclopedic catalogue of folk medicine includes rhubarb perfunctorily: W. F. Ryan, *The Bathhouse at Midnight: Magic in Russia* (University Park, PA: Pennsylvania State University Press, 1999), 279. But other scholarship omits it entirely. The rare books department of the Russian State Public Historical library contains no eighteenth-century medical titles devoted to rhubarb according to N. F. Chernisheva, *Meditsinskaia literatura v XVIII veke, Katalog kollektsii, izdaniia 1725–1800 gg.* (Moscow: Ministerstvo kultury RSFSR Gosudarstvennaia publichnaia istoricheskaia biblioteka, 1986); and Petr Bogaevskii, 'Zametka o narodnoi meditsine,' in *Etnograficheskoe obozrenie. kn. 1* ed. N. A. Ianchuka (Moscow: Russkaia tipo-litorgrafiia, 1889), 101–106 does not mention rhubarb. V. V. Pokhlebkin, probably the contemporary authority on the history of Russian food, includes rhubarb in his dictionary of Russian cuisine, but it gets no mention in his more historical work, *Kulinarnyi slovar'* (Moscow: Tsentr poligraf, 1999).

64 David A. Scott et al., 'Technical Examination of Fifteenth-Century German Illuminated Manuscript on Paper: A Study in Identification of Materials,' *Studies in Conservation* 46.2 (2001): 93–108.

65 Trusevich, *Posol'skie i torgovye snosheniia Rossii s Kitaem*, 109; Burton, *Bukharans*, 384; Raymond H. Fisher, *The Russian Fur Trade, 1550–1700*, University of California Publications in History, vol. 31 (Berkeley, CA: University of California Press, 1943), 220.

66 Miller, *The Conquest of Siberia*, 104.

67 Foust, *Rhubarb*, 18–22.

68 Ibid., 121.

69 Woodward, 'Botanical Drugs,' 413.
70 Foust, *Rhubarb*, chs. 7–8. The difficulty that Western Europeans had in the eighteenth century suggests that they had not obtained the knowledge Russians gained in the seventeenth century. A closer look into communications of Europeans in the Russian Academy of Sciences with European colleagues could illuminate intellectual exchange. See Appleby, '"Rhubarb" Mounsey and the Surinam Toad.'
71 Ibid., 243.
72 While I do highlight ways in which rhubarb was simultaneously medicine and food, the main narrative is of shifting identity.
73 William J. Bernstein, *A Splendid Exchange: How Trade Shaped the World* (New York: Grove Press, 2008), 205.
74 Jan de Vries, 'The Limits of Early Modern Globalization,' *Economic History Review* 63.3 (2010): 722; Ralph A. Austen and Woodruff D. Smith, 'Private Tooth Decay as Public Economic Virtue: The Slave-Sugar Triangle, Consumerism, and European Industrialization,' *Social Science History* 14.1 (1990): 95–115.
75 Foust, *Rhubarb*, 214. The sender referred to the recipe as an experiment.
76 *Cookbook of Ibrahim b. al-Mahdi*, trans. Charles Perry, http://daviddfriedman.com/Medieval/Cookbooks/Andalusian/andalusian7.htm, accessed April 10, 2011. NB: determining whether root or stalk is indicated is tricky because, according to translator Charles Perry, 'The word "*urûq*" can mean roots or stems/stalks. I've translated it according to what seemed to make sense.'
77 *Annals of the Caliphs' Kitchens: Ibn Sayyar al-Warraq's Tenth-Century Baghdadi Cookbook*, ed. and trans. Nawal Nasrallah (Boston, MA: Brill, 2007).
78 Ibid., 140.
79 Ibid., 156.
80 Ibid., 97, 794. From which part of the rhubarb plant – root or stalk – juice was squeezed is unspecified. The glossary, however, does specify that a 'condensed juice from rhubarb (*rubb al-ribas*) is made by first pounding the stalks of this plant to extract the juice and then boiling it down to syrup consistency. ... Poets sing praises of the pleasantly tart taste.'
81 Ibid., 282.
82 Bartolomeo Scappi, *The Opera of Bartolomeo Scappi*, trans. Terence Scully (Toronto: University of Toronto Press, 2008), 243, 574.
83 Shaw and Welch, *Marketing and Medicine in the Renaissance*, 43, n. 53, 50.
84 Moderata Fonte (Modesta Pozzo), *The Worth of Women: Wherein is Clearly Revealed Their Nobility and Their Superiority to Men*, ed. and trans. Virginia Cox (Chicago, IL: University of Chicago Press, 1997), 170.
85 Ken Albala, *Eating Right in the Renaissance* (Berkeley, CA: University of California Press, 2002), 275.
86 Richard Warner, *Antiquitates culinariae or Curious Tracts Relating to the Culinary Affairs of the Old English* (London: R. Balime Strand, 1791), 90.
87 Pamela H. Smith and Paula Findlen, eds., *Merchants and Marvels: Commerce, Science, and Art in Early Modern Europe* (New York: Routledge, 2002).
88 Foust, *Rhubarb*. For more narrativizations of evolutionary success see Michael Pollan, *The Botany of Desire: A Plant's-Eye View of the World* (New York: Random House, 2001).
89 See Michael Pollan, *The Omnivore's Dilemma: A Natural History of Four Meals* (New York: The Penguin Group, 2006), 15–122.
90 See Erika Monahan, 'Regulating Virtue and Vice: Controlling Commodities in Early Modern Siberia,' in *Tobacco in Russian History and Culture*, eds. Matthew Romaniello and Tricia Starks (New York: Routledge, 2009), 62–65.
91 Malachy Postlethwayt, *The Universal Dictionary of Trade and Commerce*, 2 vols., 4th ed., (New York: Augustus M. Kelley Publishers, 1971 [1st ed. 1774]), 2: n.p.
92 John Uri Lloyd, *Origin and History of all the Pharmacopeial Vegetable Drugs, Chemicals, and Preparations with Bibliography* (Cincinnati, OH: Caxton Press, 1921), 1: 268.

93 F. W. Tunnicliffe, 'Synthetic Purgatives: The Purgative Action of Dihydroxy-Phthalo-Phenone (Phenolphthalein, Purgen),' *The British Medical Journal* 2.2181 (1902): 1224–1227; Woodward, 'Botanical Drugs,' 410.

94 'Rhubarb Protects Teeth,' *Science News Letter* (October 18, 1947), 252.

95 Mintz, *Sweetness and Power* is a modern work, but seminal; see also Ralph S. Hattox, *Coffee and Coffeehouses: The Origins of a Social Beverage in the Medieval Near East* (Seattle, WA: University of Washington Press, 1985); Heinrich Eduard Jacob, *Coffee: The Epic of a Commodity* (New York: Viking Press, 1935); Anthony Wild, *Coffee: A Dark History* (New York: W. W. Norton & Company, 2005); Marcy Norton, *Sacred Gifts, Profane Pleasures: A History of Tobacco and Chocolate in the Atlantic World* (Ithaca, NY: Cornell University Press, 2008); Beatrice Hohenegger, *Liquid Jade: The Story of Tea from East to West* (New York: St. Martin's Press, 2006); Wolfgang Schivelbusch, *Tastes of Paradise: A Social History of Spices, Stimulants, and Intoxicants* (New York: Pantheon Books, 1992); Redcliffe N. Salaman, W. G. Burton, and J. G. Hawkes, *The History and Social Influence of the Potato* (New York: Cambridge University Press, 1985); Susan Socolow, ed., *The Atlantic Staple Trade*, 2 vols. (Brookfield, VT: Varorium, 1996).

96 Amy Butler Greenfield, *A Perfect Red: Empire, Espionage, and the Quest for the Color of Desire* (New York: HarperCollins, 2005); R. A. Donkin, *Dragon's Brain Perfume: An Historical Geography of Camphor* (Leiden: Brill, 1999); Sarah Abrevaya Stein, *Plumes: Ostrich Feathers, Jews, and a Lost World of Global Commerce* (New Haven, CT: Yale University Press, 2008). While some have become obsolete, many spices such as pepper, cinnamon, cloves, and curry are now commonplace. Andrew *Dalby, Dangerous Tastes: The Story of Spices* (Berkeley, CA: University of California Press, 2000).

97 See Jan De Vries, 'Towards a History That Counts,' Dr. A. H. Heineken Prize for History lecture, 2000, http://www.knaw.nl/Content/Internet_KNAW/prijzen/Heinekenprizes/9.pdf, accessed January 15, 2010.

98 *Narrative of the Embassy of Ruy Gonzalez de Clavijo to the Court of Timour at Samarcand, A.D. 1403–6*, trans. Clements R. Markham (London: Hakluyt Society, 1859), 171.

99 S. M. Solov'ev, 'Moskovskie kuptsy v XVII v.,' in *Sochineniie v. 18 kn.*, bk. 20, *Dopolnitel'naia raboty raznykh let*, ed. I. D. Koval'chenko (Moscow: Mysl', 1996), 511.

100 David Mungello reported that from 1552–1800, 920 European Jesuits traveled to China. See David E. Mungello, *The Great Encounter of China and the West, 1500–1800*, 3rd ed. (Lanham, MD: Rowman & Littlefield, 2009), 37.

101 Quoted in Foust, *Rhubarb*, 23.

102 Ibid., 23–24.

103 Bell, 'A Journey from St. Petersburg to Peking,' 1: ch. 2, http://www.archive.org/stream/travelsfromstpet01bell/travelsfromstpet01bell_djvu.txt.

104 For Baikov: Demidova and Miasnikov, *Pervye russkie diplomaty v Kitae*, 154; For Ides: Kazanin, 'Introduction,' 150; Foust, *Rhubarb*, 65.

105 Report of Fedor Baikov (embassy 1654–1658), reprinted in *Skazaniia russkago naroda*, compiler I. P. Sakharov, vol. 2, bk. 8 (St. Petersburg, 1849), 129.

106 Cataño had delivered the purgative mechoacan. Nicolás Monardes, *Dos Libros. El uno trata de todas las cosas q[ue] traen de n[uest]ras Indias Occiede[n]tales, que sirven al uso de Medicina* (Seville: Sebastian Trugillo, 1565), fol. Hv. I thank Marcy Norton for this reference. For more on Monardes' New World *Materia Medica* see Norton, *Sacred Gifts, Profane Pleasures*, 110–114.

107 Panciroli, *The History of Many Memorable Things*, 291–294. I thank Vera Keller for sharing this wonderful information with me. Interestingly, Panciroli was familiar with Dioscorides and ancient references to rhubarb, but he considered the medicine brought from the east so qualitatively different that, the Ancients, wise though they were, were mistaken in thinking that they had possessed rhubarb.

108 Andrew G. Little, ed., *Roger Bacon Essays* (Oxford: Clarendon Press, 1914), 314, http://www.archive.org/stream/rogerbaconessays00litt/rogerbaconessays00litt_djvu.txt, accessed April 8, 2011.

109 Marco Polo, *The Book of Ser Marco Polo, the Venetian*, trans. and ed. Henry Yule (New York: Scribner, 1903), 217.

110 See Adolph Caso, *To America and Around the World: The Logs of Christopher Columbus and Ferdinand Magellan* (Boston, MA: Branden Books, 2001), 202–203; Christopher Columbus, 'Letter to Lord Raphael Sanchez,' 14 March 1493, http://www.wise. virginia.edu/history/wciv1/ civ1ref/colum.htm, accessed July 2, 2008.

111 William Shakespeare, *MacBeth*, Act 5, Scene 3: 'What rhubarb, cyme, or what purgative drug, / Would scour these English hence? Hear'st thou of them?'

112 Carl von Linné, 'Dissertatio medico botanica, sistens rhabarbarum: quam consensu experient' (Diss., Uppsala University, 1752). I thank Vera Keller for this reference.

113 Kremers and Sonnedecker, *History of Pharmacy*, 157; Foust, *Rhubarb*, 270. In February 1773 Franklin wrote to Bartram that he was glad to hear the rhubarb was growing. Foust, *Rhubarb*, 278.

114 Lin Zixu Lin Tse-Hsü (1839 CE), 'Letter of Advice to Queen Victoria,' http://acc6. its. brooklyn.cuny.edu/~phalsall/texts/com-lin.html, accessed June 5, 2007. I thank Hal Kahn for this reference.

115 Rudyard Kipling, 'The Masque of Plenty,' http://xtf.lib.virginia.edu/xtf/view?docId= chadwyck_ep/uvaGenText/tei/chep_3.0486.xml;query=rhubarb, accessed April 8, 2011.

116 Daniel R. Headrick, *The Tools of Empire: Technology and European Imperialism in the Nineteenth Century* (New York: Oxford University Press, 1981), 71. I thank Eliza Ferguson for this reference.

117 Works devoted to the topic could fill a library. One recent contribution by a respected historian is Joyce Appleby, *The Relentless Revolution: A History of Capitalism* (New York: W. W. Norton & Co., 2011).

118 For a brief introduction to the South Sea Bubble history see Niall Ferguson, *The Ascent of Money: A Financial History of the World* (New York: Penguin Books, 2008), 138–158, 170–173.

119 For example: Henry Hobhouse, *Seeds of Change: Five Plants that Transformed Mankind* (New York: Harper & Row, 1986); Mark Kurlansky, *Cod: A Biography of the Fish That Changed the World* (New York: Walker & Co., 1997); Larry Zuckerman, *The Potato: How the Humble Spud Rescued the Western World* (New York: Northpoint Press, 1998); Tom Standage, *A History of the World in 6 Glasses* (New York: Walker & Co., 2005). For a more sober analysis in this vein see B. W. Higman, 'The Sugar Revolution,' *Economic History Review* 53.2 (2000): 213–236.

120 Martha C. Howell, *Commerce before Capitalism in Europe, 1300–1600* (New York: Cambridge University Press, 2010), 2.

10

THE WORLD IN A SHILLING

Silver coins and the challenge of political economy in the early modern Atlantic world

Mark A. Peterson

In the year 1676, two weddings took place at opposite poles of European colonial settlement in the Americas – two weddings, four thousand miles apart, but connected by a silver thread.[1] At the southern end of this thread, high in the Andes almost three miles above sea level, stood the city of Potosi in the Viceroyalty of Peru, then the largest city in the Western Hemisphere with a population comparable to London's or Amsterdam's. Here, hundreds of thousands of Native American workers dug silver out of the Cerro Rico, the giant mountain of silver that Spanish conquistadors had first encountered in the 1540s. Indian laborers often developed black lung disease from breathing the dust in the mines; the Quechua name for the Cerro Rico meant 'man-eating mountain.' Potosi became the largest single source of the stream of mineral wealth flowing to Spanish ports across the Atlantic, where giant *flotas* brought European goods to America and returned silver and gold to Cadiz, and across the Pacific, where an annual galleon carried silver to Manila in exchange for the silks and spices of Asia.[2]

In Potosi, once the silver was dug out of the Cerro Rico, still more Indian workers refined it through the use of a mercury amalgamation process (also sickening, though in a different way). Then the purified silver was minted into coins, the famous Spanish peso or eight reales piece, known throughout the Atlantic world as a Spanish dollar or a 'piece of eight' (Figure 10.1). The master of the mint at Potosi, a rich silver trader and philanthropist, was Antonio Lopez de Quiroga, a *peninsulare*, born in Galicia in northwest Spain. In the late 1640s, Quiroga came to the New World to seek his fortune, which the Cerro Rico and its forced labor provided. Under the notorious *mita* system, Indian villages for hundreds of miles around were required to send roughly one seventh of their adult male population to work in the mines each year. The Indians remained poor, sickened, and died, but the Spanish silver traders became *very* rich.

FIGURE 10.1   Spanish eight reales piece, Potosi, late sixteenth century

In October 1676, Antonio Lopez's daughter, Lorenza was getting married. The mint-master provided a handsome dowry to the intended bridegroom, Juan de Velasco, another native Spaniard and aspiring bureaucrat in the colonial service. The official value of the dowry that Lorenza brought to her marriage was 100,000 pesos, an eye-popping sum.[3] Half of this fortune consisted of exquisite objects imported from Spain, a dazzling array of goods including a gilded hardwood four-poster bed, a crimson damask bedspread embroidered in gold, a series of historical tapestries, a writing desk, a sedan chair, and a dozen paintings illustrating the months of the year, as well as upholstered chairs, oriental carpets, 7,000 pesos worth of silverware and plate for entertaining, and another 6,000 pesos worth of textiles ranging from tablecloths and napkins to dress gowns. Six African slaves (four men and two women) were included in this 'material' half of the dowry as well. But the remainder came in the form of silver coins, 50,000 pesos, twenty large sacks of the Spanish dollars produced in the mint at Potosi.[4] Each sack would have weighed about 150 pounds, perhaps as much or more than each of the slaves. With each one of those twenty sacks of 2,500 pesos, Juan de Velasco, the fortunate bridegroom, might have purchased five or six more adult male slaves.[5]

Far to the north, a small scattering of the silver that spewed forth from Potosi would occasionally wash up in Boston. New England's capital was then a town of about 4,000 people, perhaps one fiftieth the size of Potosi. There the merchant John Hull, who was born in England but moved to America in the 1630s with his family, was the town's leading silversmith, and had been employed since 1652 as master of the mint, occasionally using his skills to turn miscellaneous pieces of silver into very curious coins, the 'Pine Tree Shillings' of the Massachusetts Bay Colony. In a good year, 1679 for instance, Hull produced about 20,000 of these shillings, totaling a face value of £1,000. Over

FIGURE 10.2   Massachusetts 'Pine Tree' shilling, *c.*1652

the course of the thirty years in which he made them, he put perhaps 300,000 to 500,000 shillings into circulation[6] (Figure 10.2).

Like Antonio Lopez de Quiroga, John Hull had a daughter, Hannah, who in February 1676 was, like Lorenza, marrying an aspiring merchant and future judge. From such a wealthy and generous father-in-law, Hannah's intended bridegroom, Samuel Sewall, could expect a substantial dowry along with his bride, and John Hull did not disappoint. In fact, Hannah Hull's dowry became legendary in New England, its value repeated and exaggerated by some of the region's finest historians. The story of its disbursal was retold with inimitable flair by Nathaniel Hawthorne in a history of New England written for children, *Grandfather's Chair*. In the story, the mint-master asks his daughter to climb into one side of his commodity scales:

> 'And now,' said honest John Hull to the servants 'bring that box hither.' The box to which the mint-master pointed was a huge, square, iron-bound, oaken chest...full to the brim of bright pine-tree shillings, fresh from the mint; and Samuel Sewall began to think that his father-in-law had got possession of all the money in the Massachusetts treasury. Then the servants, at Captain Hull's command, heaped double handfuls of shillings into one side of the scales, while [Hannah] remained in the other. 'There, son Sewall!' cried the honest mint-master, resuming his seat in Grandfather's chair, 'take these shillings for my daughter's portion. Use her kindly, and thank Heaven for her. It is not every wife that's worth her weight in silver!'[7]

Hawthorne, we like to think, must have exaggerated. But no less scrupulous a historian than Thomas Hutchinson claimed that Hannah Hull's dowry amounted to £30,000, a preposterous figure (preposterous in Massachusetts, that is, though entirely believable in Potosi). The face value of all the shillings Hull ever produced for the colony might have been £25,000 at most.

Given Hutchinson's exaggeration, Hawthorne's whimsical story turns out to be surprisingly close to the truth. In 1676, John Hull, as treasurer of the colony, did have his hands on all the money in the Massachusetts treasury. But he did not bestow it all on his daughter and her future husband. From Hull's account books we learn the actual amount of Hannah's dowry: £500, paid in two separate transactions.[8] In all likelihood, John Hull probably *never* had £500 – 10,000 shillings – in his possession at any one time, given the small scale and the sporadic schedule on which he produced the coins. And yet, the actual weight of 10,000 Pine Tree Shillings would be, in modern units, roughly 105 lbs.: perhaps not so far from Hannah's actual weight in silver.

The coincidence of the simultaneous weddings and the bestowal of the mint-masters' fortunes on their daughters highlights two features of the relationship between Potosi and Boston, one a glaring contrast, the other a profound connection. First is the overwhelming difference in the scale of operations that Antonio Lopez de Quiroga and John Hull supervised. The value of Lorenza's dowry was something like eighty times as large as that of Hannah's. Yet Hannah Hull's dowry was thought to be a huge amount, large enough in New England's historical memory to become the source of extravagant legend. By any measure, the operations of Potosi's mint dwarf John Hull's trivial output in Boston. This difference in scale reflects the different kinds of colonies, and different models of political economy, that the Viceroyalty of Peru and the Commonwealth of Massachusetts represented. With its fabulously rich and immensely productive silver mines, Potosi and Peru represented the ideal colony within the mental framework of mercantilist thought: a colony ruled from the metropolis, designed to extract and export commodity wealth to the home country and to form a new consumer market for the manufactured products of the homeland.

Boston did not fit this model at all, despite the hopes of first-generation explorers that New England, too, might conceal hidden veins of mineral wealth, or at the very least, provide furs, tobacco, or some other intrinsically valuable commodity for English consumers. Boston's fortunes were made not by extracting high-value commodities from its hinterland, but by timely and ingenious forms of ocean-going trade, fueled by the humble, low-priced commodities that New England farmers and fisherman could scrape together for sale. As a consequence, the structure of the social order created by the city-state of Boston, with even its most prosperous merchants living on a modest scale and their fortunes closely intertwined with the productivity of ordinary farmers and fishermen, was far more 'middling' than that of Potosi, with its incredibly wealthy few served by hundreds of thousands of exploited Indians.

At the same time, despite the difference in scale of the minting operations in Boston and Potosi, and despite the different models of colonial economy that these cities served within their competing empires, the two operations were connected, and not only by the coincidence of these two weddings. The great majority of the silver that Hull worked into cups, spoons, buckles, and coins in his Boston shop was originally mined in Potosi.[9] And the connection was still closer than this, for besides the royally supervised mints at Potosi and Zacatecas in Mexico, Hull's mint in Boston was the only other place in the Western Hemisphere where high grade silver coins were produced to European monetary standards. In fact, the decision by the General Court of Massachusetts to initiate the minting of its own silver coins was in part a response to events that took place in Potosi in the 1640s. In monetary and fiscal terms, the Atlantic world was already sufficiently interconnected by the mid-seventeenth century that conditions at one extreme influenced events at its polar opposite.

The question that the existence of John Hull's Boston mint raises is this: why was Massachusetts, a colony with no silver deposits of its own, and no authority to produce currency from the crown, Parliament, or any other sovereign agency, engaged in this business at all? Why was John Hull making silver shillings to serve as legal tender for 'Massachusetts in New England'?

To answer this question requires an exploration of the significance of coins to the political economy of the early modern Atlantic world. In the extant scholarship on colonial British America, the concept of political economy has received much attention from historians concerned with the era of the American Revolution. But too often, the economic development of the Anglo-American colonies in the two centuries before 1776 is treated simply as prologue to the Revolution, as though North America had a brief 'political economy' moment in the late eighteenth century, but before that, simply a long period of preparatory, unpolitical, economics. Similarly, the subject has a rich literature in the historiography of the first British Empire, but the focus and the perspective in this case tends to be distinctly metropolitan. The British homeland(s) constitute the 'polity' whose economy the empire serves, and the evolution of the mercantilist doctrines that linked colonies to the metropolis through the Navigation Acts takes center stage.[10] In addition, although economic historians have paid ample attention to the volume and flow of various commodities around the Atlantic world, they seldom address the material significance of money in encouraging or restricting the making of the world of goods.

My aim here is different because Boston was different, an unusual exception to the standard model of colonial relationships to the metropolis because it produced no exotic commodities unavailable in the homeland, competed with metropolitan cities and merchants within the Atlantic carrying trade, and experimented in monetary innovations to a greater degree than any other contemporary European colony. I intend to focus on the political economy of the city-state of Boston itself, to assume that Boston was for Boston, an independent entity pursuing its own interests within the larger context of the Atlantic world. For purposes of definition, I want to borrow from Adam Smith in *The Wealth of Nations*, where he argued that the two chief purposes of political economy are 'to provide a plentiful revenue or subsistence for the people or more properly to enable them to provide such a revenue or subsistence for themselves; and...to supply the state or common-wealth with a revenue sufficient for the public services.'[11]

One of the most important things that sovereign states do to advance their political economy goals is to create and maintain a money supply. This is why it was so unusual for Massachusetts, ostensibly a colony of another state, to begin creating its own high-grade silver coinage in 1652 – no other British colony was ever so bold.[12] The right to mint coins was a royal prerogative going back to Roman times, and the penalties for uttering false coinage were those associated with *lèse-majesté* and high treason:

> [t]he punishment in Roman law and in early German law was the loss of one or both hands, but by the fourteenth century some form of gruesome death was the norm: hanging in England, burning in Venice, boiling in France.[13]

In its early years, there were many ways, and many contexts, in which Massachusetts acted as though it were an independent state, including the development of its own distinctive church polity at odds with England's; the creation of incorporated townships and the distribution of colony lands to them (usurping the crown's power to create corporations); and the formation of the United Colonies, an alliance for mutual defense with other colonies. All of these actions led to conversations on both sides of the Atlantic about whether the commonwealth was a 'perfect *res publica*' or a 'free state.'[14] But nothing Massachusetts did was quite as state-like as the creation of an independent, circulating coinage. By making its own coins, Boston made itself more like a state, and it used the coinage and the economic power, trust, and credit that the coinage accrued to advance its own vision of political economy amid the competing empires of the seventeenth-century Atlantic world.

What were the goals of the city-state of Boston? First, to preserve and develop the autonomy and self-government that were rooted in the charter of 1629, but were strengthened by subsequent achievements of the state and its agents. Boston's economic and political survival required it. Crown dependency and mercantilist complacency might have been acceptable for Virginia or Barbados, with their valuable staple crops making their utility to the home country easily visible. In the mind's eye of metropolitan consumers, Virginia *was* tobacco, and Barbados *was* sugar. But this definition of a colony's purpose was far too restrictive for Massachusetts, which built its fortunes on what economists refer to as 'invisibles' – the value found in moving goods from one place to another, and bearing the costs and risks of these ventures, thereby enhancing the overall circulation of goods within a complex economic system. As one historian of New England's economy put it, '[t]hese invisible credits in trade—the value of which contemporaries consistently underestimated—constituted the region's single most valuable export.'[15] To build these 'invisible' credits, Boston's economy required the freedom for its merchants to act as if Massachusetts were an autonomous state, trading not just within the bounds of England's colonial system, but widely across the empires of the Atlantic world, wherever a marginal profit on their cheap local products could be found.

The second goal of Boston's political economy was to extend its territorial reach beyond the tiny boundaries of the charter's original land grant, to develop access to new resources and settlement opportunities for its expanding population beyond what its initial patent allowed. This ambition, and the success with which Bostonians pursued it, also made Boston unique in seventeenth-century English America. The only comparable example involves the limited success of Barbadian planters in creating South Carolina as a colony of their colony, but the Barbados plantation of Carolina proved unable to replicate the sugar economy of the West Indies. Barbados and Carolina went separate ways while 'Boston in New England' achieved greater integration over the seventeenth and eighteenth centuries.

Third, and here I stretch Adam Smith's definition of political economy, I want to argue for the continuing importance of the colony's moral economy in the pursuit of these goals. Bostonians experienced tension between the religious and moral ideals upheld by the founders' Puritan commonwealth and the demands that engagement with Atlantic economies and empires made upon the city's leadership. The first two goals of Boston's political economy – commercial engagement in the Atlantic world, with its economies rooted in the slave-based plantation complex, and territorial expansion, with its destructive consequences to neighboring peoples – tended to undermine the commonwealth ideal. The third goal, then, involved managing these tensions, in the hope of maintaining a political economy in which the people of New England would continue to be knit together as one body. To accomplish this complex set of goals required a creative solution to a problem that had plagued European economies for centuries, a problem that was all the more difficult on the distant periphery of European settlement, and in a place where early dreams of finding gold and silver had failed to materialize.

The big problem of small change

In creating a mint, Massachusetts' leaders hoped to compensate for the absence of a local money supply that could expedite trade within the New England region and bear a stable relationship to the larger circulating currencies of the Atlantic world. This problem was not exclusive to colonial New England. For most of the second millennium of the Common Era, Western Europeans had faced a 'big problem of small change:' a shortage of reliable, government-backed coins with stable values that were nonetheless small enough for the conduct of everyday commerce. High-value precious metal coins, such as Venetian gold ducats (famously the coin loaned by Shylock to Antonio in Shakespeare's *Merchant of Venice*) or the nearly equivalent Florentine coin, the florin, circulated widely in long-distance trade. But their value was so large that individual consumers could not easily use them to buy their daily bread. In fourteenth-century Florence, the smallest available silver coin, the grosso, was enough money to purchase five liters of wine, buy a kilogram of olive oil, or pay an entire month's rent for a single working man.[16] Without the ready availability of small change, ordinary commerce on a small scale ground to a halt, and people were forced into desperate measures such as breaking coins in half or paying a whole penny for a half penny's value. In 1613, King James I recognized this problem when he issued

> Farthing Tokens…to pass between Vintners, Tapsters, Chandlers, Bakers, and other the like Tradesmen and their Customers, whereby such small portions and quantities of things vendible as the necessity and use specially of the poorer sort of People doth oftentimes require…without enforcing men to buy more ware than will serve for their use and good end.[17]

Between the year 1200, when the growth of European trade networks began to spur the production of a wider variety of coins, and the early nineteenth century, when Western governments finally worked out a reliable formula for solving the problem, most European states and their New World colonies suffered from a chronic shortage of small change. By 'small change' I do not mean fiduciary moneys – tin farthings, lead trinkets, wooden or leather tokens. Though these existed throughout Europe and its colonies, sometimes in enormous numbers, they circulated in small, confined areas (within a town, a parish, or a guild, for instance), and therefore had a local utility.[18] With no stable relationship to the larger currencies of the state or empire, and no intrinsic value as commodities, these small fiduciary moneys did not work very well to integrate local trade with larger regional, national, or international economies. The local baker might accept your tin farthings for small amounts of bread, but not the baker on the far side of town, or in the next town over. You could not buy expensive goods from an international merchant with a wheelbarrow full of them, nor could you use them to pay your taxes. What was missing were good coins, with some appreciable intrinsic value (usually silver), and with a reliable ratio to very large coins, but in small enough denominations for everyday utility, good at your local bakery *and* for the big merchant or tax collector. We might think of this as money of moderate size, but technically, economists call it small change – 'small' because it's smaller than ducats or florins, and 'change' because it can nonetheless be exchanged for big coins at a reliable rate.

In many European regions, the small change shortage was a chronic problem that common folks simply endured. It meant that the integration of larger regional or national economies proceeded at a halting pace. As far as international merchants were concerned, the problem was bearable. Their interests mainly lay in corralling the few really valuable commodities produced locally, items expensive enough to make the costs of overseas shipping worthwhile, such as the fine woolen cloth made in southeastern England, or, later, the sugar and tobacco produced in the colonies. Overseas merchants trading luxury goods tended not to care about humble foodstuffs and sundries that were bought and sold in village markets for local consumption, for which fiduciary money sufficed.

Boston, as the emergent market hub of New England in the 1640s, was different. For Boston's merchants, the necessity of participation in an Atlantic large-scale trading economy, which involved dealing in profitable goods like tobacco, sugar, and slaves, demanded that somehow, the humble goods (grain, bread, salted meat, dried or salted fish, shingles, barrel staves, and potash) that New England produced had to be used as commodities for overseas trade and converted into credits on the international market. In other words, the big merchants of Boston depended upon a steady, reliable relationship with modest goods not usually thought of as commodities at the time, and they needed small change in order to get their hands on these humble products.

The trouble with wampum

In the 1630s, the first decade of Massachusetts settlement, the Native American shell-bead strings known as wampum functioned as a form of small change. Because wampum could be used to purchase furs for export from Indian hunters, the Massachusetts government monetized it, declaring it to be legal tender at specified rates for all transactions within the colony. The furs acquired with wampum were, like sugar or tobacco, commodities with a high value in European markets, and could therefore be exchanged directly for desirable European import goods – the ultimate endpoint of Boston's Atlantic commerce in the colonial period. Had this wampum-to-fur relationship remained stable, New England might have become more like Virginia or Barbados, a staple-extracting colony with a direct trade relationship to the home country, although with little employment for its thousands of English settlers. But wampum production rose dramatically in response to this new demand, while over-hunting quickly exhausted the supply of beaver and other fur-bearing animals in southern New England. By the 1640s, wampum could no longer reliably command furs, and its prospects as a form of small change had collapsed. However, the simultaneous discovery in the 1640s that Boston merchants could compete with metropolitan merchants for the carrying trade if they could supply the West Indies with commodities like bread, salt meat, dried fish, and barrel staves, meant that Boston merchants needed a reliable money supply to encourage the farmers and fisherman of New England to produce their humble goods in sufficient quantities for export.[19]

In the first decade of colonization, when Massachusetts rapidly took off as a migrant destination for English Puritans, New England's farmers and fishermen had strong encouragement to produce more of these humble goods than they and their families consumed, because they had a steady market for the surplus in the stream of new immigrants arriving by the thousands every year.

The new arrivals desperately needed food to tide them over until they could start to produce for themselves, along with processed forest materials to build and heat their houses. The new migrants paid for these goods with money they brought from England. But with the outbreak of rebellion in Scotland in 1639 and Charles I's need to recall Parliament the following year, the heightened prospects for Puritans in England abruptly stopped, pushing Puritan migrants overseas; and therefore the market in New England for these surplus local goods bottomed out, as the supply of new customers and new money dried up. Consequently, the first Atlantic voyages attempting to vend these cheap commodities in the Caribbean were risking very little – they were selling what was now a useless surplus of not-very-valuable goods. That initial crisis, though, when local commodity prices fell to nothing around 1640, made New England farmers subsequently cautious about repeating the folly of overproduction. How might Boston merchants encourage New England farmers to return to their industrious ways?

In a barter economy, farm families have few incentives to spend their idle winter months carving barrel staves, burning potash, or slaughtering and salting down meat, especially if all their neighbors are thinking of doing the same thing. The local demand for these goods is quite limited, no more than what the locals themselves can consume. If too many people try to produce too many of these products, their local trade value is negligible. Producing surplus quantities is a waste of time and effort. But if these goods can be traded to distant markets in return for money – money of the sort that can be used to buy desirable import goods otherwise not available locally – then the incentive to engage in this kind of production becomes much greater, and it no longer matters if your neighbor does exactly the same thing. Consequently, the existence of a plentiful money supply, a stable small change currency, would be a great advantage to Boston's merchants, both to flush large quantities of humble commodities out of the countryside that they could sell in certain Atlantic markets, and to put money in the hands of potential customers who would later buy their European imports. For this reason, the collapse of the fur–wampum monetary equation was especially dire for the New England region, and the demand for an alternative small change was great.

The trouble with pieces of eight

On the face of it, the solution to New England's monetary problem seemed to be right at hand. With the inauguration of trade routes to the Caribbean, southern Europe, and the Atlantic islands, silver money began to appear in Boston. No longer were good coins arriving only in the pockets of English immigrants – now the holds of the trading ships were bringing home silver money, most of it produced by Spain's New World empire. Some of these coins were acquired in legitimate trade, when Caribbean sugar growers or wine merchants from Madeira paid for Boston's humble but necessary products in cash. More of it, though, was probably acquired in disreputable ways, when privateers or pirates captured Spanish trading vessels carrying silver, or stole slaves and sold them clandestinely to Spanish customers on the coasts of Central America, then brought their tainted money to Boston for laundering while refitting their ships for further predatory voyages.

The Spanish dollar could have been a solution to Boston's problem. In the pre-modern era, money was not 'national.' It was not generally expected that each kingdom or state should have its own exclusive monetary system.[20] If a steady supply of Spanish dollars could be had, there was no reason why they could not circulate throughout the New England region and even fill some of the necessary functions of small change. Although it was a form of silver commodity money, the eight reales coin or Spanish dollar, weighing in at one ounce of silver, was not so very large that it could not function in some everyday situations. Its commodity value was only half that of the ducat, and in Massachusetts it was valued at six English shillings, or seventy-two pence. This was an inflated value, a 'crying up' of Spanish dollars, which traded for only five shillings in England at the time. The colony of Massachusetts authorized this higher exchange value for Spanish dollars in order to encourage people to keep them circulating within New England rather than sending them directly to England as payment for imported goods.[21]

Furthermore, the fact that this single round coin's denomination was '8' reales (rather than, say '1' ducat) made it attractive to cut, like pieces of pie, into eight individual *real* 'bits' of smaller change.[22] But cutting coins was a risky practice (as any child who has ever had to share a cookie with a sibling knows), too close to other forms of physical manipulation, like clipping, that debased coins' value. Herein lay the deeper problem with Spanish money. All coins in the early modern world that were made of valuable materials like gold or silver were in jeopardy from clipping, washing, sweating, or other practices that appropriated minute amounts of precious metal while still passing the coin off at full face value. Inveterate clippers could accumulate large amounts of precious metals and seriously debase the coinage in the process. In the sixteenth and seventeenth centuries, new technologies, the screw press and the cylinder press, were developed to improve coins' resistance to these illegal debasements by making rings or markings around the edges of coins that would show off attempts to clip them. But these technologies were still imperfect, and had yet to be fully implemented in the New World.

The coins made at Potosi were known as 'cob' coins, made through a process in which the silver to be coined was rolled into long bars, a slice or 'cob' of the bar was cut off, and then the cob was hammered or pressed into a coin. These cob coins were among the most prolific coins circulating in the Atlantic world, and probably constituted the bulk of Spanish coinage arriving in Boston in the 1640s. They were crude, and the common practice of cutting pieces of eight into smaller units threatened to debase them even further (Figure 10.3). There were already reasons to be suspicious of the value of cob coins, or pieces

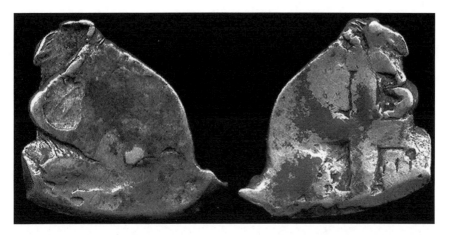

FIGURE 10.3   Image of a badly clipped and worn cob coin, front and back

thereof, circulating in Atlantic trade routes, but in the 1640s, cause for suspicion grew into outright distrust. During this decade, at the same time that Boston's merchants were establishing their foothold in the Caribbean trade, a series of scandals involving fraud at the mint in Potosi undermined public faith in Spanish money. Starting in 1633, royal officials had begun to notice that Potosi coins were low in silver content, and they warned the assayers at the mint to mind their work more carefully. The problem was engendered by the fact that the minting was actually conducted by a dozen or more silver traders in Potosi, 'mercaderes de plata,' who not only bargained with the miners to purchase their silver, but also oversaw the coining process, which included reserving one fifth of all the silver produced for the crown. It was in the pecuniary interest of the mercaderes to under-report the amount of silver produced, so as to cheat the crown, as well as to skimp on silver in the making of the coins and skim the excess for themselves.[23]

By 1645, the problem had grown severe enough that the crown took action. The public prosecutor for the Council of the Indies in Madrid claimed that people in Spain had become reluctant to accept Potosi coins, because 'there is not a patacon [piece of eight] of it that does not contain almost two reales of copper.'[24] Spanish consumers had come to expect that Potosi coins might be as much as a quarter under their face value in silver. Consequently, the prosecutor recommended the appointment of an inspector general, don Francisco de Nestares Marin, who arrived in Potosi in December 1648 and began to reform the mint. Even before his arrival, some of the mercaderes decided to improve the quality of their coins, in theory a step in the right direction, though in practice a source of still further confusion about the value of Potosi pesos, since it was difficult to tell good coins from bad without an assayer's skill. Soon, Inspector Nestares identified the three most egregious offenders among the mercaderes and determined that they owed the crown as much as a million pesos. When these three began to hide away large sums of money and then took refuge in the cathedral at Potosi to escape from prosecution, Nestares turned to violent means. After luring him out of the church with promises of clemency, Nestares arrested and executed the wealthiest of the *mercaderes* and left his corpse hanging in the plaza as an example to the town. The assayer of the mint was executed as well, and other offenders imprisoned. By 1652, only three of the dozen *mercaderes* remained in the coining business, and they now operated under a new regime, carefully designed to restore full value and public trust to the Potosi coinage.

The new plan involved two stages: first, an effort to get people to bring underweight old coins into the mint for recoinage, and second, a timetable for restoring Potosi coins to their full eight reales value. From 1649 onward, the Inspector declared that all coins minted before that date would officially be devalued – they would temporarily circulate at only six reales, three quarters of their face value. By October, 1652, all the old coins were scheduled to have been remade. The new coins, now of certified fine grade, would circulate at full face value, and the old coins would no longer be recognized as having any value as legal tender, therefore giving possessors incentive to turn them in for reminting. These draconian measures caused hardships, especially in Potosi itself, where most of the local fortunes were held in the now devalued coins. But the measures were effective in restoring trust in Potosi's coinage throughout the Spanish Empire and the Atlantic world in the years after 1652. Antonio Lopez de Quiroga had the good fortune to arrive in Potosi and begin his career as a silver trader late in the 1640s, untainted by prior scandals, and to marry into one of the few local families that the scandal had not touched. His rise to wealth as master of the mint in Potosi owed a great deal to the effective if brutal work performed by Inspector Nestares.[25]

From Spanish silver to New England shillings

It is difficult to know how widely the details of the Potosi scandal were known throughout the Atlantic world, especially beyond Spanish boundaries.[26] But in this world of scarce currencies and moneys of unknown origin, people paid close attention to the few coins that did pass their way. We know, for instance, that as Boston's traders, privateers, and pirates brought larger amounts of Spanish silver into the city, suspicion about the quality of Spanish dollars grew. Evidence can be seen by the fact that early in 1652, during the period of indeterminacy when Potosi's coins had been discounted and were being called in for reminting, the Massachusetts General Court approached John Hull with a proposal asking him to assay and stamp all silver coins for authenticity and value. Apparently, Hull and his partner Robert Sanderson (the only two men in town with the skills to carry out the work) both rejected the idea, for the records indicate that the order was repealed as being 'full of difficultjes, and unlikely to take effect in regard no p[er]sons are found willing to try & stampe the same.'[27] John Hull confirmed the general awareness of this problem, noting that the General Court was motivated 'upon occasion of much Counterfeit Coyne brought in the Countrey and much loss accruing in that respect (and that did occasion a stoppage of trade).'[28] This initial solution failed because the government offered no incentive for Hull or Sanderson to take on the work of assaying and stamping the coins.

Within months, the General Court returned with a far more ambitious proposal; the creation of a mint for issuing new high-quality silver coins under the authority of the colony's government, for which John Hull would be handsomely paid. On May 26, 1652, the House of Magistrates enacted the following measure:

> That all persons what soeuer have liberty to bring in vnto the mint howse at Boston all bulljon plate or Spannish Cojne there to be melted & brought to the allay of sterling Silver by John Hull master of the sajd mint and his sworne officers, & by him to be Cojned into 12d : 6d : & 3d peeces...[29]

This order called for Hull to begin producing coins of the plainest possible design, without any figure or image, simply its denomination in Roman numerals on one side, and the letters NE (for New England) on the other. The General Court's decision to begin coining sterling grade silver shillings expressed a desire among the colony's leaders to bridge the crippling gap between untrustworthy fiduciary moneys, like wampum or musket balls, that might possibly enhance trade and circulation of goods within New England, but were useless beyond the region, and the varieties of commodity money that were too rare, too high in purchasing power, and at the moment, too suspect in value, to function effectively as small change in the New England interior.

At the same time, the General Court avoided some of the risks of challenging the home country's monetary authority, for the act specified some other distinctive features of this new coinage:

> 3: And further the sajd master of the mint aforesjd is heereby Required to cojne all the sajd mony of good Silver and of the Just allay of new sterling English mony, & for valew to stampe [struck out: three] two pence in a shilling of lesser vallew then the p[re]sent English Cojne & the lesser peeces p[r]oportionably :

> 4: And all Such Cojne as aforesajd shall be acknowledged to be the Currant Cojne of this Commonwelth & passe from man to man in all pajments accordingly within this Jurisdiction only.[30]

In other words, John Hull was ordered to produce coins of the same quality alloy as English sterling but only about three quarters the weight of their English equivalents. Hull was to stamp the value of twelve pence, or one shilling, on a coin of fine sterling silver that actually weighed only the equivalent of nine pence in English coinage. The order itself reflects the technical difficulty in getting these matters right – the court initially wrote 'three' pence less, then crossed it out and replaced it with 'two.' But in the end, after all the adjustments were made for Hull's fees in producing the coinage and an allowance for wastage in the processing was made, the result was that the Massachusetts coins were roughly three quarters (on average, 77.5 percent) the weight of their English equivalents.[31] A Massachusetts shilling was lighter and smaller than an English one, though valued at the same rate within New England. The lighter weight was to insure that Massachusetts currency would stay in New England, as foreign merchants would not be willing to accept underweight shillings, an intention supported by the order's claim that the new shillings would be legal tender 'within this Jurisdiction only.'

In that sense, the order creating the Massachusetts coinage is striking in its similarity to the plan in Potosi to refurbish the debased Spanish dollar, though for opposite reasons. In Potosi, an enormous profusion of coins with a face value of eight reales, but a commodity weight and value suspected to be only three quarters of that amount, was seen as a serious problem, precisely because these coins were intended to circulate as widely as possible throughout Spain's expansive global empire and beyond. Common knowledge of the coins' corruption was clearly impairing that function. To begin the remedy, the government temporarily reduced the effective face value of these coins, from eight reales to six, in order to get people all over the Spanish empire to return them to Potosi for reminting.

In Boston, the problem was essentially the opposite of Potosi's. Silver was scarce, not plentiful. The objective was not to scatter this scarce coinage to the world (which happened readily enough in the general course of events, as the colonists imported goods of greater value than they had goods of their own to trade for them), but rather to keep silver coins circulating in the region. In effect, Boston's solution mimicked Potosi's problem. John Hull deliberately issued coinage that, like Potosi's, was debased, where the face value was inflated above the 'intrinsic' or commodity value of the silver the coins contained, and by roughly the same amount. But there was a key difference. Potosi's 'problem' stemmed from the fact that nobody knew the precise commodity value of any given coin because the dozen or so *mercaderes* in Potosi were not all equally corrupt – an inherently unstable situation within a commodity money system. Boston, by contrast, made sure, through the well remunerated skills of John Hull, that everyone could be certain of the precise commodity value of a Massachusetts shilling. Granted, the coin was underweight, but its alloy was of the same quality as English sterling. For that reason, it was hoped, the coins would circulate with great public confidence where it was meant to circulate – within New England – but would not be very desirable beyond New England's borders, where merchants expected a shilling to weigh a shilling, and might not want to go to the trouble and expense to convert these strange and possibly illegal coins into more familiar and universally accepted monetary forms.

The initial coins that Hull produced, following the directives of the General Court, did not last long. The design was so plain and unembellished that it positively invited clipping. Few of these coins were made, and almost none have survived. To rectify this problem, the court issued an amended order on October 19, 1652, probably with Hull's direction, 'ffor the prevention of washing or Clipping of all such peices of mony as shall be Coined within this Jurisdiction.'[32] Under this new plan, Hull produced coins with a double rim stamped around the edges on both sides of the coin, an inscription written inside each, and in the center, the image of a tree on one side and the date and coin's denomination on the other. The inscription read 'Masathusets in New England,' which, aside from the curious spelling, neatly stated the position of the colony (Massachusetts) as the dominant political power within the region (New England), and projected the intention of its makers that these coins would integrate and stimulate the economy of the entire region as well.[33]

If these purposes were not clear enough in the design of the coins, the General Court spelled it out in law two years later, when it issued an order limiting the export of Massachusetts coinage outside New England to twenty shillings per person, and appointed searchers at the ports to prevent smuggling of larger amounts:

> Whereas, the end of Coyning mony within this Commonwealth is for the more easy managing the traficque thereof within itself, & not Indended to make returnes to other Countrjes, which cannot Advance any proffitt to such as send it, but Rather a fowerth part Losse Vnlesse such persons doe oppresse & extort in the sale of theire goods to make vp the sajd losse… and vtterly frustrate the end & vse of mony amongst vs.[34]

The idea behind these coins was simple but ingenious, and curiously modern in the fiscal world of the seventeenth century. As guaranteed high-quality sterling grade alloy, the coins were trustworthy as commodities; when you had a Massachusetts shilling, you knew what you had.[35] Yet, the face value stamped on the coin, and the legal exchange value at which it circulated within New England, was higher than the commodity value of the silver within it. The coins were a hybrid, neither pure commodity money (like a Venetian ducat), nor pure fiduciary money (like a lead farthing), but something in between. In precise terms, if Spanish dollars had already been officially cried up by the Massachusetts government, trading at a face value higher than their intrinsic worth, then the Massachusetts shilling was cried up still higher – its face value was greater, per ounce of silver, than a piece of eight. This meant that Spanish dollars, rather than Massachusetts shillings, were more likely to be sent outside the colony as payment for imports, because the Massachusetts shilling had greater local purchasing power than the peso per ounce of silver. It also provided New Englanders with an incentive to have their Spanish dollars converted into Massachusetts shillings. Finally, although the coining of Massachusetts shillings would increase the money supply within New England, it remained the case that silver was scarce in the region, so that the colony was never in danger of the excessive production of coins, especially given the legal commitment to issuing them at sterling grade. In other words, wampum's problem of overproduction and plummeting value was never a concern.

What John Hull and the Massachusetts General Court had done, under the pressure of a commercial economy that demanded a surplus of humble local commodities for the purpose of overseas trade, and further motivated by a scarcity of silver money and the doubtful qualities of those coins they did encounter, was to solve the 'big problem of small change' by accident, or rather by the demands of a peculiar set of necessities. The 'standard formula' by which the small change problem was eventually resolved in Europe and North America was fully implemented only in the nineteenth century: 'In England it was not applied until 1816, and in the United States it was not accepted before 1853.' As Carlo Cipolla describes it,

> [e]very elementary textbook of economics gives the standard formula for maintaining a sound system of fractional money: to issue on government account small coins having a commodity value lower than their monetary value; to limit the quantity of these small coins in circulation; [and] to provide convertibility with unit money.[36]

Massachusetts shillings displayed all three of these qualities. The coins' commodity value was lower than their monetary value (although not as low as most small change in the modern era), they were necessarily limited in quantity by the scarcity of silver in the region, and they were 'convertible with unit money,' be it the Spanish dollar or the English pound in which Boston's merchants recorded overseas transactions in their ledgers.[37]

Conclusion

In the years after the inauguration of the mint in 1652, the political economy of Massachusetts experienced a series of remarkable successes. Over the next thirty years, Hull's mint produced enough coins that, on average, New Englanders were probably supplied at least as well with small change as their contemporaries in England. The overseas trading operations that began in the 1640s took off rapidly, once Boston's merchants could be sure of finding ways to load their ships with New England products for export. John Hull himself took great advantage of these opportunities by using his increasing wealth from the mint to finance the development of lumber mills in New Hampshire, a horse farm in Rhode Island, and other forms of vertical integration that gave him control of the goods he needed for overseas commercial ventures. By the end of the seventeenth century, the port of Boston had grown so rapidly as to be competitive with every other port city in the British Isles, save London, with respect to the volume of its carrying trade.

The internal growth of New England's population and economy matched that of its overseas trade. Despite the sudden end of immigration around 1640, the natural increase among the 20,000 colonists who arrived in that first decade was so rapid as to double the population every twenty-five years. To find land on which this growing population might settle, the Massachusetts Bay colony incorporated territory to the north and east, including parts of present-day Maine and New Hampshire, in addition to increasing expansion within its original boundaries. However, the explosive growth and economic success of the settler population had serious consequences for New England's indigenous population. By 1675, the growing friction between English settlers and Indians erupted in open warfare, a long and bloody conflict known as King Philip's War, named after the Wampanoag leader who formed an Indian coalition to drive out the English.

Hannah Hull's wedding to Samuel Sewall took place on February 28, 1676, at the height of King Philip's War, into which John Hull, his resources, and his personal credit were being ever more deeply drawn as treasurer of the colony. Three months later, Hull would oversee the sale of two hundred enemy Indian captives into the labor markets of Spain – Cadiz and Malaga – two stops among the myriad links in the expanding chain of Atlantic commercial contacts that Hull and his colleagues had forged over the preceding three decades. This brutal form of prisoner exchange offers a gruesome demonstration of how tightly consolidated the interests of English colonists in New England had become as a result of the slow and deliberate development of the region's integrated political economy. The war demonstrated the remarkable solidarity of economic and political interest groups among the region's white settler population, a solidarity made possible by an economic system that linked the productive success of the region's ordinary farmers to the mercantile interests of Boston's commercial leaders.

In fact, King Philip's War actually strengthened solidarity among colonial groups within New England. The New England Colonies successfully ran a conscription campaign, recruiting the poor from towns all over the region to fight in their cause, and raising taxes to pay the salaries of the soldiers.[38] Furthermore, the authorities in Boston never turned to the crown for assistance during the crisis. Instead, Philip and his Indian allies were defeated entirely by home-grown soldiers, both volunteers and conscripts, led by local generals (some of whom had experience in the wars in England *against* the king in the 1640s), and financed by the colony's own resources.

The sacrifice of the indigenous populations of New England to the internal expansion of the city-state of Boston is obviously the dark and bloody outcome of this process, the most flagrant and indefensible violation of the commonwealth principles that Boston otherwise espoused. But even here, despite gross injustices done to loyal Christian Indians – many of whom were interned

FIGURE 10.4 Peace medal, Boston, 1676

on Deer Island during the war, ostensibly for their safety but greatly to their misery – and despite the growing hatred of Indians in general that the bloody fighting inspired among many Englishmen and women, there were nonetheless substantial numbers of Christian Indians who had adopted English ways, allied themselves with English interests, and fought for the English colonies during the war, demonstrating the extent of their own integration into the political economy of Boston.[39]

Longtime supporters of Indian missions and peaceable relations such as John Eliot, Daniel Gookin, Thomas Danforth, and John Cotton of Plymouth lent their support to the effort to maintain distinctions among Indian groups and protect those loyal to English ways.[40] But of course, it could often be difficult to tell friend from enemy Indians, especially for those English colonists who encountered Indians less frequently. To help with this problem, the Massachusetts General Court turned to lessons well learned. On June 20, 1676, they held a council at Charlestown, across the river from Boston, and presented to Christian Indian soldiers fighting in the English cause a brass medallion, made to resemble a coin, with an image of a fighting Indian drawn from the Massachusetts Bay Company seal on one side, and a vaguely poetic inscription signed by Edward Rawson, the colony's secretary, on the other: 'In the present Warr with the Heathen Natives of this Land/They giving us peace and mercy at there hands' (Figure 10.4). To identify yourself with the city-state of Boston, it was good to wear its coin around your neck, as a sign of your willingness to circulate the goods of the commonwealth and to give back to the state what the state had given you.

Notes

1 This article builds on an earlier work; see Mark Peterson, 'Big Money Comes to Boston: The Curious History of the Pine Tree Shilling,' *Common-place.org*, 6.3 (2006), http://www.common-place.org/vol-06/no-03/peterson.

2 Lewis Hanke, *The Imperial City of Potosi: An Unwritten Chapter in the History of Spanish America* (The Hague: Nijhoff, 1956); Henry Kamen, *Empire: How Spain Became a World Power, 1492–1763* (New York: Harper Collins, 2003), 194ff.

3 100,000 pesos in this era would have been worth 40,000 sterling, a huge sum of money. In the 1640s, the entire value of the wool trade from Spain to England was roughly £200,000.

4 Peter Bakewell, *Silver and Entrepreneurship in Seventeenth-Century Potosi: The Life and Times of Antonio Lopez de Quiroga* (Albuquerque, NM: University of New Mexico Press, 1988), 121–123; for a discussion of silver mining and Indian labor at Potosi, see Bakewell, *Miners of the Red Mountain: Indian Labor in Potosi, 1545–1640* (Albuquerque, NM: University of New Mexico Press, 1984).

5 Estimate of the price of slaves in Peru is drawn from Carlos Newland and Maria Jesus san Segundo, 'Human Capital and Other Determinants of the Price Life Cycle of a Slave: Peru and La Plata in the Eighteenth Century,' *Journal of Economic History* 56.3 (1996): 694–701.

6 Estimates drawn from Louis Jordan, *John Hull, the Mint, and the Economics of Massachusetts Coinage* (Lebanon, NH: University Press of New England, 2002), 102–117.

7 Nathaniel Hawthorne, *Grandfather's Chair and Biographical Stories* (Boston, MA: Houghton Mifflin, 1896), 32–33.

8 John Hull, Account Books, MS, New England Historic and Genealogical Society, Boston, MA.

9 The other major source of New World silver in this era were the mines of Zacatecas in Mexico, but in the 17th century, Potosi's output still overshadowed that of Zacatecas. See Peter J. Bakewell, *Silver Mining and Society in Colonial Mexico: Zacatecas, 1546–1700* (New York: Cambridge University Press, 2002).

10 John J. McCusker and Russell Menard, *The Economy of British America, 1607–1789* (Chapel Hill, NC: University of North Carolina Press, 1991) offers an excellent example of this approach.

11 Adam Smith, *An Inquiry into the Nature and Causes of the Wealth of Nations* (Basil: Tourneisen, 1791), vol. 2, bk IV, 'Of Systems of Political Oeconomy,' 230.

12 See Robert Chalmers, *A History of Currency in the British Colonies* (London: HMSO, 1893), 150–151.

13 Thomas J. Sargent and Francois R. Velde, *The Big Problem of Small Change* (Princeton, NJ: Princeton University Press, 2002), 65.

14 Heated conversations on this question took place in the 1660s and 1670s, as the Restoration crown sought to curb Boston's independence; see Mark Peterson, 'Boston Pays Tribute: Autonomy and Empire in the Atlantic World,' in *Shaping the Stuart World, 1603–1714: The Atlantic Connection*, ed. Allan Macinnes and Arthur Williamson (Leiden: Brill, 2006), 311–336.

15 Margaret Newell, *From Dependency to Independence: Economic Revolution in Colonial New England* (Ithaca, NY: Cornell University Press, 1998), 75. This 'invisible' quality of Boston's economy confused many English observers, like Sir Francis Brewster, whose *Essays on Trade and Navigation* (1654) described New England as 'that unprofitable Plantation, which now brings nothing to this Nation, but to the contrary buries Numbers of Industrious People in a Wilderness, that produceth nothing but Provisions to feed them,' 88, 91, cited in Newell, *From Dependency to Independence*, 70.

16 Sargent and Velde, *The Big Problem of Small Change*, 48.

17 Deborah Valenze, *The Social Life of Money in the English Past* (Cambridge: Cambridge University Press, 2006), 35.

18 According to Sargent and Velde, 'over 12,700 different types of tokens have been catalogued for the period from 1644 to 1672, issued in 1,700 different English towns. An estimated 3,000 were issued in London alone. ... The circulation of each token was limited geographically to a few streets, but there existed in London at least one 'changer of farthings' in Drury Lane, who issued his own farthings' (*The Big Problem of Small Change*, 267). Seventeenth-century Bostonians must have been aware of these fiduciary money practices; see George Berry, *Seventeenth-Century England: Traders and their Tokens* (London: Seaby, 1988).

19 Daniel Vickers, *Farmers and Fishermen: Two Centuries of Work in Essex County, Massachusetts, 1630–1850* (Chapel Hill, NC: University of North Carolina Press, 1994).

20 This way of conceptualizing the monetary world of nation-states did not fully develop until the nineteenth century; see Eric Helleiner, *The Making of National Money: Territorial Currencies in Historical Perspective* (Ithaca, NY: Cornell University Press, 2003).

21 Curtis Putnam Nettels, *The Money Supply of the American Colonies before 1720* (Madison, WI: University of Wisconsin, 1934), 236–237; Sylvester Sage Crosby, *Early Coins of America and the Laws Governing their Issue* (Boston, MA: S. Crosby, 1875), 80; Nathaniel Shurtleff, ed., *Records of the Governor and Company of the Massachusetts Bay in New England*, 5 vols. (Boston, MA: W. White, 1853–1854), 4: part 2, 706.

22 Marc Shell writes, 'The first coin engraved with the numeral 2, insists one theorist of art, was the earliest conceptual art: it fiduciarily dissociated symbol from thing' (*Art and Money* [Chicago, IL: University of Chicago Press, 1995], 10). On clipped and cut coins in seventeenth century England, see Valenze, *The Social Life of Money*, 36.

23 Bakewell, *Silver and Entrepreneurship*, 36–44.

24 Quoted in ibid., 38. My discussion in this and the following paragraph is based on Bakewell's biography of Lopez de Quiroga in ibid., and on his *Miners of the Red Mountain*.

25 Bakewell, *Silver and Entrepreneurship*, 40–44.

26 The colonial governments in Spanish-America responded with measures to compensate for the scandal, although distance and information-control problems allowed merchants in some places, such as Buenos Aires, to hide the facts of the scandal well into the 1650s. The French government issued measures regulating the acceptance of Spanish coins as legal tender starting in the late 1640s. See Philip L. Mossman, 'The Potosi Scandal and the Massachusetts Mint,' *The Colonial Newsletter: A Research Journal in Early American Numismatics* 48.2 (2008): 3289–3309; and Sewall Menzel, *Cobs, Pieces of Eight, and Treasure Coins: The Early Spanish-American Mints and their Coinages* (New York: The American Numismatic Society, 2004).

27 Crosby, *Early Coins of America*, 30–31.

28 John Hull, 'Private Diary,' in *Transactions of the American Antiquarian Society*, 3 (1857): 145. Furthermore, an address to King Charles II written by the Massachusetts General Court in October, 1684, in an attempt to justify the Massachusetts coinage, suggests a strong awareness of the problem created by the Potosi mint scandal: 'Then comes in a considerable quantity of light, base Spanish money, whereby many people were cousened, and the Colony in danger of being undone thereby; which put us upon the project of melting it down, and stamping such pieces as aforesaid to pass in payment of debts amongst ourselves.' 'Report of a Committee appointed October 30, 1684,' Political Volume of Manuscripts, vol. 1, Massachusetts State Archives, reprinted as Appendix to Hull, 'Private Diary:' 282.

29 Crosby, *Early Coins of America*, 34.

30 Ibid.

31 For a discussion of these technical issues, see Jordan, *John Hull*, 54–73.

32 Crosby, *Early Coins of America*, 44.

33 Ibid. Crosby reprints the Massachusetts General Court legislation regarding all the significant acts in the creation of the mint, 31ff.

34 Ibid., 104, 79.
35 In fact, the Massachusetts General Court legislation went so far as to allow customers bringing silver to the mint to stay and watch the coining process and get exact receipts from Hull.
36 Carlo M. Cipolla, *Money Prices and Civilization in the Mediterranean World, Fifth to Seventeenth Century* (Princeton, NJ: Princeton University Press, 1956), 27.
37 Louis Jordan, 'On the Founding of the Hull Mint,' *The Colonial Newsletter: A Research Journal in Early American Numismatics*, 141 (2009): 3477–3488. On John Hull negotiating the difference in monetary values between Boston and London, see John Hull, Letter Book, American Antiquarian Society, Worcester, MA, ms., 237, John Hull to John Peake, January 4, 1674/75.
38 James Drake, *King Philip's War: Civil War in New England, 1675–1676* (Amherst, MA: University of Massachusetts Press, 1999), 146–147.
39 Ibid., 147–162.
40 Jenny Hale Pulsipher, *Subjects unto the Same King: Indians, English, and the Contest for Authority in Colonial New England* (Philadelphia, PA: University of Pennyslvania Press, 2006), 154–155.

11

ANATOLIAN TIMBER AND EGYPTIAN GRAIN

Things that made the Ottoman Empire

Alan Mikhail

The Ottoman Empire captured Egypt and much of the Arab Middle East from the Mamluks in 1517.[1] With this conquest came many spoils: a near doubling of the empire's territory; the inclusion of Islam's holiest sites into Ottoman domains; access to the Red Sea and Indian Ocean; strategic control of most of the eastern Mediterranean; sovereignty over some of the largest cities in the Middle East (Cairo, Aleppo, Jerusalem); and a massive influx of money, people, and resources from these newly conquered lands. All this notwithstanding, the conquest also presented the Ottomans with many logistical and administrative challenges. The most pressing from an imperial perspective was how to rule and collect taxes over such a large and widespread area, one with many already-ensconced bureaucratic and legal traditions.[2] This was a problem that the Ottomans – like all imperial states – regularly faced after the conquest and attempted absorption of new territories.

These rather conventional and routine administrative challenges aside, the Ottomans' territorial expansion of 1517 also brought them face to face with many novel challenges they had never before encountered. One of the most important of these was a logistical problem involving the movement of two strategic goods that would prove crucial in shaping much of the empire's rule after 1517 – wood and grain.[3] Concerns surrounding these goods, especially the wood, were largely a byproduct of the Ottomans' entrance into the Red Sea and Indian Ocean worlds.[4] To benefit from – never mind to attempt to control – the lucrative commerce of the Red Sea, to challenge Portuguese power in the Indian Ocean, and to provision the yearly pilgrimage to Mecca and Medina, the Ottomans needed ships in the Red Sea. To build these ships, the Ottomans needed wood.[5] Herein lies the main problem. In and around the major Ottoman Red Sea port of Suez, there was a vital lack of useable wood supplies. For all its agricultural wealth and rich soils, Egypt simply did not have adequate domestic wood supplies to feed the growing Ottoman need for shipbuilding timbers in Suez.[6] This wood thus had to be brought from elsewhere.[7]

This chapter tells the story of the enormous logistical and bureaucratic effort and organization the Ottomans undertook to overcome the problem of wood supply in Ottoman Suez by bringing lumber from Anatolia. To trace this story we must follow the wood. The wood tracked in this chapter is a group of timbers that were first harvested in the forests of southwestern Anatolia and ended up being bent to shape the hulls of three ships in Suez in 1725. These vessels would eventually sail from Egypt to the Hijaz (the region on the western coast of what is today Saudi Arabia housing the cities of Mecca and Medina) carrying massive quantities of grain to feed people across the Red Sea.[8] This is thus a story of provisioning – of what lengths the Ottomans were forced to go to make possible the movement of grain from Egypt to people in the Hijaz. The path taken by this amount of wood is important for what it illuminates about the economic history of the Ottoman Empire. The domestic markets of Egypt, Anatolia, Istanbul, or Suez alone were unable to either meet the demands for certain raw materials or undertake a massively complex and expensive logistical project like moving parts of a forest across the Mediterranean to Egypt and then overland to Suez. This sort of work could only be done by a political and organizational entity like the imperial administration of the Ottoman Empire. The example of these ships' construction thus illuminates how the early modern Ottoman Empire occasionally intervened in economic affairs and market relations in different parts of the empire to affect a desired outcome such as the undertaking of a massive infrastructural or construction project.

Grain needs ships

Most of the current scholarship on Ottoman shipbuilding and timber provisioning in the Red Sea focuses on the sixteenth century.[9] This was the period when the Ottomans first expanded into the Red Sea and captured parts of Yemen, Bahrain, and other sites on the Arabian Peninsula.[10] This was also, and perhaps more importantly from the perspective of modern scholarship, the heyday of Ottoman–Portuguese rivalry in the Indian Ocean. Our story of wood supplying, however, comes from the first half of the eighteenth century, a full 150 years after the Ottomans supposedly lost interest in the Red Sea. As we will see, however, Ottoman stakes in the Red Sea remained quite high into the eighteenth century and focused mostly on commerce and provisioning between Egypt and the Hijaz.[11]

Despite Ottoman–Portuguese high-seas imperial rivalries in the sixteenth century, the most consistent, longer-lasting, and historically more significant reason the Ottomans brought wood to Suez to build ships in the early modern period was to feed people in the Hijaz and to support transport and commerce in the region. The Hijaz was of symbolic value to the Ottomans because custodianship of the holy cities allowed them to make universalistic claims of authority, leadership, and sovereignty in the Muslim world.[12] With this symbolic power and religious status also came responsibilities. The yearly Muslim pilgrimage to Mecca and Medina was surely the largest annual gathering of people anywhere in the early modern world. It was an enormous undertaking in terms of logistics, transportation, and provisioning, which had to function smoothly if the Ottomans wanted to ensure respect and pliancy from the thousands of pilgrims who came to the Hijaz every year and who would then return to their homes in Hyderabad, Tehran, and Sofia with accounts of their experiences.

A crucial aspect of this maintenance of the yearly pilgrimage was providing pilgrims with adequate food supplies. Such provisioning was the historic duty of a pious and proper Muslim sovereign and was also in the practical interests of the Ottoman state so as to ensure the health and well-being of its visitors.[13] Egypt came to play a central role in this system of Ottoman provisioning.[14] Not only was it the largest grain-producing region in the Ottoman Empire, but it was also, quite conveniently, right across the slender Red Sea from the Hijaz. Thus throughout the imperial record of the Ottoman state, we have copious materials evidencing imperial interests in maintaining food supplies from Egypt for the yearly pilgrimage.[15] Indeed, after Istanbul, the Hijaz was the most common destination for Egyptian grains in the Ottoman period.[16] Ottoman concern for food production in Egypt often took the form of imperial orders to maintain and repair irrigation works in rural Egypt, since water was obviously the key to food production in Egypt.[17] For example, a series of orders sent to Egypt between 1709 and 1711 about the repair of a very important set of dams and dikes in the region of Fayyum made the point over and over again that grains grown in Egypt were to be sent to feed pilgrims in the Hijaz and that it was therefore imperative that these irrigation works function properly to grow the needed amounts of food.[18] Like other regions of Egypt, almost all of Fayyum's surplus grain supplies went to the Hijaz. Additionally, Fayyum also maintained its status as a major exporter of grain to the Hijaz because of the many pious endowments (*awqāf*) for the holy cities established in the region and throughout Upper Egypt more generally. The chief function of these Upper Egyptian endowments attached to the Hijaz was to provide grains for both the pilgrimage caravan and for the people of Mecca and Medina.[19]

The food grown in Fayyum and in numerous other regions in Egypt would eventually make its way to Suez to await shipment to the Hijaz. While Fayyum had always sent the majority of its export grain to Suez rather than to any other port, during the fifteenth century, just a few years before the Ottomans conquered Egypt, Suez became even more important than Egypt's southern ports (Qusayr and Aydab most prominently) as the main hub of export from the province to the Hijaz. This was chiefly due to shifts in agricultural cultivation in the period that saw the Delta emerge as Egypt's richest area of food production.[20] Whether grown in soils in Fayyum or elsewhere in rural Egypt, once food was in Suez it could only, quite obviously, continue its journey across the sea by ship. And for much of the Ottoman period, ships were readily available. Quite often, though, there were none to be had in Suez either because of disrepair, shipwreck, or needs elsewhere.[21] Such was the case in the spring of 1725 when the Ottomans had plenty of food in Suez to send to the Hijaz, but no ships to get it there.

Ships need wood

A series of cases from the archival record of Ottoman Egypt brings to life the complicated procedures involved in delivering wood to Egypt from forests in southwestern Anatolia to build three *galettas* (*kalite*) in Suez (Figure 11.1).[22] Wood was a strategic asset for the empire.[23] This was partly a function of the fact that it was available only in a few specific regions within the empire's borders (on parts of the southern Anatolian coast, around sections of the Black Sea littoral, and in Greater Syria).[24] The Ottoman Empire therefore came to manage woods supplies and their distribution and movement very closely.[25] Trees in the Ottoman Empire thus came to be controlled by the logic of the state rather than by the market. Wood – and for that matter food as well – entered into an imperial chain of demand, need, and availability in which the deficiencies of one region were met by the excesses of others. In the same way that the Hijaz relied on Egypt for food, Egypt relied on other parts of the Ottoman Empire for

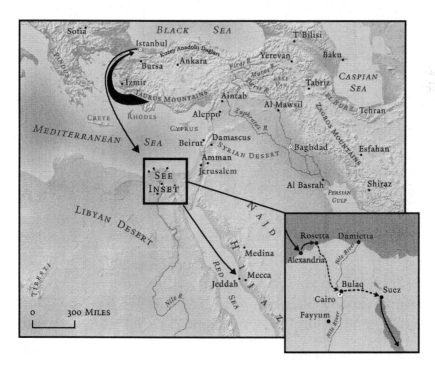

FIGURE 11.1   Map of timber transport traced in this chapter

wood. The rather complicated procedures for bringing wood to Egypt were thus Ottoman attempts to project imperial sovereignty through the management of an essential resource needed to move excess amounts of caloric energy stored in grain to be consumed elsewhere by – in this case – pilgrims from all over the Muslim world. Integral to this resource management was the fact that within the Ottoman world, it was only the imperial state itself that could undertake such a project.

Wood in the Ottoman Empire was harvested in the forests of southwestern Anatolia and parts of the southern Black Sea coast every three to four years by peasants in those areas who were hired by the Ottoman state as temporary laborers. They worked for an entire season to cut trees and to transport them to imperial storage facilities in Istanbul.[26] The organization of this labor was overseen by the *kereste emîni* (timber superintendent), who was an official in the department of the Imperial Dockyards (*Tersâne-i Âmire*), the official body responsible for the collection of wood in the empire and the institution that would store the timber for later use and distribution.[27] The *kereste emîni* managed a veritable army of laborers (*amele*) in the work of cutting and moving trees.[28] Various military cadres (*yaya, müsellem, yörük, canbaz*) and specialized craftsmen (*neccar, teksinarcı, kalafatçı*) worked to turn trees into useable wood supplies.[29] Both southwestern Anatolia and the Black Sea coast were particularly good regions for timber harvest because of their extensive forest cover and proximity to coastlines.[30] Since these trees were primarily harvested for the construction of Ottoman naval ships, it made sense that the administration of the Ottoman Imperial Dockyards oversaw forest management in the empire.

Often these trees were moved to Istanbul on merchant ships rented by the state. In the case of southwestern Anatolia, for example, numerous orders were sent to the imperial governor of the island of Rhodes to organize the renting of these ships, as this region was under his administrative purview (Figure 11.2). Given the relatively high number of orders sent to this imperial governor in the late 1710s and early 1720s, it seems likely that most of the trees going to Istanbul's timber storage facilities in these years were coming from southwestern Anatolia.[31] The important point about the empire's timber storage facilities is that they represented an attempt to monopolize the supply and control of wood as a strategic good. Other efforts at forest management included designating the vast majority of forests in the Ottoman Empire as having official (*miri*) status and promulgating numerous regulations forbidding the cutting of their trees and grazing, building, or hunting in imperial woodlands without the proper permissions.[32] By attempting to control the use of forests and by centralizing the distribution of the empire's trees in the Imperial Dockyards, an institution literally at the base of the palace, the Sultan could control how this wood was used and what projects it supported.[33]

In the cases from 1725, the palace directed that wood – again, wood mostly likely originating in southwestern Anatolia – be sent from the central Ottoman timber distribution facility in Istanbul to Alexandria on the Egyptian

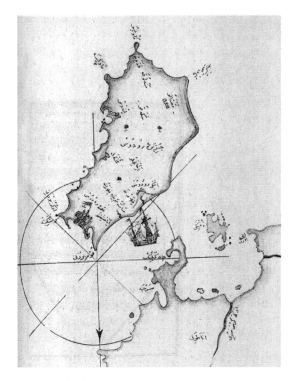

FIGURE 11.2   Ottoman Rhodes

Mediterranean coast.[34] As in many instances of moving wood from parts of the Anatolian coast to Istanbul, merchant galleys (*tüccar sefineleri*) were rented to assist a group of imperial (*miri*) ships in moving this wood from the capital to Alexandria.[35] Alexandria was central to Ottoman interests in the early modern eastern Mediterranean.[36] It was used as an Ottoman naval base for various operations around the sea. Ships from Alexandria, for example, supported Ottoman military expeditions to Chios in 1566, Malta in 1575, and Crete in 1666 and 1715. The port was also crucial as a controlling hinge of trade between the Mediterranean and Red Sea and Indian Ocean.[37] An enormous amount of the goods coming from the Indian Ocean via ship eventually made their way to Alexandria overland from Suez to be put on ships sailing to points across the Mediterranean world (essentially the opposite direction of the wood in our case).[38] Because of its military and economic importance, the Ottomans paid particularly close attention to the administration of Alexandria through a customs regime, legal and economic regulations, and a military presence.

The leg of the wood's journey from Istanbul to Alexandria was the longest (in terms of distance) of its entire itinerary from seed to ship hull.[39] It was also the most dangerous because of the Mediterranean's rough waters, threats of piracy, and various other possibilities for damage to the precious cargo. Piracy was a foremost concern of the Ottomans in the Mediterranean, and they undertook various measures over the years to try to combat it.[40] However difficult it might be for us to imagine, we must not underestimate the scale of moving such an amount of wood across the Mediterranean. Likely hundreds of very large logs that each required a dozen or so men to move were put on enormous ships and then sailed for hundreds of miles over the course of a fortnight or so, only to be taken off of those ships in another gigantic operation. There is indeed evidence of a floating crane in use in the port of Alexandria in the first half of the eighteenth century to aid in the loading and unloading of cargo and also to help in the repair of ships in port.[41] The merchant galleys that were rented to move this wood across the Mediterranean were obviously very large ships and had to be stable enough to deal with the treacheries of open sea. These ships and their captains were accustomed to this journey, as they were the ones who most often moved grains, textiles, finished goods, foodstuffs, and other products between the empire's most lucrative province and its capital. And like these other items, the wood in 1725 was entered into the customs registers of Alexandria, a requirement of all cargo entering Egypt from the Mediterranean.[42]

Once this wood had made it safely to Alexandria and had been adequately registered by the state, it had to be moved to yet another set of ships. This transfer was necessitated by concerns of both geography and technology. Getting to Suez from Alexandria – there was of course no Suez Canal in 1725 – required sailing down the Nile into the interior of Egypt.[43] In the early eighteenth century, however, there was no internal waterway connecting Alexandria to the Nile.[44] Thus, from Alexandria ships had to sail east along Egypt's Mediterranean coast to enter the Nile system either at Rosetta or Damietta, the two branches of the river forming the Nile Delta. Unless prevented by rough waters, a storm, shipwreck, or some other impediment, almost all ships from Alexandria entered the Nile through the Rosetta branch because of its proximity to Egypt's second city. Although the enormous galleys that brought the massive load of wood from Istanbul to Egypt were extremely good at navigating the Mediterranean's rough seas, they were less well suited to sailing on smaller, narrower, and curvier bodies of water like the Nile. Thus to overcome this navigational limitation, the wood in our case, like all cargo following this path, was transferred to a set of smaller, more compact and more nimble ships known as *cerîm*.[45] As with each of the transfers in this wood's journey, this one required great care, patience, and effort to move the wood and to protect it against damage and theft. Furthermore, as with some of the galleys that crossed the Mediterranean, these smaller ships were also rented by the Ottoman administration from merchants in the area.[46]

Now on the appropriate type of vessel, the wood sailed east, hugging the Egyptian coast, toward the mouth of the Rosetta branch of the Nile. Late summer and early fall were especially difficult times to enter the Rosetta mouth because of prevailing winds blowing out to sea and because of the force of the Nile's water near the end of the flood season pushing out to sea.[47] The *cerîm* ships in our case were, however, sailing in spring, so they had little trouble entering the mouth of the river's western branch. The wood's next stop was, perhaps not surprisingly, Cairo, specifically the area just to the north of the city known as Bulaq, Cairo's main economic port and commercial district.[48] Because of the unique economic status of wood as a commodity in the Ottoman Empire and because the timber in our case had already been earmarked by the state for a specific purpose, it did not enter into the business transactions that made Bulaq a hub of economic life in Egypt and the Mediterranean. The wood was noted but not traded. Instead, as before, it was transferred one last time to complete its journey to Suez.

This transfer was once again affected by Egypt's geography. For the entire journey until Cairo – from the forests to Istanbul, Istanbul to Alexandria, and Alexandria to Bulaq – the wood moved on water. Indeed, it was of the utmost importance to maximize the geographic distance traversed on water since this was clearly the easiest, cheapest, and most efficient means of moving such a heavy, unwieldy, and large quantity of wood. Between Bulaq and Suez, however, there was no waterway, only eighty miles of desert. Faced with no other option to get the wood to Suez (again, here as well, there was no canal), Ottoman authorities overseeing the project and the Egyptians they enlisted to help them arranged for the trickiest, most expensive, most complex, and most arduous part of the wood's journey. In Bulaq, they hired a convoy of camels to pull the wood through the desert.[49] Without the possibility of using ships to take advantage of water and wind power, camels were harnessed as the next best energy source affording the necessary power and stamina to move this load overland.[50]

The use of these camels, however, did not come cheap. The cost of renting the animals and of paying those who would load and unload the wood and lead the animals through the desert was the significant sum of 800 *niṣf fiḍḍa* (or *para*) – 450 *para* for the men and 350 *para* for the camels.[51] As further evidence of the cost of animal labor in transport, consider that in a list of forty-six expenses related to the pilgrimage of the year 1696 (the closest year to 1725 for which we have such figures), we find that animal labor represented nearly 10 percent of the total expended from the treasury of Egypt on the pilgrimage in that year – the impressive sum of one million *para*.[52] In the same way that historians have given much attention to the use of ships, navigation tools, and knowledge in the maritime commerce of the early modern period, so too must we recognize the importance of animals as means of transport, power, communication, commerce, and travel in the early modern world. The power, speed, and stamina provided by camels, water buffaloes, donkeys, and other animals in the Ottoman Empire made possible commercial relations, imperial governance, and agricultural production.[53] As the camels in this case show, animals – like wood – were vital commodities that allowed the state to accomplish and undertake tasks it could not do otherwise.[54] Historians estimate that camels in the Ottoman Empire could carry a quarter-ton of weight for about fifteen miles a day, 20 percent more than horses and mules and over three times more than donkeys.[55] Accepting this estimate and giving some leeway to the enormous load of wood in our case, it likely took the camels and their handlers about a week to cross the desert from Cairo to Suez.

The wood had finally reached Suez. Now that it had moved from Istanbul across the Mediterranean to the Red Sea, the work of actually building the ships needed to move food from Egypt to the Hijaz – the ultimate goal of this project, lest we have forgotten – could finally begin.[56] The journey of this wood from southwestern Anatolia, to Istanbul, to Suez, through Alexandria, Rosetta, and Cairo was long, inefficient, and difficult for numerous reasons. Even if the construction of ships in Suez was an urgent matter, it would surely take at least several weeks as in this case (or perhaps longer) before the construction materials even arrived. And, of course, this was only the first step, since it would take anywhere from another six months to two years to complete construction of the ships in port, depending on the size of the ships, the number of available laborers, unforeseen problems with the work, and other contingencies.

Another obvious problem with the wood's transport was the multiple transfers it required. Wood was packed from the royal dockyards onto ships in Istanbul, sailed to Alexandria, was then transferred to another kind of ship, sailed to Cairo via Rosetta, was packed onto the backs of camels, dragged through the desert, and was only then finally unloaded in Suez to be used for its ultimate purpose of ship construction. All of these transfers, especially the overland leg between Bulaq and Suez, exposed this lumber to damage and theft. The wood could have been dropped, lost, chipped, stolen, or damaged in any number of ways. And, of course, the wood's transport involved great financial expense: the price of ships and sailors, customs duties, camels and camel drivers, food for sailors, and so on. Despite these difficulties and costs, however, the Ottoman imperial bureaucracy had few alternatives.[57] If the goal was the construction of ships in Suez, then wood was needed, and since Egypt had no wood, it had to be brought from elsewhere. These were the realities and costs of the absence of forests in Egypt.

Economy needs state

The story of the construction of these three ships in Suez in 1725 reveals an important dimension of how certain kinds of economic resources were utilized in the Ottoman Empire. No individual, collective organization, or corporate entity in the empire could have built these ships; only the state was capable of undertaking such a project. When I use the word 'state' in this context, I do not mean merely the Sultan's imperial divan. Rather I understand the state to be the entire bureaucratic apparatus of the imperial administration, which included merchants who rented their ships to the empire, temporary forest workers hired by the Imperial Dockyards, camels used to pull wood through the desert, and shipbuilders in Suez. A project of the scale and cost involved in this case, employing so many different kinds of people in such disparate parts of the empire, could only be coordinated through imperial mechanisms – a centralized wood depot, a court system that facilitated communication across the Mediterranean, a bureaucracy with access to large amounts of cash and capital, and a network of merchants and craftsmen who knew that their goods and labor would be compensated.

By understanding what the empire could do that nothing else could, we gain a clearer understanding of what an often-vague notion of 'the empire' was at the most basic level on the ground in a place like Egypt. The Ottoman Empire was an economic mechanism for coordinating resource management that provided the materials, finances, and organization to, among other things, build ships in Suez. Again, without this political and economic administration, no other entity in Egypt, or anywhere else in the empire, could have effected the construction of these ships. This fact stands in the face of several important assumptions about the empire in this period and thus helps us understand something of Ottoman imperial governance in the first half of the eighteenth century.

First, it has long been assumed that after the seventeenth century, the Ottoman imperial administration largely gave up any attempts to control economic affairs or to directly intervene in the economy.[58] Price ceilings (*narh*) are the classic example cited in this regard. The empire did away with them at the end of the sixteenth century, and they reemerged only much later in the last two decades of the eighteenth century. The present case of the three ships, however, shows the intense involvement of the state – again, in its most capacious meaning – in market relations, resource management, and transportation networks. This shipbuilding in 1725 was, in other words, an instance of Ottoman economic interventionism. The physical resources of the market, its transportation capacities, and its available labor could not provide the wood and muscle needed to build the three ships. Thus, the state had to intervene to provide and then manage these resources.[59]

This case also shows us that the Ottoman state in the first half of the eighteenth century was still able to influence, impact, and administer areas at some distance from the capital. Historians of Egypt and of elsewhere in the empire have traditionally assumed that Istanbul largely pulled back from the provinces in the eighteenth century and was not able to provision its army and other vital organs of the state.[60] In the present case, by contrast, the state clearly comes through as an actor of enormous economic and organizational wherewithal. Importantly, as well, much of the administration of resources that took place in this case was at the very edges of the empire – not in the empire's largest cities and, indeed, at some of the furthest points from imperial nodes of power like Istanbul and Cairo. According to much of the existing literature, southwestern Anatolia and Suez would have been the kinds of places where one might expect the imperial presence in the eighteenth century to have been rather weak, but, again, just the opposite seems to have been the case. Commodity histories thus open up new possibilities for understanding the geography and function of Ottoman imperial governance. As the cases of wood and grain show, commodity acquisition, transport, and utilization created multiple kinds of linkages and connections that are otherwise difficult to trace. Following a material object, in other words, usefully allows us to push beyond established ways of thinking about the inner workings of early modern polities like the Ottoman Empire.

Finally, the building of these three ships is a wonderful example of the involvement of local actors in the day-to-day governance and operation of the empire. At every point in the journeys of both the grain and the wood to Suez, and then eventually to the Hijaz, it was peasants, small-scale actors, and local merchants, sailors, and laborers who directed the state how best to successfully meet its goals. Lumberjacks in the mountains of southwestern Anatolia knew the forests in their area better than anyone else and provided the expertise, knowledge, and experience the state needed to effectively manage and harvest wood. Likewise, sailors on the Mediterranean, who knew the best sea lanes and how to control their ships, brought the wood to Egypt. Camel drivers and their animals moved the wood across the desert, and established local shipbuilders in Suez were the ones who finally put the boats together. It was the unity and coordination of the Ottoman state that brought all these disparate actors together for the goal of building the ships. At no point in this process, however, were Ottoman imperial bureaucrats the ones actually carrying the wood, hammering the nails, and pulling the camels. Indeed, clearly the imperial administration could not have done any of this without the participation of local actors in the workings of the state.

This fact was in large part a function of the necessities and difficulties of managing and utilizing local environments and resources – forests, soils, the heat of the desert, and the flow of the river. Each of these particular environments and ecological forces demanded specific local knowledge, experience, and expertise, and the Ottomans relied on locals to help them operate in and use these natural environments, since this was the most expedient, sustainable, and efficient means of harnessing environmental resources and expertise. Thus, it was the collective knowledge and experience of local actors all across the empire that allowed the imperial state to function. At the same time, though, it was the connective administrative and economic links of the empire that tied the labor of lumberjacks in southwestern Anatolia to that of camel drivers in eastern Egypt. Neither the knowhow and experience of local actors nor the administrative acumen and integrative powers of the Ottoman administration alone, without the participation of the other, could have moved wood to Suez or, more generally, managed natural resources in the empire. This was thus a commodity utilization chain of local labor and knowledge, linked together across the Mediterranean, from one continent to another, by the Ottoman imperial administration.

State needs nature

Wood was not like any other commodity in the empire. Its scarcity and strategic value dictated much of the way the state came to manage it and many of the economic relationships forged around it. The only useable supplies of forest in the empire were in areas of southern Anatolia, around the Black Sea coast, and in Greater Syria, and the state, as already mentioned, put in place a very sophisticated forestry management system to maintain these woodlands. As with almost all natural resources, much of wood's value in the Ottoman Empire came not from human labor but from the solar energy of the sun, nutrients in the soil, and copious amounts of water. Thus, in contrast to the traditional labor theory of value, which posits that the value of most goods is a reflection of the work humans do to *produce* objects for the market, much (or perhaps most) of the utility and value of the Ottoman Empire's wood came from nonhuman nature. Clearly, human labor and energy went into the cutting, transport, and readying of wood for use in Suez over 500 miles away from its original growth site, but no amount of human labor, knowledge, or effort in Anatolia could *produce* the strong, durable, and desirable lumber that trees provided in Egypt. As William Cronon writes in reference to the American West,

> the fertility of the prairie soils and the abundance of the northern forests had far less to do with human labor than with autonomous ecological processes that people exploited on behalf of the human realm – a realm less of *production* than of *consumption*.[61]

One could make similar arguments about other natural commodities – grains or animals for example – but the case of wood nevertheless still stands out. Unlike, say, a field of wheat, a region of old growth forests would take decades, if not centuries, to reproduce itself once harvested. This is a timescale unsuited to most human endeavors.

Thus, because the use of wood was essentially a process of the relatively irreversible consumption of natural resources, the Ottoman Empire was in many ways forced to centrally manage its forest supplies if it wanted to maintain them in any kind of long-term fashion. In other words, were market forces and personal interest allowed to have free reign in how forests were used, trees would be consumed very quickly, to the detriment of populations around the empire and future populations alike. This is exactly what happened in the Great Lakes region of North America studied by Cronon. Other evidence from Ottoman Egypt further suggests the uniqueness of wood as a commodity. For example, an examination of estate inventories from the period shows that wood products were some of the most expensive items individuals owned in rural Egypt.[62] This high value of wood was again a reflection of its scarcity in Egypt.

Conclusion

Egyptian shipbuilders, camel drivers, and peasant cultivators, along with religious pilgrims from across the early modern Muslim world – all of whom had never seen Anatolia nor likely ever heard of the place – affected its history in massively important ways. As forests were cut, ecosystems were altered or destroyed, soil fertilities depleted, and animal habitats forever transformed. What do these connections between Egyptians, pious pilgrims in the Hijaz, and Anatolian forests mean for our understanding both of the environmental history of the Ottoman Empire and of the ways that the specific characteristics of certain commodities shaped that history?

First, they suggest that the imperial calculus of the Ottoman state deemed certain natural resources and environments to be more important than others. Egypt, a place of great agricultural potential – one that helped maintain food supplies and Ottoman legitimacy in the Hijaz and elsewhere – was clearly, from both an Ottoman and a local Egyptian perspective, worth the alteration and consumption of other natural landscapes to provide the Nile valley with the materials needed to achieve this rich agricultural potential and to move the products of this potential to other parts of the empire. Thus, knowingly or not – most likely not – Egyptians participated in the consumption of large sections of Anatolian forest as they worked to construct ships to move food from Egypt to the Hijaz. These histories of Anatolian forests, of the Egyptian countryside, of the sustenance of pilgrims in the Hijaz, and of Ottoman imperial administration must therefore all be taken together as parts of a single process of the coordinated and connected consumption and use of nature.

Furthermore, from the imperial perspective of the Ottoman government in Istanbul and Cairo, connecting Anatolia to Egypt made perfect sense. These connections allowed the Ottoman Empire to shift a region's excess resources to places where that excess could fill a vital need that would eventually allow Egypt to grow food to feed people in yet other places. One can easily conceive of a process, then, whereby the Ottoman bureaucracy surveyed the empire, moving different pieces around to achieve an optimal configuration of rule. Lumber went to Egypt both for shipbuilding and irrigation purposes, thereby making possible the movement of grains and other foodstuffs to Mecca and Medina (and also Istanbul and other population centers in the empire). The imperial administration was thus essentially turning Anatolian trees into caloric energy for human stomachs in the Hijaz. By concentrating the labor, skill, and expertise found in certain areas of the empire on the production (or consumption) of natural resource commodities like lumber or grain, the Ottoman Empire was consequently able to increase its overall levels of agricultural and economic productivity. For this system to work most efficiently, transportation networks – as we have seen in some detail – had to move goods quickly and with a minimal amount of energy loss. The imperial system also had to rely upon and connect the actions and expertise of hundreds of actors across three continents and two seas. Above all, this system of environmental comparative advantage and natural resource management was governed through an imperial administration that coordinated a vast system of local knowledge, autonomy, and action.

Notes

1 On the Ottoman–Mamluk confrontation and the conquest of Egypt, see Andrew C. Hess, 'The Ottoman Conquest of Egypt (1517) and the Beginning of the Sixteenth-Century World War,' *International Journal of Middle East Studies* 4 (1973): 55–76; Emire Cihan Muslu, 'Ottoman–Mamluk Relations: Diplomacy and Perceptions' (PhD diss., Harvard University, 2007); Jean-Louis Bacqué-Grammont and Anne Kroell, *Mamlouks, ottomans et portugais en Mer Rouge: l'affaire de Djedda en 1517* (Cairo: Institut français d'archéologie orientale, 1988); Michel M. Mazzaoui, 'Global Policies of Sultan Selim, 1512–1520,' in *Essays on Islamic Civilization: Presented to Niyazi Berkes*, ed. Donald P. Little (Leiden: Brill, 1976), 224–243; Michael Winter, *Egyptian Society Under Ottoman Rule, 1517–1798* (London: Routledge, 1992), 1–17.

2 On the specific case of Ottoman rule in Egypt, see Winter, *Egyptian Society under Ottoman Rule*; Stanford J. Shaw, *The Financial and Administrative Organization and Development of Ottoman Egypt, 1517–1798* (Princeton, NJ: Princeton University Press, 1962); Laylā 'Abd al-Laṭīf Aḥmad, *al-Idāra fī Miṣr fī al-'Aṣr al-'Uthmānī* (Cairo: Maṭba'at Jāmi'at 'Ayn Shams, 1978); idem, *al-Mujtama' al-Miṣrī fī al-'Aṣr al-'Uthmānī* (Cairo: Dār al-Kitāb al-Jāmi'ī, 1987); idem, *Tārīkh wa Mu'arrikhī Miṣr wa al-Shām ibbāna al-'Aṣr al-'Uthmānī* (Cairo: Maktabat al-Khānjī, 1980); 'Irāqī Yūsif Muḥammad, *al-Wujūd al-'Uthmānī fī Miṣr fī al-Qarnayn al-Sādis 'Ashar wa al-Sābi' 'Ashar (Dirāsa Wathā'iqiyya)*, vol. 1 (Cairo: Markaz Kliyūbātrā lil-Kumbiyūtar, 1996); idem, *al-Wujūd al-'Uthmānī al-Mamlūkī fī Miṣr fī al-Qarn al-Thāmin 'Ashar wa Awā'il al-Qarn al-Tāsi' 'Ashar* (Cairo: Dār al-Ma'ārif, 1985); André Raymond, *Artisans et commerçants au Caire au XVIIIe siècle*, 2 vols. (Damascus: Institut français de Damas, 1973).

3 This study necessarily builds upon a rich literature on material culture and the role of commodities in Ottoman history. Coffee, tulips, textiles, food, soap, and clothing are some of the material goods Ottoman historians have usefully studied. As even this partial list shows, the main focus of work on Ottoman material culture has been on luxury items used and consumed by mostly urban elites. This chapter takes a different tack, seeking to expand our knowledge of Ottoman objects by shifting attention to things whose histories are mostly rural and whose consumption and use were more about supporting the logistical function of the empire than they were about leisure or projecting status or wealth. For illuminating studies of Ottoman material culture, see for example: Donald Quataert, ed., *Consumption Studies and the History of the Ottoman Empire, 1550–1922: An Introduction* (Albany, NY: State University of New York Press, 2000); Suraiya Faroqhi, *Towns and Townsmen in Ottoman Anatolia: Trade, Crafts, and Food Production in an Urban Setting, 1520–1650* (Cambridge: Cambridge University Press, 1984); Dana Sajdi, ed., *Ottoman Tulips, Ottoman Coffee: Leisure and Lifestyle in the Eighteenth Century* (London: I. B. Tauris, 2007); Amy Singer, ed., *Starting with Food: Culinary Approaches to Ottoman History* (Princeton, NJ: Markus Wiener Publishers, 2011); Suraiya Faroqhi and Christoph K. Neumann, eds., *Ottoman Costumes: From Textile to Identity* (Istanbul: Eren, 2004); James Grehan, *Everyday Life and Consumer Culture in 18th-Century Damascus* (Seattle, WA: University of Washington Press, 2007).

4 Generally on the Ottomans in the Red Sea and Indian Ocean, see Salih Özbaran, *Ottoman Expansion towards the Indian Ocean in the 16th Century* (Istanbul: Bilgi University Press, 2009); idem, *The Ottoman Response to European Expansion: Studies on Ottoman–Portuguese Relations in the Indian Ocean and Ottoman Administration in the Arab Lands during the Sixteenth Century* (Istanbul: Isis Press, 1994); idem, 'A Turkish Report on the Red Sea and the Portuguese in the Indian Ocean (1525),' *Arabian Studies* 4 (1978): 81–88; idem, 'Ottoman Naval Power in the Indian Ocean in the 16th Century,' in *The Kapudan Pasha, His Office and His Domain: Halcyon Days in Crete IV*, ed. Elizabeth Zachariadou (Rethymnon: Crete University Press, 2002), 109–117; Giancarlo Casale, *The Ottoman Age of Exploration* (New York: Oxford

University Press, 2010); idem, 'The Ottoman Administration of the Spice Trade in the Sixteenth-Century Red Sea and Persian Gulf,' *Journal of the Economic and Social History of the Orient* 49 (2006): 170–198; Bacqué-Grammont and Kroell, *Mamlouks, ottomans et portugais*; Anthony Reid, 'Sixteenth-Century Turkish Influence in Western Indonesia,' *Journal of South East Asian History* 10 (1969): 395–414; Michel Tuchscherer, 'La flotte impériale de Suez de 1694 à 1719,' *Turcica* 29 (1997): 47–69.

5   On the problem of wood for Ottoman naval construction, see Palmira Brummett, *Ottoman Seapower and Levantine Diplomacy in the Age of Discovery* (Albany, NY: State University of New York Press, 1994), 96, 115–116, 144, 174; İdris Bostan, *Osmanlı Bahriye Teşkilâtı: XVII. Yüzyılda Tersâne-i Âmire* (Ankara: Türk Tarih Kurumu Basımevi, 1992), 102–118; Casale, *Ottoman Age of Exploration*, 201–202; Colin H. Imber, 'The Navy of Süleiman the Magnificent,' *Archivum Ottomanicum* 6 (1980): 211–282; Murat Çizakça, 'Ottomans and the Mediterranean: An Analysis of the Ottoman Shipbuilding Industry as Reflected by the Arsenal Registers of Istanbul, 1529–1650,' in *Le Genti del Mare Mediterraneo*, ed. Rosalba Ragosta, 2 vols. (Naples: Lucio Pironti, 1981), 773–789; Svat Soucek, 'Certain Types of Ships in Ottoman-Turkish Terminology,' *Turcica* 7 (1975): 233–249. For a useful comparative study of this problematic in early modern Venice, see Karl Appuhn, *A Forest on the Sea: Environmental Expertise in Renaissance Venice* (Baltimore, MD: Johns Hopkins University Press, 2009).

6   On the tension between Egypt's relative agricultural wealth and its dearth of domestic wood supplies, see Alan Mikhail, *Nature and Empire in Ottoman Egypt: An Environmental History* (New York: Cambridge University Press, 2011), 82–169.

7   Egypt's lack of wood, though a new problem for the Ottomans, was one that had been faced by all political powers who ruled it since antiquity. Roger S. Bagnall, *Egypt in Late Antiquity* (Princeton, NJ: Princeton University Press, 1993), 41; Russell Meiggs, *Trees and Timber in the Ancient Mediterranean World* (Oxford: Clarendon Press, 1982), 57–68; John Perlin, *A Forest Journey: The Story of Wood and Civilization* (Woodstock: Countryman Press, 2005), 131–134; J. V. Thirgood, *Man and the Mediterranean Forest: A History of Resource Depletion* (London: Academic Press, 1981), 87–94.

8   On connections between Egypt and the Hijaz in the Ottoman period, see Suraiya Faroqhi, 'Trade Controls, Provisioning Policies, and Donations: The Egypt-Hijaz Connection during the Second Half of the Sixteenth Century,' in *Süleymân the Second and His Time*, ed. Halil İnalcık and Cemal Kafadar (Istanbul: Isis Press, 1993), 131–143; idem, 'Red Sea Trade and Communications as Observed by Evliya Çelebi (1671–72),' *New Perspectives on Turkey* 5–6 (1991): 87–105; idem, 'Coffee and Spices: Official Ottoman Reactions to Egyptian Trade in the Later Sixteenth Century,' *Wiener Zeitschrift für die Kunde des Morgenlandes* 76 (1986): 87–93; Michel Tuchscherer, 'Commerce et production du café en Mer Rouge au XVIe siècle,' in *Le commerce du café avant l'ère des plantations coloniales: espaces, réseaux, sociétés (XVe-XIXe siècle)*, ed. idem (Cairo: Institut français d'archéologie orientale, 2001), 69–90; Ḥusām Muḥammad ʿAbd al-Muʿṭī, *al-ʿAlāqāt al-Miṣriyya al-Ḥijāziyya fī al-Qarn al-Thāmin ʿAshar* (Cairo: al-Hayʾa al-Miṣriyya al-ʿĀmma lil-Kitāb, 1999); Colin Heywood, 'A Red Sea Shipping Register of the 1670s for the Supply of Foodstuffs from Egyptian *Wakf* Sources to Mecca and Medina (Turkish Documents from the Archive of ʿAbdurrahman "Abdi" Pasha of Buda, I),' *Anatolia Moderna* 6 (1996): 111–174.

9   Özbaran, *Ottoman Expansion*, 77–80; Brummett, *Ottoman Seapower and Levantine Diplomacy*, 96, 115–116, 144, 174; Casale, *Ottoman Age of Exploration*, 201–202. On forestry and Ottoman shipbuilding in the Mediterranean, see Çizakça, 'Ottomans and the Mediterranean.'

10 On the Ottomans in various parts of the Arabian Peninsula and Persian Gulf, see Salih Özbaran, 'Bahrain in 1559: A Narrative of Turco-Portuguese Conflict in the Gulf,' *Osmanlı Araştırmaları* 3 (1982): 91–104; idem, *Yemen'den Basra'ya Sınırdaki Osmanlı* (Istanbul: Kitap Yayınevi, 2004); idem, 'The Ottoman Turks and the

Portuguese in the Persian Gulf, 1534–1581,' *Journal of Asian History* 6 (1972): 45–88; Jan E. Mandaville, 'The Ottoman Province of Al-Hasâ in the Sixteenth and Seventeenth Centuries,' *Journal of the American Oriental Society* 90 (1970): 486–513; Casale, *Ottoman Age of Exploration*, 63–65; Patricia Risso, 'Cross-Cultural Perceptions of Piracy: Maritime Violence in the Western Indian Ocean and Persian Gulf Region during a Long Eighteenth Century,' *Journal of World History* 12 (2001): 293–319; idem, 'Muslim Identity in Maritime Trade: General Observations and Some Evidence from the 18th Century Persian Gulf/Indian Ocean Region,' *International Journal of Middle East Studies* 21 (1989): 381–392.

11 'Abd al-Mu'ṭī, *al-ʿAlāqāt al-Miṣriyya al-Ḥijāziyya*; Alan Mikhail, 'An Irrigated Empire: The View from Ottoman Fayyum,' *International Journal of Middle East Studies* 42 (2010), 569–578.

12 Suraiya Faroqhi, *Pilgrims and Sultans: The Hajj under the Ottomans* (London: I. B. Tauris, 1994).

13 Although there is little direct evidence from the early modern period about the role of the pilgrimage in the spread of disease, there are numerous examples from the end of the nineteenth century about the diffusion of cholera resulting from the pilgrimage. One can only imagine that similar situations existed in earlier centuries as well. For the late nineteenth-century examples, see LaVerne Kuhnke, *Lives at Risk: Public Health in Nineteenth-Century Egypt* (Berkeley, CA: University of California Press, 1990), 95, 107–108; J. R. McNeill, *Something New Under the Sun: An Environmental History of the Twentieth-Century World* (New York: W. W. Norton, 2000), 196.

14 On the Ottoman provisioning of the pilgrimage from Egypt, see Mikhail, *Nature and Empire*, 113–122.

15 See for example: Prime Ministry's Ottoman Archive (Başbakanlık Osmanlı Arşivi; hereafter BOA), Mühimme-i Mısır (hereafter MM), 3: 210 (Evail Ş 1133/27 May–5 Jun. 1721); BOA, Hatt-ı Hümayun (hereafter HAT), 29/1358 (29 Z 1197/24 Nov. 1783); BOA, HAT, 28/1354 (7 Za 1198/22 Sep. 1784); BOA, HAT, 26/1256 (10 Za 1200/3 Sep. 1786). There is no internal evidence for the date of this final case. The date given is the one assigned by the BOA. Topkapı Palace Museum Archive (Topkapı Sarayı Müzesi Arşivi; hereafter TSMA), E. 3218 (n.d.); TSMA, E. 5657 (13 Ra 1204/1 Dec. 1789); TSMA, E. 664/40 (n.d.); TSMA, E. 5225/12 (Evahir S 1194/27 Feb.–7 Mar. 1780); TSMA, E. 664/51 (n.d.); TSMA, E. 2229/3 (n.d.).

16 On the provisioning of Istanbul from Egypt, see Mikhail, *Nature and Empire*, 103–113.

17 For some of this history of water management in Ottoman Egypt, see ibid., 38–81.

18 BOA, İbnülemin Umur-i Nafia, 94 (Evasıt Ra 1121/21-30 May 1709); BOA, MM, 1: 116 (Evail R 1122/30 May–8 Jun. 1710); BOA, MM, 1: 167 (Evasıt S 1123/31 Mar.–9 Apr. 1711). For a discussion of this repair work, see Mikhail, 'An Irrigated Empire,' 576–578.

19 Shaw, *Financial and Administrative Organization and Development*, 269–270. One of the most famous and lucrative of these *awqāf* in the late seventeenth century was very near Fayyum and possibly administratively connected to it. It consisted of a group of nine villages in al-Bahnasa (Beni Suef) controlled by Hasan Agha Bilifya, a Faqari leader and commander of the Gönüllüyan military bloc. Jane Hathaway, 'The Role of the Kızlar Ağası in 17th–18th Century Ottoman Egypt,' *Studia Islamica* 75 (1992), 153–158; idem, *The Politics of Households in Ottoman Egypt: The Rise of the Qazdağlıs* (Cambridge: Cambridge University Press, 1997), 157–160; idem, 'Egypt in the Seventeenth Century,' in *Modern Egypt, from 1517 to the End of the Twentieth Century*, vol. 2 of *The Cambridge History of Egypt*, ed. M. W. Daly (Cambridge: Cambridge University Press, 1998), 50.

20 On shifts in trading patterns in the fifteenth century, see Nelly Hanna, *An Urban History of Būlāq in the Mamluk and Ottoman Periods* (Cairo: Institut français d'archéologie orientale, 1983), 7–32.

21　For studies of the Red Sea shipwreck site of a particular Ottoman vessel that illuminate the ship's cargo, carrying capacity, structure, and so forth, see Cheryl Ward, 'The Sadana Island Shipwreck: An Eighteenth-Century AD Merchantman off the Red Sea Coast of Egypt,' *World Archaeology* 32 (2001): 368–382; idem, 'The Sadana Island Shipwreck: A Mideighteenth-Century Treasure Trove,' in *A Historical Archaeology of the Ottoman Empire: Breaking New Ground*, ed. Uzi Baram and Lynda Carroll (New York: Kluwer Academic/Plenum, 2000), 185–202; Cheryl Ward and Uzi Baram, 'Global Markets, Local Practice: Ottoman-Period Clay Pipes and Smoking Paraphernalia from the Red Sea Shipwreck at Sadana Island, Egypt,' *International Journal of Historical Archaeology* 10 (2006): 135–158.

22　I am relying on the following court cases from Rosetta for the story of the wood's movement: National Archives of Egypt (Dār al-Wathā'iq al-Qawmiyya; hereafter DWQ), Maḥkamat Rashīd 132, p. 88, case 140 (17 Ş 1137/30 Apr. 1725); DWQ, Maḥkamat Rashīd 132, pp. 200-201, case 311 (3 N 1137/16 May 1725); DWQ, Maḥkamat Rashīd 132, p. 199, case 308 (16 Ş 1137/29 Apr. 1725); DWQ, Maḥkamat Rashīd 132, p. 199, case 309 (17 Ş 1137/30 Apr. 1725). All of these cases are written in Ottoman Turkish. The recording of these imperial orders in Ottoman Turkish in the normally Arabic-language registers of the court of Rosetta shows both the imperial nature of this project and the way the empire used its courts to manage these kinds of imperial endeavors.

23　Earlier examples of attempts to gain access to wood from Anatolia for the construction of ships in Suez further highlight the strategic nature of this commodity. In 1510, for instance, eleven galleons were dispatched to the Anatolian port of Ayas at the very northeastern corner of the Mediterranean from the Egyptian port of Damietta to secure wood supplies for the construction of ships in Suez. Suspicious that this movement of ships to Ayas was part of an Ottoman–Mamluk plot against Rhodes, the leaders of this still-independent island territory attacked and destroyed the convoy of ships. Brummett, *Ottoman Seapower and Levantine Diplomacy*, 115–116. For another example of the transport of wood from Anatolia to build ships on the Red Sea, see also ibid., 174.

24　For a sketch of historic forest locations and coverage in the Middle East, see Carlos E. Cordova, *Millennial Landscape Change in Jordan: Geoarchaeology and Cultural Ecology* (Tucson, AZ: The University of Arizona Press, 2007), 3–4.

25　There is relatively little work on the history of Ottoman forestry. For some of the current literature, see Selçuk Dursun, 'Forest and the State: History of Forestry and Forest in the Ottoman Empire' (PhD diss., Sabancı University, 2007); Sam White, *The Climate of Rebellion in the Early Modern Ottoman Empire* (Cambridge: Cambridge University Press, 2011), 16–17, 28–31, 72, 278, 289; Mikhail, *Nature and Empire*, 124–169. See also the following very general history of Turkish forestry: Yücel Çağlar, *Türkiye Ormanları ve Ormancılık* (Istanbul: İletişim Yayınları, 1992). For useful collections of documents on Ottoman forestry, see Çevre ve Orman Bakanlığı, *Osmanlı Ormancılığı ile İlgili Belgeler*, 3 vols. (Ankara: Çevre ve Orman Bakanlığı, 1999–2003); Halil Kutluk, ed., *Türkiye Ormancılığı ile İlgili Tarihi Vesikalar, 893–1339 (1487–1923)* (Istanbul: Osmanbey Matbaası, 1948).

26　On the use of wood to construct ships in the imperial dockyards of Istanbul, see Bostan, *Tersâne-i Âmire*, 102–118.

27　On the office of the *kereste emîni*, see Çevre ve Orman Bakanlığı, *Osmanlı Ormancılığı*, 1: 94–95. For a discussion of Ottoman forestry guilds in the context of the wider early modern Mediterranean world, see J. Donald Hughes, *The Mediterranean: An Environmental History* (Santa Barbara, CA: ABC-CLIO, 2005), 97–99.

28　For cases involving the organization of laborers for the harvesting of lumber from Anatolian forests, see Çevre ve Orman Bakanlığı, *Osmanlı Ormancılığı*, 1: 8–9, 46–47, 48–49, 56–57, 60–61.

29　For more on these and other positions related to the harvesting of timber, see ibid., 1: XIII.

30 For an example of timber harvests on the southern Black Sea coast near the town of Sinop that were used to repair Egyptian vessels, see BOA, Cevdet Bahriye, 1413 (Evasıt R 1120/30 Jun.–9 Jul. 1708 and 20 Za 1124/19 Dec. 1712).

31 For a statement of the historic role of Rhodes in funneling wood to the imperial timber stores in this period, see BOA, Cevdet Nafia, 302 (23 Za 1216/28 Mar. 1802).

32 For a general discussion of Ottoman imperial forest management policies, see Çevre ve Orman Bakanlığı, *Osmanlı Ormancılığı*, 1: XI–XVI. For specific regulations, see ibid., 1: 2–3, 6–7, 18–19, 22–23, 24–25, 26–27, 38–39, 104–105, 106–107, 110–111, 114–115, 120–121, 124–125, 150–151, 172–173; 2: 2–3, 42–43, 46–47, 48–49; 3: 4–5, 6–7, 8–9, 16–17, 18–19.

33 For useful comparative examples of sustainable forest management techniques in early modern Japan, Germany, and Spain, see Conrad Totman, *The Green Archipelago: Forestry in Preindustrial Japan* (Berkeley, CA: University of California Press, 1989); idem, *The Lumber Industry in Early Modern Japan* (Honolulu, HI: University of Hawai'i Press, 1995); Paul Warde, *Ecology, Economy and State Formation in Early Modern Germany* (Cambridge: Cambridge University Press, 2006); John Thomas Wing, 'Roots of Empire: State Formation and the Politics of Timber Access in Early Modern Spain, 1556–1759' (PhD diss., University of Minnesota, 2009); John T. Wing, 'Keeping Spain Afloat: State Forestry and Imperial Defense in the Sixteenth Century,' *Environmental History* 17 (2012): 116–145.

34 DWQ, Maḥkamat Rashīd 132, p. 88, case 140 (17 Ş 1137/30 Apr. 1725); DWQ, Maḥkamat Rashīd 132, pp. 200–201, case 311 (3 N 1137/16 May 1725); DWQ, Maḥkamat Rashīd 132, p. 199, case 308 (16 Ş 1137/29 Apr. 1725); DWQ, Maḥkamat Rashīd 132, p. 199, case 309 (17 Ş 1137/30 Apr. 1725).

35 DWQ, Maḥkamat Rashīd 132, p. 88, case 140 (17 Ş 1137/30 Apr. 1725); DWQ, Maḥkamat Rashīd 132, p. 199, case 309 (17 Ş 1137/30 Apr. 1725).

36 İdris Bostan, 'An Ottoman Base in Eastern Mediterranean: Alexandria of Egypt in the 18th Century,' in *Proceedings of the International Conference on Egypt during the Ottoman Era: 26–30 November 2007, Cairo, Egypt*, ed. Research Centre for Islamic History, Art and Culture (Istanbul: IRCICA, 2010), 63–77; Michael J. Reimer, 'Ottoman Alexandria: The Paradox of Decline and the Reconfiguration of Power in Eighteenth-Century Arab Provinces,' *Journal of the Economic and Social History of the Orient* 37 (1994): 107–146.

37 Daniel Panzac, 'International and Domestic Maritime Trade in the Ottoman Empire during the 18th Century,' *International Journal of Middle East Studies* 24 (1992): 189–206.

38 On Ottoman Egypt's many trading links, see Raymond, *Artisans et commerçants*.

39 DWQ, Maḥkamat Rashīd 132, p. 88, case 140 (17 Ş 1137/30 Apr. 1725); DWQ, Maḥkamat Rashīd 132, pp. 200–201, case 311 (3 N 1137/16 May 1725).

40 On piracy and corsairs in the Ottoman Mediterranean and imperial attempts to stop them, see Brummett, *Ottoman Seapower and Levantine Diplomacy*, 94–102 and 135–136; İdris Bostan, *Kürekli ve Yelkenli Osmanlı Gemileri* (Istanbul: Bilge, 2005), 372, 376; Molly Greene, *Catholic Pirates and Greek Merchants: A Maritime History of the Mediterranean* (Princeton, NJ: Princeton University Press, 2010); idem, 'The Ottomans in the Mediterranean,' in *The Early Modern Ottomans: Remapping the Empire*, ed. Virginia Aksan and Daniel Goffman (Cambridge: Cambridge University Press, 2007), 113–116. For the case of a pirate attack near Rhodes on Egyptian grain ships on their way to Istanbul, see TSMA, E. 7008/12 (n.d.).

41 Bostan, 'An Ottoman Base in Eastern Mediterranean,' 76–77.

42 DWQ, Maḥkamat Rashīd 132, p. 88, case 140 (17 Ş 1137/30 Apr. 1725).

43 For accounts of various Ottoman plans for a Suez Canal that ultimately never materialized, see Casale, *Ottoman Age of Exploration*, 135–137, 159–170, 201–202; Colin Imber, *The Ottoman Empire, 1300–1650: The Structure of Power* (New York: Palgrave Macmillan, 2002), 62; Mustafa Bilge, 'Suez Canal in the Ottoman Sources,' in *Proceedings of the International Conference on Egypt (2007)*, 89–113.

44　The absence of such a waterway was recognized as a problem by various governments throughout Egypt's history. For accounts of attempts to build such a canal, see Isabelle Hairy and Oueded Sennoune, 'Géographie historique du canal d'Alexandrie,' *Annales Islamologiques* 40 (2006): 247–278; 'Umar Ṭūsūn, *Tārīkh Khalīj al-Iskandariyya al-Qadīm wa Tur'at al-Maḥmūdiyya* (Alexandria: Maṭba'at al-'Adl, 1942); Mikhail, *Nature and Empire*, 242–290.

45　DWQ, Maḥkamat Rashīd 132, p. 88, case 140 (17 Ş 1137/30 Apr. 1725); DWQ, Maḥkamat Rashīd 132, pp. 200–201, case 311 (3 N 1137/16 May 1725). On *cerîm* ships, see Bostan, *Osmanlı Gemileri*, 253–259. For an example of the empire's hiring of sailors of *cerîm* ships, see BOA, Cevdet Bahriye, 208 (14 Ra 1204/2 Dec. 1789).

46　DWQ, Maḥkamat Rashīd 132, p. 88, case 140 (17 Ş 1137/30 Apr. 1725).

47　For studies of the sediment load in the Nile's floodwaters that added to the force of its seaward flow, see Omran E. Frihy et al., 'Patterns of Nearshore Sediment Transport along the Nile Delta, Egypt,' *Coastal Engineering* 15 (1991): 409–429; Scot E. Smith and Adel Abdel-Kader, 'Coastal Erosion Along the Egyptian Delta,' *Journal of Coastal Research* 4 (1988): 245–255; Mohamed A. K. Elsayed et al., 'Accretion and Erosion Patterns along Rosetta Promontory, Nile Delta Coast,' *Journal of Coastal Research* 21 (May 2005): 412–420.

48　DWQ, Maḥkamat Rashīd 132, p. 88, case 140 (17 Ş 1137/30 Apr. 1725); DWQ, Maḥkamat Rashīd 132, pp. 200–201, case 311 (3 N 1137/16 May 1725). On Bulaq during the Ottoman period, see Hanna, *An Urban History of Būlāq*.

49　DWQ, Maḥkamat Rashīd 132, pp. 200–201, case 311 (3 N 1137/16 May 1725).

50　Generally on the use of camels in transport in the Middle East, see Richard W. Bulliet, *The Camel and the Wheel* (New York: Columbia University Press, 1990).

51　DWQ, Maḥkamat Rashīd 132, pp. 200–201, case 311 (3 N 1137/16 May 1725). The case lists these amounts in *niṣf fiḍḍa*, but according to Stanford J. Shaw, 'the silver coin in common use during Mamlûk and Ottoman times in Egypt was called *nıṣf fiḍḍe* colloquially and *para* officially.' Shaw, *Financial and Administrative Organization and Development*, 65 n. 169.

52　Shaw, *Financial and Administrative Organization and Development*, 264–267.

53　Alan Mikhail, 'Animals as Property in Early Modern Ottoman Egypt,' *Journal of the Economic and Social History of the Orient* 53 (2010): 621–652.

54　On the importance of camels for Ottoman transportation and military ventures, see Halil İnalcık, '"Arab" Camel Drivers in Western Anatolia in the Fifteenth Century,' *Revue d'Histoire Maghrebine* 10 (1983): 256–270; idem, 'The Ottoman State: Economy and Society, 1300–1600,' in *An Economic and Social History of the Ottoman Empire: Volume I, 1300–1600*, ed. Halil İnalcık with Donald Quataert (Cambridge: Cambridge University Press, 1994), 38–39, 62–63; Suraiya Faroqhi, 'Camels, Wagons, and the Ottoman State in the Sixteenth and Seventeenth Centuries,' *International Journal of Middle East Studies* 14 (1982): 523–539. In 1399, for example, Bayezid the Thunderbolt (r. 1389–1402) took 10,000 camels as booty from his conquest of the region of Antalya. İnalcık, '"Arab" Camel Drivers,' 265.

55　Donald Quataert, *The Ottoman Empire, 1700–1922* (Cambridge: Cambridge University Press, 2000), 119.

56　For a similar example of the movement of wood for the construction of ships in Suez in 1810, see 'Abd al-Raḥman al-Jabartī, *'Abd al-Raḥman al-Jabartī's History of Egypt: 'Ajā'ib al-Āthār fī al-Tarājim wa al-Akhbār*, ed. Thomas Philipp and Moshe Perlmann, 4 vols. (Stuttgart: Franz Steiner Verlag, 1994), 4: 146.

57　It was of course this lack of alternatives that made the project of the Suez Canal so appealing.

58　Şevket Pamuk, *A Monetary History of the Ottoman Empire* (Cambridge: Cambridge University Press, 2000); idem, 'Prices in the Ottoman Empire, 1469–1914,' *International Journal of Middle East Studies* 36 (2004): 451–468.

59　I of course do not mean to imply that the Ottoman Empire intervened in all economic relations in its realm or that somehow a Muslim polity would be more economically interventionist than a non-Muslim one. Obviously, most economic relationships in the empire did not involve the state in any way. This case of ship construction, however, is an instance in which the state did play a central role and therefore provides an opportunity to understand an important aspect of Ottoman economic history. For a discussion of the empire's selective protectionism in the sixteenth century, see Brummett, *Ottoman Seapower and Levantine Diplomacy*, 181–182.

60 For studies pointing to some of the administrative weaknesses of the empire in Egypt and in other of its provinces in the eighteenth century, see 'Abd al-Raḥīm 'Abd al-Raḥman 'Abd al-Raḥīm, *al-Rīf al-Miṣrī fī al-Qarn al-Thāmin 'Ashar* (Cairo: Maktabat Madbūlī, 1986); Albert Hourani, 'Ottoman Reforms and the Politics of Notables,' in *The Beginnings of Modernization in the Middle East: The Nineteenth Century*, ed. William R. Polk and Richard L. Chambers (Chicago, IL: University of Chicago Press, 1968), 41–68; Abdul-Karim Rafeq, 'Abd al-Ghani al-Nabulsi: Religious Tolerance and "Arabness" in Ottoman Damascus,' in *Transformed Landscapes: Essays on Palestine and the Middle East in Honor of Walid Khalidi*, ed. Camille Mansour and Leila Fawaz (Cairo: American University in Cairo Press, 2009), 1–17. For a very useful review of much of this literature, see Suraiya Faroqhi, 'Coping with the Central State, Coping with Local Power: Ottoman Regions and Notables from the Sixteenth to the Early Nineteenth Century,' in *The Ottomans and the Balkans: A Discussion of Historiography*, ed. Fikret Adanır and Suraiya Faroqhi (Leiden: Brill, 2002), 351–381. On the Ottoman army in the eighteenth century and its provisioning problems, see Virginia H. Aksan, *Ottoman Wars 1700–1870: An Empire Besieged* (Harlow: Longman-Pearson, 2007), 83–179.

61 William Cronon, *Nature's Metropolis: Chicago and the Great West* (New York: W. W. Norton, 1991), 149. Emphasis in original.

62 Mikhail, *Nature and Empire*, 128–136.

PART V

Consuming things

12

THE TOKUGAWA STOREHOUSE

Ieyasu's encounters with things

Morgan Pitelka

It is no less astonishing to see the importance that they attach to things which
they regard as the treasures of Japan, although to us such things seem trivial and
childish; they, in their turn, look upon our jewels and gems as worthless.
(Alessandro Valignano, SJ, *Historia del Principio y Progresso de la Compañia de Jesús
en las Indias Orientales*,1584)

Walter Benjamin's reading of Charles Baudelaire as the archetypal modern
poet, trash-picking through the refuse of modernity in an attempt to salvage the
language of the new urban experience, is a powerful example of the former's
archivist materialism.[1] Likewise, in his musings on the Paris Arcades, Benjamin
paid equal attention to words, images, and things, to the totality of the social
experience of being in the fractured hallways of incipient modernity. His
collection – the literary and material Benjaminian storehouse – brims with
'the idiosyncratic registrations of an author, subjective, full of gaps, unofficial.'[2]
And it is perhaps this somewhat flighty, scrapbook quality that best represents
nineteenth- and early twentieth-century urban growth and capitalist culture.
The juxtaposition of street observations and overheard utterances in *The Arcades
Project* and the picture postcards of Russian toys and Italian tourist destinations
sent to friends and collected in *Walter Benjamin's Archive*, for example, point to the
phantasmagoric dreamworld that so fascinated Benjamin: his 'City of Mirrors'
that both brought people together as the crowd and permanently isolated them
as bourgeois individuals. Both in his analysis and in the character of his choices,
Benjamin's collection is an apt representation of modernity itself.

For the historian of the early modern, Benjamin's work begs the question:
what words, images, and things fill the storehouse of early modern memory? We
should not expect to find a Benjaminian archive, of course, bursting with mass-

produced baubles and relics of early twentieth-century commodity fetishism. Rather, we might ask how a focus on early modern material culture and collecting allows us to ask new questions about the making of the period. In the case of Japan, the early modern period is usually associated with the emergence of lively urban centers such as Edo: new forms of commerce and protoindustry; increased professionalization of the bureaucracy; and the appearance of protonationalist discourses such as the National Learning movement. Much historiography has focused on explaining Japan's rapid industrialization in the late nineteenth century, reducing the study of early modern Japan to a kind of prehistory of the present; what matters, in such teleological narratives, is that which leads to modernization. Even the most prominent work on material culture in Japan before the Meiji Restoration of 1868, Susan Hanley's *Everyday Things in Premodern Japan: The Hidden Legacy of Material Culture*, is primarily focused on economic history and the role of material conditions in Japan's rapid industrialization and modernization in the late nineteenth century.[3] Recent work on Japan's long sixteenth century, however, points to the role of the 'persistent medieval'[4] in the establishment of the Tokugawa state and in diverse forms of cultural production and consumption in early modern Japan. In this chapter I will examine the collection of the founder of the Tokugawa shogunate, Tokugawa Ieyasu (1543–1616) and argue that his storehouse – which grew out of the cultural practices and predilections of late medieval, elite warriors – played a significant role in shaping the history and culture of Japan's early modern period. The particular means of acquisition, methods of use and display, and forms of probate and reproduction of Ieyasu's storehouse are themselves particularly apt representations of Japan's early modern experience.

The decision to study Ieyasu's collection is hardly arbitrary. As one of the most powerful and influential warlords of the late sixteenth century, and as the founder of the Tokugawa military government that would endure for more than 250 years, Ieyasu's access to valuable things was perhaps unmatched in his day. Furthermore, ample evidence exists that in Japanese society during the long sixteenth century, artworks and other forms of material culture functioned not merely as markers of status or objects of fetishism, but as actors in networks of information and influence that shaped the careers of men such as Ieyasu. Rather than seeing material culture as the product of a few exceptional historical subjects, or even as the result of a particular set of social or cultural conditions, we can integrate things into the overlapping collectives – the web of relations, performances, and practices – that make up history. To put it another way, material culture is not the product of an abstract entity called 'society,' external to the relations between people. Rather, things are constituent and active elements inside a messy system of relations, agents that relate as much by chance as by intentionality.[5]

One early commenter on the elite Japanese relationship with things was the Italian Jesuit Alessandro Valignano, who arrived in Japan in 1579 when the archipelago was in the throes of civil war. During this first visit he stayed for three years. He returned again for two years in 1590, and a final time for five years in 1598, long enough to witness the victory of Tokugawa Ieyasu at the Battle of Sekigahara in 1600 and the growth of the Edo settlement.[6] Valignano is a remarkable figure, not least for his articulation of a new policy for the Jesuits known as 'adaptationism' in which the cultural preferences of locals were studied, respected, and, when necessary, accommodated. He insisted on solid language training and immersion in the local culture. Above all, he demanded that Jesuits should carefully observe their surroundings in Japan, and engage in an almost ethnographic attempt to comprehend the unreflexive habits of locals. One topic on which Valignano was particularly articulate was the 'astonishing' Japanese relationship to things. In the following excerpts of a long passage, he describes the Japanese fetishization of tea utensils and swords, and contrasts this with the European lust for diamonds and rubies.

> It is no less astonishing to see the importance that they attach to things which they regard as the treasures of Japan, although to us such things seem trivial and childish; they, in their turn, look upon our jewels and gems as worthless ... The King of Bungo once showed me a small earthenware caddy for which, in all truth, we would have no other use than to put it in a bird's cage as a drinking trough; nevertheless, he had paid 9,000 silver taels (or about 14,000 ducats) for it, although I would certainly not have given two farthings for it. The surprising thing is that, although thousands of similar caddies... are made, the Japanese no more value them than we do. The prized pieces must have been made by certain ancient masters and the Japanese can immediately pick out these valuable items from among thousands of others, just as European jewelers can distinguish between genuine and false stones. I do not think that any European could acquire such an appreciation... because however much we may examine them, we can never manage to understand in what consists their value and how they are different from the others.[7]

The particular type of tea utensil that Valignano describes in this passage is the tea caddy (*chaire*), many of which were made in China during the Song Dynasty (960–1279) and brought to Japan in the fourteenth and fifteenth centuries, and which Ieyasu collected with great passion. He also acquired tea bowls, particularly well known works made in China or Korea. Valignano continues:

> They value no less their... swords. Here there seems to be greater justification because a good sword is prized in any country. However, they go to extremes here as well for they spend three, four or six thousand ducats on a blade ... When we ask them why they spend so much money on these objects, which of themselves are worthless, they answer that they do it for the same reason as we buy a diamond or a ruby for a great price, a thing which causes them no less astonishment ... Indeed, they declare

that the things that they buy and treasure at least serve some purpose and thus their desire to give so much money for them is less reprehensible than the conceit of Europeans who purchase precious stones which serve for nothing.[8]

This is in many ways a typical description of the collision of worldviews that marked the encounter between East Asians and Europeans in the sixteenth century. Valignano's realization that the value placed on things in a particular culture creates a kind of social force, however, is astute; he notes that because the Japanese appreciated not just the aesthetic and functional properties of tea utensils and swords, but in addition paid attention to the pedigree of such objects, they would pay huge sums to acquire them. It is possible to take this a step further and say that the material and symbolic qualities of certain objects compelled people to act in ways that, to this Jesuit observer, were profoundly mysterious. In short, the objects circulating through the lives of these elite Japanese of the sixteenth century had a kind of agency. Ieyasu's collection, which became an archetypal model of what warriors should want and aspire to in early modern Japan, contained many of the most famous objects of his day, things that influenced Ieyasu and his peers and continued to effect change when 'assembled under a new law,' as Benjamin put it: deployed in the particular social and cultural context of early modern Japanese society.[9]

Ieyasu's collection is also worth our attention because of the existence of supporting documentary records and significant numbers of extant works. While all elite warriors in the long sixteenth century acquired objects, ranging from commissioned artworks to imported treasures, not all of them left records of these acquisitions or worried about their fate after the death of their owners. Ieyasu, acting in ways that tell us much about his meticulous attention to the balance of power in his family and his careful establishment of his own historical and cultural legacy, did both. Perhaps the most important document for studying Ieyasu's material heritage is *The Record of Utensils Inherited from Sumpu Castle* [*Sumpu owakemono odôgu chô*]. This text was compiled according to Ieyasu's prior instructions over a period of two years from 1616 to 1618 at Sumpu Castle (contemporary Shizuoka City, Shizuoka Prefecture), Ieyasu's final base and resting place. It lists the money and objects owned by Ieyasu and records their probate. Some of these objects are still extant in the collection of the Tokugawa Art Museum in Nagoya and the collections of the Tôshôgû Shrines that were built to deify Ieyasu in the mid-seventeenth century, while others have been scattered to private and public collections or lost.

The existence of this useful document does not mean that the social biographies of extant objects can necessarily be traced; in most instances, *The Record* simply records the number of items in certain categories. Only a few named 'famous objects' (*meibutsu*) can be tracked over long periods of time as they move from one collection to the next. Still, the document allows us to read the taxonomies of objects that were significant in the lives of Ieyasu and his peers, contextualize those objects in the social and cultural practices of the day, and then speculate about the instrumentalization of these categories of material culture in new early modern configurations. This chapter will examine in particular the contexts in which two types of material culture – weapons and Chinese art – came to be widely collected by elite warriors, part of a 'struggle against dispersion,' to use Benjamin's phrase, that tells us much about the long sixteenth century.[10] In particular, three extant objects – an arquebus made by Noda Kiyotaka in 1611; a twelfth-century short sword named 'Ebina Kokaji'; and a blue and white tea bowl from Ming-dynasty China – will be situated in lesser known but significant moments in the biography of Tokugawa Ieyasu, particularly acts of alliance-building, war, and détente that prefigured the establishment of the early modern Japanese state.

Weapons of war: swords and guns in the Tokugawa storehouse

On January 31, 1543, the young warlord Matsudaira Hirotada (1526–1549) and his fourteen-year-old wife Odai no Kata (1528–1602) had their first and only child, a boy who would later take the name Tokugawa Ieyasu.[11] The couple resided in Okazaki Castle (present-day Okazaki city, Aichi Prefecture) in Mikawa province, headquarters of a relatively small territory in central Japan that was sandwiched between larger and more militarily powerful domains. Although Ieyasu was born into an elite family of warrior leaders, and possessed the type of lineage that guaranteed wealth, education, and power in times of peace, the situation of the Matsudaira in 1543 was precarious. The nominal political authority of Japan, the warrior government headed by the Ashikaga house in Kyoto, had lost much of its influence since the outbreak of war in 1467.[12] Regional warlords (daimyô) routinely formed alliances and attacked neighbors with little regard for the policies or preferences of the Ashikaga.[13] Likewise, Buddhist institutions, already significant landholders, in some cases amassed armies and challenged warrior hegemony through increasingly large acts of rebellion. In 1488, for example, followers of the True Pure Land sect of Buddhism took over Kaga province (present-day southern Ishikawa Prefecture). By 1543, similar uprisings had occurred in Sakai, Kyoto, and Osaka among other locations.[14] Therefore, as was the case for many vulnerable warlords, the leaders of the Matsudaira could rely neither on the central authority of warrior government in Kyoto nor on the steadying hand of traditional religious institutions to shield their domain from conflict among larger competing forces.

Regional conflicts and new religious uprisings were not the only ingredients in the relative instability of the mid-sixteenth century. The year of Ieyasu's birth, 1543, also marked the arrival of the first Europeans in Japan, Portuguese traders who brought new goods to sell, access to new markets overseas, a new worldview in the form of Christianity, and perhaps most significant for warriors of the period, a new and powerful weapon: the musket or arquebus. Historians have made much of the circulation of Jesuits throughout Japan beginning with the arrival of Francis Xavier and two of his compatriots in 1549, but the arrival of the early modern gun, and the ensuing changes in the material culture of warfare, not to mention the growth of the market in gunpowder and other necessary materials, surely played as significant a role in the ebb and flow of the sixteenth century and the founding of the Tokugawa military government. According to the most reliable early record of this first Japanese encounter with European firearms, *The Record of the Musket* [*Teppôki*] (1606), there were around 100 people on board the ship that arrived at the small island of Tanegashima on September 23, 1543, including two 'whose physical features differed from ours, and whose language was not understood. Those who saw them found them strange.'[15] The two Portuguese demonstrated the use of their arquebuses, and the local ruler soon ordered local artisans to study the design and mechanism and manufacture reproductions. Again, according to *The Record of the Musket*, 'in a little more than a year several tens of *teppô* [muskets] were manufactured.'[16] The use and production of the arquebus spread incrementally across the archipelago, as warriors found themselves drawn to the range and accuracy of the weapon.[17] Chinese, Japanese, and Portuguese traders provided the one ingredient in gunpowder – saltpeter – not readily available locally. This fueled the already impressive growth of Sakai, the nearest port city to the capital of Kyoto, into a thriving metropolis and cultural center (most famous, perhaps, as the birthplace of the culture of tea, or *chanoyu*), as well as a political power that would compete with warlords and religious institutions later in the sixteenth century.

Tokugawa Ieyasu, then, was born in a period of significant political and social fragmentation. He experienced this turmoil – indeed, embodied it – when he was sent to be a hostage in the household of a neighboring, more powerful warlord, at the age of five. After the death of his father and a youth spent entirely as a kind of privileged captive, Ieyasu became the ruler of Okazaki castle in 1560. He owed this abrupt change in circumstance to a neighboring warlord, a young and brash ruler named Oda Nobunaga (1534–1582) who had attacked and defeated Ieyasu's captor and who over time came to be Ieyasu's senior ally. This contingent relationship transformed Ieyasu from a potential victim of the violence of the sixteenth century to one of the leading players on the stage of national politics.

In 1568, Nobunaga occupied the capital city of Kyoto and intervened in the shogunal succession, a kind of public announcement of his intention to consolidate power. For the next fourteen years, Nobunaga waged war on various opponents, including the Enryakuji Buddhist complex on Mt. Hiei, the warlord Takeda Shingen and his son Katsuyori, and various True Pure Land uprisings.[18] Ieyasu was a central participant in these events, particularly actions against the Takeda. He moved his headquarters from Okazaki, the hereditary home of his family for generations, to Hamamatsu to the east, closer to the conflict with the Takeda.[19] I have written elsewhere about Ieyasu's fortuitous escape from death at the hands of Takeda Shingen not once but twice, and the subsequent early death of the old Takeda warlord, seemingly of natural causes, in 1573.[20] His son Katsuyori continued to resist, but Ieyasu and Nobunaga both took advantage of this surprising development by seizing portions of the Takeda domain and recruiting vassals of their former enemy whenever and wherever possible.

Around this time, Ieyasu began including arquebusiers in his army. In 1574, Ieyasu sent a letter to a military strategist who specialized in firearms usage, awarding him a stipend after witnessing what is presumed to be an arquebus display.[21] Within several years, documents also refer to Ieyasu's inclusion of arquebusier units in battle, as when his vassal Matsudaira Ietada recorded that 'Ieyasu ordered the arquebusier unit to fire quickly!' during a conflict with Takeda forces outside of Nishio Castle.[22] It should be noted that the use of firearms in this period was not sudden and revolutionary; rather, units of arquebusiers worked alongside units of archers. As Thomas Conlan demonstrates in a statistical analysis of casualty lists from the long sixteenth century, injuries from firearms only gradually increased in this period and only truly became widespread and tactically significant after 1600.[23]

Still, the use of firearms helped Nobunaga and Ieyasu to strategize against varied enemies and obstacles, as we shall see below. The guns themselves were solid and well crafted, based on Portuguese models but produced with increasing innovation by Japanese artisans. An example of an arquebus from Ieyasu's collection consists of an iron cylinder forged in an octagonal shape, with layers of native Japanese steel and imported iron to provide both strength and enough flexibility to withstand the pressure of firing. The other metal parts, such as the serpentine that held the match and the lock plate of the matchlock mechanism, are made of a copper and silver alloy (*shibuichi*). The wooden butt and stock are made of oak, though flowering plum and other woods are also found.[24] Soldiers employed the weapon by inserting the gunpowder and shot and then lighting the fuse, a somewhat time-consuming process that limited arquebusiers to a few shots per minute but allowed better penetration of armor than an arrow. For Nobunaga and Ieyasu, the arquebus represented another powerful implement in the toolkit of civil war.

The conflict with Takeda Katsuyori became increasingly heated in 1575, a development worth examining in some detail because it represents the conclusion to one of the most significant military conflicts of the period: the resistance of the Takeda to Oda Nobunaga, and the destruction of that resistance. It also involved perhaps the most famous battle in the history of firearms in Japan, at Nagashino Castle in Mikawa. Ieyasu sent his vassal Okudaira Nobumasa (1555–1615) to protect Nagashino Castle, a fortress Ieyasu had taken from the Takeda in the wake of Shingen's death. This was an interesting choice. Nobumasa was a recently acquired vassal who had once sworn fealty to Ieyasu's boyhood captors and later served Takeda Shingen. Holding Nagashino Castle, strategically located halfway between Ieyasu's old base, Okazaki, and his new base, Hamamatsu, was perhaps an opportunity for Nobumasa to prove himself to Ieyasu. This task was made easier in the following month when Nobunaga gave a substantial cache of provisions to Ieyasu, who directed that they be stored at Nagashino.[25] This illustrates the way in which successful generals like Ieyasu and Nobunaga enlisted the vassals of defeated enemies and socialized them to their new roles by giving them responsibility; such socialization was often cemented through gift giving, making material culture the glue of the expansion of the feudal and military networks that sustained long periods of warfare.

Katsuyori played his hand and launched a major invasion of Mikawa soon after Ieyasu's reinforcement of Nagashino, moving 15,000 men toward the castle and burning two towns along the way on June 9, 1575 (Tenshô 3/5/1). He divided the majority of his troops into eight groups and surrounded the castle, placing his own headquarters, with a guard of 3,000 troops, on a nearby mountain. Okudaira Nobumasa had only 500 men with which to protect the castle. Ieyasu must have received rapid warning of Katsuyori's move, as he quickly launched his army out of Okazaki Castle, where he had been staying with his son. He left 7,000 men behind as a reserve force to protect the fortress and headed toward Nagashino with a mere 5,000 men. Fortunately, Nobunaga sent a much larger force in support, seeing this battle as an opportunity to deal a fatal blow to the Takeda. Ieyasu's men joined with Nobunaga's outside of Nagashino on June 26 (Tenshô 3/5/18), bringing their joint forces to almost 38,000 men. Using a combination of quickly constructed but effective wooden barricades, superior numbers, the firepower of archers and arquebusiers, and strategic maneuvering to contain Katsuyori's cavalry, the Oda-Tokugawa force obliterated the Takeda army, with reports of the Takeda losses ranging from the thousands to the tens of thousands.[26] Arquebusiers seem to have been used to particularly good effect, with some later sources claiming that Nobunaga (and Ieyasu) pioneered the use of volley fire in this battle.[27] Katsuyori himself escaped to his home province of Kai, while Nobunaga returned to Gifu to relish his victories. Ieyasu, at Nobunaga's request, visited him there soon after to show gratitude for his decisive support. According to a later hagiography of Ieyasu, Nobunaga reportedly came out of the castle as Ieyasu and his band approached, and seeing them draw near the entryway, cried out 'You're not growing beards, are you?' to which one of the Tokugawa vassals jovially replied, 'No my Lord, this is just the stubble of Nagashino.'[28]

Ieyasu soon returned to Hamamatsu Castle, but wasted no time in taking advantage of the recent victory to go on the offensive against remaining Takeda forces. In 1575, he invaded Suruga and began burning everything in sight. He also ordered his commanders to launch assaults on a number of Takeda fortresses.[29] Meanwhile Oda Nobunaga sent Nobutada (1557–1582), his eldest son, to command an assault on a major Takeda stronghold in the mountains. Ieyasu supported the effort by dispatching Okudaira Nobumasa, who had so recently proven himself as the guardian of Nagashino Castle, to assist Nobutada, and their combined forces were successful. In 1576, Ieyasu ordered Nobumasa to repair Shinshiro Castle (present-day Shinshiro City in Aichi Prefecture) and made him lord of the keep. He also gave his oldest daughter,

Kamehime (1560–1625), to Nobumasa in marriage, effectively rewarding him and binding him to Tokugawa service in one move. Gifts of people, too, could be used to cement alliances, as in the hostage experience of Ieyasu's childhood, or in this and many similar examples of daughters trafficked in the name of marriage politics.[30]

Nobunaga decided in early 1582 to attack Katsuyori from multiple directions. He took the first step by launching his armies into Kai out of Mino. Ieyasu followed suit and launched his own forces from Hamamatsu. The neighboring house of Hôjô attacked from the east and the Oda vassals the Kanamori from the north. One by one the Takeda's fortifications fell, in some cases as a result of military action but in a few examples as a result of Takeda vassals surrendering and opening the gates wide to the invading forces. All this was, apparently, too much for Katsuyori, who ended his own life and the life of his son on April 3, 1582 (Tenshô 10/3/11). Ieyasu soon after met with Nobunaga's son Nobutada, who had been commanding the Oda forces in Kai.[31] Nobunaga then arrived to verify the Takeda defeat by examining the heads, a common practice among warlords in this period.[32] On April 18 (Tenshô 10/3/25), Ieyasu wrote to one of his vassals to share the news, noting 'Katsuyori was decisively beaten.'[33]

Having orchestrated the destruction of the Takeda, Nobunaga next turned to a review of his newly acquired territory and the division of the spoils. He rewarded Ieyasu with the entire province of Suruga, further extending Tokugawa lands to the east and giving him control over the entire coast from the edge of Owari to Suruga Bay. Ieyasu had the opportunity to thank Nobunaga on May 4 (Tenshô 10/4/12), when the latter completed his military tour of Kai (stopping along the way to take in the views of Mt. Fuji). Nobunaga came to Suruga and met Ieyasu, now officially enfeoffed by Nobunaga for the first time. Ieyasu threw a banquet and gave Nobunaga a series of gifts, including a large sword (ichimonji), a Yoshimitsu short sword, and three good horses.[34]

The inclusion of the swords among these gifts was no accident. Though swords have come to be thought of as deadly weapons and as symbols of warrior identity (or the 'soul of the samurai,' in the words of the modern Japanese author Inazô Nitobe[35]), documents from the sixteenth century clearly indicate that the primary role of swords in the lives of warriors was as gifts.[36] Ieyasu's extant letters, which probably represent only a fraction of his total output as a letter writer, mention no less than seventeen swords received as gifts; other contemporaneous sources mention additional examples as well, making Ieyasu's receipt of swords a major theme in records of his life. In addition to receiving swords, Ieyasu's letters and other sources mention more than fourteen occasions on which he gifted swords to cement alliances or improve relations. For example, in 1573 he gave a sword to his ally Uesugi Kenshin (1530–1578) to celebrate the end of their long struggle against Takeda Shingen. In 1599, Ieyasu gave swords and horses to Shimazu Yoshihiro to celebrate his return from the campaigns in Korea. Ieyasu even sent swords and horses as a gift to the King of Cambodia in 1603, in response to a request for trade and exchange.[37] In 1615, after destroying the residents of Osaka Castle and finally solidifying Tokugawa rule, he sent vassals into the rubble to retrieve the remains of objects associated with his defeated enemies, particularly famous Chinese ceramics and swords. He then commanded a sword maker to re-forge the recovered swords that had been damaged in the castle's destruction.[38]

In light of these many traces of the movement of swords in and out of Ieyasu's possession as he developed and strengthened his social networks in the years leading up to Sekigahara, it is perhaps not surprising that when he died in 1616, more than 1,000 swords were recorded in the *Record of Utensils Inherited from Sumpu Castle*. These objects represent a kind of stratigraphy of social relations between elite warriors. And although it would be pushing the evidence too far to argue a causal relationship, it is also worth noting that wearing a long and short sword became the primary marker of warrior social status throughout the early modern period. Ieyasu's large collection of swords represents this transference of the sword from its role as a kind of social lubricant to its symbolic function as a sign of samurai identity in the gradual shift from medieval to early modern Japan.

China in the Tokugawa storehouse

One of the most powerful images of early modern Japan is that of the 'closed country' (*sakoku*): a phrase that came, even in Japanese, to dominate modern discussion of Japan's ostensible insularity before the 'opening' in the 1850s. It is true that the policies of the Tokugawa government did, beginning in the 1630s, prohibit Japanese travel abroad, access to Japanese ports by most foreign merchants and dignitaries, and circulation of most Western books. However, the long sixteenth century itself, the crucible of Japan's early modernity, was the most international period in the nation's pre-modern history. In addition to the arrival of Europeans mentioned above, Ieyasu and other elite warlords of his age imagined China and Korea to be sources of civilization that could be strategically drawn upon to send certain messages about cultural authority to their peers. Collecting objects from China and Korea, using them in tea gatherings and other semi-public gatherings, and supporting new forms of cultural production modeled on Chinese and Korean antecedents all emerged as powerful methods of demonstrating cultivation among warrior elites in the long sixteenth century. As a result, the Tokugawa storehouse, far from being nativist or somehow cloistered, is a profoundly international assemblage.

The dominant power in East Asia – and, some would argue, the center of the global economy up to the sixteenth century – was of course China, and shifts in Chinese imperial regulation of trade had a major impact on Japan's international commerce and relations.[39] During the latter half of Japan's medieval period, China's Ming dynasty (1368–1644) tightly controlled trade in the region, and some of the Ashikaga shoguns managed to join this system by acknowledging Chinese suzerainty and positioning themselves, and Japan, in the context of the

Chinese tributary system. This 'tally trade' with China deteriorated in 1547, and the Ming cut off relations with Japan in 1557, partially because of the rise of piratical activities by a heterogeneous group of seafarers known as the *wakô*.[40] The withdrawal of official Ming control (and the Ming court's authorization of private trade in 1560) only opened up space for private maritime trade to occur in East Asia, with particular focus on Chinese silk and Japanese silver among many other materials.[41] It was through this somewhat unregulated seascape that European traders and missionaries sailed to Japan, often on Chinese ships; likewise, Chinese, Japanese, Korean, and *wakô* seafarers plied their trade across the waters in this period, and material traces of this international exchange can be seen throughout the Tokugawa storehouse.

While serving Oda Nobunaga, Ieyasu came into contact with foreign missionaries and traders on numerous occasions, but was far less well traveled than many of his peers. Although he did acquire a number of imported European objects – including Portuguese-manufactured helmets and other pieces of metal armor; a clock made in Spain in 1581; and a pencil from Mexico – more important in the trajectory of his career were his regular encounters with, and apparent interest in, artworks and other cultural products from China. His collection came to include many varieties of ceramics used in the culture of tea: objects that came to Japan through the trade in Buddhist material culture, or on the trading vessels that frequently docked in Sakai and which included both art from the continent and saltpeter for gunpowder. One of Ieyasu's most significant trips outside his favored haunts of his home domains and Kyoto occurred in 1582, after the defeat of the Takeda. Nobunaga, having calmed central Japan, aimed his sights on the island of Shikoku, but was distracted by news from his lieutenant Hashiba Hideyoshi, who was in the middle of a struggle against the mighty clan of Môri in southern Honshu. Hideyoshi reported that the Môri were emerging in force and that he would need reinforcements. From Nobunaga's perspective, this was a golden opportunity to crush a resilient opponent. He therefore ordered six of his generals to reinforce Hideyoshi, and he began preparations to travel to the west himself. Plans for the invasion of Shikoku also continued, meaning that he would mount two major offensives simultaneously, a clear sign of his strength and confidence. He left for Kyoto with a small group of retainers, secure in his control of the central region of the country.[42]

At this same time, Ieyasu was departing Kyoto and on his way to Sakai.[43] He arrived in the port city on June 19 (Tenshô 10/5/29), the same day that Nobunaga entered Kyoto. He soon met with two Sakai merchants and tea masters who also served as sources of information and providers of tea utensils: Imai Sôkyû and Tsuda Sôgyû.[44] Thereafter he participated in another tea gathering followed by an appearance at a dance performance and a banquet in the evening. These encounters point to the way in which material culture facilitated social and political interactions that were essential to the military actions of men like Nobunaga and Ieyasu. Tea masters like Sôkyû and Sôgyû were well connected in the city of Sakai, and therefore had news and gossip from across the archipelago. As merchants with significant incomes and with easy access to the movement of material and visual culture through the port city that was their home, they also owned substantial collections of art used in tea gatherings, including ceramic treasures originally from China and Korea as well as new varieties made in Japan. The objects enabled these sorts of meetings between men of different statuses, allowing discussions and deals around the rituals of tea preparation and consumption that were not recorded in the documentary record but which are marked in the Tokugawa storehouse by the circulation of artworks in and out of Sakai tea masters' and warlords' collections.

As Ieyasu was acquiring information from the tea masters of Sakai, his senior ally Nobunaga was relaxing in Kyoto, enjoying the prestigious attention of the imperial court. Nobunaga's vassal Akechi Mitsuhide, however, chose this moment to attempt to seize power from his lord in perhaps the most famous act of treason in Japanese history. Mitsuhide led an army of 13,000 men into the capital in the morning hours and attacked the temple in which Nobunaga was sleeping with his men. Nobunaga died, as did his son Nobutada, who was staying in another residence in Kyoto which was also attacked. The confidence of Nobunaga's vassals and allies and the sense of stability felt by many observers disappeared in a moment; many citizens of Kyoto, afraid of further violence, retreated to the imperial court in search of sanctuary. Ieyasu, hearing of the attack while in Sakai, fled to his home domain.[45]

The small decisions and chance encounters that led to Ieyasu's separation from Nobunaga at this particular historical moment had far-reaching consequences. If Ieyasu had been at Nobunaga's side in Kyoto, as he often was in those days of armed conflict and the politics of détente, he surely would have lost his life. The chance to share tea, examine fine Chinese art, and consort with knowledgeable merchants in Sakai, however, drew him down a different path. Objects such as the Chinese art desired by tea practitioners played a major role in shaping the range of possibilities in the historical past. Thus, the significance of these small moments of cultural practice are striking in the larger picture of national politics; or perhaps it is better to say that encounters such as this one prove the lie that cultural practices occur outside the realm of national politics. Historians often comment on the fact that unlike Nobunaga and Hideyoshi, who were such devoted students of tea ritual, Ieyasu was only a grudging participant. At the time of the Honnôji attack, however, it is not too much of an exaggeration to say that tea saved Ieyasu's life by drawing him away from the capital and into Sakai.

Ieyasu had numerous opportunities to acquire Chinese art from tea masters like Imai Sôkyû and Tsuda Sôgyû – as well as through other intermediaries, from vassals, and as loot – in the years after Nobunaga's assassination. His peer, the aforementioned Hideyoshi, took over the project of pacifying Japan and left Ieyasu in relative peace for several years. As an independent warlord until 1586, when he swore fealty to Hideyoshi, Ieyasu acquired artworks primarily as gifts.

FIGURE 12.1   Tea bowl named 'Araki,' sixteenth century

In fact, Ieyasu's ritualized agreement with Hideyoshi, in which he traveled to Hideyoshi's new fortress at Osaka Castle and declared his allegiance in front of an assembly of warlords, was marked by an exchange of gifts in which Ieyasu received a ceramic tea jar (either Chinese or Southeast Asian), two swords, a falcon, and a formal coat (*haori*); and Ieyasu gave Hideyoshi ten horses, one hundred gold pieces, and a long sword.[46] Two years later, as a reward for arbitrating a disagreement between Hideyoshi and warlords in northern Japan, Ieyasu received a series of valuable gifts: a Hakata tea stand; an Imogashira (potato-head) water jar; a tea caddy previously owned by the warlord Kanamori Arishige; a *temmoku* tea bowl previously owned by the tea master Sen no Rikyû (Sen Sôeki); and a large quantity of rice.[47]

The tea bowl pictured in Figure 12.1 was also previously owned by the tea master Sen no Rikyû (1522–1591), a merchant from Sakai who came to be the most influential teacher of tea practice and curator of tea utensils in Hideyoshi's employ. The bowl, made in China during the Ming Dynasty, was named 'Araki' after its previous owner, the warrior Araki Murashige (1535–1586), a retainer of Oda Nobunaga's who had fallen from grace, lost his domain, and later became an ardent tea practitioner. Araki gave the bowl to Rikyû, who presumably gave or sold it to Ieyasu. The piece consists of a shallow hemisphere on a tapered foot, with a slightly undulating lip and a largely symmetrical shape. Scrolling grass designs and an elegant exterior band appear on the surface of the bowl under a milky haze, an effect created by applying cobalt to the clay with a brush underneath a thick coat of whitish, translucent glaze. The visible lacquer repairs to the lip of the bowl were appreciated by tea practitioners as marks of the age and even the individual biography of the vessel.[48] Although this tea bowl came, over time, to be considered one of the greatest Chinese ceramic treasures in all of Japan because of its illustrious pedigree, it is only one small piece in the significant import of ceramics and other forms of visual and material culture from China in the sixteenth and early seventeenth centuries.[49]

As Ieyasu's career advanced, his interest in Chinese visual and material culture, not to mention books, only increased. It grew particularly ardent after 1590, when Hideyoshi transferred Ieyasu to the eastern provinces known as the Kantô, based in the small town of Edo. In 1593, for example, Ieyasu met with the Buddhist monk and budding China scholar Fujiwara Seika, who presented a lecture on the Chinese text *Essentials of Good Government* (Ch: *Zhenguan zhengyao*; J: *Jôgan Seiyô*; Tang Dynasty, 7th century).[50] Hideyoshi's death in 1598 presented Ieyasu with the opportunity to occupy center stage. His victory in the titanic Battle of Sekigahara in 1600 and his appointment by the imperial court to the position of shogun in 1603 empowered him to establish a new military government in Edo. After passing that position to his son Tokugawa Hidetada (1579–1632) in 1605, Ieyasu hired Seika's student Hayashi Razan in 1606 as an expert in all things Chinese. Razan lectured to Ieyasu and Hidetada on various Chinese classics; he was instructed to write diplomatic correspondence and to mind the growing Tokugawa library; and he was used, along with a range of Buddhist priests, as a kind of policy writer who drafted documents that would eventually be issued as key pieces of shogunal law.[51] Ieyasu's engagement with Chinese things therefore became the basis for early Tokugawa shogunal policy.

Ieyasu also became a collector of Chinese books, as recorded by the physician Otasaka Bokusai (1578–1655). According to Bokusai, Ieyasu's nine favorite books consisted of two Chinese Confucian works (the *Analects* and the *Doctrine of the Mean*), two Chinese historical works (*Records of the Grand Historian* and the *Book of Han*), two Chinese military guides (*The Six Secret Teachings* and *The Three Strategies*), the aforementioned Chinese text *Essentials of Good Government*, and just two Japanese texts, both focusing on governance: *Procedures of the Engi Era* (*Engishiki*) and *Mirror of the East* (*Azuma Kagami*).[52] In 1599, Ieyasu ordered the printing of six books, five of them Chinese, by the Zen monk Kanshitsu Genkitsu at Fushimi. Again in the 1610s, Ieyasu ordered underlings to print two different Chinese texts, one a compilation of canonical Buddhist extracts and the other a collection of gems from the Chinese classics.[53] The Tokugawa storehouse thus contained material and visual culture from China, part of Ieyasu's broad attempt to draw on what I have elsewhere called the institutional authority of Chinese civilization, but also an actual library of classic Chinese texts that became the foundation for shogunal policy and scholarship.[54]

Ieyasu's apotheosis and the probate of the Tokugawa storehouse

In 1616, at the age of 74, Ieyasu passed away as one of the last leaders of a generation that had fought in the endemic civil wars of the sixteenth century. He was in many ways entirely typical of a certain class of elite warriors: a difficult childhood, involving the loss of close family members and a long period spent as a hostage, was not at all uncommon in the 1530s, 40s, and 50s.[55] His struggles to put down rebellions, avoid invasions from hostile neighbors, and ally himself with strong warlords as part of a grand strategy of survival, too, were characteristic of many warlords of the age, albeit unusually successful in his case. However, unlike many warlords – such as Nobunaga betrayed in the prime of his life along with his heir, or Hideyoshi, who died with just one young son and no stable means of preserving power for him – Ieyasu had many children, successfully placed them in positions of power and influence long before his death, and in general succeeded where his predecessors had failed in setting up a political system that would perpetuate the rule of his family for generations. Although this system would come, over time, to produce socio-economic effects praised by modern observers as being distinctively early modern in their progress toward the present – urbanization, diverse commercial activities, increasingly sophisticated transportation networks, national diffusion of popular culture, and so on – Tokugawa Ieyasu's collection of things points to a wartime culture of possession and display that continued well into the Tokugawa era of peace. Ieyasu collected swords and guns because these were the tools by which he amassed and armed his armies. He collected Chinese things to legitimize his own rule, an appeal to precedent and the mythohistorical stability of China's golden past.

The influence of the Tokugawa storehouse continued well after Ieyasu's death. In 1616, he was, according to his prior arrangements, first enshrined as the deity Tôshô Daigongen ('Light of the East, the Ultimate Made Manifest') on Mt. Kunô, east of his final resting place at Sumpu Castle. Later, his grandson and the third shogun, Tokugawa Iemitsu (1604–1651), constructed a colossal shrine and temple complex on Mt. Nikkô, north of Edo. Both these shrines, as well as the many smaller shrines to Ieyasu that his descendants and other warriors built in nearly every domain in early modern Japan, became sites for the ritual storage and usage of artworks associated with Ieyasu during his life. Until the collapse of the Tokugawa regime in 1868, these shrines to Ieyasu held private rituals and in some cases public festivals at which Ieyasu's spirit was called forth, often using an inherited or donated object as ritual vessel.[56] Many shoguns made semi-annual pilgrimages to Nikkô to mark the day of Ieyasu's death.[57] Foreign embassies from Ryûkyû and Korea also made pilgrimages to Nikkô, ostensibly at their own request but in fact to emphasize Tokugawa hegemony.[58] Likewise, elite warriors from across the country petitioned the government for the right to go on pilgrimages to the main shrine at Nikkô, a privilege that was only doled out to certain applicants. This is not surprising considering the huge amounts of money the Tokugawa government spent to maintain and repair the structures at Nikkô, which amounted to more than half of all government expenditures in the late seventeenth century.[59] The objects collected by Ieyasu over the course of his life and carefully distributed to his descendants and shrines after his death therefore continued to compel and shape the actions of Japan's elites more than a century after he was buried.

Ieyasu's apotheosis and the transference of his collection into the storehouses and display rooms of shoguns, Tokugawa branch house leaders, and state-sponsored shrines represents a kind of reversal of, or perhaps an inverse precursor to, Benjamin's well known conception of the decline of the aura of the work of art in the age of mechanical reproduction.[60] Objects that had been instrumentally significant in the sixteenth century as tools of war and diplomacy – swords exchanged as gifts, arquebuses fired in battle, Chinese ceramics used in tea gatherings with informants – became mysterious again, 'parasitically dependen[t] on ritual' and infused with the cult value of the worship of a new deity.[61]

The objects that Ieyasu acquired and then bequeathed to his descendants before his own apotheosis represent a profoundly different sort of assemblage from Benjamin's haphazard collection of images, poems, postcards, and urban refuse. But these distinctions reveal the late medieval origins of Japan's early modernity, steeped in the technologies of war, built on fragile and fraught alliances among competing families and social groups, and turning always to the past and to the continent for the legitimacy and authority that would allow a government to finally stabilize Japan after a century of conflict.

Notes

1 See, for example, Walter Benjamin, *Charles Baudelaire: A Lyric Poet in the Era of High Capitalism* (London and New York: Verso, 1997); idem, *The Writer of Modern Life: Essays on Charles Baudelaire* (Cambridge, MA: The Belknap Press of Harvard University Press, 2006); and idem, *The Arcades Project* (Cambridge, MA: The Belknap Press of Harvard University Press, 1999).

2 Erdmut Wizisla, 'Preface,' in *Walter Benjamin's Archive: Images, Texts, Signs*, ed. Urusla Marx, Gudrun Schwarz, Michael Schwarz, and Erdmut Wizisla (London and New York: Verso, 2007), 2.

3 Susan B. Hanley, *Everyday Things in Premodern Japan: The Hidden Legacy of Material Culture* (Berkeley, CA: University of California Press, 1999). While many art historians have examined the history of material and visual culture in Japan's early modern period, with considerable attention to the aesthetic and formal properties of the objects themselves, few historians writing about this period in English have included things in their research. A few exceptions include Peter Kornicki, *The Book in Japan: A Cultural History from the Beginnings to the Nineteenth Century* (Leiden: Brill, 1998); Eric C. Rath, *The Ethos of Noh: Actors and Their Art* (Cambridge, MA: Harvard University Asia Center, 2004); Morgan Pitelka, *Handmade Culture: Raku Potters, Patrons, and Tea Practitioners in Japan* (Honolulu, HI: University of Hawaii Press, 2005); Mary Elizabeth Berry, *Japan in Print: Information and Nation in the Early Modern Period* (Berkeley, CA: University of California Press, 2006); and Constantine Nomikos Vaporis, *Tour of Duty: Samurai, Military Service in Edo, and the Culture of Early Modern Japan* (Honolulu, HI: University of Hawaii Press, 2008).

4 This phrase is borrowed from David Spafford, *The Persistent Medieval: Land and Place in Eastern Japan, 1450–1525* (Cambridge, MA: Harvard University Press, forthcoming). Spafford and I have worked with other historians of pre-modern Japan – David Eason, Tomoko Kitagawa, Peter Shapinsky, to name a few – on a collaborative project to rethink the 'age of unification' in less teleological terms.

5 One recent work that addresses the agency of a specific category of Japanese material culture – Buddhist objects – is Fabio Rambelli, *Buddhist Materiality: A Cultural History of Objects in Japanese Buddhism* (Stanford, CA: Stanford University Press, 2007).

6 J. F. Moran, *The Japanese and the Jesuits: Alessandro Valignano in Sixteenth-Century Japan* (London: Routledge, 1993).

7 Michael Cooper, ed., *They Came to Japan: An Anthology of European Reports on Japan, 1543–1640* (Ann Arbor, MI: Michigan Classics in Japanese Studies, 1995; first edition, 1965), 261–262.

8 Ibid.

9 Walter Benjamin, 'The Work of Art in the Age of Mechanical Reproduction,' in *Illuminations: Essays and Reflections*, ed. Hannah Arendt (New York: Schocken Books, 1978), 234.

10 Benjamin, *The Arcades Project*, 211.

11 Recorded in numerous documents, including *Kan'ei shoka keizuden*, on Tenbun 11/12/26. Ieyasu's birth year has frequently been recorded as 1542 because most of Tenbun 11 corresponds to 1542. The twelfth month, however, overlaps with the beginning of 1543, so Ieyasu's birthday in the Western calendar is actually January 31, 1543. See José Miguel Pinto do Santos, 'Ieyasu (1542–1616) Versus Ieyasu (1543–1616): Calendrical Conversion Tables for the 16th and 17th Centuries,' *Bulletin of Portuguese/Japanese Studies* 5 (2003): 9–26, for a detailed examination of this problem. I have converted the date for this entry, and all other dates used in this essay, to their equivalents in the Western calendar.

12 See Mary Elizabeth Berry, *The Culture of Civil War in Kyoto* (Berkeley, CA: University of California Press, 1997) for more on the experience of life in the capital during this period.

13 One recent study that includes information on this period of civil war is Jeroen Lamers, *Japonius Tyrannus: The Japanese Warlord Oda Nobunaga Reconsidered* (Amsterdam: Hotei Publishing, 2000).

14 See Carol Richmond Tsang, *War and Faith: Ikkô Ikki in Late Muromachi Japan* (Cambridge, MA: Harvard University Asia Center, 2007) for more information on this topic.

15 Hora Tomio, *Tanegashima jû: denrai to sono eikyô* (Tokyo: Awaji Shobô Shinsha, 1958), appendix. Here and below I quote from the English edition, *Tanegashima: The Arrival of Europe in Japan*, trans. Olof G. Lidin (Copenhagen, Denmark: NIAS Press, 2002), 36–42.

16 Tomio, *Tanegashima*, 40.

17 Thomas Conlan introduces recent Japanese findings on the history of firearms as well as his own research into the role of technology in Japanese warfare in 'Instruments of Change: Organizational Technology and the Consolidation of Regional Power in Japan, 1333–1600,' in *War and State Building in Medieval Japan*, ed. John A. Ferejohn and Frances McCall Rosenbluth (Stanford, CA: Stanford University Press, 2010), 124–158. Particularly useful is the section (145–148) that discusses the many references in the documentary record to earlier forms of East Asian firearms such as 'fire dragon spears' and 'fire arrows.' Conlan argues that the introduction of the arquebus was not particularly significant in the process of unification; rather, shifts in military tactics and military organization beginning in the fourteenth century and picking up steam in the fifteenth century proved more significant in the late sixteenth-century centralization of power. I would maintain, however, that as a new form of military material culture, the introduction of the

arquebus in 1543 and its gradual dissemination across the archipelago in the next half century deserves our attention even if it did not significantly impact tactics.

18 Again, see Lamers, *Japonius Tyrannus*, on these events.

19 This process, and his ongoing reorganization of resources in Mikawa, can be seen in a series of commendation documents issued in 1569, helpfully summarized and charted by Nakamura Kôya in *Tokugawa Ieyasu monjo no kenkyû* (Tokyo: Nihon Gakujutsu Shinkôkai, 1958), 1: 151–153.

20 Morgan Pitelka, 'Biography and Japanese History: Writing (and Contesting) the Story of Tokugawa Ieyasu (1543–1616),' in *Asia in the Classroom and the Academy: New Ideas in Scholarship and Teaching*, ed. Suzanne Barnett (forthcoming).

21 Udagawa Takehisa, *Teppô to sengoku kassen* (Tokyo: Yoshikawa Kôbunkan, 2002), 114.

22 Matsudaira Ietada, *Ietada nikki* (Kyoto: Rinsen Shoten, 1968), 1: 49.

23 Conlan, 'Instruments of Change,' 131–135.

24 Arquebus by Noda Kiyotaka, Tokugawa period, 1611, Collection of the Tokugawa Art Museum, Nagoya. See items 69–74 in Tokugawa Bijutsukan, *Ieyasu no isan: Sumpu owakemono* (Nagoya: Tokugawa Bijutsukan, 1992).

25 Most of these events are recorded in Tôkyô Daigaku Shiryô Hensanjo, ed, *Dai Nihon shiryô*, 10: 16, events of the fourth, seventh, and eighth months of Tenshô 1 (Tokyo: Shiryô Hensan Gakkari, 1968). In English, see Lamers's useful summary and analysis, *Japonius Tyrannus*, 95–98.

26 Jeroen Lamers clearly described this battle, as well as conflicting reports regarding its progress, in his study of Nobunaga: *Japonius Tyrannus*, 111–114. Also useful is the summary in Miyamoto Yoshimi, 'Nagashino no tatakai,' in *Tokugawa Ieyasu jiten*, ed. Fujino Tamotsu et al. (Tokyo: Shinjinbutsu Ôraisha, 1990), 207–211.

27 See, for example, Ôta Gyûichi, *Chronicle of Lord Nobunaga*, ed. and trans. J. S. A. Elisonas and Jeroen Lamers (Leiden: Brill, 2011), 222–227.

28 Ôkubo Hikozaemon (Tadataka), 'Mikawa monogatari,' in *Nihon shisô taikei*, ed. Ôtsuka Mitsunobu (Tokyo: Iwanami Shoten, 1974), 26: 130.

29 Ibid.

30 Mentioned in ibid. for 1575/Tenshô 4/7.

31 Matsudaira, *Ietada nikki*, 1: 125.

32 Ôkubo, 'Mikawa monogatari,' 139–140.

33 Nakamura, *Tokugawa Ieyasu monjo no kenkyû*, 1: 282–283.

34 Narushima Motonao, ed., *Tôshôgû onjikki* vol. 38 of *Tokugawa jikki*, ed. Kuroita Katsumi (Tokyo: Yoshikawa Kôbunkan, 1964), 46.

35 Inazô Nitobe, *Bushido, the Soul of Japan* (New York: G. Putnam, 1905 [originally 1900]).

36 Conlan discusses the shift in warrior usage of weapons on the battlefield from swords to pikes in 'Instruments of Change.' It is also worth noting that even when used less in combat, swords were still drawn on the battlefield for the still highly ritualized action of beheading a defeated enemy.

37 Nakamura, *Tokugawa Ieyasu monjo no kenkyû*, 3: 358.

38 Ono Shinji, ed., 'Sumpuki,' in *Ieyasu shiryô shû* (Tokyo: Jinbutsu Ôraisha, 1965), 205.

39 See Andre Gunder Frank, *ReORIENT: Global Economy in the Asian Age* (Berkeley, CA: University of California Press, 1998) and Kenneth Pomeranz, *The Great Divergence: China, Europe, and the Making of the Modern World Economy* (Princeton, NJ: Princeton University Press, 2000) on China's centrality in global trade.

40 For more on this process, see Yasunori Arano, Masatoshi Ishii, and Shôsuke Murai, eds., *Wakô to 'Nihon kokuô'* (Tokyo: Yoshikawa Kôbunkan, 2010).

41 Igawa Kenji, *Daikôkai jidai no Higashi Ajia* (Tokyo: Yoshikawa Kôbunkan, 2007); Kobata Atsushi, *Kingin bôekishi no kenkyû* (Tokyo: Hôsei Daigaku Shuppankyoku, 1976).

42 These events are described in the hagiographic but still useful Ôkubo, 'Mikawa monogatari,' and many other sources recording the events of that era. The Japanese

literature on the event at Honnôji is extensive, but Lamers's English exposition is as clear and compelling as any previous scholarship: *Japonius Tyrannus*, 215–216.

43 Ôkubo, 'Mikawa monogatari,' 140–141.

44 See Imai Sôkyû's comments in the extracts from his diary, published as Nagashima Fukutaro, ed., *Imai Sokyu chanoyu nikki nukigaki*, in *Chadô koten zenshû*, ed. Sen Soshitsu, vol. 10 (Kyoto: Tankôsha, 1957–1962; reprint, 1977), 34; and Tsuda Sôgyû's comments in Nagashima Fukutaro, ed., *Tennôjiya kaiki*, in *Chadô koten zenshû*, vols. 7 and 8 (Kyoto: Tankôsha, 1957–1962; reprint, 1977), 364. Both also note the assassination of Nobunaga the following day.

45 Okamoto Ryoichi, 'Hideyoshi no jidai,' in *Momoyama no kaika*, ed. Hayashiya Tatsusaburô, *Kyoto no rekishi*, vol. 4 (Kyoto: Kyotoshi, 1971), 234–235.

46 Matsudaira, *Ietada nikki*, 2: 27.

47 Ibid., 2: 66–67.

48 Item 166 in Tokugawa Bijutsukan, *Ieyasu no isan*, 83 and 235. See also references to this piece in the 1660 catalog of the masterpieces of the shogunal collection, 'Ganka meibutsuki,' reproduced in Tokugawa Bijutsukan and Nezu Bijutsukan, *Meibutsuki: Ganka meibutsuki to Ryûei gyobutsu* (Nagoya and Tokyo: Tokugawa Bijutsukan and Nezu Bijutsukan, 1988), 207.

49 Chuimei Ho, 'The Ceramic Trade in Asia, 1602–82,' in *Japanese Industrialization and the Asian Economy*, ed. A. J. H. Latham and Heita Kawakatsu (London: Routledge, 1994), 35–38.

50 Herman Ooms, *Tokugawa Ideology: Early Constructs, 1570–1580* (Princeton, NJ: Princeton University Press, 1985), 112. In note 3 on the same page, Ooms notes that emperors and shoguns had heard such lectures on this text on many occasions in the past. See also *Seika monjo*, Bunroku 2/12, cited in Nakamura Kôya, *Tokugawa Ieyasu kô den* (Tokyo: Kôdansha, 1965), 286; and his 'Tokugawa Ieyasu kô shôsai nempu,' in the same volume but numbered separately, 82.

51 See Boot's useful summary of Razan's services to the bakufu: Willem Jan Boot, 'The Adoption and Adaptation of Neo-Confucianism in Japan: The Role of Fujiwara Seika and Hayashi Razan,' (Dlit., University of Leiden, 1983), 184–186.

52 Ryusaku Tsunoda, William Theodore de Bary, and Donald Keene, eds., *Sources of Japanese Tradition* (New York: Columbia University Press, 1958), 1: 332.

53 Ieyasu was also active as a collector of books, a founder of libraries, and as a supporter of publishing and circulation of books. See Peter F. Kornicki, 'Books in the Service of Politics: Tokugawa Ieyasu as Custodian of the Books of Japan,' *The Journal of the Royal Asiatic Society*, Series 3, 18:1 (2008): 71–82, for more information.

54 Pitelka, 'The Empire of Things: Tokugawa Ieyasu's Material Legacy and Cultural Profile,' *Japanese Studies* 29:1 (2009): 23.

55 Umai Yûkiko, 'Kinsei shônin seido no rekishiteki zentei,' *Kokushi danwakai zasshi* 40 (1999): 1–20. Many thanks to David Eason for this reference.

56 See the discussion of swords in Nikkô, for example: Nikkô Tôshôgû, *Nikkô Tôshôgû no hômotsu* (Nikkô, Japan: Nikkô Tôshôgû Shamusho, undated booklet), 84–85.

57 Endô Jun, 'The Early Modern Period: In Search of a Shinto Identity,' in *Shinto, a Short History*, ed. Mark Teeuwen et al. (New York: Routledge, 2003), 117.

58 Ronald P. Toby, *State and Diplomacy in Early Modern Japan: Asia in the Development of the Tokugawa Bakufu* (Stanford, CA: Stanford University Press, 1984), 204.

59 Beatrice Bodart-Bailey, *The Dog Shogun: The Personality and Policies of Tokugawa Tsunayoshi* (Honolulu, HI: University of Hawaii Press, 2006), 186.

60 Benjamin, 'The Work of Art in the Age of Mechanical Reproduction'; also idem, *The Work of Art in the Age of its Technological Reproducibility and Other Writings on Media* (Cambridge, MA: Belknap Press, 2008).

61 Benjamin, 'The Work of Art in the Age of Mechanical Reproduction,' 224.

13

PORCELAIN FOR THE POOR

The material culture of tea and coffee consumption in eighteenth-century Amsterdam

Anne E. C. McCants

Few foodstuffs have influenced the diet and social habits of the modern world as much as coffee, tea, and, to a lesser extent, chocolate. All three of these plant-based beverages have, moreover, enjoyed a more-or-less constant companion in the form of sugar. The rapid spread of the consumption of these commodities across a wide spectrum of social groups worked to re-center the practices of western sociability around the ingestion of a stimulant, ultimately eclipsing the prior centrality of those more soporific elements of bread and wine. It was only within the confines of the inherently conservative realm of religion that the new groceries did not succeed in crowding out the rituals associated with the traditional staff of life. European historians have long agreed that the cultural ramifications of the adoption of hot (sweetened) caffeinated beverage consumption were multifaceted and significant. The economic significance of this shift has been less widely recognized.

In work I have done elsewhere I have sought to challenge the dominant view among economic historians that tea and coffee were luxury articles of consumption, limited in their access to only wealthy Europeans, at least prior to the nineteenth century. The particular focus of my work has been to document the experience of the broad consuming public of the urban Dutch Republic, but Maxine Berg has made a similar intervention for the British case.[1] This project to expand our understanding of the spread of colonial grocery consumption in the eighteenth century has drawn evidence from a number of different quarters, including: national trade statistics, commodity import volumes when known, falling price levels, the structure of urban excise tax programs, and, of course, the evidence about material possessions generated by the imperfect, but nonetheless quite revealing medium of household after-death inventories. What I want to do here is to explore more fully the objects themselves that were associated with tea

FIGURE 13.1 Dutchmen depicted on a seventeenth-century Japanese 'inferior' porcelain bottle with Chinese themes, designed for export

and coffee consumption: the cups, saucers, and pots that were imported from Asia for what was at first indeed the highest stratum of the social and economic elite. However, through the twin mechanisms of imitative production techniques (most importantly in the form of locally available Delftware) and increasingly the importation of ever more numerous and cheaper porcelain goods from Asia, the use of ceramic vessels for the preparation and consumption of the new hot beverages spread to the broad middle strata of Dutch society and even among the citizen working poor (Figure 13.1).

The tremendous volume of the Asiatic porcelain trade, the rapid development of imitative European industries, and the fragility of earthenware objects themselves, suggest that we need to rethink our economic history of consumption to accommodate the sweeping transformations of material life and social behavior brought about by the introduction and diffusion of tea and coffee drinking in early modern Europe. The British East India Company alone imported nearly one to two million ceramic pieces annually by the early eighteenth century, while the Dutch East India Company was at the same time fielding more than twice as many ships as the British.[2] Meanwhile, the expected useful lifespan of these objects was considerably shorter than the metal, or even wooden, wares that had preceded them.[3] Of course, hot beverages, especially acidic ones like tea, coffee, and chocolate, are not well served by the older materials. Not surprisingly then, the turn towards the consumption of colonial beverages was accompanied by a fundamental shift in people's possessions. To the extent that tea and coffee consumption had a significant impact on not only the habits and tastes of a small (but much catered to, painted, and written about) elite, but also on those of a wide swath of the European public, it should be evident in the material record they left behind. The meteoric rise in the popularity of the colonial groceries concomitant with the increasing European domination of global trade networks across the seventeenth and especially eighteenth centuries, and the socio-economic breadth of their addictive reach, both suggest that they are deserving of the prominent place they have come to occupy in the historical imagination.

My work here supports this re-evaluation of the material culture of colonial beverage consumption in the period prior to the nineteenth century by rejecting the classification of ceramic vessels as exclusively luxury goods. Evidence has already been mustered that argues for both the broad appeal of tea and coffee, and the sugar necessary to sweeten them, and more importantly, of the willingness and capacity of a wide variety of households to incorporate this consumption into their budgets. Here I will show that for many households, even of quite modest means, it was likewise important to be able to serve these beverages from new kinds of vessels that were both more decorative and novel than what they had drunk from before, but also more fragile and ephemeral. To this end, evidence mined from a number of after-death inventory studies will be presented to show that tea and coffee cups were owned by a wide spectrum of northwestern Europeans, even those living in declining economies or in individually straitened circumstances. I will also consider some evidence of very small-scale retailing of colonial commodities as it is revealed in after-death inventories from the city of Amsterdam.

Inventories with porcelain

Household inventories, drawn up at the death of a household head by either a privately hired notary or a bureaucratically interested civil servant, present historians with a wealth of both information and unanswered questions. The translation between a stock of goods left *in situ* following what would certainly have been a momentous (and often disastrous) occasion in the life of a household, and the consumer behavior of that household during its normal course of existence, is neither obvious nor straightforward. Goods can be acquired through inheritance, or from the second-hand market, thereby negating a direct link between objects found in inventories and the production and purchase of new goods. Likewise, goods, once purchased, are all too easily dispersed. Perhaps they are turned into desperately needed cash through resale or at the pawnshop; or they are hidden from public inspection to avoid taxation or redistribution. Such centrifugal forces would be especially rife in the critical period leading up to and following the death of a household head. Moreover, people are notorious borrowers and sharers, especially among the lower ranks of society where material goods are likely to be relatively scarce. What we find in a household after the fact of its demise may represent only a fraction of the goods that were actually available for its use in its heyday, given the many possible networks of community reciprocity within which it (ideally) operated. All this notwithstanding, however, after-death inventories represent a most remarkable window into the daily life of the early modern household. They allow us to gain access to the otherwise unknowable physical environment in which people across the social spectrum lived and worked. Moreover, because there is no plausible scenario under which households would have had an incentive to fraudulently *add* items to their possession just for the purposes of padding the inventory, what we find in the after-death inventories can be safely interpreted as yielding at least a minimum indication of the material world inhabited by the decedents and their households near to the time of their death. It is significant then that, on the particular subject of colonial beverage consumption, the available inventory data offer a strong corroboration of the existing trade volume and price evidence already reviewed above. Indeed, these inventories leave little room for lingering doubt that the consumption of tea and coffee was anything but widespread by the middle decades of the eighteenth century, if not in fact earlier.

As with the trade in colonial beverages, the acquisition of horticultural knowledge, and the diffusion of coffee (if not tea) cultivation throughout the tropics, we must once again look to the Dutch as precocious leaders in the consumption of these goods and in the manufacture of their accessory objects. The Delft pottery makers (Asiatic imitators all) were notoriously attentive to changes in the market. The industry emerged in the 1620s, making plates, bowls, and the like – that is, ordinary serving wares but of extraordinary fabrication and design. They produced their first specialty covered sugar dish in 1657, followed soon thereafter in 1666 by the first teapots and teacups. Delft coffee wares were not manufactured until the 1690s, mirroring precisely the moment when coffee beans achieved a regular presence on the Amsterdam wharves. These early Delftware specialty items, like their gold, silver, and Asiatic porcelain predecessors, were indisputably showpieces for the very rich.[4] An inventory dating from 1639 made for a wealthy household residing on Leiden's upmarket Rapenburg Street reveals the first Dutch 'sugar pot' to make an appearance in such a document, while a fellow resident of that same street was the possessor of the earliest surviving teapot recorded in an inventory, this one drawn up in 1673.[5] A study of seventy bourgeois and courtier inventories found in the Notarial Archives of the Hague, dating between 1660 and 1700, reveals the earliest evidence of bourgeois ownership of a teapot (porcelain in this case) in that city in an inventory of 1685, followed three years later by another bourgeois inventory containing twenty-eight coffee cups and a Japanese porcelain coffeepot. The following year, in 1689, an inventory from the provincial capital of Groningen records the first evidence of coffee wares in home use from an inland region of the Republic. However, these remain examples of rarity. Only 17 per cent of the eighty-nine seventeenth-century inventories collected so far from the well-to-do citizens of the Hague and Leiden reveal any specific evidence of tea and/or coffee drinking.[6]

This was soon to change, however. The first few decades of the eighteenth century were witness to a process of social diffusion that, once begun, proceeded with remarkable speed. Even a cursory review of the now numerous, and disparate, community studies of material culture based on after-death inventories presents us with a composite picture in remarkably sharp focus. Van Koolbergen's study of the small industrial city of Weesp (15 kilometers north-west of Amsterdam with approximately 2,500 inhabitants working primarily as beer brewers, gin distillers, and linen weavers, and as farmers in the immediate hinterland) finds no tea or coffee wares to speak of before 1700, but by the close of the 1730s, nearly 100 per cent of the inventories include at least one item relating to the consumption of these goods.[7] This study evaluates 318 inventories recorded between 1640 and 1789, with approximately two thirds of them falling after 1700. They include representation from three social classes (as determined by van Koolbergen on the basis of burial tax classification, presence of capital goods in the inventory, residence type, and occupation of the household head among other things). Not surprisingly, though, given their primary origins in the Notarial Archives and the Orphan Court records, the inventories seriously under-represent the poor (the so-called *pro Deo* tax class), by approximately 85 per cent relative to their presence in the total population.[8] Nevertheless, for those among the poor whose households were inventoried, there can be little doubt that tea and coffee drinking had become an established part of their home life before the middle of the eighteenth century. For their social betters, there is no doubt whatsoever that this was the case.

A similar picture emerges from Dibbits's comparative study of material culture in the South Holland coastal fishing village of Maassluis, and in the inland Hanseatic fortress town of Doesburg, situated at the juncture of the Oude IJssel and the IJssel rivers in a part of Gelderland known as the Achterhoek. While a place like Maassluis fits clearly into the larger picture historians have developed about the maritime economic vibrancy of the Dutch Golden Age, Doesburg, on the other hand, had reached its commercial zenith in the Middle Ages. By the time of the Republic, Doesburg served primarily as a border garrison town and a regional distribution centre for specialized craftsmen and retailers. It looked eastward towards the continent at least as much as it did westward towards the feverish activity of the Holland ports. Yet Dibbits finds no particular difference in the speed of assimilation of the material artifacts of coffee and tea consumption between the two locations. She concludes of both places that by '1750 coffee and tea wares were altogether commonplace.'[9] Once again, and in keeping with a standard reading of the social stratification of the early modern Netherlands, the inventories have been divided between three social classes. All three groups contributed (more or less quickly and numerically as expected; that is, the richest were earliest and had the most, and the poorer followed with slightly less) to the early eighteenth-century diffusion of tea and coffee wares. However, as with van Koolbergen's work, the category of the 'poor' (she uses the term *minvermogenden*; that is, of little property) remains somewhat suspect if truly widespread diffusion is the phenomenon we wish to document. Although this category includes handworkers, fishermen, domestic servants, soldiers, and day laborers, it also includes all those whose property evaluation at death totaled up to 2,000 guilders, a rather handsome sum in the context of the working poor.[10]

Before pursing the problems of social class more directly, it is worth taking a look at two cities, Delft and Antwerp, both of which were in decline and both of which are well documented. Wijsenbeek-Olthuis, in her path-breaking study of economic decline in Delft over the course of the eighteenth century, examines 300 inventories, distributed evenly between the five classificatory groups for the burial tax (from the *pro Deo* to the very rich), three quarter-century time periods (1706–1730, 1738–1762, and 1770–1794), and four household composition/life cycle groups. She documents very clearly the general process of impoverishment that affected Delft over the course of the eighteenth century, a process characterized by both relative and absolute population decline, de-industrialization, and both reductions in and redistributions of personal wealth holding as revealed in the after-death inventories. Despite these negative trends, however, the evidence for tea and coffee consumption rises markedly between the first and second quarters of the eighteenth century.[11] Her argument that 'changes in the material culture' are more 'due to trends in fashion rather than to impoverishment and the use of alternative products' is compelling.[12]

Moreover, a similar phenomenon can be found to have taken place in contemporary Antwerp, a city marked by a truly spectacular fall from the apex of international commerce in the latter part of the early modern period. Blondé and van Damme argue that despite the transformation of Antwerp from a great commercial centre to a (minor) regional city employing mostly poorly paid textile workers, 'by 1780, the material culture of Antwerp was more colorful, more diversified, and more vulnerable to changing fashion trends than it had been two centuries earlier.'[13] Tea and coffee consumption formed just one component of this larger process, albeit a noteworthy part. The authors evaluate 254 probate inventories collected from the city Notarial Archives, dividing them into six social categories on the basis of the number of rooms recorded in the inventory itself, ranging from one to in excess of sixteen. This is an extremely useful metric as it allows for a more objective treatment of the social distinctions between households which made it into the inventory sample, while simultaneously circumventing the otherwise intractable problem of our inability to make fine economic distinctions based on the burial tax system (the poorest tax class, that is the *pro Deo*, which paid no tax at all upon burial, typically encompassed between 50 and 80 per cent of the urban population, depending on the particular town or city in question, a group so large as to obfuscate much of the economic variation we wish to study). Of the eighty-six Antwerp inventories dating from 1680, none of them, regardless of social class, had equipment for making tea or coffee, although 18 per cent and 40 per cent of the 12–15 and 16+ room households respectively in that year did have equipment for making hot chocolate. By 1730, this picture had changed radically. Almost 60 per cent of even the one-room households could make tea at home, rising to 100 per cent of the most spaciously accommodated. Tea usage moved ahead of hot chocolate in every social category. Coffee equipment did not advance quite as far by 1730, but nearly caught up with that for cocoa. By 1780, both tea and coffee were everywhere ahead of hot chocolate, which among the one- and two–three-room households was still limited to only a very small minority.[14] Not surprisingly, their study also documents an accelerating increase in the number of new purveyors of tea, coffee, and chocolate throughout the 1740s, followed thereafter by more gradual increases in the number of new establishments. Over the course of the eighteenth century, tea and coffee retailers accounted for between 5 and 10 per cent of all new entrants into the Antwerp mercers' guild.[15] Thus, in spite of the radical restructuring of the local economy and the forfeiture of direct participation in global commercial exchange, Antwerpers from across the social spectrum had become regular consumers of colonial beverages at just the same time as their more prosperous northern neighbors.

The Orphanage inventories

A skeptic might still be entitled at this point to harbor lingering doubts about the true social representativeness of probate inventories culled largely from the privately contracted-for services of notaries. After all, the expertise of a notary was not without cost, and families or other heirs would have arguably avoided incurring such costs unless property was worth fighting over.[16] What is needed to confirm the picture emerging so far is evidence not tainted by the possibility of such an obvious self-selection bias. My own study of 912 probate inventories drawn up by the regents of the Amsterdam Municipal Orphanage (*Burgerweeshuis*, hereafter BWH) following the death of either a former orphan without direct heirs or a parent of a newly admitted orphan provides just such a source. The regents of the Orphanage required that inventories be drawn up for the estates of all citizen decedents leaving minor children to be cared for at municipal expense. They did this with a view to assessing the ability of those estates to contribute to the costs of maintaining the orphaned children in the institution. Thus, even the deceased parents of very poor children were evaluated, so long as they were citizens of the city and their children were eligible for residence in the BWH. As a result, this collection represents an unusually broad spectrum of the citizen working poor, as well as petty shopkeepers and craftsmen of the city. While the archive contains close to 1,500 inventories, the sample reported on here is composed of only those dated between May 1740 and April 1782.[17] A limited number of non-systematically collected orphan-household inventories have also been found which date from the latter half of the seventeenth and the early decades of the eighteenth century. Although these earlier inventories are not nearly as detailed nor are they as complete in their coverage of all households associated with the BWH, they do allow at least a glimpse at the development of colonial beverage consumption over the longer time period under consideration here.

Admittance into the BWH was open to all fully orphaned children whose parents (both of them individually) had held citizenship in the city of Amsterdam for at least seven years. There is, however, plenty of evidence to suggest that, as in many early modern communities, the well-to-do did not avail themselves of these public services, but rather found ways to care for their orphans within their own kin networks.[18]

The immigrant underclass was, on the other hand, excluded by the combined rules of citizenship and longevity. So it was that the BWH could understand itself to be primarily an institution catering to those of the middling sort. The inventories themselves can tell us more clearly exactly what that meant.

Somewhat surprisingly, given the BWH Regent's own conception of their charitable mission to the *burgerij*, that is, the respectable middle class of the city, the population that actually found its way into their bookkeeping was by any absolute measure a poor one. During a period in which the BWH itself spent 150 guilders per annum to care for each child, the median household associated with the institution had total assets at death amounting to only 69 guilders (dropping to 52 guilders if the 133 inventories recording no possessions are factored in with a value of zero).[19] Once the outstanding debts of the deceased are accounted for, the median household actually had a negative net worth. Yet some types of households were consistently poorer even than others. Male decedents enjoyed greater assets than did female decedents (with median assets of 62 and 47 guilders respectively), although they also tended to incur more and higher debts[20] (Table 13.1). This itself was a sign of men's greater economic activity in a society where bills were typically only settled at long intervals. But even greater disparities are evident across household types than can be captured by gender alone. Married couples, regardless of whether they entered the BWH books at the death of the husband or the wife, enjoyed substantially greater assets than any other group. The contrast with widows is especially great, with the experience of widowers falling in between. Even those who had never married (by necessity here, all former orphans) had higher median assets than did the widows. The median household assets of married couples were 81 guilders compared to 52, 31, and 64 guilders for widowers, widows, and the never-married respectively. Moreover, this result is not simply an artifact of age at death. The median age at death of the inventoried subjects does not vary systematically across the wealth categories, nor do the median asset figures for the various demographic groups change perceptibly when controlling for age at death.[21] The real relative strength of households headed by two adults

TABLE 13.1   Distribution of the Amsterdam BWH inventories by gender of decedent and net worth[22]

	Males	Females	Total
Positive net worth – N	109	143	252
Column percentage	26.6	28.5	27.6
Median net worth (guilders)	69.4	77.8	76.0
Negative net worth – N	251	276	527
Column percentage	61.2	55.0	57.7
Median net worth (guilders)	–3.5	–42.7	–54
Incomplete – N	50	83	133
Column percentage	12.2	16.5	14.6
Median net worth (guilders)	Not recorded	Not recorded	Not recorded

Note: Those with incomplete inventories are the so-called *per memorie* records. Typically, the family information, location of the residence, the date of the bookkeeper's visit, and the signatures of the relevant surviving family members were still recorded in the usual fashion. What is missing is the list of household belongings (presumably there were none) and the debts remaining to be paid (presumably there were more than enough of these).

should not be terribly surprising, however, given that for almost all of these families, the main source of total household assets resided in the movable goods themselves and intact households tended to be larger with more possessions than broken households, regardless of the age of the household head. Yet it is worth remembering that both widows and widowers had at one point been in such households, so there must have been some process by which they dis-acquired material possessions following the death of their spouse. Indeed, despite these local differences between the various types of families associated with the BWH, the overall sample actually occupied a fairly narrow approximate range between the second and fourth deciles of the larger distribution of social standing (estimated by a combination of housing rents, assets at death, the city income tax records, and citizenship status) in eighteenth-century Amsterdam.[23]

Tables 13.2 and 13.3 provide an overview of a select group of items and their frequency as found in the households that fell under the purview of the Orphanage's bookkeeper. What is immediately striking about the data is the absence of even basic goods in many of these homes. Nearly 15 per cent of the households examined did not have so much as a single possession recorded. Admittedly, the bookkeeper may have overlooked items he deemed of so little material consequence as to be not worth his effort to record. Nonetheless, the paucity of goods and the pathetic descriptions of some of the enumerated inventories suggest that the cut-off standard for non-reporting was very low indeed.[24] We can be fairly confident that people listed with no possessions were in fact people with not much more than the shirts on their backs. For example, just over 3 per cent of the population actually died in municipal care at either the

TABLE 13.2   Frequency of possession and number of selected goods, Amsterdam BWH inventories, 1740–1782

	N	% of inventories	Goods per inventory		
			Mean	Median	Max.
Total inventory entries	805	88.2	61.2	52	293
Total individual goods	805	88.2	218.5	134	8,129
Beds (all kinds)	652	71.5	1.8	1	14
Cupboards/wardrobes	575	60.3	1.7	1	10
Tables	577	63.3	2.2	2	15
Tea tables	66	7.2	1.2	1	2
Spoons	452	49.6	6.8	6	40
Forks	48	5.3	4.6	4	15
Beer cans/glasses	241	26.4	1.3	1	11
Delftware	492	53.9	4.1	2	73
Pewter wares	475	52.1	15.1	12	82
Pewter plates	132	14.5	6.8	6	26
China (porcelain)	341	37.4	29.0	11	412
Japanese porcelain	15	1.6	11.3	5	68
Coffee wares	482	52.8	7.4	2	199
Tea wares	360	39.5	4.5	2	94
Teapots/infusers	422	46.3	3.0	2	23
Coffee and tea (comb.)[a]	533	58.4	9.8	3	206
Sugar bowls, etc.	74	8.1	2.6	2	10
Chocolate wares	25	2.7	5.7	5	33
Pepper wares	189	20.8	1.1	1	7
Salt boxes/cellars	215	23.6	1.9	2	11
Mustard pots, etc.	68	7.5	1.1	1	3
Tobacco wares	317	34.8	2.0	1	17
Paintings	224	24.6	3.8	2	61
Prints	261	28.6	4.1	3	29
Mirrors	529	58.0	1.5	1	10
Tea trays[b]	344	37.7	3.0	3	18

Notes:

[a]   Many serving items were used interchangeably, as is confirmed by the fifty-five cases of coffee wares and three cases of tea wares specifically described as for both coffee and tea. *Trekpots* are not included here.

[b]   These appear to have been wall decorations as well as serving trays.

Delftware cannot be counted accurately because so many of the inventories enumerated this item with the terms 'small amount' or 'some.' The number of books found in the inventories may also be suspect on account of this problem, although it was not as prevalent as for Delftware. Those entries that were given imprecisely, but in the plural, were assigned a quantity of '2' for the purposes of the calculations here.

TABLE 13.3   Frequency of possession of selected goods by marital status (percentages)

	Married	Widowers	Widows	Singles
% with inventory entries	92.4	83.6	80.1	98.9
Median number of entries	(65)	(49)	(47)	(29)
Median number of goods	(184)	(112)	(122)	(94)
Beds (all kinds)	87.4	69.6	71.1	26.4
Cupboards/wardrobes	80.6	59.7	59.2	29.9
Tables	81.3	57.7	62.7	20.7
Tea tables	7.9	6.5	7.2	6.9
Spoons	66.5	43.8	48.0	14.9
Forks	5.8	6.5	4.6	3.4
Beer cans/glasses	34.2	26.4	24.9	8.0
Delftware	71.6	44.3	53.2	23.0
Pewter wares	67.3	48.8	49.4	21.8
Pewter plates	17.6	19.4	11.3	5.7
China (porcelain)	50.7	34.3	32.1	20.7
Japanese porcelain	1.8	2.0	1.1	2.3
Coffee wares	70.9	46.8	49.7	21.8
Tea wares	51.1	35.3	38.7	14.9
Teapots/infusers	61.1	42.8	42.2	23.0
Coffee and tea (comb.)	76.6	51.2	55.2	14.1
Sugar bowls, etc.	11.1	8.0	6.4	4.6
Chocolate wares	5.6	3.5	2.0	1.1
Pepper wares	28.1	19.4	19.1	6.9
Salt boxes/cellars	29.9	25.4	23.4	8.0
Mustard pots, etc.	10.4	8.0	6.4	1.1
Tobacco wares	45.3	35.8	28.6	23.0
Paintings	31.6	24.9	22.8	8.0
Prints	38.8	25.9	26.0	22.6
Mirrors	77.1	52.2	54.9	20.7
Tea trays	54.0	30.8	34.1	16.1

Pesthuis (hospital) or the *Gasthuis* (old person's home) and most of these were listed (and appropriately so) as having no possessions. Nearly 30 per cent of the inventories reveal households with not so much as a bed, or a piece of storage furniture, be it even so simple as a basket. In such a context, it is somewhat amazing that over half of the households possessed at least one item for the making of coffee (and slightly less so for the explicit making of tea, although there was a fair degree of interchangeableness here, especially for serving wares). Chocolate was a luxury almost unheard of in this population, with less than 3 per cent of the inventories listing specific goods associated with its preparation for drinking. This is entirely consistent with what we know from the qualitative literature on colonial beverages, which consistently regards chocolate as a real luxury in comparison to tea or coffee. Its near absence here is thus another indication that the BWH sample of inventories really is drawn from the poor end of the citizen spectrum.

A seemingly less expected result, especially given the strong tradition of commercial brewing in Dutch economic history, is the relative scarcity of households reporting specific drinking vessels for beer (either the *bierkan* or the *bierglas*). A scant quarter of all households had one or more of these items, and even among married heads of household the incidence rises only to one third. Of course people could consume beer in a wide variety of vessels, not all of which need have been identified for that specific purpose. Even if we expand the category to include all generic glasses (that is, items listed as *glas* and *kan* without *bier* as the prefix) the incidence rate moves only slightly upward to 30 per cent. What should we make of such low inventory numbers, knowing that beer continued to be an important source of grain calories for the poor throughout the eighteenth century?[25] One likely factor is that beer can be consumed without the benefit of single-purpose glassware. Thus the general poverty of this sample might be reflected in the inability to acquire specialized accessories. A more interesting possibility, however, is that we are seeing the culmination of a trend that historians of Dutch material culture have already located in the seventeenth century, namely the systematic substitution of fine earthenware for copper and especially pewter objects, a trend that Harm Nijboer sees as part of a 'shift from hoarding towards consumption.'[26] This broader decline in pewter ownership as a medium for storing wealth, and the simultaneous shift towards object acquisition for its decorative or functional use, seems to be well in evidence in the Orphanage population. If we consider the distribution of the remaining specified beer drinking vessels across demographic groups, especially in comparison with the comparable rates for tea and coffee ceramics, it is possible to discern ownership for use rather than 'hoarding.' For every kind of drinking vessel, households with a married head enjoy the highest rates of ownership. However, the rank ordering of widows versus widowers switches between beer and caffeinated beverage accessory ownership. Widows were less likely than their male counterparts to own specific items for drinking beer, but more likely to possess specific items for drinking or making tea and coffee, accurately reflecting the gendered nature of the two kinds of sociability. Overall rates of pewter ownership remain comparable for both male and female elderly, but beer cans and glasses specifically find more room in the inventories of men than women. It seems that the much discussed eighteenth-century transition from alcohol to caffeine as the drug of the people was indeed a phenomenon led first by women.

These gender differences aside, the high incidence of coffee and tea wares among the whole Orphanage population is entirely consistent with the argument that coffee and tea were no longer luxury commodities by the middle of the eighteenth century. But it is hardly definitive proof of that fact. In order to verify that the households with these goods represented more than just the wealthiest half of the inventoried population, it is helpful to assess the financial profiles of households sorted by their ownership of a variety of goods, not just tea and coffee wares. Table 13.4 reports a rank ordering of the wealth profiles of a variety of household groupings, determined by the presence of particular items in their inventories. The poorest grouping consists of those households that did not own so much as a bed or mattress. These 260 households had a median asset value of a scant 0.5 guilders. By contrast, the 650 households that did own a bed or mattress enjoyed substantially higher median assets of 81.3 guilders. The list continues from this point in ascending order of the median asset values associated with the different groupings of the households. (For reference, the full distribution of total assets is given for all 910 valued inventories at the bottom of the table.) Obviously, the rank order of any particular item of material culture depends somewhat on the arbitrary composition of the list itself. Nonetheless, the indication of the financial position of certain types of households relative to others is illuminating. Not surprisingly, of all the items associated with the consumption of colonial beverages, Delftware has the greatest downward reach, followed closely by tea and coffee wares generally, tea and *trekpotten* (that is, infusion pots), porcelain, and then (specifically) tea wares.

The so-called *trekpotten* are numerous and a source of potential confusion. In Table 13.2, 422 households are reported as having had at least one teapot or infuser. But the literal word teapot (*theepot*) only appears in four of the inventories, two of which date from the late 1770s, one from 1760, and the earliest from 1747. All of the remaining inventories record having at least one *trekpot*, a word that in modern usage does denote a teapot. However, its original meaning was any pot in which leaves could be infused; that is, steeped without boiling. It could be the case that all of the *trekpotten* belonging to the inventoried households were in fact already being used primarily for the steeping of tea, regardless of what might have been their usage in an earlier century. But it is worth noting that only 360 households left a record of having possession of at least one item which was used explicitly for the serving or preparation of tea; that is, these households owned items which were prefaced with the word *thee*, as in *theekop* (teacup), *theeketel* (tea kettle), or *theelepel* (teaspoon), to name the three most common examples. An additional 127 households had only a

TABLE 13.4 Quartile distribution of household assets in guilders (by possession of selected goods and rank ordered by median values)

Households by items owned	N	Household assets in guilders		
		Q1	Median	Q3
Owns no bed	260	0.0	0.5	29.3
Owns at least one bed	650	31.5	81.3	248.3
Cupboard/wardrobe	571	35.0	87.0	255.0
Delftware	492	42.8	98.9	257.7
Mirror	527	44.0	103.6	276.6
Coffee/tea wares (all)	533	50.9	114.0	319.6
Lakens (Dutch woolen)	487	53.3	116.0	323.5
Pewter wares	476	55.0	119.8	307.0
Teapot/*trekpot*	421	58.5	138.8	318.6
Cottons (Asiatic fabric)	213	62.0	142.0	332.6
China (porcelain)	341	62.5	147.0	345.1
Painting	225	53.3	150.0	335.2
Tea wares (not including *trekpots*)	360	66.5	165.5	366.1
Hanging cupboard	142	62.0	170.0	362.1
Muslin (Asiatic fabric)	165	79.0	172.1	334.0
Books (all types)	196	79.1	174.1	364.1
Bible	180	99.5	186.0	437.0
Damask (European fabric)	119	87.5	190.0	383.6
Chest of drawers	97	75.0	194.0	451.4
Tobacco wares	222	91.2	194.0	399.1
Cabinet	66	67.0	203.4	388.0
Beer cans/glasses	241	93.5	217.4	470.6
Desk	103	89.0	222.5	591.5
Silver item	226	110.5	223.5	528.8
Tea table	64	63.5	230.8	520.6
Timepiece	170	101.0	236.5	565.1
Silk (Asiatic fabric)	205	110.5	246.5	481.9
Floor mat/carpet	61	131.2	247.2	470.7
Velvet (European fabric)	62	95.0	247.4	548.3
Sugar bowl	74	140.0	268.5	651.1
Fork	48	140.5	272.0	508.6
Chintz (Asiatic fabric)	132	131.1	272.4	601.3
Gold item	112	163.0	283.5	533.7
Chocolate wares	25	150.0	297.6	591.5
Scientific instrument	30	173.5	329.7	807.0
Inkwell	44	239.7	359.1	953.6

	N	10%	Q1	Median	Q3	90%	95%	Max
Asset profile of all households	910	0.0	13.0	52.8	183.3	494.7	863.5	8,127.3

trekpot and no other specifically named tea service items. The presence of the infusion pot would have allowed them to steep tea, but need not necessarily indicate that they did so. Other kinds of leaves, particularly herbs for medicinal purposes, had been steeped prior to the introduction of tea, and this may well have been the use to which at least some of these infusion pots were employed. Much less common (only sixty-six cases) were the households that had explicit tea brewing or serving equipment, but no *trekpot*. Given the cultural hierarchy implicit in the history of the *trekpot*, it is not surprising then that the households that had specific items for use with tea ranked as wealthier than those with only an ambiguous access to colonial beverage consumption.

Mixed right in among these goods on the asset-ranking list are mirrors, pewter wares, and paintings (in every case with neither subject nor attribution): respectable commodities to be sure, but none of which would have been considered especially rare or luxurious. The households that owned books; silk and cotton chintz textiles; beer drinking vessels; precious metals; new types of furniture such as chests of drawers, cabinets, and desks; timepieces; floor carpeting; and indeed chocolate wares were much more financially substantial, even if many of these goods do not resonate for historians as particularly exotic or exciting. Given the relative position of the households containing tea and coffee service items when compared with a wide variety of other distinctive types of items, it seems reasonable to conclude that the material culture of colonial beverage consumption was no longer terribly exclusive by the middle decades of the eighteenth century.

Nonetheless, we have good reason to believe that this had not always been the case. The BWH data still need to be incorporated into the larger phenomenon of increasing specialization in consumer wares which took place over the course of the eighteenth century, of which the slow introduction of named teapots in place of the more general *trekpotten* is but one example. The complete data do not cover a long enough period of time for an extensive investigation into this question, but the archives of the BWH do include a scattering of records of this type from the period prior to 1740. I have found thiry-five inventories drawn up between 1646 and 1674, and another thirteen drawn up between 1700 and 1731. These early inventories are not at all as socially comprehensive as the systematically recorded inventories of the mid-eighteenth century. Rather, internal evidence suggests that they represent only the most prosperous end of the spectrum of households associated with the institution. While they are not all valued consistently, the ones for which asset totals can be calculated indicate that these were households which would have been located comfortably among the highest wealth category of BWH affiliates half a century later. Yet among the seventeenth-century inventories, we find not a single good specified as being for the consumption of either tea or coffee, and only one inventory that lists any kind of porcelain – in this case, a broken cup and one mustard pot. By the turn of the century, however, the picture had changed radically. Of the thirteen inventories which date from 1700–1731, six, or nearly half, record tea goods of one kind or another, and all but one of those also record coffee wares. The most materially complex of these households (dating from 1731) also includes a special cup for the drinking of hot chocolate. Clearly, by this point in time the material culture of colonial beverage consumption had begun to penetrate the upper reaches of the segment of society whose children could be found in institutional care following the death of their parents. While the exact parameters of this social segment can only be demarcated in a general way, the timing of the spread of tea and coffee wares into the records of the BWH nevertheless mirrors closely both the trade statistics reported on at the outset of this discussion, as well as the probate inventory data collected elsewhere for what were certainly more well-to-do populations.

It is, of course, also possible to look for a time trend in the more complete data from the middle of the eighteenth century onward. A simple first step is to investigate whether there was any change in the density of ownership of tea and coffee wares between the middle and the later decades of the century. Table 13.5 records the same information as Table 13.2 for the colonial beverage items (including sugar pots and beer glasses for comparison), with the inventory data divided more or less in half at January of 1760 (488 inventories were recorded from 1740–1759, and 424 from 1760–1782). Two minor but opposing trends are immediately apparent. The percentage of households participating at all in the material culture of hot beverage drinking *falls*, if only very slightly, between the two periods.[27] This is true for every item except sugar bowls and chocolate wares, which increased slightly, but of course the absolute numbers for the latter are very small indeed. Yet at the same time, the *size* of the collections for those households participating in this material culture was increasing, although not to an extent that rules out the possibility of a result generated by measurement error. It is the case that part of the fall in incidence was due to the increasing percentage of inventories completed for individuals or households that had no possessions whatsoever. In the first half of the sample, only 12 per cent of the inventories are of this type, while that share is 17.7 per cent in the second half. Yet even when we factor out the greater percentage of inventories in the latter period that had no possessions at all, participation in this particular material culture was still less common in 1760–1782 than it had been in 1740–1759. These adjusted percentages can be found in the last column of Table 13.5.

Several puzzling questions arise out of these observations. The most fundamental is concerned with the representativeness of the inventory-making process itself. Perhaps the bookkeeper's tolerance for making records of people with either few or no possessions was increasing, thereby leaving a record of Orphanage affiliates who would earlier have gone unremarked. Or perhaps the population that required the services of the BWH (and managed to become eligible for them) was increasingly drawn from lower levels of the Amsterdam social order than in earlier times. A last possibility is that the larger population of the city was getting poorer, reflecting the general economic decline and financial strain so characteristic of the second half of the century.

TABLE 13.5 Frequency of possession and number of colonial beverage goods in two time periods

	N	% of inventories	Mean	Amsterdam BWH inventories		% of inventories with enumerated goods
				Goods per inventory		
				Median	Maximum	
Panel A 1740–1759 (N = 488)						
Coffee wares	263	53.9	6.4	2	199	61.2
Tea wares	204	41.8	3.5	2	36	47.4
Teapots/infusers	245	50.2	3.2	2	23	57.0
Coffee and tea (comb.)	296	60.7	8.1	3	206	68.8
Sugar bowls, etc.	35	7.2	2.5	1	10	8.1
Chocolate wares	12	2.5	6.3	4	33	2.8
Delftware	274	56.1	2.8	2	45	63.7
China	190	38.9	32.2	12	350	44.2
Beer cans and glasses	136	27.9	1.2	1	7	31.6
Panel B 1760–1782 (N = 424)						
Coffee wares	219	51.6	8.6	3	87	62.7
Tea wares	156	36.8	5.8	2	94	44.7
Teapots/infusers	176	41.5	2.7	2	22	50.4
Coffee and tea (comb.)	232	54.7	12.0	4	120	66.5
Sugar bowls, etc.	38	9.0	2.7	2	10	10.9
Chocolate wares	13	3.1	5.2	5	12	3.7
Delftware	218	51.4	5.8	2	73	62.5
China	149	35.1	25.4	11	412	42.7
Beer cans and glasses	105	24.8	1.3	1	11	30.1

Panel C Estimation of confidence intervals for difference between proportions in 1740–1759 and 1760–1782

	Point difference	Standard error	Lower limit	Upper limit
Coffee wares	0.023	0.03314	−0.04195	0.08795
Tea wares	0.050	0.03236	−0.01342	0.11342
Teapots/infusers	0.087	0.03294	0.02244	0.15156
Coffee and tea (comb.)	0.060	0.03276	−0.00421	0.12421
Sugar bowls, etc.	−0.018	0.01817	−0.05361	0.01761
Chocolate wares	−0.006	0.01099	−0.02754	0.01554
Delftware	0.047	0.03307	−0.01782	0.11182
China	0.038	0.03201	−0.02473	0.10073
Beer cans and glasses	0.031	0.02919	−0.02621	0.08821

Enough remains unknown about changes over time in Amsterdam's wealth and income distributions that it is impossible to fully resolve this uncertainty. Nonetheless, there is plenty of corroborating evidence to suggest that the lower orders of the urban population were in fact feeling more financial strain in the last decades of the eighteenth century than they had previously. Certainly there can be no doubt about the outcome of these changes for the coffers of the BWH, for indeed, the later inventoried households are both demographically and financially weaker than their peers of only twenty years prior. The share of married couples in the collection falls by over six percentage points, while the percentage of never-marrieds almost doubles across these two time periods. Moreover, median household asset values were edging downwards over time as well, despite the increasing spread generated by the most substantial of the inventories. Yet regardless of the larger economic forces at work behind these numbers, what seems certain is that there was a threshold in the very low reaches of the social order below which it was difficult for the material culture of colonial grocery consumption to penetrate. For even while households above that threshold were clearly increasing their collections of coffee- and teacups, spoons, saucers, pots, tins, and so forth, it is likely that a narrowly increasing share of the households was shut out altogether. It seems likely then that the increasing severe financial hardships of the latter eighteenth century worked to intensify social differentiation, at least as manifested in the capacity of ordinary people to own Asiatic serving wares.

From ownership to consumption

Nonetheless the evidence yielded by the after-death inventories collected by the BWH leave little room for doubt that many economically marginal (dare we say desperately poor?) citizen households in Amsterdam had incorporated the material artifacts of tea and coffee drinking into their lives by the middle decades of the eighteenth century. But what can we say with confidence about their actual consumption of the beverages themselves? This is, of course, not typically a question for which after-death inventories are well suited.[28] Once again, however, we are aided in our quest by the remarkably unusual bookkeeping practices of the BWH. For among the items listed in these inventories, despite being of no further value to the Orphanage (hence they are always listed as *per memorie*, that is, just for the record), are the as yet unreclaimed pawnshop tickets of the deceased. While these records offer by no means a full accounting of the pawnshop activity of the inventoried population, they are nonetheless suggestive about the kinds of goods that did and did not figure importantly in people's pawning strategies.

From the total population of 912 decedents, 128 died with (a total of 960) items still at the pawnshop. The majority (61 per cent) of these outstanding pawns were for items of clothing and dress accessories, with another 14 per cent of them for jewelry. Dishes and other kitchenwares accounted for only 12 per cent of the pawns, with even smaller shares taken up by fabrics, bedding, and luxury items such as books or clocks.[29] The type of items that are likely to end up at the pawnshop is an outcome of at least two considerations: patterns of ownership of goods, and the intensity of use of those goods. Of course, households could only pawn goods they already owned, but they presumably also tried to avoid pawning those items they needed most for daily use. Perhaps the potential harm that might befall different items at the pawnshop was also a consideration; households might want to avoid pawning items especially susceptible to breakage. The relative dearth of books, timepieces, and other luxury items among this population accounts for their scarcity among the pawned goods, as likewise, the preponderance of clothing in the inventories explains the predominance of such goods at the pawnshop. But dishes and kitchen items are relatively scarce at the pawnshop. In particular, those items associated with the consumption of colonial beverages are underrepresented. No sugar accessories or porcelain of any kind appear among the pawnshop tickets, reflecting both the scarcity of the former, and perhaps the breakability of the latter. But even the more plentiful and less fragile ordinary tea and coffee goods such as cups, boxes, pots, kettles, mills, and spoons are remarkable for their limited presence at the pawnshop. Of the 121 households that did leave pawned items, but did not pawn tea or coffee goods, 81 per cent of them could have done so based on the presence of such goods in their inventories. Is this in fact evidence that people considered the items required for the consumption of colonial beverages to be essential for everyday use, and thus, despite their often obvious value, not suitable items to deposit on pawn?

One way to think about this question is to look more closely at the few households that *had* pawned tea and coffee goods. Panel A of Table 13.6 lists the seven households for which this was the case, along with a list of the items themselves and the redemption value of the tickets. As the summary financial information recorded in panel B of Table 13.6 shows, these seven households were quite prosperous by the standards of this population, and the average value of their outstanding pawns was substantially higher than for the much larger group which did not pawn any tea or coffee goods. Moreover, they pawned out of their abundance. All seven of these households had additional, indeed greater than the median number of, tea and coffee goods remaining in their inventories. Presumably these households could afford to pawn some of their tea and coffee wares without interrupting the rituals of consumption at home. If tea and coffee wares were acquired primarily for the status they imparted as items of display rather than for use, it seems likely that they would have found their way more often into the pawnshop, as we see with other discrete objects of value such as jewelry and precious metal wares. It is, of course, possible that pawn shops themselves were reluctant to take possession of tea and coffee wares, either because the resale market for them was small, or their fragility made them difficult to hold in storage. However, given the evidence presented below about people's willingness to hold onto and use damaged or broken tea and coffee

TABLE 13.6 Pawnshop evidence of tea and coffee wares

Panel A: Households with pawnshop tickets for tea and coffee wares[a]

Year	Decedent	Assets[b]	Pawned items	Value of ticket[c]
1740	Married male	82.30	1 tea kettle	2.0
1741	Married female	248.00	Set of 5 Delft cups 3 tea boxes (glass) 14 pairs of teacups/saucers 6 *trekpots* (probably teapots)	NA[c]
1741	Married male	101.50	1 tea kettle	4.0
1745	Widower	657.30	2 tea boxes	36.0
1745	Married female	13.00	2 coffee cans	1.25
1751	Widow	102.13	1 coffee can	2.0
1759	Married female	808.08	1 tea box	54.0

Panel B: Financial profile of households with pawnshop tickets

Household type	N	Assets (guilders)		Pawnshop tickets (guilders)	
		Mean	Median	Mean	Median
All with pawn tickets[d]	126	208.5	64.0	33.4	17.9
Pawn tea and coffee wares	7	287.5	102.1	113.4	63.5
Did not pawn tea or coffee[d]	119	203.8	61.8	28.7	16.5

Panel C: Possession of colonial accessories in households without tea and coffee wares among their pawned items

Type of good	N (households)	Number of goods			Potential pawn share[e]
		Mean	Min	Maxi	
Delft pottery	89	5.1	1	73	73.5%
Tea and coffee wares	98	9.2	1	120	81.0%
Porcelain	65	31.9	1	213	53.7%
Sugar pots	13	2.2	1	9	10.7%

Notes:

a No households pawned porcelain wares of any kind, nor any sugar pots.

b Household assets and the value of the pawn tickets are all given in guilders.

c These items were valued together with a number of other household items, including a porcelain chest, a cabinet, and other dish wares, for a total of 46.0 guilders. They were pawned to a private individual as surety for a cash loan.

d Two households are not included here despite having many listed possessions as well as pawnshop tickets because the inventories were not valued by the bookkeeper.

e The potential pawn share represents the number of households which did pawn something, but not tea or coffee wares, but which could have pawned the various items listed above based on their possession of them. Thus, the percentage is calculated by N/121.

wares, it seems likely that the second-hand market was in fact a thriving one. It should not have been a major impediment to the pawning of cups, saucers, pots, tea boxes, and so forth, if people had wanted to do so.

The high number of tea and coffee goods described in the inventories as old, chipped, and/or broken is yet another important indicator that the households associated with the Orphanage were indeed consumers of caffeinated beverages. To the extent that porcelain was acquired for purposes of display, it is arguable that the quality of being broken would obviate the value of holding onto the item. However, a chipped or partly broken dish could still be functional. Almost 72 per cent of all households that had porcelain of some kind or another had at least one broken piece. Moreover, most of this porcelain was chipped or broken, because for those households with any broken china at all, nearly 95 per cent of all of their porcelain was described as such. Given the material fragility of porcelain, and the economic fragility of this population, the high incidence of broken dish wares is not terribly surprising, but it is suggestive about the uses to which such dish wares were put. Display seems to have been much less important than use.[30]

Finally, what direct evidence is there of the colonial groceries themselves? Only six inventories indicate the presence of sugar, six the presence of tea, and nine the presence of coffee. All of these cases appear to be ones in which the commodity in question was part of a stock of 'shop goods'; that is, they were stocks destined primarily for retail distribution rather than personal consumption. Not surprisingly then, there was a fair degree of overlap in these inventories, with five households stocking tea along with coffee, and some of these stocking sugar as well. Table 13.7 reports summary information on the twelve inventories that held these stocks, as well as detailed information on the stocks themselves where available. Clearly, a few of the individuals in this sample were engaged in fairly sizeable retail operations (and these tended to be those who also had considerable household assets), but the majority must have been engaged at a fairly low level. Indeed, in some cases it would seem that the main activity of the inventoried shop was in other goods, with coffee distribution as a sideline. For example, Dirk Milar, who died in 1766, left a large variety of fabrics in his shop, but also a small amount of coffee beans and a mill.

Additional information on the possession of colonial groceries can also be gleaned from the debt records associated with each of the inventories. In fact, it is here that we find much more evidence of the consumption (and redistribution) of coffee and tea in particular. Sixty-five inventories record debts left outstanding at death for purchases of coffee ranging in value from 15 stuivers to 328 guilders and 5 stuivers. Forty-six inventories record debts for purchases of tea, although generally the amounts seem to have been smaller. The largest debt specifically for tea was only 21 guilders and 10 stuivers (some of this is attributable to the much lower weight of a per-cup quantity of tea leaves than coffee beans, but it also seems to be the case that larger stocks of coffee were purchased at a time). As we would expect from the information recorded among the shop goods, a

TABLE 13.7   Stocks of colonial groceries

Year	Decedent (Assets)	Grocery item	Unit price	Value of entry
1741	Married male (1,184)	200 ponden[a] coffee	@ 0.3 guild./ pond	60 guilders Valued with other goods
		20 ponden coffee		
		30 ponden tea	@ 1.25 guild./ pond	37.5 guilders Valued with other goods
		12 ponden sugar		
1742	Married male (516)	Some coffee Some tea 5 ponden tea		Valued together with thread for 14 guilders Valued with tea boxes for 7 guild.
1742	Widow (372)	4 tonnen and 50 ponden coffee 3 ponden tea 30 ponden sugar		Valued together with a mill and bins for 41 guilders
1742	Widow (251)	Small amount of sugar		Valued with some meat, beans, meal, gort, etc. for 30 guilders
1745	Married male (651)	Some coffee		Valued with other goods
1751	Married female (240)	96 ponden coffee	@ 0.3 guild./ pond	Valued at 28 guilders
		1 pond tea		Valued with other goods
1752	Widower (2,770)	Some sugar		Valued with currants for 6.5 guilders
1758	Widow (595)	Small amount of coffee Small amount of tea		Valued together with other goods
1760	Widow (864)	1 restand[b] coffee 2 restand sugar		40 guilders Valued with meal, peas, gort, soap, salt, etc.
1766	Married male (275)	Some coffee		Valued with many other goods
1770	Married male (249)	1 restand sugar		Valued with currants and candy for 5 guilders
		1.5 ponden nutmeg		Valued with other goods
1776	Widow (2,541)	220 ponden coffee	@ 0.25 guild./ pond	55 guilders

Notes:
a   Pond = 0.494 kilograms
b   Restand = remaining amount or leftover from a larger stock

majority of these cases (thirty-eight) actually left debts for both tea and coffee. Two of the cases also left debts for sugar, and an additional case had a very small debt for chocolate.

These numbers are still small, however, in comparison with the 533 inventories that listed at least one object specifically used in the preparation or serving of hot beverages. For many of the households in the sample, tea and coffee must have been acquired in very small amounts for relatively immediate consumption, and thus do not show up in the inventories. Further evidence of this pattern of purchasing can be inferred from the relatively small size of the majority of debts for tea and coffee. In this regard they are not at all unlike other everyday foodstuffs that are almost non-existent among the enumerated goods, but show up frequently among the petty debts. Dependence on the local grocer must have been widespread, particularly at the lower end of the economic spectrum. Small-scale retailers, like Aaltje van Dijk, who died in 1751 leaving a stock of ninety-six *ponden* of coffee and an additional *pond* of tea – located as she was in the low-prestige Vereenigde Oost-Indische Compagnie (VOC) warehouse district of the Eastern Islands – must have been well situated to fill that need. Given the crowded and damp conditions of most low-rent dwellings in Amsterdam, concomitant with the proximity of small retail establishments, it would hardly have made sense to act otherwise. Indeed, it seems likely that many poor households that may have consumed tea and coffee from time to time could do so only in retail establishments, because they simply did not have the equipment at home to do otherwise. Fortunately for them, they did have neighbors, who were also proximate in social distance, who could fill that need.

Conclusion

All of the evidence presented here points to the increasing consumption of colonial beverages, and their closely related material culture of ceramics, broadly across the social spectrum. Moreover, the disparate sources of evidence reassuringly point in a common direction. The widespread diffusion of a new cultural behavior is entirely consistent with the following documented phenomena: the dramatic increase in VOC and East India Company shipments of tea and coffee into Europe – not to mention the well-documented expansion of their powerful European complement, sugar; the geographical spread of bean and leaf cultivation among Dutch and English colonial possessions; the expansion of independent small-scale producers alongside the colonial plantation systems;[31] the secular decline of prices at European ports; the rapid and extensive spread of the artifacts associated with hot beverage consumption in after-death inventories drawn up in both urban and rural communities, both at the coast and at more inland locations; the emergence of local industries, first in Delft, then in England and elsewhere on the continent, to imitate the Asian manufactures associated with the preparation and service of hot beverages; and the seeming reluctance of households to part with their tea and coffee goods, even when broken, despite the temptation of their cash value at the pawnshop. These are not the likely attributes of a trade catering to a rarified and luxurious habit restricted to only a small elite.

The evidence drawn from the after-death inventories of the Amsterdam Municipal Orphanage is particularly compelling in this regard. As the household asset ranking by evidence of material possessions indicates, the consumption of colonial beverages really did extend well down into the lower reaches of society, just as many social commentators had asserted. It is perhaps not surprising that such things as timepieces, jewelry made from precious metals, and scientific instruments would only be accessible to the wealthiest of decedents. But tea and coffee wares seem to have enjoyed a wider distribution than even simple books or the Bible. They certainly were more accessible to the lower sorts than the other commodities being brought into Amsterdam by the VOC in prodigious quantities, particularly Asian textiles such as silk and cotton chintz. Perhaps the relatively different extent of the social depth of these two markets reflects the presence of suitable, if not as desirable, alternatives for the textiles. Light woolens continued to be worn in great quantity in the eighteenth century, and there were cotton and linen alternatives that were much less expensive than chintz. But in the case of colonial beverages, once someone was hooked on the sweetened and caffeinated brews, it was hard to find a substitute at any price. The meteoric rise in the share of VOC activity devoted to the transportation and ultimately cultivation of tea and coffee, both goods that began the seventeenth century with no market identity whatsoever, is certainly strong testimony to this fact.

Notes

1 Anne E. C. McCants, 'Poor Consumers as Global Consumers: the Diffusion of Tea and Coffee Drinking in the Eighteenth Century,' *The Economic History Review*, 61.S1 (2008): 172–200; and Maxine Berg, 'Britain's Asian Century: Porcelain and Global History in the Long Eighteenth Century,' in *The Birth of Europe: Culture and Economy, 1400–1800, Essays in Honor of Jan de Vries*, ed. Laura Cruz and Joel Mokyr (Leiden: Brill, 2010), 134–156.

2 Berg, 'Britain's Asian Century,' 141.

3 Harm Nijboer, 'A Product for "Feasting the Eye and Ostentation": The Market for Dutch Porcelain,' in *Pretty Dutch: 18th Century Dutch Porcelain*, ed. Ank Trumpie (Rotterdam: 010 Publishers, 2007): 25.

4 The expansion of coffee consumption in eighteenth-century Damascus spurred a similar boom in the import of Chinese porcelain, despite the fact that this region had long enjoyed a high quality indigenous tile and ceramic sector. Indeed, as the century progressed, Damascenes increasingly turned towards imports of the European imitators as their cheaper substitute for Chinese wares, allowing the local industry to decline and eventually die out. James Grehan, *Everyday Life and Consumer Culture in Eighteenth Century Damascus* (Seattle, WA: University of Washington Press, 2007), 137–139.

5 Thera Wijsenbeek-Olthuis, 'Van Medicijn tot statussymbool: koffie thuis in de zeventiende en achttiende eeuw,' in *Koffie in Nederland: vier eeuwen cultuurgeschiedenis*, ed. Pim Reinders and Thera Wijsenbeek-Olthuis (Delft: Gemeente Musea, 1994), 111.

6   Ibid.
7   Hans van Koolbergen, 'De materiele cultuur van Weesp en Weesperkarspel in de zeventiende en achttiende eeuw,' in *Aards geluk: de Nederlanders en hun spullen van 1550 tot 1850*, ed. *Anton Schuurman*, Jan de Vries, and Ad van der Woude (Amsterdam: Balans, 1997), 145.
8   Ibid., 127–128.
9   Hester Dibbits, *Vertrouwd bezit: materiele cultuur in Doesburg en Maassluis, 1650–1800* (*Nijmegen: SUN*, 2001), 160, 321–326.
10 Ibid., 18.
11 Thera Wijsenbeek-Olthuis, *Achter de gevels van Delft: bezit en bestaan van rijk en arm in een periode van achteruitgang (1700–1800)* (Hilversum: Verloren, 1987), 453–454.
12 Ibid., 346.
13 Bruno Blondé and Ilja van Damme, 'Consumer and Retail 'Revolutions': Perspectives From a Declining Urban Economy: Antwerp in the Seventeenth and Eighteenth Centuries' (paper presented at the 14th International Economic History Association Congress, Helsinki, August 21–25, 2006), accessed April 13, 2012, http://www.helsinki.fi/iehc2006/papers1/Blonde3.pdf, 4.
14 Ibid., 12.
15 Ibid., 5, 12.
16 We should, of course, never underestimate the capacity for families to squander petty as well as substantial legacies in costly legal struggles. Nonetheless, it seems safe to assume that the selection bias against very poor households appearing in the Notarial Archives was a powerful one.
17 Internal evidence suggests that household inventories had been collected prior to this date by the BWH, but the systematic record of them in bound volumes only begins in May 1740. The volumes extend forward to 1809, and an additional 600 inventories are currently being transcribed and data checked for future addition into the database.
18 Anne E. C. McCants, *Civic Charity in a Golden Age: Orphan Care in Early Modern Amsterdam* (Urbana, IL: University of Illinois Press, 1997), 22–23.
19 The city estimated the yearly cost of care per child in the BWH to be 150 guilders at the close of the eighteenth century. Ibid., 194.
20 These figures are in striking contrast to those calculated by Faber in the only other published study of probate inventory records from Amsterdam. He looked at a sample of inventories from the Notarial archives for the years 1701–1710, including individuals located across all five classes of the prevailing burial tax system. Even among those from the lowest burial tax class, the *pro Deo* group that paid nothing, the average net worth after paying the death debts was a substantial 3,334 guilders. For the highest burial tax class, it was a staggering 71,789 guilders. Johannes Faber, 'Inhabitants of Amsterdam and their Possessions, 1701–1710,' in *Probate Inventories: A New Source for the Historical Study of Wealth, Material Culture and Agricultural Development*, ed. Anton Schuurman and Ad van der Woude (Utrecht: HES Publishers, 1980), 155.
21 Anne E. C. McCants, 'Inequality Among the Poor of Eighteenth Century Amsterdam,' *Explorations in Economic History* 44 (2007): 14–15.
22 The data in all tables in this chapter are drawn from Gemeente Archief Amsterdam, particulier archief 367, oud archief 652–688.
23 For a much more thorough parsing of the wealth profiles of the families associated with the BWH, and for a complete discussion of the location of this sample within the wealth distribution of the city as a whole, see ibid.
24 'Some old worthless junk' is one such comment that appears with regularity.
25 For a discussion of beer in the diet of orphans, see McCants, *Civic Charity in a Golden Age*, ch. 3.
26 Harm Nijboer, 'Fashion and the Early Modern Consumer Evolution: A Theoretical Exploration and Some Evidence from Seventeenth Century Leeuwarden,' in

Retailers and Consumer Changes in Early Modern Europe: England, France, Italy and the Low Countries, ed. Bruno Blondé et al. (Tours: Presses universitaires François-Rabelais, 2005), 22–23.

27 It is worth noting, however, that these participation percentages from the two time periods are for the most part insufficiently different to suggest with 95 per cent confidence that they are in fact drawn from populations with fundamentally different consumer characteristics. Only the incidence of teapot possession falls sufficiently over time to generate non-overlapping confidence bounds on the two point estimates, as indicated by the fact that both the upper and the lower confidence limits reported in panel C of Table 13.5 have a positive sign.

28 For a provocative discussion of the systematic under-reporting of ceramic wares in household inventories as checked against archaeological finds, and the concomitant conclusion that consumption of beverages in ceramic vessels was even more widespread than inventories would indicate, see John Bedell, 'Archaeology and Probate Inventories in the Study of Eighteenth-Century Life,' *Journal of Interdisciplinary History,* 31 (2000): 233–238.

29 Anne E. C. McCants, 'Goods at Pawn: The Overlapping Worlds of Material Possessions and Family Finance in Early Modern Amsterdam,' *Social Science History* 31 (2007): 227.

30 This conclusion is very similar to the one reached by Overton, Whittle, Dean, and Hann in their comprehensive study of probate inventories in Kent and Cornwall, England, over the seventeenth and eighteenth centuries. They argue on the basis of evidence internal to the inventories that the acquisition of more and more varied household goods over time reflects the desire for additional comfort more than the emulation of fashion by social inferiors (Mark Overton et al., *Production and Consumption in English Households, 1600–1750* [London: Routledge, 2004]).

31 For a critique of the standard narrative of exclusive colonial expansion, see William Clarence-Smith, 'The Spread of Coffee Cultivation in Asia, from the Seventeenth to the Early Nineteenth Century,' in *Le commerce du café avant l'ère des plantations coloniales,* ed. Michel Tuchscherer (le Caire: Institut français d'archéologie orientale, 2001), 371–384.

14

FASHIONING DIFFERENCE IN GEORGIAN ENGLAND

Furniture for him and for her

Amanda Vickery

The creation and marketing of furniture specifically targeted at men and at women were decisive innovations of English manufacturers in the later eighteenth century. This chapter explores the emergence of designs for ladies' and gentlemen's objects in luxury cabinetwork in the 1760s. It confirms the penetration of 'his and hers' furniture amongst the middle market by the 1780s using upholsterers' ledgers, and charts the spread of gendered marketing to newspaper advertisements placed by upholsterers and furniture makers by the 1790s. This chapter does not claim that cabinetmakers were solely bent on manufacturing new constructions of femininity and masculinity; however, they were in the business of promoting an exploding range of needs and attributes that bespoke furniture could answer and express. Masculine business and feminine elegance were compelling design opportunities. In the catalogues and the furniture itself, masculinity was amplified, while femininity was aesthetically constrained. The solid and the dainty became design expressions of gender that are with us to this day.

The idea of gender-specific furniture owes everything to the pervasiveness of the classical rule of 'decorum' as a system of organizing the proper relationship of people to things. Decorum was built on the recognition of fundamental divisions in society, from sex and age to rank, office, and occupation, and decreed that different forms of conduct and adornment were appropriate to one's status, company, and occasion. Hence it would be indecorous for an old lady to bedeck herself in ribbons, a child to deliver a sermon, a tradesman to flounce like a lord, or a woman to ride astride. The maintenance of the traditional social and sexual hierarchy was the explicit goal of courtesy writing on decorum, good breeding, and politeness.[1] It was these customary distinctions that sumptuary laws had tried to defend, and the flood of new commodities and non-landed wealth threatened to dissolve.

A universe of difference could be read in things. *A Modern Dissertation on a Certain Necessary Piece of Household Furniture* (1752) is an elaborate joke about chamber pots, in all their infinite variety – or to be more exact, their polymorphous uniformity. The 'general utility' of chamber pots was inarguable for 'All Persons of both Sexes.' But the 'Make of these useful implements' varied across the country, petite in the metropolis 'tending rather to the fashion of a pipkin,' but larger and deeper in the regions. The material differed as much as the form.

> The most costly sort are those that are cast in silver, and used by persons of the first rank. Those that are esteemed the neatest and chiefly intended for the fair sex are wrought in China adorned with Trees, or set off with a Variety of birds, beasts and fishes. Those which are composed of white Earth and neatly glazed are generally used by the Middling sort of people… the most Inferior sort are those which carry the ordinary Colours on their Outside, which the common People claim as their sole Property.[2]

Clearly this is a piece of toilet humor: to each their own potty.

The joke inheres in the fertility of Georgian commerce and the *reductio ad absurdum* of knowing one's place. But chamber pots did indeed come in all these varieties. Even the unpretentious piss pot demonstrated innovation: white salt-glazed stoneware and naturalistic motifs on delftware and porcelain were all new. The chamber pot exemplified the burgeoning possibilities for design differentiation by gender, wealth, and rank.

Unsurprisingly, a person's house and furnishings were supposed to be suitable to their rank, thereby conforming to the rule of decorum, helping maintain social distinctions, preventing social confusion, and ensuring the payment of respect to those of superior rank. Architectural and design manuals were built on these distinctions, and borrowed freely from Vitruvius. As Isaac Ware counseled in 1756, '[t]here are apartments in which dignity, others in which neatness, and others in which shew are to be consulted.' Noble mansions should be fitted out differently from the homes of the 'genteel,' in a manner that was 'bold, substantial and magnificent' to ensure 'a very august appearance.' Genteel houses should aspire only to 'convenience, neatness and elegance.'[3]

Sumptuary legislation enshrined decorous consumption in law. Sumptuary laws existed in classical Greece and Rome, and can be found in most Western European countries in the later Middle Ages and early modern period. Yet the reign of sumptuary law was comparatively short in England: first attempted in 1336, and abandoned in 1604. English sumptuary law never applied to food or furnishings, only to apparel – limiting the use of silks and fur to the highborn, for instance. Perhaps surprisingly, there were no proclamations relating to gender. There was much fulminating about the social confusion caused by the abuse of fine apparel by the unworthy, but there is scant evidence of prosecution.[4]

A wistful and unrealistic longing for the return of sumptuary law was one Georgian response to the parade of commercial wealth and the social blurring it inevitably entailed. As late as 1776, there were attempts to pass sumptuary laws in Poland. In the same year, Adam Smith castigated such legislation as 'the highest impertinence and presumption...in kings and ministers.'[5] However attractive the idea that the lower orders should know their place and not dress or decorate above their station, English liberty could not stomach government restriction in so private a matter as a citizen's clothes. Economic common sense cautioned that government control would hinder the spread of higher living standards and depress the economy. Nevertheless a promiscuous leveling of social distinctions was a horrible prospect for most. The princely buying power of trade and industry meant that merchants' wives might literally outshine their superiors in jewels and silks, resulting in the inexorable 'prostitution of finery.'[6]

Decorum required at least a nominal acceptance of prevailing social distinctions. Maintenance of established hierarchies was its explicit goal. As a model of society, decorum was a conservative, simplistic, and static. It could not accommodate new social groups or social mobility; indeed it tried to deny them altogether. Yet decorum was philosophically more all-encompassing than simply knowing one's place. Decorum also expressed a vision of social harmony and cohesion and was the keystone of the code of manners which came to be known as politeness. And the reach of politeness was wide, from solicitors to shopkeepers.[7] Decorum married perfectly with early eighteenth-century aesthetics. Music, literature and painting, as well as architecture and design, shared the language of harmony, proportion and order. Indeed taste was often described as an innate sense of decorum. Aesthetics, manners and worldview were all of a piece. 'Behaviour is like Architecture,' opined James Forrester in the *Polite Philosopher* (1734), 'the Symmetry of the whole pleases us so much, that we examine not into its Parts.'[8] So a Palladian building, proportioned according to the golden rules of geometry, could be seen as the quintessence of flawless beauty, but also a harmoniously ordered society.

Over the course of the eighteenth century, the principle of decorum became detached from its straightforward classical manifestation, as defenses of the waving line of beauty and celebrations of the sublime loosened the hegemony of geometry over aesthetics. By 1798, Maria Edgeworth decided that since 'taste is governed by arbitrary and variable laws; the fashions of dress, of decoration, of manner, change from day to day,' so encouraging an open mind in students was the best policy. 'Show him, and you need go no farther than the Indian skreen, or the Chinese paper in your drawing-room for the illustration, that the sublime and beautiful vary at Pekin, at London, and at Westminster-bridge and on the banks of the Ganges.'[9] Nonetheless, the grammar of decorum was deeper than the expression of a passing fashion – it was about status, not style. In 1803, the designer Thomas Sheraton still urged that surroundings should mirror status: 'particular regard is to be paid to the quality of those who order a house to be furnished.'[10]

Given the obsession with fixed distinctions in conservative commentary, it is unsurprising that both producers and consumers expected femininity and masculinity to be confirmed in appearances and possessions. However, the range of available props for the performance of gender was growing exponentially from the late seventeenth century. British dominance of international trade and manufacturing innovation introduced a host of entirely new objects, while it was the business of producers and retailers to encourage new behaviors and novel consumer wants. Some gender associations were historic. Ancient commodities like linen and cooking pots were indelibly linked to virtuous housewifery, but this traditional terrain swelled enormously in the eighteenth century. New sources of supply (from Silesia, Russia, Germany, and Ireland, as well as Holland) and the elaboration of domestic ceremony triggered a dizzying diversification of linens.[11] Technical innovation in the foundry produced an array of highly specialized new metalwares for the kitchen, which demanded new technical expertise and launched new cuisine.[12] In parallel, exotic imports like tea, coffee, chocolate, and Madeira tended to be marketed towards the sex of the early adopters and stereotypical users.[13]

Dichotomies abounded in the appreciation of design. Men were more associated with classical geometry and women with its sinuous and irregular alternatives; in gardening, gentlemanly ambitions encompassed the landscape park, but her ladyship devoted herself to flowers; in furnishings elite men were seen to assert their dynastic claims in silver and mahogany, while women were credited with a discriminating eye for textiles and ceramics. Educational literature advised that young gentlemen be taught to judge architectural and landscape improvements, while girls were trained to give order and neatness, color and texture indoors. Encountering the celebrated landscape architect Lancelot 'Capability' Brown in 1767, Josiah Wedgwood 'told him that my Life was devoted to the service of the Ladys as his was to that of the Noblemen & Gent[lemen].'[14] These binary distinctions reinforced the supreme conviction that only men comprehended structure while women, like magpies, merely grasped details, a hierarchical dualism that is with us to this day in the snobberies of the male-dominated architectural profession, and the critical disparagement of the feminized world of interiors.

The femininity or masculinity of certain styles and objects was a cliché of satire. Allusion to an object could be useful as shorthand for effeminacy, or to telegraph one of life's fundamental oppositions – petticoat versus the breeches, the tea table versus the desk, the pen versus the needle. 'Women are armed with fans as men with swords, and sometimes do more execution with them' laughed *The Spectator* in 1711.[15] In a stage play of 1730, the caddish Gainlove repulsed Lady Science and married her daughter instead, appalled by her illegitimate pretensions: 'the Dressing-Room, not the Study, is the Lady's Province and a Woman makes as ridiculous a Figure, poring over Globes, or thro' a Telescope, as a Man would with a Pair of Preservers mending Lace.'[16] Key objects – the distaff, the petticoat – had long served as metonyms for woman herself.

Some journalistic clichés were grounded in repetitive consumer behavior. Account books confirm that millinery, linens, cottons, tea wares, and porcelain figurines were all bought and prized by women.[17] On the other hand, several commodities characterized as feminine in the commercial and satirical imagination – like tea, china, novels, silks, printed cottons, and haberdashery – were not the sole preserve of women, but their widespread use by men did not dispel their womanish connotations. Indeed, the perfume of femininity may even have increased the charm of novels and porcelain for male connoisseurs behind closed doors. But some common implications (like the effeminacy of French and Chinese design) were merely fantasy, unconnected to the stylistic allegiances of Englishmen and women in practice. Scientific instruments did seem to have particular allure for men who had neither been inside a laboratory nor to sea. But telescopes, globes, barometers and microscopes enjoyed a certain virile glamour by association with the glorious British navy and the adventure of exploration on the one hand, and the gradual emergence of the scientific profession, which defined any female contribution as exceptional and familial.[18] Some links between the sexes and things were re-inscribed in marketing strategy. Life-size models of sailors guarded the entrance of instrument shops, but a gent visiting a milliner's would have to fight his way through a curtain of petticoats in the doorway.[19]

A differentiation between men's and women's tasks, pleasures, tools, and ornaments is as old as civilization. The taboo against cross-dressing is antique. However, projecting the idea of a characteristic female demand was a ground-breaking departure in the history of marketing. The pioneers in Britain were the seventeenth-century booksellers and printers who addressed specialist titles to the ladies, while the post-1688 print boom saw the publication of custom-designed ladies' pocket diaries, a proliferation of female manuals of all kinds, the *Female Spectator* in the 1740s, and the long-running *Lady's Magazine* from 1770. The leap to objects was made in the new printed illustrated catalogue of the 1760s.

This was a decisive breakthrough. Books of designs for furniture produced by London cabinetmakers were published from the 1750s, led by Thomas Chippendale. The *Gentleman and Cabinet-Maker's Director* of 1754 was crucial. It had no precedents, either in Britain or France.[20] Printed lists and catalogues of manufactured goods for sale were common enough by the mid-eighteenth century, but few were illustrated. Expensive, finely engraved design illustrations were sold as single sheets for an elite audience, but books of fine designs were confined to architecture. Most famous was Colen Campbell's *Vitruvius Britannicus*, the handbook of neo-Palladianism published in 1715. Chippendale worked closely with architects, and his innovation in the *Director* was to apply the format of their illustrated publications to a book of furniture designs, commissioning finely engraved plates and soliciting a long list of aristocratic subscribers. Like books of architectural designs, the *Director* was less a trade catalogue than a vehicle for promoting Chippendale's business to an elite clientele. Most of the furniture illustrated in the *Director* could not be bought off the shelf. First and foremost, the book was a declaration of Chippendale's virtuosity as a designer and his appreciation of genteel cultural values. As a promotional vehicle for the Chippendale brand it certainly worked. Chippendale secured a much wider range of big commissions after the *Director*'s publication in 1754 than before. Not surprisingly, his competitors quickly copied him.[21]

Lists and catalogues require taxonomies. The key categories the cabinetmakers employed in these new books of furniture designs were functional and stylistic. Niche products were designed for invalids, nursing mothers, children, the elderly, and the itinerant. But a new classification by gender appeared in the 1760s – writing tables, desks, and dressing tables could now be had either for 'a lady' or for 'a gentleman.'[22] The second edition of *Genteel Household Furniture in the Present Taste*, published by 'a Society of Upholsterers, Cabinet Makers, etc.' in 1761 or 1762, included a chinoiserie 'Lady's Desk,' 'Ladies' Dressing Stools,' and a rococo 'Lady's Bookcase.'[23] The third edition of the Chippendale *Director* depicted a 'Ladies writing table and book case' (Figure 14.1) and dressing and toilet tables 'for a lady.'[24] In the same year, the London furniture makers Ince and Mayhew specified pieces for both men and women in their *Universal System of Household Furniture*. 'The Lady's Secretary' had a counterpart in the 'Gentleman's Repository,' while the 'Ladies Toiletta' (Figure 14.2) had a 'Gentleman's Dressing Table' (Figure 14.3) for its mate.[25] By 1778, an array of desks, cabinets, dressing chests, fire screens, travelling boxes, dressing stands, and tables for tasks, for him and for her, was offered in the *Cabinet-Maker's London Book of Prices*, a publication aimed at the trade and flaunting

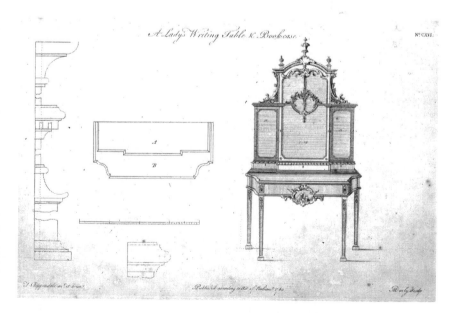

FIGURE 14.1 Thomas Chippendale, 'A Lady's Writing Table and Bookcase,' 1762

FIGURE 14.2   William Ince and John Mayhew, 'A Lady's Toiletta,' 1762

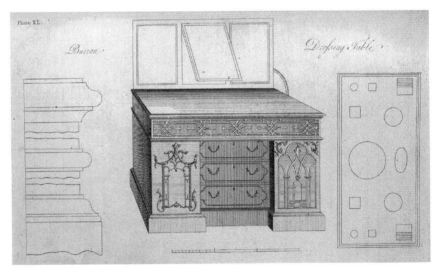

FIGURE 14.3   William Ince and John Mayhew, 'Bureau Dressing Table,' 1762

its comprehensiveness. Thomas Sheraton followed the trend in his pattern book of 1793, elaborating upon it in his *Cabinet Dictionary* of 1803, where he anticipated the lady's cabinet would be 'used to preserve their trinkets and other curious matters,' while 'the cabinets of gentlemen consist in ancient medals, manuscripts and drawing &c.'[26] Paradoxically only the survey published by a woman, the widow Alice Heppelwhite, bucked the trend.[27]

How far the birth of a marketing language of his and hers affected the construction of the objects themselves is a matter of debate. Furniture curators often see scant difference in the build, complexity, materials, finish, decorative motifs, or style of the pieces aimed at women and men. Only in scale do they differ, claims Louisa Collins of the V&A, men's furniture tending to the massive and imposing, ladies' furniture being typically more petite and compact.[28] However, their makers present very different claims. By 1803, Sheraton's secretaries for ladies were desks 'of a small size, usually with a book shelf in the top part,' while the gentleman's secretary is 'intended for standing to write at,' and was a substantial piece 'with a cupboard for a pot and slippers' and 'a place for day book, ledger, and journal, for a gentleman's own accounts' (Figure 14.4).[29] The furniture designs presume that women's writing was a delicate drawing-room performance, while men's business was altogether more important and authoritative.

Within twenty years these novel categories had reached the middle market. Suppliers of furnishings in England went by the title of upholster or upholder, but offered a more extensive range of products than the term 'upholstery' suggests, providing a full service more akin to that of a modern interior decorator.

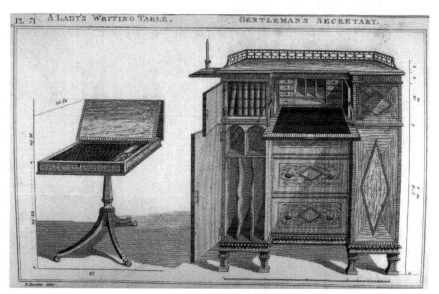

FIGURE 14.4 Thomas Sheraton, 'A Lady's Writing Table. Gentleman's Secretary,' 1803

Probably the earliest known British upholder's accounts are those of Jonathan Hall of London, whose records cover the years 1701–1735.[30] Hall makes no reference whatsoever to furniture titled a lady's this, or a gentleman's whatnot, but fifty years later the trade was warming to the new gimmick. The upholsterer and cabinetmaker James Brown was based at 29 St Paul's Churchyard in the city, the heart of London's furniture district. His ledgers survive for the years 1782–1791, and insurance records reveal a substantial business. And when the 'elegant and valuable' stock in trade was sold in 1791, *The Times* promised an Aladdin's cave of tropical wood:

> ... Beautiful Mahogany and superb inlaid modern Furniture, of the first Taste and Workmanship, in Secretaries and Bookcases, Wardrobes, Dressing, Dining, Pier, and Pembroke Tables, Commodes, Cylinder Desks, Side-boards, Dressing Glasses, large Pier Glasses and Girandoles in rich gilt Frames, Travelling Desks, Writing Boxes, Tea Trays, Tea Chests, Caddies and numerous Fancy Articles beautifully inlaid, the whole finished in a Stile of superior Taste, and in the highest Perfection.[31]

Furniture is to the fore in the sale (which could be bespoke, ready-made or second-hand), but like other upholsterers, Brown offered miscellaneous services, too, from wallpaper hanging and furniture hire, repairs and dry-cleaning, to fumigation for vermin and undertaking.[32] Brown fostered a predominantly metropolitan, professional, and mercantile clientele, with a sprinkling of provincial gentry – catering to an array of domestic needs.[33]

It was quite possible for men and women to buy furniture linked to their pleasures and tasks without recourse to an explicit language of 'lady's' and 'gentleman's.' Brown had long offered shaving stands and nursing chairs. Similarly, the workbox was a standard piece of female paraphernalia, so archetypically feminine that further specification was redundant.[34] The trappings of domestic alcohol consumption – bottle stands and bottle cases, cistern, wine cooler, and cellarets – were redolent of masculine clubbability. Of course, there was no law that prevented a widow from buying a mahogany cellaret and deal camp bed, or a bachelor a tulipwood sewing box and tea tray. Nevertheless, there were some customary differences in the patterns of male and female consumption, in so far as names in an order book are a guide.

The gender breakdown of Brown's customer base is in line with other luxury trades. Female customers are in a minority in the ledgers.[35] Married women's choices were deliberately concealed behind the names of their men in most shopkeepers' and manufacturers' accounts because women's debts were hard to recover in common law. In the order book for 1785, Brown listed 233 customers; of these 33 clients were designated only by surname, but of the remaining 200 orders only 30 were booked in a woman's name, so nominally women only accounted for barely 15 percent of the trade. The remaining 168 customers were male (84 percent), while two orders were made in both men and women's names.

Most of Brown's female customers claimed to be married or widowed (all but four of the thirty female clients in 1785 assumed the title Mrs.). Occasionally women made large orders, but most tended to commission a single piece, while men tended to make the largest orders, though they too can be seen ordering individual pieces which speak to personal needs and amusement – a chess set, backgammon table, music stool, a camp shaving stand, a bidet. Equally, there were also numerous male orders which conjured the needs and interests of a wife and bevy of daughters.

By 1782, Brown was tailoring some designs explicitly to the perceived needs of ladies (the company may have crafted lady's cabinetwork even earlier, but no order books survive). In May 1782, a Liverpool merchant, mine and canal owner, Nicholas Ashton Esq., ordered '1 Neat inlaid Ladies sattin wood secretary & Book case,' probably for his second wife and new house Woolton Hall (both acquired the previous year). Rich and pretentious, Ashton also employed leading architect Robert Adam to remodel the Liverpool manor, so he had an eye for the cutting edge of fashion. In the same year, the Brown warehouse provided a Mrs. Warner with a 'Ladys dressing case'; a Mr. Lancaster, a Cheapside lead merchant, with '1 ladies Firestick secretary 2 f 9 long'; and Sir Edward Newnham, of Suffolk Street, London, with another 'inlaid Ladies Dressing case.' The following year, 1783, Brown supplied four ladies' dressing cases, two to London women: a Mrs. Olivier in Broad Street Buildings, and a Mrs. Prevost in Little Ormond Street. By 1787, Brown had widened his range of ladies' furniture to present a matching suite. A leading Leeds woolen merchant, John Denison Esq., ordered a 'satinwood lady's secretary and bookcase, a satinwood lady's dressing table to suit, a lady's spider table, two spider chamber tables, and a vase dressing glass, tulip band.' Denison had inherited the great Leeds business not two years before, built Denison Hall in Leeds in 1786, and married in 1787. A chic feminine apartment would be just the thing for a bride of three months.[36] Whether the new Mrs. Denison actually made the choice the ledger characteristically does not reveal.

Within a year of his first ladies' pieces, Brown offered furniture avowedly designed for the gentlemen. The leading gentleman's fixture was the shaving and/or dressing table. In 1803, Sheraton suggested the dressing table could swing either way – 'a table so constructed as to accommodate a gentleman or a lady with convenience for dressing' (Figure 14.5).[37] Craftily Brown modified his ladies' prototype in 1783 for a Lawrence Cutler of Love Lane – '1 ladys dressing case with some alterations for a gent 2-5-0.' Gentlemen's dressing and shaving tables were commissioned at a rate of one or two a year thereafter, sometimes alongside other pieces aimed at the man about town, like a mahogany cordial case or cellaret.[38]

James Brown's cabinetwork was not in the vanguard of fashion like that of Chippendale and Linell, but nor was it far adrift. Fragments of evidence suggest other London cabinetmakers offered ladylike furniture around the same time.[39] Ladies' furniture in satinwood – a yellowish West-Indian timber with a satiny

FIGURE 14.5 Thomas Sheraton, 'A Gentleman's Shaving Table,' 1803

sheen – was aimed at the carriage trade. This tropical wood had only just come into fashionable use in the previous decade. Expensive male pieces tended to be crafted in darker mahogany. However, the warehouse produced ladies' and gentlemen's pieces in cheaper woods and finishes, so could adapt the concept for different segments of the market. Identifying a new niche and exploiting it is the very essence of successful trade. It is doubtful that cabinetmakers had any special investment in developing new conceptions of femininity and masculinity, but they had every interest in promoting an ever-expanding variety of perceived needs and qualities that bespoke furniture could meet and express.

Gendered marketing had spread beyond catalogues and ledgers to newspaper advertisements placed by upholsterers and furniture makers by the 1790s (Table 14.1). It was linen drapers, mercers and other dealers in clothing or textiles who were most likely to address their advertisements 'to the Ladies' or 'for the Attention of the Ladies,' or to include 'ladies' items in their lists. Furniture sellers were more sparing in the language of his and hers. Unisex categories were more common, especially the obsequious 'to the Nobility and Gentry.' Direct appeal to women was heavily concentrated in the traditionally female domains of fabrics and fashions, while men as a sex were hardly identified as addressees at all. Nevertheless, this is a departure, since a gendered language of address is almost non-existent in early eighteenth-century adverts. Moreover,

TABLE 14.1 Advertisements for goods, shops, and entertainments in four editions of *The Times*, 1796[40]

Type of advertiser	Number of advertise- ments	No addressee	Female addressee	Male addressee	Addressee not gendered
Entertainment	24	11	0	0	13
Retail	55	19	13	1*	22
Textiles/fashion	18	2	11	0	5
Furniture	9	5	1	0	3
Health	17	7	1	0	9
Other	11	5	0	1	5
Total	79	30	13	1	35

*This advertisement, which was addressed to 'Gentlemen,' was for the Portugal wine company.

The Times commanded a far wider readership than a cabinetmaker's catalogue and documents the steadily extending reach of gendered advertising.

The eighteenth century experienced the first large scale use of impersonal, widely broadcast print advertising. Newspaper and magazine adverts, handbills, and trade cards all were in limited use in the seventeenth century, but exploded after 1695, when the licensing act lapsed. Individual newspaper adverts almost certainly ran into millions in the 18th century, supplementing older methods such as shop signs and the crying of goods.[41] The authors of eighteenth-century advertising were precocious inventers of techniques for the new medium. As design historians have pointed out, 'just as the early film makers of the silent era experimented with almost all the visual techniques that have subsequently been used in the cinema, so eighteenth-century advertisers tried out many of the devices employed in modern advertising copy' (Figure 14.6).[42] Early techniques included the direct sell, unsurprisingly, but also advertorial, celebrity endorsements and testimonials, plus the use of a battery of psychological devices from patriotism to anxiety to envy. There remains a certain alchemy governing the precise workings of advertising on the audience. Both Lord Leverhulme and the Philadelphia department store magnate John Wanamaker are credited with the saying: 'Half the money I spend on advertising is wasted and the trouble is I don't know which half.'[43] Nevertheless, there is some research which confirms the effectiveness of advertising well down the social scale in Georgian England. John Styles has demonstrated that newspaper advertisements and handbills were successful in bringing offenders to trial in almost a third of horse stealing cases in the north of England in the second half of the eighteenth century.[44] One mocks the power of advertising to galvanize consumers at one's peril.

The taxonomies of catalogues would become even more significant for the Victorians. The classifications used in eighteenth-century furniture catalogues

FIGURE 14.6 Detail of a bill advertising 'The Queen's Royal Furniture Gloss,' circa 1798. In a scene comparable to modern TV advertising, two women discuss the merits of furniture polish.

provided a template for the printed catalogues circulated in far greater numbers by the new furnishing drapers of the mid-nineteenth century. Furnishing drapers were sellers, not makers, buying in furniture from specialist manufacturers to supply the burgeoning Victorian middle classes. Catalogues and showrooms were the key sales techniques for this new kind of retailing.[45] The catalogue had eclipsed the middling bespoke cabinetmaker. Classification now had a massive reach.

Of course, the sexes were not entirely the tools of the market. A belief in the passivity of the consumer is a relic of Marxist analysis. Innovative manufacturers were not so contemptuous of their customers – only too aware that consumers rejected many if not most novel products, and that the majority of exciting prototypes were not taken up. As Joss Wedgwood, son of the great potter, warned his brother Tom in 1790:

> Your black tea ware with lively colours I dare say will please the foreigners but the English I am afraid will not admire them. [W]e are not bold enough to adopt at once anything that is new and beautiful but require the sanction of fashion to give it value.

Developing new lines involved a sophisticated process of listening, translating, adapting, flattering and seducing.[46] Requests for adaptations to designs were routine. After all, the *raison d'être* of 'bespoke' was the modification of the design to suit the whims of the customer.

It is quite possible that dainty desks disciplined the women who sat at them to dainty performances. Dena Goodman claims that French femininity was forged at delicate writing desks, which proliferated from the 1740s. Ladies showed their mastery of what Mimi Hellman calls the 'work of leisure' in flawless writing at tiny tables, flourishing their props with exquisite control in a 'choreography of the quill.' It is no small matter today to sit at one of these fragile desks without knocking it over or barking your shins, but in plentiful petticoats, unwieldy hoops and frilled sleeves, fashionable letter writing was a feat of trained elegance which testified to the ultimate refinement of the French.[47] Nevertheless, furniture curators stress that French men had their *secretaires* too, along with handy mechanical tables, as well as the imposing cylinder desks associated with business and power.[48] Who's to say how many gents dashed off letters at a ladies' desk? People have ever used furniture in ways unanticipated by advertisers or interior designers. The Birmingham Unitarian Catherine Hutton was given 'a handsome chest of drawers' by her historian father 'in compensation' for his refusal to send her to boarding school in the 1760s: 'one drawer, by my especial order, being fitted up as a writing desk. This chest was my own...'[49]

It does not follow that a spindly ladies' desk and capacious gents' bureau had occult power to govern the behavior of their owners. It takes models, training, practice, and compliance to handle props as fashion expects, as manufacturers were only too aware. Tradesmen's correspondence abounds with complaints about the obtuseness of consumers. Improper use of the cellaret was a grumbling concern; there was a risk that unsophisticated guests might mistake a cellaret for a close stool and piss in it by mistake. The cabinetmaker Gillows recommended an oval temporary cellar to a Yorkshire gentleman in 1773 as 'they are always made to hold water upon occasion and are the most (nay quite) unlike a night table or close stool.'[50] Objects rely on situated knowledge to work their magic. They can mean nothing to the uninitiated.

It is not argued here that eighteenth-century marketing invented gender. Sex distinctions in clothes are as old as civilization, and the idea of furniture suited to female needs is not unprecedented (think of birthing stools), but making difference systematic and concrete by means of word, image, and object was a decisive innovation. The rapid diffusion of ladies' and gentlemen's furniture suggests gender distinctions already resonated powerfully with male and female consumers, but in the extension of the range of differentiated furniture, the projection of the trope by manufacturers thereafter, and its acceptance by consumers, a vision of masculine consequence and feminine delicacy was amplified and fixed. In the process, femininity was constrained in a specific and narrowly defined aesthetic register. The solid and the dainty emerged as design expressions of masculinity and femininity. Men were important and women were pretty – and they had the furniture to prove it.

Acknowledgments

The germ of this chapter can be found in Amanda Vickery, *Behind Closed Doors: At Home with the Georgians* (New Haven, CT: Yale University Press, 2009), 279–287, where I first noted the emergence of his and hers furniture. I have developed my thoughts on the causes and contexts of this development in conference papers at the 'Early Modern Things' workshop at Stanford; the North American Conference of British Studies, Baltimore, Maryland; the conference in honour of Penelope Corfield at the Institute of Historical Research, London; and the European University in Fiesole, Italy. I thank the audience and participants at all four events for their comments and criticisms. For advice and references, I am also indebted to Antonia Brodie, Patricia Fara, Paula Findlen, Mia Jackson, Lucy Inglis, Luca Molà, Carolyn Sargentson, John Styles, Julie Wakefield, Evelyn Welch, and Rose Wild.

Notes

1 There is a large literature on civility, courtesy literature, and conduct books, but the best survey remains: Fenela Childs, 'Prescriptions for Manners in English Courtesy Literature, 1690–1760' (DPhil diss., Oxford University, 1984). On decorum, see ch. 3.

2 Anon, *A Modern Dissertation on a Certain Necessary Piece of Household Furniture* (London: H. Kent, 1752), 8, 10, 12–13. For all you ever needed to know about chamber pots, see Ivor Noël Hume, 'Through the Lookinge Glasse: or, the Chamber Pot as a Mirror of its Time,' *Ceramics in America* (2003): 139–172.

3 Isaac Ware, *A Complete Body of Architecture* (London: T. Osborne and J. Shipton, 1756), 469; Thomas Sheraton, *The Cabinet Dictionary* (London: W. Smith, 1803), 194, 201, 217–218.

4 On sumptuary law see Negley B. Harte, 'State Control of Dress and Social Change in Pre-Industrial England,' in *Trade, Government and Economy in Pre-industrial England*, ed. D. C. Coleman and Arthur H. John (London: Weidenfeld & Nicolson, 1976), 132–165; Susan Vincent, *Dressing the Elite: Clothes in Early Modern England* (Oxford: Berg, 2003), 117–143.

5 Adam Smith, *The Wealth of Nations* (London, Methuen & Co., 1930 [first edition 1776]), 1: 328.

6 Childs, 'Manners,' 156–159.

7 There is a vast and growing literature on politeness, but see especially Lawrence Klein, 'Politeness for Plebes: Consumption and Social Identity in Early Eighteenth-Century England,' in *The Consumption of Culture, 1600–1800: Image, Object, Text*, ed. Ann Bermingham and John Brewer (London: Routledge, 1995), 362–382.

8 James Forrester, *The Polite Philosopher* (Dublin: n.p, 1734), 25.

9 Maria Edgeworth, *Essays on Practical Education*, 3 vols (London: Simpkin and Marshall, 1822), 3: 8. On changing ideals, see Walter J. Bate, *From Classic to Romantic: Premises of Taste in Eighteenth Century England* (Cambridge, MA: Harvard University Press, 1946).

10 Sheraton, *The Cabinet Dictionary*, 215–216.

11 On the production of linen, see Margaret Spufford, *The Great Reclothing of Rural England: Petty Chapmen and their Wares in the Seventeenth Century* (London: Hambledon Press, 1984), chs. 6 and 7; Negley B. Harte, 'The Rise of Protection and the English Linen Trade, 1690–1790,' in *Textile History and Economic History: Essays in Honour of Miss Julia de Lacey Mann*, ed. Negley B. Harte and Kenneth G. Ponting (Manchester: Manchester University Press, 1973), 74–112. On the expansion of quantity of linens

at home see Mark Overton et al., *Production and Consumption in English Households, 1600–1750* (London: Routledge, 2004), 108–111, 118–119, 142. For domestic rituals, see Vickery, *Behind Closed Doors*, 14, 272, 290, 294, 295, 302.

12 Nancy Cox, "'A Flesh Pott, or a Brasse Pott or a Pott to Boile in'": Changes in Metal and Fuel Technology in the Early Modern Period and the Implications for Cooking,' in *Gender and Material Culture in Historical Perspective*, ed. Moira Donald and L. M. Hurcombe (Houndmills, UK: St. Martin's Press, 2000), 143–157; Overton et al., *Production and Consumption*, 98–102; Sara Pennell, '"Pots and Pans History": The Material Culture of the Kitchen in Early Modern England,' *Journal of Design History* 11.2 (1998): 201–216; David Eveleigh, *Old Cooking Utensils* (Princes Risborough: Shire, 1986)

13 On tea and tea wares, see Elizabeth Kowaleski-Wallace, *Consuming Subjects: Women, Shopping and Business in the Eighteenth Century* (New York: Columbia University Press, 1997), 19–36; David Porter, 'A Wanton Chase in a Foreign Place: Hogarth and the Gendering of Exoticism in the Eighteenth-Century Interior,' in *Furnishing the Eighteenth Century*, ed. Dena Goodman and Kathryn Norberg (New York: Routledge, 2007), 55; Hilary Young, *English Porcelain, 1745–95: Its Makers, Design, Marketing and Consumption* (London: V&A Publications, 1999); and Sarah Richards, *Eighteenth-Century Ceramics: Products for a Civilised Society* (Manchester: Manchester University Press, 1999). On coffee and Madeira and men, see Brian Cowan, 'What was Masculine about the Public Sphere? Gender and the Coffeehouse Milieu in Post-Restoration England,' *History Workshop Journal* 51 (2001): 127–157; and David Hancock, *Oceans of Wine: Madeira and the Emergence of American Trade and Taste* (New Haven, CT: Yale University Press, 2009).

14 Josiah Wedgwood, *Correspondence of Josiah Wedgwood*, ed. Katherine E. Farrer, 3 vols (Manchester: Morten, 1903), 1: 143–144.

15 *The Spectator* 102, Wednesday, June 27, 1711.

16 James Miller, *The Humours of Oxford* (Dublin: Powell, 1730), 82. For a gloss, see Patricia Fara, *Pandora's Breeches: Women, Science and Power in the Enlightenment* (London: Pimlico, 2004), 11, who gave me this reference.

17 Amanda Vickery, 'His and Hers: Gender, Consumption and Household Accounting in 18th-Century England,' in *The Art of Survival: Gender and History in Europe, 1450–2000*, ed. Ruth Harris and Lyndal Roper (Oxford: Oxford University Press, 2006), 12–38.

18 On gender and science, see especially Fara, *Pandora's Breeches*, passim.

19 Claire Walsh, 'Shops, Shopping, and the Art of Decision Making in Eighteenth-Century England,' in *Gender, Taste and Material Culture in Britain and North America*, ed. John Styles and Amanda Vickery (New Haven, CT: Yale Center for British Art, 2006), 151–177.

20 It is difficult to prove a negative, but research so far has not turned up any equivalents either in France or Italy. Luca Molà and Carolyn Sargentson, personal communication.

21 Christopher Gilbert, *The Life and Work of Thomas Chippendale* (London: Cassell, 1978), 65–92; Clive Edwards, *Eighteenth-Century Furniture* (Manchester: Manchester University Press, 1996), 146–148.

22 The elaboration of furniture classification in catalogues has been examined by Louisa Collins, 'Elite Women, Writing and Furniture, 1750–1800' (MA diss., V&A/RCA History of Design, 2005), and Akiko Shimbo, 'Pattern Books, Showrooms and Furniture Design: Interactions between Producers and Consumers in England 1754–1851' (PhD diss., University of London, 2007).

23 Society of Upholsterers, Cabinet Makers, etc., *Genteel Household Furniture in the Present Taste* (London: R. Sayer, 1760), plates 11, 53, 54.

24 Thomas Chippendale, *Gentleman and Cabinet-Maker's Director*, 3rd ed. (London: T. Chippendale, 1762), plates 51, 'A Dressing-Table for a Lady,' and 116, 'A Writing-Table and Bookcase for a Lady.'

25 William Ince and Jonathan Mayhew, *Universal System of Household Furniture* (London: n.p., 1762), plates xviii, xxi, xxxvii, xl.

26 Thomas Sheraton, *The Cabinet-Maker and Upholsterer's Drawing Book in Three Parts* (London: T. Bensley, 1793); Sheraton, *The Cabinet Dictionary*, 115.

27 Alice Heppelwhite, *The Cabinet Maker and Upholsterer's Guide* (London: I. and J. Taylor, 1788)

28 Collins, 'Elite Women, Writing and Furniture.'

29 Sheraton, *Drawing Book*, 397, 405, 409; Sheraton, *Cabinet Dictionary*, 303.

30 West Yorkshire Archive Service, Calderdale, SH 3/AB/8-15, Jonathan Hall of Elland and London, 1701–1735.

31 *The Times*, June 9, 1791; Christopher Gilbert, *Pictorial Dictionary of Marked London Furniture 1700–1840* (London: Furniture History Society, 1996); Geoffrey Beard, *Dictionary of English Furniture Makers, 1660–1840* (London: Furniture History Society, 1986).

32 The National Archives, Kew, UK, C107/109: James Brown, 29 St Paul's Churchyard, London, upholsterer.

33 The social status of the consumer is obscure in the majority of entries for 1785 (148/233, 64 percent), however, Brown was patronized by three lords, eighteen esquires and one sir in that year, with the largest single occupational group being the professions (seventeen lawyers, clerics, army and naval officers), supplemented by provincial merchants and metropolitan tradesmen.

34 See Vickery, *Behind Closed Doors*, 231–256, 283.

35 Named female customers are in a minority in all surviving ledgers. See Louise Lippincott, *Selling Art in Georgian London: The Rise of Arthur Pond* (New Haven, CT: Yale University Press, 1983): 66–69; Judith A. Anderson, 'Derby Porcelain and the Early English Fine Ceramic Industry, c.1750–1830' (PhD diss., University of Leicester, 2002), passim; Helen Clifford, *Silver in London: The Parker and Wakelin Partnership, 1760–1776* (New Haven, CT: Yale University Press, 2004), 138.

36 Inheritance, house, marriage, furnishing is a typical sequence amongst the propertied. John Denison was probably the richest merchant in Leeds, with a partnership in a London merchant house and an estate at Ossington Hall, Nottinghamshire, as well as the new Leeds townhouse. Denison commissioned Sir John Soane to draw up plans for the improvement of Ossington, which were never realized. Denison subsequently employed William Lindley.

37 Sheraton, *Cabinet Dictionary*, 202.

38 For example, Jonathan Fryer of Wapping Dock, London ordered '1 gentleman's dressing table with a pot cupboard, washing drawer, a riddett, and shaving tackle' for £13-13-0 and '1 curious mahogany cordial case for 6 bottles, lined with velvet, strong silver handles at top. Ditto escution. Ditto hinges screws and lock and three spare bottles' for £7-7-0.

39 In 1783, Joseph Lewis, a London cabinetmaker, supplied Charlestonian Thomas Hutchinson with 'a ladies dressing table of mahogany': Elizabeth Fleming, 'Staples for Genteel Living: The Importation of London Household Furnishings in Charleston during the 1780s,' *American Furniture* (1997): 336–337.

40 *The Times*, January 23, 1796; April 23, 1796; July 23, 1796; October 24, 1796.

41 R. B. Walker, 'Advertising in London Newspapers, 1650–1750,' *Business History* 15.2 (1973): 130.

42 John Styles, 'Manufacturing, Consumption and Design in Eighteenth-Century England,' in *Consumption and the World of Goods*, ed. John Brewer and Roy Porter (London: Routledge, 1993), 540–541. A classic study of the marketing of pots and the advertizing of shaving tackle is Neil McKendrick, John Brewer and J. H. Plumb, *The Birth of the Consumer Society: The Commercialization of Eighteenth-Century England* (London: Europa, 1983), 100–194.

43 Ascribed to John Wanamaker in Martin Mayer, *Whatever Happened to Madison Avenue?: Advertising in the 90s* (Boston, MA: Little, Brown, 1991), 138; but originally

attributed to William Hesketh Lever, Viscount Leverhulme, according to Tony Augarde, *Oxford Dictionary of Modern Quotations* (Oxford: Oxford University Press, 1991), 136.

44 John Styles, 'Print and Policing: Crime Advertising in Eighteenth-Century Provincial England,' in *Police and Prosecution in Britain in the Eighteenth and Nineteenth Centuries*, ed. Douglas Hay and Francis Snyder (Oxford: Clarendon, 1989), esp. 71, 92, 111.

45 Margaret Ponsonby, *Stories from Home: English Domestic Interiors, 1750–1850* (Aldershot: Ashgate, 2007), 45.

46 Keele University Library, W/M 28 (1790 Sunday), Josiah (Joss) Wedgwood, Greek St.: 'I think you are right with respect to the impropriety of adopting the whims of customers and bringing them into use; but in this matter I believe you must not be too rigid. There are many cases in which it is necessary to humour them, especially in a business that depends almost entirely upon fashion…you must consider that it has been in a great measure owing to the taking up hints given by customers and bringing them to perfection that this manufactory has established its character for Universality.' For failed products, see John Styles, 'Product innovation in Early Modern London,' *Past and Present* 168.1 (2000): 124–169.

47 Mimi Hellman, 'Furniture, Sociability, and the Work of Leisure in Eighteenth-Century France,' *Eighteenth-Century Studies* 32.4 (1999): 415–445; Dena Goodman, *Becoming a Woman in the Age of Letters* (Ithaca, NY: Cornell University Press, 2009), passim.

48 Personal communication from Carolyn Sargentson, who is currently working on a four-volume catalogue of French furniture in the Victoria and Albert Museum, London.

49 Catherine Hutton Beale, *Reminiscences of a Gentlewoman of the Last Century: Letters of Catharine Hutton* (Birmingham: Cornish Bros., 1891), 4.

50 Susan E. Stuart, *Gillows of Lancaster and London, 1730–1840: Cabinetmakers and International Merchants: A Furniture and Business History*, 2 vols. (Woodbridge: Antique Collector's Club, 2008), 2: 98: Letter to Sir Thomas Frankland at Stockeld Park, Yorkshire, November 1773.

PART VI

Epilogue

The power of things

15

DENATURALIZING THINGS

A comment

Renata Ago

Since my task is to comment on the outcomes of these papers, the first point I would like to stress is that they have strongly contributed to 'denaturalizing' things. After decades of denaturalization of other well-established dichotomies – like nature and culture, man and woman, and so on – we have now arrived at the point of confronting the world of things and its relationship with human beings. Indeed, the more we progress in research, the more we realize how artificial a category 'things' are.

This denaturalization has gone through a long process since the seminal essay by Igor Kopytoff on the cultural biography of things, which first appeared in 1986: using the case of slaves, among other possible examples, Kopytoff clearly shows that the divide between persons and things is not as absolute and self-imposing as our common sense pretends.[1]

Sociological and philosophical research on the developments of science and technology, and the way they affect not just social relations but also the notion of human agency itself and, consequently, the clear-cut distinction between persons–subjects and things–objects have also served as important milestones in this course of action.[2] Scholars such as Michel Callon, Bruno Latour, and John Law have elaborated what they have called the 'Actor-Network Theory' or 'ANT,' that is, a theory that 'aims at describing…the very nature of societies. But to do so it does not limit itself to human individual actors but extend the word actor – or actant – to non-human, non individual entities.'[3]

Thinking beyond these developments, evidently connected to the technological Western world, we also need to consider the results of anthropological studies on the notions of property and exchange in non-Western societies, and especially those by Marilyn Strathern on Melanesian societies.[4] For example, one of Strathern's important findings, observing the Hagen of New Guinea, is that 'wealth items objectify relations by giving them the form of things; they may also objectify relations by making persons, that is positions from which people perceive one another.'[5]

The idea that persons and things are both 'made,' rather than existing unto themselves, is also shared by legal historians such as Martha Mundy and Alain Pottage. The various contributions to their edited volume on the *Constitution of the Social* all demonstrate how, from Roman law onward, legal techniques of personification and reification play an essential role in the origins of both persons and things.[6] As Pottage writes in his introduction, 'the problem is that humans are *neither* person *nor* thing, or simultaneously person *and* thing, so that law quite literally *makes* the difference.'[7]

The outcome of both these empirical studies and theoretical statements is the acknowledgment of the artificiality of the category of 'thing.' As many chapters collected here show, this very artificiality imposes a continuous process of 'translation': from things to humans; from the organic to the mechanical world and vice versa; from considering animals as subjects to their objectification; from a series of roots defined and described in different ways to the unified notion of Chinese 'ginseng,' and from the many sorts of rhubarbs to the one 'real' rhubarb in the Siberian trade. Chandra Mukerji indeed argues that in Ottoman society, clothes played an active role in fashioning the moral qualities of persons, a role that could, however, be deceptive. Jessica Riskin explains how the widely used metaphor of the clock did not necessarily signify mechanical regularity; on the contrary, clocks were frequently compared to living bodies in that they both experienced a perpetual state of disquiet. Marcy Norton clarifies how, with the Spanish expansion into the Americas, two different ways of interacting with animals, hunting and husbandry, fashioned two different ways of conceptualizing them in relation to humans: as subjects in the first case, as objects in the second.

The notion of 'things' in general and of a single thing in particular also requires a process of stabilization, be it by practice, by commodification, or by scientific definition and delimitation. Things in themselves – these chapters suggest – are more like fluxes or fluids, always moving and changing their shape, than like immutable solids. Or to adopt another metaphor, they can be compared to those solids made up of a multiplicity of particles, such as sand: they are solids and yet behave like fluids, taking a shape that is imposed from the outside. This emerges, for example, from Carla Nappi's reconstruction of the process by which Chinese ginseng finally emerged as a unified commodity through experiencing and describing the 'substance' of a discrete set of roots as a material object. Erika Monahan discusses a similar process by which rhubarb became one of the most appreciated early modern Russian commodities.

***

'Making things' may also mean singling them out, conferring on each of them its own individuality, or, on the contrary, considering them as an undifferentiated mass. And this also is a *process in context*. The case of hunting and husbandry I have already mentioned shows how both of these practices deal with the same sort of things, have almost the same goals – gaining food – and yet produce opposite effects. Hunting subjectifies the animal, allots it an agency, treats it individually; husbandry does exactly the opposite: it treats the animals as a collectivity and denies them any subjectivity, any agency.

We can observe the same sort of process, for example, in examining the relationship between an owner and his or her personal belongings, as it appears in last wills but also in account books or in correspondences, when somebody singles out one particular object among many others in his or her possession. Yet this is far from being an act of pure free will, devoid of any external constraint, on the part of the subject, as again it is a process in context: who does what and when? Who is allowed or feels allowed to treat possessions as a set of individual objects, and who tends rather to deny them any singularity and just considers them as mobile goods, invested with material value but deprived of affective or symbolic appeal?[8]

We must not forget, moreover, that singularization is a reflexive process that has very much to do with writing. Pamela Smith has explained the difficulties usually incurred in translating actual practices into writing, and reading into actual practices. Yet the very fact of writing, of describing one's sequence of acts, is a reflexive and creative endeavor, allotting agency precisely where one would think it totally absent. The wonderful manuscript Smith has presented, with its continuous corrections, insertions, etc., shows this very well.

***

A certain number of the contributions to this volume have also addressed the issue of the classical function of things, that is, their ability to make communication possible. This function is strictly connected to another crucial power of things, the power of making visible the invisible.[9] Just as Ottoman clothes reveal certain attributes of the person, the different pieces of eighteenth-century English furniture analyzed by Amanda Vickery also communicated the gender of their owner or user. In my opinion, however, this semiotic function of objects has a wider spectrum of action than we used to think. Recent research has stressed how communication is indeed performative, having an impact on the external world *and* on the human beings: gendered clothes or gendered furniture do not simply express the gender of their user; they fashion it while at the same time shaping the world within which both genders move and act. This has led many scholars to speak of 'the agency of things,' a concept that so far has primarily been discussed in regards to the active role played by technological objects.

One of the first authors to refer explicitly to the 'agency of things' and to define and circumscribe this notion was the anthropologist Alfred Gell, in 1998.[10] Where others hesitated, considering agency too closely connected with intentionality to be an attribute of non-humans, Gell instead argues: 'Social agency can be exercised relative to "things" and social agency can be exercised by "things" (and also animals).' He also confronts the connection between action and intentionality by maintaining that "'things" with their thing-ly casual properties are as essential to the exercise of agency as state of mind.'[11] For him the agency of things is no longer confined to scientific or technological artifacts and devices, but is recognized in any kind of things, though images and artifacts are mostly the focus of his analysis. Since the appearance of Gell's work over a decade ago, the idea that things may have an agency has attracted a great deal of investigation, and anthropologists, sociologists, archeologists, and cognitive scientists have all researched what they now call 'material agency.'[12]

Contributions to this book, like the one by Morgan Pitelka on the Japanese shogun Tokugawa Ieyasu, also make use of the notion of 'agency of objects,' explaining how the swords, ceramics, paintings, and books collected by the shogun 'acted' to legitimate his power both in warfare and cultural tradition. The agency of things is also evident in the chapter by Vickery, when she explains how gender identity was also fashioned by ownership and use of 'specialized' pieces of furniture.

***

Since the appearance of the seminal book by Mary Douglas and Baron Isherwood, published in 1979,[13] we have been used to associating things and consumption. Anne McCants, for example, refers to the items listed in the probate inventories of the Amsterdam Orphanage to convincingly argue for the wide diffusion of an important shift in consumption, namely from alcoholic to stimulant drinks. For his part, Giorgio Riello correctly draws our attention to the problems connected with the main source for studies on consumption, that is, probate inventories: the more historians use them, the more they become aware of their dependency on local conventions about what has to be inventoried and how. Inventories are static documents, lists of things at a moment in time, while consumption is a typically dynamic phenomenon: objects are acquired, used, alienated, etc., in a never-ending process.

Many of the chapters collected here discuss the relationship to things from the point of view of their producers. Even in the very moment in which we acknowledge and appreciate human agency through the making of things, we recognize the agency of things themselves. Corey Tazzara discusses the astonishing flexibility of things, their capacity to act alternatively as commodities or as means of exchange in the early modern Italian economy. No object is more protean than the silver shillings of seventeenth-century Boston examined by Mark Peterson; no artifacts were more infinitely useful as mediators in the relationships between the center and the periphery of an empire than timber and grain in the Ottoman Empire, as illustrated in the work of Alan Mikhail. Last but not least, things can act as treasures, absorbing a great amount of resources that they can give back when needed, thus allowing their owner to overcome short- or medium-term difficulties.[14]

The agency of things also appears, as I have said, in the prestige they offered their inventors, as we see in Smith's discussion of artisanal manuals for making things. Many of these papers emphasize the interplay between the semiotic function of things and their technical quality. I agree that these values are not opposed at all, but most of the time coexist, since one presupposes the other. The semiotic, communicative power of things emerges most forcefully in their capacity to structure the consumers' world. Yet, beyond the producers' strategies, we are continuously confronted with the customers' autonomous agency (and probably also the agency of products themselves).

*****

Finally I would like to close these comments with a reflection on the aesthetic value of objects, the communicative power of their beauty, and their ability to celebrate the virtuosity of their author, as Julie Hochstrasser's beautiful presentation of images of objects in seventeenth-century Dutch still-life painting has shown. Things communicate, they have and offer agency, reflect values, and possess many other attributes discussed in this volume, yet the ability of things to concentrate and express beauty is also an important issue that needs to be discussed by social and cultural historians, anthropologists, and literary scholars in dialogue with art historians. And, if it is undoubtedly the painter's gaze that gives value to the represented thing through an adroit use of skill and materials to capture the image of a thing, this capacity to embody beauty is yet another form of agency.

Notes

1   Igor Kopytoff, 'The Cultural Biography of Things: Commoditization as Process,' in Arjun Appadurai, ed., *The Social Life of Things: Commodities in Cultural Perspective* (Cambridge: Cambridge University Press, 1986), 64–91.
2   See for example Michel Callon, 'Éléments pour une sociologie de la traduction: la domestication des coquilles Saint-Jacques dans la Baie de Saint-Brieuc,' *L'Année sociologique* 36 (1986): 169–208; John Law, 'Notes on the Theory of the Actor Network: Ordering, Strategy, and Heterogeneity,' *Systems Practice* 5 (1992): 379–393; and Bruno Latour, *La clef de Berlin et autres leçons d'un amateur de sciences* (Paris: La Découverte, 1993).
3   Bruno Latour, 'On Actor-Network Theory: A Few Clarifications,' *Soziale Welt* 47/4 (1997): 369–381.
4   Marilyn Strathern, *Property, Substance & Effect: Anthropological Essays on Persons and Things* (London: Athlone Press, 1999).
5   Ibid., 15.
6   Alain Pottage and Martha Mundy, eds., *Law, Anthropology, and the Constitution of the Social: Making Persons and Things* (Cambridge: Cambridge University Press, 2004).
7   Alain Pottage, 'Introduction: The Fabrication of Persons and Things,' in Pottage and Mundy, *Law, Anthropology, and the Constitution of the Social*, 5.
8   Renata Ago, *Gusto for Things: A History of Objects in Seventeenth-Century Rome*, trans. Bradford Bouley and Corey Tazzara with Paula Findlen (Chicago, IL: University of Chicago Press, forthcoming).

9 Kryzstzof Pomian, *Collectors and Curiosities: Paris and Venice, 1500–1800*, trans. Elizabeth Wiles-Porter (London: Polity Press, 1990).

10 Alfred Gell, *Art and Agency: An Anthropological Theory* (Oxford: Clarendon, 1998).

11 Ibid., 17, 20.

12 See for example, Tim Dant, *Materiality and Society* (Maidenhead: Open University Press, 2005); Daniel Miller, ed., *Materiality* (Durham, NC: Duke University Press, 2005); and Carl Knappett and Lambros Malafouris, eds., *Material Agency: Towards a Non-Anthropocentric Approach* (Boston, MA: Springer, 2008).

13 Mary Douglas and Baron Isherwood, *The World of Goods: Towards an Anthropology of Consumption* (New York: Basic Books, 1979).

14 Ago, *Gusto for Things*, passim.

16

SOMETHING NEW

A comment

Timothy Brook

On June 21, 1610, by our reckoning, the artist and connoisseur Li Rihua (1565–1635) made this entry in his diary:

> I went to call on Prefect Shen and Magistrate Lu. At the prefectural guest hostel, I ran into Chen Yutong and Provincial Graduate Qiu with Wu Chihan of this prefecture, and we got talking. Wu said that in Guangdong at Macao there is a kind of human with a scaly body and black skin. When they swim underwater they can draw fish to swim with them, and when they come onto land they live alongside other people. Every prominent person in Macao has one in his care. They trick fish into entering nets, and when the nets are full, they suddenly yank them, and the men on the shore pull them in, netting a huge catch. They are called *luting*. It is said that the defeated soldiers of Lu Xun who fled south by water in the Jin dynasty (265–317) mixed with the fish, and that the various types of what came into being are hugely various. In the space between heaven and earth, strange things emerge with time. There is no original number of them that we can determine.[1]

Li Rihua at the time was in retirement at home southwest of Shanghai. He was living the charmed life enjoyed by the great gentry families of the Yangzi Delta: collecting rents, hobnobbing with officials, consorting with his social peers on the Delta, and producing a steady stream of decent landscape paintings and excellent calligraphy. A formidable art collector, Li was also his generation's most consistent diarist. His diary reveals much about what the elite at this stage of the Ming dynasty (1368–1644) thought of the circumstances in which they found themselves, and more particularly for this volume, what they thought about the things (*wu*) that thronged their world. Li had an endless curiosity for unusual things: two-headed calves and sea monsters, talking parrots and fiery clouds, red and black hailstones, roofing slates etched in an indecipherable language. The black divers of Macao – probably Andaman Islanders, possibly Africans, brought by Portuguese – were but one more case of Li's general proposition that things previously unknown could emerge within the space between heaven and earth. Those who lived in his time and place understood that there was always something new to discover and puzzle over, some arising within the Ming realm, some from beyond it.

It was not for humans to declare what was not physically possible. What was for humans to realize is that every physical thing, whether animate ('having breath,' *qi*, in Li's phrasing) or inanimate, had a particular nature that distinguished it from every other thing. When Li later that year offers another proposition – 'that things cannot come in two different sizes is fixed by their nature'[2] – he implies the more general principle of natural differentiation by which no two things can ever be the same thing. That each should have a distinctive nature had, at other times in the Chinese past, been grounds for denying there can be anything new under the sun. Li Rihua's generation believed there could be more things – and therefore more natures – than had been thought of in their predecessors' philosophy. As he concludes his entry on the black divers, there is no 'original number' of phenomena. The things of the universe are potentially infinite, every new thing simply taking its place among those already known.

Li Rihua was interested in things, for he was a keen collector. He most prized artwork, though only Chinese paintings. But he also collected curios and antiques, which gave him occasional access to foreign products. When Dealer Xia, one of his regular suppliers, drops in on March 10, 1610, he proudly shows Li a pair of earrings he claims are fragments of a rare tenth-century ceramic known as Chai ware. The knowledge of its manufacture had long been lost, and collectors were mad to get their hands on it. Once he sees them, Li knows differently. This is Venetian glass, though Li could not name it as Venetian, as his knowledge of Europe was not specific enough. As he notes in his diary, 'they were brought in a foreign ship from the south, and are things made in foreign countries by transforming [material] in forges.' Probably repeating what he told Xia, he declares that 'whatever is glass in this age is in every case made by the Europeans by melting stones, not some treasure that heaven has fashioned.' As for the earrings being made of Chai ware, 'they are not this thing.'[3] Dealer Xia may not have known that he was handling foreign material – he and Li constantly jousted over the authenticity of the things he tried to sell – but what he did know is that fragments of Chai ware sold for a lot more than fragments of Venetian glass. No sale.

What the anecdote reveals is that by the 1610s, people of the Ming inhabited a world in which 'foreign' things – from people to plants to manufactured objects – were circulating sufficiently to attract notice. They played a role in the rejection of an older version of Confucian ontology that had declared the things of the world to be finite and fixed. Li Rihua preferred old things whose age linked him to the origins of his culture. Thus elsewhere in the diary he admires an ancient two-handled ceramic goblet that comes to his attention as 'a superior thing,' praises an old zither another dealer brings for being 'an ancient thing,' and celebrates a seal from the Tang dynasty as 'an auspicious thing.'[4] But he was also passionate about collecting fine work by contemporary painters and ceramicists. The market responded to such desires. More scrolls were being painted in his era than at any earlier time in Chinese history, and porcelain pieces were coming out of Ming kilns in the millions every year. This expansion of production was part of the rapid growth of the Ming commercial economy during Li's lifetime: more commodities were produced than ever before, and more people could afford to buy them. The combination of exuberant productivity and heightened demand meant that the serious collector had to master the canons of taste that enabled him to place things accurately along the spectrum between 'vulgarity' and 'elegance.' One of Li's contemporaries on the Yangzi Delta would even compile a handbook, the wryly titled *Treatise on Superfluous Things*, to lead the uninitiated in the task of discriminating among the flood of things on offer to furnish the elegant life.[5] There were simply too many things in circulation in the last half-century of the Ming dynasty, and some of them were new.

For students of the history of early modern Europe, this situation should not be unfamiliar. The things available to Europeans in 1610 were growing in volume and variety and at a pace that beggared earlier dispensations. Many of these things were of European manufacture, such as Venetian glass, with which windows were now regularly being leaded and from which wine was being poured and beer gulped. But many came from abroad, in a dizzying range from pineapples to tulips, shells to pearls, tobacco to pepper, silks to porcelains. Europeans and Chinese alike shared the experience of coming to live within a global economy.

Their exposure to new things was different, however. Europe was a net importer, thanks to the cheap silver in the Americas, whereas China, happy to absorb the silver into its domestic markets, was a net exporter. This means that new things, many of Chinese origin, were tumbling into Europe at a far greater rate than European objects were appearing in China. This imbalance of circulation derived from the economy in which the objects moved, not as a matter of Chinese taste. The Chinese simply had less opportunity to absorb new things into their cultural practices than did the Europeans, who refurnished their homes and re-dressed themselves as new commodities flooded their markets. Their impact is immediately visible in the paintings that Julie Hochstrasser features in her chapter, the still lifes that emerged in Northern Europe just at the time Li was keeping his diary. Just as the new (and of course expensive) things were transforming the rooms in which Dutch householders lived, so too they affected the kinds of paintings they chose to pay for. These paintings leave us with a rich visual record of the things that were catching the European eye. And what the eye wanted to see, the painter knew to paint, developing a kind of distilled realism that strove to reproduce objects with visual exactitude in carefully controlled studio settings, manipulating light and distorting perspective to heighten the visual impact of treasured objects.

These new techniques are in view in the still lifes of the period, and also in the domestic genre scenes so popular with the emerging middle class which wanted art on its walls that reflected the prosperity their newly built and newly furnished rooms proclaimed. In a review of an exhibition of seventeenth-century Dutch art at the Fitzwilliam Museum in Cambridge, Julian Bell notes that the interiors they painted showed a world that was 'well lit, well furnished: a world of recent manufacture, a world that is primly modern.'[6] The primness is not universal to the genre; one has only to think of the riotous scenes that Jan Steen took delight in painting; but the newness of the objects on display certainly is. Willem Kalf did not paint familiar objects, only new and visually remarkable things: nautilus shells, Chinese pots, Turkish carpets, Venetian goblets, and imported oranges. So too Johannes Vermeer carefully selected new things to accompany his human subjects. We see the same exotic carpets, goblets, and dishes that feature in Kalf's work, but then Vermeer goes on to furnish an entire room with new furniture and costly musical instruments, and on the wall hangs recently printed maps or paintings done within his lifetime. The world Vermeer and Kalf picture is a world of entirely new things.

Hochstrasser's chapter captures changes in the things with which Europeans surrounded themselves and in the ways of representing them. These two aspects – the advent of new things, and changes in their representation – run through the chapters in this volume. The second of these aspects, representation, engages the attention of some of the authors. I shall note only three. Pamela Smith considers the inescapable gaps between what early-modern authors wrote about the making of things and the things as they actually emerged under the hands of craftsmen. She expresses this gap in terms of the 'resistance' of matter, a resistance that the experimental method was developed to get past, but can do so only by making repeated approaches. Chandra Mukerji is concerned with the gap in representation that emerged not as a material barrier between things and words, but as a distance between Ottoman things and the texts and pictures about them among Europeans, where they became not so much new things as new information. Curiously, though, in the case she analyzes of European accounts of Ottoman costumes, what at first glance looks like an Orientalizing imposition of difference ends as a domestication of the foreign achieved through the pairing of European and Ottoman modes of moral reasoning. Finally, focusing almost exclusively on the problem of representation, Carla Nappi raises problems that can arise when we go back looking for a thing for which we have a name and identification – ginseng, in her case – but for which people at the time had no stable representation. We stand on the far side of a process she calls 'objectification,' which needs to be disassembled if we are to approach what it is people in the past thought they were dealing with when they spoke of the thing we speak of. Objectification is in her view very much a process characteristic of the early-modern world. I would agree, with the additional observation – which I am sure she would endorse – that economies trade in commodities, and if commodities can't be objectified, they can't be extracted, circulated, and sold. What appears to be many processes – commodification, objectification, alienation – may in fact be a single process.

Some contributors are perhaps less concerned with representation than with 'actual' things and what these did; or more precisely, what had to be done in order that something could be done with them. Giorgio Riello introduces the reader to household inventories, drawn up on the death or bankruptcy of a head of household (the inventory drawn up when Vermeer's widow declared bankruptcy provides the only 'facts' we have about him[7]). Despite being a 'subjective representation,' as Riello puts it, these inventories provide a sense of the sorts of things a household owned and used. When Anne McCants examines household inventories from Amsterdam, she notes that the things listed vary among households depending on their wealth and complexity, yet a constant among them is the possession of ceramics dedicated to brewing coffee, chocolate, and tea. These new global products were forcing the introduction of other new objects judged necessary for their consumption, and, in so doing, altering not just what people owned but how they experienced social life within the family. Corey Tazzara turns to yet other inventories, this time of Florentine craftsmen, to explore how the makers of things managed the complex and lengthy process of transforming raw materials into the finished goods they were producing for the growing commodity markets.

I have touched on only some of the chapters in this volume, but sufficiently to underscore what this volume asserts: that things can provide the historian with a barometer of economic and social change. They tell us in the first instance about what people made, used, and consumed. They also tell us about how people acted and thought: about what they favored and refused, what they wanted to see and to be seen with, and how they represented things to produce meanings that imposed order on the natural disorder of existence. That things can be used and given meaning differently at different times indicates how they might even assist us in identifying transitions in world history. At the very least, things in history provide us with indicators of how life was managed differently between one period and another, moving from fewer things to more, expensive goods to less so, cheaper luxuries to costlier, local things to foreign, and old things to new. These shifts in consumption could tempt us into interpreting things as indicators of the onset of Bell's 'primly modern' world. Whether we want to use things to proclaim the onset of modernity depends on what other problems we are trying to solve; I shall leave the matter open.

Does Ming China offer a helpful perspective here? Yes and no. Li Rihua would not have understood why Vermeer stripped familiar domestic spaces of signs of the past and refurnished them with entirely new things. Where are the old masters? The antiquities that anchor the wobbling present to a surer past? The signs of cultural continuity stretching endlessly into a revered past while still accommodating the new things the present brought? But then he didn't have the same pressure of new objects piling up around him as did the new Dutch middle class. Nor did he have the immediate connections to a trading company as global as the Dutch East India Company. Nor were traditional forms of wealth collapsing quite as rapidly as they were in Europe.

And yet there were features of late-Ming life that suggest that a common ground of expectation was in formation. In different ways Chinese and Europeans shared the idea that the world was wider than was once thought, that it thronged with things no one had previously even imagined could exist, and that the old verities about what existed or could exist were no longer unassailable. If Li Rihua and Johannes Vermeer saw and painted the world differently – the one striving to relate to traditions stretching back a millennium to the Tang dynasty, the other refusing to refer to anything predating the late Italian Renaissance – they did so because they occupied different locations in asymmetrical networks of global circulation, which brought them different things to think with, and therefore posed different problems to solve. But both of them learned to deal with something new. This volume asks us to do the same, and how can we refuse?

Notes

1 Li Rihua, *Weishui xuan riji* (Diary from the Pavilion for Tasting Water) (Shanghai: Yuandong chubanshe, 1996), 102–103. This and the entry on earrings are noted in my *Vermeer's Hat: The Seventeenth Century and the Dawn of the Global World* (New York: Bloomsbury, 2008), 80–81, 96.
2 Li Rihua, *Weishui xuan riji*, 131.
3 Ibid., 84.
4 Ibid., 117, 121, 243.
5 This book is the subject of Craig Clunas' *Superfluous Things: Material Culture and Social Status in Early Modern China* (Cambridge: Polity, 1991).
6 Julian Bell, 'The Mysterious Women of Vermeer,' *The New York Review of Books* (December 22, 2011), 86. The exhibition was titled 'Vermeer's Women: Secrets and Silence.'
7 John Michael Montias, *Vermeer and his Milieu: A Web of Social History* (Princeton, NJ: Princeton University Press, 1989), 220–222.

17

IDENTITIES THROUGH THINGS

A comment

Erin K. Lichtenstein

The early modern era was a period of tremendous growth: of nation-states and empires; of geographic knowledge and scientific discovery; of the production and distribution of new categories and kinds of objects. Each of these changes, in its own way, created in turn new possibilities and opportunities for social identities. But even as some categories of identity shifted and blurred, others became ever more strongly delimited: a defense mechanism against these turbulent times. Of course, it is a fallacy to speak of these identity categories as acting independently; they were created and maintained by actors from both within and without. And as the chapters in this volume so astutely demonstrate, early modern things were both actants (to use the term cited by Renata Ago) and tools in this ongoing quest for identity.

The importance of objects in shaping identity was not new to the early modern period, and in fact stretched back through much of human history. Ancient rulers used myriad material tools to symbolize their might, from the pyramids of Egypt and Mesoamerica to the costly purple dyes of Roman and Chinese emperors. European nobles in the Middle Ages highlighted their rank through objects that indicated the leisure time that only they could spare, such as the hunting hawks Marcy Norton discusses. And women were so long associated with their spinning implements that a medieval compilation of women's wisdom was titled *The Distaff Gospels*, and the term 'distaff side' came to denote maternal lineage.[1]

The dawn of the early modern age, with its diversifying economies, expanding bureaucracies, and increasing mobility (both social and geographical), brought with it a new range of possible identities at precisely the same moment that a new range of objects became available to mold and reinforce them. If the phenomenon of identities through things in itself was not new, the early modern period witnessed a vast expansion of its scope.

At the most basic level, the spread of new things across space and societies served to collapse long-seated differences. Objects that had once been luxuries, available only to the most elite, became accessible to more levels of society than ever before. Improvements in the production and transportation of some goods, like the coffee and tea that Anne McCants discusses, increased supply and drove costs down. In addition, artisans and merchants discovered new ways to recreate or replicate formerly expensive goods. McCants shows how Delftware pottery and cheap imports (Figure 13.1) increasingly took the place of the costly porcelain vessels of previous generations, and were purchased and used by every level of society. Likewise silk, once the exotic fabric of kings, was now cultivated within Europe, was produced in vast quantities in cities like Venice and Lyon, and was often blended with cheaper materials like wool and cotton. The net result was that silk became more affordable for every level of society; even the poorest laborer could adorn herself with silk ribbons on special occasions.[2] Of course, some of the new luxury items that flooded the early modern marketplace remained too expensive for average families, but even then, Julie Hochstrasser explains, they could purchase a still life and hang a representation of such prosperity in their humble abodes.

In every case, the spread of such consumer goods symbolized the collapse of medieval Europe's three estates: those who prayed, those who fought, and those who worked. In this new early modern society, workers were not defined solely by their labor (though that remained essential), but also by a new middling social identity. Instead of working continually in the service of others, this group participated in the 'industrious revolution,' coordinating labor efforts to maximize both productivity and consumption.[3] They had the time to socialize over caffeinated beverages, the money to purchase non-essential goods, and the desire to project their new place in the world through things. It was no longer only the elite who could afford a bit of luxury.

Meanwhile, wealthy Europeans had to look for new ways to materially distinguish themselves, such as drinking chocolate, ordering custom wall-hangings or shoes from the artisans Corey Tazzara studies, or purchasing the rhubarb-based laxatives that Erika Monahan discusses instead of more common substitutes. True luxury products remained an essential part of the early modern economy as elites strove to find ways to demonstrate their superior taste and refinement. If consumption potentially decreased social distance, it also ensured that such differences never truly disappeared.

There were other ways in which things helped to reduce difference. Take, for example, the interactions between European explorers and native Mesoamericans that Norton details. On the eve of their encounter, these two cultures had vastly different relationships to the birds that were ubiquitous in both. After decades of interaction, these differences slowly evaporated, and parrot adoption became a point of shared identity between the two societies. Many early modern Europeans never completely abandoned their views of Native Americans as 'the Other,' and indeed debated their very humanity,[4] but material objects could still function as cultural liaisons, bridging the divide between disparate societies.

Even as things served as global ambassadors, they also never lost their local connections. Both ginseng and rhubarb, traveling across continents to reach early modern Europe, retained geographic descriptors that, if not always accurate, at least hinted at their exotic origins. This multiplicity inherent in objects in motion meant that things could act on identities in complex and manifold ways. Mark Peterson shows how New Englanders, by using the Massachusetts Pine Tree Shilling, could express loyalty to their colony while at the same time participating in the growing Atlantic economy. Similarly, Alan Mikhail demonstrates that various workers in the Ottoman Empire, each performing his own task in his own community, nevertheless became part of a larger empirical chain through his interactions with wood and grain. The global nature of early modern things ensured that no single interaction could be removed from its larger context, but the cultural specificity of material relationships also meant that the same object could play different roles in different societies.

This is especially clear in the case of material gender identities. Perhaps more than any other identity discussed above, gender is grounded in the 'thing-ness' of the body. At least on a conceptual level, one's gender directly corresponds to one's biological sex. But if these categories of male and female are relatively constant, their ascribed attributes, which we call gender, vary widely across time, space, and even subsections of the same societies.[5] Like the *renshen* discussed by Carla Nappi, sex is constantly identified and interpreted, categorized and mobilized, so that the resulting categories of 'masculinity' and 'femininity' subsume even more variation than that of 'ginseng.'

One salient example is the range of gendered identities represented by tea-making implements. In early modern Europe, caffeinated beverages and their accoutrements quickly became associated with feminine sociability. The inventories studied by McCants confirm that even at a relatively early date, widows were far more likely to own teapots than were widowers. In contrast, of the three objects Morgan Pitelka discusses from the Tokugawa storehouse, two are objects of war – a quintessentially male pursuit in nearly every pre-modern culture – and the third is a beautiful tea bowl. Pitelka tells us that for Japanese men, the tea ceremony was as essential an aspect of masculine sociability as was war. While in Europe tea elicited connotations of refined domesticity, in Japan these objects, imported from China in concept or in fact, symbolized national strength and cultural equivalency in the face of a strong foe across the sea. Men gathered over tea to exchange political information and exchanged tea objects to cement political relationships. Ieyasu's prized tea bowl (Figure 12.1) was named 'Araki' after its famous former owner, and among other objects helped to legitimate the new Shogun. While his family might be new to the shogunate, these objects said, Ieyasu was nevertheless firmly grounded in the authority of the past. Picture two cups of tea, half a world apart: both poured into porcelain crafted in China and carried across the sea; both holding deep associations of the customs that surrounded them. But one symbolized feminine domesticity while the other legitimated a masculine political regime. Things could divide as easily as they could unite.

Within the same culture, too, objects could delineate gender roles and associations. Clothing, work tools, and objects of sociability could all symbolize or even stand in place of their typical user's gender. The 'his' and 'hers' furniture discussed by Amanda Vickery is a particularly interesting example of this phenomenon. By the late eighteenth century, gendered associations attached themselves not only to literal and public manifestations of men's and women's lives, but also to objects thought to represent femininity and masculinity on a more abstract and personal level. Vickery presents us with several contrasting characteristics that British furniture makers used in their products and advertising for men versus women: structure versus detail, dark wood versus light, consequence versus delicacy. The essential function of a desk might be the same for a man or a woman, but its appearance and description were carefully crafted to 'suit' the gender of the intended user. More than ever before, objects came to symbolize not only external but also perceived *internal* characteristics of women and men. These gendered things also entered the growing private spaces of the home. Friends and neighbors might not typically encounter a husband's solid dressing table and his wife's dainty toiletta (Figures 14.2 and 14.3), but their presence still served as a personal reminder of the attributes each spouse was supposed to embody. Gender was no longer solely at play when facing the world, but also when facing oneself.

Gender difference manifests not only in these stark contrasts between men and women, but also in the subtler variations among a range of possible femininities and masculinities within a single society. Nicolas de Nicolay's *Navigations*, analyzed by Chandra Mukerji in this volume, highlights the variety of masculine identities that coexisted within the multicultural Ottoman Empire. Mukerji argues that Nicolay's depictions of various 'types' emphasize the role of clothing not only in defining social roles, but also in disciplining the morals of the body. In each case, moreover, costume is gendered masculine in particular – and various – ways. The Great Turk's Lackeys (Figure 6.1) grew fearsome facial hair that not only assimilated them into greater Ottoman culture, but also highlighted the essential masculinity of their profession. Manhood was also the literal focus of the Calenders' garb, which placed discreet but public emphasis on pierced genitalia. Meanwhile, Nicolay's description of the Janissary (Figure 6.2), with his riches won through prowess in politics and bravery in battle, strongly contrasts with the water carrier whose very lack of goods indicated his devotion to service and poverty. And yet both warfare and religious service were common paths to masculine identity in pre-modern societies. Though the men devoted themselves to distinctly disparate activities, Nicolay believed that both costumes properly contained and conveyed the *masculine* morality of their wearers.

This correspondence between external appearance and internal character did not always hold true for Nicolay. The Delli horseman he met (Figure 6.3) had a fearfully savage appearance, but upon closer interrogation Nicolay discovered that he, like the Janissaries, had earned his costume through military prowess and selfless dedication. On the other hand, the 'religious Turks' Nicolay encountered seemed to exemplify the same ideals of poverty and devotion as the water carriers, but in truth were deceitful and greedy con men who dressed as paupers but lived in luxury. As with any social identity, gender ideals could be warped and altered, mobilized and subverted. Familiar tropes – such as the Delli horseman's bellicose masculinity and moral fortitude – could become attached to new objects or costumes. Or, conversely, things that were long connected with particular values could be consciously used to capitalize on such associations, as was the case with the so-called 'religious' Turks who used their clothing and animal companions to manipulate their victims.

It is not surprising that Nicolay found it easier to assimilate new objects to an existing mindset than to accept new and nefarious uses for familiar items, for his was a culture continually faced with, in Timothy Brook's words, 'something new.' Early modern Europe was flooded with new things, and its citizens became accustomed to assigning them meaning. At the same time, the very abundance of objects left consumers and producers alike wary of fraud and imitation. Artisans and their guilds made every effort to uphold their honorable identities against those who profited from illicit conditions or unsanctioned labor.[6] Objects were part and parcel of this guild identity; guild-approved products received a special stamp or mark to denote their status,[7] while other tools, such as the how-to guide discussed by Pamela Smith, helped both preserve and promote the 'mysteries' of the craft. Thus Nicolay's aversion to the misuse of objects by the 'religious Turks' makes him very much a man of his time.

Again and again, the chapters in this volume confirm the essential connection between identities and things in the early modern world. In an age of linguistic diversity and limited literacy, the power of things to project meaning often bridged the gap between disparate groups and societies. As we have seen, the same object could hold vastly different connotations in contrasting cultural contexts. But in every case, people made things – both materially and immaterially – and things, in turn, 'made' people. From the poorest Dutch widow to the richest Boston silversmith, from the humblest Egyptian camel driver to the mightiest Japanese Shogun, early modern people relied on things to mediate between the life they wanted for themselves and the turbulent and ever-changing world in which they lived.

Notes

1 Madeleine Jeay and Katheleen Garay, eds., *The Distaff Gospels: A First Modern Edition of Les Évangiles des Quenouilles* (Ontario: Broadview Editions, 2006).
2 For Venice, see Luca Molà, *The Silk Industry in Renaissance Venice* (Baltimore, MD: Johns Hopkins University Press, 2000); for Lyon the best overview remains Étienne Pariset, *Histoire de la fabrique Lyonnaise: étude sur le régime social et économique de l'industrie de la soie à Lyon, depuis le XVIe siècle* (Lyon: A. Rey, 1901).

3 Jan de Vries, *The Industrious Revolution* (Cambridge: Cambridge University Press, 2008).

4 For example, the famous debate between Sepúlveda and de Las Casas. See Lewis Hanke, *All Mankind is One: A Study of the Disputation between Bartolomé de Las Casas and Juan Ginés de Sepúlveda in 1550 on the Intellectual and Religious Capacity of the American Indians* (DeKalb, IL: Northern Illinois University Press, 1974).

5 See Joan Scott, 'Gender: A Useful Category of Historical Analysis,' *The American Historical Review* 91.5 (1986): 1053–1075.

6 Dean Ferguson, 'The Body, the Corporate Idiom, and the Police of the Unincorporated Worker in Early Modern Lyons,' *French Historical Studies* 23.4 (2000): 545–575.

7 The textile industry in Leiden kept track of each artisan's mark in their records, e.g. Regionaal Archief Leiden (RAL) 0501A 44, after f. 650, and also printed them in guild regulations, e.g. RAL 0510 299.

INDEX